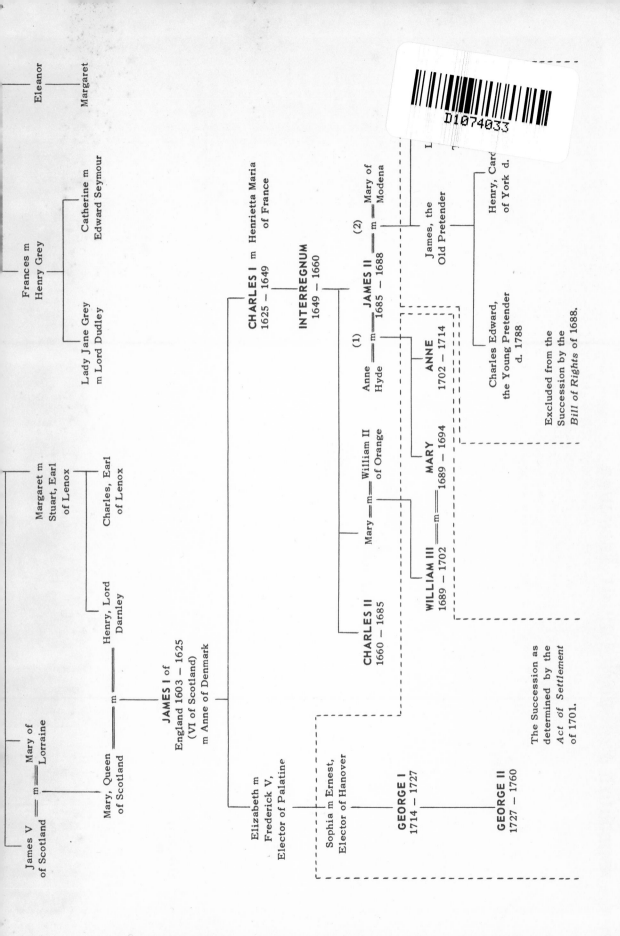

Eleanor

Margaret

Frances m
Henry Grey

Catherine m
Edward Seymour

Lady Jane Grey
m Lord Dudley

CHARLES I m Henrietta Maria
1625 – 1649 of France

INTERREGNUM
1649 – 1660

JAMES II
1685 – 1688

(1)
Anne m (2) Mary of
Hyde Modena

James, the
Old Pretender

Henry, Card
of York d.

ANNE
1702 – 1714

Charles Edward,
the Young Pretender
d. 1788

Excluded from the
Succession by the
Bill of Rights of 1688.

Margaret m
Stuart, Earl
of Lenox

Charles, Earl
of Lenox

Henry, Lord
Darnley

m

JAMES I of
England 1603 – 1625
(VI of Scotland)
m Anne of Denmark

Mary, Queen
of Scotland

CHARLES II
1660 – 1685

Mary m William II
of Orange

WILLIAM III
1689 – 1702

MARY
1689 – 1694

m

James V
of Scotland

m

Mary of
Lorraine

Elizabeth m
Frederick V,
Elector of Palatine

Sophia m Ernest,
Elector of Hanover

GEORGE I
1714 – 1727

GEORGE II
1727 – 1760

The Succession as
determined by the
Act of Settlement
of 1701.

D1074033

*Crown and Parliament*
*in Tudor-Stuart England*

*Ex Libris*

**Elston and Barbie**

# Crown and Parliament
# in Tudor-Stuart England

## A DOCUMENTARY CONSTITUTIONAL HISTORY,
## 1485-1714

*Edited and with Introductions and Commentary by*

## Paul L. Hughes    Robert F. Fries
*DePaul University*

*G. P. Putnam's Sons    New York*

# Contents

## Documents of the Reign of Edward VI

## Documents of the Reign of Mary

## Documents of the Reign of Elizabeth

## Documents of the Reign of James I

## Documents of the Reign of Charles I

## Documents of the Civil War and the Interregnum

## Documents of the Reign of Charles II

## Documents of the Reign of James II

## Documents of the Reign of William and Mary

## Documents of the Reign of Anne

# To Teacher and Student

This documentary constitutional history of Tudor-Stuart times is an outgrowth of our conviction that the study of history is truly effective only if the student has ready access to the writings of those who made and articulated it. Without access to contemporary chronicles, the study of history tends to degenerate into mere investigation of possibilities or uncritical acceptance of historical dicta. The student who has the opportunity and is encouraged to "look at the record," so to speak, is more likely to have a reasonable basis for making judgments and for evaluating interpretation. Being thus intellectually involved, his learning experience can be truly meaningful and productive.

Specialized research in political and constitutional areas has in comparatively recent years uncovered an abundance of truly significant documents relative to the development of English institutions in the period 1485-1714. Unfortunately, considerably less effort seems to have been directed toward making this material easily accessible for instructional purposes.

There are, of course, source books presently available; and although we personally have found some of them useful in our classrooms, we have also found that each has serious defects. Some of them are too broad in their overall coverage to give adequate attention to the study of Tudor-Stuart-Puritan England. Some tend to include snippets of practically every document in existence rather than to give a really sufficient expression of really significant material. Some are far too specialized, concentrating too exclusively on church history, or on political or cultural matters. Some, it seems to us, have been rather carelessly edited, and in some a paucity of explication puts too heavy a burden on the instructor.

In this volume we have tried to avoid these pitfalls and, in addition, to incorporate certain other positive improvements which we hope will enhance its value for student and instructor.

While fundamentally directed toward presenting the *documentary* evidence vital to an understanding of Tudor-Stuart times, this book was also conceived of as a general history of England from the beginning of the reign of Henry VII to the death of Queen Anne. It is constructed in such a way as to serve as both classroom text and sourcebook for courses in Tudor England, Stuart England, the Puritan Period, or all in combination, as they are offered in some institutions.

The documents pertinent to each of the twelve reigns (including the period of the Interregnum) encompassed by the years 1485 to 1715 are preceded by a general introduction, each of which presents a brief but basic outline of the political history and constitutional thought of the period, the main social, economic, and institutional problems that confronted the people and their rulers, and the attempts of monarch, parliament, and the courts to solve these problems. Each of the individual documents is, in turn, preceded by a commentary pointing out the immediate relationship of the document to the development of a particular concept or institution or, perhaps, its relationship to other documentary expressions of ideas which had been or would be given constitutional life by kings, parliaments, ministers, and clerics.

In order further to assure this volume's usefulness as something more than as well as a book of abundant primary source material, we have chosen to emphasize the accretive rather than the selective aspects of English constitutional history. For the English constitution is essentially organic. It is the product of an almost continuous process of modification, the grafting of idea upon idea, institution upon institution, rather than of conscious selection and rejection.

It is true, of course, that Englishmen in the sixteenth and seventeenth centuries often utilized the trial and error method in things political. Constitutional expedients which failed to serve were sometimes ultimately rejected, as they were in the long development of the limited monarchy, the slow growth of parliamentary prerogative, and the equally deliberate rate of the extension of liberties downward to the people. Yet little that was tried and found defective in this process of constitutional realignment was really forgotten. Perhaps nothing was truly rejected, for each expedient left its imprint on the thinking of the English people and thus helped shape England's subsequent ideas and institutions, which, in turn, helped shape our own and those of many other nations.

We believe, consequently, that this volume, with its abundance of significant source material and its editorial content informed by a broad and accretive interpretation of the constitution, provides the panoply of cause and effect which the student must have if he is to understand the political, constitutional, religious, and economic developments of Tudor-Stuart England.

In addition to its use as a sourcebook or a combined source- and text-book for students in courses dealing specifically with Tudor-Stuart-Puritan times, this volume can render much valuable service to other students and in other courses. Undergraduate and graduate students in any field of history or in a related discipline, whether they are interested in specific research problems or in the broad flow of political, economic, or cultural history, will here have ready access to the exact contemporary expression of and reasoning behind every major institutional development of the period. Students of law, too, will find much that is of interest in terms of development of legal concepts and methods and common law institutions. Nor have first and second year students been forgotten. Modern pedagogical methods call for an acquaintance with basic source materials by the neophyte as well as by the more advanced student. Teachers of introductory courses in history, political science, and the humanities will find here a variety of documents from which to choose for student reading in the areas of the development of representative political institutions, theories of governance, concepts of individual liberties, the rise of theological and ecclesiastical liberalism and radicalism, and so on.

A word, now, about the physical format of the book and something further about its editorial content.

Economy of words was not one of the marked characteristics of English constitutional literature, especially in the Stuart period. Consequently we have made every effort to pare repetitious material from each document. Such surgery has been carefully indicated by ellipses dots, and, in every case, an exact locative citation has been appended to the end of each document to direct the interested student to its full text. Further, where reference is made to a particular document (statute, decision, ordinance, decree, or so on), its full title, location, and date are immediately given (in context or within brackets), thus obviating the breaking of a train of thought by an interruptive search at the bottom of the page or the back of the book.

Whenever words or phrases are enclosed in parentheses, they should be read as part of the document. Brackets indicate an editorial clarification which the editors felt was needed to aid the student's understanding of the text. Money sums are indicated by £ (pounds), s (shillings), and d (pence). Whenever necessary for clarity, spelling has been Americanized and punctuation modernized.

Each document has been listed, numbered, and its page in the book noted in the general Table of Contents. In addition, the portion of this information that pertains to each of the sections of the book is repeated at the beginning of that section. As an additional aid to student and teacher in locating specific documents, each document has its number printed in outsize figures on the margin of the page on which it begins.

The running heads at the top of the pages of each section of the book repeat the name of the monarch whose reign is being documented and the inclusive dates of that reign. General chronology is thus effectively but unobtrusively kept to the fore.

At the end of the volume we have brought together a list of readings for teacher and student guidance. Well aware of the differential in materials available in the libraries of institutions of different sizes, we have included certain standard works that are almost everywhere available. The more specialized volumes necessary to graduate and law study are included along with certain less common works which are available to the students of most large universities. Because of its breadth this bibliography should be of help to students on every level. The "standard" works selected are not only those we considered of outstanding value but are generally those appearing on the check lists of the various academic accrediting associations—which insures their availability at least in institutions holding such accreditation. The bibliography is divided topically rather than alphabetically.

An analytical index, drawing together the references to all principal ideas, institutions, concepts, developments, and individuals has been included and will, we trust, round out the book's value to student and teacher.

## A NOTE OF ACKNOWLEDGMENT

It is hard to assess the debt that we owe to the many who have helped us along the way. The inspired teachers who first aroused our interest in the subject will no doubt recognize many of their ideas on the pages that follow. We should like to mention especially George L. Mosse, Paul A. Knaplund (now *emeritus*), and Robert L. Reynolds, of the University of Wisconsin, and Robert S. Hoyt, of the University of Minnesota. Professor N. S. Tjernagel of Concordia College gave steady aid and comfort during the course of research. Professor Mosse read the original manuscript; without his helpful suggestions the book would not have been brought to maturity in its present form. Virginia Hughes and Carol Dooner and Dorothy De Boer patiently and accurately prepared the manuscript for the printer. We feel especially grateful to the research staffs of the Newberry Library, the DePaul University Libraries, the University of Iowa Libraries, the University of Chicago Public Library, and the Huntington Library for their aid in finding and collating scores of documents.

PAUL HUGHES
ROBERT FRIES

# General Introduction

The student of English history whose interest is primarily in constitutional and related institutional developments finds himself confronted with a very real problem in the quantity of material available for study and analysis. Between the Dooms of the Kings of the Heptarchy and the legislative acts of the present House of Commons the English people have had a variety of political, constitutional, and legal experiences. In that period of more than ten centuries, this insular conglomerate of Celt, Saxon, and Norman developed and exploited many formal and informal legal-political procedures and many constitutional institutions. Some of these were merely temporary; others were lasting or left a permanent residue. Experiment and expedient have always been a very real part of the English way. The proven uselessness of trying to apply a particular item of the constitution to the many is and has been quite as weighty a factor in its final evaluation as its inherent value to the few. Still, although there was never a conscious master plan for the development of the constitution, the goals of unity, equity, and basic principle were never completely obliterated.

It is true that at times the English people reflected the characteristics of wandering Ishmaels, without purpose or hope: for example, when lost in the hideous fog of the wars of the Heptarchy, prior to the rise of Wessex to political dominance, or, again, when drifting aimlessly in the Wars of the Roses, prey to every faction and incapable of organization, and, still later when torn by the religious passions of the Reformation period. These, of course, were times of tribulation, times when both Englishmen and English institutions were submitted to the trial of ordeal by fire. When put to such tests, efficient individuals and institutions were sometimes found to be lacking. On the other hand, it often happened that men and institutions were able to meet the challenge.

The periods of crisis in English history were likely to be times when newly developing concepts and ideals, called into being by the evolving social need, were combined with worthwhile traditions and ancient, well tested, institutions. This continuous fusing process was characteristic of the Anglo-Norman peoples. Its influence is still very much evident in the constantly changing English constitution.

So far as the constitution is concerned, this characteristic Anglo-Norman approach was strengthened by the fact that it developed almost totally within an English frame of reference; domestic problems and traditions played a much more significant role in its development than did foreign problems or policies. However, although they were isolated from the continent by the channel, that waterway served the English well as a route for peaceful commerce. What was an insurmountable barrier to military invasion after 1066 was ever a broad highway for economic and cultural contact between the insular and continental peoples.

Still, the waters of the channel worked a peculiar chemistry on the continental con-

1

cepts borne by it to the English shore. The organic feudal system of the Norman conquerors was modified to fit pre-existing Saxon patterns, just as Roman and Saxon and
Danish systems were modified to adapt more easily to ways of life they were in the process of changing. This "sea-change" to which mainland concepts were subject is evident,
too, in later English history. The Reformation took on a definite English flavor when
it arrived in England almost two decades after the Lutheran disruption of the universal
church on the continent. Renaissance, mercantilism, monarchy—each was tailored to fit
English institutional and cultural patterns. England's feudalism, its expression of reformation and renaissance, its mercantile activity, and its development of monarchy, were
based on insular need rather than on continental dictation.

Each of these basically European movements (and many others as well) was to have its
particular impact on the English constitution; yet that constitution always remained
essentially English in form, purpose, and application.

Besides the abundance and eclecticism of source materials, the student of English constitutional development must face the trying fact that there is no single written document which can be called an English constitution. The multitude of materials has
never been collected and synthesized in a formalized way. Yet this technical point is no
evidence against the reality of the materials and their practical application. A convenient but, as we shall see, oversimplified definition of the English constitution, then,
might be this: the manner in which English governmental machinery is organized and
functions.

The manner of organization and function of this government has been influenced and
determined by numberless factors, which even a most minute investigation could not
possibly encompass. Celtic land laws, Anglo-Saxon superstitions, Norman cultural concepts, previous Roman civic organizational systems, and certainly the whole Christian
ethos—each played a part in the evolution of the principles and procedures of the English constitution. While we are unable to discern clearly *all* the underlying causal
factors, fortunately we are not so limited in our observation of the effects of these
phenomena as they are reflected in decisions of English courts or in the written laws,
or even in the customs of the people.

However, the constitution, although it is an instrument of regulation, consists of
more than laws, decisions, and customs, for it was never without a system of underlying principles. That these underlying principles were originally quite unrefined is
undeniable. Early Saxon law—that is, Saxon law prior to the introduction of Christianity by Augustine near the turn of the seventh century—was dedicated in great part
to the negative objective of crime prevention rather than to the positive tasks of
defining rights, insuring liberties, and securing the basic social objectives of toleration,
cooperation, and unity. Because of this, the first rough statements of Saxon law—the
Dooms—are in great part merely lists of crimes and punishments.

Yet, even though stated in negative fashion, the Dooms give evidence of social needs
and purposes. Anglo-Saxon society was primitive and savage at best; yet bloodshed and
violence were, while fairly common, not considered the *best* system of human relations.
And if not *best,* then *wrong.* This approach assumes two possibilities for social action.
One is a mode of individual action that results in destruction of objects that other

individuals have a right to enjoy as their own property. How individuals had *originally* obtained the properties (titles, lands, slaves, family, chattels) did not enter the question. The other possibility is protection of the individual's peaceful utilization of his possessions. This "right" to enjoy what is essentially one's own constituted the first approach to legal principle among the Saxons. Not that the right itself seemed warranted by God or even nature. It was a right because it came to exist in custom and tradition, because no greater prior claim to one's personal properties existed. Beyond that the Saxon in the pre-Christian period did not search for reasons. He possessed properties and felt the need for protection of this possession. Circumstance simply became part of his constitution.

In times to come, the concepts of rights and property would undergo many transformations. Limitations on the individual's free exercise of his rights would fluctuate according to society's understanding and need and would be so articulated in specific laws. The passage from the fee absolute interest of the Alfredian landowner to the limited interest of the Norman-Angevin landlord and ultimately to the considerably limited rights of today's property owner required a thousand years and the expenditure of much intellectual energy. Throughout that whole period there was a constant factor —the belief that abstract principle did exist and that the right involved rested squarely upon it, even though the rational basis for the principle itself might change, as it did, many times. Sometimes the right derived from the principle of customary practice, sometimes it rested on law; it might be held as a God-given right, or as derivable from natural law. The rational explanation made no real difference in application, for the basic principle that the individual had certain, concrete, though perhaps mutable rights, continued to exist. All this is applicable to matters other than merely those of property. Mode of government, for example, which constitutes a vital area of constitutional history, also had its constant basic principles, however variable their rationale.

Perhaps the most serious barrier to an understanding of the English constitution is a lack of precise definition for each of its parts in any period prior to the Glorious Revolution of 1688. Today's parliament, monarch, cabinet, laws, customs, and court decisions are easily defined and usually stand in logical relationship to one another. Not so those of the feudal, Tudor or Stuart periods. Indeed, they not only went undefined, they existed in a realm where rational definition was expected never to intrude.

One would suppose, for instance, that the institution of kingship, an ancient and always accepted part of the constitution, would clearly lend itself to delineation because of its antiquity, its continuity, and its dominant position among the many components of the constitution. Yet not even here may definition be applied with any hope of exactitude. The simple question, "How did the kings come to office?" at once presents a mass of dependent questions which must first be answered. What part did gender, legitimacy, factional strength, election, laudation, consecration play in the process? Did conquest by Henry VII give him legal right? Was occupancy in any way related to right? Did the *De Facto* Act remedy the possible defects in the first Henry's claim? Was inheritance sufficient to validate the claim of Henry VIII? Was that King's will and testament sufficient for Edward's claim? Did popular opinion and Council action extend the prerogative to Mary Tudor? What voice did any living monarch have in the choice of his successor? Could Henry IV negate without appeal all future Beaufort hope to the throne by insertion of the clause *excepta dignitate regali* in that family's charter of legitimacy? These are a few of the questions that cloud the issue. They resist precise answer just as kingship resists precise definition. Further, the uncertainties relative to questions of kingship are applicable, usually in more extensive way, to every other part of the Tudor constitution.

The facts of constitutional history do clearly indicate that the mode or the method or the organization of government at any given time had tremendous formative influence on the constitution, then and in succeeding periods. It is only natural that monarchy should protect the monarchial form of governance and that democratic government should tend to safeguard its future position through contemporary acts, laws, and statutes. The dictatorship of 1658, one notes, depended directly on the eight years of anticipatory legislation of the Cromwellian government.

But such protective legislation was based not so much on expedience as on principles and concepts which were acceptable both to government and people, although neither fully understood, or even attempted to rationalize, the substantive basis for them. Very often the reasoning was simply that the objective desired squared with philosophical orientation carried over from the past. For example, the Puritan government felt it had a special franchise through divine appointment. James and Charles, the first two Stuart kings, also claimed a divinely inspired liberty. Yet later Parliament, in its long struggle for legislative control of the state and against the prerogatives of kings very often fell back upon whatever ancient principles it could find to strengthen its own position, although it centered its claim to power on the basis of its representative nature.

To assume automatically that any of the parties putting forth such claims was not fully convinced of its righteousness would be unreasonable. James's conviction of a sacred duty to rule absolutely, no matter how devious the process by which he arrived at it, was to him in the nature of an immutable, God-ordained principle. To Parliament, antiquity and representation constituted inviolable principles of equal import. Further, at the beginning of the seventeenth century, the parliamentarians and common lawyers were themselves seeking to claim divine inspiration for their rights. The *Apology of the House of Commons* of 1604 constitutes an excellent statement of that body's offensive against the royal prerogatives, a manifesto which rests, not on revolutionary arguments that might easily have been extracted from new and trying social circumstances, but wholly on precedent and representation:

> Now concerning the ancient right of the subjects of this realm,
> chiefly consisting in the privileges of this house of
> parliament . . . we, the knights, citizens, and burgesses in the
> house of commons assembled in parliment, and in the name of
> the whole commons of the realm of England . . . most truly avouch
> that our privileges and liberties are our rights and due
> inheritance no less than our very lands and goods; that they
> cannot be withheld from us, denied, or impaired. . . .

Almost as an afterthought, and apparently without logical relation to the body of the document, Commons added a new and startling idea to the claims and principles set down in the preceding paragraphs: "The voice of the people in things of their knowledge is said to be as the voice of God." By 1604, apparently, Parliament, too, was reaching for that mightiest of all principles upon which to base its claim to power—Divine Right.

Such evidences of something deeper than the urge to power or the quest for regulation make it imperative that we enlarge upon our previously stated definition of constitutional history. It is now seen to be *the record of customs, court decisions, political relations, along with the principles upon which they were based and which directed their development both in form and in application.* It is apparent, then, that, an objective investigation of a social phenomenon as immersed in institutional developments and theoretical implications as is the English constitution must inevitably be accompanied by an understanding of English political and legal history. Laws do not make a constitution; they are its products. Consequently legal history is the product of constitutional development. There is, however, interaction between these elements. Very often customary laws and legislative enactment—or statute law—become the sole guide in explaining the obscurer constitutional processes.

It is clear that a constitution's principles dictate its mechanical aspect—the laws. It is not so obvious, but equally true, that application of specific statute mechanisms have influence on underlying principles. This complementary interaction between principle and law is nowhere more clearly illustrated than in the "remedies" applied in the twelfth century by King Henry II. Feudal constitutionalism had long accepted the hierarchical nature of the law. *Lex Dei,* or *God's Law,* held the ultimate position, and *Lex Naturae,* or the Law of Nature, rested directly on it. *Lex Hominis,* the Customary Law, or that portion of God's natural law within the comprehension of man, was the extension of the two others, although considered inferior to them.

Although custom functioning as man's immediate law had existed for centuries, it had never been concretely defined as a universal law guaranteeing essential and equal justice. Because of this, the old forms of the customary law often resulted in injustice, defeating their very purpose and militating against the effect of superior laws. This discrepancy between intent and effect came about because the customary law often lagged far behind rapidly changing and increasingly complex economic and political conditions. Conscious that the law led to injustice, Henry applied a series of remedial interpretations to the law in operation and inaugurated certain new legal procedures. Such innovations as itinerant justices, the warrant of General Eyre, writs, inquests, and assizes transformed usual custom into a workable universal law of the land, which was eventually integrated into the English constitutional system. These remedies tended in turn to strengthen the position of the monarchy. Thus the new methods of application made the principle underlying the process of law more effective, while the principle itself was stabilized in the minds of the English people.

One significant factor of English constitutional development is its continuity. There were no negative periods. The concept of a "Dark Age" is irrelevant to what has been essentially a story of growth and expansion. No one sovereign or representative body has had a monopoly on the creation of significant constitutional concepts. Indeed, each succeeding age from Alfred's to the present contributed out of its own experiences and knowledge of the problems of the past certain principles which found a lasting place in the English constitution.

But the changes from tribal chief to territorial king, from Witan to parliament, from feudal limitation on civil power to sovereign state, from the Saxon law of revenge to the ideals of justice, equity, and social harmony, were accompanied by genuine difficulties. Nor was the passage of time sufficient in itself to ensure even a partial discernment of the changes that had occurred. The penetrating scholarship of the modern period was not available to guide the tentative searchings of earlier ages after systems of law, jurisprudence, and governance.

For centuries custom was the only guide, and custom was insufficient, for it was geared to a stifling conservatism reinforced by a fearful mistrust of all departures from the *status quo*. In time, however, as the social organism made contact with the vast assortment of ideas and their possible combinations and with the growing abundance of material objects which might make life more pleasant and productive, it found custom confining. During its search for increasingly productive methods and more logical principles upon which to base human relationships, English political society passed through the successive stages of trial and error, scientific investigation, and philosophical rationalization. All of these phases were productive—but it is notable that no one of them produced an absolutely unique method, for each was constructed and applied within a frame of references made up of earlier principles, laws, ideals, and experiences.

One of the periods most significant to the development of the English constitution is that of the Tudor-Stuart sovereigns.

A century and almost two decades intervened between the beginning of the reign of the first Tudor monarch, Henry VII in 1485, and the end of the reign of the last, Elizabeth, in 1603. Within this period occurred the great abundance of institutional changes, procedural developments, and substantive interpretations which helped establish the legal and constitutional basis for more extensive political evolution in the period after 1603. The Tudor-Stuart period thus constituted far more than a mere time of transition between the late medieval and the modern way. The constitutional heritage of the Tudor kings, parliamentarians, judges, lawyers, and merchants was passed on to future generations stamped with a distinctive socio-political philosophy which is operative even today. Not only did these people hack away much of the deadening undergrowth of medieval conservatism, they also grafted on to what remained principles and concepts of which their medieval forebears had been completely unaware.

This was an age of expediency rather than altruism, of action rather than theory, a time of violence and crisis. Yet the age was to prove significant precisely because the perspectives of social ethics and equity were never completely forgotten. How remarkable this was becomes clear when one considers that here indeed was a land complete with every cultural, political, economic, and social problem that any frontier people had ever had to meet: the dynamic aspirations of rising economic classes, the loss of ancient, understood values which comfortably roots a people to its past, political ambitions which seem to deny the validity of ancient settlements, and a new awareness of national unity serving to weaken ancient ties.

So-called "Tudor absolutism" was a direct manifestation of the new and dynamic social ferment which was in the fifteenth and sixteenth centuries beginning to reorient English social, economic, and political aspirations. But the Tudor monarchs constituted only a single facet of a generally European pattern of change. In the same period much of Western Europe was undergoing similar throes arising from development of the national states, the centralization of authority, the struggle of representative bodies for stature, and the demands of the nascent merchant class for equal position in the political state.

Yet, other less immediate considerations must be taken into account when analyzing the growth of the constitution in this period. The often brutal and domineering personalities of the Tudor kings and queens, their manners, morals, and dynastic or religious aspirations naturally had some effect upon their actions and policies. Without being the sole shapers of English destiny, the Tudor monarchs, were in an excellent position to command and exert considerable influence on the laws and policies of the English government; and they were seldom lax in exploiting this position to the fullest degree.

This, however, is not to deny the fact that the mass of English society contributed greatly to the formation of its constitution: the concept of kingship is itself only the expression of a certain social impulse. No individual, no matter how unimportant, could exist within the framework of his society without having had some minute effect on the body of the constitution. Perhaps a man's only contribution was in being in agreement with current interpretations of principle or custom. But if so, he at least contributed to the growing political effectiveness of public opinion.

It is interesting to note how attuned the Tudors were to the opinion of the many, how finely policy was pared to fit the common need, how amenable they were to the public voice. So closely allied were the sovereigns to their subjects that it is very often difficult to know on which side the leadership lay. Objective and minute analysis of Tudor policy might well lead to the conclusion that "Tudor absolutism" was something almost diametrically opposed to the usual definition given it today.

Nevertheless it remains an historic and documentable fact that most of the Tudor sovereigns were determined and energetic in their policies and politics. If sometimes dictated to by the national will, often they were not. Yet all in all, seldom were Tudor policies deliberately hostile to the public will or welfare.

The primary objective of the Tudor dynasty was restoration of the institution of monarchy, which had been badly weakened by the political disorders of the fifteenth century. Henry VII laid the foundation for this by repairing the traditional basis of executive authority. Henry VIII and Elizabeth made the royal perogative an effective political tool. Yet here was no tyranny, no usurpation of the rights of other constitutional institutions or corporations, no general attack on the common law. All was accomplished within the accepted framework of the constitution.

The chief appeal of the Tudors was to ancient custom and law, seldom to innovation. True, there was an occasional despotic act, but despotism never developed into general policy; and even for despotic measures there is abundant evidence of some popular approval. The Tudor monarchs attempted to increase the efficiency of the institutions and principles inherent in the constitution. That such attempts bore fruit in an increasingly humane concept of the mutual responsibilities of rulers and ruled is evidence of their success.

# The Reign of Henry VII

## 1485-1509

# DOCUMENTS OF THE REIGN OF HENRY VII

# England, 1485 - 1509    Introduction

If, as has often been said, Henry Tudor found a crown on Bosworth Field, it should be added that England herself found something there of far greater intrinsic importance: the battle of Bosworth field concluded the bitterly factional and destructive Wars of the Roses and so prepared the ground for erection of a solidified *national* government.

Few English Princes after the Conquest could hope to have an undisputed claim to the throne, and fewer still to ascend to it unchallenged. The resultant shocks of revolution and civil war, draining the land of its wealth and manpower, preventing all hope of a social security conducive to progress, led eventually to a radical reappraisal of the feudal system. In theory, this system upheld the sanctity of private property and denied the right of the lord to victimize the yeoman; in practice, however, the vicious inconsistencies were glaringly apparent. The bloody climax at Bosworth brought an exhausted England to the end of her feudal adventure.

The year 1485 thus marked the beginning of a new social philosophy based upon responsibilities as well as rights. It was by putting this philosophy on an institutional basis which the English people could understand and accept that Henry VII rendered his greatest service to the nation and won for the Tudor dynasty a firm hold on the throne. His marriage to Elizabeth, the Yorkist heiress, while giving him no hereditary hold on office, signified at least a tacit truce between the old opposing factions, and thus gained him popular support for his claim to the throne. This factor loomed large in Henry's considerations, for his position on the throne was ever to rest on popular acceptance of *de facto* occupancy rather than on any legal, moral, or constitutional right.

This reliance on classes outside the nobility was not confined to the first of the Tudors. Throughout the whole of the Tudor reign such untitled names as Morton, Fox, Empson, Dudley, Cecil, Walsingham, Bacon, Cromwell, Wolsey, More and Latimore, continued to appear in high places. The basic contribution of Henry VII's reign was the setting in motion of a process which would bring to full fruition the working alliance of monarch and middle class.

But simple political homogeneity was not by itself capable of effecting the radical changes in English institutions which came with the Tudors. For this, legislative action was necessary, and legislation in the medieval period had been held beyond the legal capacity and moral competence of any political institution. Here it was that Renaissance England most deeply and surely separated itself from its past. Jealously guarding its newly won liberty from feudal precedent, it claimed complete independence for the nation and full sovereignty for the political state within the moral and physical area of its jurisdiction. Significantly, these new rights were deposited in the office of the institution of the king.

Still, legislation meant something more than mere decretory power; Henry VII never coveted that right formulated by Seneca as "the will of the Prince has the force of law." For England was a land of many interests and conflicting desires and Henry too perceptive to seek the burden of unshared decision. His awareness of the need for camouflage and caution was at least as great as his drive for power; hence Henry portioned out the responsibility for policy and law among members of the Councils and the Parliaments. Although these bodies were by no means democratic in the modern sense, and although the resultant statutes were generally articulations of the king's own desire for order, these dependent institutions did, nevertheless, speak for the ruled. And the legislation that flowed from them, freed as it was from the nagging proliferations of a king who feared he might not be heard, reflected the confident and succinct expressions of a unified government which expected to be obeyed. Each Act was dedicated to a single problem, and never was its reader uncertain as to its exact meaning. The *Act of Succession* placed, through Parliamentary action, the crown on Henry's head and gave the right of succession to his heirs, unequivocally and perpetually. In like manner, the *Star Chamber Act, Poynings Law,* and the *Treasons Act,* sometimes referred to as the *De Facto Act,* left equally little room for subsequent misunderstanding or doubt as to the intent of the legislator.

## Sir John Fortescue, *The Governance of England.* c. 1470

I.

WRITTEN before the Tudor period, Fortescue's *Governance of England* contains one of the best short definitions of the ideal political state produced by an English medieval political theorist. In substance the work compares the French and English types of monarchial government. Its most apparent implication is the superiority of the English monarchy, limited by Common Law, over the French system, in which executive arbitrariness was not restricted by any fundamental legal or constitutional principles. In the introduction to his work, Fortescue very clearly draws the distinction between royal absolutism, or *dominium regale,* unacceptable to the medieval English, and the mixed form of government, *dominium politicum et regale,* wherein the functions of government were divided between the people and the Crown. In this latter form the principle of public assent is involved as a limitation on possible arbitrary acts on the part of the Crown. Such medieval political theories did not, however, dominate English political thought at the end of the Wars of the Roses. They were rather the last whispers of a system already under attack by new social, political, and economic theories which would come to characterize the Tudor period.

There are two kinds of Kingdoms, of which one is a Lordship called in latin *dominium regale,* and the other is called *dominium politicum et regale.* And this diversion is that the first King may rule his people by such laws as he makes himself. And therefore he may set upon them *tailes* and other impositions, such as he will himself, without their assent. The second King may not rule his people by other laws than such as they assent unto. And therefore he may set upon them no impositions without their own assent.

This diversity is well taught by St. Thomas. ...(This extract from Sir John Fortescue, *The Governance of England,* is from the edition of 1887)

## Act of Succession. 1485

**2.**

AS THE FIRST significant political act of his reign, Henry VII established the pattern of personal rule legalized by statute which characterized the whole of the Tudor period. In seeking Parliamentary approbation for the new dynasty, the King tacitly admitted that Parliament, although in the "gift" of the King, was an essential part of the constitution and as such actively participated in the Tudor ascendancy. Such reliance on the voice of the national representative was by no means a departure from customary English practice, and this Act, along with Henry VIII's determined use of Parliament, had a bearing on subsequent popular conviction that Parliament's medieval claim to elective right in choice of Kings had had historic validity.

Henry, by grace of God, king of England and of France and lord of Ireland, at the Parliament holden at Westminster the seventh day of November, in the first year of the reign of King Henry VII after the Conquest. To the pleasure of Almighty God, the wealth, prosperity and surety of this realm of England, to the singular comfort of all the King's subjects of the same and in avoiding all ambiguities and questions: be it ordained, established, and enacted by authority of this present Parliament that the inheritances of the crowns of the Realms of England and of France, with all the pre-eminence and dignity royal to the same pertaining, and all other seignories to the King belonging beyond the sea, with the appurtenances thereto in any wise due or pertaining, be, rest, remain, and abide in the most royal person of our now sovereign lord, King Henry VII, and in the heirs of his body lawfully coming, perpetually with the grace of God so to endure, and in none other. (*Statutes of the Realm,* II, 499: 1 Henry VII, c.1.)

## Star Chamber Act. 1487

**3.**

CONTINUING discord and unrest among the landed classes which threatened both the King's position and the stability of the realm motivated Henry VII's institution of the court which met in the star decorated chamber of the royal palace. Contrary to custom, this court was not restricted to Common Law procedures. Guilt and degree of guilt were ascertained not through an open and public hearing where the accused was confronted by the witnesses against him, but through the process of private questioning by judges especially chosen by the King. Punishment, however, was limited by "the due order of the law." This court, tyrannical by its nature, could never rid itself of political bias and acted in each case as a group of men interested in presenting to the King the decision he desired. Nevertheless, the Star Chamber court did help to maintain civil order, particularly by enforcing the Common Law, which had been badly weakened by the Wars of the Roses.

An act giving the Court of Star Chamber authority to punish divers misdemeanors. The King, our sovereign lord, remembereth how, by unlawful maintenances, giving liveries, signs, and tokens, and retainders by indenture, promises, oaths, writings, or otherwise, embraceries of his subjects, untrue demeanings of sheriffs in making of panels and other untrue returns, by taking of money by juries, by great riots and unlawful assemblies, the policy and good rule of this realm is almost subdued, and for the non-punishment of this inconvenience and by occasion of the premises nothing or little may be found by inquiry; whereby the laws of the land in execution may take little effect, to the increase of murders, robberies, perjuries, and unsureties of all men living, and losses of their lands and goods, to the great displeasure of Almighty God: be it therefore ordained for reformation of the premises by the authority of this Parliament that the Chancellor and Treasurer of England for the time being and keeper of the King's privy seal, or two of them, calling a Bishop and temporal lord of the King's most honorable Council and the two Chief Justices of the King's bench and common pleas for the time being, or two other Justices in their absence,

upon bill or information put to the said Chancellor for the King or any other against any person for any misbehaving afore-rehearsed, have authority to call before them by writ or privy seal the said misdoers, and them and other by their discretions to whom the truth may be known to examine, and such as they find therein defective to punish them after their demerits, after the form and effect of statutes thereof made, in like manner and form as they should and ought to be punished if they were thereof convict after the due order of the law. . . . (SR, II, 509: 3 Henry VII, c.1.)

## The Bail Act. 1487

4. ALTHOUGH the notion of taking bail money to insure the future appearance in court of the accused did not originate with Henry VII, it was given its first broad recognition through this Act. Prior to 1487, the taking of bail, or its rejection in favor of incarceration, had fallen within the jurisdiction of the judge. Now the matter became a part of the fundamental law in certain cases, and the constitutional principal of the right of bail in later English procedural laws began to develop.

Where it was enacted [1 Richard III] that every Justice of the Peace, in every shire, city, or town, should have authority and power by his or their discretion to free prisoners and persons arrested for light suspicion of felony in bail; . . . by colour whereof divers persons such as were not bailable were ofttimes freed in bail by Justices of the Peace against the due form of the law, whereby many murders and felons escaped, to the great displeasure of the King and annoyance of his people: wherefore the King our sovereign Lord considering it, by the advice of his present Parliament, ordaineth, establisheth, and enacteth:

That the Justices of the Peace in every shire, city, and town, or two of them at the least whereof one to be of the Quorum, have authority and power to let any such prisoners or persons bailable by the law that be imprisoned within their several counties, city, or town, to bail unto their next general

Sessions or unto the next general Jail Delivery of the same jails in every shire, city or town . . . and that the said Justices of the Peace, or one of them, so taking any such bail do certify the same at the next general Sessions of the Peace or at the next general Jail Deliverance . . . following after such bail so taken; upon pain to forfeit unto the King for every default thereupon recorded £10. And over that, to be enacted that every sheriff, bailiff, and every other person having authority or power of keeping of jails or of prisoners for felony, in like manner and form do certify the names of every such prisoner in their keeping and of every prisoner unto them committed for such cause, at the next general Jail Delivery in any county or franchise where any such jail be or hereafter shall be, there to be recorded before the Justices of the deliverance of the same jail, whereby they may, as well for the King as for the party, proceed to make deliverance of such prisoners according the law; upon pain to forfeit unto the King, for every default thereof recorded, 100s. And that the foresaid Act giving authority and power in the premises to any one Justice of the Peace by himself, be in that behalf utterly void and of none effect by the said authority of this present Parliament. (SR, II, 512: 3 Henry VII, c.4.)

## Act for Controlling the Justices of the Peace. 1489

5·

THIS Act had dual significance. It was a measure intended to bind the administrators of local affairs more securely to the central government and to alleviate the social problems resulting from the uncertain and often laggard administration of the Justice courts. Aware of corruption in the local courts, Henry and Parliament constructed this Act so as to facilitate appealing, by plaintiff or defendant, to the king himself should justice be denied by the lower courts.

An Act for Justices of the Peace for the due execution of their Commissions.

The King our sovereign lord considereth that, by the negligence and misdemeaning, favour, and other inordinate causes of the Justice of Peace in every shire of this his realm, the laws and ordinances made for the politic and weal, peace, and good rule of the same, and for perfect security and restful living of his subjects of the same, be not duly executed according to the tenor and effect that they were made and ordained for; wherefore his subjects be grievously hurt and out of surety of their bodies and goods, to his great displeasure; for to him is nothing more joyous than to know his subjects to live peacefully under his laws and to increase in wealth and prosperity: and to avoid such enormities and injuries, so that his said subjects may live more restful under his peace and laws to their increase, he will that it be ordained and enacted by the authority of this present Parliament that every Justice of the Peace within every shire of this his said realm, within the shire where he is Justice of Peace, do cause openly and solemnly to be proclaimed yearly, four times a year in four principal sessions, the tenor of this proclamation to this bill annexed; and that every Justice of Peace being present at any of the said sessions, if they cause not the said proclamation to be made in form aforesaid, shall forfeit to our said sovereign lord at every time 20s....

And ... that the husbandry of this land may increase and be upholden, which must be had by due execution of the said laws and ordinances the King chargeth and commandeth all the Justices of the Peace to execute the said laws and ordinances ordained for subduing of the premises, as they will stand in the love and favour of his grace, and in avoiding of the pains that be ordained if they do the contrary....

And he chargeth and commandeth all manner of men, as well the poor as the rich, which be to him all one in due ministration of justice, that is hurt or grieved in anything that the said Justice of the Peace may hear or determine or execute in any wise, that he so grieved make his complaint to the Justice of the Peace that next dwelleth unto him, or to any of his fellows, and desire a remedy. And if he then have no remedy, if it be nigh such time as his Justice of Assizes come into that shire, that then he so grieved show his complaint to the same Justice. And if he then have no remedy, or if the complaint be made long before the coming of the Justice of Assize, then he so injured should come to the King's highness, or to his Chancellor for the time being, and show his grief. And his said highness then shall send for the said Justices to know the cause why his said subjects be not eased and his laws executed; whereupon, if he find any of them in default of executing of his laws in these premises according to this his high commandment, he shall do him so offending to be put out of the commission, and further to be punished according to his demerits. And over that, his said highness shall not let for any favour, affection, cost, charge, nor none other cause, but that he shall see his laws to have plain and due execution.... (SR, II, 536: 4 Henry VII, c.12.)

## Poynings Law. 1494

**6.** DETERMINED to extend peace and order to other areas dominated by the Crown, Henry VII, with Parliament, accepted the suggestion of Sir Edward Poynings, the Crown-appointed Governor of Ireland, that the legislative and judicial powers of the Parliament of Ireland be drastically limited. By this Act, the King's Council was given broader control of that country. Because of this arbitrary destruction of local rule, what had been mere discontent in Ireland soon flared into open and persistent rebellion.

An Act that no Parliament be holden in this land [Ireland] until the Acts be certified in England....

Item. At the request of the commons of the land of Ireland, be it ordained, enacted, and established that ... no Parliament be holden hereafter in the said land, but at such season as the King's lieutenant and council there first do certify the King, under the great seal of that land, the causes and considerations, and all such Acts as them seemeth should pass in the same Parliament; and such causes, considerations and Acts affirmed by the King and his council to be good and expedient for that land, and his licence thereupon, as well in affirmation of the said causes and Acts, as to summon the said Parliament under his great seal of England had and obtained ..., a Parliament to be had and holden after the form and effect above rehearsed. And if any Parliament be holden in that land hereafter contrary to the form and provision aforesaid, it [will] be deemed void and of none effect in law. (*Statutes at Large, Ireland,* I, 44: 10 Henry VII, c.4.)

## Statute of Treason. 1495

**7.** THIS statute contains elements of both political and constitutional significance. The ten years elapsed since his accession had given Henry ample opportunity to eliminate the most dangerous of those who had opposed him during the civil war or who subsequently seemed likely to prove politically troublesome. That having been accomplished, Henry extended his protection to all who would now remain faithful to him—and carefully excluded from the benefits of the statute any who might later desert his cause. By establishing the principle that the loyalty of the subject must be directed to the king *de facto,* Henry also hoped to protect the subject against punishment by a king *de jure* who might later assume the throne. Although Henry was probably not aware of it, this Act contains one of the earliest recognitions of the distinctions between the person and the office of the King.

An Act that no person going with the King to the wars shall be attaint of treason.

The King our Sovereign Lord, calling to his remembrance the duty of allegiance of his subjects of this his realm, and that they by reason of the same are bounden to serve their Prince and Sovereign Lord for the time being in his wars for the defence of him and the land against every rebellion, power, and might reared against him, and with him to enter and abide in service in battle if the case so required; and that for the same service what fortune ever fall by chance in the same battle against the mind and weal of the Prince, as in this land sometime past hath been seen, that it is not reasonable but against all laws, reason, and good conscience that the said subjects going with their Sovereign Lord in wars, attending upon him in his person, or being in other places by his commandment within this land or without, any thing should lose or forfeit for doing their true duty and service of allegiance:

It be therefore ordained, enacted, and established by the King our Sovereign Lord, by advice and assent of the lords spiritual and temporal and commons in this present Parliament assembled, and by authority of the same, that from henceforth no manner of person nor persons, whatsoever he or they be, that attend upon the King and Sovereign Lord of this land for the time being in his person, and do him true and faithful service of allegiance in the same, or be in other places by his commandment, in his wars within this land or without, that for the same deed and true service of allegiance he or they be in no wise convict or attaint of high treason nor of other offences for that cause by Act of Parliament or otherwise by any process of law, whereby he or any of them shall forfeit life, lands, tenements, rents, possessions, hereditaments, goods, chattels, or any other things, but to be for that deed and service utterly discharged of any vexation, trouble, or loss; and if any Act or Acts or other process of the law hereafter thereupon for the same happen to be made contrary to this ordinance, that then that Act or Acts or other processes of the law, whatsoever they shall be, stand and be utterly void.

Provided always that no person nor persons shall take any benefit or advantage by this Act which shall hereafter decline from his or their said allegiance. (SR, II, 568: II Henry VII, c.1.)

## Beggars Act. 1495

## 8.

NO NEW constitutional principle is to be found in the social legislation of Henry VII. The following statute, however, sets forth the pattern upon which most of the "poor laws" of England eventually were to be constructed. The superabundance of "vagabonds, idle and suspect persons" which troubled Henry—and continued to vex the government throughout the Tudor period—reflected the increasing hardships of the landless classes brought about in part by the enclosure of common land. Little of the highly regarded "benevolence" of Henry is apparent in this measure which conceives the wandering poor to be deliberate idlers and hence penalizes them on strict moral grounds. Later statutes were to treat the indigent even more harshly—without noticeably decreasing their number.

An Act against vagabonds and beggars.

Forasmuch as the King's Grace most entirely desireth amongst all earthly things the prosperity and restfulness of this his land and his subjects of the same to live quietly and surefully to the pleasure of God and according to his laws, willing and always of his pity intending to reduce them thereunto by softer means than by such extreme rigour heretofore purveyed by statute . . . , considering also the great charges that should grow to his subjects for bringing of vagabonds to the jails according to the same Statute and the long abiding of them therein, whereby by likelihood many of them should lose their lives, in easing the said Statute his Highness will by the authority of this present Parliament it be ordained and enacted:

That where such misdoers should be by examination committed to the common jail there to remain as is aforesaid, that the sheriff, mayors, bailiffs, and constables ... within three days after this Act is proclaimed, make due search, and take or cause to be taken all such vagabonds, idle and suspect persons, living suspiciously, and then so taken to set in stocks, there to remain the space of three days and three nights and there to have none other sustenance but bread and water; and after the said three days and three nights to be taken out and set at large and then to be commanded to avoid the town:

And, if again he be taken in such default in the same town or township, then he be set in the like wise in stocks the space of six days with like diet as is before rehearsed; and if any person or persons give any other meat or drink to the said misdoers being in stocks in form aforesaid, or the same prisoners favour in their misdoing, that then they forfeit for every time so doing 12s.

And also it is ordained by the said authority that all manner of beggars not able to work ... go, rest, and abide in his hundred where he last dwelled, or there where he is best known or born, there to remain or abide without begging out of the said hundred, upon pain to be punished as is beforesaid. And that no man be excused by that he is a clerk of one University or of other, without he shew the letters of the Chancellor of the University from whence he saith he cometh, nor none other calling himself a soldier, shipman, or travelling man, without he bring a letter from his captain or from the town where he landed, and that he then to be commanded to go the straight highway into his country.

. . . . .

And furthermore it is ordained and enacted ... that none apprentice nor servant of husbandry, laborer nor servant artificer, play at gambling, nor at tennis, dice, cards, bowls, nor any other unlawful game in no wise out of Christmas, and in Christmas to play only in the dwelling-house of his master or where the master of any of the said servants is present, upon pain of imprisonment by the space of a day in the stocks openly; and that the householder where ... any ... unlawful game afore rehearsed shall be used otherwise than is afore rehearsed, and that lawfully be presented before Justices of the Peace ... or by examination had afore the said Justices of the Peace, that process be made upon the same as upon indictment of trespass against the King's peace, and that the said misdoer be admitted to no fine under the sum of 6s. 8d. And that it be lawful to two of the Justices of the Peace ... within their authority to reject and put away common ale-selling in towns and places where they shall think convenient, and take surety of the keepers of alehouses of their good behaving by the discretion of the said Justices. ... (SR, II, 569: 11 Henry VII, c.2.)

## Act for the Feudal Aid. 1504

9.

PARLIAMENTARY control over taxation, clearly established by 1500, did not, according to Henry, guarantee sufficient royal income. The discrepancy between his income and requirements was made up in several time-honored ways. The Act of 1504 and the barter of £30,000 for the King's rightful claim to extraordinary aids for the knighting of his son Arthur and the marriage of his daughter Margaret were clearly within the constitutional powers of Parliament. Henry's determination to get the funds he felt he deserved is emphasized by the facts that by 1504 Arthur had been dead for two years and Margaret married for five.

Forasmuch as the King our Sovereign Lord is rightfully entitled to have two reasonable aids according to the laws of this land, the one aid for the making knight of the right noble Prince his first begotten son Arthur, late Prince of Wales deceased, whose soul God pardon, and the other aid for the marriage of the right noble Princess his first begotten daughter Margaret, now married unto the King of Scots; and also that his Highness hath sustained and borne great and inestimable charges for the defence of this his realm, and for a firm and perpetual peace with the realm of Scotland and many other countries and regions, to the great weal, comfort, and quietness of all his subjects,

The Commons in this present Parliament assembled, considering the premises, and that if the same aids should be either of them levied and had by reason of their tenures according to the ancient laws of this land, should be to them doubtful, uncertain, and great inquietness for the search and non knowledge of their several tenures and of their lands chargeable to the same, have made humble petition to his Highness graciously to accept and take of them the sum of £40,000 ... upon which petition and offer so made his Grace benignly considering the good and loving mind of his subjects ... of his mere motion and abundant grace, and for the tender zeal and love that his Highness beareth to his said nobles and subjects ... by this present Act doth remit, pardon, and release ... all his right, title, and interest which his Grace hath ... by reason of the said aids or either of them;

And also his Grace holdeth him right well pleased with the said loving offer and grant of his subjects by them so made ... and over this of his more ample grace and pity, for that the poorer people of his commons of this his land should not in any wise be contributory or chargeable to any part of the said sum of £40,000, but to be thereof discharged, hath pardoned, remitted, and released the sum of £10,000 of the £40,000, and is content to accept and take of them the sum of £30,000 only in full recompence and satisfaction of and for all the premises; which sum of £30,000 it is enacted, ordained, and established by the authority of this present Parliament to be ordered, assessed, levied, paid, and had after the manner and form ensuing.... [The assessment was to be made only against real and personal properties and chattels by a group of special assessors, the names of whom are given in the Act by Parliament.]

Provided always that no lands nor tenements nor other hereditaments nor possessions ... belonging to any College, Hospital, Hall or House of Scholars ... be charged or chargeable to or for the satisfaction of the said sum of £30,000 or any parcel of the same.... (SR, II, 675: 19 Henry VII, c.32.)

## Statute of Liveries. 1504

CONSTANT violence had attended the maintenance of private armies by wealthy subjects since the death of William I. The Tudor family, all too familiar with the perils of military factionalism and beset by a frail dynastic claim, was particularly sensitive to the fact that keeping a fighting force implied the right to use it. Henry VII took the initial and longest step in destroying this danger by abolishing the legal foundation upon which it rested. This weakening of local militarism greatly enhanced the position of the Crown and advanced the domestic peace which was to be so beneficial to the growing merchant class.

## IO.

The King our Sovereign Lord calleth to his remembrance that where before this time divers statutes for punishment of such persons that give or receive liveries, or that retain any person or persons or be retained with any person ... have been made and established, and that notwithstanding divers persons have taken upon them some to give and some to receive liveries and to retain and be retained ... and little or nothing is or hath been done for the punishment of the offenders in that behalf:

Wherefore our Sovereign Lord the King, by the advice of his Lords Spiritual and Temporal and of his Commons of his Realm in this Parliament being, and by the authority of the same, hath ordained, established, and enacted that all his statutes and ordinances afore this time made against such as make unlawful retainers and such as so to be retained, or that give or receive livery, be plainly observed and kept and put in due execution.

And over that, our said Sovereign Lord the King ordaineth, establisheth, and enacteth by the said authority, that no person, of what estate or degree or condition he be ... privily or openly give any livery or sign or retain any person, other than such as he giveth household wages unto without fraud or colour, or that he by his manual servant or his officer or man learned in the one law or in the other, by any writing, oath, promise, livery, sign, badge, token, or in any other manner wise unlawfully retain; and if any do the contrary, that then he run and fall in the pain and forfeiture for every such livery and sign, badge or token, so accepted, 100s., and the taker and acceptor of every such ... pay for such livery, badge, token, or sign so accepted, 100s., and for every month that he useth or keepeth such livery or sign, badge or token, after that he hath taken or accepted the same, to forfeit and pay 100s, and every person that by oath, writing, or promise, or in any other wise unlawfully retain, privily or openly, and also every such person that is so retained, to forfeit and pay for every month that such retainer is continued, 100s ...

And also it is ordained and enacted that no person of what estate he be ... name or cause himself to be named servant or retained to or with any person, or buy or cause to be bought or wear any gown as a livery gown,

sign, or token of the suit or livery of any person, or any badge, token, or sign of any person, upon pain of forfeiture for every day or time that he doth, 40s., and also to have imprisonment by the discretion of the judges or persons afore whom he shall be thereof convicted, and that without bail ...

Moreover the King our Sovereign Lord, by the advice, assent, and authority aforesaid, hath ordained, established, and enacted, that every person that will sue or complain before the Chancellor of England or the keeper of the King's great seal in the Star Chamber, or before the King in his Bench, or before the King and his Council attending upon his most royal person wheresoever he be, so that there be three of the same Council at the least of which two shall be Lords Spiritual or Temporal, against any person or persons offending or doing against the form of this ordinance or any other of the premises, be admitted by their discretion to give information ... And that upon the same all such persons be called by writ, subpoena, privy seal, or otherwise, and the said Chancellor or keeper of the Seal, the King in his Bench, or the said Council to have power to examine all persons defendants and every of them, as well by oath as otherwise, and to adjudge him or them convict or attaint, as well by such examination as otherwise, in such penalties as is aforesaid as the case shall require ... And also the same party, plaintiff, or informer shall have such reasonable reward of that which by his complaint shall grow to the King as shall be thought reasonable by the discretion of the said Chancellor or keeper of the Great Seal, Justices, or Council.

And also it is enacted by the said authority that the said Chancellor or keeper of the Great Seal, Justices, or Council have full authority and power by this Statute to send by writ, subpoena, privy seal, warrant, or otherwise by their discretion, for any person or persons offending or doing contrary to the premises, without any suit or information made or put before them or any of them, and the same person or persons to examine by oath or otherwise by their discretions, and to adjudge all such persons as shall be found guilty in the premises by verdict, confession, examination, proofs, or otherwise, in the said forfeitures and pains as the case shall require, as though they were condemned therein after the course of the common law, and to commit such offenders to ward and to award execution accordingly.

And that all manner of writings or indentures between any person herebefore made, whereby any person is retained contrary to this Act, that indenture or writing, as touching any such retainder only and no further, be void and of none effect: This Act to take effect after the Feast of Pentecost next coming only ... and endure during the life of our said Sovereign Lord the King that now is and no longer.

Provided also that this Act extend not to the punishment of any person or persons which by the virtue of the King's licence or writing, signed with his hand and sealed with his privy seal or signet, shall take, appoint, or indent with any persons to do and to be in a readiness to do the King service in war, or otherwise at his commandment ... and that warrant or writing to endure during the King's pleasure and no longer.

Provided also that this Act entend not to any livery to be given by any sergeants at the law at their making or creation, or to be given by any executors at the interment of any person for any mourning array, or to be given by any guild, fraternity, or craft corporate, or by the Mayor and Sheriffs of the city of London, or by any other mayor or sheriff or chief officers of any city, borough, town, or port of this realm of England, during the time of his office and by reason of the same, or to be given by any Abbot or Prior of or other chief head or governor or officer of any monastery, abbey, or priory, or other places corporate, given to their farmers or tenants or otherwise, according as it hath been used and accustomed in the same monastery, abbey, or priory. (SR, II, 658: 19 Henry VII, c.14.)

# The Reign of Henry VIII

## 1509-1547

## DOCUMENTS OF THE REIGN OF HENRY VIII

# England, 1509-1547   Introduction

Certain basic constitutional changes had become visible by the end of Henry VII's reign. The Crown now emerged as the dominant national authority, while the aristocracy had been relegated to a position of little political importance. Parliament had been given new stature, and within that body the voice of Commons, increasingly dominated by the merchant class, was beginning to be heard more clearly. Certain continental, "Roman" legal concepts had been imported to fill the gaps in the old Common Law, and these helped to consolidate the newly conceived national monarchy, which clearly was not wholly within the frame of reference of ancient English custom.

The Common Law, essentially agrarian and feudal, lacked the precedents necessary for evolutionary interpretation, and offered no real basis for self-modification. On the other hand, the unique conditions developing from the new economic and political activity of western Europe demanded concrete social and political action. Its handling of this dilemma constitutes the Tudor monarchy's most lasting influence on the English constitution.

The difficulties involved in this problem were considerable. The rights of private property and the jurisdictional claims of the Common Law courts remained in force against the centralization of political authority and no Tudor could encroach too freely on these ancient preserves. The new monarchy, though slowly evolving towards a new conception of kingship, was by no means antagonistic to the general pattern of accepted institutions and concepts, and in fact it could not have existed independently of that pattern.

Henry VIII made no more attempt than had his father to extend the royal prerogative outside the limitations imposed by the constitution. Popular acceptance was clearly preferable to antipathy aroused by a too autocratic wielding of the sceptre of state. Hence Henry VIII expanded and extended his father's policy of raising Parliament in status to the point where it could lend a voice in justifying additional constitutional changes and simultaneously directing Parliamentary action so that its statutes reflected the desires of the King.

Throughout the whole of his reign, Henry VIII never wandered far from this safe concept of "the-King-in-Parliament." The fact is that circumstances seldom were such that independent action would have been tempting. Time and the process of political ferment had brought into clear relief the growing dependence of the King on Parliament and had also isolated the Crown's most vexing problem: dynastic insecurity.

The quarter century of peace under Henry VII had dulled the memory of the misery of the Wars of the Roses. Gone with the pain was the excessive dependence of the commonwealth on the Tudor family, a dependence which the old King had capitalized upon to stabilize his position. But Henry VIII, a Renaissance monarch, could no

longer count upon a popular conception of kingship as a natural extension of God's
"right reason." The English constituency of the sixteenth century desired exact definitions of all political institutions, rights, obligations, and responsibilities. And
Henry VIII was to find that he would have to supply these definitions.

The passing of the old king placed in power a high-spirited, generous youth whose
very nature seemed to promise a whole new era of civil, political, and economic prosperity. And well might the new prince make benevolent overtures, for England was
well aware that punishment for the political sins of a usurping father could con-
ceivably be visited upon the son.

The second of the Tudor monarchs needed Parliament for several practical reasons. First, it was the only institution extant that had access to the public purse, and,
unlike Henry VII, and owing in part to the costly demands of the times, his son was
to find it impossible to "live off his own." The young King also had to rely on Parliament as an experienced helpmeet in the increasingly complex process of governing.

But more important to Henry than either of these needs was that which touched his
dynastic claims. Parliament alone, because of its representative nature, could create
a stable popular approval of his reign and dynasty. Indeed, here was the stimulation
which was to lead the English king and his subjects into a social and political revolution, for inherent in the problem of dynastic insecurity was Henry's psychological compulsion to banish all doubt from the national mind of the Tudor right to the throne.
Resulting from that need were the foolish and often futile acts of a king urged on by
fear: tempestuous courtships, unwise marriages, desperate and unsound foreign policies,
and, eventually, the English Reformation and the shattering of whatever of the ancient
bonds of universalism remained to Europe.

Of constitutional significance is the fact that each of Henry VIII's political tactics
tended to quicken the national urge toward representative institutions. Although his
reign was almost devoid of purposefully organized policy in foreign affairs, he was consistently eager, at least until the first marital crisis, to throw the English forces, in conjunction with those of Spain, against a supposedly weaker continental foe—France. Yet
any hope of victory in this venture precluded independent monarchial action; thus for
the first time Parliament was given a voice in foreign affairs. Later, the desire to quit
his Spanish wife necessitated the moral support of Parliament, and once again Parliament was admitted into an area formerly held to be royal prerogative. The Reformation presented a similar opportunity; since unilateral executive action was unconstitutional and potentially dangerous, Parliamentary consent and the good will of the nation
were essential. And so the institution of Parliament, traditionally a mere adjunct to the
monarchy, grew in power through services rendered to the Crown in effecting a settlement so revolutionary that neither party, by itself, could have accomplished it.

The Parliamentarians were, in the main, representatives of the mercantile class,
which by its very nature could feel little allegiance to the feudal past. Unsentimental,
without respect for traditional institutions, dedicated to a new materialism wherein
property and profit were superior to feudal Order and Degree, they, like the Tudor
dynasty, looked to the future for their confirmation. This confidence in times to come
was heard in the note of aggressiveness which crept into the Parliamentary voice in the

third decade of the sixteenth century. Yet this new awareness of their own worth did not lead the Parliamentarians to encroach on areas reserved for other constitutional institutions. Parliament was strictly limited by law, Crown, and the residual right of the judges of the inferior courts to interpret and apply the growing body of Parliamentary statute law. In keeping with the pervading philosophy of the late medieval and early Renaissance periods, Parliament seemed to accept such limitations as normal.

Yet there was, judging by the debates of its members, much that struck Parliament as repugnant and that cried for reform. Impatience with custom and tradition and with economic and social conditions is to be detected in the crispness of the debates, the precise structure of the statutes, and in the determined and unequivocal position taken by the legislature on issues with which the Crown, at least so far as the records show, appears not to have concerned itself. Occasionally Parliament made public display of its sense of independence. In 1534 the whole house refused to comply with Henry's request that speech critical of the Monarchy be defined as treason. On many other issues legislation was gotten only after strong, sometimes threatening, personal intervention by the Crown.

Certainly Parliament showed no servility whatever in the drawing up and passing of the *Statute of Proclamations*. As first formulated by the King's Chief Justices, Attorneys, and Solicitor-General it was utterly rejected by Commons. After the House of Lords had twice forced the Council to revise the second draft of the bill, it was finally accepted by Commons. Yet the bill as at last approved was completely new, having been in the process of debate thoroughly rewritten by the leaders of the House of Commons. A casual reading will show that the statute did not give to the King the right to legislate merely by proclaiming his will. Rather it clearly stated (as reminder and admonishment to the King) the exact limitations already existing in such matters.

On the other hand, Parliament had not as yet developed any desire for political supremacy. Stubbornly independent at times, reluctant at others, but usually amenable to the King's desires, it seems to have put its faith in time and change, fully expecting that the natural course of events would eventually raze the traditional barriers erected against its equality with the other elements of the Constitution. And it was precisely here that Parliament was truly revolutionary for its times. For the unformulated doctrine of time and change logically implied a full rejection of the doctrine of *stare decisis et non quieta movere;* that is, of the binding quality of tradition, of the medieval political dictum that only what is tried is true. The Renaissance in England had truly begun.

## Edmund Dudley, *The Tree of Commonwealth*. c. 1509

**I I .**
IF John Fortescue's *Governance of England* was a reaction to the order and degree of medieval political organization which was already outmoded in the late fifteenth century, Dudley's *Tree of Commonwealth* was the last great plea for reconsideration of the virtue of medieval social concepts and for reconciliation with that way of life now almost completely obscured by the rise of the merchant middle class in 16th century England. To Dudley the solution to all domestic social problems lay in the voluntary return of the people to the traditional system of medieval order and degree wherein each class occupied a position hallowed by divine ordination. In such a return Dudley saw the end of the social forces which to him were the chief factors destroying the efficiency and security of the constitution; for, unlike Fortescue, Dudley fully realized that the political and constitutional changes they feared were consequent to the pace and degree of social change. Thus, in Dudley's nostalgic lament is to be found a considered condemnation of the middle class, a class which was unjustly able to partake of the ease and tranquility which were rightfully the portion of the aristocracy. Although he denied the validity of the new social circumstances, Dudley was not merely a carping critic of a system he did not understand. His view was deep and penetrating. Forcefully set down in the work is his realization and fear of the growing social irresponsibility which was coming to dominate the relationship between the upper and lower classes in England, and which, if carried to its extreme would certainly result in disrupting the medieval constitution which Dudley professed to see as still in operation.

. . . . And now to speak of the Tree of Commonwealth. It is that thing, for the which all true Englishmen have great need to pray to God, that our Lord and King will thereon have a singular regard and favor, for principally by God and him it must be helped. And therefore God has ordained him to be our King and thereto is every King bound, for that is his charge. For as the subjects are bound to the Prince of their allegiance, to love, dread, serve, and obey him, or else be punished by him, [so] is the Prince bound by God to maintain and support, as far as in him lies, the Commonwealth of his subjects. . . .

The Commonwealth of this Realm, or of the subjects or inhabitants thereof, may be resembled to a fair and a great mighty tree. . . . But for a truth this tree will not long stand or grow upright in this Realm . . . without diverse strong roots sure fastened in the ground. The principal and chief root of this tree [is] . . . the love of God. . . . You will say perchance the Bishops and they of the spirituality have special charge of this root, and not the Prince. Yea, verily, the Prince is the ground out of the which this root must chiefly grow, for that it is he that does appoint and make the Bishops. . . .

Besides this principal root, this tree . . . must have four other roots, that is to say, *Justice, Truth, Concord,* and *Peace.* First [it] must have the root of Justice without which the tree of Commonwealth may not continue. And this root of Justice must needs come from our sovereign Lord, for the whole authority thereof is given to him by God to minister . . . to his subjects. . . .

But let us know when this tree, being with the four roots so surely stayed and fastened within this Realm, what fruit shall grow on the same tree? This tree shall bear four plenteous fruits, corresponding to the four roots. . . . By the virtue of the first root [Justice] this tree shall bear the fruit of honorable dignity; by the . . . second, which is Truth, this tree shall soon bear the fruit of worldly prosperity; by virtue of the third root, which is Concord, this tree shall bring forth the fruit of tranquility, and by virtue of the fourth root, which is Peace, this tree shall bring forth the fruit of good example....

But how shall these ... fruits be bestowed among our sovereign Lord and his subjects? Shall every man take or pull from this tree at his liberty of every of these fruits, ... having no regard to the state or condition the person be of? Nay, truly, these fruits must be taken discreetly, ... or else they will do more harm than good.

....As to the first of these four fruits which is honorable dignity there may be no manner of the subject ... presume to take one piece of this fruit by his own power or authority, but must have it by deliverance of his sovereign only....

As to the second fruit, which is worldly prosperity, this fruit showeth most properly for the Nobility of this Realm, which be Dukes, Earls, Barons, Knights, etc. They may take right plenteously of this fruit without deliverance. So that one of them usurp not to take his superior's part....

As for the third fruit of this tree, which is tranquility, ... it is the most necessary for the great number of the commonality.... There are two manner of fruits of tranquility; the one be tranquility in ease and pleasure, but of this fruit I do not mean for the commonality to meddle with, but utterly to refuse it, as they would ... poison.... But the other tranquility is meet for you, and that is to have tranquility to apply diligently with true labor and honest business. This fruit is ordained for your food....

What are the parings of the fruit of worldly prosperity which ye Nobility have? ... to defend the poor, to defend your Prince, the Church and the Realm.... As for the fruit of Tranquility ... to what person shall they [the commoners who become wealthy through hard work and honest business] distribute their [wealth]? To none other but to their own children and servants [to keep them in honest labor and as far as possible from the tranquility which stems from ease and pleasure].... (This extract from Edmund Dudley, *The Tree of Commonwealth,* is from the edition of 1859.)

## Tunnage and Poundage Act. 1510

# 12.

THE source of crown income lost much of its feudal character during the reign of Henry VIII. More and more the demands of the State against the national income approached the form of modern taxation. Both changing times and changing constitutional concepts were responsible for this transformation. Baronial funds, no longer expended on private armies, could find new outlets in the profitable avenues of commercial enterprise, and the ever-expanding middle class, unencumbered by feudal dues, was thought to bear an unfairly light part of the national expense. Tunnage and poundage taxation on imports presented an easy way to tap a relatively untouched source of supply. Undoubtedly the royal prerogative gave Henry VIII full right to such imposition. For it was neither opposed to tradition nor unconstitutional, having existed in some form since the time of Edward I. But to make the tax popularly acceptable Henry resorted to Parliamentary action, a step which was to have significant constitutional and political results in the next century beyond any that could have been foreseen by Henry VIII's Parliaments.

An Act for a subsidy to be granted to the King to the worship of God:

We your poor Commons by your high commandment coming to this your present Parliament for the shires, cities, and boroughs of this your noble realm, by the assent of all the Lords spiritual and temporal in this present Parliament assembled, grant by this present indenture to you our Sovereign Lord, for the defence of this your said realm and in especial for the safeguard and keeping of the sea, a subsidy called tunnage, to be taken in manner and form following, that is to say, 3s. of every tun of wine coming into this your said realm; and of every tun of sweet wine coming into the same your realm, by every alien merchant 3s. over the said 3s. afore granted, to have and to take yearly the said subsidy from the first day of this present Parliament for time of your life natural. And over that, we your said Commons, by the assent afore, grant to you our said Sovereign Lord for the safeguard and keeping of the sea another subsidy called poundage, that is to say, of all manner merchandises of every merchant, citizen and alien ... carried out of this your said realm or brought into the same by way of merchandise, of the value of every 20s., 12d., except tin, whereof the merchants strangers to pay for subsidy of the value of every 20s., 2s., and the citizen merchants 12d., and all such manner merchandises of every merchant citizen to be valued after what they cost at their first buying ... [such statement of purchase price to be given] on their oaths, or on that of their servants buyers of the said merchandises in their absence, or by their letters the which the same merchants have of such buying from their factors; all manner woolen cloth made and wrought within this your realm and by any merchant citizen not born alien to be carried out of the same realm within the time of this grant except; and all manner wool, wool fells, and hides, and every manner of corn flour, every manner of fresh fish, beasts, and wine into this realm coming also except; and beer, ale, and all manner victual going out of this your said realm for the victualling of your town of Calais and the marches there under your obeisance out of this grant always except: to have and perceive yearly the said subsidy of poundage from the first day of your most noble reign during your life.... (SR, III, 21: 1 Henry VIII, c.20.)

## Poll Tax Act. 1512

13.
THE *Poll Tax Act* of 1512 was based on a new principle of taxation—that every kind of property must bear a proportionate part of the burden of government and national defense. Heretofore some of the new types of property, ranging from domestically finished products to certain types of landed property, had been allowed to escape the financial demands made on other properties. The *Poll Tax Act* was revolutionary in that it levied taxation upon the individual rather than on specific property and in that it placed wages in the category of taxable property.

Forasmuch as it is openly and notoriously known unto all persons of Christ's Religion, that Lewis [Louis XIII] the French King, adversary unto our most dread Sovereign and natural liege lord King Henry and to this his realm of England, hath moved and stirred and daily moveth and stirreth by all the subtle means to his power to set and bring schism, variance, and as much as in him lieth studieth the means of continual error to be had in the Church of Christ. Taking of late upon him against the will and mind of our Holy Father the Pope, the whole Court of Rome, and Holy Church, to summon and call a Church Council ... and without ground, cause, or authority, in the same Council caused to be decreed, that our said Holy Father should from thenceforth be sequestered of and from all jurisdiction and administration Papal....

And our said Holy Father, for the charitable reformation of the said French King, willing the health of the soul of the said French King, hath for his said presumptions and divers other manifest offences as beforesaid, declared and published the whole realm of France [to be] interdicted and under that interdiction it yet remains.

The said French King that not regarding, but always abiding in his said indurate and pervert opinions and erroneous mind, and, the decree of the interdiction despising, will not thereby reform himself, but always erroneously defending and maintaining his said obstinate opinions against the unity of the Holy Church ... hath moved and daily moveth and maintaineth war and battle against our said Holy Father and the universal Church in such manner that our said Holy Father for the succor, maintenance, and defence of his person and of our Mother, Holy Church, and for the ceasing of the said schism and errors, hath written and sent for aid and assistance unto our said Sovereign Lord and to many other Christian princes. ...

For reformation whereof our said Sovereign Lord the King, of his blessed and Godly disposition, for the true faith that his Highness beareth unto Almighty God and to our Mother, Holy Church, as well for resisting the said malice and errors of his said adversary by the same adversary against our said Holy Father the Pope and Holy Church borne and maintained, as for that his said adversary hath of late attempted divers enterprises of war, as well by sea as by land, against his Highness and his subjects ... hath prepared and ordained, and purposeth in all hasty speed to prepare and make ready, as well by land as by water, divers and sundry great armies and navies for the intents and defences beforesaid ... which ... cannot be supported, maintained, and borne without great costs and charges:

In consideration whereof, and also for that our said Sovereign Lord many other divers and great charges for defence of this his realm in divers sundry wise of late hath borne and sustained, and for the goodness, bounteousness, liberality, favour, and tender zeal by his Highness shewed to his said Commons, as evidently is known, the same loving Commons in this present Parliament assembled, with the assent of the Lords spiritual and temporal in the same Parliament in like manner assembled, have granted unto

our said Sovereign Lord the King one whole fifteenth and tenth to be had, taken, perceived, and levied of goods, moveables, chattels, and other things to such fifteenth and tenth usually contributory and chargeable within counties, cities, boroughs, and towns, and other places of this realm of England in manner and form afore mentioned. ...

And for that the said one fifteenth and tenth ... extendeth but unto a small sum toward the said great charges, the said loving Commons [within] their powers willing a greater sum toward the said charges ... as well in shorter time as in more easy, universal, and indifferent manner to be levied than such common tax of fifteenth and tenth hath or can be according to the ancient use thereof ... have by the assent of the Lords temporal and spiritual in this Parliament assembled granted ... one subsidy to be taken and paid of every person underwritten within this realm of England in the manner and form as followeth; that is to say,

> of every Duke, £6. 13s. 4d.,
> of every Marquis, Earl, Marchioness, and Countess, £4.,
> of every Baron, Baronet, and Baroness, 40s.,
> of every other knight not being Lord of Parliament, 30s.,
> of every person, man or woman, having lands, tenements, or rents ... to the yearly value of £40 or above, 20s.; ... of £20 or above, 10s.; ... of £10 or above, 5s.; ... of 40s. or above, 2s.; ... under 40s., 12d.
> of every person, man or woman ... having goods or chattels moveable to the value of £800 or above, 80s.4d.; ... £400 or above, 40s.; ... £200 or above, 26s.8d.; ... £100 or above, 13s.4d.; ... £40 or above, 6s.8d; ... £20 or above, 3s.4d.; ... £10 or above, 20d.; ... 40s. or above, 12d. ...
> of every labourer, journeyman, artificer, handicraftman, and servant, as well men and women, above the age of 15 years, taking wages or other profits for wages

to the value of 40s. by the year or above, 12d.; ... 20s., or above, 6d.

of every servant taking any wages or other

profits under the value of 20s. ... and every other person, 4d. (SR, III, p. 74: 3 Henry VIII, c.19.)

## The Star Chamber Act. 1529

14. DETERMINED to bind the Court of Star Chamber more closely to the Council, and thereby further insure the acceptability of its future decisions, this Act modified that of Henry VII by adding the President of the King's Council to the court's personnel. The Act signifies the growing importance of that officer in a period when Council activities in administrative and judicial affairs were becoming increasingly significant in directing the political action of the central government.

An Act that the President of the King's Council shall be associate with the Chancellor and Treasurer of England and the Keeper of the King's Privy Seal.

[After restating the *Star Chamber Act* of 1487, 3 Henry VII, c.1, this act adds] ... Nevertheless in the same good and profitable statute the President of the King's most honourable Council for the time being attending upon his most noble and royal person is omitted and not named ... to be one of the said persons that should have authority to call before them such misdoers so offending the King's laws in any of the premises as is before rehearsed. Be it therefore ... enacted, that from henceforth the Chancellor, Treasurer of England, and the President of the King's most honourable Council attending upon his most honourable person for the time being, and the Keeper of the King's

Privy Seal, or two of them, calling unto them one bishop and one temporal lord of the King's most honourable Council, and the two Chief Justices of the King's Bench and the Common Pleas for the time being, or other two of the King's Justices in their absence, upon any bill or information hereafter to be put in, the Chancellor of England, Treasurer, President of the King's said most honourable Council, or Keeper of the King's Privy Seal for the time being, for any misbehaving before rehearsed, and henceforth have full power and authority to call before them by writ or privy seal such misdoers, and them and other by their discretion by whom the truth may be known to examine, and such as they shall find defective to punish them after their demerits [according to the above Act]. (SR, III, 304: 21 Henry VIII, c.20.)

## Act for the Pardon of the Clergy of Canterbury. 1531

15. THE Machiavellian aspect of Henry's Reformation legislation was already apparent before his full scale attack on the universal church. The Act of 1531 was a "pardon" given the clerics of Canterbury for having accepted Wolsey as papal legate. That Henry had been directly instrumental in Wolsey's appointment, and that clerical rejection of him would have constituted a grave offense against Church and King, were discounted. Not content with thus legislatively silencing any possible future English clerical criticism, Henry also, in his "benignity and high liberality," accepted a subsidy of £100,000 from the frightened clerics.

An Act concerning the pardon granted to the King's Spiritual Subjects of the Province of Canterbury for the *Praemunire:*

The King our Sovereign Lord, calling to his blessed and most gracious remembrance that his good and loving subjects the most

Reverend Father in God the Archbishop of Canterbury and other bishops, suffragans, prelates, and other spiritual persons of the Province of the Archbishopric of Canterbury of this his realm of England, and the ministers and underwritten which have exercised, practised, or executed in spiritual courts and other spiritual jurisdictions within the said Province, have fallen and incurred into divers dangers of his laws by things done, perpetrated, and committed contrary to the order of his laws, and especially contrary to the form of the statutes of provisors, provisions, and *praemunire,* [the specific charge against the clerics of Canterbury was that they had recognized Cardinal Wolsey's jurisdiction as papal legate] and his Highness, having always tender eye with mercy and pity and compassion towards his said spiritual subjects ... of his mere motion, benignity, and liberality, by authority of this his Parliament, hath given and granted his liberal and free pardon to his said good and loving spiritual subjects

... in manner and form ensuing, that is to wit:

The King's Highness, of his said benignity and high liberality, in consideration that the said Archbishop, Bishops, and Clergy of the said Province of Canterbury in their said Convocation now being, have given and granted to him a subsidy of one hundred thousand pounds of lawful money current in this realm ... is ... pleased that it be ordained and established ... by authority of this his said Parliament, that the most Reverend Father in God, William, Archbishop of Canterbury ... and all other Bishops and suffragans, prelates, abbots, priors, [etc.] ... shall be by authority of this present pardon acquitted, pardoned, released, and discharged ... of all and all manner offences, contempts, and trespasses committed or done against all and singular statute and statutes of provisors, provisions, and *praemunire.* ... (SR, III, 334: 22 Henry VIII, c.15.)

## Beggars Act. 1531

### 16.

THIS Act constituted an important modification of Henry VII's *Beggars Act* of 1495· In it, the Justice of the Peace is given increased authority to deal with social problems growing out of poverty. Also, contrary to the Act of 1495, this Act makes a clear distinction between those destitute individuals who needed aid and those of able body who failed to seek productive labor of their own volition. Of especial significance is the fact that the new reliance on the Justice of Peace speaks of a deep need for social reform. Here too is found what was probably the first awareness of a sense of the State's responsibility for the "impotent poor."

An Act concerning punishment of Beggars and Vagabonds.

Where in all places throughout this realm of England vagabonds and beggars have of long time increased and daily do increase in great and excessive numbers, by the occasion of idleness, mother and root of all vices, whereby hath insurged and sprung ... continual thefts, murders, and other heinous offences and great enormities, to the high displeasure of God, the inquietation and damage of the King's people, and to the marvelous disturbance of the common weal of

this realm. And whereas many and sundry good laws, statutes and ordinances, have been before this time devised and made, as well by the King our Sovereign Lord as also by divers his most noble progenitors, Kings of England, for the most necessary and due reformation of the premises, yet that, notwithstanding, the said numbers of vagabonds and beggars be not seen in any part to be diminished, but rather daily augmented and increased into great companies, as evidently and manifestly it doth and may appear:

Be it therefore enacted ... that the Justices

of the Peace . . . shall from time to time, as often as need shall require, by their discretions divide themselves within the said shires . . . and so being divided shall make diligent search and inquiry of all aged, poor, and impotent persons which live or of necessity be compelled to live by alms of the charity of the people that be or shall be hereafter abiding . . . within the limits of their division, and after and upon such search made the said Justices of Peace . . . shall have power and authority by their discretions to enable to beg, within such . . . limits as they shall appoint, such of the said impotent persons which they shall find and think most convenient within the limits of their division to live of the charity and alms of the people, and to give in commandment to every such aged and impotent beggar by them enabled that none of them shall beg without the limits to them so appointed, and shall also register and write the names of every such impotent beggar by them appointed in a bill or roll indented, [cut into two halves in an irregular manner so that the halves fitted together when and if the roll indent was later used as evidence before a court of licence to beg] the one part thereof to remain with themselves and the other part by them to be certified before the Justices of Peace at the next Sessions after such search . . . there to remain under the keeping of the Custos Rotolorum; and that the said Justices of Peace . . . shall make and deliver to every such impotent person by them enabled to beg, a letter containing the name of such impotent person and witnessing that he is authorized to beg and the limits within which he is appointed to beg, the same letter to be sealed with . . . seals . . . engraved with the name of the limit wherein such impotent person shall be appointed to beg in, and to be subscribed with the name of one of the said Justices. . . . And if any such impotent person so authorized do beg in any other place than within such limits that he shall be assigned unto, that then the Justices of Peace . . . shall . . . punish all such persons by imprisonment in the stocks by the space of two days and two nights, giving them only bread and water, and after that cause every such impotent person to be sworn to return again without delay to the [place] where they be authorized to beg.

And be it enacted, that no such impotent person . . . shall beg within any part of this realm except he be authorized by writing under seal. . . . And if any such impotent person . . . be vagrant and go begging having no such letter under seal . . . that then the constables and all other inhabitants within such town or parish where such person shall beg shall cause every such beggar to be taken and brought to the next Justice of Peace or High Constable of the Hundred; and thereupon the said Justice of Peace or High Constable shall command the said constables and other inhabitants of the town or parish which shall bring before him any such beggar that they shall strip him naked from the middle upward and cause him to be whipped within the town where he was taken, or within some other town where the same Justice or High Constable shall appoint . . . : and if not, then to command such beggar to be set in the stocks in the same town or parish where he was taken for the space of three days and three nights, there to have only bread and water; and thereupon the said Justice or High Constable afore whom such beggar shall be brought shall limit to him a place to beg in, and give to him a letter under seal in form above remembered, and swear him to depart and repair thither immediately after his punishment. . . .

And be it further enacted . . . that if any person or persons being whole in body and able to labour . . . or if any man or woman being whole in body and able to labour having no land, master, nor using any lawful merchandise, craft, or mystery, whereby he might get his living . . . be vagrant and can give none reckoning how he doth lawfully get his living, that then it shall be lawful to the constables and all other the King's officers, ministers, and subjects of every town, parish, and hamlet to arrest the said vagabonds and idle persons and them to bring to any of the Justices of Peace of the same shire ... and that every such Justice of Peace ... shall cause every such idle person so to him brought to be had to the next market town or other place where the said Justices of Peace ... shall think most convenient ... and there to be tied to the end of a cart naked and be beaten with whips throughout the same market town or other place till his body be bloody by reason of such whipping; and after such punishment and whipping had, the person so punished ... shall be enjoined upon his oath to return forthwith without delay in the next and straight way to the place where he was born, or where he last dwelled before the same punishment by the space of three years, and there put himself to labour like as a true man oweth to do; and after that done, every such person so punished and ordered shall have a letter sealed with the seal of the city, borough, town, or franchise wherein he shall be punished, witnessing that he hath been punished according to this Statute, and containing the day and place of his punishment, and the place whereunto he is limited to go, and by what time he is limited to come thither, within which time he may lawfully beg by the way, showing the same letter, and otherwise not; and if he do not accomplish the order to him appointed by the same letter, then to again be taken and whipped, and so often as any default shall be found in him contrary to the order of this Statute, in every place to be taken and whipped till he repaired where he was born or where he last dwelled by the space of three years, and there put his body to labour for his living or otherwise truly get his living without begging as long as he is able to do; and if the person so whipped be an idle person and no common beggar, then after such whipping he shall be kept in the stocks till he hath found surety to go to service or else to labour after the discretion of the said Justice of Peace ... afore whom any such idle person being no common beg-

gar shall be brought ... or else to be ordered and sworn to repair to the place where he was born or where he last dwelled by the space of three years, and to have like letter and such further punishment if he again offend this Statute.... And that the Justices of the Peace of every shire ... shall have power and authority within the limits of their Commissions to inquire of all mayors, bailiffs, constables, and other officers and persons that shall be negligent in executing of this Act: And if the constables and inhabitants within any town or parish ... be negligent ... that then the township or parish ... shall lose and forfeit for every such impotent beggar ... 3s.4d., and for every strong beggar ... 6s.8d.... And that all Justices of Peace ... shall have full power and authority as well to hear and determine every such default by presentment as by such bill of information, and upon every presentment afore them and upon every such bill of information to make process by distress against the inhabitance of every such town and parish....

And be it enacted ... that scholars of the Universities of Oxford and Cambridge that go about begging, not being authorized under the seal of the said Universities by the Commissary, Chancellor, or Vice-Chancellor of the same, and all and singular shipmen pretending losses of their ships and goods of the sea going about the country begging without sufficient authority witnessing the same, shall be punished and ordered in manner and form as is above rehearsed of strong beggars; and that all proctors [collectors of alms for charitable institutions, or who posed as such] and pardoners [sellers if supposed religious relics] going about in any country or countries without sufficient authority, and all other idle persons going about in any countries or abiding in any city, borough, or town, some of them using divers and subtile crafty and unlawful games and plays, and some of them feigning themselves to have knowledge in physic, palmistry, or other crafty sciences, whereby they [fool the people] that they can tell their destinies, diseases, and fortunes, and such other like fantastic imaginations, to the great deceit of the King's subjects, shall upon examination had before two Justices of Peace . . . if he by provable witness be found guilty of any such deceits, be punished by whipping at two days together after the manner above rehearsed; And if he again offend in the same offence or any like offence, then to be scourged two days and the third day to be put upon the pillory from nine of the clock till eleven before noon of the same day, and to have one of his ears cut off; and if he offend the third time, to have like punishment with whipping, standing in the pillory, and to have his other ear cut off; and that Justices of the Peace have like authority in every liberty and franchise within their shires where they be Justices of Peace for the execution of this Act in every part thereof as they shall have without the liberty or franchise. (SR, III, 328: 22 Henry VIII, c.12.)

## Act in Conditional Restraint of Annates. 1532

I 7.
HENRY'S first blow at the See of Rome was not intended to lead to any final breach. Contingent upon Papal nullification of the King's marriage to Catherine of Aragon, Parliament empowered Henry to interfere with the accustomed payments (annates) of the English Church to Rome if his desires were not met. Even more important than the Act's obvious purpose of placing King and Pope in a bargaining position is the fact that it laid out a carefully constructed method for consecration of Church officials without sanction from Rome and denied the power of the Pope to use the instruments of excommunication or interdict.

An Act concerning restraint of payment of Annates to the See of Rome.

Forasmuch as it is well perceived by long approved experience that great and inestimable sums of money be daily conveyed out of this realm to the impoverishment of the same, and especially such sums of money as the Pope's Holiness, his predecessors, and the Court of Rome by long time have heretofore taken of all and singular those spiritual persons which have been named, elected, presented, or postulated to be archbishops or bishops within this realm of England, under the title of annates, otherwise called firstfruits; which annates or firstfruits heretofore have been taken of every archbishopric or bishopric within this realm by restraint of the Pope's bulls for confirmations, elections, admissions, postulations, provisions, collations, dispositions, institutions, installations, investitures, orders holy, benedictions, palliums, or other things requisite and necessary to the attaining of those their promotions, and have been compelled to pay before they could attain the same great sums of money, before they might receive any part of the fruits of the said archbishopric or bishopric whereunto they were named, elected, presented, or postulated:

By occasion whereof not only the treasure of this realm hath been greatly conveyed out of the same, but also it hath happened many times by occasion of death unto such archbishops and bishops so newly promoted within two or three years after his or their consecration, that his or their friends by whom he or they have been holpen to advance and make payment of the said annates or firstfruits have been thereby utterly undone and impoverished:

And for because the said annates have risen, grown, and increased by an uncharitable custom grounded upon no just or good title, and the payments thereof obtained by restraint of bulls until the same annates or firstfruits have been paid or surety made for the same, which declareth the said payments to be exacted and taken by constraint, against all equity and justice:

The noblemen therefore of this realm and

the wise, sage, politic commons of the same assembled in this present Parliament, considering that the Court of Rome ceaseth not to tax, take, and exact the said great sums of money under the title of annates or firstfruits as is aforesaid to the great damage of the said prelates and this realm, which annates or firstfruits where first suffered to be taken ... only for the defence of Christian people against the infidels, and now they be claimed and demanded as mere duty, only for lucre, against all right and conscience, insomuch that it is evidently known that there hath passed out of this realm unto the Court of Rome since the second year of the reign of the most noble Prince of famous memory King Henry VII unto this present time, under the name of annates or firstfruits paid for the expedition of bulls of archbishoprics and bishoprics, the sum of eight hundred thousand ducats, amounting in sterling money at the least to eight score thousand pounds, besides other great and intolerable sums which have yearly been conveyed to the said Court of Rome by many other ways and means, to the great impoverishment of this realm:

And albeit that our said Sovereign Lord the King and all his natural subjects as well spiritual as temporal be as obedient, devout, Catholic, and humble children of God and Holy Church as any people be within any realm, yet the said exactions of annates or firstfruits be so intolerable and importable to this realm that it is considered and declared by the whole body of this realm now represented by all the estates of the same assembled in this present Parliament that the King's Highness before Almighty God is bound as by the duty of a good Christian prince, for the conservation and preservation of the good estate and commonwealth of this his realm, to do all that is in him to obviate, repress, and redress the said abuses and exactions of annates or firstfruits:

And because that divers prelates of this realm be now in extreme age and in other debilities of their bodies, so that of likelihood bodily death in short time shall or may succeed unto them; by reason whereof great sums of money shall shortly after their deaths be conveyed unto the Court of Rome for the unreasonable and uncharitable causes above said, to the universal damage, prejudice, and impoverishment of this realm, if speedy remedy be not in due time provided:

It is therefore ordained, established, and enacted by authority of this Parliament that the unlawful payments of annates or firstfruits ... shall from henceforth utterly cease ... and that no manner person ... hereafter to be named, elected, presented, or postulated to any archbishopric or bishopric within this realm shall pay the said annates or firstfruits ... upon pain to forfeit to our said Sovereign Lord the King ... all manner goods and chattels forever, and all the temporal lands and possessions of the same archbishopric or bishopric during the time that he or they which shall offend contrary to this Act shall have, possess, or enjoy the archbishopric or bishopric wherefore he shall so offend contrary to the form aforesaid. ... (SR, III, 385: 23 Henry VIII, c.20.)

## The Submission of the Clergy. 1532

18.

THE clergy saw clearly that the issue of the marriage annulment had grown into a struggle for control of the Church. In the *Act in Conditional Restraint of Annates* Parliament had shown its willingness to turn the entire matter over to the Crown, and the Act was also a factor in winning a minority of the churchmen to the King's side, since it implied that the moneys thus retained in England might find their way into the pockets of the churchmen.

The subsequent document, *The Submission of the Clergy,* did not signify, however, that the majority of clerics at that time were willing to alienate themselves from Rome. Rather, the clergy, unable to stand alone and unwilling to risk placing themselves in a position of having to choose one side or the other, submitted to Henry's "most excellent wisdom" in publicly placing their faith in his ability to solve the national problem.

It was, in that sense, a gesture of political expediency.

...We your most humble servants, daily orators and bedesmen of your clergy of England, having our special trust and confidence in your most excellent wisdom, your princely goodness, and fervent zeal to the promotion of God's honor and Christian religion, and also in your learning, far exceeding, in our judgment, the learning of all other kings and princes that we have read of, and doubting nothing but that the same shall still continue and daily increase in your majesty....

First, do offer and promise, on our priestly word, here unto your Highness, submitting ourselves most humbly to the same, that we will never from henceforth enact, put in use, promulge, or execute any new canons or constitutions provincial, or any other new ordinance, provincial or synodal, in our convocation or synod in time coming, which convocation is, always has been, and must be, assembled only by your Highness' commandment of writ, unless your Highness by your Royal assent shall license us to assemble our convocation, and to make, promulge, and execute such constitutions and ordinances as shall be made in the same; and thereto give your Royal assent and authority.

Secondly, that whereas divers of the constitutions, ordinances, and canons, provincial or synodal, which have been heretofore enacted, be thought to be not only much prejudicial to your prerogative Royal, but also overmuch onerous to your Highness' subjects, your clergy aforesaid is contented, if it may stand so with your Highness' pleasure, that they be committed to the examination and judgment of your grace, and of thirty-two persons, whereof sixteen to be of the upper and nether house of the temporalty, and the other sixteen of the clergy, all to be chosen and appointed by your most noble grace. So that, finally, whichsoever of the said constitutions, ordinances, or canons, provincial or synodal, shall be thought and determined by your grace and by the most part of the thirty-two persons not to stand with God's laws and the laws of the realm, the same to be abrogated and taken away by your grace and the clergy; and such of them as shall be seen by your grace, and by the most part of the said thirty-two persons, to stand with God's laws and the laws of your realm, to stand in full strength and power, your grace's most royal assent and authority once impetrate and fully given to the same. (H. Gee and W. T. Hardy, *Documents Illustrative of English Church History,* London, 1896.)

## Act in Restraint of Appeals to Rome. 1533

ALREADY declared free of his union with Catherine and married to Anne Boleyn, Henry now had to deal with an appeal to the Pope by his former wife against the English court's decision. This Act not only denied such appeals but made it treason for anyone to deny the validity of any decision made by an English court. The previous submission of the clergy enabled Henry to enforce such restraints without danger of clerical criticism.

# 19.

An act that the appeals in such cases as have been used to be pursued to the See of Rome shall not be from henceforth had nor used but within this realm.

Where, by divers sundry old authentic histories and chronicles, it is manifestly declared and expressed that this realm of England is an empire, and so hath been accepted in the world, governed by one supreme head and King having the dignity and royal estate of the imperial crown of the same, unto whom a body politic, compact of all sorts and degrees of people divided in terms and by names of spiritualty and temporalty, be bounden and owe to hear next to God a natural and humble obedience, he being instituted and furnished by the goodness ... of Almighty God with ... entire power ... and jurisdiction to render and yield justice and final determination to all manner of folk residents ... within this his realm, in all causes, matters, debates, and contentions ... occurring ... within the limits thereof, without restraint or appeal to any foreign prince or potentates of the world ... :

And whereas the King, his most noble progenitors, and the nobility and commons of this said realm, at divers ... Parliaments ... made sundry ordinances, laws, statutes, and provisions, for the entire and sure conservation of the prerogatives, liberties, and preeminences of the said imperial crown of this realm, and of the jurisdictions spiritual and temporal of the same, to keep it from the annoyance of the See of Rome as well as from that of the authority of other foreign potentates attempting the diminution or violation thereof:

And, notwithstanding the said good statutes and ordinances ... divers and sundry inconveniences and dangers not provided for plainly by the said former acts ... have risen ... by reason of appeals sued out of this realm to the See of Rome, in cases testamentary, of matrimony and divorces, right of tithes, oblations, and obventions ... :

In consideration thereof, the King's highness, his nobles, and commons, considering the great enormities, dangers, long delays, and hurts that as well to his highness as to his said nobles, commons, and residents of this his realm in the said cases ... by the assent of the lords spiritual and temporal and the commons in this Parliament assembled and by authority of the same, enact, establish, and ordain that all cases testamentary, of matrimony and divorces, rights of tithes, oblations, and obventions ... shall be from henceforth heard and adjudged within the King's jurisdiction ... and not elsewhere ...

And it is further enacted ... that, if any person do attempt, move, purchase, or procure from ... the See of Rome, or from any other foreign court out of this realm, any manner of process, inhibitions, appeals, sentences, summons, citations, suspensions, interdictions, excommunications, restraints, or judgments ... or execute any of the same process, or do any act or acts to the impediment, hindrance, or derogation of any process, sentence, judgment, or determination ... made ... in any courts of this realm ... and ... being convicted of the same, for every such default shall incur and run in the same pains, penalties, and forfeitures ordained ... by the *Statute of Provision and Praemunire,*

16 Richard II ... [Such persons were to be placed outside the King's protection and their chattels were to escheat to the crown.] (SR, III, 427: 24 Henry VIII, c.12.)

## First Succession Act. 1534

**20.** THIS was the first of Henry's four Acts for establishing the order of the royal succession. It publicly proclaimed annulment of the Spanish marriage and validation of the union with Anne Boleyn, ordered the succession in Henry's children by Anne, and made it treason to dispute the validity of the Boleyn marriage. The succession was as much a national as a dynastic problem, and Henry's actions were probably viewed with favor by a majority of the English people.

An Act for the establishment of the King's succession.

... We your said most humble and obedient subjects in this present Parliament assembled, calling to our remembrance the great divisions which in times past hath been in this realm by reason of several titles pretended to the imperial Crown of the same, which some times and for the most part ensued by occasion of ambiguity and doubts then not so perfectly declared but that men might upon froward intents expound them to every man's sinister appetite and affection after their sense, contrary to the right legality of the succession and posterity of the lawful kings and emperors of this realm, whereof hath ensued great effusion and destruction of man's blood, as well of a great number of the nobles as of other the subjects and specially inheritors in the same,

And the greatest occasion thereof hath been because no perfect and substantial provision by law hath been made within this realm of itself when doubts and questions have been moved and proponed of the certainty and legality of the succession and posterity of the Crown,

By reason whereof the Bishop of Rome and the See Apostolic, contrary to the great and inviolable grants of jurisdictions given by God immediately to emperors, kings, and princes in succession to their heirs, hath presumed in times past to invest who should please them to inherit in other men's kingdoms and dominions, which thing we your most humble subjects both spiritual and temporal do most abhor and detest,

And sometimes other foreign princes and potentates of sundry degrees, minding rather dissention and discord to continue in the realm to the utter desolation thereof then charity, equity, or unity, have many times supported wrong titles, whereby they might the more easily and facilely aspire to the superiority of the same,

The continuance and sufferance whereof deeply considered and pondered, were too dangerous and perilous to be suffered any longer within this realm, and too much contrary to the unity, peace, and tranquillity of the same, being greatly reproachable and dishonourable to the whole realm:

In consideration whereof your said most humble and obedient subjects the nobles and commons of this realm, calling further to their remembrance that the good unity, peace, and wealth of this realm and the succession of the subjects of the same most specially and principally above all worldly things consisteth and resteth in the certainty and surety of the procreation and posterity of your Highness, in whose most royal person at this present time is no manner of doubt nor question, do therefore most humbly beseech your Highness, that it may please your Majesty that it may be enacted ... that the marriage heretofore solemnized between your Highness and the Lady Catherine, being before lawful wife to Prince Arthur your elder brother, which by him was carnally known, as doth duly appear by sufficient proof in a lawful process had and made before Thomas, [Cranmer] by the sufferance of God now Archbishop of Canterbury and Metropolitan and Primate of all this realm, shall be by authority of this present Parliament definitively, clearly, and absolutely declared, deemed, and adjudged to be against the laws of Almighty God, and also accepted, reputed and taken of no value nor effect but utterly void and annulled, and the separation thereof made by the said Archbishop shall be good and effectual to all intents and purposes; ... and that the said Lady Catherine shall be from henceforth called and reputed only Dowager to Prince Arthur and not Queen of this realm. And that the lawful matrimony had and solemnized between your Highness and your most dear and entirely beloved wife Queen Anne shall be established, and taken for undoubtful, true, sincere and perfect ever hereafter, according to the just judgment of the said Thomas, Archbishop of Canterbury ... whose grounds of judgment have been confirmed as well by the whole clergy of this realm in both the Convocations, and by both the Universities thereof, as by the Universities of Bologna, Padua, Paris, Orleans, Toulouse, Angers, and divers others, and also by the private writings of many right excellent well-learned men; which grounds so confirmed. ...

And also be it enacted by authority aforesaid that all the issue had and procreate ... between your Highness and your said most dearly and entirely beloved wife Queen Anne, shall be your lawful children, and be inheritable and inherit, according to the course of inheritance and laws of this realm, the imperial Crown of the same, with all dignities, honours, preeminences, prerogatives, authorities, and jurisdictions to the same annexed or belonging, in as large and ample manner as your Highness to this present time hath; ... the inheritance thereof to be and remain to your said children and right heirs in manner and form as hereafter shall be declared:

That is to say, first the said imperial Crown and other the premises shall be to your Majesty and to your heirs of your body lawfully begotten; and for default of such heirs, then to the second son of your body and of the body of the said Queen Anne begotten, and to the heirs of the body of the said second son lawfully begotten; and so to every son of your body and of the body of the said Queen Anne begotten, and to the heirs of the body of every such son begotten, according to the course of inheritance in that behalf. And if it should happen your said dear and ... beloved wife Queen Anne to decease without issue male of the body of your Highness to be gotten, which God defend, then the same imperial Crown and all other the premises to be to your Majesty as is aforesaid, and to the son and heir male of your body lawfully begotten and to the heirs of the body of the same son and heir male lawfully begotten; and for default of such issue then to your second son of your body lawfully begotten and to the heirs of the body of the same second son lawfully begotten, and so from son and heir male to son and heir male, and to the heirs of the several bodies of every such son and heir male to be gotten, according to the course of inheritance in like manner and form as is above said,

And for default of such sons of your body begotten, and the heirs of the several bodies of every such sons lawfully begotten, that then the said imperial Crown and other the premises shall be to the issue female between your Majesty and your said most dear and entirely beloved wife Queen Anne begotten, that is to say: First to the eldest issue female, which is the Lady Elizabeth, now princess, and to the heirs of her body lawfully begotten, and for default of such issue then to the second issue female and to the heirs of her body lawfully begotten, and so from issue female to issue female and to their heirs of their bodies one after another by course of inheritance according to their ages, as the Crown of England hath been accustomed and ought to go in cases when there be heirs females to the same, and for default of such issue then the said imperial Crown and all other the premises shall be in the right heirs of your Highness for ever.

And be it further enacted by authority aforesaid, that on this side the first day of May next coming, proclamations shall be made in all shires . . . of the contents of this Act: and if any person or persons . . . after the said first day of May by writing or imprinting or by any exterior act or deed maliciously procure or do . . . any thing or things to the peril of your most royal person, or maliciously give occasion by writing, print, deed, or act whereby your Highness might be disturbed or interrupted of the Crown of this realm, or by writing, print, deed, or act procure or do, or cause to be done, anything . . . to the prejudice, slander, disturbance or derogation of the said lawful matrimony solemnized between your Majesty and the said Queen Anne, or to the peril, slander, or disherison of any the issues and heirs of your Highness being limited by this Act to inherit and to be inheritable to the Crown of this realm in such form as is aforesaid, whereby any such issues or heirs of your Highness might be destroyed, disturbed, or interrupted in body or title of inheritance to the Crown of this realm as to them is limited in this Act in form above rehearsed, that then every such person and persons, . . . for every such offence shall be adjudged high traitors, and every

such offence shall be adjudged high treason, and the offender . . . being lawfully convict of such offence . . . according to the laws and customs of this realm, shall suffer pains of death as in cases of high treason. And that also every such offender, being convict as is aforesaid, shall lose and forfeit to your Highness and to your heirs, kings of this realm, all such manors, lands, tenements, rents, annuities, and hereditaments which they had in possession . . . or were seized of. . . .

And be it further enacted by authority aforesaid, that if any person or persons, after the said first day of May, by any words without writing, or any exterior deed or act, maliciously . . . publish, divulge, or utter any thing . . . to the peril of your Highness, or to the slander or prejudice of the said matrimony solemnized between your Highness and the said Queen Anne, or to the slander or disherison of the issue and heirs of your body begotten and to be gotten of the said Queen Anne or any other your lawful heirs which shall be inheritable to the Crown of this realm as is afore limited by this Act, that then every such offence shall be taken and adjudged for misprison of treason . . . and being thereof lawfully convict . . . shall suffer imprisonment of their bodies at the King's will, and shall lose as well all their goods, chattels, and . . . hereditaments. . . . (SR, III, 471: 25 Henry VIII, c.22.)

## Treasons Act. 1534

**21.** INHERENT in all of Henry VIII's legislation on treason is the absence of any concept of ethics or justice. "Tudor absolutism" in its harshest guise can be seen in this Act, which allowed the definition of treason to hinge upon monarchial caprice. To disagree openly with the King on matters of importance became the most heinous crime under the law. This perversion of the law and the constitution to the service of the Crown was the immediate result of Henry's struggle with the Pope, and in thus seizing the most effective weapons available, Henry clearly exceeded constitutional limits.

An Act whereby divers offences be made high treason, and taking away all sanctuaries for all manner of high treasons.

Forasmuch as it is most necessary, both

for common policy and duty of subjects, above all things to prohibit, provide, restrain, and extinct all manner of shameful slanders, perils, or imminent danger or dangers which might grow, happen, or arise to their Sovereign Lord the King, the Queen, or their heirs ... or shall touch the King, his Queen, their heirs or successors, upon which dependeth the whole unity and universal well being of this realm, without providing wherefor too great a scope of unreasonable liberty should be given to all cankered and traitorous hearts, willers and workers of the same; and also the King's loving subjects should not declare unto their Sovereign Lord now being, which unto them hath been and is most entirely both beloved and esteemed, their undoubted sincerity and truth:

Be it therefore enacted ... that if any person ... after the first day of February next coming, do maliciously wish, will, or desire by words or writing, or by crafty images invent, practice, or attempt any bodily harm to be done or committed to the King's most royal person, the Queen's or their heirs apparent, or to deprive them or any of them of the dignity, title, or name of their royal estates, or slanderously and maliciously publish and pronounce, by express writing or words, that the King our Sovereign Lord should be heretic, schismatic, tyrant, infidel, or usurper of the Crown, or rebelliously do detain, keep, or withold from our said Sovereign Lord, his heirs or successors, any of his or their castles, fortresses ... or holds, within this realm ... or ... detain, keep, or withold from the King's said Highness, his heirs or successors, any of his or their ships, ordnance, artillery, or other munitions or fortifications of war, and do not humbly render and give up to our said Sovereign Lord, his heirs or successors, or to such persons as shall be deputed by them, such castles, fortresses ... holds, ships, ordnance, artillery, and other munitions ... of war rebelliously kept or detained, within six days next after they shall be commanded by our said Sovereign Lord ... by open proclamation under the great seal, then every such person ... so offending in any the premises after the said first day of February, their aiders, counsellors, consenters, and abettors, being thereof lawfully convict according to the laws and customs of this realm, shall be adjudged traitors; and that every such offence in any the premises that shall be committed or done after the said first day of February, shall be reputed, accepted, and adjudged high treason, and the offenders therein, and their aiders and abettors, being lawfully convict of any such offence as is aforesaid, shall have and suffer such pains of death and other penalties as is limited and accustomed in cases of high treason.

And to the intent that all treasons should be the more dread, hated, and detested to be done by any person ... be it therefore enacted by the authority aforesaid that none offender in any kinds of high treasons, whatsoever they be, their aiders, [etc.] ... shall be admitted to have the benefit or privilege of any manner of sanctuary; considering that matters of treasons toucheth so nigh both the surety of the King our Sovereign Lord's person and his heirs and successors. (SR, III, 508: 26 Henry VIII, c.13.)

## Act in Absolute Restraint of Annates. 1534

**22.**

HAVING failed to obtain the desired Papal approval of his marital plans with the *Act in Conditional Restraint of Annates,* Henry carried out his threat by restraining all money payments by the English Church to Rome. Naturally interested in resting the action on precedent, Parliament based this restraint on earlier legislative Acts of 1351, 1353, and 1393. From a constitutional point of view, however, the implication was very clear that regardless of precedent, depredation of private property by the State was no longer restrained by the Common Law.

An Act restraining the payment of Annates to the See of Rome.

[After restating the *Act in Conditional Restraint of Annates* the present Act continues] ... And forasmuch in the said Act it is not plainly and certainly expressed in what manner and fashion archbishops and bishops shall be elected, presented, invested, and consecrated within this realm and in all other the King's dominions:

Be it now therefore enacted ... that the said Act and everything therein contained shall be and stand in strength, virtue and effect; except only that no person nor persons hereafter shall be presented, nominated or commended to the said Bishop of Rome, otherwise called the Pope, or to the See of Rome, to or for the dignity or office of any archbishop or bishop within this realm or in any other the King's dominions, nor shall send nor procure ... any manner of bulls, briefs, palliums, or other things requisite for an archbishop or bishop, nor shall pay any sums of money for annates, firstfruits, or otherwise, for expedition of any such bulls, briefs, or palliums; but that by the authority of this Act such presenting, nominating, or commending to the said Bishop of Rome or to the See of Rome, and such bulls, briefs, palliums, annates, firstfruits, and every other sums of money heretofore limited, accustomed, or used to be paid at the said See of Rome for procuration or expedition of any such bulls, briefs, or palliums, or other thing concerning the same, shall utterly cease and no longer be used within this realm or within any the King's dominions; anything contained in the Act aforementioned, or any use, custom, or prescription to the contrary thereof notwithstanding.

And furthermore be it ordained and established by the authority aforesaid, that at every avoidance of any archbishopric or bishopric within this realm or in any other the King's dominions, the King our Sovereign Lord ... may grant unto the prior and convent or the dean and chapter of the cathedral churches or monasteries where the see of such archbishopric or bishopric shall happen to be void, a licence under the great seal, as of old time hath been accustomed, to proceed to election of an archbishop or bishop of the see so being void, with a letter permissive containing the name of the person which they shall elect and choose; by virtue of which licence the said dean and chapter or prior and convent to whom such licence and letters missives shall be directed, shall with all speed and celerity in due form elect and choose the said person named in the said letters missives ... and if they defer or delay their election above twelve days next after such licence [is] to them delivered, that then for every such default the King's Highness ... at his liberty and pleasure shall nominate and present, by his letters patents under the great seal, such a person to the said office and dignity. ...

And be it further enacted by the authority aforesaid, that if the prior and convent of any monastery or dean and chapter of any cathedral church where the see of any archbishop or bishop is within any of the King's dominions, after such licence as is afore rehearsed shall be delivered to them, proceed not to election and signify the same according to the tenor of this Act within the space of twenty days next after such licence shall come to their hands, or else if any archbishop or bishop within any of the King's dominions, after such election, nomination, or presentation shall be signified unto them by the King's letters patents, shall refuse and do not confirm, invest, and consecrate with all due circumstance as is aforesaid every such person as shall be so elected, nominated, or presented ... within twenty days next after the King's letters patents of such signification or presentation shall come into their hands ... [they] ... shall run into the dangers, pains and penalties of the statute of the provision and *praemunire* made in the twenty-fifth year of the reign of King Edward III, [*Ordinance and Statute of Praemunire. 1353. SR, I, 319: Statute of Provisers. 1351. SR, I, 317.*] and in the sixteenth year of King Richard II. [*Sec-*

*ond Statute of Praemunire.* 1393. SR, II, 85]

[Each of these three Acts speaks specifically of the consequence of disobedience: the offender is put outside the King's protection and his goods and chattels escheated to the crown.] (SR, III, 462: 25 Henry VIII, c.20.)

## Act for the Submission of the Clergy. 1534

**23.**

THIS Act merely gave formal legal substance to the prior submission of the clergy offered by the Convocation in 1532. However, in giving statute form to the previous expression, Parliament placed possible backsliders in a highly untenable legal position, since a charge of statutory treason growing out of such an offense now carried with it the equally dangerous charge of heresy.

An Act for the submission of the Clergy to the King's Majesty.

Where the King's humble and obedient subjects the clergy of this realm of England have not only acknowledged according to the truth that the Convocations of the same clergy is always, hath been, and ought to be assembled only by the King's writ, but also submitting themselves to the King's Majesty hath promised *in verbo sacerdotii* that they will never from henceforth presume to attempt, allege, claim, or put in use, or enact, promulgate, or execute any new canons, constitutions, ordinance provincial, or other ... in the Convocation, unless the King's most royal assent and licence ... be had. . . . :

And where divers constitutions, ordinance, and canons, provincial or synodal, which heretofore have been enacted, and be thought not only to be much prejudicial to the King's prerogative royal and repugnant to the laws and statutes of this realm, but also overmuch onerous to his Highness and his subjects, the said clergy hath most humbly besought the King's Highness that the said constitutions and canons may be committed to the examination of his Highness. . . . :

Be it therefore now enacted by authority of this present Parliament, according to the said submission and petition of the said clergy, that they nor any of them from henceforth shall presume to attempt, allege, claim, or put in use any constitutions or ordinances, provincial or synodal, or any other canons,

nor shall enact, promulgate, or execute any such canons, constitutions, or ordinance ... in their Convocations in time coming ... unless the same clergy may have the King's most royal assent ... upon pain ... to suffer imprisonment and make fine at the King's will. . . .

And be it further enacted ... that ... no manner of appeals shall be had, provoked, or made out of this realm or out of any of the King's dominions to the Bishop of Rome nor to the See of Rome in any causes or matters happening to be in contention ... in any of the courts within this realm ... but that all manner of appeals ... in cases of matrimony, tithes, oblations, and obventions ... shall be made after such manner as such matters are limited in this realm. . . .

And if any person or persons ... provoke or sue any manner of appeals ... to the said Bishop of Rome or to the See of Rome, or do procure or execute any manner of process from the See of Rome or by authority thereof to the derogation or let of the due execution of this Act or contrary to the same, that then every such person or persons so doing ... shall incur and run into the dangers, pains, and penalties contained and limited in the Act of Provision and *Praemunire* made in the sixteenth year of King Richard the second against such as sue to the Court of Rome against the King's crown and prerogative royal. . . . (SR, III, 460: 25 Henry VIII, c.19.)

## Act Annexing Firstfruits and Tenths to the Crown. 1534

**24.**    APPARENTLY in search of a way to rationalize its action, Parliament rested this long
and didactic statute on the poverty of the clergy. Yet the firstfruits and tenths, which,
when given to Rome had supposedly impoverished the churchmen, were now diverted
wholly to the Crown, while clerical funds remained as before. What relationship
existed in Henry's mind between the logical order of the Constitution and the rights
of private property become even more difficult to assay with the passage of this Act.

An Act concerning the payment of First Fruits of all Dignities, Benefices, and Promotions Spiritual; and also concerning one annual Pension of the tenth part of all the Possessions of the Church, Spiritual and Temporal, granted to the King's Highness and his heirs.

Forasmuch as it is and of very duty ought to be the natural inclination of all good people, like most faithful, loving, and obedient subjects, sincerely and willingly to desire to provide not only for the public weal of their native country but also for the support, maintenance, and defence of the royal estate of their most dread, benign, and gracious Sovereign Lord, upon whom and in whom dependeth all their joy and well being... ,

Wherefore his said humble and obedient subjects, as well the Lords spiritual and temporal as the Commons in this present Parliament assembled, calling to their remembrance not only the manifold and innumerable benefits daily administered by his Highness to them all, and to the residue of all other his subjects of this realm, but also how long time his Majesty hath most victoriously by his high wisdom and policy protected, defended, and governed this his realm and maintained his people and subjects of the same tranquillity, peace, unity, quietness, and welfare; and also considering what great, excessive, and inestimable charges his Highness hath heretofore been at and sustained by the space of five and twenty whole years, and also daily sustaineth for the maintenance, tuition, and defence of this his realm and his loving subjects of the same, which

cannot be sustained and borne without some honourable provision and remedy may be found, provided, and ordained for the maintenance thereof, do therefore desire and most humbly pray that for the more surety of continuance and augmentation of his Highness's royal estate, being not only now recognised ... the only Supreme Head in earth next and immediately under God of the Church of England, but also their most assured and undoubted natural sovereign liege Lord and King, having the whole governance, tuition, defence, and maintenance of this his realm and most loving, obedient subjects of the same:

It may therefore be ordained and enacted by his Highness and the Lords spiritual and temporal and the Commons in this present Parliament assembled and by authority of the same in manner and form following; that is to say, that the King's Highness, his heirs and successors kings of this realm, shall have and enjoy from time to time, to endure for ever, of every person and persons which at any time after the first day of January next coming shall be nominated, elected, prefected, presented, collated, or by any other means appointed to have any archbishopric, bishopric, abbacy, monastery, priory, college, hospital, archdeaconry, deanery, provostship, prebend, parsonage, vicarage, chantry, free chapel, or other dignity, benefice, office, or promotion spiritual within this realm ... of what name, nature, or quality soever they be or to whose foundation, patronage, or gift soever they belong, the firstfruits, revenues, and profits for one year of every such archbishopric, bishopric, abbacy, [etc.] ... whereunto any such person ... shall after the said first day of January be nominated, [etc.] ... and that every such person ... before any actual or real possession or meddling with the profits of any such archbishopric, bishopric, [etc.] ... shall satisfy, content, and pay, or compound or agree to pay to the King's use at reasonable days upon good sureties the said firstfruits and profits for one year. ... ,

And over this be it enacted by authority aforesaid that the King's Majesty, his heirs and successors kings of this realm, for more augmentation and maintenance of the royal estate of his imperial Crown and dignity of Supreme Head of the Church of England, shall yearly have, take, enjoy, and perceive, united and knit to his imperial Crown for ever, one yearly rent or pension amounting to the value of the tenth part of all the revenues, rents ... tithes, offerings, emoluments, and of all other profits, as well called spiritual as temporal, now appertaining or belonging or that hereafter shall belong to any archbishopric, bishopric, [etc.] ... within any diocese of this realm or in Wales; the said pension or annual rent to be yearly paid for ever to our said Sovereign Lord. ... (SR, III, 493: 26 Henry VIII, c.3.)

## Act of Supremacy. 1534

## 25.

EXCEPT for adding the right of visitation to Henry's list of new prerogatives in Church control, the *Act of Supremacy* has little constitutional significance. The Acts dealing with annates and appeals to Rome had already stripped the Pope of all authority in the English Church. The high-sounding title of "Supreme Head in Earth of the Church of England" was mere legalistic window dressing, intended to give Henry's Reformation measures a national tone calculated to win sympathy and hold allegiance within the realm.

An Act concerning the King's Highness to be Supreme Head of the Church of England and to have Authority to Reform and Redress all errors, heresies, and abuses in the same.

Albeit the King's Majesty justly and rightfully is and ought to be the Supreme Head of the Church of England, and so is recognised by the clergy of this realm in their Convocations; yet nevertheless for corroboration and confirmation thereof, and for increase of virtue in Christ's religion within this realm of England, and to repress and extirp all errors, heresies, and other enormities and abuses heretofore used in the same:

Be it enacted by authority of this present Parliament that the King our Sovereign Lord, his heirs and successors kings of this realm, shall be taken, accepted, and reputed the only Supreme Head in earth of the Church of England called *Anglicana Ecclesia,* and shall have and enjoy annexed and united to the imperial Crown of this realm as well the title and style thereof, as all honours, dignities, preeminences, jurisdictions, privileges, authorities, immunities, profits, and commodities, to the said dignity of Supreme Head of the same Church belonging and appertaining:

And that our said Sovereign Lord, his heirs and successors kings of this realm, shall have full power and authority from time to time to visit, repress, redress, reform, order, correct, restrain, and amend all such errors, heresies, abuses, offences, contempts, and enormities, whatsoever they be, which by any manner spiritual authority or jurisdiction ought or may lawfully be reformed, repressed, ordered, redressed, corrected, restrained, or amended, most to the pleasure of Almighty God, the increase of virtue in Christs religion, and for the conservation of the peace, unity, and tranquillity of this realm: any usage, custom, foreign laws, foreign authority, prescription, or any other thing or things to the contrary hereof notwithstanding. (SR, III, 492: 26 Henry VIII, c.1.)

## Dispensations Act. 1534

**26.** OSTENSIBLY to forbid Peter's pence payments to the Pope (they had been legally outlawed by the *Act of Annates* without specific mention), this Act shows how little doctrinal reform was originally planned. The King and his people, says the Act, do not intend "to decline or vary from the congregation of Christ's Church in any things concerning the very articles of the Catholic faith."

An Act for the exoneration from exactions paid to the See of Rome.

Most humbly beseech your most Royal Majesty your obedient and faithful subjects the Commons of this your present Parliament assembled by your most dread commandment:

That where your subjects of this your realm, and of other countries and dominions being under your obeisance, by many years past have been and yet be greatly impoverished by such intolerable exactions of great sums of money as have been claimed and taken and yet continually be claimed to be taken out of this your realm ... by the Bishop of Rome called Pope, and the See of Rome, as well in pensions, Peter pence, procurations, fruits, suits for provisions, and expeditions of bulls for archbishoprics and bishoprics and for delegacies, and rescripts in causes of contentions and appeals, jurisdictions legatine, and also for dispensations, licences, faculties, grants, relaxations, ... and other infinite sorts of bulls, briefs, and instruments of sundry natures, names, and kinds in great numbers henceforth practised and obtained ... wherein the Bishop of Rome aforesaid hath not been only to be blamed for his usurpations in the premises but also for his abusing and beguiling your subjects, pretending and persuading them that he hath full power to dispense with all human laws, uses, and customs of all realms in all causes which be called spiritual, which matter hath been usurped and practised by him and his predecessors by many years in great derogation of your imperial Crown and authority royal, contrary to right and conscience; for where this your Grace's realm, recognizing

no superior under God but only your Grace, hath been and is free from subjection to any man's laws, but only to such as have been devised, made, and ordained within this realm for the welfare of the same, or to such other as by sufferance of your Grace and your progenitors the people of this your realm have taken at their free liberty by their own consent to be used amongst them, and have bound themselves by long use and custom to the observance of the same ... as to the accustomed and ancient laws of this realm originally established as laws of the same by the said sufferance, consents, and customs, and none other:

It standeth therefore with natural equity and good reason that in all and every such laws human, made within this realm or induced into this realm by the said sufferance, consents, and customs, your Royal Majesty and your Lords spiritual and temporal and Commons, representing the whole state of your realm in this your most high Court of Parliament, have full power and authority not only to dispense but also to authorize some elect person or persons to dispense with those and all other human laws of this your realm and with every one of them....

It may therefore please your most noble Majesty for the honour of Almighty God and for the tender love, zeal, and affection that you bear and always have borne to the wealth of this your realm and subjects of the same, forasmuch as your Majesty is Supreme Head of the Church of England, as the prelates and clergy of your realm representing the said Church in their synods and convocations have recognized, [by the Submission of the Clergy] in whom consisteth full power and authority upon all such laws as have been made and used within this realm, to ordain and enact by the assent of your Lords spiritual and temporal and the Commons in this year present Parliament assembled and by authority of the same, that no person or persons of this your realm or any other your dominions shall from henceforth pay any pensions, censes, portions, Peter pence, or any other impositions to the use of the said Bishop or of the See of Rome . . . but that all such pensions, portions, and Peter pence . . . shall from henceforth clearly surcease and never more be levied, taken, perceived, nor paid to any person or persons in any manner of wise. . . .

And be it further enacted by the authority aforesaid that neither your Highness, your heirs nor successors, kings of this realm, nor any your subjects of this realm nor of any other your dominions, shall henceforth sue to the said Bishop of Rome called the Pope, or to the See of Rome, or to any person or persons having or pretending any authority by the same, for licences, dispensations, compositions, faculties, grants, rescripts, delegacies, or any other instruments or writings of what kind, name, nature, or quality so ever they be of, for any cause or matter for the which [any of the above mentioned instruments] . . . heretofore hath been used and accustomed to be had and obtained at the See of Rome or by authority thereof . . . nor for any [of these instruments] . . . that in cases of necessity may lawfully be granted without offending the Holy Scriptures and laws of God; but that from henceforth every such [instrument] . . . necessary for your Highness, your heirs and successors, and your and their people and subjects, upon the due examinations of the causes and qualities of the persons procuring such [instruments] . . . shall be granted, had, and obtained from time to time within this your realm and . . . not elsewhere in the manner and form following and none otherwise, that is to say:

The Archbishop of Canterbury for the time being and his successors shall have power and authority from time to time by their discretions to give, grant, and dispose by an instrument under the seal of the said Archbishop unto your Majesty and to your heirs and successors kings of this realm, as well all manner of licences, dispensations, [and other instruments] . . . for causes not being contrary or repugnant to the Holy Scriptures and laws of God, as heretofore hath been used and accustomed to be had and obtained by your Highness or any your most noble progenitors, or any of your or their subjects, at the See of Rome . . . so that the said Archbishop or any of his successors in no manner of wise shall grant any dispensation, licence, rescript, or any other writing afore rehearsed for any cause or matter repugnant to the law of Almighty God.

. . . . . .

Provided always that this Act nor any thing or things therein contained shall be hereafter interpreted or expounded that your Grace, your nobles and subjects, intend by the same to decline or vary from the congregation of Christ's Church in any things concerning the very articles of the Catholic Faith of Christendom; or in any other things declared by Holy Scripture and the word of God necessary for your and their salvations. . . .

Provided always that the said Archbishop of Canterbury or any other person or persons shall have no power or authority by reason of this Act to visit or vex any monasteries, abbeys, priories, colleges, hospitals, houses, or other places religious which be or were exempt [from visitation by the Bishop of the diocese] before the making of this Act . . . but that . . . visitation . . . shall be had by the King's Highness, his heirs and successors, by commission under the great seal to be directed to such persons as shall be appointed . . . for the same . . . so that no visitation nor confirmation shall from henceforth be had nor made in or at any such [of the institutions as named above] . . . by the said Bishop of Rome nor by any of his authority nor by any one out of the King's dominions; nor that any person religious or other resident in any of the King's dominions shall from henceforth depart out of the King's dominions to or for any visitation, congregation, or assembly for religion, but that all such visitations, [etc.]...shall be within the King's dominions. (SR, III, 464: 25 Henry VIII, c.21.)

## Act for the Establishing of the Court of Augmentations. 1536

**27.** THE Court of Augmentations was a unique constitutional device for overseeing and directing Crownwards the flow of wealth which would result from confiscation of Church property. Since the Court was brought into being prior to the dissolution of the greater monasteries, it is apparent that Henry's plan for destruction of the economic fabric of the Church had evolved before the series of statutes was drawn up which gave the plan its substance. This statute did not merely create the useless structure of another court system. The churchmen, realizing the extent of Henry's forthcoming expropriations, were already in the process of transferring properties and obscuring titles in order to conceal ownership.

An Act establishing the Court of Augmentations.

.... For the more surety... that the King's Majesty, his heirs and successors, shall be yearly as well as truly and justly answered, contented, and paid of the rents, ferms, issues, revenues, and profits rising, coming, and growing of the said manors, lands, tenements, and other hereditaments before specified, [in the *Act for the Dissolution of the Lesser Monasteries* which is reiterated in the first paragraph of this Act] as of goods, chattels, plate, stuff of household, debts, money, stock, store, and other whatsoever profit and commodity given, granted, or appointed to the King's Majesty by the same, in such court, place, form, manner, and condition as hereafter shall be limited, declared, and appointed:

Be it enacted... in manner and form as hereafter followeth in articles, that is to say: First, the King our said Sovereign Lord, by authority aforesaid, ordaineth, maketh, establisheth, and erecteth a certain court commonly to be called the Court of the Augmentations of the Revenues of the King's Crown; which Court by authority aforesaid continually shall be a court of record, and shall have one great seal and one privy seal to be engraved and made after such form, fashion, and manner as shall be appointed by the King's Highness, and shall remain and be ordered as hereafter shall be declared.

Also be it enacted by authority aforesaid that there shall be one certain person, to be named and assigned by the King's Highness, which shall be Chancellor of the said Court ... [who] shall have the keeping of the said great seal and privy seal to be assigned for the said Court. Also there shall be one person to be named by the King's Highness, which shall be called the King's Treasurer of the Court... and [he] shall be the second officer of the same Court.

Also it is ordained by authority aforesaid, that there shall be one person learned in the laws of the land to be named by the King's Highness, which shall be called the King's Attorney of the said Court, and [he] shall be the third officer of the same Court. Also that there shall be one person to be named by the King's Highness, which shall be called the King's Solicitor of the same Court, and [he] shall be the fourth officer of the Court. Also that there shall be ten particular auditors to be named by the King's Highness, which shall be called Auditors of the Revenues of the said Augmentations. Also there shall be 17 particular receivers to be named by the King's Highness, which shall be called Receivers of the said Revenues. Also that there shall be one person to be named by the

King's Highness, which shall be called Clerk of the said Court, and one other person which shall be Usher ... and one ... which shall be called Messenger of the same Court ... [both of] which shall be named by the King's Highness. ...

Also be it enacted by authority aforesaid, that all the said monasteries, priories, and other religious houses which be dissolved and come or shall come to the King's Highness by the Act aforesaid, and all the manors, lands, tenements, rents, services, tithes, pensions, portions, advowsons, patronages, and all hereditaments appertaining or belonging to any the said monasteries, priories, or other religious houses, shall be in the order, survey, and governance of the said Court and of the officers and ministers thereof, and all the ferms [rent income derived from leasing church land], issues, revenues, and profits coming and growing of the premises or any part thereof, shall be taken and received to the King's use by the ministers and officers of the same Court in manner and form as hereafter shall be declared. ... (SR, III, 569: 27 Henry VIII, c.27.)

## Second Succession Act. 1536

## 28.

THIS statute is significant for two reasons: it shows the extreme malleability of both constitution and Parliament in the hands of Henry VIII, and it adds the final incredible touch to the growing list of Henry's statutory treasons. In this Act, any expression of the validity of the Boleyn marriage was made a treasonable offense. However, the pattern of the royal succession here begins to assume an order. Since neither Mary, daughter of Catherine, nor Elizabeth, daughter of Anne Boleyn, were "lawfully begotten," they were excluded from the right of succession. Any threat by any of the "children or heirs" of the King to the person or position of the individual who would eventually succeed him was forejudged as treason.

An Act for the establishment of the Succession of the Imperial Crown of this Realm.

[After reciting and repealing the *First Succession Act,* and the *Act for an Oath of Succession,* this Act continues]

... And over this, most gracious Sovereign Lord, forasmuch as it hath pleased your most royal Majesty, notwithstanding the great and intolerable perils and occasions which your Highness hath suffered and sustained, as well by occasion of your first unlawful marriage between your Highness and the Lady Catherine, late Princess Dowager, as by occasion of the said unlawful marriage between your Highness and the said late Queen Anne, at the most humble petition and intercession of us your nobles of this realm, for the ardent love and fervent affection which your Highness beareth to the conservation of the peace and unity of the same and for the good and quiet governance thereof, of your most excellent goodness to enter into marriage again, and have chosen and taken a right noble, virtuous, and excellent Lady, Queen Jane, to your true and lawful wife, and have lawfully celebrated and solemnized marriage with her according to the laws of Holy Church, who for her convenient years, excellent beauty, and pureness of flesh and blood is apt, God willing, to conceive issue by your Highness, which marriage is so pure and sincere, without spot, doubt, or impediment, that the issue procreated under the same, when it shall please Almighty God to send it, cannot be lawfully, truly, nor justly interrupted or disturbed of the right and title in the succession of your Crown:

It may therefore now please your most gracious Majesty, at the most humble petition and intercession of us your Nobles and Commons in this present Parliament assembled, as well for the clear extinguishment of all ambiguities and doubts as for a pure and perfect unity of us your most humble and obedient subjects and of all our posterities, that it may be enacted:

[The royal marriage with Catherine of Spain is null and void. The child of this union is declared illegitimate and unfit for the succession. The royal marriage with Anne Boleyn is null and void and the child of that marriage is illegitimate and unfit for the succession. The succession is given to the male heirs issue of the present union with Jane Seymour. Should there be none such the crown is to go next to male heirs "by any other lawful wife," and thereafter to the female heirs issue of the present marriage in the order of their birth.]

And forasmuch as it standeth at this present time in the pleasure and will of Almighty God only whether your Majesty shall have heirs begotten and procreated between your Highness and your said most dear and beloved wife Queen Jane, or else any lawful heirs and issues hereafter of your own body begotten by any other lawful wife, and if such heirs should fail . . . and no provision made in your life who should rule and govern this realm for lack of such heirs, that then this realm after your life shall be destitute of a Governor, or else perhaps encumbered with such a person that would covet to aspire to the same whom the subjects of this realm shall not find in their hearts to love, dread, and obediently serve as their Sovereign Lord; and if your Grace, afore it may be certainly known whether ye shall have heirs or no, should suddenly name and declare any person or persons to succeed after your decease and for lack of heirs of your body lawfully begotten into the royal estate of the imperial Crown of this realm, then it is to be doubted that such person that should be so named might happen to take great heart and courage and by presumption fall into disobedience and rebellion; by occasion of which premises great division and dissension may be and is very likely to arise and spring in this realm, to the great peril and destruction of us your most humble and obedient subjects and of all our posterities,

if remedy for the same should not be provided:

For reformation and remedy whereof, we your most bounden and loving subjects, most obediently knowledging that your Majesty most victoriously, prudently, politicly, and indifferently hath maintained, defended, governed, and ruled this realm in good peace, rest, quietness, and obedience during all the time of your most gracious reign, which we most heartily desire might continue for ever, putting all our whole trust and confidence in your Highness and nothing doubting but your Majesty, if ye should fail of heirs of your body lawfully begotten . . . for the hearty love and fervent affection that ye bear to this realm, and for avoiding all the occasions of division afore rehearsed, so earnestly mindeth the wealth of the same that ye can best and most prudently provide such a Governor for us and this your realm as shall and will succeed and follow in the just and right tract of all your proceedings, and maintain, keep, and defend the same, and all the laws and ordinances established in your gracious time for the wealth of this realm, which all we desire, whereby we your most loving and obedient subjects and our heirs and successors shall and may live, as near as may be, in as good peace, unity, and obedience after your decease as we have lived in the time of your most gracious reign; do therefore most humbly beseech your Highness that it may be enacted, for avoiding of all ambiguities, doubts, divisions, and occasions in that behalf, by your most royal Majesty, by the same assent of us the Lords spiritual and temporal and the Commons in this your present Parliament assembled and by authority of the same, that your Highness shall have full and total power and authority to give, dispose, appoint, assign, declare, and limit, by your letters patents under your great seal or else by your last Will made in writing and signed with your most gracious hand, at your pleasure from time to time hereafter, the imperial Crown of this realm and all other the premises thereunto belonging, to be, remain, succeed, and come after your decease, and for lack of lawful heirs of your body to be procreated and begotten as is afore limited by this Act, to such person or persons in possession and remainder as shall please your Highness, and according to such estate and after such manner, form, fashion, order, and condition, as shall be expressed, declared, named, and limited in your said letters patents or by your said last Will. And we your most humble and obedient subjects do faithfully promise to your Majesty, by one common assent, that after your decease and for lack of heirs of your body lawfully begotten as is afore rehearsed, we our heirs and successors shall accept and take, love, dread, serve, and obey such person and persons, males, or females, as your Majesty shall give your said imperial Crown unto by authority of this Act, and to none other, and wholly to stick to them, as true and faithful subjects ought to do to their regal rulers, governors, and supreme heads. . . .

And it is further enacted by authority aforesaid, that if any of your heirs or children hereafter do usurp the one of them upon the other in the Crown of this realm, or claim or challenge your said imperial Crown in any other form or degree of descent or succession than is afore limited by this Act, or if any person or persons to whom it shall please your Highness of your most excellent goodness by authority of this Act to give and dispose your said Crown and dignity of this realm, or the heirs of any of them, do at any time hereafter demand, challenge, or claim your said Crown . . . otherwise or in any other course, form, degree, or condition than the same shall be given, disposed, and limited unto them by your Highness by virtue and authority of this Act; or if any such person or persons to whom your Majesty shall hereafter give or dispose your said Crown by authority of this Act, or any of their heirs, do interrupt or let any of the heirs of your Majesty that is or shall be begotten, born, and procreated under your . . . marriage . . . between your Highness and . . .

Queen Jane, or any other your lawful heirs hereafter to be begotten of your body by any other lawful marriage, peaceably and quietly to keep, have, and enjoy the said imperial Crown and other the premises by course of inheritance according to the limitation thereof expressed and declared by this Act, that then all and singular the offenders in any of the premises contrary to this Act . . . shall be deemed . . . high traitors to the realm; and . . . for every offence shall suffer such judgment and pains of death, losses, and forfeitures of lands, goods, and privileges of sanctuary as in any cases of high treason; and over that, as well as your said heirs and children, as every such person and persons to whom your Highness shall limit your said Crown in form as is aforesaid, and every of their heirs, for every such offence above specified by them or any of them to be committed, shall lose and forfeit as well all such right, title, and interest that they may claim . . . to the Crown of this realm. . . .

And be it further enacted . . . that if any person . . . by words, writing, imprinting, or by any exterior act or deed . . . procure . . . or cause to be done . . . to the prejudice, slander, disturbance, or derogation of the said lawful matrimony solemnized between your Majesty and the said Queen Jane or any other your lawful wife or wives hereafter by your Highness to be taken, or to the peril, slander, or disherison of any of the issues and heirs of your Highness being limited by this Act to inherit and to be inheritable to the Crown of this realm in such form as is aforesaid . . . or if any person . . . by words, writing, imprinting . . . accept or take, judge or believe, any of the marriages had and solemnized between the King's Highness and the said Lady Catherine, or between the King's Highness and the said late Queen Anne, to be good, lawful, or of any effect . . . or by words, writing, print, or any other exterior act, directly or indirectly, take, accept, name, or call . . . any of the children born and procreated under any of the said unlawful marriages to be legitimate and lawful children of your Majesty; or if any person . . . craftily imagine, invent, or attempt . . . to deprive the King's Highness, the Queen, or the heirs of their bodies begotten, or any other the heirs of the King's body lawfully begotten, or any person . . . to whom the King's Highness shall dispose, give, and limit the Crown of this realm by authority of this Act, of any of their titles, styles, names, degrees, or royal estates or regal power; or if any person . . . being required or commanded by the King's Highness or by such persons as shall be authorized by his Grace or his lawful heirs to make or take an oath to answer

such questions and interrogatories as shall be asked of them, upon any clause, article, sentence, or word contained in this Act, do . . . refuse to make or take such oath . . . that then every such person and persons . . . for every such offence afore declared shall be adjudged high traitors, and that every such offence afore specified shall be adjudged high treason. . . .

[The last paragraph of the Act states that all subjects are to abide by the Act by taking a formal oath of obedience which is appended to the Act.] (SR, III, 655: 28 Henry VIII, c.7.)

## Beggars Act. 1536

**29.** THE ACT OF 1536 has been interpreted in two ways: as a further logical step in dealing with the increasing problem of the poor, and as a direct result of the curtailing of the Church's charitable functions. Whatever the need, the Act applied a principle heretofore not active in the law; each parish became responsible for the maintenance of its own indigent. This responsibility was met through enforced local collections for the support of the poor and by putting "valiant vagabonds" to work.

[After reference to paragraph three of the *Beggars Act* of 1531, 22 Henry VIII, c.12., the present Act continues]

. . . And forasmuch as it was not provided in the said Act how . . . the said poor people and sturdy vagabonds should be ordered at their . . . coming into their own countries, nor how the inhabitants of every hundred should be charged for the relief of the same poor people, nor yet for the setting and keeping in work and labor of the aforesaid valiant vagabonds at their said repair into the hundred . . . it is therefore now ordained and established and enacted. . . .

That all the governors and ministers of cities, shires, towns, and hundreds . . . shall not only succor, find, and keep all and every of the same poor people by way of voluntary and charitable alms . . . in such wise as none of them of necessity shall be compelled to wander idly and go openly in begging to ask alms in any of the same cities, shires, towns, and parishes; but also to cause and to compel all and every the said sturdy vagabonds

and valiant beggars to be set and kept to continual labor, in such wise as by their said labors they and every of them may get their own livings with the continual labor of their own hands. . . .

It is ordained and enacted . . . that all and every the mayors, governors, and head officers of every city, borough, and town corporate and the churchwardens or two others of every parish of this realm shall in good and charitable wise take such discreet and convenient order, by gathering and procuring of such charitable and voluntary alms of the good Christian people within the same with boxes every Sunday, Holy, and other Festival Day or otherwise among themselves, in such good and discreet wise as the poor, impotent, lame, feeble, sick, and diseased people, being not able to work, may be provided, holpen, and relieved, so that in no wise they nor none of them be suffered to go openly in begging; and that such as be lusty or having their limbs strong enough to labor may be daily kept in continual labor, whereby

every one of them may get their own substance and living with their own hands. . . .

It is enacted . . . that every preacher, parson, vicar, curate of this realm, as well in all
and every their sermons . . . biddings of the
beads, as in time of all confessions, and at
the making of the wills or testaments of any
persons, at all times of the year shall exhort,
move, stir, and provoke people to be liberal,
and bountifully to extend their good and
charitable alms and contributions from time
to time for and toward the comfort and relief of the said poor, impotent, decrepit, indigent, and needy people, as for the setting
and keeping to continual work and labor of
the foresaid . . . sturdy vagabonds and valiant
beggars in every city, ward, town, hundred,
and parish of this realm as well within liberties as without.

And for the avoiding of all such inconveniences and infections as oftentime have
and daily do chance amongst the people by
common and open doles, and that most commonly unto such doles many persons do re-

sort which have no need of the same, it is
therefore enacted . . . that no manner of person . . . shall make . . . any such common or
open dole, or shall give any ready money in
alms, otherwise than to the common boxes
and common gatherings . . . upon pain to lose
and forfeit ten times the value of all such
ready money as shall be given in alms contrary to the tenor and purpose of the same.
And that every person or persons of this
realm, bodies politic, corporate, and others
that be bound or charged yearly, monthly, or
weekly to give or to distribute any ready
money, bread, victual, or other sustentation
to poor people in any place within this realm,
shall . . . give and distribute the same money
or the value of all such bread, victual, or sustentation unto such common boxes, to the
intent the same may be employed towards
the relieving of the said poor, needy, sick,
sore, and indigent persons, and also toward
the setting in work of the said sturdy and
idle vagabonds and valiant beggars. . . . (SR,
III, 558: 27 Henry VIII, c.25.)

## Act against the Papal Authority. 1536

NO constitutional concept was established or new principle applied by this Act. In
a sense it was Parliamentary "busy work," directed at relieving the domestic feeling of
frustration at having elicited so little response from Rome by previous Acts. The tone
of the Act is more petulant than legalistic. (Its conscious crudeness may be seen as a
kind of precedent for the earthy language of Puritan theological discussion in the 17th
century.)

**30.**

An Act extinguishing the authority of the
Bishop of Rome.

Forasmuch as notwithstanding the good
and wholesome laws, ordinances, and statutes
heretofore enacted, made, and established . . .
for the extirpation, abolition, and extinguishment, out of this realm and other his
Grace's dominions, seignories, and countries,
of the pretended power and usurped authority of the Bishop of Rome, by some called
the Pope, used within the same or elsewhere
concerning the same realm, dominions,
seignories, or countries, which did obfuscate
and wrest God's holy word and testament a

long season from the spiritual and true meaning thereof, to his worldly and carnal affections, as pomp, glory, avarice, ambition, and
tyranny, covering and shadowing the same
with his human and politic devices, traditions, and inventions, set forth to promote
and establish his only dominion, both upon
the souls and also the bodies and goods of all
Christian people, excluding Christ out of his
kingdom and rule of man his soul as much
as he may, and all other temporal kings and
princes out of their dominions which they
ought to have by God's law upon the bodies
and goods of their subjects; whereby he did

not only rob the King's Majesty, being only the Supreme Head of this his realm of England immediately under God, of his honor, right, and preeminence due unto him by the law of God, but spoiled this his realm yearly of innumerable treasure, and with the loss of the same deceived the King's loving and obedient subjects, persuading to them, by his laws, bulls, and other his deceivable means, such dreams, vanities, and phantasies as by the same many of them were seduced and conveyed unto superstitious and erroneous opinions; so that the King's Majesty, the Lords spiritual and temporal, and the Commons in this realm, being overwearied and fatigued with the experience of the infinite abominations and mischiefs proceeding of his impostures and craftily coloring of his deceits, to the great damage of souls, bodies, and goods, were forced of necessity for the public weal of this realm to exclude that foreign pretended power, jurisdiction, and authority, used and usurped within this realm, and to devise such remedies for their relief in the same as doth not only redound to the honor of God, the high praise and advancement of the King's Majesty and of his realm, but also to the great and inestimable utility of the same; and notwithstanding the said wholesome laws so made and heretofore established, yet it is come to the knowledge of the King's Highness and also to divers and many his loving, faithful, and obedient subjects, how that divers seditious and contentious persons, being imps [followers] of the said Bishop of Rome and his See, and in heart members of his pretended monarchy, do in corners and elsewhere, as they dare, whisper, inculcate, preach, and persuade, and from time to time instill into the ears and

heads of the poor, simple, and unlettered people the advancement and continuance of the said Bishop's feigned and pretended authority, pretending the same to have his ground and original of God's law, whereby the opinions of many be suspended, their judgments corrupted and deceived, and diversity in opinions augmented and increased, to the great displeasure of Almighty God, the high discontentation of our said most dread Sovereign Lord, and the interruption of the unity, love, charity, concord, and agreement that ought to be in a Christian region and congregation:

For avoiding whereof, and repression of the follies of such seditious persons as be the means and authors of such inconveniences, be it enacted, ordained, and established by the Lords and Commons in this present Parliament that if any person ... dwelling, inhabiting, or resident within this realm or within any other the King's dominions, [etc.] ... of whatever estate, dignity, [etc.] ... shall, by writing, printing, preaching, or teaching, deed, or act ... hold or stand with to extol, set forth, maintain, or defend the authority, jurisdiction, or power of the Bishop of Rome or of his See, heretofore used, claimed, or usurped within this realm ... for every such default and offence shall incur and run into the dangers, penalties, pains, and forfeitures ordained and provided by [the *Second Statute of Praemunire*, 1393] ... against such as attempt, procure, or make provision to the See of Rome or elsewhere for any thing ... to the derogation, or contrary to the prerogative royal or jurisdiction, of the Crown and dignity of the realm. (SR, III, 663: 28 Henry VIII, c.10.)

## Act for the Dissolution of the Lesser Monasteries. 1536

31.

THIS statute was the first blow struck at the monasteries, which were considered the centers of secret Church defiance. In it, special "visitors" were commissioned to inspect the monasteries, and these investigators knew full well what they were expected to report. The brevity of their visitations, the failure to visit more than one-quarter of the existing religious houses, and the absence of opportunity for the monks to defend themselves against charges of vice, improvidence, and "abominable living" robbed the visitations of any semblance of judicial procedure. Henry's desperate haste to complete the task of dismantling the Church forced both himself and Parliament to operate outside the constitution they claimed to defend.

An Act whereby all Religious Houses of monks, canons, and nuns which may not dispend manors, lands, tenements, and hereditaments above the clear yearly value of £200 are given to the King's Highness, his heirs and successors, for ever.

Forasmuch as manifest sin, vicious, carnal, and abominable living, is daily used and committed amongst the little and small abbeys, priories, and other religious houses of monks, canons, and nuns, where the congregation of such religious persons is under the number of twelve persons, whereby the governors of such religious houses ... spoil, destroy, consume, and utterly waste, as well their churches, monasteries, priories, principal houses, farms, granges, lands, tenements, and hereditaments, as the ornaments of their churches and their goods and chattels, to the high displeasure of Almighty God, slander of good religion, and to the great infamy of the King's Highness and the realm if redress should not be had thereof; and albeit that many continual visitations hath been heretofore had by the space of two hundred years and more for an honest and charitable reformation of such unthrifty, carnal, and abominable living, yet nevertheless little or none amendment is hitherto had, but their vicious living shamelessly increaseth and augmenteth, and by a cursed custom so rooted and infected that a great multitude of the religious persons in such small houses do rather choose to rove abroad in apostasy than to conform to the observation of good religion; so that without such small houses be utterly suppressed and the religious persons therein committed to great and honorable monasteries of religion in this realm, where they may be compelled to live religiously for reformation of their lives, there can else be no reformation in this behalf:

In consideration whereof the King's most

Royal Majesty, being supreme Head in earth under God of the Church of England, daily finding and devising the increase, advancement, and exaltation of true doctrine and virtue in the said Church, to the only glory and honor of God and the total extirpation and destruction of vice and sin, having knowledge that the premises be true, as well by the reports of his late visitations as by sundry credible informations, considering also that divers and great solemn monasteries of this realm wherein ... religion is well kept and observed, be destitute of such full numbers of religious persons as they ought and may keep, hath thought good that a plain declaration should be made of the premises as well to the Lords spiritual and temporal as to other his loving subjects of the Commons in this present Parliament assembled; whereupon the said Lords and Commons by a great deliberation finally be resolved that it is and shall be much more to the pleasure of Almighty God and for the honor of this his realm that the possessions of such spiritual religious houses, now being spent, spoiled, and wasted for increase and maintenance of sin, should be used and converted to better uses, and the unthrifty religious persons so spending the same to be compelled to reform their lives; and thereupon most humbly desire the King's Highness that it may be enacted by authority of this present Parliament, that his Majesty shall have and enjoy to him and to his heirs for ever all and singular such monasteries, priories, and other religious houses of monks, canons, and nuns, of what kinds or diversities of habits, rules, or orders so ever they be called or named, which have not in lands and tenements, rents, tithes, portions, and other hereditaments, above the clear yearly value of two hundred pounds; and in like manner shall have and enjoy all the sites and circuits of every such religious houses, and all and singular the manors, granges, . . . lands, tenements, reversions, rents, services, tithes, pensions, portions, churches, chapels, advowsons, patronages, annuities, rights, entries, conditions, and other hereditaments appertaining or belonging to every such monastery, priory, or other religious house, not having as is aforesaid above the said clear yearly value of two hundred pounds. . . . And that also his Highness shall have to him . . . all and singular such monasteries, priories, and other religious houses which, at any time within one year next afore the making of this Act, hath been given and granted to his Majesty by any abbot, prior, abbess, or prioress under their convent seals, or that otherwise had been suppressed or dissolved; and all and singular the manors, lands, tenements, [etc.] . . . to the same monasteries, abbeys, and priories or to any of them appertaining or belonging; to have and to hold all and singular the premises with all their rights, profits, jurisdictions, and commodities, unto the King's Majesty and to his heirs and assigns for ever, to do and use therewith his or their own wills to the pleasure of Almighty God and to the honor and profit of this realm.

. . . . And it is also enacted by authority aforesaid, that the King's Highness shall have and enjoy to his own proper use all the ornaments, jewels, goods, chattels, and debts which appertained to any of the chief governors of the said monasteries or religious houses. . . .

. . . . In consideration of which premises to be had to his Highness and to his heirs as is aforesaid, his Majesty is pleased and contented . . . to provide to every chief head and governor of every such religious house during their lives such yearly pensions or benefices as for their degrees and qualities shall be reasonable and convenient. . . .

And it is ordained by authority aforesaid that the chief governors and convents of such honorable great monasteries shall take and accept into their houses from time to time such number of the persons of the said convents as shall be assigned and appointed by the King's Highness, and keep them religiously during their lives. . . .

And further it is enacted, ordained, and established by authority aforesaid, that all and singular persons, bodies politic, and corporate, to whom the King's Majesty . . . shall give, grant, let, or demise any site or precinct, with the houses thereupon builded, together with the demesnes of any monasteries, priories, or other religious houses that shall be dissolved or given to the King's Highness by this Act, and the heirs, successors, executors, and assigns of every such person, body politic, and corporate, shall be bounden by authority of this Act, under the penalties hereafter ensuing, to occupy yearly as much of the same desmesnes in ploughing and tillage of husbandry . . . as . . . hath been commonly used to be kept in tillage by the governors, abbots, or priors of the same houses, monasteries, or priories, or by their farmer or farmers occupying the same, within the time of twenty years next before this Act. . . . (SR, III, 575: 27 Henry VIII, c.28.)

## Statute of Uses. 1536

32.

THE *Statute of Uses* was the last and strongest attack upon the constitutional principle that private property was beyond control of the Crown. The system of "uses" had grown up in England to circumvent both the feudal barriers to transfer of real property and the Crown's ancient claim to the obligations of wardship and marriage. In effect, "use" amounted to transfer of real property to trustees who were protected by the Common Law from payment of such obligations. The real beneficiary, even though he remained in actual possession of the property, could also escape payment to the Crown, because of the legal fiction in such cases that no real owner existed. This statute vested legal responsibility in the actual possessor, and Crown claims against that individual now became actionable in Common Law courts. After 1536 "uses" disappeared, as outright transfer of property became a legal reality.

Where, by the common laws of this realm, lands, tenements, and hereditaments be not devisable by testament, nor ought to be transferred from one to another but by solemn livery and seisin ... yet, nevertheless, divers and sundry imaginations, subtle inventions, and practices have been used whereby the hereditaments of this realm have been conveyed from one to another by fraudulent feoffments, fines, recoveries, and other assurances craftily made to secret uses, intents, and trusts, and also by wills and testaments sometime made by [oral agreements], sometime by signs and tokens, and sometime by writing. ...

For the extirping and extinguishment of all such ... and to the intent that the King's Highness or any other his subjects of this realm shall not in any wise hereafter ... be deceived, damaged, or hurt by reason of such trusts, uses, or confidences ...; it may please the King's most Royal Majesty that it may be enacted by his Highness, by the assent of the Lords spiritual and temporal and the Commons in this present Parliament assembled, and by authority of the same ... that, where any person or persons stand or be seised or at any time hereafter shall happen to be seised of and in any honors, castles, manors, lands, tenements, rents, services, reversions, remainders, or other hereditaments, to the use, confidence, or trust of any other person or persons, or of any body politic, by reason of any bargain, sale, feoffment, fine, recovery, covenant, contract, agreement, will, or otherwise ..., in every such case all and every such person and persons and bodies politic ... shall from henceforth stand and be seised, deemed, and adjudged in lawful seisin, estate, and possession of and in the same honors [etc.] ... to all intents, constructions, and purposes in the law ...; and that the estate, right, title, and possession that was in such person or persons that were or shall be hereafter seised of any lands, tenements, or hereditaments to the use, confidence, or trust of any such person or persons, or of any body politic, be from henceforth clearly deemed and adjudged to be in him or them that have or hereafter shall have such use, confidence, or trust. ... (SR, III, 539: 27 Henry VIII, c.10.)

## Act for the Court of Admiralty. 1536

PRIOR to passage of this Act the Lord High Admiral's court was of minor importance. Its proceedings were uncertain, and it was subject to the whims of the Council. Jurisdictional disputes with the Common Law courts often resulted in felons escaping punishment and in the loss of State revenue from fines. The present Act established a clear-cut area of action for the Admiralty court, gave it a definite procedure, and brought into its use the Common Law jury principle. The legal procedures and concepts developed in Henry's Admiralty courts were to become the basis of modern maritime law and judicial practices.

**33.**

An Act for punishment of Pirates and Robbers of the Sea.

Where traitors, pirates, thieves, robbers, murderers ... upon the sea many times escape unpunished because the trial of their offences hath heretofore been ordered, judged, and determined before the Admiral, or his lieutenant or commissary, after the course of the civil laws, the nature whereof is that before any judgment of death can be given against the offenders, either they must plainly confess their offences, which they will never do without torture or pains, or else their offences be so plainly and directly proved by witness indifferent, such as saw their offences committed, which cannot be gotten but by chance at few times because such offenders commit their offences upon the sea, and at many times murder and kill such persons being in the ship or boat where they commit their offences which should witness against them in that behalf, and also such as should bear witness be commonly mariners and shipmen, which because of their often voyages and passages in the seas, depart without long tarrying and protraction of time, to the great costs and charges as well of the King's Highness as such as would pursue such offenders:

For reformation whereof be it enacted . . . that all treasons, felonies, robberies and murders . . . hereafter to be committed in or upon the sea, or in any other haven, river, creek, or place where the Admiral or Admirals have or pretend to have power, authority, or jurisdiction, shall be inquired, tried, heard, determined, and judged in such shires and places in the realm as shall be limited by the King's commission or commissions to be di-

rected for the same, in like form and condition as if any such offence or offences had been committed or done in or upon the land, and such commissions shall be had under the King's great seal directed to the Admiral . . . or to his lieutenant, deputy, and to 3 or 4 such other substantial persons as shall be named or appointed by the Lord Chancellor of England . . . as often as need shall require, to hear and determine such offences after the common course of the laws of this land, used for treasons, felonies, robberies, and murders of the same done and committed upon the land within this realm.

And be it enacted . . . that such persons to whom such commissions . . . shall be directed, or 4 of them at the least, shall have full power and authority to inquire of such offences and every of them by the oaths of twelve good and lawful inhabitants in the shire limited in their commission, in such like manner and form as if such offences had been committed upon the land, within the same shire. . . . And that the trial of such offence or offences, if it be denied by the offender or offenders, shall be had by 12 lawful men inhabited in the shire limited within such commission. . . . (SR, III, 671: 28 Henry VIII, c.15.)

## Statute of Proclamations. 1539

**34.** HAVING, in order to please the King, played the part of a willing collaborator during the early Reformation period, Parliament now showed unusual determination to maintain its rightful constitutional position in the *Statute of Proclamations*. Perhaps the bullying tactics of Henry in his attacks on the Church and in the case of the *Statute of Uses* had given Parliament a warning to look to its own defenses. When Henry demanded the right to legislate independently of the representative assembly, Parliament, after careful thought, reasserted its legislative right and tactfully but firmly denied the King the full measure of independent action he desired.

An Act that Proclamations made by the King shall be obeyed.

Forasmuch as the King's most royal Majesty for divers considerations by the advice of his Council hath heretofore set forth divers and sundry articles of Christ's Religion, as for an unity and concord to be had amongst

the loving and obedient subjects of this his realm and other his dominions, and also concerning the advancement of his common wealth and good quiet of his people, which nevertheless divers and many froward, wilful, and obstinate persons have wilfully contemned and broken, not considering what a

King by his royal power may do, and for lack of a direct statute and law to coerce offenders to obey the said proclamations, which being still suffered should not only encourage offenders to the disobedience of the precepts and laws of Almighty God, but also sin too much to the great dishonor of the King's most royal Majesty, who may full ill bear it, and also give too great heart and boldness to all malefactors and offenders; considering also that sudden causes and occasions fortune many times which do require speedy remedies, and that by abiding for a Parliament in the mean time might happen great prejudice to ensue to the realm; and weighing also that his Majesty ... should not be driven to extend the liberty and supremacy of his regal power and dignity by wilfulness of froward subjects: it is therefore thought in manner more than necessary that the King's Highness of this realm for the time being, with the advice of his honorable Council, should make and set forth proclamations for the good and politic order and governance of this his realm of England ... for the defence of his regal dignity and the advancement of his common wealth and good quiet of his people, as the cases of necessity shall require, and that an ordinary law should be provided, by the assent of his Majesty and Parliament, for the due punishment, correction, and reformation of such offences and disobediences:

Be it therefore enacted by the Lords Spiritual and Temporal and the Commons in ... Parliament ... that the King ... with the advice of his Council ... or with the advice of the more part of them, may set forth at all times by authority of this Act his proclamations, under such penalties and pains and of such sort as to his Highness and his said Council or the more part of them shall see necessary and requisite; and that those same shall be obeyed, observed, and kept as though they were made by Act of Parliament for the time in them limited, unless the King's Highness dispense with them or any of them under his great seal.

Provided always that the words, meaning, and intent of this Act be not understood, interpretate, construed, or extended, that by virtue of it any of the King's liege people [as used here "liege" includes all citizens] ... should have any of his or their inheritances, lawful possessions, offices, liberties, privileges, franchises, goods, or chattels taken from them ... nor by virtue of the said Act suffer any pains of death, other than shall hereafter in this Act be declared, nor that by any proclamation to be made by virtue of the said Act, any acts, common laws, standing at this present time in strength and force, nor yet any lawful or laudable customs of this realm ... shall be infringed, broken, or subverted; and especially all those Acts standing this hour in force which have been made in the King's Highness's time; but that every such person ... shall stand and be in the same state and condition, to every respect and purpose, as if this Act or proviso had never been made.... Except ... such persons which shall offend any proclamation to be made by the King's Highness ... for and concerning any kind of heresies against Christian Religion.... (SR, III, 726: 31 Henry VIII, c.8.)

## Act Dissolving the Greater Monasteries. 1539

## 35.

SINCE no existent law gave Parliament the right to proceed against Church lands, Cromwell, Henry's Chancellor, employed threats and, on occasion, the gallows in order to bring the greater monasteries into Crown possession. Several resistant abbots were hanged on charges of treason. The great majority of religious houses, however, promptly surrendered after they unsuccessfully attempted to purchase immunity with gifts. This Statute did not in fact dissolve the monasteries; it merely recognized as legal the transfer of properties from Church to King, duly noting the "free and voluntary minds, good will, and assents, without constraint, coercion, or compulsion" of the churchmen. As a precaution against future claims against the properties, however, the Act vested legal ownership in the King and his heirs.

An act for Dissolution of Abbeys.

Where divers and sundry abbots, priors, abbesses, prioresses, and other ecclesiastical governors and governesses of divers monasteries, abbesses, priories, nunneries, colleges, hospitals, houses of friars, and other religious and ecclesiastical houses and places within this our Sovereign Lord the King's realm of England and Wales, of their own free and voluntary minds, good will, and assents, without constraint, coercion, or compulsion of any manner of person ... by the due order and course of the common laws of this his realm of England, and by their sufficient writings of record under their convent and common seals, have severally given, granted, and by the same their writings severally confirmed all their said monasteries [etc.] ... and all their sites, circuits, and precincts of the same, and all and singular their manors, lordships, granges, meses, lands, tenements, meadows, pastures, rents, reversions, services, woods, tithes, pensions, portions, churches, chapels, advowsons, patronage, annuities, rights, entries, conditions, commons, leets, courts, liberties, privileges, and franchises, appertaining or in any wise belonging to any such monastery [etc.] ..., to have and to hold all the said monasteries [etc.] ..., and all other the premises, to our said sovereign Lord, his heirs and successors, forever; and the same their said monasteries etc. ..., and other the premises, voluntarily, as is aforesaid have renounced, left, and forsaken. ...

Be it therefore enacted ... that the King, our Sovereign Lord, shall have, hold, possess, and enjoy to him, his heirs, and successors, forever all and singular such late monasteries [etc.] ... which ... have been dissolved ..., or by any other mean come to his Highness;

and by the same authority and in like manner shall have, hold, possess, and enjoy all the ... hereditaments which appertained or belonged to the said late monasteries [etc.] ... in as large and ample manner and form as the late abbots [etc.] ... of such late monasteries [etc.] ... had, held, or occupied ... their said late monasteries [etc.] ... at the time of the said dissolution ..., or by any other manner of means coming of the same to the King's Highness. ...

And it is further enacted by the authority abovesaid that, not only all the said late monasteries [etc.] ... but also all other monasteries [etc.] ... which hereafter shall happen to be dissolved ... and also all the ... hereditaments, whatsoever they be, belonging or appertaining to the same or any of them, whensoever and as soon as they shall be dissolved ... shall be vested, deemed, and adjudged by authority of this present Parliament in the very actual and real seisin and possession of the King our Sovereign Lord, his heirs, and successors, forever. ...

And be it also enacted by authority aforesaid that all the said late monasteries [etc.] ... which be dissolved ... except such thereof as be come to the King's hands by attainder or attainders of treason, and all the said monasteries [etc.] ... which hereafter shall happen to be dissolved ... and all ... hereditaments, whatsoever they be, belonging to the same or to any of them, except such thereof which shall happen to come to the King's Highness by attainder ... of treason, shall be in the order, survey, and governance of our said Sovereign Lord the King's Court of Augmentations of the revenues of his crown. ... (SR, III, 733: 31 Henry VIII, c.13.)

## Statute of the Six Articles. 1539

## 36.

ALTHOUGH primarily conceived as a means of abolishing religious diversity, this Statute was significant in other ways. It assembled, simplified, and modified the laws dealing with the definition and punishment of heresy. It also strengthened the implication of the *Dispensations Act* of 1534 that King and people did not intend to depart from the accepted principles of the Catholic faith by specifically enumerating six basic articles of faith, the acceptance of which was hereby now incorporated into the statutory law of the land. However, the view that Henry hoped to use the six articles to pave the way for an eventual return to Rome would seem incompatible with other of his actions.

An Act abolishing diversity in opinions.

Where the King's most excellent Majesty is by God's law supreme head immediately under Him of this whole Church and Congregation of England, intending the conservation of the same Church and Congregation in a true, sincere, and uniform doctrine of Christ's religion ... and ... hath therefore caused and commanded this his most high court of Parliament, for sundry and many urgent causes and considerations, to be at this time summoned, and also a Synod and Convocation of all the Archbishops, Bishops, and other learned men of the Clergy of this his realm to be in like manner assembled; and forasmuch as in the said Parliament, Synod, and Convocation there were certain articles, matters, and questions propounded and set forth touching Christian Religion ... whereupon, after a great and long deliberate and advised disputation and consultation had and made concerning the said articles, as well by the consent of the King's Highness as by the assent of the Lords Spiritual and Temporal and other learned men of his Clergy in their Convocation, and by the consent of the Commons in this present Parliament assembled, it was and is finally resolved, accorded, and agreed in manner and form following, that is to say, first, that in the most blessed Sacrament of the altar, by the strength and efficacy of Christ's mighty word, it being spoken by the Priest, is present really, under the form of bread and wine, the natural body and blood of our Saviour Jesus Christ,

conceived of the Virgin Mary, and that after the consecration there remaineth no substance of bread and wine, nor any other substance but the substance of Christ, God and man; secondly, that communion in both kinds is not necessary *ad salutem* by the law of God to all persons, and that it is to be believed and not doubted of but that in the flesh under the form of bread is the very blood, and with the blood under form of wine is the very flesh, as well apart as though they were both together; thirdly, that priests, after the order of priesthood received as afore, may not marry by the law of God; fourthly, that vows of chastity or widowhood by man or woman made to God advisedly ought to be observed by the law of God, and that it exempteth them from other liberties of Christian people which without that they might enjoy; fifthly, that it is meet and necessary that private masses to be continued and admitted in the King's English Church and Congregation, as whereby good Christian people ordering themselves accordingly do receive both Godly and goodly consolations and benefits, and it is agreeable also to God's law; sixthly, that auricular confession is expedient and necessary to be retained and continued, used, and frequented, in the Church of God....

And be it further enacted ... that, if any person or persons ... contemn or contemptuously refuse, deny, or abstain to be confessed at the time commonly accustomed within this realm and Church of England, or contemn or contemptuously refuse, deny, or abstain to receive the holy and blessed sacrament abovesaid at the time commonly used and accustomed for the same, that then every such offender ... shall suffer such imprisonment and make such fine and ransom to the King our Sovereign Lord and his heirs as by his Highness or by his or their [Privy] Council ... shall be ordered and adjudged in that behalf; and if any such offender ... do again ... refuse ... to be confessed or to be communicate ... that then every such offence shall be deemed and adjudged felony, and the offender ... shall suffer pains of death, and lose and forfeit all his ... goods, lands, and tenements, as in cases of felony. ... (SR, III, 739: 31 Henry VIII, c.14.)

## Act Dissolving the Marriage with Anne of Cleves. 1540

**37.** ON THE failure of the Cleves marriage, Henry again resorted to the device of having Parliament declare a formerly legal union to be a "pretended" marriage. Once again the number of statutory treasons was increased. Since Anne had given him no children, the problem of the succession was not mentioned in this Act.

The dissolution of the pretended marriage with the Lady Anne of Cleves.

The Lords spiritual and temporal and the Commons in this present Parliament assembled, calling to their remembrance the manifold detestable conflicts intestine, battles, mortalities of people, and disherisons which heretofore have sprang and grown in this realm by occasion of diversities of titles to the Crown of the same, which most chiefly grow and insurged by doubts of marriages and of the incertainty of the succession of the same; considering also that, thanks be to God, all manner titles be now conjoined, consolidate, united, and vested only in the King's most royal person, so that his Majesty is and standeth presently a just and undoubted, pure and perfect King of this realm, against whom no impediment or objection can or may be ... alleged, and that it appertaineth to the office and policy of all civil bodies of realms and countries, most chiefly next to their duties to God, to foresee and provide for the surety and certainty of the succession of their Kings and chief governors, forasmuch as upon the certainty thereof dependeth their whole common wealth, rest, peace, and tranquillity; and lately understanding that great ambiguities, doubts, and questions have been moved in the marriage solemnized between the King's Majesty and the Lady Anne of Cleves, whereby great troubles and inconveniences might hereafter spring and grow in this realm to the imminent danger of the destruction of the subjects thereof if remedy should not speedily be provided for the same;

The temporal Lords and Commons have therefore made their most humble intercession and petition to the King's most royal Majesty, that it may please his Highness of his accustomable goodness to commit the state of his said marriage, with all the circumstances and dependences thereof, unto the prelates and clergy of this realm to be searched, examined, defined, and determined by them according to the truth, justice, and equity, in such wise as should stand with God's pleasure, the King's honor, and the wealth and tranquillity of this realm. [Inserted in the Act at this point is the decision of the clergy of York and Canterbury against the validity of the union.]

In consideration whereof the said Lords spiritual and temporal and the Commons in this present Parliament assembled most humbly beseech the King's most royal Majesty that it may be assented, declared, and enacted by authority of this present Parliament, as well for the surety and certainty of his Highness's posterity and succession as for the wealth, quietness, rest, and tranquillity of this realm, that the marriage between his Highness and the said Lady Anne of Cleves is clearly void and of no force, value, nor effect, and that his Majesty is at his liberty and pleasure to contract matrimony and marry with any other women not prohibited by the Law of God to marry with his Highness. . . .

And be it also enacted by the authority abovesaid, that if any person . . . by writing or imprinting, or by any other exterior act, word, or deed, directly or indirectly, accept or take, judge or believe the said pretended marriage had between his Majesty and the said Lady Anne of Cleves to be good, lawful, or of any effect, or by words, writing, printing, deed, or act, procure or do, or cause to be procured or done, any thing . . . for the interruption, repeal, or annullation of this Act, or of anything therein contained, that then every such person . . . of what estate, degree, or condition soever he be, and his aiders, counsellors, maintainers, and abettors, and every of them, for every such offence before specified shall be adjudged high traitors, and every such offence shall be adjudged high treason. . . . (SR, III, 781: 32 Henry VIII, c.25.)

## Act of Attainder of Queen Katherine Howard. 1542

**38.**

BY 1542 the problem of an uncertain succession had brought Henry to the verge of desperation. Edward, ill since birth, was an uncertain peg upon which to hang the security of the realm and dynasty. Henry's two daughters, bastardized by law, were unqualified to reign, and Katherine Howard had failed to produce a male heir. Hence the Queen, her serving maid, and two innocent men were confronted with trumped up charges of adultery and put to death. Parliament and an obsequious clergy aided and abetted Henry in this act of extremity.

A Bill of Attainder of Mistress Katherine Howard, late Queen of England, and divers other persons her complices.

In their most humble wise beseechen your most royal Majesty the Lords spiritual and temporal and all other your most loving and obedient subjects the Commons of this your most High Court of Parliament assembled; that were, besides any man's expectation, such chance hath happened, your Mistress Katherine Howard which your Highness took to your wife, both to your Majesty chiefly and so consequently to us all that the like we think hath scarce been seen, the likelihoods and appearances being so far contrary to that which by evident and due proof is now found true; first, that it will please your Majesty to take it in such part as thereby arise not to us all a greater inconvenience, which is the trouble of your heart and unquietness of your mind, for that should be a shortening of that which we all should repent and most desire the contrary; secondly, that it would please your Majesty to pardon all your loving subjects which since these matters came to their knowledge have detested and abhorred her for this fact both in word, manner, and deed, and of words uttered by them of her and her adherents not maintainable in your laws, considering that they did and do it only for the great zeal and love that they bear to your Majesty and the abomination of the detestable fact; thirdly, that since it pleased your Majesty upon those likely outward appearances to take the said Mistress Katherine Howard to your wife and Queen of your most excellent goodness and for a Godly purpose, and also most liberally to endue her with great possessions for the maintenance of the same, thinking and taking her at that time to be chaste and of pure, clean, and honest living, the contrary whereof is now duly proved, both by her own confession and others also. . . .

It may therefore please your Highness of your most excellent and accustomable goodness, and for the entire love, favour, and hearty affection that your Majesty hath always heretofore borne and yet beareth to the common wealth of this your realm of England, and for the conservation of your most excellent Highness and posterity, and of the good peace, unity, and rest of us your most bounden and obedient subjects, to grant and assent at the most humble desire and petition of your loving and obedient subjects the Lords spiritual and temporal and the Commons in this present Parliament assembled, that this their lawful indictments and attainders of such as have lately suffered may be approved by the authority of this present Parliament, and that it may be enacted that the said Queen Katherine and Jane Lady Rochford, for their said abominable and detestable treasons by them and every of them most abominably and traitorously committed and done against your Majesty and this your realm, shall be by the authority of this present Parliament convicted and attainted of high treason, and that the same Queen Katherine and Jane Lady Rochford, and either of them, shall have and suffer pains of death, loss of goods, chattels, debts, ferms, and all other things as in cases of high treason by the laws of this your realm hath been accustomed, granted, and given to the Crown, and also that the said Queen Katherine, Jane Lady Rochford, Thomas Culpepper, and Francis Dereham, [Culpepper and Dereham were convicted of acts of adultery with the Queen, Lady Rochford of having acted as the Queens channel of communication with them in arranging trysts] and every of them, shall lose and forfeit to your Highness and to your heirs all such rights, title, interests, use, and possessions which they or any of them had on the 25th day of August in the 33rd year of your reign, or any time since, of, in, or to all such their honors, manors, lands, tenements, rents, reversions, remainders, uses, possessions, offices, rights, conditions, and all other their hereditaments, of what names, natures, or qualities soever they be, and that all such rights, [etc.] ... by the authority aforesaid shall be deemed vested, and judged to be in the actual and real possession of your Majesty, without any ... inquisition thereof hereafter to be taken or found according to the common laws of this your realm. . . . (SR, III, 857: 33 Henry VIII, c.21.)

## Third Succession Act. 1543

39.    HISTORY has verified the succession ordered by this Act. In it, all prior legislation concerned with the succession was nullified, and Mary and Elizabeth were returned to their rightful positions following Edward. The area of statutory treason was again broadened to include any attempt to change the order laid down by the Act. Further Henry was given the right to appoint his successor in his will and testament should the three children die before him.

An Act concerning the establishment of the King's Majesty's Succession in the Imperial Crown of the Realm.

[After restating the *Second Succession Act* the present statute continues]. . . . Since the making of which Act, the King's Majesty hath only issue of his body lawfully begotten betwixt his Highness and his said late wife Queen Jane, the noble and excellent Prince Edward . . . and also his Majesty hath now of late . . . taken to his wife the most virtuous and gracious Lady Katherine, now Queen of England, . . . by whom as yet his Majesty hath none issue, but may have full well when it shall please God, and forasmuch as our said most dread Sovereign Lord the King, upon good and just grounds and causes, intendeth by God's grace to make a voyage . . . into the realm of France against his ancient enemy the French King, [the two states were presently engaged in hostilities] his Highness most prudently and wisely considering and calling to his remembrance how this realm standeth at this present time in the case of succession ... recognizing and knowledging also that it is the only pleasure and will of Almighty God how long his Highness or his said entirely beloved son Prince Edward shall live, and whether the said Prince shall have heirs of his body lawfully begotten or not, or whether his Highness shall have heirs begotten and procreated between his Majesty and his said most dear ... wife Queen Katherine that now is, or any lawful heirs and issues hereafter of his own body begotten by any other his lawful wife, and albeit that the King's most excellent Majesty, for default of such heirs as be inheritable by the said Act, might, by the authority of the said Act, give and dispose the said imperial Crown and other the premises by his letters patents under his great seal, or by his last will in writing signed with his most gracious hand, to any person or persons of such estate therein as should please his Highness to limit and appoint, yet to the intent that his Majesty's disposition and mind therein should be openly declared and manifestly known and notified, as well to the Lords spiritual and temporal as to all other his loving and obedient subjects of this his realm, to the intent that their assent and consent might appear to concur with ... his Majesty's declaration in this behalf.

His Majesty therefore thinketh convenient afore his departure beyond the seas that it be enacted ... that in case it shall happen to the King's Majesty and the said excellent Prince his yet only son ... and heir apparent to decease without heir of either of their bodies lawfully begotten ... so that there be no such

heir male or female of any of their two bodies to have and inherit the said imperial Crown and other his dominions according and in such manner and form as in the foresaid Act and now in this is declared, that then the said Imperial Crown and all other the premises shall be to the Lady Mary the King's Highness's daughter and to the heirs of the body of the same Lady Mary lawfully begotten, with such conditions as by his Highness shall be limited by his letters patents under his great seal, or by his Majesty's last Will in writing [etc.] ... ; and for default of such issue the said imperial Crown and other the premises shall be to the Lady Elizabeth the King's second daughter and to the heirs of the body of the said Lady Elizabeth lawfully begotten, with such conditions, [etc.]. ...

And forasmuch as it standeth in the only pleasure and will of Almighty God whether the King's Majesty shall have any heirs begotten and procreated between his Highness and his said ... wife Queen Katherine or by any other his lawful wife, or whether the said Prince Edward shall have issue of his body lawfully begotten, or whether the Lady Mary and Lady Elizabeth or any of them shall have any issue of any of their several bodies lawfully begotten ... be it therefore enacted by the authority of this present Parliament, that the King's Highness shall have full power and authority to give, dispose, appoint, assign, declare, and limit, by his gracious letters patents under his great seal, or else by his Highness's last Will ... at his only pleasure from time to time hereafter, the imperial Crown of this realm ... after his decease ... to such person or persons ... as shall please his Highness. ... (SR, III, 955: 35 Henry VIII, c.1.)

# The Reign of Edward VI

## 1547-1553

# DOCUMENTS OF THE REIGN OF EDWARD VI

# England, 1547-1553    Introduction

Edward, son of Henry VIII and Jane Seymour, became King at the age of nine in 1547. His reign, cut short by death in 1553, marks a period of domestic turpitude in which the English constitution was cynically employed as a party weapon by the various factions of the Regency Council.

Much of the blame for this period must be laid to the faltering policy of Edward's father. In the final analysis, Henry had not established a nationally unified, single English Church; on the contrary, wholly intent on insuring the dynastic claim, his establishment of the Supremacy had served to promote factionalism. Thus, during Edward's reign three main groups schemed and fought for Church control: Henry's partisans, who professed to accept his settlement; the so-called "Protestant" faction, followers of Tyndale, Cranmer, and Latimer; and Stephen Gardiner's National Catholic Party, which favored a Church that was Catholic in dogma and subservient to Rome in things spiritual, but administratively and politically English. All three groups were well represented in the Council, and from the first all showed contempt for the wishes set down in Henry's last will and testament.

The political situation was no better. Somerset, the first Protector, intent on personal power, allied himself with Cranmer and Latimer, who were bidding for public approval by opposing further enclosures of common land and seeking a fairer use of church lands for the public welfare. This social reform program not only widened the gap between the English and Roman churches, but also alienated the numerous council members who, under Northumberland's lead, considered public office as an opportunity for personal gain. Northumberland's subsequent victory over Somerset and the churchmen gave rise to a period of wholesale greed at the expense of the realm by those in power which served to establish in many minds a direct connection between English Protestantism and corrupt government. The Marian reaction and the return of the Roman Church to England were the logical results of such a state of affairs.

The period of Edward's reign was also notable for tendencies in church legislation almost completely opposed to the old king's idea on the subject. Henry, as we have seen, viewed religious topics from a wholly secular bias, and the goal of all his efforts, however religiously radical they may have seemed on the surface, had been to ensure dynastic security. Hence, given the initial rupture with Rome, his subsequent religious directives had seemed faltering to sincerely Protestant eyes. While he lived, however, his massive array of threatening statutes, his increasingly broad application of the concept of treason, and his deadly determination to silence any but his own voice in church affairs had effectively prevented any open discussion of theological differences between him and Council or Parliament. His death, and Edward's political weakness, changed all this.

Of primary religious significance during the Edwardian period was the Council's attempt to unify English church policy under the guidance of continental Lutheranism, as formulated by Philip Melancthon. This reorientation was directed at fusing the doctrinal and organizational differences existing among the various English Protestant factions. Thus, in 1549, with the issuing of the first Prayerbook, the English Church accepted the latitudinarian philosophy of comprehensiveness, later to become the dominating characteristic of the Elizabethan settlement, in the hope that every Protestant group would find a place there suitable to its profession. In 1552 a second and even more comprehensive prayerbook was issued for use. These works were intentionally vague on doctrinal points, in the hope that no Protestant would find matter for disagreement in them. In 1553 the council-sponsored *Act of the Forty-Two Articles* was passed by Parliament, and Henry's settlement was completely destroyed by statute law.

Of constitutional importance in this period of uncertainty was the Parliamentary retreat from the powerful position it had enjoyed under Edward's father. Henry's problems and ambitions had necessitated his dependence on Parliament, and Parliament, eager for stature and voice, had responded to and thrived upon, the monarchial need. But Parliamentary self-confidence apparently died with Henry, and not for another generation would it appear as a power in the land, insisting, because of its representative quality, on the right of participation in governing.

## First Treasons Act of Edward VI. 1547

**40.** THE death of Henry VIII removed a strong and determined guiding hand from the affairs of State and substituted the more moderate influence of the Regency Council. Although the Council was split internally by the continuing struggle for power, the several factions were united by their mutual dread of possible future charges of treason. The broad definition given that term—and the harsh punishments meted out by Henry VIII to those convicted of such action—had approached too closely to the setting of legal precedents. To make future political action less dangerous to themselves the Council members drew up and sent to Parliament the bill which became this Act.

An Act for the Repeal of certain Statutes concerning Treasons, Felonies, etc.

Nothing being more Godly, more sure, more to be wished and desired, between a Prince the Supreme Head and Ruler and the subjects whose governor and head he is, than on the Prince's part great clemency and indulgency, and rather too much forgiveness and remission of his royal power and just punishment than exact severity and justice to be shewed, and on the subjects' behalf that they should obey rather for love, and for the necessity and love of a king and prince, than for fear of his strait and severe laws; yet such times at some time cometh in the commonwealth that it is necessary and expedient for the repressing of the insolency and unruliness of men and for the foreseeing and providing of remedies against rebellion, insurrection, or such mischiefs as God, sometime with us displeased, for our punishment doth inflict and lay upon us, or the devil at God's permission, to measure the good of God's elect, doth sow and set amongst us, the which Almighty God with His help and man's policy hath always been content and pleased to have stayed that sharper laws as a harder bridle should be made to stay those men and facts that might else be occasion, cause, and authors of further inconvenience; the which thing caused the Prince of most famous memory King Henry VIII . . . to enact certain laws and statutes which might seem and appear to men of exterior realms and many of the King's Majesty's subjects very strait, sore, extreme, and terrible, although they were then when they were made not without great consideration and policy moved and established, and for the time to the avoidance of further inconvenience very expedient and necessary; but, as in tempest or winter one garment is convenient, in calm or warm weather a more liberal or lighter garment both may and ought to be ... used, so we have seen divers strait and sore laws made in one Parliament, the time so requiring, in a more calm and quiet reign of another prince by like authority and parliament repealed and taken away; the which most high clemency and royal example of his Majesty's most noble progenitors, the King's Highness, of his tender and Godly nature most given to mercy and love of his subjects, willing to follow, and perceiving the hearty and sincere love that his most loving subjects, both the Lords and Commons, doth bear unto his Highness now in this his Majesty's tender age, willing also to gratify the same therefore, and minding further to provoke his said subjects ... to more love and kindness ... and care for his Majesty to serve his Highness . . . is contented and pleased that the severity of certain laws here following be mitigated and remitted:

Be it therefore ordained and enacted by the Lords Temporal and Spiritual and Commons in this Parliament assembled that from henceforth none act, deed, or offence being by Act of Parliament or Statute made treason or petit treason by words, writing, deeds, or otherwise whatsoever, shall be taken, had, deemed, or adjudged to be high treason or petit treason but only such as be treason or petit treason in [the *Statute of Treasons* of Edward III, 1352] and such offences as hereafter shall by this present Act be expressed and declared to be treason or petit treason, and none other, nor that any pains of death, penalty, or forfeiture in any wise ensue ... to any of the offenders for the doing or committing any treason or petit treason, other

than such as be in the said Statute made in the said ... reign of the said King Edward ... or by this present Statute ordained or provided, any Act or Acts of Parliament, Statute or Statutes, had or made at any time heretofore, or after ... the reign of the said late King Edward ... or any other declaration or matter to the contrary in any wise notwithstanding.

[The present Act here nullifies "all Acts of Parliament and Statutes touching, mentioning, or in any wise concerning religion or opinion," i.e., those of Henry VIII, along with all statutes creating felonies passed since 23 April, 1547, and all statutes giving statutory authority to royal proclamations]. ...

And be it enacted by the authority aforesaid, that if any person or persons at any time after the first day of March next coming, by open preaching, express words or sayings, do affirm or set forth that the King, his heirs or successors, kings of this realm for the time being, is not or ought not to be Supreme Head on earth of the Church of England and Ireland or of any of them immediately under God, or that the Bishop of Rome or any other person or persons other than the King of England for the time being is or ought to be by the laws of God Supreme Head of the same Churches or of any of them, or that the King, his heirs or successors kings of this realm, is not or ought not to be King of England, France, and Ireland, or of any of them, or ... do compass or imagine by open preaching, express words or sayings, to depose or deprive the King, his heirs or successors kings of this realm, from his or their royal estate or titles to or of the realms aforesaid, or do openly publish or say by express words or sayings that any other person or persons other than the King, his heirs or successors kings of this realm, of right ought to be kings of the realms aforesaid or of any of them, or to have and enjoy the same or any of them, that then every such offender, being thereof duly convicted or attainted by the laws of this realm, their aiders [etc.] ... shall suffer [for the first offence forfeiture of goods and imprisonment during the King's will; for the second offence forfeiture of lands and life imprisonment; for the third the offender shall suffer the pains of high treason].....

And be it further enacted by the authority aforesaid, that if any of the heirs of the King our said Sovereign Lord that now is, or any person or persons to whom the Crown and dignity of this realm is limited and appointed ... or the heirs of any of them, do at any time hereafter usurp the one of them upon the other in the Crown of this realm, or demand, challenge, or claim the same otherwise or in any other form or degree of descent or succession, or in any other course, form, degree, or condition but only in such manner and form as is declared ... or if any of the said heirs or persons aforesaid do interrupt ...

the King's Highness that now is peaceably and quietly to keep, have, and enjoy the said imperial Crown, then all and singular the offenders, their aiders, conforters, abettors, procurers, and counsellors therein, shall be deemed and adjudged high traitors, and shall suffer and incur the pains of death, losses, and forfeitures as is aforesaid in cases of high treason....

Provided always and be it enacted by the authority aforesaid, that no person or persons, after the first day of February next coming, shall be indicted, arraigned, condemned, or convicted [of any of the aforestated crimes] ... unless the same ... be accused by two sufficient and lawful witnesses, or shall willingly without violence confess the same. (SR, IV, 18: Edward VI, c.12.)

## Act for the Dissolution of the Chantries. 1547

41.

IF HENRY'S expropriations of the lands of the Church were in any way justified by social conditions, the Council's dissolution of the Chantries (in the name of the King's need and the building of schools) was not. The sole purpose of this Act was to increase the private wealth of the Council members, who eventually would come into possession of most of the Chantry funds. Here indeed was open theft, not of a corporate property, in which the realm as a whole might be said to have had real interest, but of private endowments which were truly the properties of private individuals and institutions.

An Act whereby certain Chantries, Colleges, Free Chapels, and the possessions of the same, be given to the King's Majesty.

The King's most loving subjects, the Lords Spiritual and Temporal and the Commons, in this present Parliament assembled, considering that a great part of superstition and errors in Christian Religion hath been brought into the minds and estimation of men by reason of the ignorance of their very true and perfect salvation through the death of Jesus Christ, and by devising and phantasing vain opinions of purgatory and masses satisfactory to [to atone for the sins of the dead] be done for them which be departed, the which doctrine and vain opinion by nothing more is maintained and upholden than by the abuse of trentals [masses], chantries,

and other provisions made for the continuance of the said blindness and ignorance; and further considering and understanding that the alteration, change, and amendment of the same, and converting to good and Godly uses, as in erecting of grammar schools to the education of youth in virtue and Godliness, the further augmenting of the Universities, and better provision for the poor and needy, cannot in this present Parliament be provided and conveniently done, nor cannot nor ought to any other manner person be committed than to the King's Highness, whose Majesty with and by the advice of his Highness's most prudent Council can and will most wisely and beneficially, both for the honor of God and the weal of this his Majesty's realm, order, alter, convert, and dispose the same; and calling further to their remembrance ... [the present Act recites the *Act for the Dissolution of the Chantries* of Henry VIII under which only a few were seized.

It is now ordained and enacted by the authority aforesaid that all manner of colleges, free chapels, and chantries, having being or *in esse* [existing] within five years next before the first day of this present Parliament, which were not in actual and real possession of the said late King, nor in the actual and real possession of the King our Sovereign Lord that now is, nor excepted in the said former Act ... , and all manors, lands, tenements, rents, tithes, pensions, portions, and other hereditaments and things above mentioned belonging to them or any of them, and also all manors, lands, tenements, rents, and other hereditaments and things above mentioned, by any manner of assurance, conveyance, will ... or otherwise had, made, suffered, knowledged, or declared, given, assigned, limited, or appointed to the finding of any priest to have continuance for ever, and wherewith or whereby any priest was sustained, maintained, or found within five years next before the first day of this present Parliament, which were not in the actual and real possession of the said late King nor in the actual and real possession of our Sovereign Lord and King that now is, and also all annual rents, profits, and emoluments at any time within five years next before the beginning of this present Parliament employed, paid, or bestowed toward or for the maintenance, supportation, or finding of any stipendiary priest intended by any act or writing to have continuance for ever, shall by authority of this present Parliament, immediately after the Feast of Easter next coming, be adjudged and deemed and also be in the very actual and real possession and seisin of the King our Sovereign Lord and his heirs and successors for ever, without any office [further legal action] or other inquisition thereof to be had or found, and in as large and ample manner and form as the priests, wardens, masters, ministers, governors, rulers, or other incumbents of them or

any of them at any time within five years next before the beginning of this present Parliament had occupied or enjoyed, or now hath, occupieth, and enjoyeth the same, and as though all and singular the said colleges, free chapels, chantries, stipends, salaries of priests, and the said manors, lands, tenements, hereditaments, and other the premises whatsoever they be, and every of them, were in this present Act specially, peculiarly, and certainly rehearsed, named, and expressed, by express words, names, surnames, corporations, titles, and faculties, and in their natures, kinds, and qualities.

And furthermore be it ordained and enacted by the authority aforesaid, that the King our Sovereign Lord shall from the said Feast of Easter next coming have and enjoy to him, his heirs and successors, for ever, all fraternities, brotherhoods, and guilds being within the realm of England and Wales and other the King's dominions, and all manors, lands, tenements, and other hereditaments belonging to them or any of them, other than such corporations, guilds, fraternities, companies, and fellowships of ... crafts, and the manors, lands, tenements, and other hereditaments pertaining to the said corporations, guilds, fraternities, companies, and fellowships ... of crafts above mentioned, and shall by virtue of this Act be judged and deemed in actual and real possession of our said Sovereign Lord the King, his heirs and successors, from the said Feast of Easter next coming for ever, without any inquisitions or office thereof to be had or found. ...

Provided always and be it ordained and enacted by the authority aforesaid that this Act ... shall not in any wise extend to any college, hostel, or hall being within either of the Universities of Cambridge and Oxford, nor to any chantry founded in any of the colleges, hostels, or halls being in the same Universities, nor to the free chapel of St. George the Martyr ... nor to the college called St. Mary College of Winchester ... nor to the College of Eton. ... (SR, IV, 24: 1 Edward VI, c.14.)

## Act for a Subsidy of Tunnage and Poundage. 1547

**42.** BARREN as was the period of Edward VI in terms of real and lasting social reform and constitutional development there were several significant attempts made during Somerset's Protectorship to alleviate the debilitating poverty of the lower classes through the medium of statute law. This subsidy act represents one such attempt. It also established one of the precedents for governmental control of one industry to the advantage of another in the name of the welfare of the commonwealth.

Expanding continental markets and increasing demand for England's wool and wool products had had a stimulating effect on the rate and extent of land enclosures. This development resulted in great material gain for the landed and corresponding loss for the landless. Somerset's attitude reflected that of the "commonweal men" who argued that the burgeoning sheep industry was creating an unbalanced national economy which would eventually fatally weaken agriculture, the traditional foundation of English life, and destroy the food-producing yeoman class. Somerset, through this act, hoped that by elevating to an almost prohibitive rate the export duty on wool, the opportunity for profit in that industry would be reduced. Enclosures would thus be made less attractive to investment capital, and the economic situation of the agrarian laborer would be improved. However, by his attempt to aid the lower classes, Somerset established himself as the champion of a radical social policy which was totally unacceptable to the upper classes.

...We...your poor Commons, as bound by duty, humbly desire your most excellent Majesty...to take, accept, and receive our poor grant hereafter ensuing...towards your great costs, charges, and expenses....

[The act here specifies a subsidy grant of three shillings per tun of wine imported by native English merchants and a duty of twice that amount per tun of wine imported by foreign merchants resident in England, as well as a shilling for each pound weight on all other merchandise exported or imported by native English merchants plus an extra shilling levy per pound weight against foreign merchants resident in England.]

...And further we your said poor Commons...give and grant...for the cause above rehearsed one other subsidy on all manner wool, woolfels, and leather carried or to be carried out of this your Realm in manner and form following, that is to say;

Of every merchant denizen, of and for every sack of wool 33s. 4d.; and of every [240 pounds weight]...woolfels 34s. 4d.; and of and for every last [bundle] of hides and backs [thick skin of the sheep's back] of every such merchant denizen 66s. 8d.; and also of every merchant stranger not born your liegeman ...of and for every sack of wool 66s. 8d.; and of and for every [240 pounds weight] 73s. 4d.; and so of all the said wool, woolfels, hides and backs and every of them after the rate [as specifically set forth]....(SR, 1 Edward VI, c.13.)

## Act for Punishing Vagabonds. 1547

**43.** THE painful social results of the political, religious, and economic policies of the two Henrys had become constitutionally significant by the beginning of Somerset's Protectorship. This act was an irrational and savage attempt, early in the reign of Edward VI, to cope with the social ills of poverty and unemployment which were the immediate consequences of enclosures, inflation, and the loss of the social services to the poor heretofore rendered by the monasteries.

It is difficult to understand Somerset's reliance on an instrument of this type; its nature was foreign to his usual humanitarianism (as seen in subsequent Council decrees and Parliamentary statutes), his compassion for the lower classes and his desire to protect them against the designs of the monied classes. Be that as it may, with this act Somerset partially alienated himself from the general populace. The ferocity of the government in crushing the rebellion in Cornwall and Devon further widened the breach between Somerset and the common people, and a short time later, Robert Ket's rebellion in Norfolk completely isolated him from the landed gentry, whose support was vitally necessary to his continued domination of the Regency Council.

While both of these short-lived rebellions were largely consequent to the prevalent economic instability, the religious issues of the period were almost as significant in the destruction of Somerset and his replacement by Northumberland. On the one hand the more conservative people of the outlying shires, convinced of the constitutionality of the Henrician church, rejected Edward's *Book of Common Prayer* and excoriated Somerset for the heresy of its publication. On the other hand, the inhabitants of the larger towns, which were the centers of the "new learning," were disappointed that the church settlement was less radical (or "German") than they had expected. By the time of Ket's rebellion, virtually every group believed it had reason to be less than friendly to Somerset.

In the end, however, it was the growing hostility of the landed classes to the Protector's policy of social reform which dislodged him from control of the Regency Council.

Those groups, already fearful of Somerset's radical sense of social responsibility, were further disquieted by his attitude of conciliation toward Ket's followers. To the landed classes conciliation implied sympathy with insidious social revolution.

Yet—and of overriding significance at the time of Edward's death—Somerset's policies would soon come to be compared favorably by the people with the arrogant and cynical excesses of Northumberland, a comparison which would open the way to the throne for Mary Tudor and to the block for Lady Jane Grey; for it became increasingly obvious to the English people that Protestantism and the irresponsible and exploitative forces of the Council, which Somerset and Cranmer had been able to repress temporarily, were now in league.

An act for the Punishing of Vagabonds and for the Relief of the Poor and Impotent Persons.

For as much as idleness and vagabondage is the mother and root of all thefts, robberies, and all evil acts and other mischiefs and the multitude of people given thereto hath always been within this Realm very great ... to the great impoverishment of the Realm and danger of the King's ... subjects, the which idleness and vagabondage all the King's noble progenitors, kings of this Realm, and the high Court of Parliament hath often ... gone about and assayed with Godly acts and statutes to repress, yet ... it hath not had that success which hath been wished, partly by foolish pity and mercy of them which should have seen ... the laws executed ... ,

the said statutes hitherto have had small effect, and idle and vagabond persons being unprofitable members, or rather enemies of the commonwealth, have been suffered to remain and increase and yet so do, who ... should be punished by death, whipping, and imprisonment:

Be it therefore enacted ... first, that all statutes and acts of Parliament heretofore made for the punishment of vagabonds and sturdy beggars ... shall from henceforth be repealed ... :

Secondly that whosoever after the first day of April next following, man or woman not being lame, impotent or so aged or diseased with sickness that he or she cannot work, not having lands, tenements, fees, annuities, or any other yearly revenues or profits ... be lurking in any house ... or idly wander by the highway's side or in streets of cities, towns, or villages, not applying themselves to some honest and allowed art, science, service, or labour, and so do continue by the space of three days ... and not offer themselves to labour with any who will take them according to their faculty [ability to labor], and if no man ... will take them ... to work for meat and drink ... that then every such person shall be taken for a vagabond. ...

[Any person may apprehend a vagabond and cause the vagabond to be charged before a Justice of Peace who] ... shall cause the said idle loiterer to be marked with a hot iron in the breast the mark of V and adjudge the said person living so idle to such person [as shall have made the charge against him] to be his slave, to have and to hold the said slave to him ... for the space of two years ... and only give the said slave bread and water

... and cause the said slave to work by beating, chaining, or otherwise. ...

And if any manner of slave ... shall within the space of the said two years appointed run away, depart, or absent him from his said master by the space of fourteen days ... it shall not only be lawful to his said master to pursue and fetch him again ... but also to punish such fault by chains or beating ... ; and further every such master showing and proving by two sufficient witnesses the said offence or fault of his running away before two Justices of Peace ... the same Justice shall cause such slave ... to be marked on the forehead or on the ball of the cheek with a hot iron with the sign of an S ... and he shall adjudge the ... runaway to be the said master's slave for ever. ...

[Upon the second attempt at escape the slave was to be indicted as a felon and put to death.] (SR, 1 Edward VI, c.3.)

## First Act of Uniformity. 1549

44.

ALTHOUGH Edwardian reformation represented a conscious and systematic move toward continental Protestantism, this Act established a precedent for denying that the Monarch had a constitutional right to establish a permanent religious settlement. (And it thereby perhaps contributed to the eventual destruction of Edward's church by succeeding governments.) The "uniformity" here imposed was limited to the service of the Mass and had no bearing on the temporal form of the Church or its administration by the State. Hereafter, however, the whim of the King or the desire of the Council would constitute sufficient ground for altering the position of the Church within the constitution.

An Act for the Uniformity of Service and Administration of the Sacraments throughout the Realm.

Where of long time there hath been had in this realm of England and Wales divers forms of common prayer commonly called the service of the Church, that is to say, the use of Sarum, of York, of Bangor, and of Lincoln; and besides the same now of late much more divers and sundry forms and fashions have been used in the cathedral and parish churches of England and Wales, as well concerning the matins or morning prayer and the evensong, as also concerning the Holy

Communion commonly called the Mass, with divers and sundry rites and ceremonies concerning the same, and in the administration of other sacraments of the Church; and as the doers and executors of the said rites and ceremonies in other form than of late years they have been used were pleased therewith, so others not using the same rites and ceremonies were thereby greatly offended, and albeit the King's Majesty, with the advice of his most entirely beloved uncle the Lord Protector and others of his Highness's Council, hath heretofore divers times assayed to stay innovations or new rites concerning the premises, yet the same hath not had such good success as his Highness required in that behalf; whereupon his Highness by the most prudent advice aforesaid, being pleased to bear with the frailty and weakness of his subjects in that behalf, of his great clemency hath not been only content to abstain from punishment of those that have offended in that behalf, for that his Highness taketh that they did it of a good zeal, but also to the intent a uniform, quiet, and Godly order should be had concerning the premises, hath appointed the Archbishop of Canterbury and certain of the most learned and discreet bishops and other learned men of this realm to consider and ponder the premises, and thereupon having as well eye and respect to the most sincere and pure Christian Religion taught by the Scripture as to the usages in the primitive Church, should draw and make one convenient and meet order, rite, and fashion of common and open prayer and administration of the sacraments, to be had and used in his Majesty's realm of England and in Wales; the which at this time, by the aid of the Holy Ghost, with one uniform agreement is of them concluded, set forth, and delivered to his Highness, to his great comfort and quietness of mind, in a book entitled *The Book of the Common Prayer and Administration of the Sacraments and other Rites and Ceremonies of the Church after the Use of the Church of England:*

Wherefore the Lords Spiritual and Temporal and the Commons in this present Parliament assembled, considering as well the most Godly travail of the King's Highness, of the Lord Protector, and others of his Highness's Council, in gathering and collecting the said archbishop, bishops, and learned men together, as the Godly prayers, orders, rites, and ceremonies in the said book mentioned, and the considerations of altering those things which be altered and retaining those things which be retained in the said book, but also the honor of God, and great quietness which by the grace of God shall ensue upon the one and uniform rite and order

in such common prayer and rites and external ceremonies, to be used throughout England and in Wales, at Calais, and the marches of the same, do give to his Highness most hearty and lowly thanks for the same, and humbly pray that it may be ordained and enacted by his Majesty, with the assent of the Lords and Commons in this present Parliament assembled and by the authority of the same, that all and singular person and persons that have offended concerning the premises, other than such person and persons as now be and remain in ward in the Tower of London or in the Fleet, may be pardoned thereof; and that all and singular ministers in any cathedral or parish church, or other place within this realm of England, Wales, Calais, and marches of the same, or other the King's dominions, shall from and after the Feast of Pentecost next coming be bounden to say and use the matins, evensong, celebration of the Lord's Supper commonly called the Mass, and administration of each of the sacraments, and all their common and open prayer, in such order and form as is mentioned in the said book and none other or otherwise.

And albeit that the same be so Godly and good that they give occasion to every honest and conformable man most willingly to embrace them, yet lest any obstinate person who willingly would disturb so Godly order and quiet in this realm should not go unpunished, that it may also be ordained and enacted by the authority aforesaid, that if any manner of parson, vicar, or other whatsoever minister that ought or should sing or say common prayer mentioned in the said book or minister the sacraments, shall after the said Feast of Pentecost next coming refuse to use the said common prayers or to minister the sacraments in such cathedral or parish church or other places as he should use or minister the same, in such order and form as they be mentioned and set forth in the said book, or shall use, wilfully and obstinately standing in the same, any other rite, ceremony, order, form, or manner of mass, openly or privily, or matins, evensong, administration of the sacraments, or other open prayer than is mentioned and set forth in the said book ... or shall preach, declare, or speak anything in the derogation or disapproval of the said book or anything therein contained or of any part thereof, and shall be thereof lawfully convicted according to the laws of this realm by verdict of twelve men, or by his own confession, or by the notorious evidence of the fact, shall lose and forfeit ... [the Act lists various punishments to be applied to first, second, and third offences].

And it is ordained and enacted by the authority above-said, that if any person or persons whatsoever, after the said Feast of Pentecost next coming, shall in any interludes, plays, songs, rhymes, or by other open words, declare or speak anything in the derogation, depraving, or despising of the same book or of anything therein contained ... or shall by open act, deed, or by open threatenings compel or cause ... any parson, vicar, or other minister, in any cathedral or parish church or in any chapel or other place, to sing or say any common and open prayer or to minister any sacrament otherwise or in any other manner or form than is mentioned in the said book, or that by any of the said means shall unlawfully interrupt or stop any parson, vicar, or other ministers in any cathedral or parish church, chapel, or any other place to sing or say common and open prayer or to minister the sacraments or any of them in any such manner and form as is mentioned in the said book, that then every person being thereof lawfully convicted in form above-said shall forfeit to the King ... [the Act lists the various punishments to be applied to first, second, and third offences]. ...

Provided always that it shall be lawful to any man that understandeth the Greek, Latin, and Hebrew tongue, or other strange tongue, to say and have the said prayers heretofore specified of matins and evensong in Latin or any such other tongue, saying the same privately as they do understand: And for the further encouraging of learning in the tongues in the Universities of Cambridge and Oxford, to use and exercise in their common and open prayer in their chapels, being no parish churches or other places of prayer, the matins, evensong, litany, and all other prayers, the Holy Communion commonly called the Mass excepted, prescribed in the said book, in Greek, Latin, or Hebrew, anything in this present Act to the contrary notwithstanding. (SR, IV, 37: 2 & 3 Edward VI, c.1.)

## Act Concerning the Improvement of Commons and Waste Grounds. 1550

**45.** THE rebellions which doomed Somerset's Protectorship, and with it the hope of the "commonweal men" who had aspired to a long-term program of state-sponsored social reform, brought to the fore in the Council those forces which openly favored an unrestricted policy of self-aggrandizement. Somerset's policies of moderation and social justice were repudiated and the *Subsidy Act* of 1547 was repealed. The Enclosure Commission, a body activated by Somerset to study the results of land enclosing in the midlands, was disbanded. Parliament, coerced by Northumberland and the landed gentry, in the present act re-enacted the *Statute of Merton,* an ancient law of the reign of Henry III which defined as treason any effort on the part of any group to oppose the enclosure action of anyone having a writ to that end.

This act marked perhaps the nadir of the ideal of social responsibility in sixteenth-century England. Alone, and in vain, the followers of Cranmer and Latimer and the remnants of the "commonweal men" fought in press and pulpit against the rising tide of greed and cynicism. In discrediting the Council, however, they were in reality destroying themselves, for by 1550 it was too late for the church leaders and the men of the "new learning" to make clear their repudiation of the Council; they were too firmly associated with it in the eyes of the people. Edward's death thus brought about a church reformation by popular subscription and led to what almost amounted to the popular election of an English monarch, Mary Tudor.

Wherein the Parliament holden at Merton in the twentieth year of the reign of King Henry the Third it is contained that because many great men of England ... did complain that they might not make their profits of the residue of their manors ... [because of the use of the common and waste land by the tenants of the manor for agricultural purposes] than then they should recover their seisen by view [investigation and trial] of the [Justice of Peace]. ...

[The Act here recites the provisions of the *Statue of Merton*, 20 Henry III, c.4., wherein Parliament had encouraged the lords of manors to repossess common, wood, and waste land which the tenants, residents of the manor, could not show either legal title to, or absolute necessity for. The lord's plea for repossession was to be made before a Justice of Peace and the burden of proof was placed on the tenant or villager].

And ... also in the Parliament holden in Westminster after Easter the thirteenth year of the reign of King Edward the First, it was ordained ... that lords of wastes, woods, and pastures might approve themselves of their waste, woods, and pastures, notwithstanding the gainsayings and contradictions of their tenants ... [the act here recites as further

precedent, the *Statute of Westminster*, 13 Edward I, c.46., which upholds and expands the right of the lord of the manor to exclude the tenants from common land by ditching or hedging the portion he wished to set aside for his own use].

... And foreasmuch as it happens sometimes that some men having right to approve to himself [claim common land according to the above mentioned statutes] hath made ... a ditch or a hedge, and other [men] by night ... do or will cast down the same ditch or hedge, and it cannot be known ... who did cast down the same..., nor will the men of the next towns indict them that be guilty of the same deed, then the next townships adjoining ... shall be distrained to levy or make up the same ditch or hedge at their proper cost. ...

And foreasmuch as the aforesaid Statutes be thought beneficial for the commonwealth of this Realm of England, be it enacted ... that all and every the said Statutes [of Merton and Westminster] and all branches, clauses, articles, sentences, matters and points contained and specified in them and every of them now not repealed ... stand and be in their full strength, force, and effect. ... (SR, 3 & 4 Edward VI, c.3.)

## Second Act of Uniformity. 1552

HAVING destroyed Henry's settlement with the Act of 1549, Cranmer and the Council now began the real work of reconstructing the English Church along continental lines. A new Prayer Book was brought into use which contained Lutheran, Calvinist, and Zwinglian influences. The form of the Mass was completely changed, and the communion service lost its sacramental significance, becoming merely a commemorative ritual. (However, the truly revolutionary aspect of the Edwardian reformation was its emphasis on the Lutheran concept of "whose territory—his religion.")

**46.**

An Act for the Uniformity of Common Prayer and Administration of the Sacraments.
Where there hath been a very Godly order

set forth by authority of Parliament for common prayer and the administration of the sacraments, to be used in the mother tongue within the Church of England, agreeable to the word of God and the primitive Church, very comfortable to all good people desiring to live in Christian conversation, and most profitable to the estate of this realm, upon the which the mercy, favor, and blessing of Almighty God is in no wise so readily and plenteously poured as by common prayers, due using of the sacraments, and often preaching of Gospel, with the devotion of the hearers; and yet this notwithstanding, a great number of people in divers parts of this realm, following their own sensuality and living either without knowledge or due fear of God, do wilfully and damnably before Almighty God abstain and refuse to come to their parish churches and other places where common prayer, administration of the sacraments, and preaching of the word of God is used, upon the Sundays and other days ordained to be holy days:

For reformation hereof be it enacted by authority of the Lords Spiritual and Temporal and Commons in this present Parliament assembled, that from and after the Feast of All Saints next coming, all and every person and persons inhabiting within this realm or any other the King's Majesty's dominions, shall diligently and faithfully, having no lawful or reasonable excuse to be absent . . . resort to their parish church or chapel accustomed . . . upon every Sunday and other days ordained and used to be kept as holy days, and then and there to abide orderly and soberly during the time of the common prayer, preachings, or other service of God there to be used and ministered; upon pain of punishment by the censures of the Church.

And for the due execution hereof the King's most excellent Majesty, the Lords Temporal, and all the Commons in this present Parliament assembled, doth in God's name earnestly require and charge all the archbishops, bishops, and other ordinaries that they shall endeavor themselves to the uttermost of their knowledge that the due and true execution hereof may be had throughout their dioceses and charges, as they will answer before God for such evils and plagues wherewith Almighty God may justly punish his people for neglecting this good and wholesome law.

And for their authority in this behalf, be it further likewise enacted by the authority aforesaid, that all and singular the same archbishops, bishops, and all other their officers exercising ecclesiastical jurisdiction, as well in place exempt as not exempt within their diocese, shall have full power and authority by this Act to reform, correct, and punish by censures of the Church all and singular persons which shall offend within any their jurisdictions or dioceses after the said Feast of All Saints next coming against this Act and Statute; any other law, statute, privilege, liberty, or provision heretofore made, had, or suffered to the contrary notwithstanding.

And because there hath arisen in the use and exercise of the foresaid common service in the Church heretofore set forth, divers doubts for the fashion and manner of the ministration of the same, rather by the curiosity of the minister, and mistakers, than of any other worthy cause; therefore as well for the more plain and manifest explanation hereof as for the more perfection of the said order of common service, in some places where it is necessary to make the same prayers and fashion of service more earnest and fit to stir Christian people to the true honoring of Almighty God; the King's most excellent Majesty, with the assent of the Lords and Commons in this present Parliament assembled and by the authority of the same, hath caused the foresaid order of common service entitled *The Book of Common Prayer* to be faithfully and Godly perused, explained, and made fully perfect, and by the foresaid authority hath annexed and joined it so explained and perfected to this present statute, adding also a form and manner of making and consecrating archbishops, bishops, priests, and deacons, to be of like force, authority, and value as the same like foresaid book entitled *The Book of Common*

*Prayer* was before, and to be accepted, received, used, and esteemed in like sort and manner, and with the same clauses of provisions and exceptions to all intents, constructions, and purposes, as by the Act of Parliament made in the second year of the King's Majesty's reign was ordained and limited, expressed and appointed, for the uniformity of service and administration of the sacraments throughout the Realm, upon such several pains as in the said Act of Parliament is expressed; and the said former Act to stand in full force and strength to all intents and constructions, and to be applied, practiced, and put in use to and for the establishing of *The Book of Common Prayer* now explained and hereunto annexed, and also the said form of making archbishops, bishops, priests, and deacons hereunto annexed, as it was for the former book.

And by the authority aforesaid it is now further enacted, that if any manner of person or persons inhabiting and being within this realm or any other the King's Majesty's dominions shall after the said Feast of All Saints willingly and wittingly hear and be present at any other manner or form of common prayer, of administration of the sacraments, of making ministers in the churches,

or of any other rites contained in the book annexed to this Act than is mentioned and set forth in the said book or that is contrary to the form of sundry provisions and exceptions contained in the foresaid former statute, and shall be thereof convicted according to the laws of this realm ... by the verdict of twelve men or by his own confession or otherwise ... [here follow the degrees of punishment to be meted out for the first, second, and third offences].

And for the more knowledge to be given hereof and better observation of this law, be it enacted by the authority aforesaid that all and singular curates shall upon one Sunday every quarter of the year, during ... the Feast of All Saints ... read this present Act in the Church at the time of the most assembly ... at the same time declaring unto the people by the authority of the Scripture how the mercy and goodness of God hath in all ages been showed to his people in their necessities and extremities by means of hearty and faithful prayers made to Almighty God; especially where people be gathered together with one faith and mind to offer up their hearts by prayer, as the best sacrifices that Christian men can yield. (SR, IV, 130: 5 & 6 Edward VI, c.1.)

## Second Treasons Act of Edward VI. 1552

POPULAR discontent following Edward's legislative acts in things religious made necessary certain changes in the *First Treasons Act* of 1547. This revision was characterized by a return to the inclusive concept of treason established by Henry VIII. Once again any words, acts, or deeds against the King were to be considered high treason. Since protest against the policies of the Council was logically the same as criticism of the King, the Act mainly indicates the Council's defensive attitude.

**47.**

An Act for the punishment of divers Treasons.

Forasmuch as it is most necessary for common policy and duty of subjects above all things to prohibit, restrain, and extinct all manner of shameful slanders which might grow, happen, or arise to their Sovereign Lord the King's Majesty, which when they be heard, seen, or understood cannot be but

... abhorred of all those sorts that be true and loving subjects, if in any point they may, do, or shall touch his Majesty, upon whom dependeth the whole unity and universal weal of this realm, without providing wherefore too great a scope of unreasonable liberty should be given to all cankered and traitorous hearts, and the King's loving subjects should not declare unto their Sovereign Lord now being, which unto them hath been and is most entirely both beloved and esteemed, their undoubted sincerity and truth:

Be it therefore enacted by the Lords Spiritual and Temporal and the Commons in this present Parliament assembled that if any person or persons, after the first day of June next coming, by open preaching, express words or sayings, do expressly, directly, and advisedly set forth and affirm that the King that now is is an heretic, schismatic, tyrant, infidel, or usurper of the Crown, or that any his heirs or successors to whom the Crown of this realm is limited [by the *Third Succession Act* of Henry VIII] being in lawful possession of the Crown, is an heretic [etc.] . . . that then every such offender, being thereof duly convicted or attainted by the laws of this realm, their abettors, procurers, and counsellors, and all and every their aiders and comforters, knowing the said offences or any of them to be done shall suffer [the same punishments as stated in the *First Treasons Act* of Edward VI.]

And be it further enacted by the authority aforesaid, that if any person or persons, at any time . . . by writing, printing, painting, carving, or graving, do directly, expressly, and advisedly publish, set forth and affirm that the King that now is, or any his heirs or successors limited as is beforesaid, is an heretic [etc.] . . . , that then every such offence and offences shall be deemed and adjudged high treason, and the offender and offenders, their abettors, procurers, [etc.] . . . being thereof convicted or attainted . . . shall be deemed and adjudged high traitors, and shall suffer pains of death, and lose and forfeit all their goods and chattels, lands and tenements, to the King as in cases of high treason. . . .

[Detaining royal ships or forts is treason].

Provided always and be it enacted by the authority aforesaid, that no person or persons . . . shall be indicted . . . condemned, convicted, or attained for any of the treasons or offences aforesaid, or for any other treasons that now be or hereafter shall be, which shall hereafter be perpetrated . . . unless the same offender . . . be thereof accused by two lawful accusers, which said accusers at the time of the arraignment of the party accused, if they be then living, shall be brought in person before the party so accused, and avow and maintain that [what] they have to say against the said party to prove him guilty of the treasons or offences contained in the bill of indictment laid against the party arraigned [be true], unless the said party arraigned shall willingly without violence confess the same. (SR, IV, 144: 5 Edward VI, c.11.)

# The Reign of Mary

## 1553-1558

## DOCUMENTS OF THE REIGN OF MARY

# England, 1553-1558 Introduction

In terms of constitutional development, Mary Tudor's reign, despite its social, religious, and political ferment, was, with Edward's, an interlude between two well defined periods of constitutional growth. The reason for this is to be found partly in Mary's inability to gauge the opinions and desires of her people, who were motivated more by political and economic ambitions than by the theological interest which determined Mary's political actions. But this failure was only one aspect of a much greater misunderstanding: she never comprehended the *sine qua non* of monarchial political power in England. Unlike her father and grandfather, Mary placed her faith in statute law, assuming that her desires would be undoubted and indestructible once given statutory existence. Not that Mary denied or ever consciously transgressed the common law; rather she failed to realize that popular opinion and public agreement, not monarchial voice, were the real and vital forces in making national policy.

Mary assumed, as many have since, that Henry VII had literally instituted the modern English monarchy and that Henry VIII had broken the ties between the Roman and English Churches. Hence, the lessons she learned from the past seemed to demonstrate the crucial importance of vigorous and independent monarchial action—her attempt to conform to this fallacious notion cost her popular good will and the support of Commons. For Mary did not realize that the English people had made the Reformation, had created and conditioned both the constitution and Tudor absolutism, and had, for that matter, placed her on the throne. Fatally, she elevated *her* law and *her* sense of moral righteousness above the general will.

It is often said that Mary Tudor was the most honest of all Tudor monarchs. Certainly she was constitutionally averse to political obscurantism or cynicism: her goals were ever clearly and publicly articulated. Her enmity to Henry's religious settlement and her hope for marriage into the Catholic royal family of Spain were never hidden. Her repudiation of Gardiner's diluted Romanism was forcefully expressed in the first year of her reign. Unlike her predecessors, Mary had a single program, the revival of the ancient ties between Rome and Westminster, and she held to it with the determination of one totally innocent of knowledge of things political, economic, or historical. That her hopes came to nothing should not be laid to inconsistency or vacillation.

This is not to say that Mary was above compromise. Students of Marian legislation might wonder at a religious settlement which returned to the Catholic Church every right and prerogative enjoyed by that institution prior to 1520—except the lands and properties which had been taken from it by her father. The answer lies in the need for compromise. English sentiment was opposed in overwhelming way to such material restitution of the Roman Church in England. Mary was forced (in the *Second Statute of Repeal*) to grant the legal right of the holders of former Church lands to their possessions in order to secure popular acceptance of the rest of her religious program.

Unfortunately, Mary's willingness to compromise on the single issue of Church and Chantry lands led her to believe she had thereby purchased the right of independent and even arbitrary action on other issues. Perhaps she misjudged the real meaning of the wave of enthusiasm which had swept her to the throne. It was as much a manifestation of popular hatred for the violence and greed of her enemies as of accord for her own constitutional claim which had prevented Northumberland's attempt to usurp the crown for Lady Jane Grey. Had her perception been keener she might have foreseen the political dangers inherent in her marriage to Philip of Spain. Half Spanish by blood, a sincere Roman Catholic, broodingly resentful of the treatment of her mother at the hands of Henry VIII and his subjects, it is no wonder that Mary turned, in the time of her misery, to Spain for consolation. Nor is it strange that later, when contemplating marriage with Philip, she neglected the mutterings of obvious popular disapproval and unrest. Peter Carew's insurrection in Devonshire and Thomas Wyatt's march on London would have served notice on a more alert government that the forces of social discontent were deep and abiding.

The marriage, the violent application of the heresy laws, and the loss of Calais in the Franco-Spanish war constituted the triple prelude to the public rejection of the queen's will. These events impressed most deeply on the English mind the belief that her policy meant absolute submission to Spain and to the See of Rome—things as objectionable to Parliament and people in 1555 as they had been in 1535.

The last year of Mary's life was tragic. Childless and disillusioned by the calculated coldness of Philip and without the good will of her people, knowing that Elizabeth would never attempt to stem the determined renaissance of English Protestantism, Mary sought solace in religious mysticism, and, as Professor Trevelyan has said, "turned her face away to die."

Yet Mary's ill-fated reign did render a tremendous and lasting service to the English people. By her very indifference to it, Mary forced the popular will into an offensive role from which it would not easily retreat. As a consequence, it began to realize its own strength and its ability to influence governmental policy. Indeed, the public will was now to become operative in the English constitution and a force which no King or Parliament would ever again dare to ignore.

## First Treasons Act of Mary. 1553

**48.** DETERMINED from the beginning of her reign to adhere to a program of peaceful persuasion in consolidating her position, Mary identified herself with the conservative policies of Henry VIII prior to his break with Rome. In the name of common humanitarianism, all the measures of Henry and Edward relative to treason were stricken from the statute books, and treason was redefined in the medieval and much less comprehensive terms of Edward III's *Statute of Treasons* of 1352.

An Act repealing certain Treasons, Felonies, and *Praemunire*.

Forasmuch as the state of every king, ruler, and governor of any realm, dominion, or commonalty standeth and consisteth more assured by the love and favor of the subject toward their sovereign ruler and governor than in the dread and fear of laws made with rigorous pains and extreme punishment for not obeying of their sovereign ruler and governor; and laws also justly made for the preservation of the common weal, without extreme punishment or great penalty, are more often for the most part obeyed and kept than laws and statutes made with great and extreme punishments, and in especial such laws and statutes so made, whereby not only the ignorant and rude, unlearned people, but also learned and expert people minding honesty, are often and many times trapped and snared, yea, many times for words only, without other fact or deed done or perpetrated:

The Queen's most excellent Majesty, calling to remembrance that many, as well honourable and noble persons as other of good reputation within this her Grace's realm of England, have of late, for words only without other opinion, fact, or deed, suffered shameful death not accustomed to nobles; Her Highness therefore, of her accustomed clemency and mercy, minding to avoid and put away the occasion and cause of like chances hereafter to ensue, trusting her loving subjects will, for her clemency to them showed, love, serve, and obey her Grace the more

heartily and faithfully than for dread or fear of pains of body, is contented and pleased that the severity of suchlike extreme dangerous and painful laws shall be abolished, annulled, and made frustrate and void:

Be it therefore ordained and enacted by the Lords Spiritual and Temporal and the Commons in this present Parliament assembled [that no act be adjudged treason or petty treason by the courts or punished as such by the government except such as are defined as treason by 25 Edward III. Thus the present Act nullifies all precedent statutes relative to treason since that of Edward III and reestablishes statutory treason on a purely medieval basis. According to the *Statute of Treasons* of Edward III (1352) as stated in the French in SR I, 319f, treason could *only* consist of hoping for the death of the King or Queen or the heir apparent, copulation with the Queen or the wife of the heir apparent, committing acts of war against the King or comforting the King's enemies anywhere, counterfeiting the great seal or the money of the realm, or murdering the Chancellor, Treasurer, or the Chief Justice while they stood and acted in office.] (SR, IV, 198: 1 Mary, c.1.)

## First Statute of Repeal. 1553

**49.**

DURING the first two years of her reign Mary was content with a program of statutory nullification of the Church legislation of Edward VI. Here, and later, her purpose was clear: to invalidate the religious settlements of her Protestant predecessors, and, by thus severing the bonds between the English Church and continental Protestantism, to return to the ancient ties with Rome. It is noteworthy that Mary relied entirely on constitutional processes to effect her program of counter-reformation.

An Act for the Repeal of certain Statutes made in the time of the Reign of King Edward the Sixth.

Forasmuch as by divers and several Acts hereafter mentioned, as well the divine service and good administration of the sacraments as divers other matters of religion which we and our forefathers found in this Church of England to us left by the authority of the Catholic Church, be partly altered and

in some part taken from us, and in place thereof new things imagined and set forth by the said Acts, such as a few of singularity have of themselves devised, whereof hath ensued amongst us in very short time numbers of divers and strange opinions and diversities of sects, and thereby grown great unquietness and much discord, to the great disturbance of the common wealth of this realm, and in very short time like to grow to extreme peril and utter confusion of the same, unless some remedy be in that behalf provided, which thing all true, loving, and obedient subjects ought and are bounded to foresee and provide to the uttermost of their power:

In consideration whereof be it enacted by the authority of this present Parliament assembled ... [the Act here provides for the repeal the Edwardian statutes concerning: the *Sacrament of the Altar;* the *Election of Bishops; First Act of Uniformity; Marriage of Priests; Images; For the Ordering of Ecclesiastical Ministers; Second Act of Uniformity; For the Keeping of Holy Days and Fasting Days*].

And be it further enacted by the authority aforesaid, that all such Divine Service and administration of Sacraments as were most commonly used in the realm of England in the last year of the reign of our late Sovereign Lord King Henry the Eighth, shall be, from and after the twentieth day of December in this present year of our Lord God one thousand five hundred fifty and three, used and frequented through the whole realm of England and all other the Queen's Majesty's dominions, and that no other kind nor order of Divine Service nor administration of Sacraments be after the said twentieth day of December used or ministered in any other manner, form, or degree within the said realm of England or other the Queen's dominions than was most commonly used, ministered, and frequented in the said last year of the reign of the said late King Henry the Eighth. (SR, IV, 202: I Mary, c.2.)

## Act Reviving the Heresy Laws. 1554

50.    IN THE first phase of the destruction of Protestantism, Mary was less enthusiastic about burning heretics than were the Catholic Parliamentarians. In the end, however, her scruples were obscured by a fanatical religious ardor. The following Act shows the extent to which both Crown and Parliament were willing to go in order to effect the return of England to the Papal fold.

An Act for the renewing of three Statutes made for the punishment of Heresies.

For the eschewing and avoiding of errors and heresies which of late have risen, grown, and much increased within this realm, for that the ordinaries [church officials] have wanted [lacked] authority to proceed against those that were infected therewith:

Be it therefore ordained and enacted by the authority of this present Parliament, that the statute made in the fifth year of the reign of King Richard the Second concerning the arresting and apprehension of erroneous and heretical preachers, [Richard's *Statute of Heresies* authorized justices and sheriffs to imprison suspected heretics when so charged by a bishop] and one other statute made in the second year of the reign of King Henry the Fourth concerning the repressing of heresies and punishment of heretics, [the statute here referred to charged the secular authorities with the burning of nonrepentant heretics] and also one other statute made in the second year of the reign of King Henry the Fifth concerning the suppression of heresy and Lollardy, [this statute authorized crown courts to accept indictments for heresy and to deliver persons so indicted to canon law courts for trial] and every article, branch, and sentence contained in the same three several acts and every of them, shall from the 20th day of January next coming be revived and be in full force, strength, and effect, to all intents, constructions, and purposes for ever. (SR, IV, 244: 1 & 2 Philip & Mary, c.6.)

## Act Concerning the Regal Power. 1554

DISSATISFACTION with the Spanish marriage and fear of foreign intervention in English domestic affairs impelled Mary's enemies to seek a weakness in her claim to the throne. The most obvious defect was her sex; and, since no precedent existed for a female monarch, it was the one first exploited. Thus, the reactions of Carew and Wyatt against Mary were rationalized in terms of her constitutional right to the throne. In the Queen's defense, Parliament formulated the idea that the sex of a monarch was of secondary importance to right of inheritance. This Act was of supreme importance to the development of English Constitution.

**5 I.**

An Act declaring that the Regal Power of this Realm is in the Queen's Majesty as fully and absolutely as ever it was in any of her most noble Progenitors, Kings of this Realm.

Forasmuch as the imperial Crown of this realm, with all dignities, honors, prerogatives, authorities, jurisdictions, and preeminences thereunto annexed, united, and belonging, by the Divine Providence of Almighty God is most lawfully, justly, and rightfully descended and come unto the Queen's Highness that now is, being the very true and undoubted heir and inheritrix thereof, and invested in her most Royal Person, according unto the laws of this realm; and by force and virtue of the same all regal power, dignity, honor, authority, prerogative, preeminence, and jurisdictions doth appertain, and of right ought to appertain and belong unto her Highness, as to the sovereign supreme Governor and Queen of this realm and the dominions thereof, in as full, large, and ample manner as it hath done heretofore to any other her most noble progenitors, kings of this realm:

Nevertheless the most ancient statutes of this realm being made by kings then reigning, do not only attribute and refer all prerogative, preeminence, power, and jurisdiction royal unto the name of king, but also do give, assign, and appoint the correction and punishment of all offenders against the regality and dignity of the Crown and the laws of this realm unto the king; by occasion whereof the malicious and ignorant persons may be hereafter induced and persuaded

unto this error and folly, to think that her Highness could nor should have, enjoy, and use such like royal authority, power, preeminence, prerogative, and jurisdiction, nor do nor execute and use all privilege of the same, nor correct and punish offenders against her most Royal Person and the regality and dignity of the Crown of this realm and the dominions thereof, as the kings of this realm her most noble progenitors have heretofore done, enjoyed, used, and exercised:

For the avoiding and clear extinguishment of which said error or doubt, and for a plain declaration of the laws of this realm in that behalf; be it declared and enacted . . . that the law of this realm is and ever has been and ought to be understood, that the kingly or regal office of the realm, and all dignities, [etc.] . . . thereto annexed, united, or belonging, being invested either in male or female, are and be and ought to be as fully, wholly, absolutely, and entirely deemed, judged, accepted, invested, and taken in the one as in the other, so that what and whensoever statute or law doth limit and appoint that the king of this realm may or shall have, execute, and do anything as king, or doth give any profit or commodity to the king, or doth limit or appoint any pains or punishment for the correction of offenders or transgressors against the regality and dignity of the king or of the Crown, the same the Queen (being supreme Governess, possessor, and inheritor to the imperial Crown of this realm as our said Sovereign Lady the Queen most justly presently is) may by the same authority and power likewise have exercise, execute, punish, correct, and do, to all intents, constructions, and purposes, without doubt, ambiguity, scruple, or question: any custom, use, or scruple, or any other thing whatsoever to be made to the contrary notwithstanding. (SR, IV, 222: 1 Mary, c.1.)

## Second Statute of Repeal. 1555

52. THE following Act repeals all anti-Catholic laws passed since 1528 with the exception of the laws concerning the dissolution of the monasteries and Crown assumption of Papal incomes. In time, no doubt, Mary hoped to make legal restitution for every property alienated from the Church. In the meanwhile, however, in order that the upper classes would consent to return to Rome, she was forced to pay their passage by letting them retain whatever wealth they had received during the seizures.

An Act repealing all Statutes, Articles, and Provisions made against the See Apostolic of Rome since the 20th year of King Henry the Eight, and also for the establishment of all Spiritual and Ecclesiastical Possessions and Hereditaments conveyed to the Laity.

Whereas since the 20th year of King Henry the Eight of famous memory, father unto your Majesty our most natural Sovereign and Gracious Lady and Queen, much false and erroneous doctrine hath been taught, preached, and written, partly by divers and natural-born subjects of this realm, and partly being brought in hither from sundry other foreign countries, hath been sown and spread abroad within the same; by reason whereof as well the spiritualty as the temporalty of your Highness's realms and dominions have swerved from the obedience of the See Apostolic and declined from the unity of Christ's Church, and so have continued, until such time as your Majesty being first raised up by God and set in the royal seat over us, and then by his divine and gracious Providence knit in marriage with the most noble and virtuous prince, the King our Sovereign Lord your husband, the Pope's Holiness and the See Apostolic sent hither unto your Majesties ... and to the whole realm, the most Reverend Father in God the Lord Cardinal Pole, Legate *de latere,* to call us home again into the right way, from whence we have all this long while wandered and strayed abroad; and we after sundry long and grievous plagues and calamities, seeing by the goodness of God our own errors, have acknowledged the same unto the said most Reverend Father, and by him have been and are ... at the contemplation of your Majesties received and embraced into the unity and bosom of Christ's Church; and upon our humble submission and promise made, for a declaration of our repentance, to repeal and abrogate such acts and statutes as had been made in Parliament since the said 20th year of the said King Henry the Eighth against the supremacy of the See Apostolic, as in our submission exhibited to the said most Reverend Father in God by your Majesties appeareth: The tenor whereof ensueth:

We the Lords Spiritual and Temporal and the Commons assembled in this present Parliament, representing the whole body of the realm of England and the dominions of the same, in the name of ourselves particularly and also of the said body universally in this our supplication directed to your Majesties, with most humble suit that it may by your Graces' intercession ... be exhibited to the most Reverend Father in God the Lord Cardinal Pole, Legate sent specially hither from our most Holy Father the Pope Julius the Third and the See Apostolic of Rome, do declare ourselves very sorry and repentant of the schism and disobedience committed in this realm and dominions aforesaid against the said See Apostolic, either by making, agreeing, or executing any laws, ordinances, or commandments against the supremacy of the said See, or otherwise doing or speaking that might impugn the same; offering ourselves and promising by this our supplication that for a token and knowledge of our said repentance we be and shall be always ready, under and with the authorities of your Majesties, to the utmost of our powers, to do that shall lie in us for the abrogation and repealing of the said laws and ordinances in this present Parliament as well for ourselves as for the whole body whom we represent:

Whereupon we most humbly desire your Majesties, as personages undefiled in the offence of this body towards the See, which nevertheless God by his Providence hath made subject to you, so set forth this our most humble suit that we may obtain from the See Apostolic by the said most Reverend Father, as well particularly as generally, absolution, release, and discharge from all danger of such censures and sentences as by the laws of the Church we be fallen into; and that we may as children repentant be received into the bosom and unity of Christ's Church, so as this noble realm with all the members thereof may in this unity and perfect obedience to the See Apostolic and Popes for the time being serve God and your Majesties to the furtherance and advancement of His honor and glory, we are at the intercession of your Majesties by the authority of our Holy Father Pope Julius the Third and of the See Apostolic assoiled, discharged, and delivered from excommunication, interdictions, and other censures ecclesiastical which hath hanged over our heads for our said defaults since the time of the said schism mentioned in our supplication. It may now like your Majesties that for the accomplishment of our promise made in the said supplication, that is to repeal all laws and statutes made contrary to the said supremacy and See Apostolic during the said schism, the which is to be understood since the 20th year of the reign of the said late King Henry the Eighth, and so the said Lord Legate doth accept and recognize the same.

[This Act here repeals 21 Henry VIII, c.13; 23 Henry VIII, c.9; 24 Henry VIII, c.12; 23 Henry VIII, c.20; 25 Henry VIII, c.19; 25 Henry VIII, c.20; 25 Henry VIII, c.21; 26 Henry VIII, c.1; 26 Henry VIII, c.14; 27 Henry VIII, c.15; 28 Henry VIII, c.10; 28 Henry VIII, c.16; 28 Henry VIII, c.7, paragraph 7; 31 Henry VIII, c.9; 32 Henry VIII, c.38; 35 Henry VIII, c.3; 35 Henry VIII, c.1, paragraph 7; 37 Henry VIII, c.17; 1 Edward VI, c.12, paragraph 5 and 6].

And be it further enacted by the authority aforesaid, that all clauses, sentences, and articles of every other statute or act of Parliament made since the said 20th year of the reign of King Henry the Eighth against the supreme authority of the Pope's Holiness or See Apostolic of Rome, or containing any other matter of the same effect only, that is repealed in any of the statutes aforesaid, shall be also by authority hereof from henceforth utterly void, frustrate, and none effect. . . .

. . . . And finally, where certain acts and statutes have been made in the time of the late schism concerning the lands and hereditaments of archbishoprics and bishoprics, the suppression and dissolution of monasteries, abbeys, priories, chantries, colleges, and all other the goods and chattels of religious houses, since the which time the right and dominion of certain lands and hereditaments, goods and chattels, belonging to the same be dispersed abroad and come to the hands and possessions of divers and sundry persons who by gift, purchase, exchange, and other means, according to the order of the laws and statutes of this realm for the time being, have the same; for the avoiding of all scruples that might grow by any the occasions aforesaid or by any other ways or means whatsoever, it may please your Majesties to be intercessors and mediators to the said most Reverend Father Cardinal Pole, that all such causes and quarrels as by pretence of the said schism or by any other occasion or mean whatsoever might be moved, by the Pope's Holiness or See Apostolic or by any other jurisdiction ecclesiastical, may be utterly removed and taken away; so as all persons having sufficient conveyance of the said lands and hereditaments, goods and chattels, as is aforesaid by the common laws, acts, or statutes of this realm, may without scruple of conscience enjoy them, without impeachment or trouble by pretence of any General Council, canons, or ecclesiastical laws, and clear from all dangers of censures of the Church.... (SR, IV, 246: 1 and 2 Philip and Mary, c.8.)

## Second Treasons Act of Mary. 1555

**53.** THE measure of domestic discontent with Mary's policy of submission to Rome and with the Spanish marriage is indicated by her return to the defense of statutory treason. Just as Henry VIII had used Parliamentary legislation to protect his several marriages, so Mary in 1555 resorted to manipulation of constitutional law to protect Philip from "such shameful slanders."

An Act whereby certain Offences be made Treasons; and also for the Government of the King's and Queen's Majesties' Issue.

Forasmuch as the great mercy and clemency heretofore declared by the Queen's Highness, in releasing the penal laws made by her progenitors, hath given occasion to many cankered and traitorous hearts to imagine, practice, and attempt things stirring the people to disobedience and rebellion against her Highness; common policy and duty of subjects require that some law be again established to restrain the malice of such wicked and evil doers, whereby they may be prohibited to blow abroad such shameful slanders and lies as they daily invent and imagine of her Highness and of the King's Majesty her most lawful husband, which when they be heard cannot be but disliked and detested of all good men, considering they touch their Majesties, upon whom dependeth the whole unity and universal wealth of this realm:

In consideration whereof be it ordained and enacted by the authority of this present Parliament assembled, that if any person ... during the marriage between the King and the Queen's Majesties, do compass or imagine to deprive the King's Majesty that now is from the having and enjoying jointly together with the Queen's Highness the style, honor, and kingly name of the realms and dominions unto our said Sovereign Lady the Queen's Highness appertaining, or to destroy the King that now is during the said matrimony, or to destroy the Queen's Majesty that now is, or the heirs of her body begotten being kings or queens of this realm, or to levy war ... against [any of them] ... or to depose the Queen ... or the heirs of her body ... from the imperial Crown ..., or if any person ... by preaching, express words or sayings, shall maliciously, advisedly, and directly say, publish, declare, maintain, or hold opinion that the King's Majesty that now is, during the said matrimony, ought not to have or enjoy jointly together with the Queen's Majesty the style, honor, and kingly name of this realm, or that any person or persons, being neither the King or the Queen's Majesty that now are, during the said matrimony between them, ought to have or enjoy the style, [etc.] ... or that the Queen's Majesty that now is during her life is not or of right ought not to be Queen of this realm, or after her death that the heirs of her Highness's body being kings or queens of this realm of right ought not to be kings or queens of this realm or to have and enjoy the same, or that any person or persons other than the Queen's Majesty that now is, during her life, ought to be Queen of this realm, or after her death other than the heirs of her body being kings or queens of this realm, as long as any of her said heirs of her body begotten shall be in life, of right ought to have and enjoy the imperial Crown of this Realm; that then every such offender, being thereof duly convicted or attainted by the laws of this realm, their abettors, procurers, and counsellors, and all and every one their comforters, knowing the said offences or any of them be done, and being thereof convicted or attainted as is above said, for his or their such offence shall forfeit and lose to the Queen's Highness, her heirs and successors, all his and their goods and chattels and the whole issues and profits of his and their lands, tenements, and other hereditaments for term of the life of every such offender ... and shall ... suffer during his or their lives perpetual imprisonment....

And be it further enacted by the said authority, that if any person or persons, at any time after the said first day of February next to come, during the said marriage, compass or imagine the death of the King's Majesty that now is and the same maliciously, advisedly, and directly shall utter and attempt by any writing, printing, overt deed or act, or if any person ... shall maliciously, advisedly, and directly, by writing, printing, overt deed or act, [deny the title of either the King or Queen or their issue shall be guilty of treason]....

And be it further enacted by the authority aforesaid, that if any persons, during the time that our said Sovereign Lord the King that now is shall and ought to have the order, rule, education, and government of such issue or issues, being king or queen of this realm, according to the order and provision aforesaid, maliciously, advisedly, and directly, by writing, printing, or deed or act, do compass, attempt, and go about to destroy the person of our said Sovereign Lord, or to deprive or remove his said Highness from the order, rule, education, and government of the same issue or issues, being king or queen of this realm, contrary to the tenor, intent, and true meaning of this present Act, that then every such person ... so offending, their procurers and abettors, being thereof lawfully convict or attainted by the laws of this realm, shall be deemed and adjudged high traitors, and that all and every such offence and offences shall be deemed and adjudged high treason....

Provided always and be it enacted by the authority aforesaid, that upon the arraignment of any person which hereafter shall fortune to be arraigned for any treason mentioned in this Act, all and every such person and persons, or two of them at the least, as shall hereafter write, declare, confess, or depose any thing or things against the person to be arraigned, shall, if they be then living and within the realm, be brought forth in person before the party arraigned, if he require the same, and object and say openly in his hearing what they or any of them can against him for or concerning any the treasons contained in the indictment whereupon the party shall be so arraigned, unless the party arraigned for any such treason shall willingly confess the same at the time of his or their arraignment. (SR, IV, 255: 1 and 2 Philip and Mary, c.10.)

## Act Against Traitorous Words. 1555

# 54.

THIS statute is dramatic evidence of the absolute rejection of Mary by a portion of her subjects; it shows, too, her ultimate rejection of moderation. For the first time in English history it became treason for the subject to pray to God for anything but what the Monarch desired, an example of the incredible length to which repressive legislation could be carried in time of high passion. Mary's ultimate reliance on her father's method of silencing his opposition is clearly demonstrated.

An Act for the punishment of Traitorous Words against the Queen's Majesty.

Forasmuch as now of late divers naughty, seditious, malicious, and heretical persons, not having the fear of God before their eyes, but in a devilish sort, contrary to the duty of their allegiance, have congregated themselves together in conventicles in divers and sundry profane places within the city of London, esteeming themselves to be in the true faith where indeed they are in errors and heresies and out of the true road of Christ's Catholic Religion, and in the same places at several times using their fantastical and schismatical services lately taken away and abolished by authority of Parliament, have of their most malicious and cankered stomachs prayed against the Queen's Majesty that God would turn her heart from idolatry to the true faith or else to shorten her days or take her quickly out of the way; which prayer was never heard nor read to have been used by any good Christian man against any prince though he were a pagan and infidel, and much less against any Christian prince, and especially so virtuous a Princess as our Sovereign Lady that now is known to be, whose faith is and always hath been most true and Catholic, and consonant and agreeing with Christ's Catholic Church throughout the world dispersed:

For reformation whereof, be it enacted by the authority of this present Parliament, that every such person and persons which, since the beginning of this present Parliament, have by express words and sayings prayed, required, or desired as is aforesaid, or hereafter shall pray by express words or sayings that God should shorten her days or take her out of the way ... or any such like malicious prayer amounting to the same effect, their procurers and abettors therein, shall be taken, reputed, and judged traitors, and every such praying, requiring, or desiring shall be judged, taken, and reputed high treason, and the offenders therein, [etc.] ... being lawfully convict according to the laws of this realm, shall have, suffer, and forfeit as in cases of high treason.... (SR, IV, 254: 1 and 2 Philip and Mary, c.9.)

# The Reign of Elizabeth

## 1558-1603

# England 1558-1603  Introduction

The coronation of Elizabeth in 1558 inaugurated an era of significant change in the patterns of English life. The swift acceleration in intellectual, artistic, and economic activity which characterized the Renaissance generally and her reign in particular had a lasting effect on the English constitution. Committed, as part of her inheritance, to the fortunes of that merchant middle class which had risen to economic and political eminence under her father, Elizabeth joined the class in seeking validation in the future rather than in the feudal past.

Yet the rejection of the ancient ways and acceptance of political pragmatism and realism was not a panacea, for the new monarchy of Henry VII and the Reformation of Henry VIII had, while solving few problems, created a multitude of them for reigns to come. By exploiting the inevitable public uncertainties in times of national crisis, the two Henrys had established not only the new dynasty but a whole new concept of English kingship; moreover, they had accomplished this to the satisfaction of the national constituency. But with the beginning of Elizabeth's reign, the emotional leverage of immediate domestic crisis was no longer available. The institutional novelties of Tudor absolutism were endangered by their very newness: they had no background in popular tradition or common law. Moreover, popular belief in a disinterested monarchy had been considerably shaken by the many questionable procedures occurring in the reigns of Edward and Mary. At the same time the concept of political resistance to authority had lost its medieval semi-heretical overtones and had acquired moral status, in certain cases, as a Christian duty against immoral political authority. Hence Elizabeth's primary problem was to evaluate and define the proper politic *rôle* of the monarchy in the light of current public concepts and opinions.

Since Henry VII, four monarchs, including Elizabeth, had uprooted Church settlements which had been previously in each case popularly accepted as legally, constitutionally, and morally valid. Four times in twenty-five years English subjects had been boldly notified that the previous settlement had been in error—sufficiently so for drastic reform to be necessary. Each radical change in religious organization had necessitated like social innovations in the distribution of land, wealth, political power, and social positions. The cumulative effect of this apparently patternless series of upheavals made redefinition in the area of church-state relationships particularly urgent.

In scrutinizing the intricate patterns of statute law and constitutional evolution from 1558 to 1603 it is clear that Elizabeth, as administrator of the English government, was gifted with exceptional insight in certain respects and suffered from political myopia in others. Yet it should be remembered in her favor that her chief failures involved forces and factors which governments of later periods, having (unlike her) precedents and a fund of human knowledge and experience to aid them, were still unable to order. Again, the rapid acceleration of social and economic change in western Europe had direct, and often violent influence on one or another aspect of English life. The Huguenot problem in France, Spain's unlimited importation of American gold, the doctrines of John Calvin, the shifting balance of power on the continent, and the political rationalizations of Jean Bodin were as crucial to English development as they were to any continental state.

The England of Henry VIII's day had been less closely bound to the continent than was that of Elizabeth's, for commercial activity in the earlier period had been less encompassing. Hence, Henry's problems had been proportionately smaller and his makeshift solutions were in the long run inadequate. The single example of social legislation illustrates the major differences in the legislative programs of the two administrations, and also shows to what extent the uncertain formulations of Henry's reign became a problem for his daughter. It will be recalled that Henry's attack on the Church almost entirely demolished the ancient pattern of poor-relief in England. Prior to this, the Church had been the only social institution concerned with extending moral and material aid to the indigent of the land, not only giving alms but, in times of economic crisis, caring for widows and dependent children, supporting the mentally feeble, and maintaining wage levels through moral persuasion. Disagreements between employer and employee had been generally worked out in the local courts where clerical influence was most keenly felt. Traditionally, the state had seldom interfered with Church action in these matters.

The Reformation occurred at the moment when capitalistic development in western Europe was becoming an important factor in forcing a transition in England from a purely agrarian to a partially commercial economy. But while Reformation legislation gave the Crown use and control of Church wealth, it neglected to include in the transfer the concurrent social responsibilities which had been traditional functions of that wealth. Furthermore, no other institution assumed the burden of protecting that growing portion of society incapable of competing successfully in economic life.

The social legislation of Henry's Parliaments was not only scant but brutal and demoralizing in that it reflected a puritanical callousness in assessing poverty as the just desert of sloth and evildoing. The Edwardian churchmen, Cranmer and Latimer, were apparently aware of economic cause and effect in indigence but were never able to develop effective remedies because of self-centered factionalism in the council. Mary, intent on reconstructing the Roman Catholic Church in England, although not indifferent, had neither time nor energy to spare for such matters.

Thus Elizabeth inherited the problem of widespread poverty with her crown; and her legislative program was immediate, massive, and positive. The Acts of 1563 (*Statute of Apprentices*), 1571 (*Tillage Act*), 1576 (*Poor Relief Act*), and 1598 (*Poor Relief Act* and *Beggars Act*) show growing awareness of economic causation as well as compassion. Gauged by modern standards of treatment, the methods employed in Elizabeth's reforms were somewhat crude. Yet basically her legislation was sympathetic and was based on the assumptions that poverty was the responsibility of the social organism and that it had to be cured at its source by increasing both the productive and consumptive potentials of the nation. The complex provisions of the *Statute of Apprentices* and the simpler expressions of the *Acts of Poor Relief* were clear statements of Elizabeth's attempt to reactivate through governmental agencies the sense of social responsibility which had formerly guided the Church. The statutory methods utilized by Elizabeth in shifting the care of the poor from the impoverished Church to the more capable agency of the social whole was characteristic of all of her social legislation. Constitutional, humane, and strictly applied, such legislation was at once of extreme importance in the development of the constitution and one of the most significant legacies to humanity bequeathed by the Tudor dynasty.

When the full measure of Elizabethan legislation is studied in relation to constitutional evolution it is clear, however, that it was the Queen's attitudes of compromise and procrastination which influenced the process most heavily. As a case in point, one might consider the changing status of the House of Commons in the Tudor period. Henry VII, in return for the moral and financial support of that class, had dignified Commons' electoral constituency. Henry VIII added institutional permanence to Commons for the same reasons. Elizabeth carried recognition to the point of allowing the growth and expression of independent parliamentary will and voice—just at the time when Commons' full realization of the political strength and moral power it derived from its representative qualities gave it added confidence. In the case of all three monarchs, Commons was given privileges in return for reasonable toleration and financial aid in the Crown's management of an increasingly complex and expanding realm. Thus Elizabeth's flirtatious policy with Parliament, Puritans, merchants, and common lawyers, is more accurately to be thought of as an expedient, common-sense solution to an unescapable problem at a time when constitutional rigidity might have fatally crippled the entire social structure.

Finally, it is necessary to note the significant difference in monarchial attitude toward resistance to authority during Elizabeth's reign. Some few individuals had attempted to controvert the poltical prerogatives of Henry VII, and some had questioned Henry VIII's Reformation settlement. In each case the monarchial reaction had been immediate and severe, for the mere toleration of opposition was thought to encourage its further expression. Mary's reign, short though it was, stands alongside the Puritan interregnum in the destructive quality of its efforts against resistant minorities. The Elizabethan period, on the other hand, saw the unimpeded return of the Marian exiles into England. These exiles brought with them the Calvinistic concept of the Divine Right of theological governance, and here, in her failure to counteract such an ambitious claim, was Elizabeth's most significant constitutional failure. Because of the Queen's sturdy belief in the idea that the English Monarchy "stands highest in our Parliament," she never fully understood that the deterministic, theologically dominated ideology of the Puritans was essentially opposed to her own. Moreover, Elizabeth's toleration of the doctrine was itself defective in Puritan eyes on the grounds that any toleration was tacit recognition of virtue and, further, that toleration was in any case merely a political expedient employed to retain political power against divinely inspired political Calvinism.

Thus, all the explosive moral and theological arguments regarding political power were in Puritan possession, while the Crown continued its customary courtship of Parliament—although even in Elizabeth's time this institution was coming more and more under the domination of the opposition. Within a half-century of her reign all this would result in the destruction of the institution of the monarchy, the total subversion of the common law, and in the ignominious death of an English king.

## Sir Thomas Smith, *De Republica Anglorum.* 1589

**55.**

SIR THOMAS SMITH shows more clearly than any other Elizabethan theorist the changes in the function of constitutional institutions and in the application of political techniques resulting from a century of Tudor rule. Smith, concerned with the actual rather than the ideal, set down a true picture of the political developments of the past hundred years. It is interesting to compare his concepts with those of John Fortescue.

Fortescue had had a dual view of the natural law which for him was the ligament binding the elements of the constitution into a functionable unity. Under natural law, also, King, Parliament, and the people each had certain areas reserved to them and those areas were secured against the interference of other constitutional components. Thus, Fortescue, in full accord with medieval socio-political theory argued that absolute sovereignty could not exist in the political state.

Sir Thomas Smith, on the other hand, did not look to any fundamental law to guarantee or protect rights or limit political action. Sovereignty *did* exist—in Parliament—and Smith pointed to its proofs. "Parliament abrogates old laws, makes new . . . changes rights, and possessions of private men . . . establishes forms of religion . . . gives forms of succession to the Crown." Nor did Smith dig into the distant past or distort present circumstances in order to bulwark his contentions. Parliament had proven its right to act in each of those areas during his own lifetime.

However, while Smith's ideas symbolize the pace and extent of progressive constitutional change during the Tudor period, those same ideas will serve to underline the continuity of medieval concepts in the late Elizabethan period. With Fortescue, Smith held that the King was a part of Parliament and that in changing the vital alignments within the constitutional pattern neither the King nor the body of representatives could act alone. Parliament, therefore, existed in its active capacity only when King and people met together to "advertise, consult, and show what is good and necessary for the Commonwealth. . . ."

It is sometimes said that Smith imported the concept of political sovereignty from France into England. But that Smith's theories originated at home is proven by the fact that medieval political theories were already deteriorating in England before any clearly worked out concept of sovereignty was visible on the continent. His writings constitute one of the landmarks of English realism in political theory.

Of the parliament and authority thereof.

The most high and absolute power of the Realm of England consists in the Parliament. For as in war where the King himself in person, the nobility, the rest of the gentility, and the yeomen are, is the force and power of England: so in peace and consultation where the Prince is to give life, and the last and highest commandment, the Barony for the nobility and higher, the knights, esquires, gentlemen and commons for the lower part of the Commonwealth, the Bishops for the clergy be present to advertise, consult and show what is good and necessary for the Commonwealth, and to consult together, and upon mature deliberation every bill or law being thrice read and disputed upon in either House, . . . and after the Prince himself in the presence of both parties does consent unto and allow. That is the Prince's and the whole Realm's deed; whereupon justly no man can complain, but must accommodate himself to find it good and obey it.

That which is done by this consent is called firm, stable, and *sanctum,* and is taken for law. The Parliament abrogates old laws, makes new, gives orders for things past, and for things hereafter to be followed, changes rights, and possessions of private men, ... establishes forms of religion, ... gives forms of succession to the Crown, ... appoints subsidies, tailes, taxes, and impositions ... : and to be short, all that ever the people of Rome might do either in *Centuriatis Comitiis* or *tributis,* the same may be done by the Parliament of England, which represents and has the power of the whole Realm both head and body. For every Englishman is intended to be there present, either in person or by procuration or attorneys, of what preeminence, state, dignity, or quality soever he be, from the Prince (be he King or Queen) to the lowest person in England. And the consent of the Parliament is taken to be every man's consent.

Of the monarchy of England.

The Prince ... has absolutely in his power the authority of war and peace. ...

The Prince [has] also absolute power in crying and decreeing the money of the Realm by his proclamation only. ...

The Prince uses also to dispense with laws made, where equity requires a moderation to be had. ...

The Prince gives all the chief and highest offices or magistracies of the Realm, be it of judgment or dignity, temporal or spiritual. ...

All writs, executions and commandments be done in the Prince's name. ...

To be short the Prince is the life, the head, and the authority of all things that be done in the Realm of England. ... (Sir Thomas Smith, *De Republica Anglorum,* Edition of 1635, pp. 48-49, 61-63.)

## Richard Hooker, *The Laws of Ecclesiastical Polity.* c. 1597

IN HIS *Laws of Ecclesiastical Polity* Richard Hooker applied the reasoning of Sir Thomas Smith to a specific case: the Puritan rejection of Parliament's power to legislate in Church matters. Although Hooker was in broad agreement with Fortescue and Smith in denying the power of either King or Parliament to act independently of each other, he also thought that King and Parliament, in concert, had the right to absolute voice in Church as well as political affairs. It followed from this that all men, including Puritans, were bound by the natural law and by right reason to obey whatever laws were promulgated by the King in his Parliament, unless, of course, those regulations were inimical to the law of God. To Hooker the law of nature was a fundamental and operative law to which obedience was enjoined by God. Again, he conceived the rights and security of the whole society to exceed the rights of the individual in importance and sanctity. This latter aspect of his thought seems to agree with the doctrine of Reason of State set down in *The Prince* by Niccolo Machiavelli in 1514, and foreshadows the doctrine of social utilitarianism defined by Thomas Hobbes in his *Leviathan* in 1651.

**56.**

There are those which wonder that we should count any statute a law, which the High Court of Parliament in England has established about the matter of Church regiment; the Prince and Court of Parliament having, as they suppose, no more lawful means to give order to the Church and clergy in these things, than they have to make laws for the ... angels in heaven; that Parliament

being a mere temporal court, can neither by the law of nature, nor of God, have competent power to define of such matters; that supremacy of power in this kind cannot belong unto Kings, as Kings, because pagan emperors, whose princely power was notwithstanding true sovereignty, never challenged thus much over the Church. ...

We hold, that seeing there is not any man

of the Church of England but the same man is also a member of the Commonwealth, nor any member of the Commonwealth which is not also of the Church of England, therefore as in a figure triangle the base does differ from the sides thereof, and yet one and the selfsame line is both a base and also a side...; so albeit properties and actions of one do cause the name of a Commonwealth, qualities and functions of another sort, the name of the Church to be given to a multitude, yet one and the selfsame multitude may in such sort be both. Nay, it is so with us, that no person appertaining to the one can be denied also to be of the other: contrariwise, unless they against us shall hold, that the Church and the Commonwealth are two, both distinct and separate societies; of which two one comprehends always persons not belonging to the other,... they could not conclude out of the difference between the Church and the Commonwealth, namely, that the Bishops may not meddle with the affairs of the Commonwealth, because they are the governors of another corporation, which is the Church; nor Kings, with making laws for the Church, because they have government, not of this corporation, but of another divided from it, the Commonwealth....

.    .    .    .    .    .    .    .

Without order there is no living in public society, because the want thereof is mother to confusion, whereupon division of necessity followeth; and out of division destruction. ... This order of things and persons in public societies is the work of policy, and the proper instrument thereof in every degree is power.... If the action which we have to perform be conversant about matters of mere religion, the power of performing of it is then spiritual; and if that power be such as has not any other to overrule it, we term it *dominium,* or power supreme.... When therefore Christian Kings are said to have spiritual *dominium* or supreme power in ecclesiastical affairs and causes, the meaning is, that within their own precincts and territories they have an authority and power to command, even in matters of Christian Religion, and that there is no higher nor greater [power] that can in those cases over-command them....

.... *Where the King has power of dominium ... there no foreign state, or potentate, no state or potentate domestic, whether it consists of one or many, can possibly have ... authority higher than the King....*

.... *On the other side; the King alone has no right to do without consent of his Lords and Commons in Parliament: the King himself cannot change the nature of pleas, nor courts, no not so much as restore [corrupted] blood, because the law is a bar unto him....* (This extract from Richard Hooker, *The Laws of Ecclesiastical Polity,* is from the edition of 1820, Book VIII.)

## Act of Supremacy. 1559

57.
THIS Act was one of the most significant actions of Elizabeth's first Parliament. It nullified some of Mary's legislation and revived eight of Henry's reformation statutes, thereby establishing the Elizabethan Church settlement on the foundations constructed by Henry. However, aware of the constitutional difficulty of giving the title of Supreme Head of the Church to a female, Parliament substituted a less potentially offensive one: "Supreme Governor of this Realm ... in all things spiritual ... [and] temporal."

An Act restoring to the Crown the ancient Jurisdiction over the State Ecclesiastical and Spiritual, and abolishing all Foreign Power repugnant to the same.

Most humbly beseech your most excellent Majesty your faithful and obedient subjects the Lords Spiritual and Temporal and the Commons in this your present Parliament assembled:

That where in time of the reign of your most dear father of worthy memory, King Henry the Eighth, divers good laws and statutes were made and established, as well for the utter extinguishment and putting away of all usurped and foreign powers and authorities out of this your realm and other your Highness's dominions and countries, as also for the restoring and uniting to the imperial Crown of this realm the ancient jurisdictions, authorities, superiorities, and preeminences to the same of right belonging and appertaining; by reason whereof we your most humble and obedient subjects, from the five and twentieth year of the reign of your said dear father, were continually kept in good order, and were disburdened of divers great and intolerable charges and exactions before that time unlawfully taken and exacted by such foreign power and authority as before that was usurped, until such time as all the said good laws and statutes by one Act of Parliament made in the first and second years of the reigns of the late King Philip and Queen Mary, your Highness's sister, entitled *An Act repealing all Statutes, Articles, and Provisions made against the See Apostolic of Rome since the twentieth year of King Henry the Eighth, and also for the Establishment of all Spiritual and Ecclesiastical Possessions and Hereditaments conveyed to the Laity,* [Mary's second *Act of Repeal*] were all clearly repealed and made void, as by the same *Act of Repeal* more at large doth and may appear; by reason of which *Act of Repeal* your said humble subjects were again brought under an usurped foreign power and authority, and yet do remain in that bondage, to the intolerable charges of your loving subjects if some redress by the authority of this your High Court of Parliament with the assent of your Highness be not had and provided:

May it therefore please your Highness, for the repressing of the said usurped foreign power and the restoring of the rights, jurisdictions, and preeminences appertaining to the imperial Crown of this your realm, that it may be enacted by the authority of this present Parliament, that the said Act and all and every branch, clauses, and articles therein contained, other than such branches, clauses, and sentences as hereafter shall be excepted, may ... by the authority of this present Parliament, be repealed, and shall from thenceforth be utterly void and of none effect.

And that also for the reviving of divers of the said good laws and statutes made in the time of your said dear father, it may also please your Highness that ... [this Act reactivates here the reformation statutes of Henry VIII which had been nullified by Mary's acts of repeal: 23 Henry VIII, c.9; 24 Henry VIII, c.12; 23 Henry VIII, c.20; 25 Henry VIII, c.19; 25 Henry VIII, c.20; 25 Henry VIII, c.21, 26 Henry VIII, c.14; 28 Henry VIII, c.16] ... and all and every branches, words, and sentences in the said several Acts and Statutes contained, by authority of this present Parliament from and at all times after the last day of this session of Parliament, shall be revived and shall stand and be in full force and strength to all intents, constructions, and purposes. ...

And that it may also please your Highness that it may be further enacted by the authority aforesaid, that all other laws and statutes, and the branches and clauses of any act or statute, repealed and made void by the said *Act of Repeal* ... and not in this present Act specially mentioned and revived, shall stand, remain, and be repealed and void, in such like manner and form as they were before the making of this Act, anything herein contained to the contrary notwithstanding.

[At this point the Act revives 1 Edward VI, c.1, and repeals Mary's heresy laws]. ...

And to the intent that all usurped and foreign power and authority, spiritual and temporal, may for ever be clearly extinguished and never to be used nor obeyed within this realm or any other your Majesty's dominions or countries, may it please your Highness that it may be further enacted by the authority aforesaid, that no foreign prince, person, prelate, state, or potentate, spiritual or temporal, shall at any time after the last day of this session of Parliament use, enjoy, or exercise any manner of power, jurisdiction, superiority, authority, preeminence, or privilege, spiritual or ecclesiastical, within this realm or within any other your Majesty's dominions or countries that now be or hereafter shall be, but from thenceforth the same shall be clearly abolished out of this realm and all other your Highness's dominions for ever. . . .

And also that it may likewise please your Highness that it may be established and enacted by the authority aforesaid, that such jurisdictions, privileges, superiorities, and preeminences, spiritual and ecclesiastical, as by any spiritual or ecclesiastical power or authority hath heretofore been or may lawfully be exercised or used for the visitation of the ecclesiastical state and persons, and for reformation, order, and correction of the same, and of all manner of errors, heresies, schism, abuses, offences, contempts, and enormities, shall for ever by authority of this present Parliament be united and annexed to the imperial Crown of this realm; and that your Highness, your heirs and successors, kings or queens of this realm, shall have full power and authority, by virtue of this Act, by letters patents under the great seal of England to assign, name, and authorize, when and as often as your Highness, your heirs or successors, shall think meet and convenient, and for such and so long time as shall please your Highness, your heirs or successors, such person or persons being natural born subjects to your Highness, your heirs or successors, as your Majesty, your heirs or successors, shall think meet, to exercise, use, occupy, and execute under your Highness, your heirs and successors, all manner of jurisdictions, privileges, and preeminences in any wise touching or concerning any spiritual or ecclesiastical jurisdiction within these your realms . . . and to visit, reform, redress, order, correct, and amend all such errors, heresies,

schisms, abuses, offences, contempts, and enormities whatsoever which by any manner spiritual or ecclesiastical power, authority, or jurisdictions can or may lawfully be reformed, ordered, redressed, corrected, restrained, or amended, to the pleasure of Almighty God, the increase of virtue, and the conservation of the peace and unity of this realm; and that such person or persons so to be named, assigned, authorized, and appointed by your Highness, your heirs or successors . . . shall have full power and authority, by virtue of this Act and of the said letters patents, under your Highness . . . to exercise, use, and execute all the premises according to the tenor and effect of the said letters patents. . . .

And for the better observation and maintenance of this Act, may it please your Highness that it may be further enacted by the authority aforesaid, that all and every archbishop, bishop, and all and every other ecclesiastical person and other ecclesiastical officer and minister, of what estate, dignity, preeminence, or degree soever he or they be or shall be, and all and every temporal judge, justice, mayor, and other lay or temporal officer and minister, and every other person having your Highness's dominions, shall make, take, and receive a corporal oath [an oath sworn while the swearer holds the bible] upon the Evangelist, before such person or persons as shall please your Highness, your heirs or successors, under the great seal of England to assign and name to accept and take the same, according to the tenor and effect hereafter following, that is to say:

I, (name), do utterly testify and declare in my conscience that the Queen's Highness is the only Supreme Governor of this realm and of all other her Highness's dominions and countries, as well in all spiritual things or causes as temporal, and that no foreign prince, person, prelate, state, or potentate hath or ought to have any jurisdiction, power, superiority, preeminence, or authority, ecclesiastical or spiritual, within this realm, and therefore I do utterly renounce and forsake all foreign jurisdictions, powers, superiorities, and authorities, and do promise that from henceforth I shall bear faith and true allegiance to the Queen's Highness, her heirs and lawful successors, and to my power shall assist and defend all jurisdictions, preeminences, privileges, and authorities granted or belonging to the Queen's Highness, her heirs and successors, or united or annexed to the imperial Crown of this realm: so help me God and by the contents of this Book.

[The Act here establishes the penalties for refusal to take the above oath of allegiance, all of which act to debar the person so refusing the oath from holding any office, spiritual or ecclesiastical.]

.... Provided always and be it enacted by the authority aforesaid, that such persons to whom your Highness, your heirs or successors, shall hereafter by letters patents under the great seal of England give authority to have or execute any jurisdiction, power, or authority spiritual, or to visit, reform, order, or correct any errors, heresies, schisms, abuses, or enormities by virtue of this Act, shall not in any wise have authority or power to order, determine, or adjudge any matter or cause to be heresy but only such as heretofore have been determined, ordered, or adjudged to be heresy by the authority of the canonical Scriptures, or by the first four General Councils [Nicaea in 325, which decided against the doctrine of Arias; Constantinople in 381, which accepted as dogma the divinity of the Holy Ghost as the Third Person of the Trinity; Ephesus in 431, which rejected the Nestorian and Pelagian doctrines; and the Chalcedon which, in the year 451 defined the dual nature of Christ] or any of them, or by any other General Council wherein the same was declared heresy by the express and plain words of the said canonical Scriptures, or such as hereafter shall be ordered, judged, or determined to be heresy by the High Court of Parliament of this realm with the assent of the Clergy in their Convocation.... (SR, IV, 350: 1 Elizabeth c.1.)

## Act of Uniformity. 1559

## 58.

ALTHOUGH this Act required uniformity in worship and Church procedures, it also originated the policy of inclusive broadness which came to be typical of the Elizabethan Church. The Queen's reasoning on this point was sound. In extending to everyone, from the old Catholics to the new groups infected with Lutheran and Calvinistic teachings, something they could accept, she pacified a majority of those who rejected the Established Church, which, under Edward and Mary, had been prohibitively narrow.

An Act for the Uniformity of Common Prayer and Divine Service in the Church, and the Administration of the Sacraments.

Where at the death of our late Sovereign Lord King Edward the Sixth there remained one uniform order of common service and prayer and of the administration of sacraments, rites, and ceremonies in the Church of England, which was set forth in one book entitled *The Book of Common Prayer and Administration of Sacraments and other Rites and Ceremonies in the Church of England,* [the second *Prayer Book of Edward VI,* issued in 1552] authorized by Act of Parliament holden in the fifth and sixth years of our said late Sovereign Lord King Edward the Sixth, entitled *An Act for the Uniformity of Common Prayer and Administration of the Sacraments;* [Edward's second *Act of Uniformity*] the which was repealed and taken away by Act of Parliament in the first year of the reign of our late Sovereign Lady Queen Mary, [Mary's first *Statute of Repeal*] to the great decay of the due honor of God and discomfort to the professors of the truth of Christ's Religion:

Be it therefore enacted by the authority of this present Parliament, that the said Statute of Repeal and everything therein contained only concerning the said book and the service, administration of sacraments, rites, and ceremonies contained or appointed in or by the said book shall be void and of none effect . . . and that the said book with the order of service and of the administration of sacraments, rites, and ceremonies, with the alteration and additions therein added and appointed by this Statute shall stand . . . in full force and effect according to the tenor and effect of this Statute. . . .

And further be it enacted by the Queen's Highness, with the assent of the Lords and Commons in this present Parliament assembled and by authority of the same, that all and singular ministers in any cathedral or parish church or other place within this realm of England, Wales, and the marches of the same, or other the Queen's dominions, shall . . . be bounden to say and use the matins, evensong, celebration of the Lord's Supper and administration of each of the sacraments, and all their common and open prayer, in such order and form as is mentioned in the said book so authorized by Parliament in the said fifth and sixth year of the reign of King Edward the Sixth, with one alteration or addition of certain lessons to be used on every Sunday in the year, and the form of the Litany altered and corrected, and two sentences only added in the delivery of the sacrament to the communicants. [The sentences here referred to established the Elizabethan compromise between the exclusive concepts of the nature of the sacrament of Communion as found in Edward's first and second prayerbooks. The first book followed the Henrician, and therefore the Roman, belief that the Communion contained truly the flesh and blood of Christ. The second issue of the book denied this, accepting instead the "German" or Zwinglian doctrine that the Communion was symbolic only. In seeking broadness or comprehension Elizabeth included both doctrines].

And that if any manner of parson, vicar, or other whatsoever minister that ought or should sing or say common prayer mentioned in the said book, or minister the sacraments . . . refuse to use the said common prayers or to minister the sacraments in such cathedral or parish church or other places as he should use to minister the same, in such order and form as they be mentioned and set forth in the said book, or shall wilfully or obstinately . . . use any other rite, ceremony, order, form, or manner of celebrating of the Lord's Supper openly or privily, or matins, evensong, administration of the sacraments, or other open prayers than is mentioned and set forth in the said book . . . or shall preach, declare, or speak anything in the derogation or depraving of the said book or anything therein contained, or of any part thereof, and shall be thereof lawfully convicted according to the laws of this realm or by verdict of twelve men, or by his own confession, or by the notorious evidence of the fact . . . he shall . . . [suffer penalties. The Act here states the degrees of punishment to be meted out for first, second, and third offences, ending with life imprisonment for the third offence]. . . .

. . . And . . . all and every person and persons inhabiting within this realm or any other the Queen's Majesty's dominions, shall diligently and faithfully, having no lawful or reasonable excuse to be absent, endeavor themselves to resort to their parish church or chapel accustomed . . . upon every Sunday and other days ordained and used to be kept as Holy Days, and then and there to abide orderly and soberly during the time of the common prayer, preachings, or other service of God there to be used and ministered; upon pain of punishment by the censures of the Church, and also upon pain that every person so offending shall forfeit for every such offence twelve pence to be levied by the Churchwardens of the parish where such offence shall be done, to the use of the poor of the same parish, of the goods, lands, and tenements of such offender by way of distress. . . .
(SR, IV, 355: 1 Elizabeth, c.2.)

## Statute of Apprentices. 1563

THE sense of social responsibility of the State toward the lower classes was first for-
mally admitted by legislative action in Henry's *Beggars Act* of 1536. That Act was
the direct precedent for this one. One of the longest and most detailed statutes of the
Tudor period, it was the immediate result of Elizabeth's keen sense of the political
effects of economic causes. Prior to its enactment, the destructive effects of continued
common land enclosures were increasingly noticeable in the flow of labor from countryside to city and from city to city. Determined to maintain the balance between wages
and prices and to stabilize industry, and although the royal prerogative legally encompassed all such regulation, Elizabeth reasoned that the general voice in such significant
action was far better than proclamation. Hence, she resorted to the use of Parliamentary process in order to insure popular acceptance. Of all the social legislation in
this period, this was by far the most important, both in intent and result.

**59.**

An Act touching divers Orders for Artificers, Laborers, Servants of Husbandry, and
Apprentices.

Although there remain and stand in force
presently a great number of acts and statutes concerning the retaining, departing,
wages, and orders of apprentices, servants,
and laborers, as well husbandry as in divers
other arts, mysteries [trades], and occupa-
tions, yet partly for the imperfection and
contrariety that is found and do appear in
sundry of the said laws, and for the variety
and number of them, and chiefly for that the
wages and allowances limited and rated in
many of the said statutes are in divers places
too small and not answerable to this time,
respecting the advancement of prices of all
things belonging to the said servants and
laborers, the said laws cannot conveniently
without the great grief and burden of the
poor laborer and hired man be put in good
and due execution: and as the said several
acts and statutes were at the time of the
making of them thought to be very good and
beneficial for the common wealth of this
realm, as divers of them yet are, so if the
substance of as many of the said laws as are
meet to be continued shall be digested and
reduced into one sole law and statute, and
in the same an uniform order prescribed and
limited concerning the wages and other orders for apprentices, servants, and laborers,

there is good hope that it will come to pass
that the same law, being duly executed,
should banish idleness, advance husbandry,
and yield unto the hired person both in the
time of scarcity and the time of plenty a
convenient proportion of wages:

Be it therefore enacted by this present Parliament assembled, that as much of the statutes heretofore made, and every branch of
them as touch or concern the hiring, keeping,
departing, or working wages or order of
servants, workmen, artificers, apprentices,
and laborers, or any of them, and the penalties and forfeitures concerning the same, shall
be ... repealed and utterly void ... and that
all the said statutes ... not repealed by this
Statute, shall remain in full force. ...

And be it further enacted ... that no
manner of person or persons ... shall retain,
hire, or take into service, or cause to be retained, hired, or taken into service, nor any
person shall be retained, [etc.] ... by any
means or color, to work for any less time than
for one whole year, in any of the sciences,
crafts, mysteries, or arts of clothiers, woolen
cloth, weavers, tuckers, fullers, clothworkers,
shearmen, dyers, hosiers, tailors, shoemakers,
tanners, pewterers, bakers, brewers, glovers,
cutlers, smiths, farriers, curriers, sadlers, spur-
riers, turners, coppers, hatmakers, or felt-
makers, bowyers, fletchers, arrowheadmakers,
butchers, cooks or millers.

And be it further enacted, that every person being unmarried, and every other person being under the age of thirty years that after the feast of Easter next shall marry, and having been brought up in any of the said arts, crafts, or sciences, or that hath used or exercised any of them by the space of three years or more, and not having lands, tenements, rents, or hereditaments, copyhold, or freehold of an estate of inheritance or for term of life or lives of the clear yearly value of 40s., nor ... goods the clear value of 10£, and so allowed by two justices of the peace of the counties where he hath most commonly inhabited by the space of one whole year and under their hands and seals, or by the mayor or other head officer of the city, borough, or town corporate where such person hath most commonly dwelled ... one whole year ... not being retained with any person in husbandry or in any of the aforesaid arts and sciences according to this Statute ... nor being lawfully retained in households or in any office with any noble gentleman or others ... nor having a convenient farm or other holding in tillage whereupon he may employ his labor, shall, (during the time that he or they shall so be unmarried or under the said age of thirty years, upon request made by any person using the art or mystery wherein the said person so required hath been exercised as is aforesaid), be retained and shall not refuse to serve according to the tenor of this Statute, upon the pain and penalty hereafter mentioned.

And be it further enacted, that no person which shall retain any servant shall put away his or her said servant, and that no person retained according to this Statute shall depart from his master, mistress, or dame before the end of his or her term ... unless it be for some reasonable and sufficient cause or matter to be allowed before two Justices of Peace, or one at the least, within the said county, or before the Mayor or other chief officer of the city, [etc.] ... wherein the said master, mistress, or dame inhabiteth, to whom any of the parties grieved shall com-

plain; which said Justice, Mayor, [etc.] ... shall have and take upon them or him the hearing and ordering of the matter between the said master, mistress, or dame, and servant according to the equity of the case....

And be it further enacted, that every person between the age of twelve and thirty years, not being lawfully retained, nor apprentice with an fisherman or mariner ... nor being in service with any ... carrier of grain or meal for the provision of the city of London, nor with any husbandman ... nor in any city, town, or corporate or market town, in any of the arts or sciences limited and appointed in this Statute to have or take apprentices, nor being retained by the year or half year at the least, for the digging, seeking, finding, getting, melting, fining, working, or making of any silver, tin, lead, iron, copper, stone, sea coal, stone coal, moor coal or cherk coal, nor being occupied in or about the making of any glass, nor being a gentleman born, nor being a student or scholar in any of the Universities, or in any school, nor having lands, rents, or hereditaments of the clear yearly value of 40s ... nor being worth in goods and chattels to the value of 10£, nor having a father or mother then living, or other ancestor whose heir apparent he is, then having lands, [etc.] ... to the clear yearly value of 40£, ... not being now lawfully retained or retained according to the true meaning of this Statute, shall ... be compelled to be retained to serve in husbandry by the year, with any person that keepeth husbandry, and will require any such person so to serve within the same shire where he shall be so situate.

And be it further enacted ... that if any person after he hath retained any servant shall put away the same servant before the end of his term, unless it be for some reasonable and sufficient cause to be allowed as is aforesaid, or if any such master, mistress, or dame shall put away any such servant at the end of his term without one quarter's warning given before the said end as is above remembered, and then every such master, mistress, or dame so offending, unless he or they be able to prove by two sufficient witnesses such reasonable and sufficient cause of putting away of their servant or servants during their term, or a quarter's warning given before the end of the said term as is aforesaid, before the Justices ... of the Peace in the Quarter Sessions ... shall forfeit the sum of 40s., and if any servant [leaves his appointed position or refuses to serve in it he is to suffer imprisonment until he agrees to fulfill his responsibility]. ...

And be it likewise enacted ... that none of the said retained persons in husbandry or in any the arts or sciences above remembered, after the term of his retaining has expired, shall depart forth of one city, town, or parish for another ... nor out of the county or shire where he last served, to serve in any other city or town unless he have a Testimonial under the seal of the city ... or of the constable ... of the city, town, or parish where he last served, declaring his lawful departure, and the name of the shire and place where he dwelled last before his departure. [The form of the Testimonial is here stated]. ...

[The Statute here orders the punishment for those who depart from their appointed tasks unlawfully or who refuse to show testimonial evidence of the legality of their departure. In every case the culprit was to be punished as a vagabond, whipped and imprisoned].

And be it further enacted ... that all artificers and laborers being hired for wages by the day and the week shall between the middle of the months of March and September, be and continue at their work at or before five o'clock in the morning, and continue at work and not depart until between seven and eight ... at night, except [for eating, drinking, etc., which time altogether shall not exceed two and one-half hours daily]. ...

And all the said artificers and laborers, between the middle of September and the middle of March, shall be and continue at their work from the spring [first light] of the day in the morning until the night of the

same day, except it be in time afore appointed [for meals] ..., upon pain to lose and forfeit one penny for every hours absence. ...

And for the declaration and limitation what wages servants, laborers, and artificers, either by the year or day or otherwise, shall have and receive:

Be it enacted ... that the Justices of Peace ... shall yearly at every general Sessions first to be holden and kept after Easter ... assemble themselves together, and they so assembled calling unto them such grave and discreet persons of the said county or of the said city or town corporate ... and conferring together respecting the plenty or scarcity of the time and other circumstances necessary to be considered, shall have authority ... to limit, rate, and appoint the wages ... of artificers, handicraftsmen, husbandmen, or any other laborer, servant, or workman ... and shall ... certify the same engrossed in parchment, with the considerations and causes thereof, under their hands and seals into the Queen's most honorable Court of Chancery, whereupon it shall be lawful to the Lord Chancellor of England ... upon declaration thereof to the Queen's Majesty ... to cause to be printed and sent down ... into every county to the Sheriff and Justices of Peace ... proclamations ... containing in them the several rates appointed by the said Justices. ... :

And if the said ... Justices ... shall at their said general Sessions ... upon their assembly and conference together think it convenient to retain and keep for the year then to come the rates and proportion of wages that they certified the year before, or to change or reform them or some part of them, then they shall ... yearly certify into the said Court of Chancery their resolutions and determinations therein, to the intent that proclamations may accordingly be renewed and sent down. ...

And be it further enacted ... that if the said Justice of the Peace resident within the counties ... do not before the tenth day of

June, and afterwards yearly, appear at the said general Sessions ... and limit the rate of wages of the said servants and laborers, or shall not consider whether the former rates made be meet to be continued, or to be altered and reformed in manner and form ... or be negligent or remiss in the certificate thereof ... that then ... [he or they] ... for such default ... forfeit unto the Queen's Majesty ... 10£ in lawful English money. . . .

And be it further enacted ... that if any person, after the said proclamation shall be so ... published, shall by any secret ways or means directly or indirectly retain or keep any servant, workman, or laborer, or shall give more or greater wages or other commodity contrary to the true intent and purport of this Statute ... and shall be lawfully convicted ... shall suffer imprisonment by the space of ten days without bail ... and shall lose and forfeit 5£ ... , and [every person taking wages in excess of the established rates, being convicted, shall suffer imprisonment twenty-one days without bail]. . . .

Provided always and be it enacted ... that in the time of hay or corn harvest, the Justices of Peace and every of them, and also the constable or other head officer of every township, upon request and for avoiding of loss of any corn, grain, or hay, shall and may cause all such artificers and persons as be meet to labor ... to serve by the day for the mowing, reaping, shearing, getting, or inning of corn, grain, or hay, according to the skill and quality of the person; and that none of the said persons shall refuse so to do, upon pain to suffer imprisonment in the stocks by the space of two days and one night. . . .

And be it enacted ... that if any servant, workman, or laborer shall willfully or maliciously make assault ... upon his master or mistress ... or upon any other that shall ... have charge or oversight of such servant, [etc.] ... and being convicted ... that then every such offender shall suffer imprisonment by the space of one whole year or less, by the discretion of two Justices of Peace. . . .

And be it further enacted ... that two Jus-

tices of Peace, the Mayor ... of any city, borough, or town corporate and two Aldermen ... shall and may by virtue hereof appoint any such woman as is of the age of twelve years and under the age of forty years and unmarried to service as they shall think meet to serve, to be retained or serve by the year or by the week or day, for such wages and in such reasonable sort and manner as they shall think meet. . . .

And for the better advancement of husbandry and tillage, and to the intent that such as are fit to be made apprentices to husbandry may be bounded thereto: Be it enacted ... that every person, being a householder [having land in tillage] ... may have and receive as an apprentice any person above the age of ten years and under eighteen years to serve ... until his age of one and twenty years at the least. . . .

And be it further enacted that every householder ... using any art, mystery, or manual occupation ... [shall] ... have and retain the son of any freeman not occupying husbandry nor being a laborer ... to serve and be bound as an apprentice ... for seven years. . . .

And be it further enacted ... it shall not be lawful to any person or persons, other than now do lawfully use or exercise any art, craft, [etc.] ... to set up, occupy, use, or exercise any art, craft, [etc.] ... except he shall have been brought up therein seven years ... as apprentice. . . .

And be it further enacted, that if any person [as within this Act described] shall be required by any householder having and using half a ploughland at the least in tillage to be an apprentice and to serve in husbandry or in any other kind of art, mystery, or science before expressed, and shall refuse so to do, that then upon the complaint of such housekeeper made to one Justice of Peace of the county wherein the said refusal is or shall be made, or [in any city or town corporate to the Mayor] ... they shall have full power and authority by virtue hereof to send for the same person so refusing; and if the said Justice or the said Mayor ... shall think the said person meet and convenient to serve as an apprentice in that art, labor, science, or mystery wherein he shall be so then required to serve, that they the said Justice or the said Mayor . . . shall have power and authority by virtue hereof, if the said person refuse to be bound as an apprentice, to commit him unto ward, there to remain until he be contented and will be bounden to serve as an apprentice should serve, according to the true intent and meaning of this present Act; and if any such master shall misuse or evil intreat his apprentice, or that the said apprentice shall have any just cause to complain, or the apprentice do not his duty to his master, then the said master or prentice being grieved and having just cause to complain shall repair unto one Justice of Peace within the said county or to the Mayor . . . of the city, town corporate, market town, or other place where the said master dwelleth, who shall by his wisdom and discretion take such order and direction between the said master and his apprentice as the equity of the case shall require; and if for want of good conformity in the said master, the . . . Justice . . . or Mayor . . . cannot compound and agree the matter between him and his apprentice, then the said Justice or . . . Mayor . . . shall take bond of the said master to appear at the next Sessions then to be holden in the said county or . . . town . . . and upon his appearance and hearing of the matter before the said Justices . . . if it be thought meet unto them to discharge the said apprentice of his apprenticehood, that then the said Justices or four of them at the least . . . or the said Mayor . . . with the consent of three other of his brethern or men of best reputation within the said . . . town . . . shall have power by authority hereof in writing under their hands and seals to pronounce and declare that they have discharged the said apprentice of his apprenticehood, and the cause thereof, and the said writing so being made and enrolled by the Clerk of the Peace or Town Clerk amongst the records that he keepeth, shall be a sufficient discharge for the said apprentice against his master, his executors and administrators . . . and if the default shall be found to be in the apprentice, then the said Justices or Mayor . . . with the assistants aforesaid, shall cause such due correction and punishment to be ministered unto him as by their wisdom and discretions shall be thought meet. . . .

And be it further enacted by authority aforesaid, that if any servant, [etc.] . . . unlawfully depart or fly into any other shire, that it shall be lawful to the said Justice of Peace, [or other responsible officer] . . . to make and grant writs of *capias* [warrant commanding arrest], so many and such as shall be needful, to be directed to the sheriffs of the counties . . . whither such apprentice shall fly, to take their bodies . . . that they be put in prison till they find sufficient surety well and honestly to serve. . . . (SR, IV, 414: 5 Elizabeth, c.4.)

## Second Treasons Act of Elizabeth. 1571

AN EARLIER treasons Act by Elizabeth's first Parliament in 1559 was superseded by this Act. In several respects the present statute bespeaks a clearer concept of treason than those of Henry, Edward, or Mary. It is difficult to say whether this was due to the advance in legal thought in Parliament or to the painstaking efforts of the Council to arrive at a workable definition.

**60.**

An Act whereby certain Offences be made Treason.

Forasmuch as it is by some doubted whether the laws and statutes of this realm remaining at this present in force are strong and sufficient enough for the surety and preservation of the Queen's most royal person, in whom consisteth all the happiness and comfort of the whole state and subjects of the realm, which thing all faithful, loving, and dutiful subjects ought and will with all careful study and zeal consider, foresee, and provided for, by the neglecting and passing over whereof with winking eyes there might happen to grow the subversion and ruin of the quiet and most happy state and present government of this realm. . . .

Therefore at the humble suit and petition of the Lords and Commons in this present Parliament assembled, be it enacted, declared, and established by authority of the same Parliament, that if any person or persons whatsoever . . . during the natural life of our most gracious Sovereign Lady Elizabeth . . . shall, within the realm or without, compass, imagine, invent, devise, or intend the death or destruction, or any bodily harm tending to death, destruction, maim, or wounding of the royal person of the same our Sovereign Lady Queen Elizabeth; or to deprive or depose her of or from the style, honor, or kingly name of the imperial Crown of this realm or of any other realm or dominion to her Majesty belonging, or to levy war against her Majesty within this realm or without, or to move or to stir any foreigners or strangers with force to invade this realm or the realm of Ireland or any other her Majesty's dominions being under her Majesty's obedience; and such compasses, imaginations, inventions, devices, or intentions or any of them shall maliciously, advisedly, and expressly utter or declare by any printing, writing, ciphering, speech, words, or sayings, or if any person or persons whatsoever . . . shall maliciously, advisedly, and directly publish, declare, hold opinion, affirm, or say by any speech, express words or sayings, that our said Sovereign Lady Queen Elizabeth during her life is not or ought not to be Queen of this realm of England and also of the realms of France and Ireland; or that any other person or persons ought of right to be king or queen of the said realms of England and Ireland or of any other her Majesty's dominions being under her Majesty's obedience, during her Majesty's life, or shall by writing, printing, preaching, speech, express words or say-

ings, maliciously, advisedly, and directly publish, set forth, and affirm that the Queen our said Sovereign Lady Queen Elizabeth is an heretic, schismatic, tyrant, infidel, or an usurper of the Crown of the said realms or any of them, that then all and every such said offence or offences shall be taken, deemed, and declared, by the authority of this Act of Parliament, to be high treason, and that as well the principal offender or offenders therein as all and every the abettors, counsellors, and procurers to the same offence or offences, and all and every aiders and comforters of the same offender or offenders, knowing the same offence or offences to be done and committed in any place within this realm or without, being thereof lawfully and duly indicted, convicted, and attainted, according to the usual order and course of the common laws of this realm, or [shall be tried before a King's Bench Court or before a special Commission] . . . and as the case shall require, shall be deemed, declared, and adjudged traitors to the Queen and the realm, and shall suffer pains of death and also forfeit unto the Queen's Majesty, her heirs and successors, all and singular lands, tenements, and hereditaments, goods, and chattels, as in cases of high treason by the laws and statutes of this realm at this day of right ought to be forfeited and lost.

And be it also enacted by the authority aforesaid, that all and every person and persons, of what degree, condition, place, nation, or estate soever they be, which shall . . . at any time in the life of our Sovereign Lady Elizabeth in any wise claim, pretend, utter, declare, affirm, or publish themselves or any of them, or any other than our said Sovereign Lady Elizabeth the Queen's Majesty that now is, to have right or title to have or enjoy the Crown of England during or in the life of our said Sovereign Lady, or shall usurp the same Crown or the royal style, title, or dignity of the Crown or realm of England during or in the life of our said Sovereign Lady, or shall hold and affirm that our said Sovereign Lady hath not right to hold and enjoy the said Crown and realm, style, title, or dignity, or shall not, after any demand on our said Sovereign Lady's part to be made, effectually acknowledge our said Sovereign Lady to be in right true and lawful Queen of this realm, they and every of them so offending shall be utterly disabled, during their natural lives only, to have or enjoy the Crown or realm of England, or the style, title, or dignity thereof, at any time in succession, inheritance, or otherwise after the decease of our said Sovereign Lady as if such person were naturally dead....

And be it further enacted, that if any person shall, during the Queen's Majesty's life, in any wise hold, affirm, or maintain any right, title, interest, or possibility in succession or inheritance in or to the Crown of England, after our said Sovereign Lady the Queen, to be rightfully in or lawfully due or belonging unto any such claimer, pretender, usurper, utterer, declarer, affirmer, publisher, or not-acknowledger, so that our said Sovereign Lady the Queen shall, by proclamation to be published through the realm, or else in the more part of those shires of this realm, as well on the south side as the north side of Trent, and also in the Dominion of Wales, in which shires no war or rebellion then shall be, set forth, notify, or declare such claiming, pretence, uttering, declaration, affirming, publishing, usurpation, or not-acknowledging, then every person which after such proclamation shall during the Queen's Majesty's life maintain, hold, or affirm any right in succession, inheritance, or possibility in or to the Crown or realm of England or the rights thereof to be in or to any such claimer, pretender, utterer, declarer, affirmer, usurper, publisher, or not-acknowledger, shall be a high traitor and suffer and forfeit as in cases of high treason is accustomed.

And be it further enacted, that if any person shall in any wise hold and affirm or maintain that the common laws of this realm not altered by Parliament ought not to direct the right of the Crown of England, or that our said Sovereign Lady Elizabeth the Queen's Majesty that now is, with and by the authority of the Parliament of England, is not able to make laws and statutes of sufficient force and validity to limit and bind the Crown of this realm and the descent, limitation, inheritance, and government thereof, or that this present Statute, or any part thereof, or any other statute to be made by authority of the Parliament of England with the royal assent of our said Sovereign Lady the Queen for limiting of the Crown, or any statute for recognizing the right of the said Crown and realm to be justly and lawfully in the most royal person of our said Sovereign Lady the Queen, is not, are not, or shall not, or ought not to be for ever of good and sufficient force and validity to bind, limit, restrain, and govern all persons, their rights and titles, that in any wise may or might claim any interest or possibility in or to the Crown of England in possession, remainder, inheritance, succession, or otherwise howsoever, and all other persons whatsoever, every such person so holding, affirming, or maintaining during the life of the Queen's Majesty shall be judged a high traitor and suffer and forfeit as in cases of high treason is accustomed....

And for the avoiding of contentious and seditious spreading abroad of titles to the succession of the Crown of this realm, to the disturbing of the common quiet of the realm; be it enacted by the authority aforesaid, that whosoever shall hereafter, during the life of our said Sovereign Lady, by any book or work, printed or written, directly and expressly declare and affirm, at any time before the same be by act of Parliament of this realm established and affirmed, that any one particular person, whosoever it be, is or ought to be the right heir and successor to the Queen's Majesty that now is ... except the same by the natural issue of her Majesty's body, or shall wilfully set up in open place, publish, or spread any books or scrolls to that effect, or shall print, bind, or put to sale, or utter, or cause to be printed, bound, or put to sale, or uttered, any such book or writing wittingly, that he or they, their abettors and counsellors, and every of them, shall for the first offence suffer imprisonment of one whole year and forfeit half his goods, whereof the one moiety to the Queen's Majesty, the other moiety to him or them that will sue for the same by bill, action, plaint, information, or otherwise in any of the Queen's Majesty's Courts, wherein no ... protection shall be allowed, and if any shall again offend therein, then they and every of them ... shall incur the pains and forfeitures which in the Statutes of Provisions or Praemunire are appointed and limited. . . .

[Proof is limited to two witnesses making their public accusation in the presence of the person charged.] (SR, IV, 526: 13 Elizabeth, c.1.)

## Act against Bulls from Rome. 1571

**61.** EXCOMMUNICATED by the Papal Bull of 1570 and badly frightened by the Catholic uprisings in the north of England, Elizabeth acted logically in forbidding foreign publications access to England and in making it high treason for anyone to aid the import or dissemination of such publications. In preparing this Act for acceptance, Parliament added to it certain new passages which reflect an increasing hostility toward Catholics.

An Act against bringing in and putting in execution of Bulls and other Instruments from the See of Rome.

Where in the Parliament holden at Westminster in the fifth year of the reign of our Sovereign Lady the Queen's Majesty that now is, by one act and statute then and there made, entitled *An Act for the Assurance of the Queen's Majesty's Royal Power over all States and Subjects within her Highness's dominions,* it is among other things very well ordained and provided, for the abolishing of the usurped power and jurisdiction of the Bishop of Rome and of the See of Rome heretofore unlawfully claimed and usurped within this realm and other the dominions to the Queen's Majesty belonging, that no person or persons shall hold or stand with to set forth, maintain, defend, or extol the same usurped power, or attribute any manner jurisdiction, authority, or preeminence to the same, to be had or used within this realm or any the said dominions, upon pain to incur the danger, penalties, and forfeitures ordained and provided by the *Statute of Provision and Praemunire* made in the sixteenth year of the reign of King Richard the Second, as by the same Act more at large it doth and may appear; and yet nevertheless divers seditious and very evil disposed people, without respect of their duty to Almighty God or of the faith and allegiance which they ought to bear and have to our said Sovereign Lady the Queen, and without all fear or regard had to the said good law and statute or the pains therein limited, but minding as it should seem very seditiously and unnaturally, not only to bring this realm and the imperial Crown thereof, being in ... itself most free, into the thraldom and subjection of that foreign usurped, and unlawful jurisdiction, preeminence, and authority claimed by the said See of Rome, but also to estrange and alienate the minds and hearts of sundry her Majesty's subjects from their dutiful obedience, and to raise and stir sedition and rebellion within this realm, to the disturbance of the most happy peace thereof, have lately procured and obtained to themselves from the said Bishop of Rome and his said See divers bulls and writings, the effect whereof hath been and is to absolve and reconcile all those that will be contented to forsake their due obedience to our most gracious Sovereign Lady the Queen's Majesty, and to yield and subject themselves to the said feigned, unlawful, and usurped authority, and by color of the said bulls and writings the said wicked persons very secretly and most seditiously in such parts of this realm where the people for want of good instruction are most weak, simple, and ignorant, and thereby farthest from the good understanding of their duties towards God and the Queen's Majesty, have by their lewd and subtle practices and persuasions so far forth wrought that sundry simple and ignorant persons have been contented to be reconciled to the said usurped authority of the See of Rome and to take absolution at the hands of the said naughty and subtle practicers, [the Jesuits] whereby hath grown great disobedience and boldness in many, not only to withdraw and absent themselves from all Divine Service now most Godly set forth and used within this realm, but also have thought themselves discharged of and from all obedience, duty, and allegiance to her Majesty, whereby most wicked and unnatural rebellion hath ensued, and to the further danger of this realm is hereafter very like to be renewed if the ungodly and wicked attempts in that behalf be not by severity of laws in time restrained and bridled:

For remedy and redress whereof, and to prevent the great mischiefs and inconveniences that thereby may ensue, be it enacted ... that if any person or persons ... shall use or put in use in any place within this realm or in any the Queen's dominions any such bull, writing, or instrument written or printed, of absolution or reconciliation at any time heretofore obtained and gotten, or at any time hereafter to be obtained and gotten, from the said Bishop of Rome or any his successors, or from any other person or persons authorized or claiming authority by or from the said Bishop of Rome, his predecessors or successors, or See of Rome, or if any person or persons ... shall take upon him or them by color of any such bull, writing, instrument, or authority to absolve or reconcile any person or persons, or to grant or promise to any person or persons within this realm or any other the Queen's Majesty's dominions any such absolution or reconcilia-

tion by any speech, preaching, teaching, writing, or any other open deed, or if any person or persons within this realm or any the Queen's dominions ... shall willingly receive and take any such absolution or reconciliation, or else if any person or persons have obtained or gotten since the last day of the Parliament holden in the first year of the Queen's Majesty's reign, or ... shall obtain or get from the said Bishop of Rome or any his successors or See of Rome any manner of bull, writing, or instrument written or printed, containing any thing, matter, or cause whatsoever, or shall publish or by any ways or means put in use any such bull, writing, or instrument, that then all and every such act and acts, offence and offences, shall be deemed and adjudged by the authority of this Act to be high treason, and the offender and offenders therein, their procurers, abettors, and counsellors to the fact and committing of the said offence or offences, shall be deemed and adjudged high traitors to the Queen and the realm, and being thereof lawfully indicted and attainted, according to the course of the laws of this realm, shall suffer pains of death, and also lose and forfeit all their lands, [etc.]. ...

Provided always and be it further enacted by the authority aforesaid, that if any person or persons to whom any such absolution, reconciliation, bull, writing, or instrument as is aforesaid shall ... be offered, moved, or persuaded to be used, put in use, or executed, shall conceal the same offer, motion, or persuasion, and not disclose and signify the same by writing or otherwise within six weeks then next following to some of the Queen's Majesty's Privy Council or else to the President or Vice-President of the Queen's Majesty's Council established in the north or in the marches of Wales for the time being, that then the same person or persons so concealing and not disclosing or not signifying the said offer, motion, or persuasion, shall incur the loss, danger, penalty, and forfeiture of misprision of high treason. ...

And be it further enacted by the authority

aforesaid, that if any person or persons shall ... bring into this realm of England or any the dominions of the same any token or tokens, thing or things, called by the name of an *Agnus Dei,* or any crosses, pictures, beads, or suchlike vain and superstitious things from the Bishop or See of Rome, or from any person or persons authorized or claiming authority by or from the said Bishop or See of Rome to consecrate or hallow the same, which said *Agnus Dei* is used to be specially hallowed and consecrated, as it is termed, by the said Bishop in his own person, and the said crosses, pictures, beads, and suchlike superstitious things be also hallowed either by the said Bishop or by others having power or pretending to have power for the same, by or from him or his said See, and divers pardons, immunities, and exemptions granted by the authority of the said See to such as shall receive and use the same, and that if the same person or persons so bringing in as is aforesaid such *Agnus Dei* and other like things as be before specified shall deliver or offer or cause to be delivered the same or any of them to any subject of this realm or any of the dominions of the same to be worn or used in any wise, that then as well the same person and persons so doing, as also all and every other person and persons so doing, as also all and every other person or persons which shall receive and take the same to the intent to use or wear the same, being thereof lawfully convicted and attainted by the order of the common laws of this realm, shall incur into the dangers, penalties, pains, and forfeitures ordained and provided by the *Statute of Praemunire and Provision* made in the sixteenth year of the reign of King Richard Second. . . . (SR, IV, 528: 13 Elizabeth, c.2.)

## Act for the Relief of the Poor. 1576

**62.** THIS ACT was a further development of Elizabeth's use of statute law to cure the social evils of poverty and crime. Somewhat harsher in tone than the *Act of Apprentices,* it developed the policy of overseership of the indigent by locally appointed officers, and clarified the system of placing the idle in productive labor by the setting aside of stores of raw materials for their use. Although the people of Elizabeth's time were beginning to consider crime to be the result of poverty, there was as yet little notion of the responsibility of the economic system as a whole for social ills. Thus poverty was accepted as something to be cured rather than prevented.

An Act for setting of the Poor on Work, and for the avoiding of Idleness.

For some better explanation and for some needful addition to the statute concerning punishment of vagabonds and relief of the poor [14 Elizabeth, c.5] ... be it ordained and enacted ... in manner and form following:

First, concerning bastards begotten and born out of lawful matrimony ... the said bastard being now left to be kept at the charge of the parish where they be born, to the great burden of the same parish and in defrauding of the relief of the impotent and aged true poor of the same parish, and to the evil encouragement of lewd life:

It is ordained and enacted by this present Parliament assembled, that two Justices of Peace ... in or next unto the limits where the parish church is, within which parish such bastard shall be born, upon examination of the cause and circumstance, shall and may by their discretion take order as well for the punishment of the mother and reputed father of such bastard child, as also for the better relief of every such parish ... and ... shall ... take order for the keeping of every such bastard child by charging such mother or reputed father with the payment of money weekly or other sustentation for the relief of such child, in such way as they shall think meet and convenient. And if after the same order by them ... the mother or reputed father default in performance of the said order [they are] to be committed to . . . the common jail without bail.

Also concerning rogues; inasmuch as by [the statute above referred to] . . . they are to be conveyed to the jail or prison by the constable . . . at the charges of the parish where such rogue is apprehended, for avoiding of great travail and charges rising thereby many are suffered to pass and are winked at:

Be it ordained and enacted . . . that from henceforth every such rogue apprehended shall be conveyed by the constable . . . of the parish where such apprehension shall be, but [only] to the constable . . . of the next township or parish in the next hundred, and so from one hundred to another by the constables . . . of every such township or parish which shall be next in every such hundred, and so from one hundred to another . . . to the jail or prison appointed. . . .

Also to the intent youth may be accustomed and brought up in labor and work, and then not like to grow to be idle rogues, and to the intent also that such as be already grown up in idleness, and so rogues at this present, may not have any just excuse in saying that they cannot get any service or work and then without any favor or toleration worthy to be executed, and that other poor and needy persons being willing to work may be set on work:

Be it ordained and enacted . . . that in every city and town corporate within this realm a competent store and stock of wool, hemp, flax, iron, or other stuff [goods] by the appointment and order of the Mayor, Bailiffs, Justices, or other head officers having rule in the said cities or towns corporate (of themselves and all others the inhabitants within their several authorities to be taxed, levied, and gathered) shall be provided; and that likewise in every other market town or other place within every county of this realm (where to the Justices of Peace or greater part of them in their general Sessions yearly next after Easter within every limit shall be thought most meet and convenient) a like

competent store and stock of wool, hemp, flax, iron, or other stuff, as the country is most meet for, by appointment and order of the said Justices of Peace or the greater part of them in their said general Sessions (of all the inhabitants within their several authorities to be taxed, levied, and gathered) shall be provided, the said stores and stocks in such cities and towns corporate to be committed to the hands and custody of such persons as shall by the Mayor, Bailiffs, [etc.] . . . be appointed, and in other towns and places to such persons as to the said Justices of Peace or the greater part of them in their said general Sessions of the Peace in their several counties shall be by them appointed; which said persons so appointed as aforesaid shall have power and authority (by the advice of them who do appoint them) to dispose, order, and give rules for the division and manner of working of the said stocks and stores, who shall from henceforth be called the Collectors and Governors of the Poor, to the intent every such poor and needy person, old or young, able to do any work, standing in necessity of relief, shall not for want of work go abroad either begging or committing pilferings or other misdemeanors, living in idleness; which Collectors and Governors of the Poor from time to time, as cause requireth, shall and may of the same stock and store deliver to such poor and needy person a competent portion to be wrought into yarn or other matter within such time and in such sort as in their discretions shall be from time to time limited and prefixed, and the same afterwards being wrought, to be from time to time delivered to the said Collectors and Governors of the Poor, for which they shall make payment to them which work the same according to the desert of the work, and of new deliver more to be wrought; and so from time to time to deliver stuff unwrought and receive the same again wrought as often as cause shall require, which hemp, wool, flax, or other stuff wrought from time to time shall be sold by the said Collectors and Governors of the Poor either at some market or other place, and at such time as they shall think meet, and with the money coming of the sale to buy more stuff in such wise as the stocks or store shall not be decayed in value; and if hereafter any such person able to do any such work shall refuse to work, or shall go abroad begging or live idly, or taking such work shall spoil or embezzle the same in such wise that after monition given the minister and churchwardens of the parish and Collectors and Governors of the Poor, or the more part of them, shall think the same person not meet to have any more work delivered out of the same store and stock, that then upon certificate thereof made under their hands and brought by one of the said Collectors and Governors of the Poor to the hands of such person or persons as shall in that county have the oversight and government of one of the Houses of Correction hereafter mentioned in this Act, in convenient apparel meet for such a body to wear, he, she, or they from such town, place, or parish shall be received into such House of Correction, there to be straitly kept, as well in diet as in work, and also punished from time to time as to the said persons having the oversight and government of the said House of Correction shall be appointed, as hereafter in this Act is declared; all which stocks and stores shall be provided and delivered into the hands of the said Collectors and Governors of the Poor before the first day of November next coming, and at all times hereafter as occasion shall serve; and that every person refusing to pay or not paying such sum of money towards the said stocks and stores as upon them or any of them shall

be by order aforesaid taxed, and at such time as by the same order shall be appointed, shall for every default forfeit double so much as he or they shall be so taxed unto.

And moreover be it ordained and enacted ... that within every county of this realm, one, two, or more abiding-houses or places convenient in some market town or corporate town or other place or places, by purchase, lease, building, or otherwise, by the appointment and order of the Justices of Peace or the more part of them in their said general Sessions (of the inhabitants within their several authorities to be taxed, levied, and gathered) shall be provided, and called the Houses of Correction, and also stock and store and implements to be in like sort also provided for setting on work and punishing not only of those which by the Collectors and Governors of the Poor for causes aforesaid to the said Houses of Correction shall be brought, but also of such as be or shall be inhabiting in no parish, or be or shall be taken as rogues, or once punished as rogues, and by reason of the uncertainty of their birth or of their dwelling by the space of three years, or for any other cause, ought to be abiding and kept within the same county ... and that every person refusing to pay or not paying such sum of money towards the making, obtaining, and furnishing of the said Houses of Correction, as upon them or any of them shall be by order aforesaid taxed, and at such time as by the same order shall be appointed, shall for every default forfeit double so much as he or they shall be taxed unto....

[Justices to appoint wardens of houses of poor] (SR, IV, 610: 18 Elizabeth, c.3.)

## Act against Reconciliation with Rome. 1581

63.

THIS ACT, enforcing the subjects' obedience to the Queen in ecclesiastical affairs, was intended as a measure against the Catholic revival which first became strong in the northern counties about 1575. In this period, the colleges of Douay and Rome, supported by continental Catholic contributions, secretly and continuously sent messages and priests into England. In 1579 the Jesuits began to direct those activities. If the threatened assassinations and political plots on the part of the Catholic leaders were meant merely to create unrest in England, they succeeded; but the English Catholics suffered most from such tactics. This Act established so high a financial penalty for not attending religious services of the Established Church that many of the wealthy Catholic families were ruined.

An Act to retain the Queen's Majesty's Subjects in their due Obedience.

Where since the Statute made in the thirteenth year of the reign of the Queen our Sovereign Lady, entitled *An Act against the Bringing in and putting in Execution of Bulls, Writings, and Instruments, and other Superstitious things from the See of Rome,* [13 Elizabeth, c.2.] divers evil affected persons have practiced, [attempted] contrary to the meaning of the said Statute, by other means than by bulls or instruments written or printed, to withdraw divers the Queen's Majesty's subjects from their natural obedience to her Majesty to obey the said usurped authority of Rome, and in respect of the same to persuade great numbers to withdraw their due obedience to her Majesty's laws established for the due service of Almighty God:

For reformation whereof, and to declare the true meaning of the said law, be it declared and enacted by the authority of this present Parliament, that all persons whatsoever which have, or shall have, or shall pretend to have power, or shall by any ways or means put into practice to absolve, persuade, or withdraw any of the Queen's Majesty's subjects or any within her Highness's realms and dominions from their natural obedience to her Majesty, or to withdraw them for the intent from the religion now by her Highness's authority established within her Highness's dominions to the Romish religion, or to move them or any of them to promise any obedience to any pretended authority of the See of Rome, or of any other prince, state, or potentate, or be had or used within her dominions, or shall do any overt act to the intent or purpose, and every of them, shall be to all intents adjudged to be traitors, and

being thereof lawfully convicted shall have judgment, suffer, and forfeit as in case of high treason, and if any person shall, after the end of this session of Parliament, by any means be willingly absolved or withdrawn as aforesaid, or willingly be reconciled, or shall promise any obedience to any such pretended authority, prince, state or potentate as is aforesaid, that then every such person, their procurers and counsellors thereunto, being thereof lawfully convicted, shall be taken, tried, and judged, and shall suffer and forfeit as in cases of high treason. . . .

And be it likewise enacted, that every person which shall say or sing mass, being thereof lawfully convicted, shall forfeit the sum of two hundred marks and be committed to prison in the next jail, there to remain by the space of one year, and from thenceforth till he have paid the said sum of two hundred marks; and that every person which shall willingly hear mass shall forfeit the sum of one hundred marks and suffer imprisonment for a year.

Be it also further enacted by the authority aforesaid, that every person above the age of sixteen years which shall not repair to some church, chapel, or usual place of common prayer, but forbear the same contrary to the tenor of a Statute made in the first year of her Majesty's reign for uniformity of common prayer, [*Act of Uniformity,* 1 Elizabeth, c.2.] and being thereof lawfully convicted, shall forfeit to the Queen's Majesty for every month after the end of this session of Parliament which he or she shall so forbear, twenty pounds of lawful English money; and that over and besides the said forfeitures, every person so forbearing by the space of twelve months as aforesaid shall for his or her obstinacy, after certificate thereof in writing made into the Court commonly called the King's Bench by the ordinary of the diocese, a Justice of Assize and Jail Delivery, or a Justice of Peace of the county where such offender shall dwell or be, be bound with two sufficient sureties in the sum of two hundred pound at the least to the good behavior, and so to continue bound until such time as the persons so bound do conform themselves and come to the church, according to the true meaning of the said Statute made in the first year of the Queen's Majesty's reign. . . .

Provided also, that every person which usually on the Sunday shall have in his or their house the Divine Service which is established by the law in this realm, and be thereat himself or herself usually or most commonly present, and shall not obstinately refuse to come to church and there to do as is aforesaid, and shall also four times in the year at the least be present at the Divine Service in the church of the parish where he or she shall be resident, or in some other open common church or such chapel . . . shall not incur any pain or penalty limited by this Act for not repairing to church. . . . (SR, IV, 657: 23 Elizabeth, c.1.)

## Act for the Surety of the Queen's Person. 1585

**64.** THE provisions contained in this Act grew out of the fear generated by the assassination of William the Silent and by the intrigues of Mary Stuart against Elizabeth's throne. It marks the beginning of the Council's determined attempt to stay Elizabeth from further protection of Mary, who was presently confined in the Tower.

An Act for Provision to be made for the Surety of the Queen's Majesty's most Royal Person, and the continuance of the Realm in Peace.

Forasmuch as the good felicity and comfort of the whole estate of this realm consisteth . . . in the surety and preservation of the Queen's most excellent Majesty; and for that it hath manifestly appeared that sundry wicked plots and means have of late been devised and laid, as well in foreign parts beyond the seas as also within this realm, to the great endangering of her Highness's most royal person and to the utter ruin of the whole common weal. . . .

Therefore for preventing of such great perils as might hereafter otherwise grow by the like detestable and devilish practices . . . be it enacted and ordained, if at any time after the end of this present session of Parliament any open invasion or rebellion shall be had or made into or within any of her Majesty's realms or dominions, or any act attempted tending to the hurt of her Majesty's most royal person, by or for any person that shall or may pretend any title to the Crown of this realm after her Majesty's decease, or if anything shall be compassed or imagined tending to the hurt of her Majesty's royal person by any person or with the privity [guilty knowledge] of any person that shall or may pretend title to the Crown of this realm, that then by her Majesty's commission under her great seal the Lords and others of her Highness's Privy Council and such other Lords of Parliament to be named by her Majesty as with the said Privy Council shall make up the number of twenty-four at the least, having with them for their assistance in that behalf such of the Judges of the Courts of Record at Westminster as her Highness shall for that purpose assign and appoint, or the more part of the same Council, Lords, and Judges, shall by virtue of this Act have authority to examine all and every the offences aforesaid and all circumstances thereof, and thereupon to give sentence or judgment as upon good proof the matter shall appear unto them; and that after such sentence or judgment given and declaration thereof made and published by her Majesty's proclamation under the great seal of England all persons against whom such sentence or judgment shall be so given and published shall be excluded and disabled for ever to have or claim, or to pretend to have or claim, the Crown of this realm or of any her Majesty's dominions . . . and that thereupon all her Highness's subjects shall and may lawfully, by virtue of this Act and her Majesty's direction in that behalf, by all forcible and possible means pursue to death every such wicked person by whom or by whose means, assent, or privity any such invasion or rebellion shall be in form aforesaid denounced to have been made, or such wicked act attempted, or other thing compassed or imagined against her Majesty's person, and all their aiders, comforters, and abettors. And if any such detestable act shall be executed against her Highness's most royal person whereby her Majesty's life shall be taken away . . . that then every such person by or for whom any such act shall be executed, and their issues being any wise assenting or privy to the same, shall by virtue of this Act be excluded and disabled for ever to have or claim . . . the said Crown of this realm or any other her Highness's dominions. . . . And that all the subjects of this realm and all other her Majesty's dominions shall and may lawfully, by virtue of this Act, by all forcible and possible means pursue to death every such wicked person by whom or by whose means any such detestable fact shall be, in form hereafter expressed, denounced to have been committed, and also their issues. . . .

And to the end that the intention of this law may be effectually executed, if her Majesty's life shall be taken away by any violent or unnatural means. . . .

Be it further enacted by the authority aforesaid, that the Lords and others which shall be of her Majesty's Privy Council at the time of such her decease, or the more part of the same Council, joining unto them for their better assistance five other Earls and seven other Lords of Parliament at the least (foreseeing that none of the said Earls, Lords, or Council be known to be persons that may make any title to the Crown), those persons which were Chief Justices of every Bench, Master of the Rolls, and Chief Baron of the Exchequer at the time of her Majesty's death, or in default of the said Justices, Master of the Rolls, and Chief Baron, some other of those which were Justices of some of the Courts of Record at Westminster at the time of her Highness's decease to supply their places, or any twenty-four or more of them, whereof eight to be Lords of Parliament not being of the Privy Council, shall to the uttermost of their power and skill examine the cause and manner of such her Majesty's death, and what persons shall be any way guilty thereof, and all circumstances concerning the same, according to the true meaning of this Act; and thereupon shall by open proclamation publish the same, and without any delay by all forcible and possible means prosecute to death all such as shall be found to be offenders therein and all their aiders and abettors; and for the doing thereof, and for the withstanding and suppressing of all such power and force as shall any way be levied or stirred in disturbance of the due execution of this law, shall by virtue of this Act have power and authority not only to raise and use such forces as shall in that behalf be needful and convenient, but also to use all other means and things possible and necessary for the maintenance of the same forces and prosecution of the said offenders; and if any such power and force shall be levied or stirred in disturbance of the due execution of this law by any person that shall or may pretend any title to the Crown of this realm, whereby this law in all things may not be fully executed according to the effect and true meaning of the same, that then every such person shall by virtue of this Act be therefore excluded and disabled for ever to have or claim, or to pretend to have or claim, the Crown of this realm or of any other her Highness's dominions. . . .

And be it further enacted by the authority

aforesaid, that all and every the subjects of all her Majesty's realms and dominions shall, to the uttermost of their power, aid and assist the said Council and all other the Lords and other persons to be adjoined unto them for assistance as is aforesaid in all things to be done and executed according to the effect and intention of this law; and that no subject of this realm shall in any wise be impeached in body, lands, or goods at any time hereafter for any thing to be done or executed according to the tenor of this law. . . .

And whereas of late many of her Majesty's good and faithful subjects have, in the name of God and with the testimony of good consciences, by one uniform manner of writing under their hands and seals and by their several oaths voluntarily taken, joined themselves together in one Bond and Association [this group of private persons, sworn to defend and protect the life of the Queen, and voluntarily associated, is here given legal recognition by the Act] to withstand and revenge to the uttermost all such malicious actions and attempts against her Majesty's most royal person. Now for the full explaining of all such ambiguities and questions as otherwise might happen to grow by reason of any sinister or wrong construction or interpretation to be made or inferred of or upon the words or meanings thereof, be it declared and enacted by the authority of this present Parliament, that the same Association and every article and sentence therein contained, as well concerning the disallowing, excluding, or disabling of any person that may or shall pretend any title to come to the Crown of this realm, and also for the pursuing and taking revenge of any person for any such wicked act or attempt as is mentioned in the same Association, shall and ought to be in all things expounded and adjudged according to the true intent and meaning of this Act, and not otherwise nor against any other person or persons. (SR, IV, 704: 27 Elizabeth, c.1.)

## Act for the Redress of Erroneous Judgments. 1585

**65.**  THE constitutional significance of this Act lies in the fact that it took from Parliament part of its appellate jurisdiction. Heretofore decisions from the Courts of King's Bench could be appealed only to Parliament. In thus establishing a special court to hear such pleas, Elizabeth took away one of Parliament's ancient rights, but the Parliament of 1585 took no exception to this since it felt itself already overburdened with legislative matters. Thus Parliament gladly gave away a right that it would struggle bitterly to repossess in the next century.

An Act for Redress of Erroneous Judgments in the Court commonly called the King's Bench.

Forasmuch as erroneous judgments given in the court called the King's Bench are only to be reformed by the High Court of Parliament, which Court of Parliament is not in these days so often holden as in ancient time it hath been, neither yet in respect of greater affairs of this realm such erroneous judgments can be well considered of and determined during the time of Parliament, whereby the subjects of this realm are greatly hindered and delayed of justice in such cases:

Be it therefore enacted by the authority of this present Parliament, that, where any judgment shall at any time hereafter be given in the said Court of the King's Bench in any suit or action of debt, detinue [legal action for repossessing personal property wrongfully withheld], covenant [contract], account, action upon the case, ejection, wrongful assumption of real property, ferm [rent for real property], or trespass, first commenced or to be first commenced there, other than such only where the Queen's Majesty shall be a party, the party, plaintiff or defendant, against whom any such judgment shall be given, may at his election sue forth out of the Court of Chancery a special writ of error, to be devised in the said Court of Chancery, directed to the Chief Justice of the said Court of the King's Bench for the time being, commanding him to cause the said record and all things concerning the said judgment to be brought before the Justices of the Common Bench and the Barons of the Exchequer into the Exchequer Chamber, there to be examined by the said Justices of the Common Bench and Barons aforesaid; which said Justices of the Common Bench and such Barons of the Exchequer as are of the degree of the coif [serjeants-at-law], or six of them at the least, by virtue of this present Act shall thereupon have full power and authority to examine all such errors as shall be assigned or found in or upon any such judgment, and thereupon to reverse or affirm the said judg-

ment as the law shall require, other than for errors to be assigned or found for or concerning the jurisdiction of the said Court of King's Bench, or for any want of form in any writ, return, plaint, bill, declaration, or other pleading, process, verdict, or proceeding whatsoever; and that after that the said judgment shall be affirmed or reversed, the said record and all things concerning the same shall be removed and brought back into the said Court of the King's Bench, that such further proceeding may be thereupon as well for execution or otherwise as shall appertain.

And be it further enacted, that such reversal or affirmation of any such former judgment shall not be so final but that the party who findeth him grieved therewith shall and may sue in the High Court of Parliament for the further and due examination of the said judgment in such sort as is now used upon erroneous judgments in the said Court of King's Bench. (SR, IV, 714: 27 Elizabeth, c.8.)

## Act against Jesuits and Seminary Priests. 1585

**66.**

ALTHOUGH confined in the Tower, Mary of Scotland was still the heir apparent and still a Catholic. Should one of the plots against Elizabeth's life succeed, the entire law would at once be ranged on the side of Mary's Catholic friends. The danger to the Church settlement and to those who maintained it was more than clear. However, this Act, in banishing Catholic priests from the Realm, distinguished between those born in England and those who were foreigners. Elizabeth was still determined, as late as 1585, to win over English Catholics to the Established Church by measures of firmness and kindness.

An Act against Jesuits, Seminary Priests, and such other like disobedient Persons.

Whereas divers persons called or professed Jesuits, seminary priests, and other priests, which have been and from time to time are made in the parts beyond the seas by or according to the order and rites of the Romish Church, have of late years come and been sent, and daily do come and are sent, into this realm of England and other the Queen's Majesty's dominions, of purpose ... not only to withdraw her Highness's subjects from their due obedience to her Majesty but also

to stir up and move sedition, rebellion, and open hostility within her Highness's realms and dominions, to the great dangering of the safety of her most royal person and to the utter ruin, desolation, and overthrow of the whole realm, if the same be not the sooner by some good means forseen and prevented:

For reformation whereof be it ordained, established, and enacted by the Queen's most excellent Majesty and ... [by] ... this present Parliament assembled ... that all and every Jesuits, seminary priests, and other priests whatsoever, made or ordained out of the realm of England or other her Highness's dominions or within any of her Majesty's realms or dominions by any authority, power, or jurisdiction derived, challenged, or pretended from the See of Rome since the Feast of the Nativity of St. John Baptist in the first year of her Highness's reign, shall within forty days next after the end of this present session of Parliament depart out of this realm of England and out of all other her Highness's realms and dominions. . . .

And be it further enacted . . . that it shall not be lawful to or for any Jesuit, seminary priest, or other such priest, deacon, or any religious person whatsoever, being born within this realm or any other her Highness's dominions, and heretofore since the said Feast of the Nativity of St. John Baptist in the first year of her Majesty's reign made, ordained, or professed, or hereafter to be made, ordained, or professed, by any authority or jurisdiction derived, challenged, or pretended from the See of Rome, by or of what name, title, or degree soever the same shall be called or known, to come into, be, or remain in any part of this realm or any other her Highness's dominion after the end of the same forty days, other than in such special cases and upon such special occasions only and for such time only as is expressed in this Act; and if he do, that then every such offence shall be taken and adjudged to be high treason, and every person so offending shall for his offence be adjudged a traitor, and shall suffer, lose, and forfeit as in case of high treason; and every person which after the end of the same forty days, and after such time of departure as is before limited and appointed, shall wittingly and willingly receive, relieve, comfort, aid, or maintain any such Jesuit, seminary priest, or other priest, deacon, or religious or ecclesiastical person as is aforesaid, being at liberty or out of hold, knowing him to be a Jesuit, [etc.] . . . shall also for such offence be adjudged a felon without benefit of clergy, and suffer death, lose, and forfeit as in case of one attainted of felony.

And be it further enacted . . . if any of her Majesty's subjects, not being a Jesuit, [etc.] . . . now being or which hereafter shall be of or brought up in any college of Jesuits or seminary already erected or ordained or hereafter to be erected or ordained . . . beyond the seas or out of this realm in any foreign parts, shall not within six months next after proclamation in that behalf to be made in the city of London under the great seal of England, return into this realm, and thereupon, within two days next after such return, before the bishop of the diocese or two Justices of Peace of the county where he shall arrive, submit himself to her Majesty and her laws, and take the oath set forth by Act in the first year of her reign [*Act of Supremacy*, 1 Elizabeth, c.1.], that then every such person which shall otherwise return, come into, or be in this realm or any other her Highness's dominions, for such offence of returning or being in this realm or any other her Highness's dominions without submission as aforesaid, shall also be adjudged a traitor, and shall suffer, lose, and forfeit as in case of high treason.

And be it further enacted . . . if any person under her Majesty's subjection or obedience shall at any time after the end of the said forty days by way of exchange or by any other shift, way, or means whatsoever, wittingly and willingly, either directly or indirectly, convey, deliver, or send, or cause or procure to be conveyed or delivered to be sent, over the seas or out of this realm or out of any other her Majesty's dominions or territories into any foreign parts, or shall otherwise wittingly and willingly yield, give, or contribute any money or other relief to or for any Jesuit, [etc.] . . . or to or for the maintenance or relief of any college of Jesuits or seminary already erected or ordained or hereafter to be erected or ordained in any the parts beyond the seas or out of this realm in any foreign parts, or of any person then being of or in any the same colleges or seminaries and not returned into this realm with submission as in this Act is expressed, and continuing in the same realm, that then every such person so offending, for the same offence shall incur the danger and penalty of *praemunire* mentioned in the *Statute of Praemunire* made in the sixteenth year of the reign of King Richard the Second.

And be it further enacted... that it shall not be lawful for any person of or under her Highness's obedience, at any time after the said forty days, during her Majesty's life... to send his or her child or other person being under his or her government into any the parts beyond the seas out of her Highness's obedience without the special license of her Majesty, except merchants engaged in foreign trade who reside abroad for purposes of trade... upon pain to forfeit and lose for every such their offence the sum of one hundred pounds....

Provided also, that this Act or anything therein contained shall not in any wise extend to any such Jesuit, seminary priest, or after such priest, deacon, or religious or ecclesiastical person as is before mentioned, as shall at any time within the said forty days, or within three days after that he shall hereafter come into this realm or any other her Highness's dominions, submit himself to some archbishop or bishop of this realm, or to some Justice of Peace within the county where he shall arrive or land, and do thereupon truly and sincerely before the same archbishop, bishop, or such Justice of Peace, take the said oath set forth *in anno primo,* and by writing under his hand confess and acknowledge and from thenceforth continue his due obedience unto her Highness's laws, statutes, and ordinances made and provided, or to be made or provided, in causes of religion....

And be it also further enacted... that every person or persons being subject of this realm which after the said forty days shall know and understand that any such Jesuit, seminary priest, or other priest abovesaid shall abide, stay, tarry, or be within this realm or other the Queen's dominions and countries, contrary to the true meaning of this Act, and shall not discover the same unto some Justice of Peace or other higher officer within twelve days next after his said knowledge, but willingly conceal his knowledge therein; that every such offender shall make fine and be imprisoned at the Queen's pleasure, and that if such Justice of Peace or other such officer to whom such matter shall be so discovered do not within twenty-eight days then next following give information thereof to some of the Queen's Privy Council or to the President or Vice-President of the Queen's Council established in the north or in the marches of Wales for the time being, that then he or they so offending shall for every such offence forfeit the sum of two hundred marks.

. . . . . .

And be it also enacted, that all such oaths, bonds, and submissions as shall be made by force of this Act as aforesaid, shall be certified into the Chancery by such parties before whom the same shall be made, within three months after such submission, upon pain to forfeit and lose for every such offence an hundred pounds of lawful English money, the said forfeiture to be to the Queen, her heirs and successors; and that if any person submitting himself as aforesaid do at any time within the space of ten years after such submission come within ten miles of such place where her Majesty shall be, without especial license from her Majesty in that behalf to be obtained in writing under her hand, that then and from thenceforth such person shall take no benefit of the said submission, but that the said submission shall be void as if the same had never been. (SR, IV, 706: 27 Elizabeth, c.2.)

## Act against Discontinuance of Writs. 1589

**67.** THIS ACT was meant to ensure fairer judicial procedures. A fourteenth-century statute of Edward III had directed appeals from decisions of the Exchequer to the Chancellor and Treasurer. In the sixteenth century those "great officers of the Realm" were usually too overburdened with the affairs of State to act in appellate capacity. Hence the old pleas, unheard on the day appointed, had to be reinitiated from the beginning, and such cases were usually assigned a later date of hearing. This often resulted in overly expensive justice or outright injustice to the litigants. By this Act, such cases were hereafter not to be discontinued, but to be heard immediately by the two Chief Justices.

An Act against Discontinuances of Writs of Error in the Court of Exchequer and King's Bench.

Whereas by a statute in the one and thirtieth year of the reign of King Edward the Third [31 Ed. III, c.12.] it is enacted, that upon complaint concerning error made in the Exchequer touching the King or other persons, the Lord Chancellor and Lord Treasurer shall do to [cause] come before them in any Chamber of Council near the Exchequer the record and process of the Exchequer, and taking to them such Justices and other sage persons as to them shall be thought meet, shall hear and determine such errors.... And whereas those two, being great officers of the realm, are employed, not only in their several offices and places of justice elsewhere but also for the other weighty affairs of the realm in Council attendant on the Queen's Majesty's person, and otherwise they be many times upon sudden warning called away, in such wise as they both many times and sometimes neither of them can be present in the Exchequer at the day of adjournment in such suit of error; and then by not coming of them at the day of adjournment every such writ of error depending is by the laws of the realm discontinued, and the party cannot proceed but must begin his suit of new, to the great loss of the party and hindrance of justice:

For remedy whereof, be it ordained and enacted ... that the not coming of the Lord Chancellor and Lord Treasurer or of either of them at the day of adjournment in such suit of error depending by virtue of the said former statute shall not [cause] discontinuance of any such writ or error; but if both the Chief Justices of either Bench, or any one of the said great officers the Lord Chancellor or Lord Treasurer, shall come to the Exchequer Chamber and there be present at the day of adjournment in such suit of error, it shall be no discontinuance, but the suit shall proceed in law to all intents and purposes as if both the Lord Chancellor and Lord Treasurer had come and been present at the day and place of adjournment: Provided always that no judgment shall be given in such suit or writ of error unless both the Lord Chancellor and Lord Treasurer shall be present thereat.

[After reciting 27 Elizabeth, c.8., *Act for Redress of Erroneous Judgments,* the Act continues].... Forasmuch as it doth many times fall out [happen] that the full number of the said Justices of the Common Bench and Barons of the Exchequer so authorized by the said statute, sometimes for want of health, sometimes through other weighty services and earnest occasions, cannot be present at the days and times of the returns and continuances of the same writs of error; and by reason of their absence and not coming the said writs of error are discontinued, justice delayed, and the parties put to begin new suit, to their great charges and prejudice:

For remedy thereof be it also enacted ... that from henceforth, if the full number of

Justices and Barons authorized by the said Act come not at the day or time of return or continuance of any such writ of error, that it shall be lawful for any three of the said Justices and Barons, at every of the said days and times, to receive writs of error, to award process thereupon, to make and prefix [assign] days from time to time of and for the continuance of all such writs of error as shall be there returned certified or depending; and the same shall be to these respects as good and available as if all the Justices and Barons authorized by the same Act were present ... provided, nevertheless, that no judgment shall be given in any such suit or error unless it be by such full number of the said Justices and Barons as are in that behalf authorized and appointed by the said Act.

Provided also, and be it nevertheless enacted ... that the party, plaintiff or defendant, against whom any such judgment hath been heretofore or hereafter shall be given in the said Court of King's Bench, may at his election sue in the High Court of Parliament for the reversal of any such judgment, as heretofore hath been usual or accustomed, anything in ... the former act notwithstanding. (SR, IV, 799: 31 Elizabeth, c.1.)

## Act against Popish Recusants. 1593

## 68.

THE "five mile" principle of law wherein non-conformists (in this case Catholics) were confined to a specific geographic area was incorporated into statute law by this Act. Such a method of controlling religious enemies became a fundamental weapon in the struggle against religious non-conformity by later English governments, and was most effectively applied after the Restoration by the Clarendon Code.

An Act against Popish Recusants. [As used in this Act the term describes a person who refused to comply with state regulations relative to church affairs because of sympathy for or connection with the Roman Catholic church. The same term was occasionally, but not customarily used in reference to Puritans and other non-conformists.]

For the better discovering and avoiding of all such traitorous and most dangerous conspiracies and attempts as are daily devised and practised against our most gracious Sovereign Lady the Queen's Majesty and the happy estate of this common weal by sundry wicked and seditious persons, who terming themselves Catholics and being indeed spies and intelligencers, nor only for her Majesty's foreign enemies but also for rebellious and traitorous subjects born within her Highness's realms and dominions, and hiding their most detestable and devilish purposes under a false pretext of religious conscience do secretly wander and shift from place to place within this realm to corrupt and seduce her Majesty's subjects and to stir them to sedition and rebellion:

Be it ordained and enacted ... that every person above the age of sixteen years, born within any the Queen's Majesty's realms or dominions or made denizen, being a Popish recusant and before the end of this session of Parliament convicted for not repairing to some church, chapel, or usual place of common prayer to hear Divine Service there, but forbearing the same contrary to the tenor of the laws and statutes heretofore made and provided in that behalf, and having any certain place of dwelling and abode within this realm, shall within forty days next after the end of this session of Parliament if they be within this realm and not restrained or stayed, either by imprisonment, or by her Majesty's commandment, or by order and direction of some six or more of the Privy Council, or by such sickness or infirmity of body as they shall not be able to travel without imminent danger of life, and in such cases of absence out of the realm, restraint, or stay, then within twenty days next after they shall return into the realm, and be enlarged freed of such imprisonment or restraint, and shall be able to travel repair to their place of dwelling where they usually heretofore made their common abode, and shall not at any time after pass or remove above five miles from thence; and also that every person being above the age of sixteen years born within any her Majesty's realms or dominions or made denizen, and having or which hereafter shall have any certain place of dwelling and abode within this realm, which being then a Popish recusant shall at any time hereafter be lawfully convicted for not repairing to some church, chapel, or usual place of common prayer to hear Divine Service there, but forbearing the same contrary to the said laws and statutes, and being within this realm at the time that they shall be convicted, shall within forty days next after the same conviction, (if they be not restrained or stayed by imprisonment or otherwise as is aforesaid, and in such cases of restraint and stay then within twenty days next after they shall be enlarged of such imprisonment or restraint and shall be able to travel) repair to their place of usual dwelling and abode, and shall not at any time after pass or remove above five miles from thence; upon pain that every person and persons that shall offend against the tenor and intent of this Act in any thing before mentioned shall lose and forfeit all his and their goods and chattels, and shall also forfeit to the Queen's Majesty all the lands, tenements, and hereditaments, and all the rents and annuities of every such person so doing or offending, during the life of the same offender. . . .

Provided always and be it further enacted by the authority aforesaid, that all such persons as by the intent and true meaning of this Act are to make their repair to their place of dwelling and abode, or to the place where they were born, or where their father or mother shall be dwelling, and not to remove or pass above five miles from thence as is aforesaid, shall within twenty days next after

their coming to any of the said places, as the case shall happen, notify their coming thither and present themselves and deliver their true names in writing to the minister or curate of the same parish and to the constable . . . of the town; and thereupon the said minister or curate shall presently enter the same into a book to be kept in every parish for that purpose; and afterward the said minister or curate and the said constable . . . shall certify the same in writing to the Justices of the Peace of the same county at the next general or quarter Sessions to be holden in the said county; and the said Justices shall cause the same to be entered by the clerk of the peace in the rolls of the same Sessions.

And to the end that the realm be not pestered and overcharged with the multitude of such seditious and dangerous people as is aforesaid, who having little or no ability to answer or satisfy any competent penalty for their contempt and disobedience of the said laws and statutes, and being committed to prison for the same do live for the most part in better case there than they could if they were abroad at their own liberty; the Lords Spiritual and Temporal and the Commons in this present Parliament assembled do most humbly . . . beseech the Queen's Majesty that it may be further enacted, that if any such person or persons being a Popish recusant . . . not having lands, tenements, rents, or annuities of an absolute estate of inheritance or freehold of the clear yearly value of twenty marks above all charges, to their own use and behalf and not upon any secret trust or confidence for any other, or goods and chattels in their own right and to their own proper use and behalf, and not upon any secret trust or confidence for any other, above the value of forty pounds, shall not within the time before in this Act in that behalf limited and appointed repair to their place of usual dwelling and abode, if they have any, or else to the place where they were born or where their father or mother shall be dwelling, according to the tenor and meaning of this present Act, and thereupon notify their coming and present themselves and deliver their true names in writing to the minister or curate of the parish and to the constable . . . of the town within such time and in such manner and form as is aforesaid; or at any time after such their repairing to any such place as is before appointed shall pass or remove above five miles from the same, and shall not within three months next after such person shall be apprehended or taken for offending as is aforesaid conform themselves to the obedience of the laws and statutes of this realm in coming usually to the church to hear Divine Service, and in making such public confession and submission as hereafter in this Act is appointed and expressed, being thereunto required by the bishop of the diocese, or any Justice of Peace of the county where the said person shall happen to be, or by the minister or curate of the parish; that in every such case every such offender, being thereunto warned or required by any two Justices of the Peace or coroner of the same county where such offender shall then be, shall upon his or their corporal oath before any two Justices of the Peace or coroner of the same county abjure [leave] this realm of England and all other the Queen's Majesty's dominions for ever; and thereupon shall depart out of this realm at such haven and port and within such time as shall in that behalf be assigned and appointed by the said Justices of Peace or coroner before whom such abjuration shall be made, unless the same offenders be letter or stayed by such lawful and reasonable means or causes as by the common laws of this realm are permitted and allowed in cases of abjuration for felony, and in such cases of let or stay, then within such reasonable and convenient time after as the common law requireth in case of abjuration for felony as is aforesaid: and that every Justice of Peace and coroner before whom any such abjuration shall happen to be made as is aforesaid, shall cause the same presently to be entered of record before them, and shall certify the same to the Justices of Assizes and Jail De-

livery of the said county at the next Assizes or Jail Delivery to be holden in the same county: and if any such offender which by the tenor and intent of this Act is to be abjured as is aforesaid shall refuse to make such abjuration as is aforesaid, or after such abjuration made shall not go to such haven and within such time as is before appointed and from thence depart out of this realm according to this present Act, or after such his departure shall return or come again into any her Majesty's realms or dominions without her Majesty's special license in that behalf first had and obtained, that then in every such case the person so offending shall be adjudged a felon and shall suffer and lose as in case of felony without benefit of clergy.

And be it further enacted and ordained by the authority aforesaid, that if any person which shall be suspected to be a Jesuit, seminary, or massing priest, being examined by any person having lawful authority in that behalf to examine such person which shall be so suspected, shall refuse to answer directly and truly whether he be a Jesuit or seminary or massing priest, as is aforesaid, every such person so refusing to answer shall for his disobedience and contempt in that behalf be committed to prison by such as shall examine him as is aforesaid, and thereupon shall remain and continue in prison without bail . . . until he shall make direct and true answer to the said questions. . . .

Provided nevertheless and be it further enacted . . . that if any of the persons which are hereby limited and appointed to continue and abide within five miles of their usual dwelling place, or of such place where they were born or where their father or mother shall be dwelling . . . shall have necessary occasion or business to go and travel out of the compass of the said five miles, that then and in every such case upon license in that behalf to be gotten under the hands of two of the Justices of the Peace of the same county, with the . . . assent in writing of the bishop of the diocese, or of the lieutenant or of any deputy lieutenant of the . . . county, under their hands, it shall and may be lawful for every such person to go and travel about such their necessary business, and for such time only for their travelling, attending, and returning as shall be comprised in the same license.... (SR, IV, 843: 35 Elizabeth, c.2.)

## Act against Seditious Sectaries. 1593

69.

ELIZABETH'S efforts to include the Protestant extremists in the Established Church had proven a marked failure by 1593. This Act paved the way for their withdrawal from England and thereby relieved the Bishops of the duty of suppression, which now was delegated to the civil courts.

An Act to retain the Queen's Subjects in Obedience.

For the preventing and avoiding of such great inconveniences and perils as might happen and grow by the wicked and dangerous practices of seditious sectaries and disloyal persons:

Be it enacted... that if any person or persons above the age of sixteen years which shall obstinately refuse to repair to some church, chapel, or usual place of common prayer to hear Divine Service established by her Majesty's laws and statutes in that behalf made, and shall forbear to do the same by the space of a month next after without lawful cause, shall at any time after forty days next after the end of this session of Parliament, by printing, writing, or express words or speeches, advisedly and purposely practice or go about to move or persuade any of her Majesty's subjects or any other within her Highness's realms or dominions to deny, withstand, and impugn her Majesty's power and authority in causes ecclesiastical united and annexed to the imperial Crown of this realm; or to that end or purpose shall advisedly and maliciously move or persuade any other person whatsoever to forbear or abstain from coming to church to hear Divine Service or to receive the communion according to her Majesty's laws and statutes aforesaid, or to come to or to be present at any unlawful assemblies, conventicles, or meetings under color or pretence of any exercise of religion, contrary to her Majesty's said laws and statutes; or if any person or persons which shall obstinately refuse to repair to some church, chapel, or usual place of common prayer and shall forbear by the space of a month to hear Divine Service as is aforesaid, shall after the said forty days either of him or themselves, or by the motion, persuasion, enticement, or allurement of any other, willingly join or be present at any such assemblies, conventicles, or meetings under color or pretence of any such exercise of religion, contrary to the laws and statutes of this realm as is aforesaid; that then every such person so offending... and being thereof lawfully convicted, shall be committed to prison, there to remain without bail... until they shall conform and yield themselves to come to some church, chapel, or usual place of common prayer and hear Divine Service, according to her Majesty's laws and statutes aforesaid, and to make such open submission and declaration of their said conformity as hereafter in this Act is declared and appointed.

[The Act here provides the same punishments for obdurate nonconformists as was extended to Popish recusants by 35 Elizabeth, c.2., *Act against Popish Recusants*.]

[Convicted offenders might make public submission by oral statement in the parish church during services and escape punishment.]

And for every person having house and family is in duty bounden to have special regard of the good government and ordering of the same:

Be it enacted... that if any person or persons shall at any time hereafter relieve, maintain, retain, or keep in his or their house or otherwise any person which shall obstinately refuse to come to some church, chapel, or usual place of common prayer to hear Divine Service, and shall forbear the same by the space of a month together, contrary to the laws and statutes of this realm, that then every person which shall so relieve, maintain, [etc.] ... any such person offending as aforesaid, after notice thereof to him or them given by the ordinary of the diocese, or any Justice of Assizes of the circuit, or any Justice of Peace of the county, or the minister, curate, or churchwardens of the parish where such person shall then be, or by any of them, shall forfeit to the Queen's Majesty for every person so relieved, maintained, [etc.] ... ten pounds for every month that he or they shall so relieve, maintain, [etc.] ... any such person so offending.

Provided nevertheless, that this Act shall not in any wise extend to punish or impeach any person or persons for relieving, maintaining, [etc.] ... his or their wife, father, mother, child or children, ward, brother or sister, or his wife's father or mother, not having any

certain place of habitation of their own, or the husbands or wives of any of them, or for relieving, maintaining, [etc.] ... any such person as shall be committed by authority to the custody of any by whom they shall be so relieved, maintained, or kept; anything in this Act ... to the contrary notwithstanding.

Provided also, that every person that shall abjure by force of this Act, or refuse to abjure being thereunto required as aforesaid, shall forfeit and lose to her Majesty all his goods and chattels for ever, and should further lose all his lands, tenements, and hereditaments for and during the life only of such offender and no longer; and that the wife of any offender by force of this Act shall not lose her dower; nor that any corruption of blood shall grow or be by reason of any offence mentioned in this Act; but that the heir of every such offender by force of this Act shall and may after the death of every offender have and enjoy the lands, [etc.] ... of such offender as if this Act had not been made. And this Act to continue no longer than to the end of the next session of Parliament. (SR, IV, 841: 35 Elizabeth, c.1.)

## Act to Relieve the Poor. 1598

### 70.

ELIZABETHAN social legislation reached its highest development in this Act. Although previous legislation had approached the concept of the poor as a helpless product of the economic system, no specific Act presented such a well-considered plan for local maintenance of the poor as did this. The Justice of the Peace, heretofore with no important voice in the matter of poor relief, now was given almost absolute power to tax for their support. The domiciling of the indigent in houses erected for that purpose became one of the lasting principles of English care of the "impotent poor."

An Act for the Relief of the Poor.

Be it enacted by the authority of this present Parliament, that the churchwardens of every parish, and four substantial householders there ... who shall be nominated yearly in Easter week, under the hand and seal of two or more Justices of the Peace in the same county ... shall be called Overseers of the Poor of the same parish; and they or the greater part of them shall take order from time to time by and with the consent of two

or more such Justices of Peace for setting to work of the children of all such whose parents shall not by the said persons be thought able to keep and maintain their children, and also all such persons married or unmarried as having no means to maintain them use no ordinary and daily trade of life to get their living by; and also to raise weekly or otherwise (by taxation of every inhabitant and every occupier of lands in the said parish in such competent sum and sums of money as they shall think fit) a convenient stock of flax, hemp, wool, thread, iron, and other necessary ware and stuff to set the poor on work, and also competent sums of money for and towards the necessary relief of the lame, impotent, old, blind, and such other among them being poor and not able to work, and also for the putting out of such children to be apprentices, to be gathered out of the same parish according to the ability of the said parish; and to do and execute all other things, as well for disposing of the said stock as otherwise concerning the premises, as to them shall seem convenient.

. . . . [The] churchwardens, and Overseers so to be nominated, or such of them as shall not be let [prevented] by sickness or other just excuse to be allowed by such two justices of peace or more, shall meet together at the least once every month in the church of the said parish, upon the Sunday in the after-noon after divine service, there to consider of some good course to be taken and of some meet orders to be set down in the premises; and shall within four days after the end of their year, and after other overseers nomi-nated as aforesaid, make and yield up to such two justices of peace a true and perfect ac-count of all sums of money by them received, or rated and cessed [assessed] and not re-ceived, and also of such stock as shall be in their hands or in the hands of any of the poor to work, and of all other things con-cerning their said office, and such sum or sums of money as shall be in their hands shall pay and deliver over to the said church-wardens and overseers newly nominated and appointed as aforesaid: upon pain that every one of them absenting themselves without lawful cause as aforesaid from such monthly meeting for the purpose aforesaid, or being negligent in their office or in the execution of the orders aforesaid being made by and with the assent of the said justices of peace, to for-feit for every such default twenty shillings.

And be it also enacted, that if the said justices of peace do perceive that the in-habitants of any parish are not able to levy among themselves sufficient sums of money for the purposes aforesaid, that then the said justices shall and may tax, rate, and assess as aforesaid any other of other parishes, or out of any parish within the hundred where the said parish is, to pay such sum and sums of money to the churchwardens and overseers of the said poor parish for the said purposes as the said justices shall think fit, according to the intent of this law; and if the said hundred shall not be thought to the said justices able and fit to relieve the said several parishes not able to provide for themselves as aforesaid, then the justices of peace at their general Quarter Sessions, or the greater num-ber of them, shall rate and assess as aforesaid . . . other parishes . . . as in their discretion shall seem fit.

And that it shall be lawful for the said churchwardens and overseers or any of them, by warrant from any such two justices of peace, to levy as well the said sums of money of every one that shall refuse to contribute according as they shall be assessed, by distress and sale of the offender's goods, as the sums of money or stock which shall be behind upon any account to be made as aforesaid, rendering to the party the overplus [surplus]; and in defect of such distress, it shall be law-ful for any such two justices of the peace to commit him to prison, there to remain with-out bail . . . till payment of the said sum or stock; and the said justices of peace or any one of them to send to the House of Correc-tion such as shall not employ themselves to work being appointed thereunto as afore-said; and also any two such justices of peace to commit to prison every one of the said churchwardens and overseers which shall re-fuse to account, there to remain without bail . . . till he have made a true account and satisfied and paid so much as upon the said account shall be remaining in his hands.

And be it further enacted, that it shall be lawful for the said churchwardens and over-seers or the greater part of them, by the as-sent of any two justices of peace, to bind any such children as aforesaid to be apprentices where they shall seem convenient, till such man-child shall come to the age of four and twenty years, and such woman-child to the age of one and twenty years; the same to be as effectual to all purposes as if such child were of full age and by indenture of covenant bound him or herself.

And to the intent that necessary places of habitation may more conveniently be provided for such poor impotent people, be it enacted ... that it shall and may be lawful for the said churchwardens and overseers or the greater part of them, by the leave of the lord or lords of the manor whereof any waste or common, within their parish is or shall be ... to erect, build, and set up in fit and convenient places of habitation in such waste or common, at the general charges of the parish or otherwise of the hundred or county as aforesaid, to be taxed, rated, and gathered in manner before expressed, convenient houses of dwelling for the said impotent poor; and also to place inmates or more families than one in one cottage or house. ...

Provided always, that if any person or persons shall find themselves grieved with any cess or tax or other act done by the said churchwardens and other persons or by the said justices of peace, that then it shall be lawful for the justices of peace at their general Quarter Sessions, or the greater number of them, to take such order therein as to them shall be thought convenient, and the same to conclude and bind all the said parties.

And be it further enacted, that the parents or children of every poor, old, blind, lame, and impotent person, or other poor person not able to work, being of sufficient ability, shall at their own charges relieve and maintain every such poor person in that manner and according to that rate as by the justices of peace of that county where such sufficient persons dwell, or the greater number of them, at their general Quarter Sessions shall be assessed; upon pain that every one of them to forfeit twenty shillings for every month which they shall fail therein.

And be it further enacted, that the mayors,

bailiffs, or other head officers of every corporate town within this realm being justice or justices of peace, shall have the same authority by virtue of this act within the limits and precincts of their corporations, as well out of Sessions as at their Sessions, as in herein limited, prescribed, and appointed to any of the justices of peace in the county for all the uses and purposes in this act prescribed, and no other justice of peace to enter or meddle there.

And be it further enacted ... that ... no person or persons whatsoever shall go wandering abroad and beg in any place whatsoever, by licence or without, upon pain to be esteemed, taken, and punished as a rogue; provided always, that this present Act shall not extend to any poor people which shall ask relief of victuals only in the same parish where such poor people do dwell, so the same be in such time only and according to such order and direction as shall be made and appointed by the churchwardens and overseers of the poor of the same parish according to the true intent and meaning of this Act.

And forasmuch as all begging is forbidden by this present Act, be it further enacted ... that the justices of peace of every county or place corporate, or the more part of them, in their general Sessions to be holden next after the end of this session of Parliament, or in default thereof at the Quarter Sessions to be holden about the feast of Easter next, shall rate every parish to such a weekly sum of money as they shall think convenient, so as no parish be rated above the sum of six pence nor under the sum of an half-penny weekly to be paid, and so as the total sum of such taxation of the parishes in every county amount not above the rate of two pence for every parish in the said county; which sums so taxed shall be yearly assessed by the agreement of the parishioners within themselves, or in default thereof by the churchwardens and constables of the same parish or the more part of them, or in default of their agreement by the order of such justice or justices of peace as shall dwell in the same parish or (if none be there dwelling) in the parts next adjoining; and if any person shall refuse or neglect to pay any such portion of money so taxed, it shall be lawful for the said churchwardens and constables, or in their default for the justices of peace, to levy the same by distress and sale of the goods of the party so refusing or neglecting, rendering to the party the overplus, and in default of such distress it shall be lawful to any justice of that limit to commit such persons to prison, there to abide without bail ... till he have paid the same.

And be it also enacted, that the said justices of the peace at their general Quarter Sessions to be holden at the time of such taxation, shall set down what competent sum of money shall be sent quarterly out of every county or place corporate for the relief of the poor prisoners of the King's Bench ... and also of such hospitals and almshouses as shall be in the said county, and what sums of money shall be sent to every one of the said hospitals and almshouses, so as there be sent out of every county yearly twenty shillings at the least to the prisoners of the King's Bench ... which sums, rateably to be assessed upon every parish, the churchwardens of every parish shall truly collect and pay over to the high constable in whose division such parish shall be situate ... and every such constable at every such Quarter Sessions in such county shall pay over the same to two such justices of peace, or to one of them, as shall be by the more part of the justices of peace of the county elected to be treasurers of the said collection; which treasurers in every county so chosen shall continue but for the space of one whole year, and then give up their charge with a due account of their receipts and disbursements at their meeting in the Quarter Sessions to be holden after the feast of Easter in every year to such others as shall from year to year in form aforesaid successively be elected; which said treasurers or one of them shall pay over the same to the Lord Chief Justice of England and Knight Marshal for the time being, equally to be divided to the

use aforesaid, taking their acquittances for the same, or in default of the said Chief Justice to the next ancientest justice of the King's Bench as aforesaid: and if any churchwarden or high constable or his executors or administrators shall fail to make payment in form above specified, then every churchwarden, his executors or administrators, so offending shall forfeit for every time the sum of ten shillings; and every high constable, his executors or administrators, shall forfeit for every time the sum of twenty shillings; the same forfeitures, together with the sums behind, to be levied by the said treasurer ... by way of distress and sale of goods ... and by them to be employed towards the charitable uses comprised in this Act.

And be it further enacted, that all the surplusage of money which shall be remaining in the said stock of any county shall by the discretion of the more part of the justices of peace in their Quarter Sessions be ordered, distributed, and bestowed for the relief of the poor hospitals of that county, and of those that shall sustain losses by fire, water, the sea, or other casualties, and to such other charitable purposes for the relief of the poor as to the more part of the said justices of peace shall seem convenient.

And be it further enacted, that if any treasurer shall wilfully refuse to take upon him the said office of treasurership, or refuse to distribute and give relief according to such form as shall be appointed by the more part of the said justices of peace, that then it shall be lawful for the justices of peace in their Quarter Sessions, or in their default for the justices of assize at the assizes to be holden in the same county, to fine the same treasurer by their discretion; the same fine to be levied by sale of his goods, and to be prosecuted by any two of the said justices of peace whom they shall authorize.

·    ·    ·    ·    ·

Provided always, that this Act shall endure no longer than to the end of the next Session of Parliament. (SR, IV, 896: 39 Elizabeth, c.3.)

## Lay Subsidy Act. 1601

**71.**

THROUGHOUT the Tudor period Parliament's hold on the right of taxation, the "power of the purse," had grown very strong. By the beginning of the seventeenth century parliamentary subsidies had evolved a special form in which purpose, amount, and method of collection were clearly established. The present Act is included both *for its form and its strong statement of Parliament's realization of its rights in the area of taxation. Later, during the early Stuart period when the Monarchy challenged this ancient right, conflicts were touched off which were to result in a century-long struggle.*

An Act for the Grant of Four entire Subsidies and Eight Fifteenths and Tenths granted by the Temporalty.

Most excellent and most gracious Sovereign, where we your Majesty's humble, faithful, and loving subjects being here ... assembled in your High Court of Parliament, have entered into due consideration of the great and weighty causes which ought at this time, more than at any other time [due to a rebellion in Ireland which was encouraged and aided by Spanish troops and money], to stir up the heart of all that are either well affected in religion towards God, loyalty towards you their dear Sovereign, or care of their own safety and their posterities, to consult timely and provide effectually for all such means as are or may be necessary to preserve both you and us from those apparent dangers wherein this State may fall through lack of so much care and providence as agreeth with the rules of nature and common reason ... we do most humbly beseech your Majesty that it may be enacted by the authority of this present Parliament in manner and form following, that is to say:

That your Majesty shall have eight whole fifteenths and tenths, to be paid, taken, and levied of the moveable goods, chattels, and other things usual to such fifteenths and tenths to be contributory and chargeable, within the shires, cities, boroughs, towns, and other places of this your Majesty's realm, in manner and form aforetime used. ...

And be it further enacted ... that the knights elected and returned of and for the

shires within this realm for this present Parliament, citizens of cities, burgesses of boroughs and towns, where collectors have been used to be named and appointed for the collection of any fifteenth and tenth before this time granted, shall name and appoint ... sufficient and able persons to be collectors . . . [those appointed to have] . . . lands, tenements, and other hereditaments in their own right of an estate of inheritance of the yearly value of 40£, or in goods worth 400£ at the least, each of them, after such rate and value as he or they shall be assessed and rated at in the Subsidy Book. ...

And furthermore ... we the Lords spiritual and temporal, and the Commons of this present Parliament assembled ... give and grant to your Highness ... four entire subsidies, to be rated, taxed, levied, and paid ... of every person spiritual and temporal ... in manner and form following, that is to say; as well that every person born within ... the Queen's dominions, as all and every fraternity, guild, corporation, mystery, brotherhood, and commonalty, corporated or not corporated ... being worth three pounds, for every one pound as well in coin ... as also plate, stock of merchandise, all manner of corn and grain, household stuff, and all other goods moveable, as well within this realm as without, and of all such sums of money as to him or them is or shall be owing, whereof he or they trust in his or their conscience surely to be paid (except and out of the premises deducted such sums of money as he or they owe and in his or their consciences intendeth truly to pay, and except also the apparel of every such person their wives and children belonging to their own bodies, saving jewels, gold, silver, stone, and pearl), shall pay [for each of the four subsidies mentioned above, 2s.8d. for every pound value of commodities as enumerated]. . . .

And be it further enacted by the authority aforesaid, that every person born under the Queen's obeisance, and every corporation, fraternity, [etc.] . . . for every pound that every of the same . . . has in fee simple, fee tail, for term of life, term of years, by execution, wardship, or by copy of court roll, and in any honors, castles, manors, lands, tenements, rents, services, heritaments, annuities, fees . . . or other yearly profits of the yearly value of twenty shillings, as well within ancient demesne and other places of privileged as elsewhere, and so upward, shall

pay . . . [for each of the above-mentioned subsidies, 4s. on the pound]. . . .

And further be it enacted by the said authority, that the said commissioners . . . shall for every of the said payments of the said subsidies, name such sufficient and able persons which then shall have and possess lands and other hereditaments in their own right of the . . . yearly value of forty pounds, or goods to the value of four hundred pounds . . . as he shall be taxed in the Subsidy Book, if any such be in the said limits, and for want of such so assessed, than those to be appointed collectors that then shall be sufficient, and rated and taxed in the Subsidy Books in lands or goods nearest to the values aforesaid, as by their discretion shall be thought good, in shires . . . cities, towns, corporate, and other . . . places . . . to be high collectors. . . . (SR, IV, 991: 43 Elizabeth, c.18.)

## Clerical Subsidy Act. 1601

**72.** IN THE Convocation of 1601 the clergy had signified its willingness to grant a subsidy to the Crown, and had worked out the rates against individual clerics and clerical holdings. It was necessary, however, to formulate this bequest in statute form, since Parliament was unwilling to allow any Crown income independent of its control. The political implications of this are very clear: by the end of Elizabeth's reign Parliament had located the weakness in the position of the Monarchy—its economic dependence on the Houses of Parliament.

An Act for the Confirmation of the Subsidies granted by the Clergy.

Where the prelates and clergy of the Province of Canterbury have for certain considerations lovingly and liberally given and granted to the Queen's most excellent Majesty four subsidies of four shillings in the pound, to be taken and levied of all and singular their promotions spiritual within the same Province, as such days and times and in such certain manner and form, and with such exceptions and provisions, as be specified and declared in a certain instrument by them thereof made, and delivered to the Queen's Highness, under the seal of the most Reverend Father in God, John [Whitgift], now Archbishop of Canterbury and Primate of

all England, which instrument is now exhibited in this present Parliament to be ratified and confirmed; the tenor whereof ensueth in these words: [The instrument of subsidy is here stated in full]. . . .

Most excellent and most gracious Sovereign, your Majesty's most humble subjects the prelates and clergy of the Province of Canterbury, called together by your Highness's authority and now lawfully assembled and met together in a Convocation or Synod . . . with one uniform consent, accord, and agreement, have given and granted and by these presents do give and grant to your Highness, your heirs and successors, four whole and entire subsidies in manner and form following, that is to say; that every archbishop, bishop, dean, archdeacon, provost, master of college, prebendary, parson, and vicar, and every other person and persons of whatsoever name and degree he or they be within the Province of Canterbury, having and enjoying any spiritual promotion or other temporal possession to the same spiritual promotion annexed, now not divided or separated by act of Parliament or otherwise from the possession of the clergy, shall pay to your Highness, your heirs and successors, for every pound that he may yearly dispend by reason of the said spiritual promotion, the sum of four shillings for every of the said four subsidies; and for the true and certain value of all the promotions and every of them ... the rate, taxation, valuation, and estimation now remaining of record in your Majesty's Court of Exchequer for the payment of a perpetual dime or tenth granted unto your Majesty's most noble father in the six and twentieth year of his reign, concerning such promotions as now be in the possession of the clergy [26 Henry VIII, c.3: SR, III, 493], shall only be followed and observed, without making any valuation, rate, taxation, or estimation other than in the said record is comprised:

Provided always, that forasmuch as the tenth part of the said rate and valuation before mentioned is yearly paid to your Highness for the said perpetual dime, so as there remaineth only nine parts yearly to the incumbent clear, these four subsidies of four shillings the pound shall be understood and meant only of every full pound of the said nine parts and no more. . . .

. . . . [Also], your said prelates and clergy do grant, that every archbishop and bishop . . . shall be collectors of these subsidies within their proper diocese . . . and . . . shall certify into your Majesty's Court of Exchequer under their seals and names and surnames of all such stipendiary priests, deacons, and ministers within their diocese as be chargeable by this Act. . . .

. . . . Wherefore for the true and sure payment of the said subsidies granted by the said prelates and clergy of the said Province of Canterbury according to the tenor, effect, and true meaning of the said instrument, be it enacted by the Queen's most excellent Majesty, with the assent of the Lords spiritual and temporal and the Commons in this present Parliament assembled, and by the authority of the same, that the said gift, grant, and every matter, sum of money, petition, provision, clause, and sentence in the same instrument contained shall stand and be ratified, established, and confirmed by the authority of this present Parliament. . . .

And be it further enacted by the authority aforesaid, that all and every grant and grants of all and every sum and sums of money granted, or which hereafter shall be granted, to the Queen's Majesty by the clergy of the Province of York, shall be of the same strength, force, and effect in all things as the said grant made by the said Province of Canterbury; and shall be taxed, certified, collected, levied, gathered, and paid according to the tenor, form, and effect of this present Act of Parliament. . . . (SR, IV, 984: 43 Elizabeth, c.17.)

# The Reign of James I

## 1603-1625

# DOCUMENTS OF THE REIGN OF JAMES I

# England, 1603-1625 *Introduction*

The stages of constitutional, economic, and political development which constitute the framework on which the fabric of history is draped are seldom sharply distinguishable from one decade, or even one century, to another. Ideas and institutions which come eventually to characterize one historic period and give it aspect apart from preceding times can usually be traced to earlier times, where they existed in embryonic form. Again, concepts which were detrimental to the social development of an earlier age are seldom later completely obliterated; they continue, but with diminishing influence on the intellectual and institutional preoccupations of the social organism. Hence it is seldom safe to nominate a single period as being so different from preceding ones as to call it "a new age." But a revolutionary era in English constitutional development can truly be said to have come into being with the beginning of the Stuart period.

This is not to say that Tudor concepts and problems disappeared, or that Stuart-dominated England faced forces and problems which were altogether unknown to the Tudors. Yet there were real and dramatic differences between the sixteenth and seventeenth centuries in England, particularly in the area of constitutional development and in the problems which stimulated the growth of that institution.

There was, first of all, a shifting of the constitutional basis of monarchial authority from that of tenurial right and Parliamentary warrant, as understood by Elizabeth, to that of divine commission, as understood by James I. This relocation of the basis of authority was clearly not the result of the application of any particular Stuart principle; rather, the concept developed as the result of certain conflicting historic forces which guided political thought in that direction. Its later evolution indirectly resulted in the maturation of the Divine Rights concept, demonstrably a Stuart ideal, which went far beyond the medieval theory of authority which held the divine election of kings to be an irrefutable limitation on the office as well as the holder's most valid claim to it.

In medieval practice it was assumed that God's choice of rulers was made known to man through tenurial inheritance. However, neither the tenurial nor the Parliamentary basis of the Tudor warrant to kingship could compete against the divine delegation claimed by the Calvinists, to which James added his own particular sense of divinely ordained leadership. To James, and to the whole social order of the seventeenth century, the Parliamentary basis of the monarchy appeared not only archaic and useless, but positively distasteful. Such a basis, after all, could only be defined in terms of limitations as well as specified rights and prerogatives, and this would seem a barrier to the idea of political sovereignty, which, though practically unrecognized in sixteenth-century political thought, had become a familiar part of political philosophy early in the seventeenth century.

Secondly, the medieval framework of social organization, which in the early Tudor period had allowed considerable power to the aristocracy and Church in local areas, was already a thing of the past upon Elizabeth's accession. The social revolution in which the industrial and economic strength of the towns had destroyed the guilds and monasteries had ended by draining the political strength of the first two estates. Political power was now concentrated in the central government. More and more it was apparent to the new commercial classes of the seventeenth century that the struggle led by the Tudors against the medieval corporations was completed; the immediate necessity was for a concrete settlement which would secure the rights and properties of the individual against the aggression and possible tyranny of the new monarchy. Thus, Tudor developments in the sixteenth century had precipitated a problem which was only to be solved in the next century, when the English people, having experimentally constructed and defined political sovereignty, finished by locating it not in the monarch but in Parliament.

The third major difference between the two periods was in the religious sphere. The powers of the Roman Church had been limited, and finally rejected and destroyed by the Tudors. This process had resulted in aligning Protestantism and English nationalism against Catholicism and Spanish intrigue, which, it was popularly believed, was aimed at reviving the universalism of the late medieval period and relegating England to its former status as a Spanish satellite. Cut adrift from Spain by patriotic and religious motives, England was also isolated from France by traditional differences, while continental Protestantism was not strong enough in the Elizabethan period to offer a firm foundation for English foreign policy. Hence the predominant interest of the English monarchy during the last half of the sixteenth century had been chiefly concerned with problems of national security in the area of foreign affairs.

The years from 1588 to 1603 had tremendous importance for English domestic affairs and constitutional development; in that period conditions affecting the security of the nation changed rapidly and positively. The defeat of the Spanish attempt at invasion, the success of Elizabeth's strong measures in securing Ireland against infiltration by Spanish money and leadership, the loss of Spanish hegemony in the Low Countries, and the ascension of James VI of Scotland brought to an end the possibility of future French-sponsored Scottish invasions and pointed to the cessation of the heretofore ever-present possibility of foreign exploitation of English domestic weakness, whether by political, economic, or military means.

The first result of this new-found freedom from fear was the growth of England's concern with her home affairs. James's inheritance of the throne was not only the last step in the winning of national security; it was the beginning of a new and violent revolution within England. Constitutional and domestic issues, hitherto the silent concern of classes and interests seeking new liberties and greater political stature, could now be safely brought out for inspection and debate. This, more than any other factor, contributed to the rapid and unique acceleration of constitutional movement and institutional growth in the Stuart period.

However, in analyzing the differences between the sixteenth and seventeenth centuries it is necessary to recall that while domestic issues had not been the major determinants of national policy and constitutional development in Elizabeth's time, she did not entirely escape from them. The growing sense of security after 1588 had unleashed the latent forces of Puritanism and had encouraged both the merchants and the Parliamentarians to formulate forcefully their determinations to gain their desired objectives. Those growing demands had accelerated the policy of compromise for which Elizabeth is so often reprimanded by historians. The Stuarts had to face these demands in a period when the chastening fear of foreign antagonisms no longer existed and compromise was out of date.

Conflict was not long in coming after Elizabeth's death. Unruly but respectful under the old Queen, the three most significant opposition groups were prepared in advance to present their grievances and demands for redress to the new King. This opposition chose not to struggle over petty issues where the stakes were small. In the debates at Hampdon Court following the *Millenary Petition* the Calvinists presented what amounted to their fullest demands: complete restructure of the state church in accordance with Calvin's *Institutes of the Christian Religion.* In the *Apology* of 1604 Parliament openly declared itself hostile to James's political philosophy of divinely inspired sovereignty and demanded equality with the Crown in matters of national policy and control of the realm. The principle backing such demands was absolute: the voice of the people was as the voice of God—and Parliament was the voice of the people. The merchants at the same time sought the elimination of monopolies with the tenuous but appealing argument that they created idleness "which the Common Law knoweth not."

It is to be noticed that each of the three reforms demanded were of a constitutional rather than a mere administrative nature. In terms of possible results, monarchial retreat on any one of the issues could have serious reverberations in the areas of the others; each of the three interests was aggressively and consciously seeking reapportionment of power and authority under the constitution and, therefore, drastic rearrangement of the constitution itself.

It is often said of James that his mode of treatment of those opposed to him was unrealistic or narrow because of his pedantic manner. The charge, however, is not borne out by the record of his relationships with his opponents or his resistance to their demands. That he was learned beyond the intellectual attainment of most men of his day is true; yet the resort to discussion rather than repression could hardly be claimed as an ostentatious or vain display of sterile booklearning. But in his dependence on debate and reason James opened the way to louder protest and more grotesque demands, the very volume and distortion of which encouraged more forceful action. Here the first of the Stuart kings may have committed his greatest disservice to his successors; certainly it was here that he weakened the resistance of the constitution to the forces of change. Henry VII had simply destroyed such opposition, an example followed by Henry VIII whenever threat or bribe failed to generate compliance. Elizabeth had ignored or retreated from, or cajoled or charmed her opponents into submission, seldom allowing political events or developments to force her into a posture so rigid that it could not be gracefully modified as conditions made change necessary. James, with his bitter memories of the brutal school of Scottish power-politics, attempted to find a middle ground of moderation to stand upon. His political methods eschewed force; unfortunately, his arguments were arrogant and obviously the products of an egocentric personality. He attempted fully and logically to explain his own concepts and purposes without ever admitting the slightest justification or virtue in those of his opponents. In short he showered a vast and variable talent for reason and logic upon an unappreciative and pedestrian opposition only interested in gaining its own ends. A clash of egocentricities ensued, with each party stone-deaf to the merits of the other.

Of great constitutional significance in the early Stuart period, then, were the arguments concerning the division of political power. Prior to the death of James in 1625 none of his opponents could be justly called anti-monarchial. The institution of kingship was too firmly rooted in the English constitution and political way of life to need rationalization; never was the necessity for the office questioned, although the form of monarchy was many times the subject of enlightened political discussion and analysis. But what James did not realize was that his people made a clear distinction between the King's office and the personality temporarily inhabiting the throne, and that each act of his which seemed to the subjects to be an attempt to modify or change in any way the rights or prerogatives of that office was interpreted as an attack on something as sacrosanct as private property. The result was that James, in trying to strengthen the institution of the monarchy, actually weakened himself and his entire dynasty in the struggle for power which would continue long after the seventeenth century had ended.

During the early part of that century, after the long reign of Elizabeth, in which the English monarchy had reached its peak of popular acceptance and reverence, there is indisputable evidence of a reaction in which certain forces were fashioning the tools to be used in eventually forcing the monarch to disgorge part of his traditional powers. It follows from this that James's struggle was primarily defensive, geared to retain rather than expand the prerogatives of the crown he had inherited. Being deeply conscious of the sacred responsibilities of his office and convinced of the righteousness of his cause, James carried his struggle in defense of monarchial prerogative into the area of the rights of the people—and eventually encroached upon the preserve of the common law. In so doing he weakened to the point of eventual breakdown the most important protective device for the monarchy offered by the English constitution. It would have been more fitting for Charles I on the scaffold to forgive his father for committing this blunder than his enemies for taking his life.

In one sense the prolonged struggle between King and Parliament in the early seventeenth century was the direct result of the failure of those two constitutional elements to respect the traditional position and significance of a third, the common law.

Modern students of English constitutional history have at times been puzzled because this simple fact has been obscured by the conflicting analyses of the pro-Parliament "Whig" historians and historians favoring the royalist cause. Each party has charged the other with denigrating the established order of the period. The first group emphasizes James's disregard of English institutions to justify its case in behalf of the Parliamentary rejection of his ideals. The second group attempts to prove the unwarranted aggression of Commons against the established institutions and limitations which guaranteed the smooth functioning of the political order. Both arguments are weakened by a tendency to deny the complexity of seventeenth-century political realities and the significance of sixteenth-century causal factors.

The truth of the matter is that neither the King nor Parliament acted entirely within or without the limitations imposed by the common law and the constitution. At times both stood in contempt of accepted political institutions and procedures, while at other times each held to points of view which were, despite their mutually exclusive natures, both logical and moral in light of the looseness of a constitution which permitted conflicting differences in interpretation. Thus in the final analysis it would be historically inaccurate to assert either side to have been categorically right or wrong. The problems they faced were their legacy from earlier times. In a crucial period, without the guide of applicable precedents, each party struggled desperately to maintain its footing against the rising tide of problems, forces, and factors which seemed to threaten the entire social order. Both, each in its own way, were in quest of order and harmony, and neither as yet denied the moral or constitutional basis of the other. That mutual repudiation would come after 1625 to upset the balance of political powers necessary for domestic harmony, but in James's time, at least, the struggle was between two mutually dependent parts of government seeking primacy within the accepted political pattern.

## John Calvin, *The Institutes of the Christian Religion.* 1559

JOHN CALVIN'S influence on the ideal of individual liberty expressed by the English constitution is difficult to assess with any real exactness. Seldom do present day historians find ground for complete agreement when analyzing Calvin's political thought. Some tend to deny any causal relationship between Calvin and later democratic civil institutions; others vigorously affirm it.

## 73.

The excerpt from the *Institutes of the Christian Religion* included here seems in part to support both attitudes. Very clearly, in the first section Calvin reaffirms the idea of strict obedience to magistrates whose powers are derived from divine commission. But, later, he denies the magistrate's right to require actions of the subject which are not in conformity with divine law. This apparent ambiguity is perhaps attributable to the erroneous quest for modern definitions in a century where they could not possibly have existed. The fundamental problem would seem to be to ascertain the extent to which Calvin influenced political and constitutional thought in sixteenth and seventeenth century political struggles, bearing in mind that the new liberalism resulting from these struggles did not begin to develop in the modern direction for another century.

The denial of political Calvinism as a source of modern liberal concepts appears to be based on Calvin's intent rather than ultimate effect. No doubt, John Calvin did not conceive the prerogative of political regulation to be a right vested in the people. To him no less than to Sir Robert Filmer political authority was delegated by God to the magistrate, and obedience to legitimate authority was thus the religious duty of every subject.

Again, by the beginning of the seventeenth century, having been attacked violently by civil government both on the continent and in England, Calvinism had constructed a formidable political theory in addition to its purely theological doctrines. His statement was later taken to imply active measures rather than mere passive resistance. This sentence alone gave rise to a variety of explosive interpretations and applications by English Puritans and Scottish Presbyterians in the middle of the seventeenth century: "If they [Kings] command anything against Him, it ought not to have the least attention; nor, in this case, ought we to pay any attention to all that dignity attached to magistrates."

Nor was Calvin's contribution to English constitutional thought limited to the stimulation of Puritan revolutionary thought. Inherent in his theories is the concept of social contract so significant to John Locke, as well as the idea of the natural virtue of aristocratic rule which the English gentry modified to validate its own position after 1688. These developments, however, had never clearly been enunciated by Calvin himself.

Civil government is designed, as long as we live in this world, to cherish and support the external worship of God, to preserve the pure doctrine of religion, to defend the constitution of the Church, to regulate our lives in a manner requisite for the society of men, to form our manners to civil justice, to promote our concord with each other, and to establish general peace and tranquility....

If we direct our attention to the word of God, it will carry us even to submit to the government, not only of those princes who discharge their duty to us with becoming integrity and fidelity, but of all who possess the sovereignty, even though they perform none of the duties of their function. For, though the Lord testifies that the magistrate is an eminent gift of his liberality to preserve the safety of men, and prescribes to magistrates themselves the extent of their duty, yet he at the same time declares, that whatever be their characters, they have their government only from Him; that those who govern for the public good are true specimens and mirrors of his beneficence; and that those who rule in an unjust and tyrannical manner are raised up by him to punish the iniquity of the people; that all equally possess that sacred majesty with which He has invested legitimate authority....

But in the obedience which we have shown to be due to the authority of governors, it is always necessary to make one exception, and that is entitled to our first attention—that it do not seduce us from obedience to Him, to whose will the desires of all kings ought to be subject, to whose decrees all their commands ought to be subject, to whose decrees all their commands ought to yield, to whose majesty all their sceptres ought to submit. And, indeed, how preposterous it would be for us, with a view to satisfy men, to incur the displeasure of God on whose account we yield obedience to kings! The Lord, therefore, is the King of Kings; who, when he has opened his sacred mouth is to be heard alone, above all, for all, and before all; in the next place, we are subject to those men who preside over us; but not otherwise than in Him. If they command anything against Him, it ought not to have the least attention; nor, in this case, ought we to pay any regard to all that dignity attached to magistrates; to which no injury is done when it is subjected to the unrivalled and supreme power of God. (John Calvin, *The Institutes of the Christian Religion,* ed. of 1559.)

## John Knox, *The History of the Reformation in Scotland.* 1566

74.

EVEN before the returning Marian exiles could organize to defend themselves against the religious policies of the young Queen Elizabeth in England, John Knox was carrying the Calvinist doctrine of the righteousness of resistance to civil authority to its ultimate end in Scotland. Without denying that the subject was commanded by God to obey the magistrate, Knox clearly limited the prerogative to secular affairs. Nor did Knox depend on the scriptural evidences so vital to Calvin's theories in showing that the magistrate had no right to authority in the framing of religious regulations. To Knox the word of God "is plain in the self." When Queen Mary Stuart demanded to know how she could ascertain whose interpretation of scripture was authoritative,

Knox's answer exemplified the arbitrariness which caused Oliver Cromwell to exclaim almost a century later, "New Presbyter is but old priest writ large." "You," Knox answered the Queen, "shall believe God that plainly speaketh in his Word." Since God's word was channeled through the Elect there was no doubt but that Knox felt himself to speak with divine meaning. Should the civil authority refuse to conform to the dictates of the Elect in matters of religious organization it was at once guilty of tyranny, and, said Knox to the Queen, "If Princes exceed their bounds, it is no doubt but that they may be resisted, even by power."

The Queen spoke with John Knox, and had long reasoning with him ... the sum of their discussion being this....

"But yet," she said, "ye have taught the people to receive another religion than their prince can allow; and how can that doctrine be of God, seeing that God commands subjects to obey their prince?"

"Madam," said he, "as that right religion takes neither origin nor authority from worldly princes, but from the eternal God alone, so are not subjects bound to frame their religion according to the appetite of their princes; for oft it is, that princes are the most ignorant of all others in God's true religion, as we may read well in the histories before the death of Christ Jesus, and after, ... and so, Madam, ye may perceive, that subjects are not bound to the religion of their princes, albeit they are commanded to give them obedience."

"Yea," said she, "none of these men raised the sword against their princes."

"Yet madam," said he, "ye cannot deny but that they resisted; for these that obey not the commandments that are given, in some part they resist...."

"Think ye," said she, "that subjects having power may resist their princes?"

"If their princes exceed their bounds," said he, "... it is no doubt but they may be resisted, even by power...."

At these words, the queen stood as if amazed, more than quarter of an hour; her countenance altered.... At length she said, "Well then, I perceive, that my subjects shall obey you and not me; and shall do what they list, and not what I command; and so must I be subject to them, and not they to me."

"... Kings," said he, "... be, as it were, foster-fathers to His Kirk...."

"Yea," said she, "but ye are not the Kirk that I will nurse. I will defend the Kirk of Rome, for it is, I think, the true Kirk of God."

"Your will," said he, "madam, is no reason; neither doth your thought make that Roman harlot to be the true and immaculate spouse of Jesus Christ...."

"My opinion," said she, "is not so."

"Opinion," said he, "requires knowledge; and I fear that right knowledge you have none."

"Ye interpret the scriptures," said she, "in one manner, and they in another; whom shall I believe, and who shall be judge?"

"You shall believe God," said he, "that plainly speaketh in His word.... The word of God is plain in the self ... so that there can remain no doubt, but unto such as will remain obstinately ignorant." (This is an extract from John Knox, *The History of the Reformation in Scotland,* from the edition of 1832, pp. 232-33.)

## The Millenary Petition. 1603

EVEN before his English coronation James was made aware of the problems of religious dispute which unsettled his new realm. Supposedly signed by a thousand Puritan churchmen this *Petition* presented their desired reforms within the Church. As a mere list of proposed alterations in such ecclesiastical matters as baptism, Church discipline,

75.

the Prayer Book, and preaching, the document has small constitutional significance. But as the instrument which brought about the debates at Hampden Court wherein James placed himself firmly on the side of the Bishops against religious reform, the document is of extreme importance. It was at Hampden Court that James defined the Church as a political institution necessary to the maintenance of the political state, rejecting Puritan demands for destruction of the Bishops' powers with the statement, "No Bishop—No King."

Most gracious and dread Sovereign:

Seeing it has pleased the Divine Majesty, to the great comfort of all good Christians, to advance your Highness, according to your just title, to the peaceable government of this Church and Commonwealth of England, we, the ministers of the gospel in this land, neither as factious men affecting a popular parity in the Church, nor as schismatics aiming at the dissolution of the State Ecclesiastical, but as the faithful servants of Christ and loyal subjects to your Majesty, desiring and longing for the redress of divers abuses of the Church, could do no less in our obedience to God, service to your Majesty, love to His Church, than acquaint your princely Majesty with our particular griefs; for as your princely pen writeth, "the King, as a good physician, must first know what peccant humors his patient naturally is most subject unto, before he can begin his cure," and although divers of us that sue for reformation have formerly, in respect of the times, subscribed to the book, some upon protestation, some upon exposition given them, some with condition rather than the Church should have been deprived of their labor and ministry; yet now we, to the number of more than a thousand of your majesty's subjects and ministers, all groaning as under a common burden of human rites and ceremonies, do with one joint consent humble ourselves at your Majesty's feet, to be eased and relieved in this behalf. Our humble suit, then, unto your majesty is that these offences following, some may be removed, some amended, some qualified:

In the Church Service:

That the cross in baptism, interrogatories ministered to infants, confirmation, as superfluous, may be taken away; baptism not to be ministered by women, and so explained; the cap and surplice not urged; that examination may go before the communion; that it be ministered with a sermon; that divers terms of priests, and absolution, and some other used, with the ring in marriage, and other such like in the book, may be corrected; the longsomeness of service abridged, Church songs and music moderated to better edification; that the Lord's Day be not profaned; the rest upon holy days not so strictly urged; that there may be a uniformity of doctrine prescribed; no Popish opinion to be any more taught or defended; no ministers charged to teach their people to bow at the name of Jesus; that the canonical Scriptures only be read in the Church.

Concerning Church ministers:

That none hereafter be admitted into the ministry but able and sufficient men, and those to preach diligently and especially upon the Lord's day; that such as be already entered and cannot preach, may either be removed, and some charitable course taken with them for their relief, or else be forced, according to the value of their livings, to maintain preachers; that non-residency be not permitted; that King Edward's statute for the lawfulness of ministers' marriages be revived; that ministers be not urged to subscribe, but according to the law, to the *Articles of Religion,* and the King's supremacy only.

For Church livings and maintenance:

That bishops leave their commendams [benefices], some holding parsonages, some prebends, some vicarages, with their bishoprics; that double-beneficed men be not suffered to hold some two, some three benefices with cure, and some two, three, or four dignities besides; that impropriations [Church lands transferred to lay holders] ... be demised [given over to] only ... the preachers incumbents, for the old rent; that the impropriations of laymen's fees be charged, with a sixth or seventh part of their worth, to the maintenance of the preaching minister.

For Church discipline:

That the discipline and excommunication may be administered according to Christ's own institution, or, at the least, that enormities may be redressed, as namely, that excommunication come not forth under the name of lay persons, chancellors, officials, etc.; that men be not excommunicated without consent of their pastor; that the officers be not suffered to extort unreasonable fees; that none having jurisdiction or registers' places, put out the same to farm; that divers Popish canons (as for restraint of marriage at certain times) be reversed; that the longsomeness of suits in ecclesiastical courts (which hang sometimes two, three, four, five, six, or seven years) may be restrained; that the oath *Ex Officio,* whereby men are forced to accuse themselves, be more sparingly used; that licenses for marriages without banns asked, be more cautiously granted:

These, with such other abuses yet remaining and practised in the Church of England, we are able to show not to be agreeable to the Scriptures, if it shall please your highness further to hear us, or more at large by writing to be informed, or by conference among the learned to be resolved; and yet we doubt not but that, without any further process, your Majesty (of whose Christian judgment we have received so good a taste already) is able of yourself to judge of the equity of these causes. God, we trust, has appointed your highness our physician to heal these diseases; and we say with Mordecai to Esther, "Who knoweth whether you are come to the kingdom for such a time?" Thus your Majesty shall do that which we are persuaded shall be acceptable to God, honorable to your Majesty in all succeeding ages, profitable to His Church, which shall be thereby increased, comfortable to your ministers, which shall be no more suspended, silenced, disgraced, imprisoned for men's traditions, and prejudical to none but to those that seek their own quiet, credit and profit in the world.

Thus, with all dutiful submission, referring ourselves to your Majesty's pleasure for your gracious answer, as God shall direct you, we most humbly recommend your highness to Divine majesty, whom we beseech, for Christ His sake, to dispose your royal heart to do herein what shall be to His glory, the good of His Church, and your endless comfort.

Your Majesty's most humble subjects, the ministers of the Gospel that desire not a disorderly innovation, but a due and Godly reformation. (Thomas Fuller, *Church History,* 1655, X, p. 21.)

## Act Concerning Jesuits and Seminary Priests. 1604

76.

THE anti-Catholicism which brought this Act to passage was not fundamental to James's policy. Although the King accepted the Act and even spoke in its defense, he showed a marked tendency to disregard the punitive measures which it established. Had the minority of faithful Catholics been as willing to pursue quietly their religious activities as James was to allow them, the few passionate Protestant leaders who stood for harshness would have been isolated in Parliament. The Bye Plot and the Main Treason, both of which failed to accomplish anything positive for the Catholics, aroused their enemies and rendered James's position of tactful neutrality incompatible with his office.

An Act for the due execution of the Statutes against Jesuits, Seminary Priests, Recusants, etc.

For the better and due execution of the Statutes heretofore made as well against Jesuits, seminary priests, and other such like priests as also against all manner of recusants:

Be it ordained and enacted . . . that all and every the Statutes heretofore made in the reign of the late Queen of famous memory, Elizabeth, as well against Jesuits, seminary priests, and other priests, deacons, religious and ecclesiastical persons whatsoever, made, ordained, or professed, or to be made, ordained, or professed, by any authority or jurisdiction derived, challenged, or pretended from the See of Rome, as those which do in any wise concern the withdrawing of the King's subjects from their due obedience and the religion now professed, and the taking of the oath of obedience unto the King's Majesty his heirs and successors, together with all those made in the said late Queen's time against any manner of recusants, shall be put in due and exact execution. . . .

And be it further enacted . . . that where any seizure shall be had of the two parts of any lands . . . for the not payment of the twenty pounds due and payable for each month, according to the Statute in that case lately made and provided [*Act against Reconcilliation to Rome,* 23 Elizabeth, c.1.], that in every such case every such two parts shall, according to the extent thereof, go towards the satisfaction and payment of the twenty pounds due and payable for each month and unpaid by any such recusant, and that the third part thereof shall not be taken or seized by the King's Majesty his heirs or successors. . . . And where any such seizure shall be had of the two parts of the lands . . . of any such recusant as is aforesaid and such recusant shall die [without having satisfied the debt] . . . that in every such case the same two parts shall continue in his Majesty's possession until the residue or remainder of the said debt or duty be thereby or otherwise paid, satisfied, or discharged, and that his

Majesty his heirs or successors shall not seize or take any third part descending to any such heirs, or any part thereof, either by reason of the recusancy of his or her ancestor or of the recusancy of any such heir.

And be it further enacted . . . that all and every person and persons under the King's obedience which at any time . . . shall pass or go, or shall send or cause to be sent any child or other person under their or any of their government, into any the parts beyond the seas out of the King's obedience, to the intent to enter into . . . any college, seminary, or house of Jesuits, priests, or any other Popish order, profession, or calling whatsoever, or repair in or to any the same to be instructed, persuaded, or strengthened in the Popish religion, or in any sort so to profess the same, every such person . . . shall for every such offence forfeit to his Majesty . . . the sum of one hundred pounds; and every such person so passing or being sent beyond the seas to any such intent or purpose as is aforesaid, shall by authority of this present Act, as in respect of him or her self only and not to or in respect of any of his heirs or posterity, be disabled and made incapable to inherit, purchase, take, have, or enjoy any manors, lands, tenements, annuities, profits, commodities, hereditaments, goods, chattels, debts, duties, legacies, or sums of money within this realm of England or any other his Majesty's dominions, and that all and singular estates, terms, and other interests whatsoever hereafter to be made, suffered, or done to or for the use or behoof of any such person or persons, or upon any trust or confidence mediately or immediately, to or for the benefit or relief of any such person or persons, shall be utterly void and of none effect to all intents, constructions, and purposes.

And be it further enacted . . . that if any person born within this realm or any the King's Majesty's dominions be at this present in any college, seminary, house, or place in any parts beyond the seas, to the end to be instructed or strengthened in the Popish religion, which shall not make return into this realm or some part of his Majesty's dominions within one year next coming after the end of this session of Parliament and submit himself ... shall be, in respect of himself only and not to or in respect of any of his heirs or posterity, utterly disabled and uncapable to inherit, have, or enjoy any manors, [etc.] ... provided always that if any such person or child so passing ... shall after become conformable and obedient unto the laws and ordinances of the Church of England, and shall repair to the church and there remain and be as is aforesaid, and continue in such conformity according to the true intent and meaning of the said statutes and ordinances; that in every such case every such person and child, for and during such time as he or she shall so continue in such conformity and obedience, shall be freed and discharged of all and every such disability and incapacity as is before mentioned.

And be it further enacted ... that no woman, nor any child under the age of one and twenty years, except sailors or ship-boys or the apprentice or factor of some merchant in trade of merchandise, shall be permitted to pass over the seas ... upon pain that the officers of the port that shall willingly or negligently suffer any such to so pass, or shall not enter the names of such passengers licenced, shall forfeit his office and all his goods and chattels; and upon pain that the owner of any ship or vessel that shall wittingly or willingly carry any such over the seas without licence as is aforesaid shall forfeit his ship or vessel and all the tackle; and every master or mariner of or in any ship or vessel offending as aforesaid shall forfeit all their goods and suffer imprisonment by the space of twelve months, without bail. ... (SR, IV, 1020: 1 and 2 James I, c.4.)

## Act of Succession. 1604

## 77.

AS Edward VI's legislation had destroyed Henry VIII's ecclesiastical settlement, so the *Act of Succession* of 1604 repudiated his will in the matter of the royal succession. When James VI of Scotland was declared the rightful successor to Elizabeth, England was for the first time since the death of Henry VII freed from the dangers of a disputed succession. However, James brought new problems to England to replace those solved by his accession, not the least of which was his interpretation of the meaning of the English constitution.

A most joyful and just recognition of the immediate, lawful, and undoubted Succession, Descent, and Right of the Crown.

Great and manifold were the benefits, most dread and most gracious Sovereign, wherewith Almighty God blessed this kingdom and nation by the happy union and conjunction of the two noble Houses of York and Lancaster, thereby preserving this noble realm, formerly torn and almost wasted with long and miserable dissension and bloody civil war; but more inestimable and unspeakable blessings are thereby poured upon us because there is derived and grown from and out of that union of those two princely families a more famous and greater union, or rather a reuniting, of two mighty, famous, and ancient kingdoms, though anciently but one, of England and Scotland under one Imperial Crown in your most Royal Person, who is lineally, rightfully, and lawfully descended of the body of the most excellent Lady Margaret, eldest daughter of the most renowned King Henry VII and the high and noble Princess, Queen Elizabeth his wife, eldest daughter of King Edward the Fourth, the said Lady Margaret being eldest sister of King Henry VIII, father of the high and mighty Princess of famous memory, Elizabeth, late Queen of England:

In consideration whereof, albeit we your Majesty's loyal and faithful subjects, of all estates and degrees, with all possible and public joy and acclamation, by open proclamations within five hours after the decease of our late Sovereign Queen, acknowledging thereby with one full voice of tongue and heart that your Majesty was our only lawful and rightful liege Lord and Sovereign, by our unspeakable and general rejoicing and applause at your Majesty's most happy inauguration and coronation, by the affectionate desire of infinite numbers of us of all degrees to see your Royal Person, and by all possible outward means have endeavoured to make demonstration of our inward love, zeal, and devotion to your most excellent Majesty our undoubted rightful liege Sovereign Lord and King... in this High Court of Parliament, where all the whole body of the realm, and every individual member thereof, either in person or by representation upon their own free elections, are by the laws of this realm deemed to be personally present [and express gratitude for the King's actions]...

We therefore your most humble and loyal subjects the Lords Spiritual and Temporal and the Commons in this present Parliament assembled, do from the bottom of our hearts ... beseech your most excellent Majesty that ... it may be published and declared in this High Court of Parliament, and enacted by authority of the same, that we, being bound thereunto by both the laws of God and man,

do recognize and acknowledge... that immediately upon the dissolution and death of Elizabeth, late Queen of England, the Imperial Crown of the realm of England, and of all the kingdoms, dominions, and rights belonging to the same, did by inherent birthright and lawful and undoubted succession descend and come to your most excellent Majesty, as being lineally, justly, and lawfully next and sole heir of the blood royal of this realm as is aforesaid, and that by the goodness of God Almighty and lawful right of descent under one Imperial Crown your Majesty is of the realms and kingdoms of England, Scotland, France, and Ireland the most potent and mighty King, and by God's goodness more able to protect and govern us your loving subjects in all peace and plenty than any of your noble progenitors; and thereunto we most humbly and faithfully do submit and oblige ourselves, our heirs and posterities, for ever, until the last drop of our bloods be spent, and do beseech your Majesty to accept the same as the first-fruits in this High Court of Parliament of our loyalty and faith to your Majesty and your royal progeny and posterity for ever. Which if your Majesty shall be pleased... to adorn with your Majesty's royal assent, [signature] without which it [this Act] can neither be complete and perfect.... (SR, IV, 1017: 1 James I, c.1.)

## Act for Commissioners of Union. 1604

78. ONE of the goals fundamental to James's political policy—the union of England and Scotland—was not realized until the reign of the last of the Stuarts. In 1604 James first broached the plan to Parliament. At first the House of Commons seemed to favor the idea, but nothing was done because of the resistance of a small minority, centered in London, who feared that the economic competition of the Scots would be detrimental to English trade. Later, as political, constitutional, and ecclesiastical issues more widely split Crown and legislature, James's hopes for the union faded until nothing remained but the bitterness and hostility engendered by the Parliamentary denial.

An Act authorizing certain Commissioners of the Realm of England to treat with Commissioners of Scotland for the benefit of both Kingdoms.

Whereas his most excellent Majesty hath been pleased, out of his great wisdom and judgment, not only to represent unto us by his own prudent and princely speech on the first day of this Parliament how much he desired, in regard of his inward and gracious affection to both the famous and ancient realms of England and Scotland, now united in allegiance and loyal subjection in his Royal Person to his Majesty and his posterity for ever, that by a speedy, mature, and sound deliberation such a further union might follow us should make perfect that mutual love and uniformity of manners and customs which Almighty God in his Providence, for the strength and safety of both realms, hath already so far begun in apparent sight of all the world, but also hath vouchsafed to express many ways how far it is and ever shall be from his royal and sincere care and affection to the subjects of England to alter and innovate the fundamental and ancient laws, privileges, and good customs of this kingdom, whereby not only his regal authority but the people's security of lands, livings, and privileges both in general and particular are preserved and maintained. . . .

Forasmuch as his Majesty's humble, faithful, and loving subjects have not only conceived the weight of his Majesty's reasons, but apprehend to their unspeakable joy and comfort his plain, clear, and gracious intention to seek no other changes or alteration but of such particular, temporary, or indifferent manner of statutes and customs as may both prevent and extinguish all and every future questions or unhappy accidents by which the perfect and constant love and friendship and quietness between the subjects of both the realms aforesaid may be completed and confirmed, and also perform and accomplish that real and affectual union already inherent in his Majesty's Royal Blood and Person, and now desired by his Majesty to be performed and brought to an end for the benefit of both kingdoms of this course following:

Be it enacted by the King's most excellent Majesty, by and with the assent and consent of the Lords Spiritual . . . [etc.] . . . , and by the authority of the same, [that the commissioners here named] . . . shall by force of this Act from and after the end of this present session of Parliament have full power, liberty, commission, and authority at any time or times before the next session of this Parliament to assemble and meet, and thereupon to treat and consult with certain selected commissioners to be nominated and authorized by authority of Parliament of the realm of Scotland, according to the tenor . . . of their authority or commission in that behalf, of and concerning such an union of the said realms of England and Scotland, and of and concerning such other matters, causes, and things whatsoever as upon mature deliberation and consideration [the two bodies of Commissioners] . . . shall . . . think and deem convenient and necessary for the honor of his Majesty and the benefit and common good of both the said realms during his Majesty's life . . . and under all his royal progeny and posterity for ever. . . . (SR, IV, 1018: 1 and 2 James I, c.2.)

## Act for New Executions against Members of Parliament. 1604

79.

THE legal meaning and extent of Parliamentary privilege was gradually clarified in the sixteenth and seventeenth centuries. Since Parliamentary practices had accrued by usage there were no specific precedents or statutes for the legislature to fall back upon in attempting to define its rights. Consequently all actions which attempted to limit Parliamentary freedom had to be approached in general and ordinarily unsatisfactory ways. The Act of 1604 grew out of Sir Thomas Shirley's arrest for debt after his election to Commons. As a member of the lower House he was held by Parliament to be exempt from legal actions against private persons, and his release was obtained by writ on that ground. However, the Act specifically stated that in such cases "the party at . . . whose suit such writ of execution was pursued ... after such time as the privilege of that session of Parliament in which such privilege ... be ... granted shall cease, may sue forth ... a new writ." Not stated but nonetheless implicit was the contention that Parliament was the sole judge in disciplining its members.

An Act for new executions to be sued against any which shall hereafter be delivered out of execution by Privilege of Parliament, and for discharge of them out of whose custody such persons shall be delivered.

Forasmuch as heretofore doubt hath been made if any person being arrested in execution, and by privilege of either of the Houses of Parliament set at liberty, whether the party at whose suit such execution was pursued be for ever after barred and disabled to sue forth a new writ of execution [a judicial writ to carry a judgment into effect] in that case:

For the avoiding of all further doubt and trouble which in like cases may hereafter ensue, be it enacted by the King's most excellent Majesty, by the Lords Spiritual and Temporal, and by the Commons in this present Parliament assembled, that from henceforth the party at or by whose suit such writ of execution was pursued, his executors or administrators, after such time as the privilege of that session of Parliament in which such privilege shall be so granted shall cease, may sue forth and execute a new writ or writs of execution in such manner and form as by the law of this realm he or they might have done if no such former execution had been taken forth or served: and that from henceforth no sheriff, bailiff, or other officer from whose arrest or custody any such person so arrested in execution shall be delivered by any such privilege shall be charged or chargeable with or by any action whatsoever for delivering out of execution any such privileged person so as is aforesaid by such privilege of Parliament set at liberty; any law, custom, or privilege heretofore to the contrary notwithstanding. Provided always, that this Act or anything therein contained shall not extend to the diminishing of any punishment to be hereafter by censure in Parliament inflicted upon any person which hereafter shall make or procure to be made any such arrest as is aforesaid. (SR, IV, 1029: 1 and 2 James I, c.13.)

## The Apology and Satisfaction of the House of Commons. 1604

80.

THE *Apology* of 1604 is perhaps the most significant single constitutional document of the first quarter of the seventeenth century. A thorough study of both context and implication is requisite for an understanding of the development of Parliament's concept of its position in the constitution in that period. Of the many significant statements by the legislators in this document, two are of great importance. The first is relative to Parliament's capacity and right, as the representative of the realm, to debate and decide on all matters pertaining to the general commonwealth. This is no less than a claim to superior power in matters of government and polity. The second, "the voice of the people in things of their knowledge is said to be as the voice of God," attempts to claim for Parliament as much "Divine Right" as was claimed for the King. James may have smiled at such naïveté, but Commons was quite in earnest—which would be made painfully clear to his successor.

To the King's most excellent Majesty: From the House of Commons assembled in Parliament.

Most gracious Sovereign, we cannot but with much joy and thankfulness of mind acknowledge your Majesty's great graciousness in declaring lately unto us by the mouth of our Speaker that you rested now satisfied with our doings.

Which satisfaction notwithstanding, though most desired and dear unto us, yet proceeding merely from your Majesty's most gracious disposition and not from any justification which on our behalf hath been made, we found this joy intermingled with no small grief, and could not, dread Sovereign, in our dutiful love to your Majesty and in our ardent desire of the continuance of your favor towards us, but tender in humble sort this farther satisfaction, being careful to stand right not only in the eye of your Majesty's Grace but also, and that much more, in the balance of your princely judgment, on which all assuredness of love and grace is founded. Into which course of proceedings we have not been rashly carried by vain humor of curiosity, of contradiction, of presumption, or of love of our own devices or doings; unworthy affections in a Council of Parliament, and more unworthy in subjects towards their Lord and Sovereign.

But, as the searcher and judge of all hearts doth know, for these and for no other undue ends in the world: to increase and nourish your Majesty's gracious affection towards your loyal and most loving people; to assure and knit all your subjects' hearts most firmly to your Majesty; to take away all cause of jealousy on either part, and diffidence for times ensuing; and to prevent and control all sinister reports which might be unreasonably spread, either at home or abroad, with prejudice to your Majesty or the good state of your kingdom.

With these minds, dread Sovereign, your Commons of England, represented in us their knights, citizens, and burgesses, do come with this humble declaration to your Highness, and in great affiance of your most gracious disposition, that your Majesty, with benignity of mind correspondent to our dutifulness, will be pleased to pursue it.

We know, and with great thankfulness to God acknowledge, that he hath given us a King of such understanding and wisdom as is rare to find in any prince in the world.

Howbeit, seeing no human wisdom, how great soever, can pierce into the particularities of the rights and customs of people or of the sayings and doings of particular persons but by tract of experience and faithful report of such as know them, which it has pleased your Majesty . . . to deliver, what grief, what anguish of mind hath it been unto us at some time in presence to hear, and so in other things to find and feel by effect, your gracious Majesty, to the extreme prejudice of all your subjects of England, and in particular of this House of the Commons thereof, so greatly wronged by misinformation as well touching the estate of the one as the privileges of the other, and their several proceedings during this Parliament: which misinformations, though apparent in themselves and to your subjects most injurious, yet have we in some humble and dutiful respect rather hitherto complained of amongst ourselves than presumed to discover and oppose against your Majesty.

But now, no other help or redress appearing, and finding those misinformations to have been the first, yea, the chief and almost the sole cause of all the discontentful and troublesome proceedings so much blamed in this Parliament, and that they might be again the cause of like or greater discontents and troubles hereafter . . . we have been constrained, as well in duty to your royal Majesty whom we serve as to our dear native country for which we serve in this Parliament, to break our silence, and freely to disclose unto your Majesty the truth of such matters concerning your subjects the Commons as hitherto by misinformation hath been suppressed or perverted: wherein that we may more plainly proceed . . . we shall reduce these misinformations to three principal heads.

First, touching the cause of the joyful receiving of your Majesty into this your kingdom.

Secondly, concerning the rights and liberties of your subjects of England, and the privileges of this House.

Thirdly, touching the several actions and speeches passed in the House, it has been told us to our faces by some of no small place, and the same spoken also in the presence of your Majesty, that on the 24th of March [of 1603, the day of Elizabeth's death] ... we stood in so great fear that we would have given half we were worth for the security wherein we now stand.

Whereby some misunderstanders of things might perhaps conjecture that fear of our own misery had more prevailed with us in the duty which on that day was performed [Parliament's proclamation of James' succession], than love of your Majesty's virtues and hope of your goodness towards us.

We contrariwise most truly protest the contrary, that we stood not at that time, nor of many a day before, in any doubt or fear at all.

We all professing true religion by law established ... standing clear in our consciences touching your Majesty's right, were both resolute with our lives and all other our abilities to have maintained the same against all the world, and vigilant also in all parts to have suppressed such tumult as, but in regard of our poor united minds and readiness, by the malcontented and turbulent might have attempted.

But the true cause of our extraordinary great cheerfulness and joy in performing that day's duty, was the great and extraordinary love which we bear towards your Majesty's most royal and renowned person, and a longing thirst to enjoy the happy fruits of your Majesty's most wise, religious, just, virtuous, and gracious heart; whereof not rumor but your Majesty's own writings have given us a strong and undoubted assurance.

For from hence, dread Sovereign, a general hope was raised in the minds of all your people that under your Majesty's reign religion, peace, justice, and all virtue should renew again and flourish; that the better sort should be cherished, the bad reformed or repressed, and some moderate ease should be given us of those burdens and sore oppressions under which the whole land did groan.

This hope being so generally and so firmly settled in the minds of all your most loyal and most loving people, recounting what great alienation of men's hearts and defeating of great hopes doth usually breed, we could not in duty as well unto your Majesty as to our country, cities, bouroughs, who hath sent us hither not ignorant or uninstructed of their griefs, of their desires, and hopes, but according to the ancient use and liberty of Parliaments, present our several humble petitions to your Majesty of different nature, some for right and some for grace, to the easing and relieving of us of some just burdens and of other some unjust oppressions, wherein what due care and what respect we have had that your Majesty's honor and profit should be enjoyed with the content and satisfaction of your people, shall afterwards in their several due places appear.

Now concerning the ancient rights of the subjects of this realm, chiefly consisting in the privileges of this House of Parliament, the misinformation openly delivered to your Majesty hath been in three things:

First, that we held not privileges of right, but of grace only, renewed every Parliament by way of donature [the King's gift] upon petition, and so to be limited.

Secondly, that we are no Court of Record, nor yet a Court that can command view of records, but that our proceedings here are only to acts and memorials, and that the attendance with the records is courtesy, not duty.

Thirdly, that the examination of the return of writs for knights and burgesses is without our compass, and due to the Chancery.

Against which assertions, most gracious Sovereign, tending directly and apparently to the utter overthrow of the very fundamental privileges of our House, and therein of the rights and liberties of the whole Commons of your realm of England which they and their ancestors from time immemorable have undoubtedly enjoyed under your Majesty's most noble progenitors, we, the knights, citizens, and burgesses of the House of Commons assembled in Parliament, and in the name of the whole commons of the realm of England, with uniform consent for ourselves and our posterity, do expressly protest, as being derogatory in the highest degree to the true dignity, liberty, and authority of your Majesty's high Court of Parliament, and consequently to the rights of all your Majesty's said subjects and the whole body of this your kingdom; and desire that this our protestation may be recorded to all posterity.

And contrariwise, with all humble and due respect to your Majesty our Sovereign Lord and Head, against those misinformations we most truly avouch:

First, that our privileges and liberties are our right and due inheritance, no less than our very lands and goods.

Secondly, that they cannot be withheld from us, denied, or impaired, but with apparent wrong to the whole state of the realm.

Thirdly, and that our making of request in the entrance of Parliament to enjoy our privilege is an act only of manners, and doth weaken our right no more than our suing to the King for our lands by petition. . . .

Fourthly, we avouch also, that our House is a Court of Record, and so ever esteemed.

Fifthly, that there is not the highest standing court in this land that ought to enter into competition, either for dignity or authority, with this High Court of Parliament, which with your Majesty's royal assent gives laws to other courts but from other courts receives neither laws nor orders.

Sixthly, we avouch that the House of Commons is the sole proper judge of returns of all such writs and of the election of all such members as belong to it, without which the freedom of election were not entire, and that the Chancery, though a standing court under your Majesty, be to send out those writs and receive the returns and to preserve them, yet the same is done only for the use of the Parliament, over which neither the Chancery nor any other court ever had or ought to have any manner of jurisdiction.

From these misinformed positions, most gracious Sovereign, the greatest part of our troubles, distrusts, and jealousies have risen; having apparently found that in the first Parliament of the happy reign of your Majesty the privileges of our House, and therein the liberties and stability of the whole kingdom, have been more universally and dangerously impugned than ever, as we suppose, since the beginnings of Parliaments. For although it may be true that in the latter times of Queen Elizabeth some one privilege now and then were by some particular act attempted against . . . yet was not the same ever by so public speech nor by positions in general denounced against our privileges.

Besides that in regard of her sex and age which we had great cause to tender, and much more upon care to avoid all trouble which by wicked practice might have been drawn to impeach the quiet of your Majesty's right in the succession, those actions were then passed over which we hoped, in succeeding times of freer access to your Highness of renowned grace and justice, to redress, restore, and rectify. Whereas contrariwise in this Parliament which your Majesty in great grace . . . intended to be a precedent for all Parliaments that should succeed, clean contrary to your Majesty's so gracious desire, by reason of these misinformations not privileges but the whole freedom of the Parliament and realm have from time to time upon all occasions been mainly hewed at;

First, the freedom of persons in our election hath been impeached,

Secondly, the freedom of our speech prejudiced by often reproofs,

Thirdly, particular persons noted with taunt and disgrace who have spoken their consciences in matters proposed to the House, but with all due respect and reverence to your Majesty.

Whereby we have been in the end subject to so extreme contempt as a jailer durst so obstinately withstand the decrees of our House. [The Warden of the Fleet had refused to set free Thomas Shirley whose arrest on a court writ had followed his election to Commons.] Some of the higher clergy to write a book against us, even sitting [in] the Parliament. [The Bishop of Bristol had publicly attacked Commons in his pamphlet published earlier in the year, *A Discourse Plainly Proving the Evident Utility and Urgent Necessity of the Desired Happy Union of England and Scotland*]. The inferior clergy to inveigh against us in pulpits, yea, to publish their protestations, tending to the impeachment of our most ancient and undoubted rights in treating of matters for the peace and good order of the Church.

What cause we your poor Commons have to watch over our privileges is manifest in itself to all men. The prerogatives of princes may easily and do daily grow; the privileges of the subject are for the most part at an everlasting stand. They may be by good providence and care preserved, but being once lost are not recovered but with much disquiet. If good kings were immortal as well as kingdoms, to strive so for privilege were but vanity perhaps and folly; but seeing the same God who in his great mercy hath given us a wise King ... doth also sometimes permit hypocrites and tyrants in his displeasure and for the sins of the people, from hence hath the desire of rights, liberties, and privileges, both for nobles and commons, had its just original, by which an harmonious and stable State is framed, each member under the Head enjoying that right and performing that duty which for the honor of the Head and happiness of the whole is requisite.

Thus much touching the wrong done to your Majesty by misinformation touching our privileges. The last kind of misinformation made to your Majesty hath been touching the actions and speeches of particular persons used in the House. Which imputation notwithstanding, seeing it reacheth the whole House in general, who neither ought, neither have, at any time suffered any speech

touching your Majesty other than respectful, dutiful, and as become loyal subjects of a King so gracious; and foreasmuch as it is very clear unto us by the effect that divers things spoken in the House have been perverted and very untruly reported to your Majesty, if it might seem so fit in your Majesty's wisdom and were seemingly for us to crave, we should be most glad if, for our better justification and for your further satisfaction which we principally desire, the accusers and the accused might be confronted.

And now, most gracious Sovereign, these necessary grounds of our causes and defences being truly laid, and presented sincerely to your Majesty's grace and wisdom, the justification of such particulars wherein your Highness seemed doubtful of our dutiful carriage ... we trust will be plain; and to expedite which particulars we find them to have been of three different natures:

The first sort, concerning the dignity and privileges of our House.

The second, the good estate of the realm and Church.

The third was for ease of certain grievances and oppressions....

The right of the liberties of the Commons of England consists chiefly in these three parts:

First, that the shires, cities, and boroughs of England, by representation to be present, have free choice of such persons as they shall put in trust to represent them.

Secondly, that the persons chosen, during the time of the Parliament as also of their access and recess, be free from restraint, arrest, and imprisonment.

Thirdly, that in Parliament they may speak freely their consciences without check and controlment, doing the same with due reverence to the Sovereign Court of Parliament, that is, to your Majesty and both the Houses, who all in this case make but one politic body whereof your Highness is the Head.

These three several branches of the ancient inheritance of our liberty were in three matters ensuing apparently injured: the freedom of election in the case of Sir Francis Goodwin; the freedom of the person elected in Sir Thomas Shirley's imprisonment; the freedom of our speech, as by divers other reproofs, so also in some sort by the Bishop of Bristol's invective.

For the matter of Sir Francis Goodwin, the knight chosen for Buckinghamshire, we were and still are of a clear opinion that the freedom of election was in that action extremely injured; that by the same right it might be at all times in a Lord Chancellor's power to reverse, defeat . . . and substitute, all the elections and persons elected over all the realm. Neither thought we that the Judges's opinion, which yet in due place we greatly reverence, being delivered what the Common Law was, which extends only to inferior and standing Courts, ought to bring any prejudice to this High Court of Parliament, whose power being above the law is not founded on the Common Law but have their rights and privileges peculiar to themselves.

For the manner of our proceeding, which your Majesty seemed to blame in that, the second writ going out in your Majesty's name, we presumed to censure it without first craving access to acquaint your Highness with our reasons therein, we trust our defence shall appear just and reasonable. It is the form of the Court of Chancery, as of divers other Courts, that writs going out in your Majesty's name are returned also as to your Majesty in that Court from whence they issue; howbeit therefore no man ever repaireth to your Majesty's person, but proceeds according to law notwithstanding the writ. This being the universal custom of this kingdom, it was not nor could be admitted into our conceits that the difference was between your Majesty and us . . . but it always was and still is conceived that the controversy was between the Court of Chancery and our Court, an usual controversy between courts about their preeminences and privileges; and that the question was, whether the Chancery or our House of the Commons were judge of the members returned for it. Wherein though we supposed the wrong done to be most apparent, and extremely prejudicial for the rights and liberties of this realm, yet such and so great was our willingness to please your Majesty as to yield to a middle course proposed by your Highness, preserving only our privileges by voluntary cessions of the lawful right. And this course as it were of deceiving of ourselves and yielding in our apparent right, wheresoever we could but invent such ways of escape as that the precedent might not be hurtful, we have held, dread Sovereign, more than once this Parliament, upon desire to avoid that which in your Majesty by misinformation, whereof we have had cause always to stand in doubt, might be distasteful or not approvable, so dear hath your Majesty's gracious favor been unto us.

In the delivery of Sir Thomas Shirley our proceedings were long; our defence of them shall be brief. We had to do with a man, the Warden of the Fleet, so intractable and of so resolved obstinacy as that nothing we could do, no, not your Majesty's royal word for confirmation thereof, could satisfy him for his own security. This was the cause of the length of that business; our privileges were so shaken before, and so extremely vilified, as that we held it not fit in so unreasonable a time and against so mean a subject to seek our right by any other course of law or by any strength than by our own.

The Bishop of Bristol's book was injurious and grievous to us, being written expressly with contempt of the Parliament and of both the Houses in the highest degree; undertaking to deface the reasons proposed by the Commons, approved by the honorable Lords, confirmed by the Judges, and finally by your royal Majesty not disassented to. And to increase the wrong, with strange untruths he had perverted those reasons in their main drift and scope, pretending that they were devised to impugn the union [between England and Scotland] itself; whereas both by their title and by themselves it was clear and evident that they were only used against alteration of name, and that not simply, but before the union of both realms in substance were perfected. This book being thus written and published to the world, containing moreover sundry slanderous passages and tending to murmurs, distractions, and sedition, we could not do less against the writer thereof than to complain of the injury to the Lords of the higher House, whereof he had now attained to be a member.

These wrongs were to the dignity of our House and privileges. Touching the causes appertaining to State and Church, true it is we were long in treating and debating the matter of union. The propositions were new, the importance great, the consequences far reaching and not discoverable but by long disputes; our numbers also are large, and each hath liberty to speak. But the doubts and difficulties once cleared or removed, how far we are from opposing to the just desires of your Majesty, as some evil-disposed minds would perhaps insinuate who live by division and prosper by disgrace of other men, the great expedition, alacrity, and unanimity which was used and showed in passing the Bill [*Act for Commissioners of Union.* 1604] may sufficiently testify.

For matter of religion, it will appear by examination of truth and right that your Majesty should be misinformed if any man should deliver that the Kings of England have any absolute power in themselves either to alter Religion ... or to make any laws concerning the same otherwise than in temporal causes, by consent of Parliament. We have and shall at all times by our oaths acknowledge that your Majesty is Sovereign Lord and Supreme Governor in both. Touching our own desires and proceedings therein, they have not been a little misconceived and misreported. We have not come in any Puritan or Brownist spirit, to introduce their party [represent radical religious causes] or to work the subversion of the state ecclesiastical as now it standeth; things so far and so clearly from our meaning as that with uniform con-

sent in the beginning of this Parliament we committed to the Tower a man who out of that humor in a petition exhibited to our House had slandered the Bishops. But according to the tenor of your Majesty's writ of summons directed to the counties from whence we came, and according to the ancient and long continued use of Parliaments as by many records from time to time appeareth, we came with another spirit, even with the spirit of peace. We disputed not of matters of faith and doctrine; our desire was peace only and our device of unity, how this lamentable and longlasting dissension amongst the ministers, from which both atheism, sects, and all ill life have received such encouragement and so dangerous increase, might at length, before help came too late, be extinguished. And for the ways of this peace, we are not all addicted to our own inventions but ready to embrace any fit way that may be offered; neither desire we so much that any man in regard of weakness of conscience may be exempted by Parliament from obedience unto laws established, as that in this Parliament such laws may be enacted as by the relinquishment of some few ceremonies of small importance, or by any way better, a perpetual uniformity may be enjoined and observed.

Our desire hath also been to reform certain abuses crept into the ecclesiastical state even as into the temporal. And lastly, that the land might be furnished with a learned, religious, and Godly ministry, for the maintenance of whom we would have granted no small contributions, if in these as we trust just and religious desires we had found that correspondency from others which was expected. These minds and hearts we in secret present to that Sovereign Lord who gave them, and in public profess to your gracious Majesty who we trust will so esteem them. . . .

And therefore we come, lastly, to the matter of wards and such other burdens ... as to the tenures of *capite* and knight's service are incident. We cannot forget ... how your Majesty in a former most gracious speech in your Gallery at Whitehall advised us for unjust burdens to proceed against them by Bill, but for such as were just, if we desired any ease that we should come to yourself by way of petition, with tender of such countervailable composition in profit as for the supporting of your royal estate was requisite. According unto which your Majesty's most favorable grant and direction, we prepared a petition to your most excellent Majesty for leave to treat with your Highness touching a perpetual composition to be raised by yearly revenue out of the lands of your subjects for wardships and other burdens depending upon them or springing with them; wherein we first entered into this dutiful consideration, that this prerogative of the Crown which we desire to compound for was matter of mere profit, and not of any honor at all or princely dignity. For it could not then, neither yet can, by any means sink into our understandings that these economical matters of education and marrying of children, which are common also to subjects, should bring any renown or reputation to a potent monarch whose honor is settled on a higher and stronger foundation. Faithful and loving subjects, valiant soldiers, an honorable nobility, wise counsellors, a learned and religious clergy, and a contended and a happy people are the true honor of a King; and contrariwise, that it would be an exceeding great honor and of memorable renown to your Majesty with all posterity, and in present an assured bond of the hearts of all your people, to remit unto them this burden under which our children are born.

This prerogative then appearing to be a mere matter of great profit, we entered into a second degree of consideration: with how great grievance and damage of the subject, to the decay of many houses and disabling of them to serve their Prince and country; with how great mischief also by occasion of many forced and ill-suited marriages; and lastly, with how great contempt and reproach of our nation in foreign countries; how small a commodity now was raised to the Crown in respect of that which with great love and joy and thankfulness, for the restitution of this original right in disposing of our children, we would be content and glad to assure unto your Majesty.

We fell also from hence into a third degree of consideration: that it might be that in regard that the original of these wardships was serving of the King in his wars against Scotland, which cause we hope now to be at an everlasting end, and in regard, moreover, of that general hope which at your Majesty's first entry by the whole land was embraced . . . that they should be now for ever eased of this burden, Your Majesty, out of your most noble and gracious disposition and desire to overcome our expectation with your goodness, may be pleased to accept the offer of a perpetual and certain revenue, not only proportionable to the uttermost benefit that any of your progenitors ever reaped thereby but also with such an overplus and large addition as in great part to supply your Majesty's other occasions, that our ease might breed you plenty.

There remaineth, dread Sovereign, yet one part of our duty at this present. . . . We stand not in place to speak or do things pleasing; our care is and must be to confirm the love and tie the hearts of your subjects the commons most firmly to your Majesty. Herein lieth the means of our well deserving of both. . . . Let your Majesty be pleased to receive public information from your Commons in Parliament as to the civil estate and government, for private informations pass often by practice: the voice of the people, in the things of their knowledge, is said to be as the voice of God. And if your Majesty shall vouchsafe, at your best pleasure and leisure, to enter into your gracious consideration of our petition for the ease of these burdens under which your whole people have of long time mourned, hoping for relief by your Majesty, then may you be assured to be possessed of their hearts, and if of their hearts, of all they can do or have. . . . (*Journals of the House of Commons*, I, 243.)

## James I: Speech to Parliament Concerning Union with Scotland. 1607

**81.**

ALTHOUGH, by establishing a commission to study the matter, Parliament had taken the first step in preparing for the union of England and Scotland in 1604, nothing further of a constructive nature had followed. And though James spoke with high eloquence concerning his hope of union an underlying tone of frustration and disappointment is to be found in this speech. Yet it is possible that James asked too much, that he did not appreciate the excessive popular hostility to his proposals, or that the community of interest he presumed to see between the two peoples did not really exist.

Though united under a single King, England and Scotland were still far apart in many ways. Bishops and Presbyters were antithetical. England's common law concepts could not compromise with Scotland's Roman Law, and economically the English felt they could not compete successfully with the canny Scottish merchants. While James's request for union was never rejected outright, Parliament was guilty of the charges made by James of "long disputations, strange questions, and nothing done."

....For myself, I protest unto you all when I first propounded the union I thought there could have been no more question of it than of your declaration and acknowledgment of my right unto this Crown, and that as two twins they would have grown up together. The error was my mistaking; I knew mine own end but not others' fears. But now, finding many crossings, long disputations, strange questions, and nothing done, I must needs think it proceeds either of mistaking of the errand, or else from some jealousy of me the propounder, that you so add delay unto delay, searching out as it were the very bowels of curiosity, and conclude nothing....

I desire a perfect union of laws and persons, and such a naturalizing as may make one body of both kingdoms under me your King, that I and my posterity...may rule over you to the world's end...for no more possible is it for one King to govern two countries contiguous, the one a great the other a less, a richer and a poorer, the greater drawing like an adamant the lesser to the commodities thereof, than for one head to govern two bodies or one man to be husband of two wives....

But in the general union you must observe two things, for I will discover my thoughts plainly unto you; I study clearness, not eloquence. And therefore with the old philosophers I would heartily wish my breast were a transparent glass for you all to see through, that you might look into my heart and then would you be satisfied of my meaning. For when I speak of a perfect union, I mean not confusion of all things; you must not take from Scotland those particular privileges that may stand as well with this union as in England many particular customs in particular shires...do with the common law of the kingdom, for every particular shire almost, and much more every county, have some particular customs that are as it were naturally most fit for that people. But I mean of such a general union of laws as may reduce the whole island, that as they live already under one march, so they may all be governed by one law....

There is a conceit entertained, and a double jealousy possesseth many, wherein I am misjudged.

First, that this union will be the crisis to the overthrow of England and setting up of Scotland; England will then be overwhelmed by the swarming of the Scots, who if the union were effected would reign and rule all.

The second is, my profuse liberality to the Scottish men more than the English, and that with this union all things shall be given to them and you turned out of all; to you shall be left the sweat and labor, to them shall be given the fruit and sweet; and that my forbearance is but till this union may be gained. . . . Some think that I will draw the Scottish nation hither, talking idly of transporting of trees out of a barren ground into a better, and of lean cattle out of bad pasture into a more fertile soil. Can any man displant you unless you will? Can any man think Scotland is so strong to pull you out of your houses? Do you think I know not that England hath more people, Scotland more waste ground? . . . .

For the matter of the union presently desired, it standeth in three parts. The first, taking away of hostile laws, for since there can be now no wars betwixt you, is it not reason hostile laws should cease? . . . . The second is community of commerce. . . . For the third point, of naturalization, all you agree that they are no aliens, and yet will not allow them to be natural. . . .

. . . . For my part, when I have two nations under my government, can you imagine I will respect the lesser and neglect the greater? Would I not think it a less evil and hazard to me that the plague were at Northampton or Berwick than at London, so near Westminster, the seat of my habitation and of my wife and children? Will not a man be more careful to quench the fire taken in his nearest neighbor's house than if a whole town were afire far from him? You know that I am careful to preserve the woods and game through all England, nay through all the isle; yet none of you doubts but that I would be more offended with any disorder in the Forest of Waltham for stealing of a stag there, which lieth as it were under my nose and in a manner joineth with my garden,

than with cutting of timber or stealing of a deer in any forest of the north parts of Yorkshire. . . . Think you that I will prefer them that be absent, less powerful, and farther off to do me good or hurt, before you with whom my security and living must be and where I desire to plant my posterity? . . . I need speak no more of this with protestations. . . . To doubt of my intention in this were more than devilish. . . .

Now to conclude. . . . I pray you, the truth and sincerity of my meaning, which in seeking union is only to advance the greatness of your empire seated here in England; and yet with such caution I wish it as may stand with the weal of both States. What is now desired hath oft before been sought when it could not be obtained; to refuse it now, then, were double iniquity. Strengthen your own felicity; London must be the seat of your King, and Scotland joined to this kingdom by a golden conquest but cemented with love . . . which within will make you strong against all civil and intestine rebellion, as without we will be compassed and guarded with our walls of brass. Judge me charitably, since in this I seek your equal good, that so both of you might be made fearful to your enemies, powerful in yourselves, and available to your friends. Study therefore hereafter to make a good conclusion, avoid all delays, cut off all vain questions, that your King may have his lawful desire and be not disgraced in his just ends. And for your security in such reasonable points of restrictions whereunto I am to agree, ye need never doubt of my inclination; for I will not say anything which I will not promise, nor promise anything which I will not swear; what I swear I will sign, and what I sign I shall, with God's grace, ever perform. (James I, *Works,* ed. of 1616, pp. 509-25.)

## James I: Speech to Parliament Concerning Regal Power. 1610

**82.**

THE reign of James I marked the beginning of a new era of political thought in England. There were several reasons for this. Vexing contradictions in the ecclesiastical legislation of the four preceding monarchs had inculcated a national mood of unrest and rejection, and at times open defiance. More people came to be directly involved in the religious problems of the realm because of the practice of equating differences in religious belief with political treason. Also, as the middle class was increasingly incorporated into political life its voice began to be more distinctly heard in the area of law and policy making. Finally, owing to the general propagation of information characterizing the Renaissance, more people were interested in political and theological debate and were becoming more capable of logically ordered processes of thought. In short, national problems and their solutions were no longer the sole property of a small class of traditional leaders. These considerations were fundamental to the development of the divine right theory as set forth by James in his speech to Parliament in 1610.

In this speech James enumerated three broad categories of evidence to justify his divinely ordained right to absolute voice in all state matters. God, nature, and philosophy all directed and legitimized his right to exist, politically, above the Common Law. In asserting this theory James did not speak as an individual whose ambition ran counter to the will of the people. The divine right theory was not his invention. Indeed, it represented the thinking of a majority of the responsible English political and theological spokesmen who had been instrumental in placing him on the throne. More than that, it would remain the most acceptable of many possible rationalizations of monarchial rights until the need for overawing disaffected elements in England and dangerous foes abroad no longer existed. Thus, while James resorted to the broad generalizations of theology, nature, and philosophy to prove his inherent right, it is more than plain that the divine right theory was rooted as well in the exigencies of politics.

. . . . As you made me a fair present indeed in presenting your thanks and loving duties unto me; so have I now called you here, to recompence you again with a great and a rare present, which is a fair and a crystal mirror; not such a mirror wherein you may see your own faces, or shadows, but such a mirror . . . as through the transparentness thereof, you may see the heart of your King. The philosophers wish, that every man's breast were a crystal, wherethrough his heart might be seen, is vulgarly known, and I touched it in one of my former speeches unto you; but though that were impossible in the general, yet will I now perform this for my part, that as it is a true axiom in divinity, that *Cor Regis* is *in manu Domini,* so will I now set *Cor Regis in oculis populi.* I know that I can say nothing at this time, whereof some of you that are here, have not at one time or other, heard me say the like already: yet as corporal food nourishes and maintains the body, so does *Reminiscentia* nourish and maintain memory.

I will reduce to three general and main grounds, the principal things that have been agitated in this Parliament, and whereof I will now speak:

First, the errand for which you were called by me; and that was, for supporting of my state, and necessities.

The second is, that which the people are to move unto the King: to represent unto him such things, whereby the subjects are vexed, or wherein the state of the commonwealth is to be redressed; and that is the thing which you call grievance.

The third ground that hath been handled amongst you, and not only in talk amongst you in Parliament, but even in many other people's mouths, as well within, as without the Parliament, is of a higher nature than any of the former (though it be but an incident?) and the reason is, because it concerns a higher point; and this is a doubt, which hath been in the heads of some, of my intention in two things.

First, whether I was resolved in the general, to continue still my government according to the ancient form of this State, and the laws of this Kingdom: or if I had an intention not to limit my self within those bounds, but to alter the same when I thought convenient, by the absolute power of a King.

The other branch is about the Common Law, which some had a conceit I disliked, and, in respect that I was born where another form of law was established, that I would have wished the Civil Law to have been put in place of the Common Law for the government of this people. And the complaint made among you of a book written by Doctor Cowell, was a part of the occasion of this incident: but as touching my censure of that book, I made it already to be delivered unto you by the Treasurer here sitting, which he did out of my own directions and notes; and what he said in my name, that had he directly from me: but what he spoke of himself therein without my direction, I shall always make good; for you may be sure I will be loth to make so honest a man a liar, or deceive your expectations: ... within a very few days my edict shall come forth about that matter, which shall fully discover my meaning.

.... And now to the matter. As it is a Christian duty in every man, *Reddere rationem fidei,* not to be ashamed to give an account of his possessions before men, and Angels, as oft as occasion shall require: so did I ever hold it a necessity of honor in a just and wise king, though not to give an account to his people of his actions, yet clearly to deliver his heart and intention unto them upon every occasion....

The state of monarchy is the supremest thing upon earth: for kings are not only God's lieutenants upon earth, and sit upon God's throne, but even by God himself they are called gods. There be three principal similitudes that illustrate the state of monarchy: one taken out of the word of God; and the two other out of the grounds of policy and philosophy. In the scriptures kings are called gods, and so their power after a certain relation compared to the Divine power. Kings are also compared to fathers of families: for a king is truly *Parens patriae,* the political father of his people. And lastly, kings are compared to the head of this microcosm of the body of man.

Kings are justly called gods, for that they exercise a manner or resemblance of Divine power upon earth: for if you will consider the attributes to God, you shall see how they agree in the person of a king. God hath power to create, or destroy, make, or unmake at his pleasure, to give life, or send death, to judge all, and to be judged nor accountable to none: to raise low things, and to make high things low at his pleasure, and to God are both soul and body due. And the like power have kings: they make and unmake their subjects: they have power of raising, and casting down; of life, and of death: judges over all their subjects, and in all causes, and yet accountable to none but God only. They have power to exalt low things, and abase high things, and make of their subjects like men at chess; a pawn to take a bishop or a knight, and to cry up, or down any of their subjects, as they do their money. And to the king is due both the affection of the soul, and the service of the body of his subjects; and therefore that reverend Bishop here amongst you, though I hear that by divers he was mistaken or not well understood, yet did he preach both learnedly and truly annent this point concerning the power of a king: for what he spoke of a king's power in *abstracto,* is most true in Divinity; for to emperors, or kings that are monarchs, their subjects bodies and goods are due for their defence and maintenance....

As for the father of a family, they had of

old under the law of nature *Patriam potestatem,* which was *Potestatem vitae* and *necis,* over their children or family (I mean such fathers of families as were the lineal heirs of those families whereof kings did originally come:) for kings had their first original from them, who planted and spread themselves in colonies through the world. Now a father may dispose of his inheritance to his children, at his pleasure; yea, even disinherit the eldest upon just occasions, and prefer the youngest, according to his liking; make them beggars, or rich at his pleasure; restrain, or banish out of his presence, as he finds them give cause of offence, or restore them in favor again with the penitent sinner: so may the king deal with his subjects.

And lastly, as for the head of the natural body, the head hath the power of directing all the members of the body to that use which the judgment in the head thinks most convenient. It may apply sharp cures, or cut off corrupt members, let blood in what proportion it thinks fit, and as the body may spare, but yet is all this power ordained by God *Ad aedificationem, non ad destructionem.* For although God have power as well of destruction, as of creation or maintenance; yet will it not agree with the wisdom of God, to exercise His power in the destruction of nature, and overturning the whole frame of things, since His creatures were made, that His glory might thereby be the better expressed: so were he a foolish father that would disinherit or destroy his children without cause, or leave off the careful education of them; and it were an idle head that would in place of physic so poison the body as might breed a dangerous distemper or destruction thereof. . . .

I conclude then this point touching the power of kings, with this axiom of Divinity, that as to dispute what God may do, is blasphemy; but *quid vult Deus,* that Divines may lawfully, and do ordinarily dispute and discuss; for to dispute *A Posse ad Esse* is both against logic and Divinity: so is it sedition in

subjects, to dispute what a king may do in the height of his power: but just kings will ever be willing to declare what they will do, if they will not incur the curse of God. I will not be content that my power be disputed upon: but I shall ever be willing to make the reason appear of all my doings, and rule my actions according to my laws.

The other branch of this incident is concerning the Common Law, being conceived by some, that I condemned it, and preferred the Civil Law thereunto. As I have already said, king's actions . . . are as the actions of those that are set upon the stage . . . : and I hope never to speak that in private, which I shall not avow in public, and print it if need be, as I said in my *Basilicon Doron.* For it is true, that within these few days I spoke freely my mind touching the Common Law in my Privy Chamber, at the time of my dinner, which is come to all your ears; and the same was likewise related unto you by my Treasurer, and now I will again repeat and confirm the same my self unto you. First, as a King I have least cause of any man to dislike the Common Law: for no law can be more favorable and advantageous for a king, and extendeth further his prerogative, then it does: and for a King of England to despise the Common Law, it is to neglect his own Crown. It is true, that I do greatly esteem the Civil Law, the profession thereof serving more for general learning and being most necessary for matters of treaty with all foreign nations: and I think that if it should be taken away, it would make an entry to barbarism in this Kingdom, and would blemish the honor of England: for it is in a manner *Lex Gentium,* and maintaineth intercourse with all foreign nations: but I only allow it to have course here, according to those limits of jurisdiction, which the Common Law itself doth allow it: and therefore though it be not fit for the general government of the people here; it doth not follow, it should be extinct, no more, then because the Latin tongue is not the mother or radical language of any nation in the world at this time, that therefore the English tongue should alone be learned in this kingdom, which would bring in barbarism. My meaning therefore is not to prefer the Civil Law before the Common Law; but only that it should not be extinguished, and yet so bounded, (I mean to such Courts and cases) as have been in ancient use; ....

Now the second general ground whereof I am to speak, concerns the matter of grievances: there are two special causes of the peoples presenting grievances to their King in time of Parliament. First, for that the King cannot at other times be so well informed of all the grievances of his people, as in time of Parliament, which is the representative body of the whole realm. Secondly, the Parliament is the highest Court of Justice, and therefore the fittest place where divers natures of grievances may have their proper remedy, by the establishment of good and wholesome laws. But though my speech was before directed to the whole body of Parliament; yet in this case I must address my speech in special to you of the lower House.

I am now then to recommend unto your considerations the matter and manner of your handling and presenting of grievances. As for the manner, though I will not deny, but that you, representing the body of the people, may as it were both *opportune* and *inopportune* (I mean either in Parliament as a body, or out of Parliament as private men) present your grievances unto me; yet would I have you to use this caution in your behavior in this point: which is, that your grievances be not as it were greedily sought out by you, or taken up in the streets ... thereby to show a willingness that you would have a show made, that there are many abuses in the government, and many causes of complaint: but that according to your first institution, you should only meddle with such grievances, as your selves do know had need of reformation, or had informations thereof in your counties for which you serve,

and not so to multiply them, as might make it noised amongst the people, that all things in the government were amiss and out of frame: for even at the beginning of this very session of Parliament, the general name of grievance being mentioned among you, such a concept came in the heads of many, that you had a desire to multiply and make a great muster of them, as every one exhibited what his particular spleen stirred him unto. Indeed there fell out an accident upon this occasion, for which I have reason to thank you of the lower House, I mean for your fire work ... for having one afternoon found many grievances ... divers of them proceeding from grudging and murmuring spirits; you, upon the hearing read two or three of the first lines of divers of them, were not content with a public consent to condemn them, but you also made a public bonfire of them. ... You ... know how kindly I take your dutiful behavior in this case. But since this was a good effect of an evil cause, I must not omit also to admonish you upon the other part, to take course amongst yourselves, to prevent the like accident in all times hereafter; otherwise the lower House may become a place for *Pasquils,* and at another time such grievances may be cast in amongst you, as may contain treason or scandal against me, or my posterity. Therefore in this case, look over your ancient orders, and follow them, and suffer not hereafter any petitions or grievances to be delivered obscurely or in the dark, but openly and avowedly in your public house, and there to be presented to the Speaker. ...

First then, I am not to find fault that you inform yourselves of the particular just grievances of the people, nay, I must tell you, you can neither be just faithful to me, or to your counties that trust and employ you, if you do it not: for true plaints proceed not from the persons employed, but from the body represented, which is the people. And it may very well be, that many directions and commissions justly given forth by me, may be abused in the execution thereof, upon the people: and yet I never to receive information, except it come by your means, at such a time as this is.... But I would wish you to be careful to avoid three things in the matter of grievances.

First, that you do not meddle with the main points of government; that is my craft: *tractent fabrilia fabri;* to meddle with that, were to lesson me: I am now an old King; for six and thirty years I have governed in Scotland personally, and now I have accomplished my apprenticeship of seven years here; and seven years is a great time for a King's experience in Government: therefore there would not be too many Phormios to teach Hannibal: I must not be taught my office.

Secondly, I would not have you meddle with such ancient rights of mine, as I have received from my predecessors ... such things I would be sorry should be accounted for grievances....

And lastly, I pray you beware to exhibit for grievances any thing that is established by a settled law, and whereunto, as you have already had a proof, you know I will never give a plausible answer: for it is an undutiful part in subjects to press their King, wherein they know beforehand he will refuse them. Now, if any law or statute be not convenient, let it be amended by Parliament, but in the meantime term it not a grievance: for

to be grieved with the law, is to be grieved with the King, who is sworn to be the patron and maintainer thereof. But as all men are flesh, and may err in the execution of laws; so may you justly make a grievance of any abuse of the law, distinguishing wisely between the faults of the person, and the thing itself. As for example, complaints may be made unto you of the high commissioners: if so be, try the abuse, and spare not to complain upon it, but say not there shall be no Commission; for that were to abridge the power that is in me....

And now to conclude this purpose of grievances, I have one general grievance to commend unto you, and that in behalf of the counties from whence you come. And this is, to pray you to beware that your grievances savor not of particular men's thoughts, but of the general griefs rising out of the minds of the people, and not out of the humor of the propounder. And therefore I would wish you to take heed carefully, and consider of the party that propounds the grievance: for ye may easily discern whether it be his own passion, or the people's grief, that makes him to speak: for many a man will in your House propound a grievance out of his own humor, because he accounts highly of that matter: and yet the county that employs him, may perhaps either be of a contrary mind, or little care for it.... (James I, *Works*, pp. 528-33.)

## Act for the Better Execution of Justice. 1610

**83.** JAMES'S numerous communications to Parliament concerning his plan for unifying Scotland and England were inconsistent in tone. Some were petulant and others as forceful and ordered as his speech of 1607, wherein the King plainly told the Parliamentarians that his purpose in seeking the union was "only to advance the greatness of your empire seated here in England." However, James's perennial return to the subject placed him in the undignified position of a suppliant for favor. Kingship could ill afford to lose its awesome dignity in dealing with an institution as aggressively inclined as was Parliament in the seventeenth century. Hence the occasional harshness. The Act of 1610 was one of the few sops the legislature gave the King. James accepted the statute as evidence of progress, but in reality it added little to the prospects of union.

An Act for the better execution of justice and suppressing of criminal offenders in the north parts of the Kingdom of England.

Whereas in a Statute made in the third session of this present Parliament, entitled *An Act for the Utter Abolition of all memory of Hostility and the Dependences thereof between England and Scotland*... [4 and 5 James I, c.1.] it was amongst other things enacted that no natural born subject of the Realm of England or the dominions of the same should for any high treason, misprision or concealment of high treason, petty treason, or any other whatsoever offence or cause committed within Scotland, be sent out of England where he is apprehended to receive his trial until such time as both realms should be made one in laws and government, which is the thing so much desired as that wherein the full perfection of the blessed union already begun in his Majesty's Royal Person consisteth:

Since the making of which statute, although those parts of the Kingdom of England adjoining and lying near unto the realm and Kingdom of Scotland have been and are by his Majesty's incessant care and princely policy reduced to a more civil and peaceable estate than could in short time have been expected or hoped for; yet experience teacheth that malefactors of either realm having committed their offences in the other realm do forthwith fly and escape into their own country thereby to purchase their impunity, to the great and manifest grievance of the one realm and the dishonor of the other:

By means whereof very many great and heinous offences since the making of the said Statute have been and are still likely to be committed without ... punishment; for that since the making of the said Statute there hath not been any one offender committing any the offences aforesaid in Scotland that hath been prosecuted to his trial, judgment, or execution in England by reason or upon any the branches, laws, or ordinances in the said Statute mentioned or contained:

Whereby it manifestly appeareth that the said clause in the said Statute contained, and before in this present Act expressly mentioned, concerning the not sending out of England any natural born subject of the realm or dominions of the same for any whatsoever offence committed within the realm of Scotland to receive his trial for any the said offences, hath not brought forth that good effect as was hoped for and by the said law intended, to the great prejudice and dishonor of both realms:

For the preventing of which apparent and two manifest mischief and inconvenience be it enacted and by the authority of this present Parliament established, that if at any time or times after the end of this present session of Parliament any person or persons shall commit any offence or offences within the realm of Scotland which by the laws of this realm of England is, are, or shall be declared or adjudged to be petty treason, murder, manslaughter, felonious burning of houses and corn, burglary, robbing of houses by day, robbery, theft, or rape, and do or shall fly or escape into the realm of England, and be or shall be apprehended within any the counties of Northumberland, Cumberland, Westmorland, or any parts or members of the same, or within the parts or places lying on the north side of the river of Tyne commonly called or known by the names of Bedlingtonshire, Norhamshire, and Islandshire, the town and county of Newcastle upon Tyne, and the town of Berwick upon Tweed, with the bounds and liberties thereof, that then it shall and may be lawful to and for the Justices of Assize or any one of them in the absence of the other, the Justices of Jail Delivery at their jail delivery or any four of them, or the Justices of Peace in their General or Quarter Sessions or any four of them, upon due and mature examination of the said offence or offences in open sessions and pregnant proofs of the same, by warrant under their hands and seals to remand and send all and every such offender and offenders into the realm of Scotland, there to receive their trial for any the offences aforesaid by them there committed; anything in the said Statute contained to the contrary thereof notwithstanding; this law to continue to the end of the first session of the next Parliament.

Provided nevertheless and be it enacted by the authority aforesaid, that this Statute nor any clause therein contained shall take effect ... until a law by Act of Parliament be made and established within the realm of Scot-land for the remanding and sending out of the realm of Scotland into the realm of England all and every person and persons born within the realm of Scotland or the dominions of the same which shall at any time hereafter commit any the offences aforesaid within the realm of England, to receive his and their trial in the realm of England for all and every the said offences by them committed in the said realm of England. (SR, IV, 1156: 7 and 8 James I, c.1.)

## The Oaths Act. 1610

**84.** JAMES'S neutrality in the Catholic problem, which had already motivated Parliament's passage of several anti-Catholic statutes, now gave rise to the *Oaths Act*. Its significance is not in its severity so much as in its effect on the prerogative. James's laxness regarding national religious problems and his suspected leniency toward wealthy and aristocratic Catholic families eventually inaugurated stronger remonstrances and harsher legislative actions in the House of Commons.

Although the *Oaths Act* was not intended by Commons as an attack on the prerogative, it was one of the many minor actions wherein Parliament asserted its right to a voice in Church affairs. It is doubtful that the King was really the Supreme Head of the English Church in 1610.

An Act for administering the Oath of Allegiance, and reformation of Married Women Recusants.

[After reference to the oath of loyalty set forth in 3 James I, c.4, *An Act for the Better Discovery and Repression of Popish Recusants,* which was to be administered to "any person of the age of 18 or above, being or which shall be convict or indicted of or for any recusancy" the present Act states "that all and every person and persons, as well ecclesiastical as temporal, of what estate, dignity, preeminence, sex, quality, or degree soever ... above the age of 18 years, being hereafter mentioned in this Act ... shall make, take, and receive a corporal oath" of allegiance, loyalty, and non-recusancy. Included were all administrative, military, and naval personnel, all churchmen, the Houses of Parliament, the King's children, all officers of the judiciary, all local officials, all doctors, lawyers, clerks and teachers, all scholars and collegiate officials, and "every other person ... that doth or shall receive any fee of your Highness your heirs and successors"].

And be it further enacted ... that it shall and may be lawful to and for any one of the Privy Council ... and to and for every Bishop within his diocese to require any baron or baroness of the age of 18 or above to take the said oath, and to and for any two Justices of Peace within any county, city, or town ... to require any person or persons of the age of 18 years or above under the degree of a baron or baroness to take the said oath; and if any person or persons of or above the said age and degree ... be presented, indicted, or convicted for not coming to church or not receiving the Holy Communion ... then three of the Privy Council ... shall require such person ... to take the said oath; and if any other person ... be presented, indicted, or convicted ... or if the minister, petty constable, and churchwardens, or any two of them, shall … complain to any Justice of Peace near adjoining to the place where any person complained of shall dwell, and the said Justices shall find cause of suspicion; that then any one Justice of Peace … shall upon notice thereof require such person … to take the said oath; and that if any person or persons being of the age of 18 years or above shall refuse to take the said oath … that then the persons authorized by this law to give the said oath shall and may commit the same offender to the common jail … until the next Assizes or General Quarter Sessions … where the said oath shall be again … required of such person … : and if the said person … shall refuse to take the said oath [he] … shall incur … the penalty of *Praemunire.* …

And be it further enacted, that every person refusing to take the said oath as above shall be disabled … to execute any public place of judicature or bear any other office … within this your Highness's realm of England, or to use or practice the Common Law or Civil Law, or the science of physic or surgery, or the art of an apothecary, or any liberal science for his or their gain within this realm, until such time as the same person shall receive the same oath according to the intent of this Statute.

And be it further enacted, that if any married woman, being lawfully convicted as a Popish recusant for not coming to church, shall not within three months next after such conviction conform herself and repair to the church and receive the Sacrament of the Lords Supper … that then she shall be committed to prison by one of the Privy Council … or by the Bishop of the diocese if she be a baroness, or if she be under that degree, by two Justices of the Peace … , there to remain without bail … until she shall conform herself … , unless the husband of such wife shall pay to the King's Majesty … for the offence of his said wife for every month ten pounds of lawful money of England, or else the third part … of all his lands and tenements, at the choice of the husband whose wife is so convicted as aforesaid, for and during so long time as she remaining a recusant convicted shall continue out of prison, during which time, and no longer, she may be at liberty. (SR, IV, 1162: 7 & 8 James I, c.6.)

## The House of Commons Petition of Right. 1610

THE *Petition* was not an attack on the Crown's right in matters of impositions. As part of the ancient prerogative such imposts were still beyond the direct attack of Parliament in 1610. Instead, the *Petition* extended the *Apology of 1604* to include Parliamentary right to greater voice in matters of extra-Parliamentary Crown income. From the generalization that it was "an ancient, general, and undoubted right of Parliament to debate freely all matters which do properly concern the subject and his right" Parliament arrived at the conclusion that it could demand that the Crown explain the full extent of the prerogative in money matters. The *Petition,* then, attempted to force the King into explanation and definition which would allow Parliament to shift its debate easily from the prerogative to matters pertaining to Parliamentary rights in general.

**85.**

To the King's most Excellent Majesty.

Most gracious Sovereign, whereas your Majesty's most humble subjects the Commons assembled in Parliament have received, first by message and since by speech from your Majesty, a commandment of restraint from debating in Parliament your Majesty's right of imposing upon your subjects' goods exported or imported out of or into this realm, yet allowing us to examine the grievance of those impositions in regard of quantity, time, and other circumstances of disproportion thereto incident; we your said humble subjects, nothing doubting but that your Majesty had no intent by that commandment to infringe the ancient and fundamental right of the liberty of the Parliament in point of exact discussing of all matters concerning them and their possessions, goods, and rights whatsoever, which yet we cannot but conceive to be done in effect by this commandment; do with all humble duty make this remonstrance to your Majesty.

First, we hold it an ancient, general, and undoubted right of Parliament to debate freely all matters which do properly concern the subject and his right or state; which freedom of debate being once foreclosed, the essence of the liberty of Parliaments is withal dissolved.

And whereas in this case the subjects' right on the one side and your Majesty's prerogative on the other cannot possibly be served in debate of either, we allege that your Majesty's prerogatives of that kind concerning directly the subject's right and interest are daily handled and discussed in all Courts at Westminster, and have been ever freely debated upon all fit occasions, both in this and all former Parliaments, without restraint: which being forbidden, it is impossible for the subject either to know or to maintain his right and property to his own lands and goods, though never so just and manifest.

It may further please your most excellent Majesty to understand that we have no mind to impugn, but a desire to inform ourselves of, your Highness's prerogative in that point, which, if ever, is now most necessary to be known; and though it were to no other purpose, yet to satisfy the generality of your Majesty's subjects, who finding themselves much grieved by these new impositions do languish in much sorrow and discomfort.

These reasons, dread Sovereign, being the proper reasons of Parliament, do plead for the upholding of this our ancient right and liberty. Howbeit, seeing it hath pleased your

Majesty to insist upon that judgment in the Exchequer as being direction sufficient for us without further examination, upon great desire of leaving your Majesty unsatisfied in no one point of our intents and proceedings, we profess touching that judgment that we neither do nor will take upon us to reverse it; but our desire is, to know the reasons whereupon the same was grounded, and the rather for that a general conceit is had that the reasons of that judgment may be extended much further, even to the utter ruin of the ancient liberty of this kingdom and of your subjects' right of property of their lands and goods.

Then for the judgment itself, being the first and last that ever was given in that kind, for ought appearing unto us, and being only in one case and against one man, it can bind in law no other but that person, and is also reversible by writ of error granted heretofore by Act of Parliament, and neither he nor any other subject is debarred by it from trying his right in the same or like case in any of your Majesty's Courts of Record at Westminster.

Lastly, we nothing doubt but our intended proceeding in a full examination of the right, nature, and measure of these new impositions (if this restraint had not come between) should have been so orderly and moderately carried, and so applied to the manifold necessity of these times, and given your Majesty so true a view of the state and right of your subjects, that it would have been much to your Majesty's content and satisfaction . . . and removed all cause of fears and jealousies from the loyal hearts of your subjects, which is . . . our careful endeavor; whereas, contrariwise, in that other way directed by your Majesty we cannot safely proceed without concluding forever the right of the subject, which without due examination thereof we may not do.

We therefore, your Highness's loyal and dutiful Commons, not swerving from the approved steps of our ancestors, most humbly and instantly beseech your gracious Majesty that without offence to the same we may, according to the undoubted right and liberty of Parliament, proceed in our intended course of a full examination of these new impositions; that so we may cheerfully pass on to your Majesty's business, from which this stop hath by diversion so long withheld us. And we your Majesty's most humble, faithful, and loyal subjects shall ever, according to our bounden duty, pray for your Majesty's long and happy reign over us. (*Journals of the House of Commons*, I, 431.)

## James I: Letter to the House of Commons. 1621

**86.**

BY 1621 the relations between King and Commons were strained almost irretrievably. On the continent the Thirty Years War had brought into clear focus the antithetical natures of the goals of Parliament and Crown in foreign policy. The proposed marriage of Prince Charles with the Spanish Princess reactivated all the ancient fears of foreign intrigue and intervention in English affairs. James's unwillingness to debate his every policy and action with Parliament stimulated that body to more determined restatement of its aims. James's letter to Commons was a frank threat, and one which drew immediate response from Commons in the *Protestation of 1621*.

Mr. Speaker:

We have heard by divers reports, to our great grief, that our distance from the Houses of Parliament, caused by our indisposition of health, has emboldened some fiery and popular spirits of some of the House of Commons to argue and debate publicly of the matters far above their reach and capacity, tending to our high dishonor and breach of prerogative royal. These are therefore to command you to make known, in our name, unto the House that none therein shall presume henceforth to meddle with anything concerning our government or deep matters of State; and, namely, not to deal with our dearest son's match with the daughter of Spain, nor to touch the honor of that King or any other our friends and confederates, and also not to meddle with any man's particulars which have their due motion in our ordinary courts of justice. And whereas we hear they have sent a message to Sir Edwin Sandys to know the reasons of his late restraint, you shall in our name resolve them that it was not for any misdemeanor of his in Parliament. But, to put them out of doubt of any question of that nature that may arise among them hereafter, you shall resolve them, in our name, that we think ourself very free and able to punish any man's misdemeanors in Parliament, as well during their sitting as after: which we mean not to spare hereafter upon any occasion of any man's insolent behavior there that shall be ministered unto us. And if they have already touched any of these points, which we have forbidden, in any petition of theirs which is to be sent unto us, it is our pleasure that you shall tell them that, except they reform it before it come to our hands, we will not deign the hearing nor answering of it. (Rushworth, *Historical Collections*, I, p. 43.)

## The Debate in Commons Relative to the Privileges of that House. 1621

**87.** JAMES'S letter of 1621 to Commons concerning the content and tone of the House debates only added fuel to Commons' determination to resist what were thought to be unconstitutional and arbitrary limitations on the freedom of Parliamentary speech. Sir Edward Coke's suggestion that a sub-committee be appointed to consider the specific items mentioned in the King's letter also indirectly rejected one of the main contentions of that letter, the King's claim that his authority over Parliament extended to the punishment of "any man's misdemeanors in Parliament." For, said Coke, the committee was to consider "of our liberty of speech and of our power to punish those that speak too lavishly."

Mr. Alford: [he] would have a select committee appointed to consider of the points of such of our privileges as are impeached, and to draw a protestation for the same privileges in particular and also of all the rest in general.

Mr. Thomas Crewe: [he] saith that, though the calling of a Parliament and the continuing, prorogation, and dissolving of it be in the King's sole power, yet, when we are called, we are without limitation to deal in what business ourselves think best; for otherwise shall we not be able to do their business for whom we come here, which is that of the people of the country. He would not have this committee to insist so much on particulars as on the generality of our privileges.

Sir Edward Coke: [he] would not have us here at this time, in the handling and debating of our privileges, to meddle with war or marriage; and would have a sub-committee appointed for this; and this committee should consider of all those matters which are mentioned in the Writ of Parliament, and also of our liberty of speech and of our power to punish those that speak too lavishly, and of our power to meddle and debate of what we shall of ourselves think fit.

The heads to be considered by the sub-committee for privileges:

Concerning freedom of speech; and therein to treat *de arduis et urgentibus negotiis regni* according to the writ of summons, whether it be concerning the King or not,

Touching the liberty of this House to punish the misdemeanors of any Parliament-man in Parliament for things whereof this House hath cognizance, whether he ought not to be censured here by the House only,

Whether, when we receive commandment from the King, the House shall thereon desist, and not proceed notwithstanding such command in any business,

Whether our privileges be not our right and inheritance,

That the sub-committee shall consider of anything else incident to the liberty of the House,

That the sub-committee shall consider whether it be not fit for us to make an expression here in the House, that it is an ancient privilege of Parliament that no member of this House shall presume to acquaint the King with any business in debate here but by order from the whole House or from the Speaker.

It is ordered . . . that the sub-committee shall reduce all these heads which have been propounded into the form of a protestation; and that they shall render an account and their reasons of such things as they shall think not fit to be reduced into a protestation. And the sub-committee is appointed accordingly, and is to sit this afternoon in the committee chamber.

The Speaker . . . is ordered . . . [to] attend here at four o'clock this afternoon; that, the sub-committee having drawn the foresaid heads into the form of a protestation and made a report thereof to the grand committee, the House may, if occasion be, confirm the protestation; because otherwise it may be the King will command the House to be adjourned before such protestation be made in the House, and so may we endanger the validity of our privileges and liberties in those points wherein they have seemed to be impeached at this our meeting.... (E. Nicholas, *Proceedings and Debates in the House of Commons in 1620 and 1621*, 1766, p. 356.)

## The Protestation of the House of Commons. 1621

### 88.

THE *Protestation* is the report of the sub-committee suggested by Sir Edward Coke in the preceding document. It explicitly denied the King's right to censure the House for its debates or to molest any individual member for anything said or done in Parliament. In short, Parliament attempted to destroy all limitations on its privilege of free speech. Subsequently James tore the *Protestation* from the Journal and declared it void and of no effect. However, distasteful as the document was to James, it did not actually extend Parliament's claims beyond those already recorded in the *Apology of 1604*. The mood of defiance in which the document was constructed was far more significant to constitutional development than its contents. The King might treat the revolutionary symptom by angrily ripping the offending work from the Journal but he could not erase its words from the minds of those who were to serve in future Parliaments.

The Commons now assembled in Parliament, being justly occasioned thereunto concerning sundry liberties, franchises, and privileges of Parliament, amongst others here mentioned, do make this Protestation following:

That the liberties, franchises, privileges, and jurisdictions of Parliament are the ancient and undoubted birthright and inheritance of the subjects of England; and that the arduous and urgent affairs concerning the King, State, and defence of the Realm and of the Church of England, and the maintenance and making of laws, and redress of mischiefs and grievances which daily happen within this Realm, are proper subjects and matter of counsel and debate in Parliament; and that in the handling and proceeding of those businesses every member of the House of Parliament hath, and of right ought to have, freedom of speech to propound, treat, reason, and bring to conclusion the same; and that the Commons in Parliament have like liberty and freedom to treat of these matters in such order as in their judgments shall seem fittest; and that every member of the said House hath like freedom from all impeachment, imprisonment, and molestation (other than by censure of the House itself) for or concerning any speaking, reasoning, or declaring of any matter or matters touching the Parliament or Parliament-business; and that if any of the said members be complained of and questioned for anything done or said in Parliament, the same is to be showed to the King by the advice and assent of all the Commons assembled in Parliament, before the King give credence to any private information. (Rushworth, *Historical Collections*, I, 53.)

## The Proclamation of James I Dissolving Parliament. 1622

**89.** HAVING removed the *Protestation* from the Journal, James proceeded to dissolve the offending Parliament. In the *Proclamation* of January, 1622, therefore, is a detailed summary of the reasons for the discord between King and legislature. With some justice James placed the onus for his act on the House of Commons, which had acted in arbitrary and revolutionary way in entering the *Protestation* in the Journal. Despite James's anger at the *Protestation*, it is evident from the *Proclamation* that the dissolution was really based on Parliament's niggardly withholding of supply.

*De Proclamatione Regia pro Dissolutione Conventionis Parliamenti.*

Albeit the assembling, continuing, and dissolving of Parliaments be a prerogative so peculiarly belonging to our Imperial Crown, and the times and seasons thereof so absolutely in our own power that we need not give account thereof unto any man; yet according to our continual custom to make our good subjects acquainted with the reasons of all our public resolutions and actions, we have thought it expedient at this time to declare not only our pleasure and resolution therein, grounded upon mature deliberation, with the advice and uniform consent of our whole Privy Council, but therewith also to note some especial proceedings moving us to this resolution, and that chiefly to this end: that as God so also the world may witness with us that it was our intent to have made this the happiest Parliament that ever was in our time, and that the let and impediment thereof being discerned, all misunderstandings and jealousies might be removed, and all our people may know and believe that we are as far from imputing any of those ill accidents that have happened in Parliament to any want or neglect of duty or good affection toward us by them in general, or by the greater or better number of Parliament men, as we are confident, the true causes discovered, they will be far from imputing it to any default in us, there having in the beginning of this late assembly passed greater and more infallible tokens of love and duty from our subjects to us their Sovereign, and more remarkable testimonies

from us of our princely care and zeal of their welfare than have been in any Parliament met in any former age.

The Parliament was by us called as for making good and profitable laws, so more especially in this time of miserable distraction throughout Christendom [the Thirty Years War] for the better settling of peace and religion and restoring our children [James's daughter, Elizabeth, and her husband, the continental Protestant spokesman, Frederick, the Elector of Palatine] to their ancient and lawful patrimony, which we attempted to procure by peaceable treaty at our own excessive charge, thereby to save and prevent the effusion of Christian blood, the miserable effect of war and dissension; yet with full purpose, if that succeeded not, to recover it by the sword, and therefore as a necessary means conducing to those ends the supply of our treasures was to be provided for.

This Parliament, beginning in January last, proceeded some months with such harmony between us and our people as cannot be paralleled by any former time . . . [yet] after their first recess at Easter, we found that they mis-spent a great deal of time rather upon the enlarging of the limits of their liberties, and divers other curious and unprofitable things, than upon the framing and proposing of good and profitable laws, yet we gave them time and scope for their Parliamentary proceedings and prolonged the session to an unusual length, continuing it until the eight and twentieth day of May before we signified our purpose for their recess, and then we declared that we would make a recess on the fourth day of June next following, but only for a time, and in such manner as might be without disturbance to any their businesses at hand; expressing out of our grace, though we needed not, the causes of that our purpose, which were; the season of the year, usually hot and unfit for great assemblies; our progress [travels throughout the realm] approaching, the necessity we had to make use of our Council attending in both Houses both to settle our weighty affairs of State before we went and to attend us when we went on our progress; the disfurnishing our ordinary Courts of Justice so many terms together; the long absence of Justices of Peace and Deputy-Lieutenants whose presence was needful for making and returning of musters and for subordinate government of the country; and therefore we appointed to adjourn the Parliament on the fourth day of June, giving that warning longer than usual that they might set in order their business and prepare their grievances, which we promised both to hear and answer before that recess, for presenting whereof we appointed them a time.

This message, graciously intended by us, was not so well entertained by some who in a short time dispersed and spread their jealousies unto others, and thereby occasioned discontentment in the House for being adjourned without passing of bills, yet made not their address to us [as they should have done] but desired a conference with the Lords, and at that conference the nine and twentieth of May, under color of desiring to petition us for some further time to perfect and pass some special bills, were emboldened not only to dispute but to deny all the reasons that we had given for the adjournment; which being made known unto us, we again signified our pleasure to both Houses that on the fourth day of June the Parliament should rise, but we would then give our royal assent to such bills as were or should be ready and fit to be then passed, continu-

ing all other businesses as they were by a special Act to be framed for that purpose.

The Lords with all duty and respect submitted to our resolution, passed the Act, and sent it with special recommendation to the House of Commons, but they neither read it nor proceeded with business but, forgetting that the time was ours and not theirs, continued their discontent as they pretended for being so soon dismissed.

We, though it were strange to observe such averseness for our resolving upon such weighty reasons that wherein we needed not be measured by any other rule but our own princely will, yet were contented to descend from our right to alter our resolution and to continue the session for a fortnight more, wherein they might perfect such public bills as were esteemed of most importance, for which purpose we ourself came in person unto the Higher House of Parliament and made offer thereof unto them, which being in effect as much as the Commons had formerly desired, was no sooner offered but, yielding thanks to us, the said Commons resolved the same day, directly contrary to their former desire, to refuse it, and to accept our first resolution of an adjournment, but attending us at Greenwich, presented no grievances.

This inconstancy as we passed by with a gentle admonition, so for the matter of grievances as well of England as Ireland we promised to take them into our own care though not presented to us, and really performed the same so far forth as time and the advice of our Council of each kingdom could enable us, as is witnessed by our several proclamations published in both realms, as likewise in granting at the same time those three suits which were propounded unto us by the Archbishop of Canterbury at the request and in the name of both the Houses; but in conclusion the House of Commons making it their choice, we made a recess by adjournment of the Parliament the fourth day of June, though indeed we must do them this right that at the said recess, taking into their serious consideration the present estate of our children abroad and the general afflicted estate of the true professors of religion in foreign parts, they did with one unanimous consent, in the name of themselves and the whole body of the kingdom, make a most dutiful and solemn protestation that if our pious endeavours by treaty to procure their peace and safety should not take that good effect which was desired in the treaty, whereof they humbly besought us not to suffer any long delay, then upon signification of our pleasure in Parliament, they would be ready to the uttermost of their powers, both with lives and fortunes, to assist us, so as that, by the divine help of Almighty God, we might be able to do that by our sword which by peaceable courses should not be effected.

But during the time of this long recess, having to our great charges mediated with the Emperor by the means of our Ambassador the Lord Digby, and having found those hopes to fail which we had to prevail by treaty, we in confidence of the assistance of our people, thus freely promised and protested in Parliament, did instantly shorten the time of the recess, which we had before appointed to continue until the eighth day of February, and did reassemble our Parliament the twentieth day of November last, and made known unto them the true state and necessity of our children's affairs; declaring our resolution unto them of taking upon us the defence of our children's patrimony by way of arms since we could not compass it by an amicable treaty, and therefore expected the fruit of that their declaration whereby we were invited unto this course.

Wherein, howbeit we are well satisfied of the good inclination of most part of our House of Commons, testified by their ready assent to the speedy payment of a subsidy newly to be granted, yet upon this occasion some particular members of that House took such inordinate liberty, not only to treat of our high prerogatives and of sundry things that without our special direction were no fit subjects to be treated of in Parliament, but

also to speak with less respect of foreign princes our allies than were fit for any subject to do of any anointed King, though in enmity and hostility with us.

And when upon this occasion we used some reprehension towards those miscarriages, requiring them not to proceed but in such things as were within the capacity of that House according to the continual custom of our predecessors, then by the means of some evil-affected and discontented persons such heat and distemper was raised in the House that, albeit themselves had sued unto us for a session and for a general pardon, unto both which at their earnest suit we assented, yet after this fire kindled they rejected both, and setting apart all businesses of consequence and weight notwithstanding our admonition and earnest pressing them to go forward, they either sat as silent or spent the time in disputing of privileges, discussing the words and syllables of our letters and messages, which for better clearing of truth and satisfaction of all men we are about to publish in print so soon as possibly we can; and although in our answer to their petition we gave them full assurance that we would be as careful of the preservation of their privileges as of our own royal prerogative, and in our explanation after sent unto them by our letters written unto our secretary we told them that we never meant to deny them any lawful privileges that ever that House enjoyed in our predecessors's times, and that whatsoever privileges or liberties they enjoyed by any law or statute should ever be inviolably preserved by us, and we hoped our posterity would imitate our footsteps therein, and whatsoever privileges they enjoyed by long custom and uncontrolled and lawful precedents we would likewise be as careful to preserve them, and transmit the care thereof to our posterity, confessing ourselves in justice to be bound to maintain them in their rights, and in grace that we were rather minded to increase than infringe any of them if they should so deserve at our hands, which might satisfy any reasonable man that we were far from violating their privileges.

And although by our letters written to their Speaker we advised them to proceed and make this a session, to the end our good and loving subjects might have some taste as well of our grace and goodness towards them by our free pardon and good laws to be passed as they had both by the great and unusual examples of justice since this meeting and the so many cases and comforts given unto them by proclamation, and although we had given order for the pardon to go on, and that in a more gracious and liberal manner than had passed in many years before, and signified our willingness that, rather than time should be misspent, they might lay aside the thought of the subsidy and go on with an Act for continuance of statutes and the general pardon; but all this prevailed not to satisfy them, either for their pretended privileges or to persuade them to proceed with bills for the good of themselves and those that sent them. But as the session and pardon were by them well desired at first, so were they as ill rejected at the last, and notwithstanding the sincerity of our protestations not to invade their privileges, yet by persuasion of such as had been the cause of all these distempers they fall to carve for themselves, and pretending causelessly to be occasioned thereunto, in an unseasonable hour of the day and a very thin House, contrary to their own customs in all matters of weight, conclude and enter a protestation for their liberties in such ambiguous and general words as might serve for future times to invade most of our inseparable rights and prerogatives annexed to our Imperial Crown whereof, not only in the times of other our progenitors but in the blessed reign of our late predecessor the renowned Queen Elizabeth, we found our Crown actually possessed, an usurpation that the majesty of a King can by no means endure.

By all which may appear that howsoever in the general proceedings of that House there are many footsteps of loving and well-affected duty towards us, yet some ill-tempered spirits have sowed tares among the corn, and thereby frustrated the hope of that plentiful and good harvest which might have multiplied the wealth and welfare of this whole land, and by their cunning diversions have imposed upon us a necessity of discontinuing this present Parliament without putting unto it the name or period of a session.

And therefore, whereas the said assembly of Parliament was by our commission adjourned until the eighth day of February now next ensuing, we minding not to continue the same any longer, and therefore not holding it fit to cause the prelates, noblemen, and states of this our realm or the knights, citizens, and burgesses of the same Parliament to travail thereabout, have thought fit to signify this our resolution with the reasons thereof unto all our subjects inhabiting in all parts of this realm, willing and requiring the said prelates, noblemen, [etc.] ... and all others to whom in this case it shall appertain, that they forbear to attend at the day and place prefixed by the said adjournment, and in so doing they are and shall be discharged thereof against us; and we do hereby further declare that the said convention of Parliament neither is, nor after the dissolution and breaking thereof shall be nor ought, to be esteemed, adjudged, or taken to be or make any session of Parliament.

And albeit we are at this time enforced to break off this convention of Parliament, yet our will and desire is that all our subjects should take notice, for avoiding of all sinister suspicions and jealousies, that our intent and full resolution is to govern our people in the same manner as our progenitors and predecessors, kings and queens of this realm, of best government have heretofore done, and that we shall be careful, both in our own person and by charging our Privy Council, our Judges, and other our ministers in their several places respectively, to distribute true justice and right unto all our people, and that we shall be as glad to lay hold on the first occasion in due and convenient time, which we hope shall not be long, to call and assemble our Parliament with confidence of the true and hearty love and affection of our subjects as either we or any of our progenitors have at any time heretofore.

Given at our Palace of Westminster the sixth day of January. (T. Rymer, ed., *Foedera, conventiones, Litterae . . .*, 1710, XVII, pp. 344-47.)

## Act Voiding Monopolies. 1624

**90.** THE new Parliament of 1624—the first after the dissolution of 1622—was inclined toward cooperation with the King. The proposed marriage of Charles with the Spanish Princess had come to naught with the failure of Buckingham's trip to Spain, and the alliance with Spain had ended with the failure of the marriage plan. At Buckingham's and Charles's insistence, James now was moving in the direction of involvement in the Thirty Years War.

While this Parliament was ready to furnish supply more generously than any of its predecessors, it was not willing to do so for nothing. Monopolies had been a long-term cause for discontent. Although James had paid a certain amount of lip service to their abolition, he had remained adamant in his refusal to recognize their inconsistency with the common law. More than likely his attitude toward monopolies was shaped by his desire to use them as a future pawn in his Parliamentary relations. In accepting this Act, which placed control of monopolies in the Common Law Courts, James secured the supply necessary for English participation in the war at the cost of losing a prerogative which the Crown would never be able to regain.

An Act concerning Monopolies and Dispensations with penal laws and the forfeiture thereof.

Forasmuch as your most excellent Majesty . . . did, in the year of our Lord God one thousand six hundred and ten, publish in print to the whole realm and to all posterity that all grants of monopolies . . . are contrary to your Majesty's laws, which your Majesty's declaration is truly consonant and agreeable to the ancient and fundamental laws of this your realm:

And whereas your Majesty was further graciously pleased expressly to command that no suitor should presume to move your Majesty for matters of that nature; yet nevertheless upon misinformations and untrue pretences of public good many such grants have been unduly obtained and unlawfully put in execution, to the great grievance and inconvenience of your Majesty's subjects, contrary to the laws of this your realm and contrary to your Majesty's royal and blessed intentions so published as aforesaid:

For avoiding whereof, and preventing of the like in time to come, may it please your most excellent Majesty, at the humble suit of . . . this present Parliament assembled, that it may be declared and enacted . . . that all monopolies and all commissions, grants, licences, charters, and letters patents heretofore made or granted, or hereafter to be made or granted, to any person or persons, bodies politic or corporate whatsoever, of or for the sole buying, selling, making, working, or using of anything within this realm or the dominion of Wales, or of any other monopolies, or of power, liberty, or faculty to dispense with any others, or to give licence or toleration to do, use, or exercise anything against the tenor or purport of any law or statute, or to give or make any warrant for any such dispensation, licence, or toleration to be had or made, or to agree or compound with any others for any penalty, or sum of money that is or shall be due by any statute before judgment thereupon had, and all proclamations, inhibitions, restraints, warrants of assistance, and all other matters and things whatsoever any way tending to the instituting, erecting, strengthening, furthering, or countenancing of the same or any of them, are altogether contrary to the laws of this realm, and so are and shall be utterly void and of none effect, and in no wise to be put in use or execution.

And be it further declared and enacted ... that all monopolies ... and the force and validity of them ... ought to be and shall be for ever hereafter examined, heard, tried, and determined by and according to the common laws of this realm, and not otherwise.

And be it further enacted ... that all person and persons, bodies politic and corporate whatsoever which now are or hereafter shall be, shall stand and be disabled and uncapable to have, use, exercise, or put in use any monopoly, or any such commission, grant, licence, charters, letters patents, proclamation, inhibition, restraint, warrant of assistance, or other matter or thing tending as aforesaid, or any liberty, power, or faculty grounded or pretended to be grounded upon them or any of them.

And be it further enacted ... that if any person ... shall be hindered, grieved, disturbed, or disquieted, or his ... goods or chattels any way seized, attached, distrained, taken, carried away, or detained by occasion or pretext of any monopoly ... and will sue to be relieved ... that then ... the same person ... shall and may have his ... remedy for the same at the Common Law by any action or actions to be grounded upon this Statute, the same action and actions to be heard and determined in the Courts of King's Bench, Common Pleas, and Exchequer or in any of them, against him or them by whom he ... shall be so hindered, [etc.] ... or against him or them by whom his ... goods or chattels shall be so seized, [etc.] ... wherein ... every such person ... shall recover three times so much as the damages which he ... sustained, ... and double costs. ...

Provided nevertheless, and be it declared and enacted, that any declaration before mentioned shall not extend to any letters patents and grants of privilege for the term of one and twenty years or under heretofore made, of the sole working or making of any manner of new manufacture within this realm, to the first and true inventor or inventors of such manufactures which others at the time of the making of such letters patents and grants did not use, so they be not contrary to the law nor mischievous to the State by raising of the prices of commodities at home, or hurt of trade, or generally inconvenient. ...

Provided also, and be it declared and enacted, that any declaration before mentioned shall not extend to any letters patents and grants of privilege for the term of fourteen years or under hereafter to be made for the sole working or making of any manner of new manufactures within this realm to the true and first inventor and inventors of such manufactures. ...

Provided also, and it is hereby further intended, declared, and enacted, that this Act or anything therein contained shall not in any wise extend or be prejudicial unto the city of London, or to any city, borough, or town corporate within this realm for or concerning any grants, charters, or letters patents to them or any of them made or granted, or for or concerning any custom or customs used by or within them or any of them, or unto any corporations, companies, or fellowships of any trade, art, occupation, or mystery, or to any companies or societies of merchants within this realm erected for the maintenance, enlargement, or ordering of any trade of merchandise, but that the same charters, customs, corporations, companies, fellowships, and societies and their liberties, privileges, power, and immunities, shall be and continue of such force and effect as they were before the making of this Act. ... (SR, IV, 1212: 21 and 22 James I, c.3.)

## Subsidy Act. 1624

**91.**
THE *Subsidy Act* fulfilled part of the agreement between Crown and legislature relative to monopolies. Moreover, the Act itself was of great constitutional significance
because of the devices it adopted to insure the expenditure of the supply advanced
according to the desire of Parliament. Surely James must have realized the precedent-
setting nature of the Act; in dire immediate need, however, he was in no position to
reject either the money or the mode of its offer. The Act introduced two novel provisions: that Parliament-appointed treasurers release the money only on warrants
presented by the Council of War, and that the treasurers and the Council of War be
directly responsible to Parliament for all expenditures. The evidences in this Act of
Parliament's increasing stature are too numerous and significant to overlook. Primary
among them is that Parliament had established itself as very nearly equal to the
monarchy in the area of foreign affairs.

An Act for payment of Three Subsidies
and Three Fifteenths by the Temporalty.

Most gracious Sovereign, we your Majesty's most humble, faithful, and loving subjects, by your royal authority now assembled
in your High Court of Parliament, having
entered into serious and due consideration
of the weighty and most important causes
which at this time more than at any other
time heretofore do press your Majesty to a
much greater expense and charge than your
own treasure alone can at this present support and maintain, and likewise of the injuries and indignities which have been lately
offered to your Majesty and your children,
under color and during the time of the
treaties for the marriage with Spain and the
restitution of the Palatinate, which in this
Parliament have been clearly discovered and
laid open unto us; and withal what humble
advice with one consent and voice we have
given unto your Majesty to dissolve those
treaties, which your Majesty hath been graciously pleased, to our exceeding joy and
comfort, fully to yield unto, and accordingly
have made your public declaration for the
real and utter dissolution of them, by means
whereof your Majesty may be engaged in a
sudden war: we in all humbleness most ready
and willing to give unto your Majesty and
the whole world an ample testimony of our
dutiful affections and sincere intentions to
assist you therein for the maintenance of that

war that may hereupon ensue, and more particularly for the defence of this your realm of
England, the securing of your kingdom of
Ireland, the assistance of your neighbors the
States of the United Provinces and other your
Majesty's friends and allies, and for the setting forth of your royal navy, we have resolved to give for the present the greatest
Aid which ever was granted in Parliament to
be levied in so short a time; and therefore
we do humbly beseech your Majesty that it
may be declared and enacted ... that the said
two treaties are by your Majesty utterly dissolved; and for the maintenance of the war
which may come thereupon, and for the
causes aforesaid, be it enacted that three
whole fifteenths and tenths shall be paid,
taken, and levied of the moveable goods,
chattels, and other things usual to such fifteenths and tenths to be contributory and
chargeable within the shires, cities, boroughs,
towns, and other places of this your Majesty's realm, in manner and form aforetime
used; ... and the same three fifteenths and
tenths [are] to be paid unto the hands of
[eight men are here named as treasurers for
the receiving of the subsidy]. ...

And be it further enacted ... that the
knights elected and returned of and for the
shires within this realm for this present Parliament, citizens of cities, burgesses of
boroughs and towns, where collectors have
used to be named and appointed for the col-

lection of any fifteenth and tenth before this time granted, shall name and appoint... sufficient and able persons to be collectors [in their own areas]....

And furthermore, for the great and weighty considerations aforesaid, we the Lords Spiritual etc.... do... give and grant to your Highness... three entire subsidies, to be... levied... in manner and form following: .... As well that every person born within... the King's dominions as all and every fraternity, guild, corporation, mystery, brotherhood, and corporate body... being worth three pounds, for every pound as well in coin... as also plate, stock of merchandise, all manner of corn and grain, household stuff, and of all other goods movable... and of all such sums of money as to him or them is or shall be owing whereof he or they trust in his or their conscience surely to be paid, except and out of the said premises deducted such sums of money as he or they owe and in his or their consciences intendeth truly to pay, and except also the apparel of every such person, their wives, and children, belonging to their own bodies, saving jewels, gold, silver, stone, and pearl, shall pay [for each of the three subsidies 2s. 8d. on each pound value of goods]....

And to the end that all and every the sums of money by this present Act granted as aforesaid... may be truly expended for and towards the uses aforesaid and not otherwise ... be it further enacted, that the moneys to be received by the said Treasurers by virtue of this Act shall be issued out and expended for or towards the uses aforesaid to such person and persons in such manner and form as by the warrant of [ten men are named here as responsible for all expenditures]... which ten persons... his Majesty hath already nominated and hath made choice of to be of his Council for War, or any five or more of them, whereof two of them to be of his Majesty's most honorable Privy Council, under their hands and seals shall be directed and not otherwise; and such warrant and warrants of the said Councillors of War or of any five of

them, whereof two to be of the Privy Council as aforesaid, together with the acquittances of those persons who shall receive those moneys according to those warrants or the inrolment thereof to be for that purpose likewise kept by his Majesty's Remembrancer of the said Court of Exchequer, shall be unto the said Treasurers and every of them their heirs, executors, and administrators a full and sufficient discharge....

And be it further enacted, that as well the said treasurers as the said persons appointed for the Council of War as aforesaid, and all other persons who shall be trusted with the receiving, issuing, bestowing, and employing of these moneys or any part thereof, their heirs, executors, and administrators, shall be answerable and accountable for their doings or proceedings herein to the Commons in Parliament when they shall be thereunto required by warrant under the hand of the Speaker of the House of Commons for the time being, and there they and every of them, according to their several places and employments, shall give a true and a real declaration and account of their several and respective dealings, doings, and proceedings therein; and that the said Commons in Parliament shall have power by this Act to hear and determine the said account and all things thereto appertaining.

And be it further enacted, that for the better preparation of these things for the examination of the House of Commons, and for the more frugal expending of the moneys given by this Act, that the said Council of War or any five or more of them as aforesaid, or such person or persons as they or any five or more of them shall under their hands nominate and appoint, shall by virtue of this Act have power, and by virtue of this Act are required, from time to time to take account of all person and persons of and for all such sums of money as shall be issued to any person or persons to the uses aforesaid, and how they have expended and bestowed the same: provided always, that such account taken by the said Council of War as aforesaid shall not exclude the power of the House of Commons to examine the said accounts and determine the same as aforesaid.

And be it further enacted, that when the Commons in Parliament have heard, examined, and determined the dealings, doings, and proceedings of any the persons aforesaid according to the true intent and meaning of this Act, that then and in every such case the offender or offenders being no Lord or Lords of Parliament shall by the House of Commons be committed to the Tower of London, there to remain close prisoners until by order of the House of Commons they be delivered; and if any the Lords of Parliament shall be found offenders, then the Commons in Parliament shall present their offence to the Lords in Parliament, and thereupon the Lords in Parliament shall have power by virtue of this Act to hear, examine, and determine the offence so presented, and to commit them . . . to the Tower . . . until by order of that House they shall be delivered. . . .

And be it further enacted, that for all and every the several services or purposes mentioned in this Act to be performed in any part beyond the seas, the charge thereof shall be defrayed from time to time out of the treasure raised and given by this Act and not otherwise, either for arms, coat [military uniforms and dress], or conduct [transportation cost] money, or otherwise; and that no part of this money shall be disposed of but for the ends mentioned in this Act, and not for the satisfying of any arrearages due before the beginning of this Parliament; and because these moneys are given for the public service of the whole kingdom and not for any private end, that therefore there shall be no fees required by any person whatsoever for the collecting, receiving, issuing, expending or disposing of any part of these moneys given or granted by this Act, but that the same shall be done freely, without any fee, reward, or allowance. . . . (SR, IV, 1247: 21 and 22 James I, c.33.)

# The Reign of Charles I

# 1625-1642

# England, 1625-1642    Introduction

Prior to the momentous events of 1641 the conflict between the first two Stuart Kings and their Parliaments had resulted in little significant modification of English political institutions or of the administrative forms of government. Due to the constitutional strength of the Common Law, which had served as an effective barrier against encroachment by either side on the traditional rights of the other, Crown and legislature had been restrained from making overly forceful demands which might have precipitated a more violent conflict. The buffer quality of the law, however, only served to augment its vulnerability in the last years of the reign of Charles when the Long Parliament was called into being.

The documents relating to this period of the history of the constitution show that the Parliamentarians were already bent upon destruction of the King's prerogative, that they had decided on bold usurpation of the executive powers, and that they were determined to nullify those aspects of the law and the constitution which might prevent them from achieving these ends. It is within the available evidence to suggest that as early as Charles's first Parliament in 1625, his opposition had decided upon the most effective method to attack both constitution and Crown: that is, exploitation of the customary financial weaknesses of the Monarchy in such a way as to force the King into actions not in accord with the constitution, which, in turn, because of their apparent immorality, would alienate public opinion from the King and establish him as a tyrant bent upon using the theory of Divine Right to attack the rights of private property. Such a plan was, of course, consciously revolutionary and unconstitutional.

Yet the struggle for political sovereignty and control of the constitution was not to be resolved in Parliament's favor through the mere expedient of denying the Crown necessary financial support; the causes of this mutual hostility were too many and complex for that. Thus the contest for control and dominion had to be fought out in every constitutional, political, administrative, and jurisdictional area. It should be ever kept in mind, however, that both sides, Crown and Parliament, regardless of their convictions of personal agency in this conflict, functioned mainly in response to stimulations which had their roots in the rapidly changing political, cultural, and theological conditions of seventeenth-century Europe.

One of the primary causes for Charles's unpopularity with the Parliamentarians was his blind insistence on the immutable quality of his divine right to rule, a theory which ruled out all compromise with either a rapidly changing social order or with other opposing theories. To James Divine Right had been mainly an intellectual conception, documentable when necessary from Scripture, philosophy, and ancient customs; his political actions had reflected a modicum of expedient elasticity reminiscent of Elizabeth's tactical maneuvering. To his son, however, Divine Right was an article of faith imposed by God's will; hence any rationalization was unnecessary. Indeed, all demands for explanation seemed blasphemous to this political mystic, for they questioned, by implication, that divinely revealed Right upon which the well-being and all other rights of the realm rested.

This theory, new as it was to England and efficient as it promised to be, was already outmoded and unacceptable by the time Charles came to the throne. Seventeenth-century political theory was by then already beginning to group itself around two opposed concepts—one based on the principle that the whole people was the repository of political authority and power, and the narrower theory of political Calvinism which held to the sanctity of sovereign control by the elect or saints of God. Hostility to the royal prerogative and the overlapping (though basically diverse) purposes of the Puritans and the upper middle class Parliamentarian made them for a time strange but cooperative political bedfellows. In failing to placate either minority, Charles solidified the alliance against himself and made possible an attack on the constitution which would eventually result in his own ignominious and unnecessary execution.

The question which arises at this point, is, then, one of political method. How could Charles have avoided the consolidation of his opposition—or, more precisely, what were the alternatives, under the constitution, to absolute refusal to negotiate the demands of the two groups. An acute assessment of the various documentary demands such as the *Apology of 1604,* the *Protestation of 1621,* the *Petition of Right,* the *"Three Resolutions,"* the *Grand Remonstrance,* the *Declaration of Purpose,* and the *Nineteen Propositions of 1642,* and the legislative acts relative to the militia, the Church, taxation, tunnage and poundage, and the privileges of Parliament, in the period between the *Apology* and the *Nineteen Propositions,* clearly shows the goals of the opposition. These were two in number: such extreme right of jurisdiction in the several prerogative areas as to destroy the real meaning of kingship, and the right to regulate Church affairs in such a way as to destroy all Anglican and Arminian opposition to domination of the Church by the Puritan minority. Yet the inference that Commons was Puritan-dominated in 1640 is only apparent. A majority of the House, bent on resistance to Charles, was willing to court the support of religious radicalism in a time of immediate crisis and aligned itself with Puritanism for the political nonce. When the extent of Puritan purpose was made clear at the outbreak of hostilities, some who were previously irreconcilable with Charles accepted his cause as their own in order to protect the Common Law from final destruction.

Charles's possible alternatives to negotiation with Parliament and its ardent Puritan supporters prior to mid-summer of 1641 were limited to retreats and compromises which would have gained him nothing and given the opposition stimulation to press forward. Charles was doomed to failure when he ascended the throne in 1625 because the disaffected elements had shifted the ground and purpose of their attack. By 1640 these elements had sufficient public support to rationalize or override all opposition, while Charles, unimaginative in appeal and unsubtle in his theory, held only his obsolete weapon of Divine Right.

Charles's misreading of English history also played a part in his undoing. In Elizabeth's day Parliament had relied upon its ancient position under the constitution which had given it certain rights in formulating policy and law, and in administrative jurisdiction. After 1600, however, that body, realizing the decrepit quality of such anti-quarian arguments, fell back increasingly on utilitarian theories of popular rights for the purpose of attaining equality with the monarchy. By the time of Charles's accession the classes and interests represented in Parliament had proposed to themselves the total destruction of all monarchial claim to power. Charles's arguments and defensive postures, on the other hand, were generally directed at countering the Parliamentary claims of the Elizabethan period; thus the realities of the situation were completely different from what he thought they were. The documents of his reign make it clear that Parliament, and especially the lower House, no longer wished to appear as the defender of the constitution or the law, nor even cared to gild its drive for power with the arguments of the Natural Law, antiquity, and right reason. Charles's lonely vigil by the body of the dying constitution is a measure of his innocence of the political actuality.

Nevertheless, for all of Commons's planning and intrigue, it was Charles's errors in judgment as well as the incapacity of the common law to maintain and protect the political *status quo* which decided the issue. The magnitude of Charles's errors is demonstrable in every area of his administrative action, beginning with his inability to estimate correctly the capacity and disinterestedness of his chosen ministers, and ending with his inopportune and clumsy attempts at foreign policy. Charles conducted most of his affairs with an identical lack of perception. His marriage to Henrietta Maria, sister of Louis XIII, involved him in a contract to allow the maintenance of a Catholic religious group in the royal court. His desire to assume the mantle of Gustavus Adolphus as the protector of continental Protestantism forced him into friction with the French King, who was, like Charles, seeking a solution to the problem of the denial of traditional political authority by a religious minority (in Louis's case the Calvinistically inclined Huguenots). Perhaps Charles's greatest blunder in foreign affairs, judged in terms of domestic results, was in allowing Buckingham to match wits with Cardinal Richelieu. This was especially distasteful to Parliament since Buckingham had already proven his inability to cope with the Spanish King—a person far less gifted in the fine art of international political trickery than the clever and determined French Minister.

None of these errors escaped Parliamentary attention and each in turn stirred a deeper resentment not only toward the King but toward a constitutional system which made it necessary for the many to run the risk of treason charges in attempting to prevent or remedy the unreasoned acts of the one. Throughout the whole of his reign, until the meeting of Long Parliament, Charles foolishly brandished the desperate legal weapon of dissolution against the Parliamentarians who blindly insisted on debating matters of privilege while the war against France—which Parliament had earlier insisted on—continued to go badly for England, and while the King's lack of supply assumed the proportions of a national catastrophe.

The impasse between Crown and Parliament was rationalized by each side on grounds of the general welfare of the realm, an obscure and uncertain justification even in its own time. Neither side was above exploiting the national emergency of war, with all its adverse domestic, economic, and sociological by-products, as a mechanism for boosting itself in the public esteem at the other's expense. Unbending, nursing principles and theories of polity that few but he appreciated, Charles was never able to evaluate objectively the factors involved in the general welfare he defended. Consequently, he could not think of placing the common good on a higher plane than his mystical adoration of the royal prerogative.

Similar subjectivism destroyed much of the potential value of Parliament in the period prior to 1641, for it, too, was unable to set the general welfare above its own political aims. Thus, while each side employed all the rhetorical paraphernalia of ancient custom, public utility, and divinely inspired obligation in its pronouncements, both made clear, in actual practice, their real social irresponsibility.

It is unnecessary to point out the quality or duration or results of the evils which beset the nation as a result of the failure of the King and his Parliaments to come to terms. War, successful or not, and the daily attrition of governmental administrative action, must be paid for. Without funds from Parliament, Charles was thrown back upon constitutional devices of questionable morality—forced loans, tunnage and poundage assessments, quartering of soldiers on private persons, and imprisonment of any who resisted these measures. Professing to see in this fiscal program the actions of a tyrant but mainly afraid of losing its financial hold on the Crown should these measures be allowed to stand as precedents, Commons counselled resistance by lending its support to those who refused the King's demands, by expression of sympathy toward the victims, and by public statements that only Parliament had the right to take money from the people for governmental use. One case of this support was that of the five knights who refused to pay a forced loan to the King in 1627 and who, when imprisoned, appealed to the judges of the King's Bench for the right of release on bail. Justice Hyde's decision in this case must stand as a constitutional milestone in English history, for he rejected the Parliamentary stand against the prerogative when he told the knights, "The precedents are all against you." Clearly Parliament's plea against the King was not in accord with the Common Law; and the judges, as the final arbiters of the law in its application, established themselves as the next most important barrier to Parliamentary conquest of political dominance. Future legislation was to render the judges accountable to Parliament and thus destroy their independent operation within the constitution.

However, the documentary evidence of Parliament's aggressive intentions against the constitutional settlement goes beyond this first and most obvious example. The area of religious debate provided that institution with another field for violent attack wherein it could appeal for popular support against the alleged despotism of the King, this time in the field of religion.

By 1628 Charles had already dissolved two Parliaments for failing to provide the funds necessary to government. At that time, being unwilling to risk greater discontent by increasing extra-parliamentary revenues, Charles again issued writs of election for the calling of a third meeting. The time was most inopportune, for by 1628 another grievance had caught the popular fancy—the question of Arminianism.

Arminius, a theologian at Leyden, had some years previously given the continental reformation a new shock by preaching a doctrine opposed to Calvinist dogma. Arminius rejected the concept of predestination in favor of the idea that man was a creature of free will, that is, free to accept or reject the Divine grace necessary to salvation. Anglicanism,

having never disavowed the Catholic acceptance of free will, found Arminius's teachings stimulating, and English interest in this theological point served to emphasize the
main differences between the established Church and the Puritan sects, who were convinced that Arminius was a heretic. But this man's doctrines had gone even further. He
denied one of the basic premises of the entire Protestant movement in holding that
Church tradition and good works were almost equal to Scripture as aids to salvation,
and, further, that images, religious music, and rituals had real spiritual value, and that
the priest was a necessary adjunct to Christianity.

The clergy of the established Church, already on the defensive against the growing
demands of Puritanism, and fearful of any reform in the direction of Calvinism which
would threaten their own security, were forced into even closer political alliance with
the King, an alliance which King James had clearly defined in the Hampden Court debates: "No Bishop, no King." The clergy further took it upon themselves to defend the
King from the pulpit against his enemies, for such enemies were certainly capable of
crushing the clergy as well unless practical steps were taken. This was by no means an
alliance of equals. Even more than Charles the clergy realized the strength of the Puritans and the danger to the established order—and the greater the fear, the more abject
the retreat of the churchmen to the protection of the King. Hence there developed
within the Church a cult of non-resistance to the monarchial will and voice, which
raised the King, that "minor magistrate in the eyes of God," to a position of undoubted
supremacy in the Church.

Thus, to the Puritans, King and Church were identical mockeries of God's word as
revealed through the true Church. Yet as long as the Crown maintained its preference
for Anglicanism they could not hope to inaugurate constitutionally a program of
change. Quite clearly, by the time of the Arminian dispute, the Puritans were disposed
to revamp James's phrase to read "No King, no Bishop," and it was plainly recognized by
the middle of Charles's reign that any hopes of constitutional alterations were idle fan-
cies, while the new danger was looming that the Anglican Church might move, under
Arminian influence, towards the right and Rome.

Yet Arminianism was not Catholicism and Charles had small inclination to despotism. At the opening of the Parliament of 1628 he agreed that some action in religious
affairs was necessary; and sensing an easy victory the House of Commons turned
again to the question of its grievances and brought forth the *Petition of Right* with
its purely negative resolutions against forced loans, arbitrary imprisonment, quartering
of soldiers on private persons, and issuance of warrants and commissions of martial law.

Some students of the period feel that the *Petition* remedied many of the evils resulting from the King's overly enthusiastic use of the prerogative. However, a closer look
will show that the *Petition* was spectacularly defective in that it represented a victory of
unchecked and politically motivated emotionalism over objective consideration. Basically this document was a negation of authority rather than a creative solution to existing problems, and it finally brought King and Parliament to a constitutional stalemate
from which neither could retreat. Further, it bared a glaring defect in the Parliamentary
program inasmuch as with its enactment the constitutional thought of the Parliamentary
leaders came to an end. The King's powers were checked, but a vacuum was created

through Parliament's failure to create any system of executive authority to take the place of what was destroyed.

From the *Petition* to the civil war was not a difficult step, for with Parliament's dissolution in 1629 the King once again confronted the dilemma of governing without funds. The ensuing eleven-year period of Charles's personal government, usually but inadequately described as a time of despotism, gave the opposition time to consolidate its public support and prepare the ground for its final attack on the prerogative when next Parliament should be called into being. That it would have to be called seemed certain to the Parliamentarians since Charles's policies would either eventually necessitate his asking for funds or would so deeply stir popular resentment as to force him to seek the validation of the legislature. In the end their prognostications proved correct— for Strafford's policy of "thorough" and Bishop Laud's program of harshly enforced religious uniformity generated extreme domestic discontent. The King's use of the royal Councils of Wales and the North to enforce social justice in favor of the yeoman impoverished by enclosures further strengthened the middle class suspicion of Charles's planned tyranny, and the war with the Scottish Covenantors in 1638 came to stand as final proof.

Yet Charles's determination to fortify the monarchy might not have proven disastrous had he not made the ultimate miscalculation of underestimating the strength of the Covenantors—or conversely, had he realized that he could not cope with an armed and aroused Scotland without the funds for war, and that to obtain these he must call Parliament into session. Thus, the Short Parliament, dissolved after only three weeks, met in an unyielding mood, and after dismissing the Crown's plea for supply fell at once to discussing the misuse of the prerogative and its own grievances. Clearly the realm had deserted Charles. In the face of invasion by the Scottish armies Parliament had refused his leadership. Yet he had no choice but to assemble once more the institution which was openly hostile to his very existence. In November of 1640 the Long Parliament was called by the King—and its members met with the intention of dismantling the Monarchy. Strafford was destroyed, a *Triennial Act* insured periodic meetings of Parliament, the collection of revenue became by statute the sole right of Parliament, the prerogative courts were abolished along with the Councils of the North and Wales, ship-money was declared illegal, and forced loans and distraint of knighthood forbidden.

Charles, having given up Strafford and Laud to their enemies, passively accepted all the bills placed before him and signed away his powers. Yet there remained the problem of the *Grand Remonstrance*. Parliament and the Puritans, with all political authority in their hands, were determined to impose a religious settlement and discipline on England of a far harsher nature than ever Laud's had been, and the *Remonstrance* was the instrument of their purpose. No doubt Charles would have accepted this bill as statute as he had the others if the moderates in both Houses had not rejected it and demanded that the King take active measures for its denial. Their resistance to the extreme intolerance expressed by the *Remonstrance* gave the King a party and set him on a course of reinstating the monarchic constitutional rights, a course which made civil war inevitable.

## Thomas Hobbes, *The Leviathan*. 1651

IN HIS *Leviathan* Hobbes erected perhaps the most formidable political theory of
the entire Tudor-Stuart period. That its impact on English constitutional thought in
the last half of the seventeenth century was great cannot be denied—although its
actual influence can only be surmised. This uncertainty is due in large part to the
mixed public reaction to the work in its own day.

92.

Hobbes's main intent appears on the surface to have been defense of the sovereign
rights of the Crown. Yet his ideas were not well received by the royalists of England,
because his fundamental principles were as much in opposition to the claims of the
Stuarts as they were to those of the Puritans and Parliamentarians whom he meant to
refute. Clearly Hobbes's defense of royal absolutism was superficial, for indeed, his
real purpose was the defense of *de facto* government no matter what its form.

The abiding significance of Hobbes's political theories is centered in three main
concepts: his individualism, his utilitarianism, and his acceptance of the need for
political sovereignty. Since the alternative to anarchy or a "state of nature," where
man's life would be "solitary, poor, nasty, brutish, and short," was association in a
political state, individual men chose—and continue to choose by passive acceptance—
to form societies by compact or contract wherein each surrendered to a chosen authority
his individual right to use force in protecting his life, property, and happiness. This
act of association was freely made by man for his own selfish ends. No principle repos-
ing in nature, no divine inspiration, no higher force drove man into society, but only his
desire for greater security. The results derived from this association are plainly utilitarian
in that it satisfied an urgent need for security. It is, according to Hobbes, only for
that reason that man established government and appointed governors to whom was
given the sovereign power.

It was this individualism and utilitarianism which was so distasteful to the royalists.
According to Robert Filmer, James I had received his patent to rule by way of direct
genealogical succession from Adam, and, according to the Divine Rights theory, each
king was directly appointed by God. In Hobbes's concept self-interest, not divine
inspiration, was basic to social union and the king was the result rather than the
initiator of civil union.

The third significant concept found in Hobbes's works was the overriding validity
of political sovereignty. Since the Stuarts claimed the sovereign power, this might
appear as an aid to them. Yet even this was illusory. Sovereignty, popularly established,
was not limited to any particular form of government. Hobbes broadened the category
of reasonable governments to include any type of social regulation which was capable
of defending its own existence; and its *de facto* status was more important to him than
its *de jure* claim.

This was certainly one of the most revolutionary formulations in all seventeenth-
century England. Not even the most radical of the sectarian theorists of the Cromwellian period could have deviated so far from precedent and tradition as to place
free choice in political affairs in man's hands alone. Nevertheless, in its use as a
propaganda device the idea of popular sovereignty appealed to the Puritans of that
time.

.... In the nature of man we find three
principal causes of quarrel. First, competition; second, diffidence; thirdly, glory.

The first maketh men invade for gain; the
second for safety; and the third for reputation. The first use violence to make themselves masters of other men's persons, wives,
children, and cattle; the second to defend

them; the third for trifles such as a word, a smile, a different opinion, and any other sign of undervalue, either direct in their persons, or by reflection in their kindred, their friends, their nation, their profession, or their name.

. . . . It is manifest that during the time men lived without a common power to keep them all in awe they were in that condition which is called war; and such a war as is of every man against every man. For WAR consists not in battle only, or the act of fighting; but in a tract of time wherein the will to contend by battle is sufficiently known, and therefore the notion of TIME is to be considered in the nature of war as it is in the nature of weather. For as the nature of foul weather lies not in a shower or two of rain, but in an inclination thereto of many days together, so the nature of war consists not in actual fighting, but in the known disposition thereto, during all the time there is no assurance to the contrary. All other time is PEACE.

Whatsoever therefore is consequent to a time of war, where every man is enemy to every man; the same is consequent to the time, wherein men live without other security, than what their own strength, and their own invention shall furnish them withal. In such condition there is no place for industry, because the fruit thereof is uncertain, and consequently no culture of the earth, no navigation, nor use of the commodities that may be imported by sea, no force, no knowledge of the face of the earth, no account of time, no arts, no letters, no society, and which is worst of all, continual fear, and danger of violent death, and the life of man, solitary, poor, nasty, brutish, and short.

A *commonwealth* is said to be *instituted* when a *multitude* of men do agree and *covenant, every one, with every one,* that to whatsoever, *man,* or *assembly of men,* shall be given by the major part, the *right* to *present* the person of them all, that is to say, to be their *representative:* every one, as well he that *voted for it* as he that *voted against*

*it,* shall *authorize* all the actions and judgments of that man or assembly of men, in the same manner, as if they were his own, to the end to live peaceably amongst themselves, and be protected against other men.

From this institution of a commonwealth are derived all the *rights,* and *faculties* of him, or them, on whom sovereign power is conferred by the consent of the people assembled.

First, because they covenant, it is to be understood they are not obliged by former covenant to anything repugnant hereunto. And consequently they that have already instituted a commonwealth, being thereby bound by covenant, to own the actions and judgments of one, cannot lawfully make a new covenant amongst themselves to be obedient to any other in anything whatsoever without his permission. And therefore, they that are subject to a monarch cannot without his leave cast off monarchy, and return to the confusion of a disunited multitude, or transfer their person from him that bears in to another man or other assembly of men, for they are bound, every man to every man, to own, and be reputed author of all, that . . . their sovereign, shall do, . . . so that any one man dissenting, all the rest should break their covenant made to that man, which is injustice: and they have also every man given the sovereignty to him that bears their person; and therefore if they depose him, they take from him that which is his own, and so again it is injustice. . . .

. . . . That he which is made sovereign makes no covenant with his subjects beforehand is manifest; because either he must make it with the whole multitude, as one party to the covenant, or he must make a several covenant with every man. With the whole, as one part, it is impossible; because as yet they are not one person: and if he make so many several covenants as there be men, those covenants after he has the sovereignty are void; because what act soever can be pretended by any one of them for breach thereof, is the act both of himself and of all the rest, because done in the person, and by the right of every one of them in particular. Besides, if any one, or more of them, pretend a breach of the covenant made by the sovereign at his institution; and others, or one other of his subjects, or himself alone, pretend there was no such breach, there is in this case, no judge to decide the controversy; it returns therefore to the sword again; and every man recovers the right of protecting himself by his own strength, contrary to the design they had in the institution. It is therefore in vain to grant sovereignty by way of precedent covenant. The opinion that any monarch receives his power by covenant, that is to say, on condition, proceeds from want of understanding this easy truth, that covenants being but words and breath, have no force to oblige, contain, constrain, or protect any man, but what it has from the public sword; . . . .

Thirdly, because the major part has by consenting voices declared a sovereign; he that dissented must now consent with the rest; . . . .

Fourthly, because every subject is by this institution author of all the actions and judgments of the sovereign instituted; it follows, that whatsoever he does, it can be no injury to any of his subjects; nor ought he to be by any of them accused of injustice. . . .

Fifthly, and consequently to what was last said, no man that has sovereign power can justly be put to death, . . . for seeing every subject is author of the actions of his sovereign, he punishes another for the actions committed by himself. . . .

Sixthly, it is annexed to the sovereignty, to be judge of what opinions and doctrines are averse, and what conducing to peace. . . .

Seventhly, it is annexed to the sovereignty, the whole power of prescribing the rules, whereby every man may know what goods he may enjoy, and what actions he may do . . . and this it is men call *propriety*. . . . These rules of propriety . . . are the civil laws; that is to say, the laws of each commonwealth in particular; . . . .

Eighthly, is annexed to the sovereignty, the right of judicature; that is to say, of hearing and deciding all controversies, which may arise concerning law, either civil, or natural, or concerning fact. . . .

Ninthly, is annexed to the sovereignty, the right of making war and peace with other nations, and commonwealths; that is to say, of judging when it is for the public good, . . . .

Tenthly, . . . the choosing of all counselors, ministers, magistrates, and officers both in peace and war. . . .

. . . . Lastly, considering what value men are naturally apt to set upon themselves, what respect they look for from others, and how little they value other men; from whence continually arise among them, emulation, quarrels, factions, and at last war, to the destroying of one another, and diminution of their strength against a common enemy; it is necessary that there be laws. . . . To the sovereign, therefore, it belongs also to give titles of honor, and to appoint what order of place and dignity each man shall hold, and what signs of respect, in public or private meetings, they shall give to one another. . . . (Thomas Hobbes, *The Leviathan*, 1651, ed. of 1849.)

## Charles I: Letter to the House of Commons Concerning Subsidies. 1626

THE following letter was the first of the King's numerous pleas to Commons to perform the constitutional task for which it had been called into being. Such documents and the records of House debates make it clear that Parliament's main objective in delaying supply during the first five years of Charles's reign was to force him into some arbitrary action which would make it possible for Parliament to reopen the question of its own privileges and popular rights.

93.

Trusty and well-beloved, we greet you well.

Our House of Commons cannot forget how often and how earnestly we have called upon them for the speeding of that aid which they intended unto us [tunnage and poundage, a traditional subsidy] for our great and weighty affairs concerning the safety and honor of us and our Kingdoms; and now, in the time being so far spent that, unless it be presently concluded, it can neither bring us money nor credit by the time which themselves have prefixed; which is the last of this month— and being further deferred would be of little use. We being daily advertised from all parts of the great preparations of the enemy, ready to assail us, we hold it necessary by these our letters to give them our last and final admonition, and let them know that we shall account all further delays and excuses to be express denials.

And therefore we will and require you to signify unto them that we do expect that they forthwith bring forth their bill of subsidy to be passed without delay or condition, so as it may fully pass that House by the end of the next week at the furthest;—which if they do not, it will force us to take other resolutions. But let them know that, if they finish this according to our desire, that we are resolved to let them sit together for the dispatch of their other affairs and, after their recess, to bring them together again the next winter. And if by their denial or delay anything of ill consequences shall fall out either at home or abroad, we may call God and man to witness that we have done our part to prevent it by calling our people together to advise with us, by opening the weight of our occasions unto them, and by requiring their timely help and assistance in those actions wherein we stand engaged by their own counsels. And we will and command you that this letter be publicly read in the House. (*Journals of the House of Lords,* III, 670)

## Charles I: Ordinance for the Levying of Customs. 1626

**94.** PARLIAMENT'S hope that Charles, made desperate by need, would resort to the arbitrary tactics of his predecessor was fully satisfied by this ordinance, which reinstated all the "customs, subsidy, and imposts ... as the same were levied, collected, and received in the time of our late dear father." Some of the duties enumerated here had fallen into disuse and some had been foresworn by James in bargaining for Parliamentary supply. Charles's action was especially dangerous because it took cases arising out of non-payment of the customs from the Common Law Courts and turned them over to the Privy Council.

Charles, by the Grace of God King of England, [etc.] ... to whom these presents shall come, greeting:

Whereas the Lords and others of our Privy Council have taken into their serious consideration the present state of our revenue arising by customs, subsidy, and impost upon goods and merchandise to be exported and imported out of and into this our Realm of England and dominion of Wales and port and town of Berwick, and finding that it hath been constantly continued for many ages, and is now a principal part of the revenue of our Crown and is of necessity to be so continued for the supportation thereof, and which in the two last Parliaments hath been thought upon, but could not there be settled by authority of Parliament as from time to time by many ages and descents past it hath been by reason of the dissolution of those Parliaments before those things which were there treated of could be perfected—have therefore ... especially ordered that all those duties upon goods and merchandise, called by the several names of customs, subsidy, and imposts, should be levied, collected, and received for our use in such manner and form as the same were levied, collected, and received in the time of our late dear father, King James of blessed memory ... and forasmuch as, through the want of a Parliamentary course to settle the payment of those duties, many inconveniences may arise which would tend to the impairing of our revenue of that nature, if in convenient time some settled course should not be taken for the prevention thereof:

.... We ... by the advice of the Lords and others of our Privy Council, do by these presents declare our will and pleasure to be that all those duties upon goods and merchandises ... shall be levied, collected, and received in such manner and form as the same were levied, collected, and received at the time of the decease of our said late father.

.... And if any person or persons whatsoever shall refuse or neglect to pay the duties, customs, subsidies, or imposts aforesaid ... we do further grant by these presents unto the Lords and others of our Privy Council ... or unto the Lord Treasurer of England or Chancellor of our Exchequer ... full power and authority to commit all and every such person ... to prison. ... (T. Rymer, *Foedera, Conventiones, Litterae, et ... Acta Publica,* XVIII, 737.)

## Chief Justice Hyde's Decision and Reasoning in the Case of the Five Knights. 1627

CONSEQUENT to their refusal to comply with Charles's demand for a forced loan, a number of individuals were imprisoned. Five among them sued in the Court of the King's Bench for writs of *habeas corpus*. When the Warden of the Fleet Prison refused to comply with the writs and release the prisoners, the case was appealed to Chief Justice Hyde who exonerated the warden, rejected the writs, and remanded the five to prison. The reasoning of the Chief Justice in this case was brought under attack by Parliament's *Petition of Right* the following year.

**95.**

.... We [the judges] are sworn to maintain all prerogatives of the King; that is one branch of our oath. And we are likewise sworn to administer justice equally to all people. ...

That which is now to be judged by us is this: whether any one that is committed by the King's authority, and [with] no cause declared of his commitment ... we ought to deliver him by bail or to remand him back [to prison]. ...

The exceptions which have been taken to this return were two: the one for the form, the other for the substance. ... In our case the cause of the detention is sufficiently answered, which is the demand of the writ; and therefore we resolve that the form of this return is good. The next thing is the main point in law, whether the substance or matter of the return be good or no—wherein the substance is this: he [the warden of the Fleet]

doth certify that they are detained in prison by the special command of the King. [The five knights, having refused the King's demand for a forced loan, were imprisoned in the Fleet by the King. Their suit to activate writs of *habeas corpus* which had been refused by the warden resulted in the decision here rendered.] Whether this be good in law or not, that is the question. ...

The precedents are all against you, every one of them. And what shall guide our judgments, since there is nothing alleged in this case but precedents? That, if no cause of the commitment be expressed, it is presumed to be a matter of State, which we cannot take notice of. You see we find none—no, not one that hath been delivered by bail in the like cases, but by the hand of the King or his direction.

.... The common custom of the law is the Common Law of the land, and that hath been the continual common custom of the law, to which we are to submit; for we come not to change the law, but to submit to it....

But the question now is whether we may deliver this gentleman or not.... Mr. Attorney hath told you that the King hath done it, and we trust him in great matters. And he is bound by law, and he bids us proceed by

law as we are sworn to do, and so is the King. And we make no doubt but the King, if you seek him ... will have mercy. But we leave that. If in justice we ought to deliver you, we would do it; but upon these grounds and these records, and the precedents and resolutions, we cannot deliver you.... (T. B. Howell, *State Trials*, III, 51)

## The Petition of Right. 1628

**96.**

THE judgment of Chief Justice Hyde in the case of the five knights rested upon the pleading of the Warden of the Fleet Prison that he could not relinquish custody of the knights since he held them "by the special command of his Majesty." Here indeed was something for the members of Commons to think upon, for it brought several things into clearer focus. The Common Law defenses of private property were nullified and Charles had the legal right to continue to exact forced loans. Providing Charles had the courage to take sufficient money by this method he would be free of the most important Parliamentary limitations on his liberty to act in matters of foreign and domestic policy.

Beyond the matter of private property the decision placed the King above the law. It also made clear to Parliament that the Courts were allied with the Crown and in the present circumstances would interpret any law in such a way as to defeat every Parliamentary purpose.

But in Hyde's decision there was a hint for possible future Parliamentary action. Speaking of the several elements of the case the Chief Justice pointed out that "Mr. Attorney ... is bound by the law, and he bade us [the judges] to proceed by the law as we are sworn to do, and so is the King." The *Petition of Right* was a logical elaboration of Hyde's argument. If the King was bound by the law and the Judges would enforce the law, then Parliament must make the law concrete by giving it statute form and by making the King accept it. With this thought before them the Parliamentarians were very careful in the *Petition* not to render another loosely and subjectively constructed instrument such as the *Apology of 1604*. Instead both Lords and Commons were closely attentive to the compiling of legal precedents and sound arguments which would strengthen their cause.

The *Petition* is often referred to as one of the three most important English constitutional documents limiting the power of the Monarch, being given almost equal place with *Magna Carta* and the *Bill of Rights*. Although there is some justification for this, it should not be forgotten that Parliament in constructing the *Petition* was more interested in protecting traditional rights and liberties than in attempting to establish revolutionary limitations on the power of the King. Yet since the Crown had every right to expect from Parliament an income sufficient to orderly government and national security, it is clear that that body departed from accepted constitutional practices in using Crown poverty as a method of forcing Charles's acceptance of the document. Political expediency was by no means a Crown monopoly.

The Petition exhibited to his Majesty by the Lords Spiritual and Temporal, and Commons in this present Parliament assembled, concerning divers rights and liberties of the subjects....

To the King's most excellent Majesty:

Humbly show unto our Sovereign Lord the King the Lords Spiritual and Temporal, and Commons in Parliament assembled, that, whereas it is declared and enacted by a statute made in the time of the reign of King Edward I, commonly called *Statutum de Tallagio non Concedendo,* that no tallage or aid should be laid or levied by the King or his heirs in this Realm without the goodwill and assent of the archbishops, bishops, earls, barons, knights, burgesses, and other the freemen of the commonalty of this Realm; and, by authority of Parliament holden in the five and twentieth year of the reign of King Edward III, it is declared and enacted that from thenceforth no person should be compelled to make any loans to the King against his will, because such loans were against reason and the franchise of the land; and by other laws of this Realm it is provided that none should be charged by any charge or imposition, called a benevolence, or by such like charge; by which the statutes before mentioned, and other the good laws and statutes of this Realm, your subjects have inherited this freedom, that they should not be compelled to contribute to any tax, tallage, aid, or other like charge not set by common consent in Parliament; yet, nevertheless, of late divers commissions directed to sundry commissioners in several counties with instructions have issued, by means whereof your people have been in divers places assembled and required to lend certain sums of money unto your Majesty; and many of them, upon their refusal to do so, have had an oath administered unto them, not warrantable by the laws or statutes of this Realm, and have been constrained to become bound to make appearance and give attendance before your Privy Council and in other places; and others of them have been therefor imprisoned, confined, and sundry other ways molested and disquieted; and divers other charges have been laid and levied upon your people in several counties by lord lieutenants, deputy lieutenants, commissioners for musters, Justices of Peace, and others, by command or direction from your Majesty or your Privy Council, against the laws and free customs of this Realm.

And where also, by the statute called the Great Charter of the Liberties of England, it is declared and enacted that no freeman may be taken or imprisoned, or be disseised of his freehold or liberties or his free customs, or be outlawed or exiled or in any manner destroyed, but by the lawful judgment of his peers or by the law of the land; and in the eight and twentieth year of the reign of King Edward III it was declared and enacted by authority of Parliament that no man, of what estate or condition that he be, should be put out of his land or tenements, nor taken, nor imprisoned, nor disherited, nor put to death, without being brought to answer by due process of law:

Nevertheless, against the tenor of the said statutes and other the good laws and statutes of your Realm to that end provided, divers of your subjects have of late been imprisoned without any cause showed; and when for their deliverance they were brought before your Justices by your Majesty's writs of *habeas corpus,* there to undergo and receive as the court should order, and their keepers commanded to certify the causes of their detainer, no cause was certified, but that they were detained by your Majesty's special command, signified by the Lords of your Privy Council; and yet were returned back to several prisons, without being charged with anything to which they might make answer according to the law.

And whereas of late great companies of soldiers and mariners have been dispersed into divers counties of the Realm, and the inhabitants against their wills have been compelled to receive them into their houses, and there to suffer them to sojourn, against the laws and customs of this Realm, and to the great grievance and vexation of the people: and whereas also, by authority of Parliament in the five and twentieth year of the reign of King Edward III, it is declared and enacted that no man should be forejudged of life or limb against the form of the Great Charter and law of the land; and, by the said Great Charter and other the laws and statutes of this your realm, no man ought to be adjudged to death but by the laws established in this your realm, either by the customs of the same Realm or by acts of Parliament; and whereas no offender of what kind soever is exempted from the proceedings to be used, and punishments to be inflicted by the laws and statutes of this your Realm: nevertheless of late divers commissions under your Majesty's great seal have issued forth, by which certain persons have been assigned and appointed commissioners, with power and authority to proceed within the land according to the justice of martial law against such soldiers or mariners, or other dissolute persons joining with them, as should commit any murder, robbery, felony, mutiny, or other outrage or misdemeanor whatsoever, and by such summary course and order as is agreeable to martial law and as is used in armies in time of war, to proceed to the trial and condemnation of such offenders, and then to cause to be executed and put to death according to the law martial; by pretext whereof some of your Majesty's subjects have been by some of the said commissioners put to death, when and where, if by the laws and statutes of the land they had deserved death, by the same laws and statutes also they might, and by no other ought to have been, adjudged and executed; and also sundry grievous offenders, by color thereof claiming an exemption, have escaped the punishments due to them by the laws and statutes of this your Realm, by reason that divers of your officers and ministers of justice have unjustly refused or forborne to proceed against such offenders ... upon pretence that ... offenders were punishable only by martial law and by authority of such commissions as aforesaid; which commissions and all other of like nature are wholly and directly contrary to the said laws and statutes of this your Realm.

They do therefore humbly pray your most excellent Majesty that no man hereafter be compelled to make or yield any gift, loan, benevolence, tax, or such like charge without common consent by act of Parliament, and that none be called to make answer, or take such oath, or to give attendance, or be confined, or otherwise molested or disquieted concerning the same, or for refusal thereof; and that no freeman, in any such manner as is before mentioned, be imprisoned or detained; and that your Majesty would be pleased to remove the said soldiers and mariners; and that your people may not be so burdened in time to come; and that the foresaid commissions for proceeding by martial law may be revoked and annulled; and that hereafter no commissions of like nature may issue forth to any person or persons whatsoever, to be executed as aforesaid, lest by color of them any of your Majesty's subjects be destroyed or put to death, contrary to the laws and franchise of the land ... and that your Majesty would also vouchsafe and declare that the awards, doings, and proceedings to the prejudice of your people in any of the premises shall not be drawn hereafter into consequence or example; and that your Majesty would be also graciously pleased, for the further comfort and safety of your people, to declare your Royal will and pleasure that in the things aforesaid all your officers and ministers shall serve you according to the laws and statutes of this Realm, as they tender the honor of your Majesty and the prosperity of this kingdom. (*Statutes of the Realm*, V, 23.)

## Charles I: Speech to Commons in Answer to the Petition of Right. 1628

PARLIAMENT'S immediate reaction to the King's acceptance of the *Petition of Right* was one of broad and almost irresponsible interpretation. Limitations on the King's power not incorporated in the bill were now treated as political realities in the debates of Commons, while further limitations were prepared in a new petition. Chief among the new demands to be made was that the King publicly confirm his willingness to discontinue tunnage and poundage impositions.

## 97.

In desperation Charles closed the session with the avowal that "I owe an account of my actions to none but God alone." However, the interruption of Parliamentary proceedings worked against the King in two ways. First, supply was absolutely curtailed as long as Parliament was inactive, and second, the members, returned to their constituencies, were in an even better position to appeal for popular support.

My Lords and Gentlemen:

It may seem strange that I come so suddenly to end this session. Wherefore, before I give my assent to the bills, I will tell you the cause; though I must avow that I owe an account of my actions to none but to God alone. It is known to every one that a while ago the House of Commons gave me a remonstrance. How acceptable it is every man may judge. And for the merit of it, I will not call that in question; for I am sure no wise man can justify it. Now, since I am certainly informed that a second remonstrance is preparing for me, to take away my profit of tunnage and poundage, one of the chief maintenances of the crown, by alleging that I have given away my right thereof by my answer to your petition, this is so prejudicial unto me that I am forced to end this session some few hours before I meant it, being willing not to receive any more remonstrances to which I must give an harsh answer. And since I see that even the House of Commons begins already to make false constructions of what I granted in your petition; lest it might be worse interpreted in the country, I will now make a declaration concerning the true meaning thereof.

The profession in both Houses, in time of constructing this petition, was by no ways to entrench upon my prerogative, saying they had neither intention or power to hurt it. Therefore it must needs be conceived that I have granted no new, but only confirmed the ancient, liberties of my subjects. Yet, to show the clearness of my intentions, that I neither repent nor mean to recede from anything I have promised you, I do here declare that those things which have been done—whereby men had some cause to suspect the liberty of the subjects to be trenched upon, which indeed was the first and true ground of the petition—shall not hereafter be drawn into example for your prejudice; and in time to come—on the word of a King—you shall not have the like cause to complain. But as for tunnage and poundage, it is a thing I cannot want and was never intended by you to ask, never meant, I am sure, by me to grant. To conclude, I command you all that are here to take notice of what I have spoken at this time, to be the true intent and meaning of what I granted you in your petition. But you, my Lords and judges... to you only under me belongs the interpretation of the laws; for none of the House of Commons, joint or separate, what new doctrine soever may be raised, have any power either to make or declare a law without my consent. (*Journals of the House of Lords*, III, 835.)

## The "Three Resolutions" Passed by the House of Commons in Defiance of the King's Dissolution of Parliament. 1629.

**98.**  CHARLES'S speech to Parliament in 1628 and his termination of that session were both in part intended to prevent the formulation of a more precise petition against his tunnage and poundage impositions. Subsequently Charles continued to make them on the grounds that they were part of the ancient custom. When, in 1629, the King ordered Parliament dissolved for its insistence on discussing the matter, served members, in open defiance of the King's wishes, forcefully held the Speaker in his chair while the three resolutions were passed amid great tumult.

While there is no mistaking the hostility of the resolutions, their constitutional significance lies in their fundamental purpose: they constitute Parliament's first clear statement in the long struggle for ministerial responsibility. Unable to control the King through the direct methods of political action, the Parliamentarians chose the oblique but effective means of attempting to control the members of his Council. The "Three Resolutions" dimly foreshadowed the Cabinet form of government, which was not to be fully stabilized until the middle of the next century.

Whosoever shall bring in innovation of religion, or by favor or countenance seek to extend or introduce popery or Arminianism, or other opinion disagreeing from the true and orthodox Church, shall be ... capital enemy to this Kingdom and commonwealth.

Whosoever shall counsel or advise the taking and levying of the subsidies of tunnage and poundage, not being granted by Parliament, or shall be an actor or instrument therein, shall be likewise reputed an innovator in the government, and a capital enemy to the Kingdom and commonwealth.

If any merchant or person whatsoever shall voluntarily yield or pay the said subsidies of tunnage and poundage, not being granted by Parliament, he shall likewise be reputed a betrayer of the liberties of England, and an enemy to the same. (Rushworth, *Historical Collections,* I, 660.)

## Writ of the King for the Collection of Ship Money. 1634

**99.**  HAVING dissolved Parliament in 1629, Charles was forced to locate new sources of Crown income. Ship money, a tax traditionally levied only on certain ports for the support of the Navy in time of war, was now made into a general levy on the theory that the Navy protected the entire realm, and that therefore every area should bear part of the burden. Charles's need was real and he employed the money for naval purposes. To his subjects however this seemed a further denial of the *Petition of Right* as well as a direct attack on private property. Two main constitutional questions grew from the problem of ship money. Did the King have the legal right to demand the tax without Parliamentary agreement? If the King had that right, could he legally reapportion the levy so as to include those areas traditionally not affected by it?

Charles, King [etc.] ... to the mayor, commonalty, and citizens of our city of London, and to the sheriffs of the same city and good men in the said city and in the [various parts of the same city] ... greeting:

Because we are given to understand that certain thieves, pirates, and robbers of the sea, as well Turks, enemies of the Christian name, as others ... are wickedly taking by force and spoiling the ships and goods and merchandises, not only of our subjects, but also of the subjects of our friends in the sea, which has been accustomed anciently to be defended by the English nation . . . and also in consideration of the dangers which do hang over our heads, [it behooves] . . . us and our subjects to hasten to the defence of the sea and Kingdom with all expedition or speed that we can . . . and, although that charge of defence which concerns all men ought to be supported by all . . . you, constituted in the sea-coasts . . . are chiefly bound to set your helping hand:

We command firmly, enjoining you . . . that you cause to be prepared and brought to the port of Portsmouth before the first day of March now next ensuing one ship of war of the burden of 900 tons, with 350 men at the least, as well expert masters as very able and skilful mariners; and one other ship of war of the burden of 800 tons, with 260 men at

the least; and four other ships of war, every of them of the burden of 500 tons and every of them with at least 200 men; and one other ship of war of the burden of 300 tons, with 150 men . . . and also every of the said ships [are to be fully outfitted] with ordnance, as well greater as lesser, gunpowder and spears and weapons and other necessary arms sufficient for war, and with double tackling and victuals until the said first of March competent for so many men; and from that time for twenty-six weeks at your charges as well in victuals as men's wages and other things necessary for war. . . . Also we have assigned you, the aforesaid mayor and aldermen of the city aforesaid . . . to assess all men in the said city and its parts of the same . . . to contribute to the expenses about the necessary provision of the premises. . . . [and to commit any who refuse payment] (Rushworth, *Historical Collections*, II, 257.)

## King Charles's Appeal to the Judges for an Opinion Regarding the Legality of a General Ship Money Levy. 1637

REALIZING the danger inherent in taxing the entire realm for an item which had been traditionally limited to a particular geographic area, Charles appealed to the judges for a decision on the legal right of the Crown to force payment of the tax. He hoped by this act to prevent protracted pleadings in the Courts and to make the tax legally impregnable. The judges' decision, reminiscent of its findings in the case of the Five Knights a decade earlier, gave Charles the unqualified right to levy and collect the tax. However, the decision once again placed the Courts on the side of the Crown and made it inevitable that Parliament must one day dispute the principle of judicial review.

**100.**

Charles, King: [to the Judges] . . . desirous to avoid such inconveniences, and out of our princely love and affection to all our subjects, being willing to prevent such errors as any of our loving subjects may happen to run into, have thought fit in a case of this nature to advise with our Judges, who . . . are all well studied and informed in the right of our Sovereignty. And because . . . trial in our . . . courts, by the formality in pleading, will require a long protraction, we have thought it expedient, by this our letter directed to you . . . to require your judgments in the case, as

is set down in the enclosed paper, which will not only gain time but also be of more authority to overrule any prejudiced opinions of others in the point.

*The Decision of the Judges.*

May it please your most excellent Majesty:

We have, according to your Majesty's command . . . taken into consideration the case and question signed by your Majesty and enclosed in your royal letter. And we are of the opinion, that, when the good and safety of the Kingdom in general is concerned and the whole Kingdom is in danger, your Majesty may, by writ under the Great Seal of England, command all the subjects of this your Kingdom at their charge to provide ... such number of ships, with men, munition, and victuals, and for such time as your Majesty shall think fit, for the defence ... from such danger and peril; and that by law your Majesty may compel the doing thereof in case of refusal or refractoriness. And we are also of the opinion that in such case your Majesty is the sole judge both of the danger and when and how the same is to be prevented and avoided. (Howell, *State Trials,* III, 843.)

## Charles I: Speech to the Two Houses of the Short Parliament. 1640

**IOI.** ELEVEN YEARS of governing without Parliament only increased Charles's financial and political problems. During this period royal income continued to be the main problem for both sides. The King was never able to acquire sufficient funds to adopt determined foreign or domestic policies, while the Parliamentary party grew increasingly bitter at his methods. By 1640, the sole alternative to complete executive failure was the calling of Parliament. But when the House of Commons was convened it was evident that, contrary to the King's optimistic hopes, nothing had been either forgiven or forgotten. The time elapsed since the last Parliament had only served to aggravate Parliament's resentments, both real and imagined, while Charles had proved beyond a doubt that Parliament was vital to the well-being of the nation. Henceforth the newly elected House of Commons was unwilling to function in the matter of supply without a definite understanding with the King. The King's opening speech answered few questions and made no clear promises, but the temper of this "Short Parliament" was such as to demand both answers and promises in considerable quantity.

My Lords: The necessity of calling this Parliament makes me to come this day hither contrary to expectation. You remember what the Lord Keeper said concerning the occasion of this meeting the first and second days ... [ ... "the cause of the calling of this Parliament ... was for the supply of His Majesty"....]. The House of Commons did not seem to take into consideration my weighty affairs; but they have in a manner concluded the contrary and, instead of preferring my occasions in the first place, they have held consultation of innovation of religion, property of goods, and privileges of Parliament, and so have put the cart before the horse.

If it were a time to dispute, I should not much stand upon it; but my necessities are so urgent that there can be no delay. If the House of Commons will trust me, I will make good what I have promised by my Lord Keeper. As for religion, my heart and conscience with the religion now established in the Church of England shall go together. For the ship money, God is my witness I never converted any of it to my own profit, but to the end of preserving the dominion of the seas. ... As for property of goods, it is a thing I never but intended; and it is my desire to be King of a free and rich people; and if no property in goods, no rich people. I told the Commons that, if they would speedily supply my occasions for the present, I would give them further time at winter to present and debate all their just grievances. If they will not trust me first, all my business this summer will be lost; and before the year goeth about I must be trusted at last, for in the winter I must call them to give me a greater supply. If the House of Commons will not join to prefer my occasions before their grievances, I conjure your Lordships to consider your own honors and mine, and the preposterous course of the House of Commons; and desire that your Lordships will not join with them, but leave them to themselves. . . .

If the supply come not in time, I will not say what mischief may and must follow. (*Journals of the House of Lords,* IV, 66.)

## Dissolution of the Short Parliament. 1640

SHORT Parliament lasted only for three weeks of the spring of 1640. Few of the members had forgotten that Sir John Eliot, the author of the "Three Resolutions" of 1629, had died in prison for having submitted them to the House. Again, all were aware that while the King had accepted the *Petition of Right* he had made every attempt to circumvent the principal limitations specified in it. Thus it was inevitable that the main aim of Parliament was to secure recognition and protection for its own privileges. In dissolving this Parliament Charles laid the blame for the distemper of Commons on "some few cunning and some ill-affectioned men that have been the cause of this misunderstanding." However, it was clear to the most hopeful of the King's friends that his view was far too narrow. The spirit of defiance in Commons was in fact a majority expression of rejection of Crown policy.

**102.**

Time and political circumstance were on the side of Parliament; it could afford to wait, while the King could not. With the dissolution of this Parliament, the King's cause was already lost.

My Lords: For my own part, I hope you remember what the first day of the Parliament the Lord Keeper said to you in my name . . . and what I said the last day myself. I named it to you, not in any doubt that you do not remember, but to show you that I never said anything that way in favor of my people but, by the grace of God, I will fully and really perform it. . . . My Lords, you know at the first I expressed myself . . . that delay [in giving supply] was worse danger than refusing. I would not put this fault on all the whole House . . . But it hath been some few cunning and some ill-affectioned men that have been the cause of this misunderstanding. I shall only end as I began, giving your Lordships thanks for the care you have had of my honor and affairs, desiring you to go on and assist me for the maintaining of government and the liberties of the people that they so much start at. For, my Lords, no king in the world shall be more careful to maintain the propriety of their goods, and liberties of their persons, and true religion than I shall be. And now, my Lord Keeper, do as I have commanded you! [dissolve the Parliament]. (*Journals of the House of Lords,* IV, 81.)

## The Triennial Act. 1641

THE King's capitulation came in November of 1640 with the calling of the "Long Parliament." An elated Parliament now set in motion legislative processes intended to prevent a repetition of the events of the past decade. The *Triennial Act* was only the first of a series of laws which cut away a significant part of the King's power. Henceforth Parliament was to meet at least once every three years. Should the Crown fail to summon the legislature other officials were designated, under pain of treason, to issue the necessary summons for local elections. This latter point constituted a clear infringement on the executive prerogative as well as the destruction of the Crown's last control of the national representative except for adjournment and dissolution.

**103.**

Act for the Preventing of Inconveniences happening by the long Intermission of Parliaments.

Whereas by the laws and statutes of this Realm the Parliament ought to be holden at least once every year for the redress of grievances, but the appointment of the time and place for the holding thereof has always belonged, as it ought, to his Majesty ... and whereas it is by experience found that the not holding of Parliaments accordingly has produced sundry and great mischiefs and inconveniences to the King's Majesty, the Church, and Commonwealth:

For the prevention of the like mischiefs and inconveniences in time to come, be it enacted by the King's most Excellent Majesty, with the consent of ... this present Parliament assembled, that the said laws and statutes be from henceforth duly kept and observed. And your Majesty's loyal and obedient subjects, in this present Parliament now assembled, do humbly pray that it be enacted, and be it enacted accordingly by the authority of this present Parliament, that in case there be not a Parliament summoned by writ under the Great Seal of England and assembled and held before the 10th day of September which shall be in the third year next after the last day of the last meeting and sitting in this present Parliament ... and so from time to time and in all times hereafter, if there shall not be a Parliament assembled and held before the 10th day of September which shall be in the third year next after the last day of the last meeting and sitting in Parliament before that time assembled and held ... that then ... the Parliament shall assemble and be held in the usual place at Westminster in such manner and by such means only as is hereafter in this present Act declared and enacted, and not otherwise, on the second Monday which shall be in the month of November then next ensuing. And in case this present Parliament now assembled and held, or any other Parliament which shall at any time hereafter be assembled and held ... shall be prorogued or adjourned ... until the 10th day of September which shall be in the third year next after the last day of the last meeting and sitting in Parliament ... that then ... every such Parliament so prorogued or adjourned ... shall from the said 10th day of September be thenceforth clearly and absolutely dissolved, and the Lord Chancellor of England, the Lord Keeper of the Great Seal of England, and every commissioner and commissioners for the keeping of the Great Seal of England, for the time being, shall within six days after the said 10th day of September, in every such third year as aforesaid, in due form of law and without further warrant or direction from his Majesty ... seal, issue forth, and send abroad several and respective writs to the several and respective peers of this realm, commanding every such peer that he personally be at the Parliament to be held at Westminster on the second Monday which shall be in November next following the said 10th day of September ... and shall also seal and issue forth ... several and respective writs to the several and respective sheriffs of the ... counties ... of England and Wales ... and to all and every other officers and persons to whom writs have used to be directed, for the electing of the knights, citizens, barons, and burgesses of and for the said counties ... in the accustomed form, to appear and serve in Parliament to be held at Westminster on the said second Monday, which shall be in November aforesaid; which said peers, after the said writs received, and which said knights, citizens, barons, and burgesses chosen by virtue of the said writs, shall then and there appear and serve in Parliament accordingly. And the said Lord Chancellor, Lord Keeper, commissioner and commissioners aforesaid, shall respectively take a solemn oath upon the Holy Evangelists for the due issuing of writs according to the tenor of this Act. ...

[Provisions are here set forth for the calling of Parliament in case the above nominated officials fail to carry out the general provisions of this Act. Penalties for such failure are established, and it is enacted that the whole of the present Act be orally recited once each year in all local courts.]

And it is ... enacted, that his Majesty's royal assent to this bill shall not hereby determine this present session of Parliament, and that all statutes and acts of Parliament which are to have continuance unto the end of this present session shall be of full force after his Majesty's assent, until this present session be fully ended and determined. And if this present session shall determine by dissolution of this present Parliament, then all the acts and statutes aforesaid shall be continued until the end of the first session of the next Parliament. (SR, V, 54: 16 Charles I, c.1.)

## Act to Continue the Existing Parliament. 1641

THE defect in the *Triennial Act* by which the King retained the power to dissolve Parliament was corrected by this statute. In order to have sufficient time to achieve its program of transferring power from the Monarchy to itself, Parliament once again invaded the area of the prerogative. Although this Act was to remain in force only until the end of the current session, it established a precedent for future action should the need arise.

**104.**

An act to prevent inconveniences ... by the untimely adjourning, proroguing, or dissolving of this present Parliament.

Be it declared and enacted by the King our Sovereign Lord with the assent of ... this present Parliament assembled ... that this present Parliament now assembled shall not be dissolved unless it be by Act of Parliament to be passed for that purpose, nor shall be, at any time or times during the continuance thereof, prorogued or adjourned, unless it be by Act of Parliament to be likewise passed for that purpose; and that the House of Lords shall not at any time or times during this present Parliament be adjourned, unless it be by themselves or by their own order; and in like manner, that the House of Commons shall not, at any time or times during this present Parliament, be adjourned, unless it be by themselves or by their own order; and that all and every thing or things whatsoever done or to be done for the adjournment, proroguing, or dissolving of this present Parliament contrary to this Act shall be utterly void and of none effect. (SR, V, 103: 16 Charles I, c.7.)

## Act for the Subsidy of Tunnage and Poundage. 1641

THE passing of political power from the King to Parliament was accompanied by a transfer of political and social responsibility which placed Parliament in a difficult position. In their violent denunciations of the King's arbitrary taking of subsidies and impositions the Parliamentarians had unwittingly encouraged popular resentment of the general institution of taxation. Ironically, however, their newly found authority in matters of state welfare put them in the uncomfortable position of having to resume the detested exploitation of tunnage and poundage.

In a sense, the return to the use of impositions in the name of the national security characterized much of the constitutional history of the next fifty years. Each political vacuum created by the destruction of a specific monarchial power was filled by the reconstitution of that power in a slightly different form under Parliamentary direction.

**105.**

A subsidy granted to the King of tunnage, poundage, and other sums of money payable upon merchandise exported and imported.

Whereas, upon examination in this present Parliament of divers of the farmers, customers, and collectors of the customs upon merchandise, and likewise upon their own confession, it appeared that they have taken divers great sums of money of his Majesty's subjects, and likewise of merchants aliens for goods imported and exported by the names of subsidy of tunnage and poundage, and by color of divers other impositions laid upon merchandise, which have been taken and received against the laws of the realm, in regard the said sums of money and impositions were not granted by common consent in Parliament....

Be it therefore declared and enacted by the King's most excellent Majesty and ... this present Parliament assembled, and it is hereby declared and enacted, that it is and has been the ancient right of the subjects of this realm that no subsidy, custom, impost, or other charge whatsoever ought or may be laid or imposed upon any merchandise exported or imported by subjects, denizens, or aliens without ... consent in Parliament.

Yet ... the [House of] Commons ... taking into their consideration the great peril that might ensue to this realm by the not guarding of the seas and the other inconveniences which might follow in case the said sums of money should upon the sudden be forborne to be paid, by and with the advice of the Lords in this present Parliament assembled and by the authority of the same, do give and grant to our supreme liege Lord and Sovereign one subsidy called tunnage—that is to say, of every tun of wine that is or shall come into this realm or any his Majesty's dominions by way of merchandise the sum of 3s. ... And also one other subsidy called poundage—that is to say, of all manner of goods and merchandise of every merchant, denizen, and alien carried or to be carried out of this realm, or any his Majesty's dominions, or to be brought into the same by way of merchandise, of the value of every 20s. of the same goods and merchandise 12d. ...

[Woolen goods were excepted from the above provisions and special rates set for them. Tobacco exported from English colonies was to be taxed at the rate of 2d. to the pound value.] (SR, V, 104: 16 Charles I, c.8.)

## Act Abolishing the Arbitrary (Prerogative) Courts. 1641

106.    THE most permanent and significant work of Long Parliament was accomplished in 1641 through a series of Acts intended to dismantle the institution of the English Monarchy. Star Chamber, symbolic of the King's prerogative of justice, along with the Councils of the North and Wales and the Court of the Exchequer, were hereby abolished as being contrary to the Common Law.

An Act for the regulating of the Privy Council and for taking away the Court commonly called the Star Chamber.

Forasmuch as all matters examinable or determinable ... in the court commonly called the Star Chamber may have their proper remedy and redress and their due punishment and correction by the Common Law of the land and in the ordinary course of justice elsewhere; and forasmuch as the

reasons and motives inducing the erection and continuance of that court do now cease, and the proceedings, censures and decrees of that court have by experience been found to be an intolerable burden to the subjects and the means to introduce an arbitrary power and government; and forasmuch as the council table hath of late times assumed unto itself a power to intermeddle in civil causes and matters only of private interest between party and party, and have adventured to determine of the estates and liberties of the subject contrary to the law of the land and the rights and privileges of the subject, by which great and manifold mischiefs and inconveniences have arisen and happened, and much uncertainty by means of such proceedings hath been conceived concerning men's rights and estates:

For settling whereof and preventing the like in time to come, be it ordained and enacted by the authority of this present Parliament that the said court commonly called the Star Chamber, and all jurisdiction, power, and authority belonging unto or exercised in the same court, or by any the judges, officers, or ministers thereof, be from the first day of August, in the year of our Lord God 1641, clearly and absolutely dissolved, taken away, and determined.

.... And be it likewise enacted that the like jurisdiction now used and exercised in the court before the president and council in the Marches of Wales; and also in the court before the president and council established in the northern parts; and also in the court commonly called the Court of the Duchy of Lancaster, held before the Chancellor and council of the court; and also in the Court of the Exchequer of the county palatine of Chester, held before the chamberlain and council of that court ... shall ... be also repealed and absolutely revoked and made void. . . .

Be it likewise declared and enacted by authority of this present Parliament, that neither his Majesty nor his Privy Council have or ought to have any jurisdiction, power, or authority by English bill, petition, articles, libel, or any other arbitrary way whatsoever, to examine or draw into question, determine, or dispose of the lands, tenements, hereditaments, goods, or chattels of any the subjects of this Kingdom, but that the same ought to be tried and determined in the ordinary courts of justice and by the ordinary course of the law. (SR, V, 110: 16 Charles I, c.10.)

## Act Abolishing the Court of High Commission. 1641

THE destruction of the Court of High Commission by this Act ended the authority of both King and Bishop in the established Church. Parliament however, was far from unanimous in this decision. The moderates, fearful that the rate of change in Church affairs and political matters might result in destructive licence, began to withhold their support from John Pym's radical faction. By the time the *Grand Remonstrance* was presented to the lower House for final debate the breach between the radical Puritans and the moderates in Parliament was complete.

**107.**

An Act for the repeal of a branch [clause] of a statute ... concerning commissioners for causes ecclesiastical.

Whereas in the Parliament holden in the first year of the reign of the late Queen Elizabeth ... there was an Act made [*Act of Supremacy*, 1 Elizabeth, c.1., which brought into being the Court of High Commission] ... and whereas, by color of some words in this ... Act whereby commissioners are authorized to execute their commission according to the tenor and effect of the King's letters patents and by letters patents grounded thereupon, the said commissioners have, to the great and insufferable wrong and oppression of the King's subjects, used to fine and imprison them, and to exercise other authority not belonging to ecclesiastical jurisdiction restored by that Act, and divers other great mischiefs and inconveniences have also ensued to the King's subjects by occasion of the ... commissions issued thereupon and the executions thereof:

Therefore, for the repressing and preventing of the foresaid abuses, mischiefs, and inconveniences in time to come, be it enacted by the King's most excellent Majesty and the Lords and Commons in this present Parliament assembled ... that the foresaid branch, clause, article, or sentence contained in the said Act ... shall ... be repealed. ...

And be it also enacted ... that no archbishop, bishop ... nor any other person ... whatsoever exercising spiritual or ecclesiastical power, authority, or jurisdiction ... shall ... award, impose or inflict any pain, penalty, fine, amercement, imprisonment, or other corporal punishment upon any of the King's subjects for any contempt, misdemeanor, crime, offence, matter, or thing whatsoever belonging to spiritual or ecclesiastical cognizance or jurisdiction, or shall *ex officio,* or at the instance or promotion of any other person whatsoever ... minister unto any ... person whatsoever any corporal oath, whereby he ... shall or may be charged or

obliged to make any presentment of any crime or offence, or to confess or to accuse himself ... of any crime, offence, delinquency, or misdemeanor, or any neglect ... or thing whereby ... he ... shall or may be liable or exposed to any censure, pain, penalty, or punishment. ...

And be it further enacted that ... no new court shall be erected, ordained, or appointed within this realm of England or dominion of Wales which shall or may have the like power, jurisdiction, or authority as the said High Commission Court now hath or pretends to have; but that all and every such letters patents, commissions, and grants made or to be made by his Majesty ... and all powers and authorities granted or pretended or mentioned to be granted thereby, and all acts, sentences, and decrees to be made by virtue or color thereof shall be utterly void and of none effect. (SR, V, 112: 16 Charles I, c.11.)

## The House of Commons "Grand Remonstrance." 1641

108. THE *Grand Remonstrance* marked the real beginning of civil war between the Royalists and the Puritans. The party of John Pym, having alienated the moderates in the debates on the passage of the *Act Abolishing the Arbitrary Courts* and other measures aimed at total destruction of the King's executive and judicial powers, now forced that large minority in Parliament into a defensive alliance with the King. Thus the Royalist party was born. In victory Parliament was unable to maintain that homogeneity of purpose and action which was the only security against civil war.

The *Remonstrance,* despite its form of a petition to the King, was really a popular appeal against the growing strength of the moderate party which was daily drawing closer to the Crown and commanding increasing public support. The content of the *Remonstrance* was significant only in that it stated the plans of the radicals for additional changes in the Church. These proposed changes were beyond compromise; the moderates had no choice but to repudiate the leadership of Pym. The result was to give Charles a sufficiently strong following (both in and outside Parliament) to resist the radicals.

The Commons in this present Parliament assembled having, with much earnestness and faithfulness of affection and zeal to the public good of this Kingdom and his Majesty's honor and service, for the space of twelve months, wrestled with great dangers

and fears, the pressing miseries and calamities, the various distempers and disorders which had not only assaulted but even overwhelmed and extinguished the liberty, peace, and prosperity of this great Kingdom, the comfort and hopes of all his Majesty's good

subjects, and exceedingly weakened and un-
dermined the foundation and strength of his
own royal throne, do yet find an abounding
malignity and opposition in those parties and
factions who have been the cause of those
evils and do still labor to cast aspersions
upon that which hath been done, and to raise
many difficulties for the hindrance of that
which remains yet undone, and to foment
jealousies between the King and Parliament,
that so they may deprive him and his people
of the fruit of his own gracious intentions,
and their humble desires of procuring the
public peace, safety, and happiness of this
Realm.

For the preventing of those miserable effects, which such malicious endeavors may
produce, we have thought good to declare
the root and the growth of these mischievous
designs; the maturity and ripeness to which
they have attained before the beginning of
the Parliament; the effectual means which
have been used for the extirpation of those
dangerous evils, and the progress which hath
therein been made by his Majesty's goodness
and the wisdom of the Parliament; the ways
of obstruction and opposition by which that
progress has been interrupted; the courses to
be taken for the removing those obstacles,
and for the accomplishing of our most dutiful and faithful intentions and endeavors of
restoring and establishing the ancient honor,
greatness, and security of this crown and
nation.

The root of all this mischief we find to be
a malignant and pernicious design of subverting the fundamental laws and principles
of government, upon which the religion and
justice of this Kingdom are firmly established. The actors and promoters hereof have
been:

First: the bishops and the corrupt part of
the clergy, who cherish formality and superstition as the natural effects and more prob-
able supports of their own ecclesiastical
tyranny and usurpation.

Second: such councilors and courtiers as
for private ends have engaged themselves to
further the interests of some foreign princes
or states to the prejudice of his Majesty and
the state at home. . . .

Third: the Jesuited papists, who hate the
laws as the obstacles of that change and subversion of religion which they so much long
for. . . .

In the beginning of his Majesty's reign, the
Catholic party began to revive and flourish
again, having been somewhat damped by the
breach with Spain in the last year of King
James, and by his Majesty's marriage with
France . . . the papists of England, having
ever been more addicted to Spain than
France; yet they still retained a purpose and
resolution to weaken the Protestant parties
in all parts, and even in France, whereby to
make way for the change of religion which
they intended at home. . . .

[The results of the growing strength of
the Catholics are to be seen in the following:]

The *Petition of Right,* which was granted
in full Parliament, blasted with an illegal
declaration to make it destructive to itself, to
the power of Parliament, to the liberty of
the subject, and to that purpose printed with
it, and the *Petition* made of no use but to
show the bold and presumptuous injustice
of such ministers as durst break the laws and
suppress the liberties of the Kingdom, after
they had been so solemnly and evidently
declared. . . .

After the breach of the Parliament in the
fourth year of his Majesty, injustice, oppression, and violence broke in upon us without
any restraint or moderation, and yet the first
project was the great sums exacted through
the whole Kingdom for the default of knighthood, which seemed to have some color and
shadow of a law, yet if it be rightly examined by that obsolete law which was pretended for it, it will be found to be against
all the rules of justice. . . .

Tunnage and poundage has been taken
without color or pretense of law; many other
heavy impositions continued against law, and
some so unreasonable that the sum of the
charge exceeds the value of the goods. . . .

And although all this was taken upon pretense of guarding the seas, yet a new unheard-of tax of ship money was devised, and upon the same pretense, by both which there was charged upon the subject nearly £700,000 some years; and yet the merchants have been left so naked to the violence of the Turkish pirates that many great ships of value and thousands of his Majesty's subjects have been taken by them, and do still remain in miserable slavery.

.... The monopolies of soap, salt, wine, leather, sea coal, and in a manner of all things of most common and necessary use. ...

The Court of Star Chamber hath abounded in extravagant censures not only for the maintenance and improvement of monopolies and other unlawful taxes, but for divers other causes where there hath been no offense, or very small; whereby his Majesty's subjects have been oppressed by grievous fines, imprisonments, stigmatizings, mutilations, whippings, pillories, gags, confinements, banishments; after so rigid a manner as hath not only deprived men of the society of their friends, exercise of their professions, comfort of books, use of paper and ink, but even violated that near union which God hath established between men and their wives, by forced and constrained separation, whereby they have been bereaved of the comfort and conversation one of another for many years together, without hope of relief, if God had not, by His overruling providence, given some interruption to the prevailing power and counsel of those who were the authors and promoters of such pre-emptory and heady courses. ...

The High Commission grew to such excess of sharpness and severity as was not much less than the Romish Inquisition. ... The bishops and their courts were as eager in the counties; although their jurisdiction could

not reach so high in rigor and extremity of punishment, yet were they no less grievous in respect of the generality and multiplicity of vexations, which, lighting upon the meaner sort of tradesmen and artificers, did impoverish many thousands, and so afflict and trouble others that great numbers, to avoid their miseries, departed out of the Kingdom, some into New England and other parts of America, others into Holland. ...

This faction was grown to that height and entireness of power that now they began to think of finishing their work, which consisted of these three parts:

First: the government must be set free from all restraint of laws concerning our persons and estates.

Second: there must be a conjunction between Papists and Protestants in doctrine, discipline, and ceremonies, only it must not yet be called Popery.

Third: the Puritans, under which name they include all that desire to preserve the laws and liberties of the Kingdom and to maintain religion in the power of it, must be either rooted out of the Kingdom with force or driven out with fear.

For the affecting of this it was thought necessary to reduce Scotland to such Popish superstitions and innovations as might make them apt to join with England in that great change which was intended. Whereupon new canons and a new liturgy were pressed upon them, and when they refused to admit of them an army was raised to force them to it, towards, which the clergy and the Papists were very forward in their contribution.

[After reviewing many more charged abuses Parliament here restates the legislative measures it has carried out for the establishing of the government on a firm basis.] (S. R. Gardiner, *Constitutional Documents*, 297.)

## Act Abolishing the Temporal Power of the Clergy. 1641

**109.**

LIKE James I, the radical Puritan majority in Parliament realized that the security of the Monarchy rested largely on the preeminence of the Bishops in the Established Church. As a first step toward the church reforms demanded by the *Remonstrance* the present Act relieved the churchmen of all temporal jurisdiction and authority on the grounds that "their intermeddling with secular jurisdictions hath occasioned great mischiefs and scandals both to Church and State." Politically the Act further strengthened the moderates' resistance to the next statutory attack on the Monarchy, the *Militia Ordinance* of 1642.

An Act for disenabling all persons in holy orders to exercise any temporal jurisdiction or authority.

Whereas bishops and other persons in holy orders ought not to be entangled with secular jurisdiction, the office of the ministry being of such great importance that it will take up the whole man; and for that it is found by long experience that their intermeddling with secular jurisdictions hath occasioned great mischiefs and scandals both to Church and State:

His Majesty, out of his religious care of the Church, and souls of his people, is graciously pleased that it be enacted, and by authority of this present Parliament be it enacted, that no archbishop or bishop or other person that now is or hereafter shall be in holy orders, shall ... have any seat or place, suffrage, or voice, or use, or execute any power or authority in the Parliaments of this Realm, nor shall be of the Privy Council of his Majesty, ... or justice of the peace ... or execute any temporal authority by virtue of any commission; but shall be wholly disabled and be incapable to have, receive, use, or execute any of the said offices, places, powers, authorities, and things aforesaid. ... (SR, V, 138: 16 Charles I, c.27.)

## The Militia Ordinance. 1642

**110.**

IN THE winter of 1642 the greatest fear of the radicals was realized when the King's attempt to arrest several of the most outspoken of their leaders underlined the fact that the army was still loyal to him. On the other hand, Charles's resort to force was interpreted as an arbitrary and unjustified attack on Parliamentary privilege and hence weakened the Royalist cause. Charles's action in this instance threatened to set a precedent for the future, and Parliament was frightened into attempting (unconstitutionally) to appoint its own commanders and officers for the militia.

In its first passage the *Ordinance* was formulated as a bill which the majority expected the King to accept as he had several previous bills. However, with the growing strength of the Royalist party's demands for resistance, the King rejected the *Militia Bill* and forced Parliament to decide between dropping the matter altogether or acting in such a frankly unconstitutional way as to alienate some of its followers.

An ordinance of Parliament for the safety and defence of the Kingdom of England. ...

Whereas there hath been of late a most dangerous and desperate design upon the House of Commons, which we have just cause to believe to be an effect of the bloody counsels of papists and other ill-affected persons, who have already raised a rebellion in the Kingdom of Ireland; and by reason of many discoveries we cannot but fear they will proceed not only to stir up the like rebellion and insurrections in this Kingdom of England but also to back them with forces from abroad:

For the safety, therefore, of his Majesty's person, the Parliament, and Kingdom in this time of imminent danger, it is ordained by the Lords and Commons now in Parliament assembled, that [Lieutenants of militia are here appointed in the several counties]. . . . And [those Lieutenants] shall . . . have power to assemble and call together all and singular his Majesty's subjects within the said several and respective counties and places . . . that are meet and fit for the wars, and them to train and exercise and put in readiness, and them after their abilities and faculties well and sufficiently from time to time to cause to be arrayed and weaponed, and to take the muster of them in places most fit for that purpose; and [they] shall severally and respectively have power . . . to nominate and appoint such persons of quality as to them shall seem meet to be their deputy lieutenants, to be approved of by both Houses of Parliament; and [they] shall have power to make colonels and captains and other officers . . . as they shall think fit for that purpose; and . . . power to lead, conduct and employ the persons aforesaid arrayed and weaponed, for the suppression of all rebellions, insurrections, and invasions that may happen within the several and respective counties and places; and shall have power and authority to lead, conduct, and employ the persons aforesaid arrayed and weaponed, as well within their said several and respective counties and places as within any other part of this realm of England or dominion of Wales, for the suppression of all rebellions, insurrections, and invasions that may happen, according as they from time to time shall receive directions. . . . (*Journals of the Lords,* IV, 587.)

## Royal Proclamation Concerning the Militia Ordinance. 1642

**I I I.**   CHARLES'S immediate reaction to the *Militia Ordinance* was to declare it contrary to the law. The local officials chosen by Parliament to call together, outfit, and train local bands of militiamen were warned that the King would not accept the *Ordinance* because it clearly invaded the royal prerogative. Since no bill could become law without the King's assent, any men who armed or trained in defiance of the King's prohibition would be liable to charges of treason. Thus what had been heretofore a purely governmental struggle of little interest to the great body of subjects now began to have very real personal meaning for each individual. All citizens were commanded to bear arms by Parliament, and all were forbidden to do so by the King.

. . . . Whereas we understand that, expressly contrary to the . . . laws of this our Kingdom, under color . . . of an ordinance of Parliament [the *Militia Ordinance*], without our consent or any . . . warrant from us, the trained bands and militia of this Kingdom have been lately, and are intended to be, put in arms and drawn into companies in a warlike manner, whereby the peace and quiet of our subjects is or may be disturbed:

We, being desirous . . . to prevent that some malignant persons in this our Kingdom do not by degrees seduce our good subjects from their due obedience to us and the laws of this our Kingdom . . . do therefore, by this our proclamation, expressly charge and command all our sheriffs, and all colonels, lieutenant-colonels, sergeant-majors, captains, officers, and soldiers belonging to the trained bands of this our Kingdom, and likewise all high and petty constables and other our officers and subjects whatsoever, upon their allegiance and as they tender the peace of this our Kingdom, not to muster, levy, raise, or march, or to summon or warn, upon any warrant, order or ordinance from one or both our Houses of Parliament, whereunto we have not, or shall not, give our express consent, any of our trained bands or other forces to rise, muster, march, or exercise without express warrant under our hand or warrant from our sheriff of the county, grounded upon a particular writ to that purpose under our great seal. And in case any of our trained bands shall rise or gather together contrary to this our command, we shall then call them in due time to a strict account and proceed legally against them as violators of the laws and disturbers of the peace of this Kingdom. (*Journals of the House of Lords*, V, 111.)

## The Declaration of Purpose of Lords and Commons. 1642

WHEN Charles refused to sanction the *Ordinance* and threatened legal reprisal against those who armed under it, the Parliamentary party had little choice but to defy him. The *Declaration* declared that Parliament had the power to speak for the King and established the *Militia Ordinance* as the law of the land without royal signature. Hereafter whatever the two Houses of Parliament "do herein hath the stamp of the royal authority although his Majesty, seduced by evil council, do in his person oppose or interrupt the same."

Such flagrantly subjective and irrational grounds had never before been offered by Parliament to justify an unconstitutional act. If the Houses could legislate without the King, it followed that there was no logical place for a King in the constitution, except as a mere minister to Parliament.

## 112.

The Lords and Commons, having perused his Majesty's proclamation forbidding all his Majesty's subjects belonging to the trained bands or militia of this Kingdom, to rise, march, [etc.] ... by virtue of any order or ordinance of one or both Houses of Parliament without consent or warrant from his Majesty, upon pain of punishment according to the laws, do thereupon declare that ... it is acknowledged that the King is the fountain of justice and protection; but the acts of justice and protection are not exercised in his own person, nor depend upon his pleasure, but by his courts and by his ministers, who must do their duty therein though the King in his own person should forbid them. And therefore, if judgments should be given by them against the King's will and personal command, yet are they the King's judgments. The High Court of Parliament is not only a court of judicature, enabled by the laws to adjudge and determine the rights and liberties of the Kingdom against such patents and grants of his Majesty as are prejudicial thereunto, although strengthened both by his personal command and by his proclamation under the Great Seal; but it is likewise a council to provide for the necessities, prevent the imminent dangers and preserve the public peace and safety of this Kingdom, and to declare the King's pleasure in those things as are requisite thereunto. And what they do herein hath the stamp of the royal authority although his Majesty, seduced by evil counsel, do in his own person oppose or interrupt the same; for the King's supreme and royal pleasure is exercised and declared in this High Court of law and council, after a more eminent and obligatory manner than it can be by personal act or resolution of his own.

Seeing therefore the Lords and Commons, which are his Majesty's great and high council, have ordained that, for the present and necessary defence of the realm, the trained bands and militia of this Kingdom should be ordered according to that ordinance ... the Lords and Commons do require and command all constables, petty constables, and all other his Majesty's officers and subjects whatsoever to muster, levy, raise, march, and exercise, or to summon or warn any, upon warrants from the lieutenants, deputy lieutenants, captains, or other officers of the trained bands, and all others, according to the said ordinance of both Houses; and [those officers] shall not presume to muster, levy, raise, march, or exercise by virtue of any commission or other authority whatsoever, as they will answer the contrary at their perils. And in their so doing they do further declare that they shall be protected by the power and authority of both Houses of Parliament; and that whosoever shall oppose, question, or hinder them in the execution of the said ordinance, [The *Militia Ordinance*] shall be proceeded against as violators of the laws and disturbers of the peace of the Kingdom. (*Journals of the House of Lords*, V, 112.)

## The Nineteen Propositions. 1642

**I I 3.**  CHARLES'S rejection of the *Militia Ordinance* completed the process of separation between Crown and Parliament. Thereafter Parliament assumed full executive power by promulgating its ordinances as the statute law of the land. During the spring of 1642, exasperated by Charles's withdrawal from the capital and his absolute refusal to communicate with them, the two Houses drew up the *Nineteen Propositions*. The nineteen items (in essence a broad claim to sovereign political power) attempted to justify all previous Parliamentary actions and demanded that all issues be settled immediately according to Parliament's desires. Had Charles accepted the instrument— and governed according to its expression—the Monarchy of 1642 would have been relegated to a position far less significant in the constitution than would be that of the English Monarch after 1689.

Your Majesty's most humble and faithful subjects, the Lords and Commons in Parliament, having nothing in their thoughts and desires more precious and of higher esteem, next to the honor and immediate service of God, than the just and faithful performance of their duty to your Majesty and this Kingdom ... do in all humility and sincerity present to your Majesty their most dutiful petition and advice, that out of your princely wisdom ... you will be pleased to grant and accept these their humble ... propositions, as the most necessary effectual means, through God's blessing, of removing those jealousies and differences which have unhappily fallen betwixt you and your people. ...

That the Lords and others of your Majesty's Privy Council and other the great officers and ministers of state, either at home or beyond the seas, may be put from your Privy Council and from those offices and employments, excepting such as shall be approved of by both Houses of Parliament; and that the persons put into the places and employments of those that are removed may be approved of by both Houses of Parliament; and that all Privy Councillors shall take an oath for the due execution of their places in such form as shall be agreed upon by both Houses of Parliament.

That the great affairs of the Kingdom may not be concluded or transacted by the advice of private men, or by any unknown or unsworn councillors; but that such matters as concern the public and are proper for the High Court of Parliament, which is your Majesty's great and supreme council, may be debated, resolved, and transacted only in Parliament, and not elsewhere. And such as shall presume to do anything to the contrary shall be reserved to the censure and judgment of Parliament. And such other matters of state as are proper for your Majesty's Privy Council shall be debated and concluded by such of the nobility and others as shall from time to time be chosen for that place, by approbation of both Houses of Parliament. And that no public act concerning the affairs of the Kingdom, which are proper for your Privy Council, may be esteemed of any validity, as proceeding from the royal authority, unless it be done by the advice and consent of the major part of your council, attested under their hands. And that your council may be limited to a certain number, not exceeding twenty-five, nor under fifteen. And if any councillor's place happen to be void in the intervals of Parliament, it shall not be supplied without the assent of the major part of the council; which choice shall be confirmed at the next sitting of Parliament, or else to be void.

That the Lord High Steward of England, Lord High Constable, Lord Chancellor, or Lord Keeper of the Great Seal, Lord Treasurer, Lord Privy Seal, Earl Marshal, Lord Admiral, Warden of the Cinque Ports, the Wards, Secretaries of State, two Chief Justices, and Chief Baron, may always be chosen with the approbation of both Houses of Parliament....

That he or they unto whom the government and education of the King's children shall be committed shall be approved of by both Houses of Parliament

.... That no marriage shall be concluded or treated for any of the King's children with any foreign prince or other person whatsoever, abroad or at home, without the consent of Parliament....

That the laws in force against Jesuits, priests, and popish recusants be strictly put in execution, without any toleration or dispensation....

That the votes of popish lords in the House of Lords may be taken away....

That your Majesty would be pleased to consent that such a reformation be made of the Church government and liturgy as both Houses of Parliament shall advise....

That your Majesty will be pleased to rest satisfied with that course that the Lords and Commons have appointed for ordering the militia until the same shall be further settled by a bill; and that your Majesty will recall your declarations and proclamations against the ordinance made by the Lords and Commons concerning it.

That such members of either House of Parliament as have, during this present session, been put out of any place and office may either be restored to that place and office or otherwise have satisfaction for the same, upon the petition of that House whereof he or they are members.

That all Privy Councillors and judges may take an oath, the form whereof to be agreed on and settled by Act of Parliament, for the maintaining of the *Petition of Right* and of certain statutes made by this Parliament, which shall be mentioned by both Houses of Parliament.

That all the judges and all the officers placed by approbation of both Houses of Parliament may hold their places [during good behavior]....

That the justice of Parliament may pass upon all delinquents, whether they be within the Kingdom or fled out of it....

That the general pardon offered by your Majesty may be granted, with such exceptions as shall be advised by both Houses of Parliament.

That the forts and castles of this Kingdom may be put under the command and custody of such persons as your Majesty shall appoint with the approbation of your Parliament....

That the extraordinary guards and military forces now attending your Majesty may be removed and discharged; and that for the future you will raise no such guards or extraordinary forces, but according to the law, in case of actual rebellion or invasion.

That your Majesty will be pleased to enter

into a more strict alliance with the states of the United Provinces, and other neighboring princes and states of the Protestant religion. . . .

That your Majesty will be pleased, by Act of Parliament, to clear the lord Kimbolton and the five members of the House of Commons in such manner that future Parliaments may be secured from the consequences of that evil precedent.

That your Majesty will be graciously pleased to pass a bill for restraining peers made hereafter from sitting or voting in Parliament, unless they be admitted thereunto with the consent of both Houses of Parliament.

And these our humble desires being granted by your Majesty, we shall forthwith apply ourselves to regulate your present revenue in such sort as may be for your best advantage; and likewise to settle such an ordinary and constant increase of it as shall be sufficient to support your royal dignity in honor and plenty, beyond the proportion of any former grants of the subjects of this Kingdom to your Majesty's royal predecessors. . . . (*Journals of the House of Lords,* V, 97.)

# The Civil War and the Interregnum

## 1642-1660

## DOCUMENTS OF THE CIVIL WAR
## AND THE INTERREGNUM

# England, 1642-1660    Introduction

The constitutional documents of the Interregnum, though few, are of extreme significance. Not only are they evidence of radical shifts in the traditional balance of governmental powers in that period, they also illustrate important changes in the patterns of English political thought which were to have abiding influence on further constitutional development.

The Civil War, which brought the House of Commons to power and Charles I to the executioner's block, was one of the results of the long conflict between two apparently exclusive concepts of the English constitution. The one—the monarchial—held that political authority was a divinely instituted property of kingship, and that, since God was the basis of that power, no mortal institution could legitimately limit or control it. The second insisted that the people, as the natural repository of power and authority, were entitled to self-regulation through their chosen representatives in Parliament.

Such fundamentally different basic assumptions would seem to make these concepts irreconcilable. On the other hand, critical analysis will show striking similarities between the two which exemplify the evolutionary socio-political nature of the constitution.

Of the many characteristics common to these theories of government two may be singled out for examination. The concept of political authority based on divine right was actually common to both King and Parliamentarian. The Stuarts' constant public reiteration of the divine basis of their power provides ample evidence of their sincerity but tends to obscure the almost identical but less dramatic arguments of Commons as expressed in its bills, petitions, and debates. As early as 1604 in the *Apology of Commons* the lower House had stated that "the voice of the people in things of their knowledge is said to be as the voice of God." Subsequent Parliamentary expression on this score, while less bold in design and language, was aimed at strengthening the claim in the minds of King and populace. The ordinances of the Interregnum contain tactfully worded rationalizations of the theory designed to appeal to both friends and foes of Commons.

It should be noted that while both King and Parliament claimed divine sanction, each offered opposing and exclusive evidence in justification. The Stuarts found proof of the validity of their claims in Scripture. The Parliamentarians, on the other hand, attempted to smother such mystical grounds under an avalanche of complex claims. They referred to Common Law to prove that Parliament was the ancient defender of the people's rights and properties, while the immutable law of nature was made to show that God's design intended multiple rather than single voice in governance and policy. When historical events made the alliance of Parliament with political Calvinism possible, an even more versatile theological proposition was added to Commons's evidence of its divine right to authority. Not only were Kings mere minor magistrates in the eyes of God, but the elect of both God and the people were, by happy chance, joined in the same political institution. This argument was devastating to monarchial claims in an age when men searched diligently and sincerely for God's will in political manifestations.

The second significant similarity between these two theories of political government is to be found in the problem of sovereignty. The medieval constitution had denied that sovereign power could reside in any political institution. Such elements of the constitution as the law, popular rights, the rights of private property, and the various governing bodies had theoretically provided effective and mutual protection for all against trespass by the few. The Tudors, with their debasing of property rights, their going beyond customary limitations, and their several church settlements had gradually disintegrated the medieval scheme of things and conditioned public opinion to other ideas. Henry VII had given Parliament new status and Henry VIII had imbued it with new purpose. Under Elizabeth that institution had shown an increasingly aggressive independence and in the reign of James I had demanded equality in the affairs of the State. Finally, under Charles I, Parliament made its bid for absolute control, disrupting normal constitutional procedures, turning class against class, and eventually taking up arms in order to achieve its ends.

Thus the problem after 1625 was never centered around the moral aspect of political sovereignty. By the time of the Civil War both King and Parliament had accepted the proposition that political power must be absolute to be effective. The purpose of the conflict was to decide which side was to possess such power.

Parliament's victory was due more to Charles's defective leadership and the weary defeatism of the royalist forces than to the brilliance of Parliamentary strategy or to broad popular acceptance of its political theories. And while the King was executed and the concept of kingship humiliated, the result was not a triumph for the Parliamentary program. The people's representatives discovered eventually that they had been treating a symptom rather than the disease itself; that the political, theological, and economic distemper of the period was the result of institutional and historical development rather than the Machiavellian designs of Charles against the liberties and property of his subjects. In terms of achieving any of its promised rewards (such as religious unity, political order, extensive liberty, security of property, or social equanimity) the Interregnum must be judged a failure. Within ten years of the King's death three dictatorships laid violent hands on the English government, each denying the very liberty of act and conscience by which the anti-monarchial party had sanctioned its moral right to assault traditional institutions of government and authority.

The failure of the Interregnum governments might also be gauged by other measures. One of the basic beliefs of the victorious sectarian, economic, and political groups was that all problems would automatically cease upon the promulgation of a written constitution. Yet such a document was to be composed by men of differing political views, religious preferences, and social backgrounds, inexperienced in governing, largely intolerant of differing views and interests. Existing records of Parliamentary disagreements, of unending disputes between soldiers and officers, between ministers in the churches and merchants in the market place, show this to have been a period of heated and fanatical debate. Such a chaotic situation was all the more tragic owing to the intense sincerity of all concerned. The sense of divinely imposed mission felt by each group blinded them to the human necessity for compromise.

Indeed, compromise with the desires, rights, and traditional aspirations of opposed groups had no meaning for most Puritan sectarians. As untutored in political history as in civil administration, they did not realize that laws, constitutions, and systems of policy are the fruits of countless generations of social interaction, of necessary and studied compromises. Thus men whose chief claim to ability in the constitutional area was based on intuitive perception of the needs and desires of the people, or on a divinely inspired ability to ascertain all truth and justice, dominated English political life in this period. The profuse variety of their legislation shows that this was a decade of wild experimentation with the rights of other men by a sectarian minority.

In essence, the sectarian's concept of freedom meant absolute political liberty for his own group to realize its messianic mission. Under such a scheme the liberty of the average individual was simply the fact of existence under a God-appointed minority which regulated rights according to its conception of God's will. Thus the English radical of the mid-seventeenth century went beyond even Thomas Hobbes in anticipating the theories of modern collectivist societies, since, although "God's will" has given way to "historical process," the political fact remains the same.

It would seem safe to assume that to the sectarian minorities of the Interregnum the building of the earthly City of God was not as important as the necessity for its being constructed by the properly inspired architects. Yet, could such an ideal state actually exist in view of the Calvinistic concept of man's total depravity? Here was the frustrating dilemma of English Puritanism, for the City of God on earth was conceived as a theocratic Utopia, where perfection was to be enforced by the state operating in the area of social regulation under franchise from the Church. To be enforced, perfection first had to exist—and it could not exist in light of the doctrine of depravity. Confronted by this philosophical problem which was beyond its limited capacity to rationalize, the sectarian movement in England turned to petulant disinclination to political cooperation in a time of unsurpassed political crisis. The frustrations inherent in this uncompromising posture held by conflicting groups left a lasting imprint of negativism on the Puritan political movement and was largely responsible for its failure in the time of its supreme political opportunity.

## The Solemn League and Covenant. 1643

THE *Covenant* was intended as a political instrument for fusing the military forces and public opinion of Parliamentary England and Scotland into an effective unit for resistance against the Cavalier armies. Charles's early victories in central England forced this action by which the Puritans were brought, by military expedience, to agree tentatively to the establishment of the Scottish form of Presbyterianism in England, though many of them compared it with popery in its harsh tyranny.

It is important to note that, although armies were in the field and Parliament was willing to include the "foreign" Scots in English domestic affairs, no expression is to be found of any desire to do more than protect the King from evil advisors and

114.

maintain the "Reformed Religion." In actual fact the *Covenant* bound Parliament morally to a religious settlement not in accord with the more tolerant principles of the radical sects. The attempted enforcement of the items of the document in England eventually paved the way for Oliver Cromwell's entry into political affairs.

A solemn League and Covenant for reformation and defence of religion, the honor and happiness of the King, and the peace and safety of the three Kingdoms of England, Scotland, and Ireland.

We, noblemen, barons, knights, gentlemen, citizens, burgesses, ministers of the Gospel, and commons of all sorts in the Kingdoms of England, Scotland, and Ireland, by the Providence of God living under one King and being of one Reformed Religion. . . . :

For the preservation of ourselves and our religion from utter ruin and destruction according to the commendable practice of these Kingdoms in former times and the example of God's people in other nations, after mature deliberation, resolved and determined to enter into a mutual and solemn League and Covenant wherein we all subscribe; and each one of us for himself, with our hands lifted up to the most high God, do swear:

That we shall sincerely, really, and constantly, through the grace of God, endeavor in our several places and callings the preservation of the Reform Religion. . . .

That we shall endeavor to bring the Churches of God in the three Kingdoms to the nearest conjunction and uniformity in religion, confession of faith, form of church government, directory for worship, and catechising. . . .

That we shall . . . endeavor the extirpation of popery, prelacy, (that is, church government by archbishops, bishops, their chancellors and commissaries, deans, deans and chapters, archdeacons, and all other ecclesiastical officers depending on that hierarchy, superstition) . . . and whatsoever shall be found to be contrary to sound doctrine and power of Godliness. . . .

That we shall . . . endeavor . . . to preserve the rights and privileges of the Parliaments and the liberties of the Kingdoms, and to preserve and defend the King's Majesty's person and authority in the preservation and defence of the true religion and liberties of the Kingdoms, that the world may bear witness . . . that we have no thoughts or intentions to diminish his Majesty's power and greatness. . . .

And whereas the happiness of a blessed peace between these Kingdoms . . . is by the good providence of God granted to us, and hath been lately concluded and settled by both Parliaments, we shall . . . endeavor that they may remain conjoined in a firm peace and union. . . . (Rushworth, *Historical Collections*, V, 478.)

## Parliamentary Ordinance Appointing the Committee for Cooperation with Scotland. 1644

**115.**  THIS ordinance was a further step toward Parliament's abdication of rights and flight from responsibility which preceded the dictatorship of Oliver Cromwell. The *Covenant* of 1643 had sworn away the right of the English people to control the reorganization of the Church in favor of a religious form completely foreign and unacceptable to a majority of the sectarians. The present ordinance placed in the hands of an uncommonly small committee absolute direction of the war and a large amount of liberty in the conduct of foreign affairs. If the *Covenant* was the entryway for Cromwell, the spokesmen of the Independent sects, into political life, the *Ordinance* of 1644 provided the requisite political atmosphere for Parliament's future acceptance of his dictatorship.

An ordinance for the appointing a committee of both Houses of Parliament to join with the committees and commissioners of Scotland for the better managing the affairs of both nations in the common cause, according to the ends expressed in the late *Covenant and Treaty between the two nations of England and Scotland.*

Whereas, by the *Covenant and Treaty* ratified and established between the two Kingdoms, both nations are engaged in one common cause against the enemies of their religion and liberties, and ... are firmly united in a joint posture of arms for their own necessary defence, and for the attaining the ends expressed in the *Covenant and Treaty;* and whereas both Kingdoms have thought it necessary that they should be joined in their counsels as well as in their forces, and in pursuance thereof the convention of the estates of Scotland have appointed committees residing in Scotland and in the Scottish army, and have sent some of the said committees as commissioners for the purposes aforesaid to repair unto and to reside near the Parliament. ...

In consideration hereof the Lords and Commons do nominate, ordain, and appoint [twenty-one members of both houses] ... to treat with the committees and commissioners appointed by our brethren of Scotland in such things as shall by them be propounded from and in the name of the Kingdom of Scotland for the ends aforesaid; as likewise to propound to the committees and commissioners of Scotland whatever they shall receive in charge from both Houses, and from time to time to advise and consult concerning the same and report the results to both Houses. And further power and authority is hereby given to them ... as a joint committee with the committee and commissioners of Scotland, to advise, consult, order, and direct concerning the carrying on and managing of the war for the best advantage of the three Kingdoms, and the keeping a good intelligence between the three Kingdoms, their forces, committees, and counsels; and likewise with power to hold good correspondence and intelligence with foreign states, and further to advise and consult of all things in pursuance to the ends in the late *Covenant and Treaty.*

Provided always that nothing in this ordinance shall authorize the committee hereby appointed to advise, treat, or consult concerning any cessation of arms or making peace, without express directions from both Houses of Parliament. ... (*Journals of the House of Lords,* VI, 430.)

## The Self-denying Ordinance. 1645

## 116.

IT WAS apparent after the events of 1644, which culminated in Cromwell's decisive victory at Marston Moor, that the Royalist cause was a lost one. The King's armies, listless and without supplies, were led by officers less gifted in tactics and strategy than Cromwell, Lambert, and Fairfax. Assured of eventual victory Parliament had only to wait for the King to accept the situation and agree to the terms of peace. However, the unity urged by common purpose and hope for victory disintegrated early in 1645, and two opposed groups emerged once again to rob Parliament of its effectiveness. One group desired peace by way of arbitration and mutual compromise. The other, determined to increase the military pressures on the King and win a clear and undisputed victory, wished to rid the army of officers whose incompetence was known or whose willingness to arbitrate the struggle was suspected. The *Ordinance* was a compromise between the two extremes. All members of Parliament were required to resign their military commands. This retirement opened the way for Cromwell's reorganization of Parliament's military forces around the New Model army.

An ordinance of the Lords and Commons assembled in Parliament for the discharging of the members of both Houses and all officers, both military and civil.

Be it ordained by the Lords and the Commons assembled in Parliament that all and every of the members of either House of Parliament shall be and by authority of this ordinance are discharged, at the end of forty days after the passing of this ordinance... from every office or command, military or civil... conferred by both or either of the said Houses of this present Parliament, or by any authority derived from both or either of them since the twentieth day of November, 1640.

And be it further ordained that all other governors and commanders of any island, town, castle, or fort, and all other colonels and officers inferior to colonels in the several armies, not being members of either of the Houses of Parliament, shall, according to their respective commissions, continue in their several places and commands wherein they were employed and entrusted the twentieth day of March, as if this ordinance had not been made.

Provided always, and it is further ordained and declared, that during this war the bene-fit of all offices, being neither military nor judicial, hereafter to be granted or any way to be appointed to any person or persons by both or either House of Parliament... shall go and inure to such public uses as both Houses of Parliament shall appoint. And the grantees and persons executing all such offices shall be accountable to the Parliament for all the profits and perquisites thereof, and shall have no profit out of any such office, other than a competent salary for the execution of the same, in such manner as both Houses of Parliament shall order....

Provided that this ordinance shall not extend to take away the power and authority of any lieutenancy or deputy-lieutenancy in the several counties, cities, or places, or of any... commission for Justice of Peace

.... Provided always, and it is hereby declared, that those members of either House, who had offices by grant from his Majesty before this Parliament [met], and were by his Majesty displaced [during]... this Parliament, and have since by authority of both Houses been restored, shall not by this ordinance be discharged from their said offices or profits thereof.... (Rushworth, *Historical Collections*, VI, 16.)

## The Heads of Proposals. 1647

**117.** THIS document, drawn up after long and furious debate between the more radical of the independent groups and those who favored a more conservative settlement of the issue of the civil war, was the first of the Puritan experiments with a written constitution.

The fact that it was Oliver Cromwell who persuaded the army officers, by and large a moderate group, to offer these compromises to the King, illustrates the growth of the new conservatism. As a property holder of genteel family background Cromwell apparently saw danger in the radicals' demands. Having consistently taken a stand against all extremes, such as the claimed absolute right of the Crown, the arbitrariness of the Presbyterians, and the self-seeking interests of Parliament, Cromwell now tried his powers of persuasion in behalf of the political regeneration of the Monarchy. Although apparently almost every demand made in the document seemed to reiterate one or another of the earlier claims of Parliament, in reality the *Proposals* would have checked the King's powers under a written constitution without essentially changing them. The King's rejection of the demands made in the document isolated Cromwell from the radical Levellers who saw in the offer an attempt by the conservative army officers to attain their own selfish political ends.

The heads of the proposals agreed upon by his excellency Sir Thomas Fairfax and the Council of the Army, to be tendered to the commissioners of Parliament residing with the army and with them to be treated on by the Commissioners of the Army... that a certain period may by act of Parliament be set for the ending of this Parliament, such period to be put within a year at most, and in the same act provision to be made for the succession and constitution of Parliaments in the future, as follows:—

1. That Parliaments may biennially be called and meet at a certain day, with such provision for the certainty thereof as in the late Act was made for triennial Parliaments [*Triennial Act,* 16 Charles I], and what further or other provision shall be found needful by the Parliament to reduce it to more certainty. And upon the passing of this, the said Act for triennial Parliaments to be repealed.

2. Each biennial Parliament to sit 120 days certain, unless adjourned or dissolved sooner by their own consent; afterwards to be adjournable or dissolvable by the King. And no Parliament to sit past 240 days from their first meeting, or some other limited number of days to be agreed on; upon the expiration whereof each Parliament is to dissolve of course, if not otherwise dissolved sooner.

3. The King, upon advice of the Council of State, in the intervals between biennial Parliaments, to call a Parliament extraordinary; provided it meet above 70 days before the next biennial day and be dissolved at least 60 days before the same, so as the course of biennial elections may never be interrupted.

4. That this Parliament and each succeeding biennial Parliament, on or before adjournment or dissolution thereof, may appoint committees to continue during the interval for such purposes as are in any of these proposals referred to such committees.

5. That the elections of the commons for succeeding Parliaments may be distributed to all counties, or other parts or divisions of the Kingdom, according to some rule of equality of proportion; so as all counties may have a number of Parliament members allowed to their choice proportionable to the respective rates they bear in the common charges and burdens of the Kingdom, or according to some other rule of equality or proportion, to render the House of Commons, as near as may be, an equal representative of the whole. And in order thereunto, that a present consideration be had to take off the elections of burgesses for poor, decayed, or inconsiderable towns, and to give some present addition to the number of Parliament members for great counties that have now less than their due proportion, to bring all ... as near as may be, to such a rule of proportion as is aforesaid.

6. That effectual provision be made for future freedom of elections, and certainty of due returns.

7. That the House of Commons alone have the power from time to time to set down further orders and rules for the ends expressed in the last two preceding articles, so as to reduce the elections of members for that House to more and more perfection of equality in the distribution, freedom in the election, order in the proceeding thereof, and certainty in the returns....

8. That there be a liberty for entering dissents in the House of Commons, with provision that no member be censurable for anything said or voted in the House further than to exclusion from that trust; and that only by the judgment of the House itself.

9. That the judicial power, or power of final judgment in the Lords and Commons ... may be cleared; and that no officer of justice, minister of state, or other person adjudged by them, may be capable of protection or pardon from the King without their advice or consent.

10. That the right and liberty of the Commons of England may be cleared and vindicated as to a due exemption from any judgment, trial, or other proceeding against

them by the House of Lords, without the concurring judgment of the House of Commons, as also from any other judgment, sentence, or proceeding against them, other than by their equals or according to the law of the land.

11. The same Act [should] provide that grand-jurymen may be chosen by and for several parts or divisions of each county respectively, in some equal way ... and that such grand-jurymen for their respective counties may at each assize present the names of persons to be made Justices of the Peace from time to time, as the county has need for any to be added to the commission; and at the summer assize to present the names of three persons, out of whom the King may pick one to be sheriff for the next year.

For the future security of Parliament and the militia in general, in order thereunto, that it be provided by act of Parliament:

1. That the power of the militia by sea and land during the space of ten years next ensuing shall be ordered ... by the Lords and Commons assembled ... in the Parliament ... of England by such persons as they shall ... appoint for that purpose....

2. That the said power shall not be ordered, disposed, or exercised by the King's majesty that now is, or by any person or persons by any authority derived from him, during the said space; or at any time hereafter by his said majesty without the ... consent of the said Lords and Commons....

3. That during the same space of ten years the said Lords and Commons may by bills or ordinance raise and dispose of what moneys and for what forces they shall from time to time find necessary, as also for payment of the public debts and damages, and for all other the public uses of the Kingdom.

4. And to the end the temporary security intended by the three particulars last precedent may be the better assured, it may therefore be provided that no subjects that have been in hostility against the Parliament in the late war shall be capable of bearing any office of power or public trust in the Com-

monwealth during the space of five years without the consent of Parliament or of the Council of State; or to sit as members or assistants of either House of Parliament until the second biennial Parliament be passed.

For the present form of disposing the militia in order to the peace and safety of this Kingdom and the service of Ireland:

1. That there be commissioners for the admiralty, with the vice-admiral and rear-admiral now to be agreed on, with power for the forming, regulating, appointing of officers and providing for the navy....

2. That there be a general for command of the land forces that are to be in pay both in England, Ireland, and Wales, both for field and garrison.

3. That there be commissioners in the several counties for the standing militia of the respective counties ... with power for the proportioning, forming, regulating, training, and disciplining of them.

4. That there be a Council of State, with power to superintend and direct the several and particular powers of the militia last mentioned for the peace and safety of this Kingdom and of Ireland.

5. That the same Council may have power, as the King's Privy Council, for and in all foreign negotiations; provided that the making of war and peace with any other Kingdom or State shall not be without the advice and consent of Parliament.

6. That the said power of the Council of State be put into the hands of trusty and able persons now to be agreed on, and the same persons to continue in that power ... for the certain term not exceeding seven years.

7. That there be a sufficient establishment now provided for the salary of forces both in England and Ireland, the establishment to continue until two months after the meeting of the first biennial Parliament.

That an act be passed for disposing the great offices for ten years by the Lords and Commons in Parliament ... and after ten years they to nominate three and the King out of that number to appoint one for the succession upon any vacancy. . . .

That an act be passed for confirmation of the treaties between the two Kingdoms of England and Scotland, and for appointing conservators of the peace between them. . . .

And an act to be passed to take away all coercive power, authority, and jurisdiction of bishops and all other ecclesiastical officers whatsoever extending to any civil penalties. . . .

That there be a repeal of all acts or clauses in any act enjoining the use of the *Book of Common Prayer* and imposing any penalties for neglect thereof; as also of all acts or clauses in any act imposing any penalty for not coming to church, or for meetings elsewhere for prayer or other religious duties, exercises, or ordinances; and some other provision to be made for discovering all papists and popish recusants, and for disabling of them and of all Jesuits or priests from disturbing the State.

That the taking of the Covenant be not enforced upon any, nor any penalties imposed on the refusers, whereby men might be restrained to take it against their judgments or conscience. . . .

That—the things herebefore proposed being provided, for settling and securing the rights, liberties, peace and safety of the Kingdom—his Majesty's person, his queen, and royal issue may be restored to a condition of safety, honor, and freedom in this nation, without diminuation to their personal rights, or further limitation to the exercises of the regal power than according to the particulars foregoing. . . .

Next to the proposals aforesaid for the present settling of a peace, we shall desire that no time may be lost by the Parliament for dispatch of other things tending to the welfare, ease, and just satisfaction of the Kingdom, and in special manner that the just and necessary liberty of the people to represent their grievances and desires by way of petition, may be cleared and vindicated. . . .

That the common grievances of this people may be speedily considered of and effectually redressed, and in particular; that the excise may be taken from such commodities whereon the poor people of the land do ordinarily live, and a certain time to be limited for taking of the whole; that the oppressions and encroachments of forest laws may be prevented for the future; all monopolies, old or new, and restraints to the freedom of trade to be taken off; that a course may be taken and commissioners appointed to settle the proportion for land rates to more equality throughout the Kingdom; the present unequal, troublesome, and contentious way of ministers' maintenance by tithes to be considered of, and some remedy applied; that the rules and course of law, and the officers of it, may be so reduced and reformed as that all suits and questions of right may be more clear and certain in the issues, and not so tedious nor chargeable in the proceedings as now; that the estates of all men may be some way made liable to their debts . . . whether they be imprisoned for it or not; some provision to be made that none may be compelled by penalty or otherwise to answer unto questions tending to the accusing of themselves or their nearest relations in criminal causes, and no man's life to be taken away under two witnesses; that consideration may be had of all statutes, and the laws or customs of corporations, imposing any oaths, either to repeal or else to qualify the same, so far as they may extend . . . to the molestation or ensnaring of religious and peaceable people merely for nonconformity in religion. . . .

That provision may be made for payment of arrears to the army and the rest of the soldiers of the Kingdom who have concurred with the army in the late desires and proceedings thereof; and in the next place for payment of the public debts and damages of the Kingdom; and that to be performed, first to such persons whose debt or damages . . . are great, and their estates small, so as they are thereby reduced to a difficulty of subsistence. . . . (Rushworth, *Historical Collections*, VII, 731.)

## An Agreement of the People. 1649

I I 8.    SEVEN years of growing radical strength added to the confidence of the Levellers, a group which held that the distribution of property should not be the sole determinant of the composition of Parliament or the nature of government. The *Agreement* was the product of the Levellers' determination to shape the perfect civil constitution—and their answer to the *Heads of Proposals*. And, although the conservative officers led by Cromwell and Ireton rejected the *Agreement* as utopian and impractical, it nevertheless was an almost exact statement of the political ideals of the majority of the lower class sectarians. It demanded abolition of the Monarchy and the House of Lords. Religious toleration was to be extended to all, even Catholics, and all elections were to be decided by universal manhood suffrage. The high point of progressive political philosophy was reached in the bill of rights incorporated into the *Agreement*, enumerating man's fundamental liberties based on the laws of reason and nature. Those rights, and all the laws limiting the powers of government, were to be enforced by the courts, which received their power to act by delegation from the sovereignty of the entire people. These concepts—the sovereignty of the people, a written constitution based on man's natural and inalienable rights, and the limitations imposed on the powers of the State—were not necessarily unique to the radicals of mid-seventeenth century England. It was, however, radical determination which placed those concepts in the mainstream of English constitutional development.

An agreement of the people of England and the places therewith incorporated for a secure and present peace upon grounds of common right, freedom, and safety.

Having, by our late labors and hazards, made it appear to the world at how high a rate we value our just freedom, and God having so far owned our cause as to deliver the enemies thereof into our hands, we do now hold ourselves bound, in mutual duty to each other, to take the best care we can for the future to avoid both the danger of returning into a slavish condition and the chargeable remedy of another war. For, as it cannot be imagined that so many of our countrymen would have opposed us in this quarrel if they had understood their own good, so may we hopefully promise to ourselves that, when our common rights and liberties shall be cleared, their endeavors will be disappointed that seek to make themselves our masters. Since, therefore, our former oppressions and not yet ended troubles have been occasioned, either by want of frequent national meetings in council, or by the undue or unequal constitution

thereof, or by rendering those meetings ineffectual, we are fully agreed and resolved, God willing, to provide that hereafter our Representatives [Parliaments] be neither left to an uncertainty for times nor be unequally constituted, nor made useless to the ends for which they are intended. In order whereunto we declare and agree:

First, that, to prevent the many inconveniences apparently arising from the long continuance of the same persons in supreme authority, this present Parliament end and dissolve upon or before the last day of April, 1649.

Secondly, that the people of England, being at this day very unequally distributed by counties, cities, and boroughs for the election of their Representatives, be indifferently proportioned; and, to this end, that the Representative of the whole nation shall consist of 400 persons, or not above; and in each county and the places thereto subjoined there shall be chosen, to make up the said Representative at all times, the several numbers here mentioned; [each constituency in Wales and England is here assigned the number of its representatives.] **Provided that the first or second Representative may**, if they see cause, assign the remainder of the 400 representers, not hereby assigned, or so many of them as they shall see cause for, unto such counties as shall appear in this present distribution to have less than their due proportion. Provided also that, where any city or borough, to which one representer or more is assigned, shall be found in a due proportion not competent alone to elect a representer or the number of representers assigned thereto, it is left to future Representatives to assign such a number of parishes or villages near adjoining to such city or borough, to be joined therewith in the elections, as may make the same proportionable.

Thirdly, that the people do of course choose themselves a Representative once in two years, and shall meet for the purpose upon the first Thursday in every second May, by eleven in the morning; and the Representatives so chosen to meet upon the second Thursday in the June following at the usual place in Westminster, or such other place as, by the foregoing Representative or the Council of State in the interval, shall be from time to time appointed and published to the people, at the least twenty days before the time of election; and [they are] to continue their sessions there or elsewhere until the second Thursday in December following, unless they shall adjourn or dissolve themselves sooner, but not to continue longer. The election of the first Representative to be on the first Thursday in May, 1649; and that and all future elections to be according to the rules prescribed for the same purpose in this agreement; i.e.,

(1) That the electors in every division shall be natives or denizens of England; not persons receiving alms, but such as are assessed ordinarily towards the relief of the poor; not servants to, and receiving wages from, any particular person; and in all elections, except for the Universities,

they shall be men of twenty-one years of age ... and house-holders, dwelling within the division for which the election is [held] ... [any person who sided with the King in the civil war should be debarred from political participation for seven years]. ...
(2) That, to the end all officers of State may be certainly accountable and no factions made to maintain corrupt interests, no member of a Council of State, nor any officer of any salary-forces in army or garrison, nor any treasurer or receiver of public money, shall, while such, be elected to be of a Representative; and in case any such election shall be, the same to be void; and in case any lawyer shall be chosen into any Representative or Council of State, then he shall be incapable of practice as a lawyer during that trust.
(3) For the more convenient election of Representatives, each county wherein more than three representers are to be chosen, with the towns corporate and cities ... within the compass thereof to which no representers are herein assigned, shall be divided by a due proportion into so many and such parts as each part may elect two, and no part above three representers. ...

Fourthly, that 150 members at least be always present in each sitting of the Representative, at the passing of any law or doing of any act whereby the people are to be bound; saving that the number of 60 may make a House for debates or resolutions that are preparatory thereunto.

Fifthly, that each Representative shall, within twenty days after their first meeting, appoint a Council of State for the managing of public affairs until the tenth day after the meeting of the next Representative, unless that next Representative think fit to put an end to that trust sooner. And the same Council to act and proceed therein according to such instructions and limitations as the Representative shall give, and not otherwise.

Sixthly, that in each interval between biennial Representatives the Council of State, in case of imminent danger or extreme necessity, may summon a Representative to be forthwith chosen and to meet; so as the session thereof continue not above eighty days, and so as it dissolve at least fifty days before the appointed time for the next biennial Representative. And upon the fiftieth day so preceding it shall dissolve of course, if not otherwise dissolved sooner.

Seventhly, that no member of any Representative be made either receiver, treasurer, or other officer during that employment, saving to be a member of the Council of State.

Eighthly, that the Representatives have ... the supreme trust in order to the preservation and government of the whole; and that their power extend, without the consent or concurrence of any other person or persons, to the erecting and abolishing of courts of justice and public offices, and to the enacting, altering, repealing, and declaring of laws, and the highest and final judgment concerning all natural or civil things, but not concerning things spiritual.... Provided that, even in things natural and civil, these six particulars next following are ... excepted and reserved from our Representatives:

(1) We do not empower them to impress or constrain any person to serve in foreign war, either by sea or land, nor for any military service within the kingdom; save that they may take order for the forming, training, and exercising of the people in a military way, to be in readiness for resisting of foreign invasions, suppressing of sudden insurrections, or for assisting in execution of the laws. And [the Representative] may take order for the employing and conducting of them for those ends, provided that, even in such cases, none be compellable to go out of the county he lives in, if he procure another to serve in his place.

(2) That, after the time herein limited for the commencement of the first Representative, none of the people may be in any time questioned for anything said or done in relation to the late wars or public differences, otherwise than in execution or pursuance of the determinations of the present House of Commons, against such as have adhered to the King or his interests against the people; and saving that accountants for public moneys received, shall remain accountable for the same.

(3) That no securities given or to be given by the public faith of the nation, nor any engagements of the public faith for satisfaction of debts and damages, shall be made void or invalid by the next or any future Representatives; except to such creditors as have or shall have justly forfeited the same; and saving that the next Representative may confirm or make null, in part or in whole, all gifts of lands, moneys, offices, or otherwise, made by the present Parliament to any member or attendant of either House.

(4) That, in any laws hereafter to be made, no person, by virtue of any tenure, grant, charter, patent, degree, or birth, shall be privileged from subjection thereto, or from being bound thereby....

(5) That the Representative may not give judgment upon any man's person or estate, where no law has before provided; save only in calling to account and punishing public officers for abusing or failing in their trust.

(6) That no Representative may in any way render up or give or take away any of the foundations of common right, liberty, and safety contained in this agreement, nor level men's estates, destroy property, or make all things common; and that, in all matters of such fundamental concernment, there shall be a liberty to particular members of the said Representatives to enter their dissents from the major vote.

Ninthly, concerning religion, we agree as follows:

(1) It is intended that the Christian religion be held forth and recommended as the public profession in this nation; which we desire may, by the grace of God, be reformed to the greatest purity in doctrine, worship, and discipline, according to the word of God. The instructing the people thereunto in a public way, so it be not compulsive, as also the maintaining of able teachers for that end and for the confutation or discovery of heresy, error, and whatsoever is contrary to sound doctrine, is allowed to be provided for by our Representatives; the maintenance of which teachers may be out of a public treasury, and we desire, not by tithes—provided that popery or prelacy be not held forth as the public way or profession in this nation.

(2) That to the public profession so held forth, none be compelled by penalties or otherwise, but only may be endeavored to be won by sound doctrine and the example of a good conversation.

(3) That such as profess faith in God by Jesus Christ, however differing in judgment from the doctrine, worship, or discipline publicly held forth, as aforesaid, shall not be restrained from, but shall be protected in, the profession of their faith and exercise of religion according to their consciences in any place except such as shall be set apart for the public worship ...so as they abuse not this liberty to the civil injury of others or to actual disturbance of the public peace on their parts. Nevertheless, it is not intended to be hereby provided that this liberty shall necessarily extend to popery or prelacy.

(4) That all laws, ordinances, statutes, and clauses in any such law, statute, or ordinance to the contrary of the liberty herein provided for, in the two particulars next preceding concerning religion, be and are hereby repealed and made void.

Tenthly, it is agreed that whosoever shall by force of arms resist the orders of the next or any future Representative—except in case where such Representative shall evidently render up, or give, or take away the foundations of common right, liberty, and safety contained in this agreement—he shall forthwith ... lose the benefit and protection of the laws and shall be punishable with death as an enemy and traitor to the nation.

.... The things expressed in [Articles 1, 2, 3 (1) and (2), 4, 6, 8 (1-6), 9 (2) and (3), and 10] we do account and declare to be fundamental to our common right, liberty, and safety; and therefore do both agree thereunto and resolve to maintain the same.... The rest of the matters in this agreement we account to be useful and good for the public. And the particular circumstance of numbers, times, and places expressed in the several Articles we account not fundamental; but we find them necessary to be here determined for the making the agreement certain and practicable, and do hold these most convenient that are here set down, and therefore do positively agree thereunto.... (W. Cobbett, *Parliamentary History of England,* III, 1267.)

## Act Abolishing the House of Lords. 1649

THE abolition of the Upper House of Parliament by Commons was both a sop to the radicals and a political expedient aimed at eliminating from the government one of the continuing centers of resistance to Cromwell's growing political power.

**119.**

An Act for the abolishing the House of Peers.

The Commons of England assembled in Parliament, finding by too long experience that the House of Lords is useless and dangerous to the people of England to be continued, have thought fit to ordain and en-act ... that from henceforth the House of Lords in Parliament shall be and is hereby wholly abolished and taken away; and that the Lords shall not from henceforth meet or sit in the said House called the Lords' House, or in any other house or place whatsoever, as a House of Lords, nor shall sit, vote, advise, adjudge, or determine of any matter or thing ... as a House of Lords in Parliament.

Nevertheless it is hereby declared that neither such Lords as have demeaned themselves with honor, courage, and fidelity to the Commonwealth, nor their posterities who shall continue so, shall be excluded from the public councils of the nation; but shall be admitted thereunto and have their free vote in Parliament, if they shall be thereunto elected.... (H. Scobell, *Collections,* 16.)

## Act Abolishing Kingship. 1649

**120.** HAVING vested all power in its own hands and having declared England to be a Commonwealth, Parliament paved the way for the execution of Charles by abolishing the institution of kingship. The Act was a mere formality although its constitutional implications were extremely significant. By legally disposing of the office of the King Parliament insured its own position as sole arbiter of English political life. The struggle for sovereign power was brought to an end; but the national representative had come finally to accept the Stuart theory that sovereign power was necessary to the welfare of the State.

An Act for the abolishing the Kingly office in England, Ireland, and the dominions thereunto belonging.

Whereas it is and has been found by experience that the office of a King in this nation and Ireland ... is unnecessary, burdensome, and dangerous to the liberty, safety, and public interest of the people; and that for the most part use has been made of the regal power and prerogative to oppress and impoverish and enslave the subject; and that usually and naturally any one person in such power makes it his interest to encroach upon the just freedom and liberty of the people and to promote the setting up of their own will and power above the laws....

Be it therefore enacted and ordained by this present Parliament ... that the office of a King in this nation shall not henceforth reside in or be exercised by any one single person....

And whereas, by the abolition of the kingly office provided for in this Act, a most happy way is made for this nation ... to return to its just and ancient right of being governed by its own representatives ... chosen and entrusted for that purpose by the people: it is therefore resolved and declared by the Commons assembled in Parliament that they will put a period to the sitting of this present Parliament and dissolve the same so soon as may possibly stand with the safety of the people that has betrusted them, and with what is absolutely necessary for the preserving ... the government now settled in the way of a Commonwealth; and that they will carefully provide for the certain choosing, meeting, and sitting of the next and future Representatives, with such other circumstances of freedom in choice and equality in distribution of members to be selected.... (H. Scobell, *Collections,* 12.)

## Act Establishing the Commonwealth. 1649

NO longer fearful of the influence of a King free to roam the countryside at the head
of an army, Commons—constituting itself as Parliament—proclaimed England a Commonwealth and vested supreme authority in itself "without any King or House of
Lords."

### I 2 I.

An Act declaring and constituting the people of England to be a Commonwealth and free state.

Be it declared and enacted by this present Parliament . . . that the people of England, and of all the dominions and territories thereto belonging, are and shall be, and are hereby constituted, made, established, and confirmed, to be a Commonwealth and free state, and shall from henceforth be governed as a Commonwealth and free state by the supreme authority of this nation—the representatives of the people in Parliament, and by such as they shall appoint and constitute as officers and ministers under them for the good of the people, and without any King or House of Lords. (Scobell, *Acts and Ordinances*, II, 30.)

## Act Erecting a High Court of Justice for the Trial of Charles I. 1649

### I 2 2.

HAVING dismantled the Monarchy, Parliament and Cromwell faced the problem of disposing of a useless and dangerous King. The present Act was also Charles's indict- ment, for it charged the King with a "wicked design totally to subvert the ancient and fundamental laws and liberties of this nation," and in their place to introduce an arbitrary and tyrannical government. Completely disregarding legal precedent, the judges were also the prosecutors and the chief witnesses against the King. Parliament was apparently unaware that by its nature tyranny is not limited to monarchs alone.

The Act of the Commons of England as- sembled in Parliament for erecting of a High Court of Justice for the trying and judging of Charles Stuart, King of England.

Whereas it is known that Charles Stuart, the now King of England, not content with those many encroachments which his prede- cessors had made upon the people in their rights and freedoms, has had a wicked design totally to subvert the ancient and funda- mental laws and liberties of this nation and in their place to introduce an arbitrary and tyrannical government, and that, besides all other evil ways and means to bring this de- sign to pass, he has prosecuted it with fire and sword, levied and maintained a cruel war in the land against the Parliament and Kingdom. . . .

For prevention therefore of the like or greater inconveniences, and to the end no chief officer or magistrate whatsoever may hereafter presume traitorously and mali- ciously to imagine or contrive the enslaving or destroying of the English nation, and to expect immunity for so doing:

Be it ordained and enacted by the Com- mons in Parliament, and it is hereby or- dained and enacted by the authority thereof, that Thomas Lord Fairfax, Oliver Crom- well, Henry Ireton and others . . . shall be . . . appointed and required to be commissioners and judges for the hearing, trying, and ad- judging of the said Charles Stuart. And the said commissioners, or any twenty or more of them, shall be . . . constituted a High Court of Justice to meet and sit at such convenient time and place as by the said commissioners ... shall be appointed ... and to take order for the charging of the said Charles Stuart, with the crimes and treasons above mentioned, and for the receiving of his personal answer thereunto, and for the examination of witnesses upon oath ... and taking any other evidence concerning the same; and thereupon, or in default of such answer, to proceed to final sentence according to justice and the merit of the case, and such final sentence to execute or cause to be executed speedily and impartially. ... (Gardiner, *Constitutional Documents*, 268.)

## King Charles's Statement to the Trial Court. 1649

123.

CHARLES'S statement was in effect a refusal to recognize the legal jurisdiction of the court constituted by Commons for his trial. The brevity, clarity, and preciseness of the King's refusal and his command of logic and legal reason showed Charles— when it was finally too late for compromise—to be as gifted as his father in perception and ability. Yet the statement, while excellent proof of the King's command of the fine points of law, was also evidence of the extreme poverty of his ability to accept political reality. The Stuart constitution under which a King could do no wrong had perished with Cromwell's victory at Marston Moor. Under the new constitution the abolition of the Kingship logically necessitated the elimination of its embodiment: the person of the King.

Having already made my protestations, not only against the illegality of this pretended court, but also that no earthly power can justly call me, who am your King, in question as a delinquent, I would not any more open my mouth upon this occasion more than to refer myself to what I have spoken, were I in this case alone concerned; but the duty I owe to God in the preservation of the true liberty of my people will not suffer me at this time to be silent. For how can any free-born subject of England call life or anything he possesses his own, if power without right daily make new and abrogate the old fundamental laws of the land—which I take to be the present case? ....

There is no proceeding justly against any man but what is warranted either by God's laws or the municipal laws of the country where he lives. Now I am most confident this day's proceeding cannot be warranted by God's laws; for, on the contrary, the authority of obedience unto Kings is clearly warranted and strictly commanded in both the Old and New Testament. ... [As] for the law of this land, I am no less confident that no learned lawyer will affirm that an impeachment can lie against the King, they all going in his name. And one of their maxims is that the King can do no wrong. ...

How the House of Commons can erect a court of judicature, which was never one itself, as is well-known to all lawyers, I leave to God and the world to judge. And it were full as strange that they should pretend to make laws without King or Lord's House, to any that have heard speak of the laws of England. And admitting, but not granting, that the people of England's commission could grant your pretended power, I see nothing you can show for that; for certainly you never asked the question of the tenth man in the Kingdom; and in this way you manifestly wrong even the poorest ploughman, if you demand not his free consent. ...

Thus you see that I speak not for my own right alone ... but also for the true liberty of all my subjects, which consists, not in the power of government, but in living under such laws, such a government, as may give them the best assurance of their lives and property. ... Besides all this, the peace of the

Kingdom is not the least in my thoughts. And what hope of settlement is there so long as power reigns without rule of law, changing the whole frame of that government under which this Kingdom has flourished for many hundred years? . . . . And believe it, the common people of England will not thank you for this . . . for they will remember how happy they have been of late years under the reigns of Queen Elizabeth, the King my father, and myself, until the beginning of these unhappy troubles, and will have cause to doubt that they shall never be so happy under any new. And by this time it will be too sensibly evident that the arms I took up were only to defend the fundamental laws of this Kingdom against those who have supposed my power has changed the ancient government.

Thus, having showed you briefly the reasons why I cannot submit to your pretended authority without violating the trust which I have from God for the welfare and liberty of my people, I expect from you either clear reasons to convince my judgment, or that you will withdraw your proceedings. . . . (Rushworth, *Historical Collections,* VII, 1403.)

## Act for the Control of Trade and Navigation. 1651

THE methods of trade control which were contributing so generously to the wealth of the continental states were not overlooked by the Commonwealth government of England. Although certain "navigation" laws had been enforced by Elizabeth and James, the present statute was a clear departure from earlier methods of trade regulation which had been of a definite monopolistic cast. Having successfully attacked the principle of control upon which trade monopolies had traditionally rested, the Puritans now reestablished governmental control of trade while simultaneously opening the way to the later development of free trade.

**124.**

An Act for increase of shipping and encouragement of the navigation of this nation.

For the increase of the shipping and the encouragement of the navigation of this nation, which under the good providence . . . of God is so great a means of the welfare and safety of this Commonwealth, be it enacted by this present Parliament . . . that . . . no goods or commodities whatsoever of the growth, production, or manufacture of Asia, Africa, or America, or of any part thereof, or of any islands belonging to them . . . as well of the English plantations as others, shall be imported or brought into this Commonwealth of England, or into Ireland, or any other lands, islands, plantations, or territories to this Commonwealth belonging . . . in any other ship . . . but only in such as do . . . belong only to the people of this Commonwealth or the plantations thereof . . . and whereof the master and mariners are also for the most part of them of the people of this Commonwealth, under the penalty of . . . forfeiture. . . .

And it is further enacted . . . that no goods or commodities of the growth, production, or manufacture of Europe . . . shall . . . be imported . . . into this Commonwealth . . . or into Ireland, or any other [possessions] of this Commonwealth . . . in any ship or ships . . . whatsoever, but in such as do truly and without fraud belong only to the people of this Commonwealth . . . and in no other, except only such foreign ships and vessels as do truly . . . belong to the people of that country or place of which the said goods are the growth, . . . or manufacture, or to such ports where the said goods can only be or most usually are first shipped for transportation. . . . (Scobell, *Acts and Ordinances,* II, 165.)

## The Instrument of Government. 1653

**125.** AFTER Cromwell's dissolution of the Nominated Parliament the English people once again turned to experimentation with a written constitution. The *Instrument of Government,* although applied effectively for only a few years, left a lasting imprint on the constitutional thought and methods of the English people. The main objectives of the *Instrument* were to balance the legislative and executive powers and to prevent the expression of arbitrarily assumed authority by any individual or group. Yet, advanced as it was as a statement of political theory and as a sincere effort to formulate ethical political principles for government, the *Instrument* was fatally defective in its omissions. If executive and legislature, evenly balanced in political power, should disagree or quarrel, there was no authorized or sufficiently powerful institution to arbitrate the dispute. One side or the other must eventually be forced to maintain its way by resorting to force.

Fundamentally the *Instrument* was the product of the conservative Independents. The right to vote for members of Parliament was limited to possessors of at least two hundred pounds in real or personal property. In short the franchise was extended to those who, because of their economic position, would almost certainly favor a republican form of government, yet who would not be sympathetic to the leveling tendencies of the more radical sectarians.

The government of the Commonwealth of England, Scotland, and Ireland, and the dominions thereunto belonging:

That the supreme legislative authority of the Commonwealth of England, Scotland, and Ireland, and the dominions thereunto belonging, shall be and reside in one person and the people assembled in Parliament; the style of which person shall be the Lord Protector of the Commonwealth of England, Scotland, and Ireland.

That the exercise of the chief magistracy and the administration of the government over the said countries and dominions, and the people thereof, shall be in the Lord Protector, assisted with a Council the number whereof shall not exceed twenty-one nor be less than thirteen.

That all writs, process, commissions, patents, grants, and other things, which now run in the name and style of the keepers of the liberty of England by authority of Parliament, shall run in the name and style of the Lord Protector; from whom for the future, shall be derived all magistracy and honors in these three nations. And [the Protector] have the power of pardons, except in case of murders and treason, and benefit of all forfeitures for the public use; and shall **govern**

the said countries and dominions in all things by the advice of the Council, and according to these presents and the laws.

That the Lord Protector, [with] the Parliament sitting, shall dispose and order the militia and forces, both by sea and land, for the peace and good of the three nations by consent of Parliament; and that the Lord Protector, with the advice and consent of the major part of the Council, shall dispose and order the militia for the ends aforesaid in the intervals of Parliament.

That the Lord Protector, by the advice aforesaid, shall direct in all things concerning the keeping and holding of a good correspondency with foreign kings, princes, and states; and also, with the consent of the major part of the Council, have the power of war and peace.

That the laws shall not be altered, suspended, abrogated, or repealed, nor any new law made, nor any tax, charge, or imposition laid upon the people, but by common consent in Parliament....

That there shall be a Parliament summoned to meet at Westminster upon the third day of September, 1654, and that successively a Parliament shall be summoned once in every third year....

That neither the Parliament to be next summoned nor any successive Parliaments shall, during the time of five months to be accounted from the day of their first meeting, be adjourned, prolonged, or dissolved, without their own consent.

That as well the next as all other successive Parliaments shall be summoned and elected in manner hereafter expressed: that is to say, the persons to be chosen within England, Wales, the isles of Jersey, Guernsey, and the town of Berwick-upon-Tweed to sit and serve in Parliament shall be, and not exceed, the number of 400; the persons to be chosen within Scotland . . . 30; . . . for Ireland . . . 30.

That all . . . persons who have aided, advised, assisted, or abetted in any war against Parliament since the first day of January, 1641—unless they have been since in the service of the Parliament and given signal testimony proof of their good affection thereunto—shall be disabled and incapable to be elected or to give any vote in the election of any members to serve in the next Parliament or in the three succeeding triennial Parliaments.

That all such who have advised, assisted, or abetted the rebellion of Ireland shall be disabled and incapable forever to be elected or give any vote in the election of any member to serve in Parliament; as also all such who do or shall profess the Roman Catholic religion. . . .

That the persons who shall be elected to serve in Parliament shall be such . . . as are . . . of known integrity, fearing God, and of good conversation, and being of the age of twenty-one years.

That all and every person . . . seised or possessed to his own use, of any estate, real or personal, to the value of £200, and not within the aforesaid exceptions, shall be capable to vote for members to serve in Parliament. . . .

That the Lord Protector, with the advice of the major part of the Council, shall at any other time than is before expressed, when the necessities of the State shall require

it, summon Parliaments in manner before expressed; which shall not be adjourned, prorogued, or dissolved without their own consent during the first three months of their sitting. And in case of future war with any foreign state a Parliament shall be forthwith summoned for their advice concerning the same.

That all bills agreed unto by the Parliament shall be presented to the Lord Protector for his consent; and in case he shall not give his consent thereto within twenty days after they shall be presented to him, or give satisfaction to the Parliament within the time limited, that then, upon declaration of the Parliament that the Lord Protector has not consented nor given satisfaction, such bills shall pass into and become laws, although he shall not give his consent thereunto; provided such bills contain nothing in them contrary to the matters contained in these presents.

That Henry Lawrence and 14 others here nominated . . . or any seven of them, shall be a Council for the purposes expressed in this writing. And upon the death or other removal of any of them, the Parliament shall nominate six persons of ability, integrity, and fearing God, for every one that is dead or removed, out of which the major part of the Council shall elect two, and present them to the Lord Protector, of which he shall elect one. . . . And in case of . . . miscarriage in any of the Council in their trust, the Parliament shall appoint seven of their number, and the Council six, who, together with the lord chancellor, lord keeper, or commissioners of the great seal for the time being, shall have power to hear and determine such corruption and miscarriage, and to award and inflict punishment, as the nature of the offence shall deserve; which punishment shall not be pardoned or remitted by the Lord Protector. . . .

That the Lord Protector and the major part of the Council aforesaid may, at any time before the meeting of the next Parliament, add to the Council such persons as they shall think fit, provided the number of the Council be not made thereby to exceed twenty-one, and the quorum to be proportioned accordingly by the Lord Protector and the major part of the Council.

That a constant yearly revenue shall be raised, settled, and established for maintaining of 10,000 horse and dragoons and 20,000 foot in England, Scotland, and Ireland, for the defence and security thereof; and also for a convenient number of ships for guarding of the seas; besides £200,000 yearly for defraying the other necessary charges of administration of justice and other expenses of the government; which revenue shall be raised by the customs, and such other ways and means as shall be agreed upon by the Lord Protector and the Council, and shall not be taken away or diminished, nor the way agreed upon for raising the same altered, but by the consent of the Lord Protector and the Parliament.

That the raising of money for defraying the charge of the present extraordinary forces ... in respect of the present wars, shall be by consent of Parliament and not otherwise; save only that the Lord Protector, with the consent of the major part of the Council, for preventing the disorders and dangers which might otherwise fall out both by sea and land, shall have power, until the meeting of the first Parliament, to raise money for the purposes aforesaid; and also to make laws and ordinances for the peace and welfare of these nations where it shall be necessary, which shall be binding and in force until order shall be taken in Parliament concerning the same....

That the office of Lord Protector over these nations shall be elective and not hereditary and, upon the death of the Lord Protector, another fit person shall be forthwith elected to succeed him in the government; which election shall be by the Council.... And until the aforesaid election be past, the Council shall take care of the government and administer in all things....

That Oliver Cromwell ... shall be and is hereby declared to be Lord Protector of the Commonwealth of England, Scotland, [etc.] ... for his life.

That the chancellor, keeper or commissioners of the great seal, the treasurer, admiral, chief governors of Ireland and Scotland, and the chief justices of the benches, shall be chosen by the approbation of Parliament; and, in the intervals of Parliament, by the approbation of the major part of the Council, to be afterwards approved by the Parliament.

That the Christian religion, as contained in the Scriptures, be held forth and recommended as the public profession of these nations; and that, as soon as may be, a provision less subject to scruple and contention, and more certain than the present, be made for the encouragement and maintenance of able ... teachers, for instructing the people, and for discovery and confutation of error, heresy, and whatever is contrary to sound doctrine; and that, until such provision be made, the present maintenance shall not be taken away nor impeached.

That to the public profession held forth none shall be compelled by penalties or otherwise; but that endeavors be used to win them by sound doctrine and the example of a good conversation.

That such as profess faith in God by Jesus Christ, though differing in judgment from the doctrine, worship, or discipline publicly held forth, shall not be restrained from, but shall be protected in, the profession of the faith and exercise of their religion; so as they abuse not this liberty to the civil injury of others and to the actual disturbance of the public peace on their parts; provided this liberty be not extended to popery nor prelacy, nor to such as, under the profession of Christ, hold forth and practice licentiousness....

That every successive Lord Protector ... shall take and subscribe a solemn oath, in the presence of the Council and such others as they shall call to them, that he will seek the peace, quiet, and welfare of these nations, cause law and justice to be equally administered, and that he will not violate or infringe the matters and things contained in this writing, and in all other things will, to his power and to the best of his understanding, govern these nations according to the laws, statutes, and customs thereof.

That each person of the Council shall, before they enter upon their trust, take and subscribe an oath, that they will be true and faithful in their trust, according to the best of their knowledge, and that in the election of every successive Lord Protector they shall proceed therein impartially, and do nothing therein for any promise, fear, favor, or reward. (Gardiner, *Constitutional Documents*, 314.)

## Gerard Winstanley, *An Humble Request to the Ministers of Both Universities and to All Lawyers in Every Inns-A-Court.* 1656

SUCCESSFUL as it was in destroying the civil authority of the Monarchy in the name of the liberty of the individual, the Puritan movement was theologically and ideologically split in the five-year period preceding the Restoration. The end of Stuart rule brought to the fore a series of social problems and crises which were without precedent. Freed from the old censorship laws, the Levellers demanded political reform in an almost endless flow of printed pamphlets, the Anabaptists demanded radical religious changes, and the Diggers economic reforms, while a host of less important sects and individuals sought other changes in church, constitution, and economic system.

126.

The Diggers' spokesman, Winstanley, was the first to interject the socialist concept of economic equality into the national debate. Although this particular facet of the Diggers' social concept was received with a marked lack of enthusiasm by the propertied Puritan leaders, it is certain that the Diggers' liberal ideals and demands for social consideration of the poor, as well as for the development of a sense of social responsibility, had some effect on political thought in 17th century England. And it is of more than passing interest to note that to the Digger sectarians the change of governments from Monarchial to Commonwealth republicanism did not necessarily indicate a basic change in political organization. In fact, Winstanley in this document interpreted the change to mean no more than the transference of tyrannical power from one master to another, neither of which was fundamentally interested in the wellbeing of the entire people.

True religion, and undefiled, is to let everyone quietly have earth to manure, that they may live in freedom by their labors; for it is earth that everyone seeks after, that they may live in peace....

The practice of the gentry is to have the earth to themselves: It is that the army fights for: It is that the clergy preaches for; ....

Nay, is it not the bottom of all national laws, to dispose of the earth: And does not this appear to be true, by the practice of lords of manors and the gentry, that cannot be at rest for raving and fretting, because poor men begin to see their creation-freedom, and begin to build upon, and plant the commons.

And men ... are like lions and devils, ready to kill and destroy these poor diggers; and not only the gentry, but the clergy generally are mad against this work....

And seeing the Scriptures confirms this creation-right to whole mankind, then in the next place it follows,

That all the title and power which the lords of manors have to the common land, whereby they beat the people off from this their freedom, is no other but the will of kings, who were conquerors and ruled ... by swordly power, enslaving mankind ...

First then consider, that King CHARLES and his laws was the successor of the person and power of WILLIAM the CON-QUEROR; for he did not rule by law of creation, suffering every one to enjoy their creation-right on the earth: but by the laws of a conquest which entitles some to the earth and shuts out others....

The first Parliament law, which encourages the poor commoners of England, to plant the commons and waste land, is this; wherein they declare England to be a free Commonwealth: This law breaks in pieces the kingly yoke, and the laws of the Conqueror, and gives a common freedom to every Englishman, to have a comfortable livelihood in this their own land, or else it cannot be a Commonwealth....

Therefore in reason and justice, I conceive, that if the poor people do build houses, and plant corn upon the commons of England, for a livelihood, they are protected and warranted both by Scriptures, and the laws of the present Commonwealth....

And whereas some Justices do say, that for poor men to dig and plant upon the commons, they do bring themselves within the statute, to be punished for vagrants, idle or wandering rogues: To this I answer,

That the Justices cannot call these men vagrants ... for by the law it is no vagrancy to dig and work.... They are *Englishmen* upon the commons of *England*,....

*Ministers* and *lawyers,* will you all stand looking on, and see the *lords* of *manors* exercise *kingly* power over the poor men that claim their creation-right in the earth, and be silent?

You would be called dispensers of justice; here is a point of justice for you to decide: This is a point upon which you shall either stand or fall, be saved or damned; for you are put upon the trial.... (Gerard Winstanley, *An Humble Request to the Ministers of Both Universities and to All Lawyers in Every Inns-A-Court,* 1656, 7-13.)

## The Humble Petition and Advice. 1657

**127.** THE *Humble Petition and Advice* symbolized two things that were apparent by 1657, the failure of Republicanism and the beginning of the return to the monarchial form of government. John Ashe, who submitted the document to Parliament, referred to its adoption as a renewal of the "ancient constitution." The document nominated Cromwell as King with power to choose his successor, reinstituted the House of Lords, and authorized a very large fixed revenue (not under Parliamentary control) for use of the executive. Cromwell refused the crown but accepted the rest of the *Humble Petition and Advice* for two reasons. Fear of rejection by the army of any kind of monarchial government made him wary of alienating his staunchest ally, while monarchy itself was alien to his fundamental political principles by that time.

However, the instrument opened the way to a new and more violent wave of political distemper. The broadening of toleration opened the doors of Parliament to men of many theological creeds and political programs—each bound more closely to his party than to Parliament itself. The bickering, uncertainty, and political intrigue led the Protector to the high-handed treatment of Parliament reminiscent of the Stuart Kings. In dismissing the legislature in 1657 Cromwell sounded strangely like James I: "I think it high time that an end be put to your sitting and I do dissolve this Parliament. And let God judge between you and me."

To his highness, the Lord Protector of the Commonwealth of England, Scotland, [etc.] ... the humble petition and advice of the knights, citizens, and burgesses now assembled in the Parliament of this Commonwealth.

We, the knights, citizens, and burgesses in this present Parliament assembled, taking into our most serious consideration the present state of these three nations, joined and united under your highness' protection cannot but in the first place ... acknowledge the ... mercy of Almighty God in delivering us from that tyranny and bondage ... which the late King and his party designed to bring us under ... and also that it has pleased ... God to preserve your person in many battles, to make you an instrument for preserving our peace. ... We consider likewise the continual danger which your life is in from the ... malignant and discontented party ... it being a ... principle amongst them that, no order being settled in your lifetime for the succession in the government, nothing is wanting to bring us into blood and confusion, and them to their desired ends, but the destruction of your person. ... Upon these considerations, we have judged it a duty incumbent upon us to present and declare these our most just and necessary desires to your highness:

That your highness will be pleased, by and under the name and style of Lord Protector ... to hold and exercise the office of chief magistrate of these nations, and to govern, according to this petition and advice, in all things therein contained, and in all other things according to the laws of these nations, and not otherwise; that your highness will be pleased during your lifetime to appoint and declare the person who shall immediately after your death succeed you in the government of these nations.

That your highness will for the future be pleased to call Parliaments consisting of two Houses, in such manner and way as shall be more particularly afterwards agreed and declared in this petition and advice, once in three years at furthest, or oftener as the affairs of the nation shall require. ...

That the ancient and undoubted liberties and privileges of Parliament ... be preserved and maintained; and that you will not break or interrupt the same, nor suffer them to be broken or interrupted; and, particularly, that those persons who are legally chosen by a free election of the people to serve in Par-

liament may not be excluded from sitting in Parliament to do their duties, but by judgment and consent of that House whereof they are members.

... . [All who sided with the King in the Civil War and all who aided the Irish rebellion should be excluded from all participation in public life along with all civil criminals, drunkards, and persons married to Roman Catholic wives or who permit their children to be taught Catholic doctrine]. And that these qualifications may be observed, and yet the privilege of Parliament maintained, we desire that it may be by your highness' consent ordained that forty-one commissioners be appointed by Act of Parliament, who ... shall be authorized to examine and try whether the members to be elected for the House of Commons in future Parliament be capable to sit, according to the qualifications mentioned in this petition ... and in case they find them not qualified accordingly, then to suspend them from sitting until the House of Commons shall, upon hearing their particular cases, admit them to sit. ... That the number of persons to be elected and chosen to sit ... in Parliament ... and the distribution of the persons chosen ... may be according to such propositions as shall be agreed upon and declared in this present Parliament.

That your highness will consent that none be called to sit and vote in the other House, but such as are not disabled, but qualified according to the qualifications mentioned in the former article, being such as shall be nominated by your highness, and approved by this House, and that they exceed not seventy in number, nor be under the number of forty ... and that, as any of them do die or be legally removed, no new ones be admitted to sit and vote in their rooms, but by consent of the House itself. That the other House do not proceed in any civil causes, except in writs of error, in cases adjourned from inferior courts into the Parliament for difficulty, in cases of petitions against proceedings in courts of equity, and in cases of privileges of their own House;

that they do not proceed in any criminal causes whatsoever against any person criminally, but upon an impeachment of the Commons assembled in Parliament, and by their consent; that they do not proceed in any case, either civil or criminal, but according to the known laws of the land, and the due course and custom of Parliament; that no final determinations or judgments be by any members of that House, in any case there depending, either civil, criminal, or mixed, as commissioners or delegates, to be nominated by that House; but all such final determinations and judgments to be by the House itself. . . .

That in all other particulars which concern the calling and holding of Parliaments, your highness will be pleased that the laws and statutes of the land be observed and kept; and that no laws be altered, suspended, abrogated, or repealed, or new law made but by Act of Parliament.

And to the end there may be a constant revenue for support of the government, and for the safety and defence of these nations by sea and land, we declare our willingness to settle forthwith a yearly revenue of £1,300,-000 whereof £1,000,000 for the navy and army, and £300,000 for the support of the government, and no part thereof to be raised by a land tax; and this not to be altered without the consent of the three estates in Parliament; and to grant such other temporary supplies, according as the Commons assembled in Parliament shall from time to time adjudge the necessities of these nations to require. And [the petitioners] do pray your highness that it be enacted and declared that no charge be laid, nor no person be compelled to contribute to any gift, benevolence, tax, tallage, aid, or any other like charge without common consent by Act of Parliament. . . .

That none may be added or admitted to the Privy Council of your highness or successors, but such as are of known piety and undoubted affection to the rights of these nations and a just Christian liberty in matters

of religion, nor without consent of the Council to be afterwards approved by both Houses of Parliament . . . after your highness' death, the commander-in-chief under your successors of such army or armies as shall be necessary to be kept in England, Scotland, or Ireland, as also all such field officers at land or generals at sea which, after that time, shall be newly made and constituted by your successors, be [appointed] by the consent of the Council and not otherwise. And that the standing forces of his Commonwealth shall be disposed of by the chief magistrate, by the consent of both Houses of Parliament, sitting the Parliament; and in the intervals of Parliament, by the chief magistrate, by the advice of the Council. And also that your highness and successors will be pleased to exercise your government over these nations by the advice of your Council.

And that the chancellor, keeper or commissioners of the great seal of England, the treasurer or commissioners of the treasury there, the admiral, the chief governor of Ireland, the chancellor, keeper or commissioners of the great seal of Ireland, the chief justices of both the benches, and the chief baron in England and Ireland, the commander-in-chief of the forces in Scotland, and such officers of State there as by Act of Parliament in Scotland are to be approved by Parliament, and the judges in Scotland hereafter to be made, shall be approved of by both Houses of Parliament. . . .

That the true Protestant Christian religion, as it is contained in the Holy Scriptures of the Old and New Testament, and no other, be held forth and asserted for the public profession of these nations; and that a confession of faith, to be agreed by your highness and the Parliament, according to the rule and warrant of the Scriptures, be asserted, held forth, and recommended to the people of these nations; that none may be suffered or permitted, by opprobrious words or writing, maliciously . . . to revile . . . the confession of faith to be agreed on . . .
(Scobell, *Acts and Ordinances*, II, 378.)

# The Reign of Charles II

## 1660-1685

# England, 1660-1685    Introduction

The death of Oliver Cromwell and the almost simultaneous collapse of the Puritan-sponsored absolute state aided in restoring the Stuart Monarchy to its former position and prerogatives; yet these events were not the sole causes of the Restoration in 1660. Rather they were the ultimate elements of a violent struggle between opposed forces, each seeking to direct the function and application of the constitution to its own ends. The disagreements between the sectarian factions had drained the Puritan movement of vital energies of direction, purpose, and leadership by the time the *Humble Petition and Advice* was drawn up to give to Cromwell the office of hereditary ruler of England. That such a solution was conceivable illustrates the Puritans' despairing realization that the pace of constitutional change during the preceding decade had not been in agreement with the prevailing tone of English political thought.

While the Puritan movement failed, it would not be accurate to discount the real and lasting gains it produced in the areas of political thought and institutional modification. The sixteen-year period of political uncertainty, erratic foreign policy, and social tension had certain positive results in that it served, by the very failure of its experimental methods, to re-emphasize the basic virtue of evolutionary change inherent in the nature of the constitution. Keenly aware of their presumed divine mission to establish the City of God in England, the sectarians had denied this traditional conservatism when they feverishly set about to demolish ideas and institutions opposed to their intended way. Churches, laws, rights, and the King, as products of the erroneous past, were attacked with calculated determination, and one by one the surface evidences of those institutions were obliterated. However, the sectarians, having terminated the ancient constitution, did not intend to construct another without sufficient guarantees of its continuing ability to withstand all onslaughts that might be brought to bear against it. The surest warrant of its durability was to be in its written form. In a frenzy of creation the Puritan factions marked out the road to their promised Utopia with written constitutions of every color and degree of political promise—only to find that the road led to a bondage more severe than that of the Stuart Kings. And yet, frustrating as it was, this was not an entirely barren experience for the English people; in future crises they were carefully to avoid committing themselves to written constitutions based on so-called first principles, which by their immutable nature were antithetical to both compromise and growth.

In the minds of the people the war had been fought to maintain and protect their liberties, their Protestant Church, and the accepted position of Parliament in the constitution. When the war was over and popular objectives appeared to have been attained, normal conservatism began to reassert itself against a Protectorship which seemed, by its arbitrary mode of governing, to take on the threatening outlines of the old monarchy. Thus the Puritan leadership was made uneasy by the very ideal of resistance to authority which Calvinism itself had inculcated. It had committed the error of allowing itself to be identified in the public mind with these very vices it had previously charged against Charles.

Charles II and the royalist party, whiling away the time on the continent until the political methods of the Puritans should prove their own undoing, were well prepared to launch a psychological attack even before General Monk's invasion of southern England. The *Declaration of Breda* was not a spontaneous statement of the King's political purpose but a cleverly constructed appeal to the variant groups and interests in England which had reason to desire a return of the old ways of stable institutions. More important, the *Declaration* made many attractive promises: pardon for the King's enemies, pay for the army, acceptance of all peaceful Protestant expressions, and a just and orderly settlement of the land problems caused by the alienation or sale of aristocrat's estates during the Interregnum. These promises were made even more appealing by Charles's added stipulation that they would be carried out by Parliament—a masterstroke of policy which established his respect for Parliamentary government and furnished a ready-made scape-goat should acceptable solutions to the enumerated problems fail to materialize. Thus Charles repudiated none of the prerogatives or rights of the monarchy while Parliament was given the responsibility of working out political and economic solutions to problems complicated by the uncompromising natures of its various groupings.

Charles's first—or "Cavalier"—Parliament, overwhelmingly Royalist and Anglican, in session from 1661 to 1679, assumed the task of putting in legal form the settlement upon whch the restored monarchy was to function. Since less than fifty sectarian spokesmen were elected to the House of Commons it is clear that at least the traditional electoral class welcomed the return of the old and familiar system of government which was to be administered by a hereditary monarch with the aid of a hereditary governing class.

It was soon obvious, however, that Parliament was not going to be submissive to the Crown—and that, while the restored monarch might claim the full prerogatives of his father and grandfather, he would have to wield them with extreme tact. The documents of the period show the steadily growing Parliamentary control of the executive functions of the Crown by virtue of Commons's control of the royal purse. By emphasizing, for their own purposes, the position of the King as unlimited and uncontrolled, the Parliamentarians attempted to make the actual curbs written into legislation so unobtrusive and palatable as to insure their general acceptance.

Under the constitution as reconstructed by the Cavalier Parliament the King had many apparent powers and rights: the appointment of his own ministers, the right to veto Parliament's bills and to dissolve that institution, command of the armed forces of the state, and diplomatic control in the making of war and peace. Yet these powers were curtailed in their possible application in ways which brought the King into immediate dependence on the will of Commons. Without necessary funds Charles dared not act independently in making any policy. Thus he was forced to seek funds, and thereby approval, from Parliament. In this way the two Houses controlled the executive while avoiding popular criticism when particular Crown programs were either unpopular at home or failures abroad. In short, Parliament effectively employed Charles's tactic of the *Declaration of Breda* which had allowed him to pose as forgiving and magnanimous while placing the onus of fulfillment of promises on Parliament.

Parliament's second limiting power was equally paralyzing in its effect on the King. The legislation of the Long Parliament which had been approved by Charles I was accepted as part of the constitution. Those earlier Acts had destroyed the prerogative courts, taken criminal jurisdiction out of the Privy Council, relieved the Crown of all feudal money-raising rights, and denied the suspending and dispensing powers, while the newly imposed Clarendon Code made it clear that the King was no longer even the effective head of the Church. In thus falling back on what it piously and publicly assumed was tradition the Cavalier Parliament insured effective operation of all the limitations on monarchial power at no risk to itself.

The third control of the Crown's executive function was in the area of ministerial responsibility. Although the King appointed his own Council and advisers they were open to attack and even punishment should Parliament become hostile to them. As yet the concept of ministerial responsibility was only imperfectly worked out, it is true, but it was certain that should a minister overstep the unwritten limits or lose the confidence of Parliament he lost his usefulness to the Crown. And should the Crown extend its protection to any minister not acceptable to the legislature that institution had alternative methods of reprisal: use of the processes of the law in cases where the minister had clearly broken the law, impeachment, attainder, or the less direct method of cutting off Crown incomes.

In this carefully constructed Parliamentary program is to be seen the end of the Divine Rights theory as a practical political concept in England. In the rejoicing at the end of austere and incompetent Puritan rule and the prospect of return to the known, comfortable, and understood ways of social and political life, the Divine Rights concept had reached perhaps its highest point in popular acceptance—and Charles II *had* been accepted almost without limiting qualifications by the English people. Yet little by little as the problems and contradictions of workaday politics gave evidence of growing distrust of such a settlement, Parliament found ways of hedging against a recurrence of the actions and conditions of 1642. Instead of attempting to construct a modified theory of Divine Rights in a constitutionally limited area of action, which would have been agreeable to such earlier Parliamentary leaders as John Pym and even Sir Edward Coke, the ruling class, logically enough, turned toward the establishment of a method of non-resistance to the King. Resistance, having gotten out of the control of the ruling class in 1642, had produced many things never intended when first that class took up weapons against Charles I. Radical sectarianism, in the beginning a minor partner in the early struggle for power and meant only as a threat, had given both mass and moral basis to resistance to legitimate authority and in that way had grown to be the dominant power in the alliance. The results were painfully obvious to the traditional class of power, which, too late, attempting to stay the process of revolution, had declared against it and, like the King became its victim. So now, in 1660, having eschewed dangerous resistance, parson and squire were forced to build anew a place for the Monarchy in the constitution that prevented any expression of arbitrary action but that was yet above the possibility of popular resistance. Therefore nonresistance had a definite and limited purpose—to shape Kingship into the chief bulwark shoring up the position of the old ruling class which had now returned to its original position of competition with the Monarchy. It was for this reason that nonresistance insisted that the King could do no wrong. This by no means implied that the King could deny or disdain the limitations placed on his office by the constitution, for that office was precisely defined and absolutely limited by the law, which was in the full possession of a Parliament which represented a single class, the squirearchy. Thus Parliament returned to the principle of the rule of law in vesting the Crown with a definable and limited position under the constitution.

No matter what the negative and inhumane consequences of the Puritan use of force had been, it cannot be denied that sincere religious motives were the chief source of their inspiration. The same depth of altruistic purpose is not apparent in the settlement of the revolution by the ruling class. The Clarendon Code, ostensibly intended to cure the worst abuses of the radical and non-conforming groups, was far less religious than social in purpose, and no more humane in the final analysis than the narrowest church legislation of the Commonwealth government. To the Puritan, intolerance was a sacred duty owed to God. The Clarendon Code was inspired by the firm belief that intolerance was a duty owed by the ruling class to itself, and even in its own day it was not defended by its proponents as having ethical or reasonable basis. The argument that the Code was the result of Parliament's fear of a sectarian reassertion is quite insufficient and indefensible when viewed in relation to the events following the death of Oliver Cromwell. That the Code was "logical retribution" comes nearer to reality—for, in fact, the Code was pure class legislation in the interests of revenge. Revenge for what specific wrongs? The sectarians *had* destroyed the Anglican Church, they *had* accepted intolerance as a guiding principle, and they *had* destroyed a King and undone a Kingdom. Yet strangely enough none of these charges constituted major points of discussion during the debates on the several bills which became the Code—which ironically bears the name of the person who, next to Charles II, did the most to promote an atmosphere of goodwill and to protect the non-conformists. Nor was the Code dedicated to resurrecting the Elizabethan Church, nor to denying the validity of intolerance, nor to reconstituting Kingship on its former basis. It was actually an arbitrary device for punishing the groups which had challenged the social prerogatives of the semi-feudal squirearchy, a class which had found that if no bishop meant no king, it also meant no squire. Parliament's determination to champion the cause of the established Church was as cynical as Puritan intolerance had been sincere and was intended to continue only so long as Anglicanism played its part as the pulpit-defender of the social position of the ruling class.

Charles' attempt to stand between this vengeful alliance and the shattered forces of non-conformity and the quietly prospering Catholics precipitated the next phase of the constitutional struggle. Having lost the position of head of the Church won by Henry VIII for the King, Charles possessed only the potentially explosive suspending power and royal decree. When the King tried these methods, in suspending the *Act of Supremacy* and in decreeing indulgence to non-conformist groups, bishop, parson, and squire combined their righteous indignation in the voice of the House of Commons to protest against such latitudinarian attempts against the exclusiveness of the Anglican Church. Clearly theirs was not the church conceived by Elizabeth, spread wide to encompass all insular Protestantism. Anglicanism was now a legally constituted sect which best answered the political purposes of the social class that was its sponsor and its master—an institution of pure secular purpose without a trace of spiritual idealism.

Yet, the fear of Catholic revival was not altogether groundless after the Restoration, since the Duke of York, the heir apparent, had already made clear his affinity with Rome, and his succession was assured since Charles refused to divorce his barren wife and take another. Thus many factors were combined in the period of the seventies to infuse new intensity into the struggle for control of the constitution. The alliance between scheming Titus Oates and Shaftesbury, the Whig whose career of political intrigue would have better fitted the decade of the forties, was highly significant to the new constitutional struggle. Another factor was Charles's stubborn refusal to allow the office of Kingship to be reshaped into an elective office wholly reliant on the will of Parliament. A third factor was the diplomatic agility of Louis XIV of France in maintaining England's ineffective policy in foreign affairs, a policy primarily the result of conflict of purpose between the anti-Dutch King and the anti-French Parliamentarians. This situation produced the "Exclusion Crisis," which widened further the breach between King and people.

The Exclusion group represented many English interests: the Anglican primates who were convinced that if they did not firmly exclude York from the succession they would eventually become the first victims of his restored Catholic friends; Puritan sectarians who had made their peace with the established Church; the Whigs who used the crisis as a club for battering at the remnant of the royal power; the Parliamentarians who pleaded the cause of a constitutionally limited monarchy; the violent dissenters and nonconformists who used the crisis to weaken further the sanctions of the *Clarendon Code* against themselves. These militant groups hoped, by excluding York, to win the franchise of electing Kings—which would bring to an end the tedious practices of the constitutional institutions which protected the Monarchy from Parliamentary whims.

In his last effort to maintain the monarchy intact against the encroachment of the legislature Charles did not clearly lose—or win. Exclusion was defeated, the Whig leaders brought to bay, and Shaftesbury sent into exile. Yet the monarch's victory in these things had its price; for Charles, whether he realized it or not, had become a constitutional monarch in fact if not in name. He saved the succession for his brother but only by trading for it whatever independence of action there remained to him. He turned, in time of need, to the Anglican Church—and was forced by the primates to cast away his ideal of toleration in return for their meager but necessary support against the enemies of his younger brother. Thus the King's victory was really a victory for the Tory Party and the Anglican Churchmen—a victory which insured the rule of Parliamentary law, the position of the King under that law, and the security of the Established Church. Yet these fruits of compromise could be gathered only so long as the dominant party's interest and that of the King were identical; and York's religious preference, sense of toleration, and inability to learn from vicarious experience could never be shaped to fit the political scene he was soon to dominate.

## The Declaration of Breda. 1660

**128.** LONG Parliament voluntarily dissolved itself in March of 1660 and shortly afterward Charles II's declaration of purpose was published in Breda. Although, according to General Monk, 1660 was a time for healing, and although the Stuart King appeared willing to forego revenge in favor of peace and harmony, it was clearly indicated in the *Declaration of Breda* that the forces of high passion and bitter vengeance had not run their full course. In the document the King promised pardon to all former enemies except such persons "as shall hereafter be excepted by Parliament." That the Restoration Parliament would be predominantly Royalist, Anglican, and anti-sectarian was certain, and that some would suffer for their actions during the past eighteen years was just as certain. However, the problems of the promised land settlement were left by Charles to Parliament as were many other financial, political, and constitutional problems. In thus accepting Parliament as the arbiter of the future the King placed the onus for fulfilling of his promises on other shoulders. Should his program fail, Parliament, not the Crown, would bear the blame.

Charles, by the grace of God, King of England, Scotland, France, and Ireland, defender of the faith, etc., to all our loving subjects of what degree or quality soever, greeting.

If the general distraction and confusion which is spread over the whole kingdom doth not awaken all men to a desire and longing that those wounds which have so many years together been kept bleeding, may be bound up, all we can say will be to no purpose; however, after this long silence, we have thought it our duty to declare how much we desire to contribute thereunto; and that as we can never give over the hope, in good time, to obtain the possession of that right which God and nature has made our due, so we do make it our daily suit to the Divine Providence, that He will, in compassion to us and our subjects after so long misery and sufferings, remit and put us into a quiet and peaceable possession of that our right, with as little blood and damage to our people as is possible; nor do we desire more to enjoy what is ours, than that all our subjects may enjoy what by law is theirs, by a full and entire administration of justice throughout the land, and by extending our mercy where it is wanted and deserved.

And to the end that the fear of punishment may not engage any, conscious to themselves of what is past, to a perseverance in guilt for the future, by opposing the quiet and happiness of their country, in the restoration both of King, peers, and people to their just, ancient, and fundamental rights, we do, by these presents declare that we do grant a free and general pardon, which we are ready, upon demand, to pass under our great seal of England, to all our subjects, of what degree or quality soever, who, within forty days after the publishing hereof, shall lay hold upon this our grace and favor, and shall, by any public act, declare their doing so, and that they return to the loyalty and obedience of good subjects; excepting only such persons as shall hereafter be excepted by Parliament.

Those only excepted, let all our subjects, how faulty soever, rely upon the word of a King, solemnly given by this present declaration, that no crime whatsoever, committed against us or our royal father before the publication of this, shall ever rise in judgment, or be brought in question, against any of them, to the least endamagement of them, either in their lives, liberties, or estates, or (as far forth as lies in our power) so much as to the prejudice of their reputations, by any reproach or term of distinction from the rest of our best subjects; we desiring and ordaining that henceforth all notes of discord, separation, and difference of parties be utterly abolished among all our subjects, whom we invite and conjure to a perfect union among themselves, under our protection, for the re-settlement of our just rights and theirs in a free Parliament, by which, upon the word of a King, we will be advised.

And because the passion and uncharitableness of the times have produced several opinions in religion, by which men are engaged in parties and animosities against each other (which, when they shall hereafter unite in a freedom of conversation, will be composed or better understood), we do declare a liberty to tender consciences, and that no man shall be disquieted or called in question for differences of opinion in matter of religion, which do not disturb the peace of the kingdom; and that we shall be ready to consent to such an Act of Parliament as, upon mature deliberation, shall be offered to us, for the full granting that indulgence.

And because, in the continued distractions of so many years, and so many and great revolutions, many grants and purchases of estates have been made to and by many officers, soldiers and others, who are now possessed of the same, and who may be liable to actions at law upon several titles, we are likewise willing that all such differences, and all things relating to such grants, sales, and purchases, shall be determined in Parliament, which can best provide for the just satisfaction of all men who are concerned.

And we do further declare that we will be ready to consent to any Act or Acts of Parliament to the purposes aforesaid, and for the full satisfaction of all arrears due to the officers and soldiers of the army under the command of General Monk; and that they shall be received into our service upon as good pay and conditions as they now enjoy. ... (*Journals of the House of Lords*, XI, 7.)

## Act Legalizing the Convention Parliament. 1660

THE first statutory movement toward restoration of the Stuart Monarchy was the Act which gave legal existence to the Convention Parliament that received Charles as King. The Act provided for the Crown's power of dissolution "after the usual manner," a constitutional device by Parliament to insure against any possible lasting radical control of the legislature in the future.

**129.**

An Act for Removing and Preventing all Questions and Disputes Concerning the Assembling and Sitting of this Present Parliament.

For the preventing all doubts and scruples concerning the assembling, sitting and proceeding of this present Parliament, be it declared and enacted, and it is declared and enacted by the King our Sovereign Lord, and by the Lords and Commons in Parliament assembled and by authority of the same, that the Parliament begun and holden at Westminster the third day of November in the sixteenth year of the reign of the late King Charles of blessed memory is fully dis-

solved and determined; and that the Lords and Commons now sitting at Westminster in this present Parliament are the two Houses of Parliament, and so shall be and are hereby declared, enacted and adjudged to be to all intents, constructions and purposes whatsoever, notwithstanding any want of the King's Majesty's writ or writs of summons, or any defect or alteration of or in any writ or writs of summons, or any other defect or default whatsoever; as if this Parliament had been summoned by writ or writs in his Majesty's name according to the usual form, and as if his Majesty had been present in person at the assembling and commencement of this present Parliament. Provided always that this present Parliament may be dissolved by his Majesty after the usual manner, as if . . . summoned by writ or writs in his Majesty's name.

Provided also, and it is hereby enacted, that his Majesty's royal assent to this bill shall not determine this present session of Parliament. (SR, V, 179: 12 Charles II, c.1.)

## Parliament's Proclamation of Charles II as King. 1660

130.

IN May of 1660 Parliament proclaimed Charles II King of England and the Restoration process was legally completed. However Parliament carefully refrained in the document from claiming any elective right. Charles's "right and title to his Crowns and Kingdoms is and was every way completed by the death of his most royal father." Thus the cult of non-resistance fostered the concept of the evil of opposition to the Crown.

A Proclamation of both Houses of Parliament for Proclaiming of His Majesty King of England, Scotland, France, and Ireland, and Defender of the Faith, etc.

Although it can no way be doubted but that his Majesty's right and title to his crowns and Kingdoms is and was every way completed by the death of his most royal father of glorious memory, without the ceremony or solemnity of a proclamation, yet since proclamations in such cases have been always used, to the end that all good subjects might upon this occasion testify their duty and respects, and since the armed violence and other the calamities of these many years last past have hitherto deprived us of any such opportunity wherein we might express our loyalty and allegiance to his Majesty, we, therefore, the Lords and Commons now assembled in Parliament, together with the lord mayor, aldermen and commons of the

city of London and other freemen of this Kingdom now present, do, according to our duty and allegiance, heartily, joyfully, and unanimously acknowledge and proclaim that immediately upon the decease of our late Sovereign Lord King Charles the imperial crown of the Realm of England, and of all the Kingdoms, dominions and rights belonging to the same, did by inheritance, birthright and lawful and undoubted succession descend and come to his most excellent Majesty Charles the Second, as being lineally, justly, and lawfully next heir of the blood royal of this Realm, and . . . he is of England, Scotland, France and Ireland . . . the undoubted King, defender of the faith, etc. And thereunto we most humbly and faithfully submit and oblige ourselves, our heirs and posterities for ever. The 8th day of May 1660. (*Journals of the House of Lords*, XI, 19.)

## Act of Indemnity and Oblivion. 1660

131.

FOLLOWING the promise made in the *Declaration of Breda* to allow Parliament to seek out and punish those responsible for the more violent actions of the civil war, Charles did not openly encourage reprisal. Parliament—and more particularly the House of Lords—was neither inclined toward leniency nor bound by any public promise to forgive and forget. This Act, while pardoning certain felonies and treasons committed since the beginning of 1637, reserved certain individuals and actions for Parliamentary punishment.

An Act of Free and General Pardon, Indemnity and Oblivion.

The King's most excellent Majesty, taking into his gracious and serious consideration the long and great troubles, discords and wars that have for many years past been in this Kingdom, and that divers of his subjects are by occasion thereof and otherwise fallen into, and be obnoxious to, great pains and penalties, out of a hearty and pious desire to put an end to all suits and controversies that by occasion of the late distractions have arisen and may arise between all his subjects, and to the intent that no crime whatsoever committed against his Majesty or his royal father shall hereafter rise in judgment or be brought in question against any of them to the least endamagement of them, either in their lives, liberties, estates, or to the prejudice of their reputations, by any reproach or term of distinction, and to bury all seeds of future discords and remembrance of the former as well in his own breast as in the breasts of his subjects one towards another, and in performance of his royal and gracious word signified by his letters to the several Houses of Parliament now assembled, ... is pleased that it may be enacted, and be it enacted by the King's most excellent Majesty, with the advice and consent of the Lords and Commons in this present Parliament assembled, first, that all and all manner of treasons, misprision of treasons, murders,

felonies, offences, crimes, contempts and misdemeanors, counselled, commanded, acted or done since [1 January 1637] ... by any person or persons before [24 June 1660] ... other than the persons hereafter by name excepted in such manner as they are hereafter excepted, by virtue or color of any command, power, authority, commission, warrant or instructions from his late Majesty King Charles, or his Majesty that now is, or from any other person or persons deriving or pretending to derive authority, mediately or immediately, from both or either of their Majesties, or by virtue or color of any authority derived, mediately or immediately, of or from both Houses or House of Parliament, or of or from any convention or assembly called, or reputed, or taking on them the name of, a Parliament, or by, from or under any authority styled or known by the name of the keepers of the liberty of England by authority of Parliament, or by virtue or color of any writ, commission, letters patents, instruction ... of or from any person or persons tituled, reputed or taken to be Lord Protector of the Commonwealth of England, Scotland and Ireland, and the dominions thereunto belonging ... or from any person or persons whatsoever deriving or pretending to derive authority from them or any of them, be pardoned, released, indemnified, discharged and put in utter oblivion. ... (SR, V, 226: 12 Charles II, c.11.)

## Navigation Act. 1660

THE *Navigation Act* of 1660 expanded and refined the provisions of the Act of 1651, thus reinforcing the power of the State in matters of the regulation of commerce. That the Act was in some part directed at French shipping is indicated by the heavy retaliatory duty levied on ships of that nation.

## 132.

An Act for the Encouraging and Increasing of Shipping and Navigation.

For the increase of shipping and encouragement of navigation of this nation ... be it enacted ... that from and after the first

day of December [1660] ... no goods or commodities whatsoever shall be imported into or exported out of any lands, islands, plantations, or territories to his Majesty belonging or in his possession ... in Asia, Africa, or

America, in any other ship or ships, vessel or vessels whatsoever, but in such ships or vessels as do truly and without fraud belong only to the people of England or Ireland, dominion of Wales or town of Berwick-upon-Tweed, or are of the build of and belonging to any of the said lands, islands, plantations, or territories as the proprietors and right owners thereof, and whereof the master and three fourths of the mariners at least are English, under the penalty of the forfeiture and loss of all the goods and commodities which shall be imported into, or exported out of, any the aforesaid places in any other ship or vessel, as also of the ship or vessel with all its guns, furniture, tackle, ammunition and apparel. . . . And all admirals and other commanders at sea of any the ships of war or other ship having commission from his Majesty, or from his heirs or successors, are hereby authorized and strictly required to seize and bring in as prize all such ships or vessels as shall have offended contrary hereunto, and deliver them to the Court of Admiralty, there to be proceeded against [as is usual with ships taken prize]. . . .

And be it enacted, that no alien or person not born within the allegiance of our Sovereign Lord the King . . . or naturalized or made a free denizen, shall from and after the first day of February [1661] . . . exercise the trade or occupation of a merchant or factor in any the said places, upon pain of the forfeiture and loss of all his goods and chattels, or which are in his possession. . . .

And it is further enacted . . . that no goods or commodities whatsoever of the growth, production or manufacture of Africa, Asia, or America, or of any part thereof . . . be imported into England, Ireland, or Wales, islands of Guernsey or Jersey or town of Berwick-upon-Tweed, in any other ship or ships than [as specified above] . . . under the penalty of forfeiture. . . .

And it is further enacted . . . that no goods or commodities that are of foreign growth, production, or manufacture, and which are to be brought into England, Ireland, Wales,

the islands of Guernsey and Jersey or town of Berwick-upon-Tweed in English-built shipping, or other shipping belonging to some of the aforesaid places, and navigated by English mariners as abovesaid, shall be shipped or brought from any other place or places, country or countries, but only from those of their said growth, production, or manufacture, or from those posts where the said goods and commodities can only or are or usually have been first shipped for transportation. . . .

And it is further enacted . . . that any sort of ling, stockfish, pil, chard or any other kind of dried or salted fish usually fished for and caught by the people of England, [etc.] . . . or any sort of cod-fish or herring, or any oil or blubber made or that shall be made of any kind of fish whatsoever, or any whale fins or whale bones which shall be imported into England, [etc.] . . . not having been caught in vessels truly and properly belonging thereunto as proprietors and right owners thereof, and the said fish cured, saved or dried, and the oil and blubber aforesaid . . . not made by the people thereof, and shall be imported into England, Ireland, [etc.] . . . shall pay double aliens' customs.

And be it further enacted . . . that from henceforth it shall not be lawful to any person or persons whatsoever to load or cause to be loaded and carried in any bottom or bottoms, ship or ships, vessel or vessels whatsoever, whereof any stranger or strangers born, (unless such shall be denizens or naturalized), be owners, part owners or master, and whereof three fourths of the mariners at least shall not be English, any fish, victual, wares, goods, commodities or things of what kind or nature soever the same shall be, from one port or creek of England, [etc.] . . . to another port or creek of the same or of any of them. . . .

And it is further enacted . . . that where any ease, abatement or privilege is given in the Book of Rates [the list of tax rates established in the Act *A Subsidy granted to the King of Tunnage and Poundage and other*

*Sums of Money Payable upon Merchandise Exported and Imported.* 12 Charles II, c.4.] to goods or commodities imported or exported in English-built shipping, that is to say shipping built in England, Ireland, Wales, islands, dominions or territories to his Majesty in Africa, Asia, or America belonging or in his possession, that it is always to be understood and provided that the master and three fourths of the mariners of the said ships at least be also English. . . .

And it is further enacted . . . that no goods or commodities of the growth, production, or manufacture of Muscovy, or of any the countries, dominions or territories to the great Duke or Emperor of Muscovy or Russia belonging, as also that no sorts of masts, timber or boards, no foreign salt, pitch, tar rosin, hemp or flax, raisins, figs, prunes, olive oils, no sort of corn or grain, sugar potashes, wines, vinegar or spirits called *aqua vitae* or brandy wine, shall from and after the first day of April 1661 be imported into England, Ireland, Wales or town of Berwick-upon-Tweed in any ship or ships, vessel or vessels whatsoever, but in such as do truly and without fraud belong to the people thereof or of some of them as the true owners and proprietors thereof, and whereof the master and three fourths of the mariners at least are English; and that no currants nor commodities of the growth, production, or manufacture of any the countries, islands, dominions or territories to the Ottoman or Turkish Empire belonging shall from and after the first day of September 1661 be imported into any the fore-mentioned places in any ship or vessel but which is of English build and navigated as aforesaid and in no other, except only such foreign ships and vessels as are of the build of that country or place of which the said goods are the growth, production, or manufacture, respectively, or of such port where the said goods can only be, or most usually are, first shipped for transportation, and whereof the master and three fourths of the mariners at least are of the said country or place. . . .

Provided also, that it shall and may be lawful to and for any of the people of England, Ireland, Wales, islands of Guernsey or Jersey or town of Berwick-upon-Tweed, in vessels or ships to them belonging and whereof the master and three fourths of the mariners at least are English, to load and bring in from any of the ports of Spain or Portugal or western islands, commonly called Azores or Madeira or Canary Islands, all sorts of goods or commodities of the growth, production or manufacture of the plantations or dominions of either of them respectively. . . .

Provided always, that this Act or anything therein contained shall not extend or be construed to extend to lay aliens' duties upon any corn of the growth of Scotland, or to any salt made in Scotland, or to any fish caught, saved and cured by the people of Scotland and imported directly from Scotland in Scotch-built ships, and whereof the master and three fourths of the mariners are of his Majesty's subjects, nor to any seal oil of Russia imported from thence into England, Ireland, Wales or town of Berwick-upon-Tweed in shipping *bona fide* to some of the said places belonging, and whereof the master and three fourths of the mariners at least are English.

Provided also . . . that every ship or vessel belonging to any the subjects of the French King which from and after the twentieth day of October [1660] shall come into any port, creek, harbor or road of England, Ireland, [etc.] . . . and shall there load or unload any goods or commodities, or take in or set on shore any passengers, shall pay to the collector of his Majesty's customs in such port, creek, harbor or road for every ton of which the said ship or vessel is of burden, to be computed by such officer of the customs as shall be thereunto appointed, the sum of five shillings current money of England . . . and that this duty shall continue to be collected, levied and paid for such time as a certain duty of fifty *sols* per ton lately imposed by the French King or any part thereof shall continue to be collected upon the shipping of England . . . and three months after and no longer.

And it is further enacted . . . that from and after the first day of April [1661] no sugars, tobacco, cotton-wool, indigos, ginger, fustic or other dyeing wood of the growth, production, or manufacture of any English plantation in America, Asia, or Africa, shall be shipped, carried, conveyed or transported from any of the said English plantations to any land, island, territory, dominion, port or place whatsoever other than to such other English plantations as do belong to his Majesty . . . or to the Kingdom of England or Ireland, [etc.] . . . there to be laid on shore, under penalty of . . . forfeiture. . . . (SR, V, 246: 12 Charles II, c.18.)

## Corporation Act. 1661

133.

THE strong Anglican sympathies of the Cavalier Parliament colored most of its early legislative actions. The Clarendon Code—which quite unjustly took its name from Edward Hyde, the Earl of Clarendon, Charles's Lord Chancellor—was inaugurated by the *Corporation Act* and terminated the toleration promised in the *Declaration of Breda* by enjoining religious conformity and imposing a narrow Anglicanism on the people. The Act also placed the counties under control of the Anglican Churchmen, required all municipal officers to take an oath of allegiance to the King and to receive the Anglican communion. All non-Anglicans were thus barred from public office.

[An Act] for the Well Governing and Regulating of Corporations.

Whereas questions are likely to arise concerning the validity of elections of magistrates and other officers and members of corporations, as well in respect of removing some as placing others during the late troubles, contrary to the true intent and meaning of their charters and liberties, and to the end that the succession in such corporations may be most probably perpetuated in the hands of persons well affected to his Majesty and the established government, it being too well known that, notwithstanding all his Majesty's endeavors and unparalleled indulgence in pardoning all that is past, nevertheless many evil spirits are still working; wherefore for prevention of the like mischief for the time to come, and for preservation of the public peace . . . be it enacted . . . that commissions shall before the twentieth day of February next be issued forth under the great seal of England unto such persons as his Majesty shall appoint for the executing of the powers and authorities hereinafter expressed, and that all and every the persons to be named commissioners in the said commissions respectively shall by virtue of this Act be commissioners respectively for and within the several cities, corporations and boroughs, and cinque ports and their members and other port towns within the Kingdom of England, dominion of Wales and town of Berwick-upon-Tweed, for which they shall be respectively nominated and appointed.

And be it further enacted . . . that no charter of any corporation, cities, towns, boroughs, cinque ports and their members and other port towns in England [etc.] . . . shall at any time hereafter be avoided for or by reason of any act or thing done or omitted before the first day of this present Parliament.

And be it further enacted . . . that all persons who upon [24 December 1661] shall be mayors, aldermen, recorders, bailiffs, town clerks, common council men and other persons then bearing any office or offices of magistracy, or places or trusts or other employment relating to or concerning the government of the said respective cities, corporations and boroughs, and cinque ports and their members and other port towns, shall, at any time before [25 March 1663], when they shall be thereunto required by the said respective commissioners or any three or more of them, take the oaths of allegiance and supremacy and this oath following:

I, (name), do declare and believe that it is not lawful upon any pretence whatsoever to take arms against the King, and that I do abhor that traitorous position of taking arms by his authority against his person, or against those that are commissioned by him. So help me God.

And also at the same time shall publicly subscribe before the said commissioners or any three of them this following declaration:

I, (name), to declare that I hold that there lies no obligation upon me or any other person from the oath commonly called the Solemn League and Covenant, and that the same was in itself an unlawful oath, and imposed upon the subjects of this realm against the known laws and liberties of the Kingdom.

And that all such of the said mayors and other the persons aforesaid, by whom the said oaths are to be taken and declaration subscribed as aforesaid, who shall refuse to take and subscribe the same within the time and in manner aforesaid, shall from and immediately after such refusal by authority of this Act *ipso facto* be removed and displaced of and from the said offices and places respectively....

And nevertheless be it further enacted ... that the said commissioners or any five or more of them shall have full power by virtue of this Act, by order and warrant under their hands and seals, to displace or remove any of the persons aforesaid from the said respective offices and places or trusts aforesaid, if the said commissioners or the major part of them then present shall deem it expedient for the public safety, although such persons shall have taken and subscribed ... the said oaths and declarations.

And be it also enacted, that the said respective commissioners ... shall have power to restore such persons as have been illegally or unduly removed into the places out of which he or they were removed.... (SR, V, 321: 13 Charles II, Stat. II, c.1.)

## Act Amending the Poor Laws. 1662

HAVING regained their former dominant political position, the Tory-Anglican country gentry extended their policy of planned intolerance from Church and political to economic and social affairs. The present Act, designed piously for "the better relief of the poor," was one of the harshest pieces of social legislation of the entire Restoration period. In the minds of the gentry there was an obvious correlation between economic poverty and political and religious radicalism. Individually dangerous, their combination compounded their distastefulness. The Justices of the Peace, upon the approbation of the Privy Council, were given almost unlimited powers in dealing with the indigent. Workhouses—more nearly prisons—were established in certain cities and counties where the poor were herded without regard for age, sex, or state of health and morals. Transportation to the colonies and plantations, a system which was little more than legalized slavery, was encouraged by Parliament, and no method of appeal against the methods or decisions of the Justices was established for the protection of the poor.

I 34.

An Act for the Better Relief of the Poor of this Kingdom.

Whereas the necessity, number and continual increase of the poor . . . through the whole Kingdom of England and dominion of Wales, is very great and exceeding burdensome, being occasioned by reason of some defects in the law concerning the settling of the poor, and for want of a due provision of the regulations of relief and employment in such parishes or places where they are legally settled, which does force many to turn incorrigible rogues and others to perish for want, together with the neglect of the faithful execution of such laws and statutes as have formerly been made for the apprehending of rogues and vagabonds and for the good of the poor; for remedy whereof, and for the preventing the perishing of any of the poor, whether young or old, for want of such supplies as are necessary, may it please your most excellent Majesty that it may be enacted . . . that whereas by reason of some defects in the law poor people are not restrained from going from one parish to another, and therefore do endeavor to settle themselves in those parishes where there is the best stock, the largest commons or wastes to build cottages, and the most woods for them to burn and destroy, and when they have consumed it then to another parish, and at last become rogues and vagabonds, to the great discouragement of parishes to provide stocks where it is liable to be devoured by strangers, be it therefore enacted . . . that it shall and may be lawful, upon complaint made by the churchwardens or overseers of the poor of any parish to any justice of peace within forty days after any such person or persons coming so to settle as aforesaid in any tenement under the yearly value of ten pounds, for any two Justices of the Peace, whereof one to be of the quorum, of the division where any person or persons that are likely to be chargeable to the parish shall come to inhabit, by their warrant to remove and convey such person or persons to such parish where he or they were last legally

settled, either as a native, householder, sojourner, apprentice or servant, for the space of forty days at the least, unless he or they give sufficient security for the discharge of the said parish, to be allowed by the said Justices. . . .

Provided also, that . . . it shall and may be lawful for any person or persons to go into any county, parish or place to work in time of harvest, or at any time to work at any other work, so that he or they carry with him or them a certificate from the minister of the parish and one of the churchwardens and one of the overseers for the poor for the said year, that he or they have a dwelling-house or place in which he or they inhabit [unemployed persons to return to legal habitation].

And for the further redress of the mischiefs intended to be hereby remedied, be it enacted . . . that from thenceforth there be and shall be one or more corporation or corporations, workhouse or workhouses within the cities of London and Westminster, and within the boroughs, towns and places of the county of Middlesex and Surrey. . . .

And it is further enacted . . . that it shall . . . be lawful to and for the said president and governors of the said corporations . . . or any two of them, or to or for any person authorized and appointed by them . . . from time to time to apprehend . . . any rogues, vagrants, sturdy beggars or idle or disorderly persons within the said cities and liberties, places, divisions and precincts, and to cause them to be kept and set to work in the several and respective corporations or workhouses; and it shall and may be lawful for the major part of the Justices of Peace in their quarter-sessions to signify unto his Majesty's Privy Council the names of such rogues, vagabonds, [etc.] . . . as they shall think fit to be transported to the English plantations, and upon the approbation of his Majesty's Privy Council to the said Justices of Peace signified which persons shall be transported it shall and may be lawful for any two or more of the Justices of the Peace to transport, or cause to be transported, from time to time during the space of three years next ensuing the end of this present session of Parliament to any of the English plantations beyond the seas, there to be disposed in the usual way of servants for a term not exceeding seven years....

And whereas for want of some encouragement to such person or persons as shall apprehend rogues, vagabonds and sturdy beggars, the statutes [39 Elizabeth, c.4., and 1 James 1, c.7.]... in which statutes the constable, headborough or tithing-man of every parish that shall not apprehend such rogues, [etc.]... which shall pass through or be found in their said parish unapprehended... shall forfeit as in the said statutes is expressed;... be it therefore enacted... that it shall... be lawful to and for any Justice of Peace to whom any rogue, vagabond or sturdy beggar so apprehended shall be brought, to reward any person or persons that shall apprehend any rogue, [etc.]... by granting unto such person... an order or warrant under his hand and seal to the constable, headborough, or tithing-man of such parish where such rogue, vagabond, or sturdy beggar passed through unapprehended, requiring him to pay such person or persons the sum of two shillings for every rogue, vagabond, or sturdy beggar which shall be so apprehended.... (SR, V, 401: 14 Charles II, c.12.)

## Act of Uniformity. 1662

NON-CONFORMITY was dealt another legal blow by the new *Act of Uniformity.* However, because of its harsh insistence on no compromise in matters of conscience, over eighteen-hundred vicars, rectors, and ministers of the established Church refused to comply with its tenets and were severed from their parishes by the government. Thus the Clarendon Code began to consume its own supporters, a fact which was to have extreme political significance after the turn of the decade.

135.

An Act for the Uniformity of Public Prayers, and Administration of Sacraments, and other Rites and Ceremonies; and for Establishing the Form of making, ordaining and consecrating Bishops, Priests, and Deacons in the Church of England.

Whereas in the first year of the late Queen Elizabeth there was one uniform order of common service and prayer, and of the administration of sacraments, rites and ceremonies in the Church of England... compiled by the reverend bishops and clergy, set forth in one book entitled, *The Book of Common Prayer and Administration of Sacraments and other Rites and Ceremonies in the Church of England,* and enjoined to be used by Act of Parliament holden in the said first year of the said late Queen entitled, *An Act for the Uniformity of Common Prayer and Service in the Church and Administra-tion of the Sacraments* [1 Eliz. c.2.]... and yet, this notwithstanding, a great number of people in divers parts of this Realm, following their own sensuality, and living without knowledge and due fear of God, do wilfully and schismatically abstain and refuse to come to their parish churches and other public places where common prayer, administration of the sacraments and preaching of the word of God is used upon the Sundays and other days ordained and appointed to be kept and observed as holy days; and whereas by the great and scandalous neglect of ministers in using the said order or liturgy so set forth and enjoined as aforesaid great mischiefs and inconveniences during the times of the late unhappy troubles have arisen and grown, and many people have been led into factions and schism, to the great decay and scandal of the reformed religion of the Church of England, and to the hazard of many souls; for prevention whereof in time to come, for settling the peace of the Church, and for allaying the present distempers which the indisposition of the time has contracted, the King's Majesty, according to his declaration of [25 October 1660], granted his commission under the great seal of England to several bishops and other divines to review the *Book of Common Prayer* and to prepare such alterations and additions as they thought fit to offer; and afterwards the convocations of both the provinces of Canterbury and York being by his Majesty called and assembled and now sitting, his Majesty has been pleased to authorize and require the presidents of the said convocations and other the bishops and clergy of the same to review the said *Book of Common Prayer* and the book of the form and manner of the making and consecrating of bishops, priests and deacons, and that after mature consideration they should make such additions and alterations in the said books respectively as to them should seem meet and convenient, and should exhibit and present the same to his Majesty in writing for his further allowance or confirmation; since which time, upon full and mature deliberation, they the said presidents, bishops and clergy of both provinces have accordingly reviewed the said books, and have made some alterations which they think fit to be inserted to the same, and some additional prayers to the said *Book of Common Prayer* to be used upon proper and emergent occasions, and have exhibited and presented the same unto his Majesty in writing in one book entitled, *The Book of Common Prayer and Administration of the Sacraments and other Rites and Ceremonies of the Church according to the use of the Church of England, together with the Psalter of Psalms of David, pointed as they are to be Sung or Said in Churches, and the form and manner of Making, Ordaining and Consecrating of Bishops, Priests, and Deacons;* all of which his Majesty, having duly considered, hath

fully approved and the same hath recommended to his present Parliament. . . .

Now in regard that nothing conduceth more to the settling of the peace of this nation . . . nor to the honor of our religion and the propagation thereof, than an universal agreement in the public worship of Almighty God . . . be it enacted . . . that all and singular ministers in any cathedral, collegiate or parish church or chapel or other place of public worship within this Realm of England . . . shall be bound to say and use the morning prayer, evening prayer, celebration and administration of both the sacraments and all other the public and common prayer in such order and form as is mentioned in the said book annexed and joined to this present Act, and entitled [as above], . . . and that the morning and evening prayers therein contained shall upon every Lord's Day, and upon all other days and occasions and at the times therein appointed, be openly and solemnly read by all and every minister or curate in every church, chapel or other place of public worship within this Realm of England and places aforesaid.

And to the end that uniformity in the public worship of God . . . may be speedily effected, be it further enacted . . . that every parson, vicar or other minister whatsoever, who now has and enjoys any ecclesiastical benefice or promotion within this Realm of England or places aforesaid, shall in the church, chapel or place of public worship belonging to his said benefice or promotion, upon some Lord's day before the Feast of Saint Bartholomew [1662] . . . openly, publicly and solemnly read the morning and evening prayer appointed to be read by and according to the said *Book of Common Prayer* at the times thereby appointed, and after such reading thereof shall openly and publicly before the congregation there assembled declare his unfeigned assent and consent to the use of all things in the said book contained and prescribed, in these words and no other:

I, (name), do declare my unfeigned assent and consent to all and every thing contained and prescribed in and by the book entitled, *The Book of Common Prayer and Administration* [etc.]. . . .

And that all and every such person who shall . . . neglect or refuse to do the same within the time aforesaid . . . shall *ipso facto* be deprived of all his spiritual promotions. . . .

And be it further enacted . . . that every dean, canon and prebendary of every cathedral or collegiate church, and all masters and other heads, fellows, chaplains and tutors of or in any college, school, house of learning or hospital, and every public professor and reader in either of the universities and in every college elsewhere, and every parson, vicar, curate, lecturer and every other person in Holy Orders, and every schoolmaster keeping any public or private school, and every person instructing or teaching any youth in any house or private family as a tutor or schoolmaster, who upon the first day of May 1662 . . . or at any time thereafter, shall be incumbent or have possession of any deanery, canonry, [etc.] . . . shall . . . subscribe the declaration or acknowledgment following:

I, (name), do declare that it is not lawful upon any pretence whatsoever to take arms against the King, and that I do abhor that traitorous position of taking arms by his authority against his person or against those that are commissionated by him, and that I will conform to the liturgy of the Church of England as it now is by law established; and I do declare that I do hold there lies no obligation upon me or on any other person from the oath commonly called the Solemn League and Covenant to endeavor any change or alteration of government either in Church or State, and that the same was in itself an unlawful oath, and imposed upon the subjects of this realm against the known laws and liberties of the Kingdom.

. . . . And be it further enacted . . . that no form or order of common prayers, administration of sacraments, rites or ceremonies, shall be openly used in any church, chapel or other public place of or in any college or hall in either of the universities, the colleges of Westminster, Winchester or Eton or any of them, other than what is prescribed and appointed to be used in and by the said book; and that the present governor or head of every college and hall in the said universities and of the said colleges . . . within one month after the Feast of St. Bartholomew . . . in the year [1662] . . . shall openly and publicly in the church, chapel or other public place . . . and in the presence of the fellows and scholars of the same . . . subscribe unto the Nine and Thirty Articles of religion mentioned in the statute made in [13 Eliz. c.2.] . . . and unto the said book, and declare his unfeigned assent and consent unto and approbation of the said articles and of the same book, and to the use of all the prayers, rites and ceremonies, forms and orders in the said book prescribed and contained according to the form aforesaid; and that all such governors or heads of the said colleges and halls or any of them as are or shall be in Holy Orders shall once at least in every quarter of the year . . . openly and publicly read the morning prayer and service in and by the said book appointed to be read in the church, chapel, or other public place of the same college or hall, upon pain to lose and be suspended of and from all the benefits and profits belonging to the same government or headship by the space of six months. . . . (SR, V, 364: 14 Charles II, c.4.)

## Second Militia Act. 1662

136.

THE *Second Militia Act* reestablished the control of the executive in army affairs. Officers chosen by the King were given wide power in choosing additional officers, in levying and collecting a special tax for army support, and in using imprisonment to punish mutineers. So long as Crown and Parliament were in agreement as to the excluding of Catholics from the army there was little cause to fear the re-alignment of King and army, but when James II later attempted to use the authority specified in this Act to incorporate officers of Catholic preference into the army, Parliament found it had given away one of its best methods of controlling the actions of the King.

An Act for ordering the Forces in the several Counties of this Kingdom.

Forasmuch as within all his Majesty's realms and dominions the sole supreme government, command and disposition of the militia, and of all forces by sea and land, and of all forts and places of strength, is, and by the laws of England ever was, the undoubted right of his Majesty and his royal predecessors, kings and queens of England; and that both or either of the Houses of Parliament cannot, nor ought to, pretend to the same, nor can, nor lawfully may, raise or levy any war, offensive or defensive, against his Majesty, his heirs or lawful successors; and yet the contrary thereof has of late years been practised almost to the ruin and destruction of this Kingdom, and during the late usurped governments many evil and rebellious principles have been distilled into the minds of the people of this Kingdom, which unless prevented may break forth to the disturbance of the peace and quiet thereof; be it therefore declared and enacted . . . that the King's most excellent Majesty . . . shall and may, from time to time as occasion shall require, issue forth several commissions of lieutenancy to such persons as his Majesty . . . shall think fit to be his Majesty's lieutenants for the several and respective counties, cities and places of England and dominion of Wales and town of Berwick-upon-Tweed, which lieutenants shall have full power and authority to call together all such persons at such times, and to arm and array them in such manner, as is

hereafter expressed and declared, and to form them into companies, troop and regiments, and in case of insurrection, rebellion or invasion them to lead, conduct and employ . . . as well within the said several counties, cities and places for which they shall be commissionated respectively, as also into any other the counties and places aforesaid, for suppressing of all such insurrections and rebellions and repelling of invasions . . . according as they shall from time to time receive directions from his Majesty . . . and that the said respective lieutenants shall have full power and authority from time to time to constitute, appoint and give commissions to such persons as they shall think fit to be colonels, majors, captains and other commission officers of the said persons so to be armed, arrayed and weaponed, and to present to his Majesty . . . the names of such persons as they shall think fit to be deputy lieutenants, and upon his Majesty's approbation of them shall give them deputations accordingly; always understood that his Majesty . . . have power and authority to direct and order otherwise, and accordingly at his and their pleasure may appoint and commissionate or displace such officers. . . .

And for the providing horse and arms and furniture thereunto belonging for the arming and weaponing the persons aforesaid, and also for the defraying and paying the necessary charges thereunto belonging in manner as hereafter follows, be it further enacted, that the said respective lieutenants . . . have hereby full power and authority to charge any person with horse, horseman and arms, or with foot-soldier and arms, in the same county, shire, city, borough or town corporate where his, her or their estates lie, having respect unto and not exceeding the limitations and proportions hereafter mentioned, that is to say: no person shall be charged with finding a horse, horseman and arms unless such person ... have a revenue of five hundred pounds by the year in possession, or have an estate of six thousand pounds in goods or money besides the furniture of his or their houses, and so proportionably for a greater estate in lands in possession or goods as the respective lieutenants ... in their discretions shall see cause and think reasonable; and they are not to charge any person with finding a foot-soldier and arms that has not a yearly revenue of fifty pounds in possession, or a personal estate of six hundred pounds in goods and moneys. ...

And be it enacted, that the said lieutenants ... shall require and direct all persons so charged as aforesaid with horse, horseman and arms to allow two shillings by the day to the troopers that serve with their horse and arms for the maintenance of the man and horse, and twelve pence a day for the foot-soldiers ... for so many days as they shall be absent from their dwellings and callings by occasion of muster or exercise. ...

And be it enacted ... that the said lieutenants ... shall and may imprison mutineers and such soldiers as do not their duties as soldiers on the day of their musters and training, and shall and may inflict for punishment for every such offence any pecuniary mulct not exceeding five shillings, or the penalty of imprisonment without bail ... not exceeding twenty days. ...

Provided also that no person [shall be capable of acting or serving as lieutenant unless he first make the oaths of allegiance and supremacy before six of the Lords of his Majesty's Privy Council and also make the following oath]: I, (name) do declare and believe that it is not lawful upon any pretence whatsoever to take arms against the King, and that I do abhor that traitorous position that arms may be taken by his authority against his person or against those that are commissioned by him in pursuance of such military commissions. ... (SR, V, 358: 14 Charles II, c.3.)

### The Triennial Act. 1664

### 137.

ROYALIST as it was in sympathy, Parliament was unwilling to place its future fully in the hands of the Crown. This Act settled once and for all the question of regular Parliamentary meetings by stating that the King must issue writs of election "once in three years at least." Thus already in 1664 the philosophy of non-resistance to the Crown began to show the effects of political stress and strain. Parliament was beginning to realize that, while its fundamental interests were essentially identical with those of Charles, there were sufficient differences of opinion between them in political and theological matters to necessitate regular meetings of the legislature as a check.

An Act for the Assembling and Holding of Parliaments once in three years at the least, and for the Repeal of an Act entitled *An Act for the Preventing of Inconveniences happening by the Long Intermission of Parliaments* [16 Charles I].

Whereas the Act made in the Parliament begun at Westminster the third day of November in the sixteenth year of the reign of our late Sovereign Lord King Charles ... entitled, *An Act* [etc.] ... is in derogation of his Majesty's just rights and prerogative inherent to the imperial Crown of this Realm for the calling and assembling of Parliaments, and may be an occasion of manifold mischiefs and inconveniences and much endanger the peace and safety of his Majesty and all his ... people of this Realm, be it therefore enacted . . . that the said Act . . . and all . . . things therein contained is, shall be and are hereby wholly repealed, annulled and utterly made void, and are hereby declared to be null and void to all intents and purposes whatsoever, as if the said Act had never been had or made, anything in the said Act contained to the contrary in any wise notwithstanding.

And because by the ancient laws and statutes of this Realm made in the reign of King Edward III Parliaments are to be held very often, your Majesty's humble and loyal subjects the Lords Spiritual [etc.] . . . most humbly do beseech your most excellent Maj-

esty that it may be declared and enacted . . . that hereafter the sitting and holding of Parliaments shall not be intermitted or discontinued above three years at the most, but that within three years from and after the determination of this present Parliament, and so from time to time within three years after the determination of any other Parliament . . . or if there be no occasion more often, your Majesty . . . do issue out writs for calling, assembling and holding of another Parliament, to the end there may be frequent calling, assembling and holding of Parliaments once in three years at the least. (SR, V, 513: 16 Charles II, c.1.)

## The Five Mile Act. 1664

I38.
THIS ACT was another addition to the Clarendon Code. The method of excluding non-conformist and Catholic ministers and priests from towns and villages, with the hope that they would not be able to hold religious meetings, was not unique in English legal procedure. Yet, since most of the meetings and conventicles the Act attempted to prevent were clandestine, it was of little value in forcing conformity. Conversely, the non-conforming groups, driven underground, became more highly organized and closely associated and in the end more efficient in their various modes of resistance.

An Act for Restraining Nonconformists from Inhabiting in Corporations.

Whereas divers parsons, vicars, curates, lecturers and other persons in Holy Orders have not declared their unfeigned assent and consent to the use of all things contained and prescribed in the *Book of Common Prayer and Administration of the Sacraments and other Rites and Ceremonies of the Church according to the Use of the Church of England,* or have not subscribed the declaration or acknowledgment contained in a certain Act of Parliament made in the fourteenth year of his Majesty's reign and entitled, *An Act for the Uniformity of public Prayers* [etc.] . . . according to the said Act or any other subsequent Act; and whereas they or some of them, and divers other persons not ordained according to the form of the Church of England, and as have since the

*Act of Oblivion* [12 Charles II] taken upon them to preach in unlawful assemblies, conventicles or meetings under color or pretence of exercise of religion, contrary to the laws and statutes of this Kingdom, have settled themselves in divers corporations in England, sometimes three or more of them in a place, thereby taking an opportunity to distil the poisonous principles of schism and rebellion into the hearts of his Majesty's subjects, to the great danger of the Church and Kingdom:

Be it therefore enacted . . . that the said parsons, vicars, curates, lecturers and other persons in Holy Orders, or pretended Holy Orders, . . . and all . . . other persons who have been possessed of any ecclesiastical or spiritual promotion, and every of them, who have not declared their unfeigned assent and consent as aforesaid, and subscribed the declaration aforesaid, and shall not take and subscribe the oath following:

I, (name), do swear that it is not lawful upon any pretence whatsoever to take arms against the King, and that I do abhor that traitorous position of taking arms by his authority against his person, or against those that are commissionated by him, in pursuance of such commissions, and that I will not at any time endeavor any alteration of government either in Church or State.

And all such persons as shall take upon them to preach in any unlawful assembly, conventicle or meeting under color or pretense of any exercise of religion, contrary to the laws and statutes of this Kingdom, shall not at any time from and after [24 March 1665] ... unless only in passing upon the road, come or be within five miles of any city, or town corporate, or borough that sends burgesses to the Parliament, within his Majesty's Kingdom of England ... or within five miles of any parish, town or place wherein he or they have since the *Act of Oblivion* been parson, vicar, curate, sti-

pendiary or lecturer, or taken upon them to preach in any unlawful assembly, conventicle or meeting under color or pretence of any exercise of religion, contrary to the laws and statutes of this Kingdom, before he or they have taken and subscribed the oath aforesaid before the Justices of Peace at their quarter-sessions ... upon forfeiture for every such offence the sum of forty pounds of lawful English money....

Provided always, and be it further enacted ... that it shall not be lawful for any person ... restrained from coming into any city, town corporate, borough, parish, town or place as aforesaid, or for any other person or persons as shall not first take and subscribe the said oath, and as shall not frequent divine service established by the laws of this Kingdom, and carry him or herself reverently, decently and orderly there, to teach any public or private school, or take any boarders or tablers that are taught or instructed by him or herself or any other, upon pain for every such offence to forfeit the sum of forty pounds.... (SR, V, 575: 17 Charles II, c.2.)

## Articles of Impeachment against the Earl of Clarendon. 1667

**I 39.**

THE fall of Edward Hyde, Earl of Clarendon, from power was due to a combination of political, constitutional, and personal reasons. His constitutional policies were obsolete—being far better suited to the Tudor than the Stuart period—and his political theories were not acceptable to the new generation of spokesmen being brought into Parliament by the increasing number of by-elections resulting from Parliament's long session. His impeachment and dismissal, however, are of great significance in documenting the rising determination of Parliament to make unmistakably clear its power and right to control the actions of the Crown through control of its ministers.

I. That the Earl of Clarendon has designed a standing army to be raised, and to govern the Kingdom thereby; advised the King to dissolve this present Parliament, to lay aside all thoughts of Parliaments for the future, to govern by a military power, and to maintain the same by free quarter and contribution.

II. That he has in the hearing of many of his Majesty's subjects falsely and seditiously said that the King was in his heart a papist, popishly affected, or words to that effect.

III. That he has received great sums of money for passing the Canary patent and other illegal patents, and granted illegal injunctions to stop proceedings at law against them and other illegal patents formerly granted.

IV. That he has advised and procured divers of his Majesty's subjects to be imprisoned, against law, in remote islands, garrisons and other places, thereby to prevent them from the benefit of the law, and to introduce precedents for imprisoning many other of his Majesty's subjects in like manner.

V. That he has corruptly sold several offices, contrary to law.

VI. That he procured his Majesty's customs to be farmed at under-rates, knowing the same, and great pretended debts to be paid by his Majesty, to the payment which his Majesty was not in strictness bound, and has received great sums of money for procuring the same.

VII. That he received great sums of money from the Company of Vintners, or some of them, or their agents, for enhancing the prices of wines, and for freeing of them from the payments of legal penalties which they had incurred.

VIII. That he has in short time gained to himself a greater estate than can be imagined to be lawfully gained in so short a time, and contrary to his oath has procured several grants under the great seal from his Majesty to himself and his relations of several of his Majesty's lands, hereditaments and leases, to the disprofit of his Majesty.

IX. That he introduced an arbitrary government in his Majesty's plantations, and has caused such as complained thereof before his Majesty and Council to be long imprisoned for so doing.

X. That he did reject and frustrate a proposal and undertaking approved by his Majesty, for the preservation of Nevis and St. Christopher's and reducing the French plantations to his Majesty's obedience, after the commissions were drawn up for that

purpose, which was the occasion of our great losses and damages in those parts.

XI. That he advised and effected the sale of Dunkirk to the French King, being part of his Majesty's dominions, together with the ammunition, artillery and all sorts of stores there, and for no greater value than the said ammunition, artillery and stores were worth.

XII. That the said Earl did unduly cause his Majesty's letters patents under the great seal to one Dr. Crowther to be altered, and the enrolment thereof to be unduly razed.

XIII. That he has in an arbitrary way examined and drawn into question divers of his Majesty's subjects concerning their lands, tenements, goods, and chattels and properties, determined thereof at the Council table, and stopped proceedings at law by order of the Council table, and threatened some that pleaded the statutes of 17 Charles I.

XIV. That he has caused *quo warrantos* [writs demanding that the holders of charters show proof of the validity of their claim] to be issued out against most of the corporations of England immediately after their charters were confirmed by Act of Parliament, to the intent he might receive great sums of money from them for renewing their charters, which when they complied withal he caused the said *quo warrantos* to be discharged, or prosecution thereupon to cease.

XV. That he procured the bills of settlement for Ireland, and received great sums of money for the same, in most corrupt and unlawful manner.

XVI. That he has deluded and betrayed his Majesty and the nation in foreign treaties and negotiations relating to the late war, and discovered and betrayed his secret counsels to his enemies.

XVII. That he was a principal author of the fatal counsel of dividing the fleet about June 1666. (*Journals of the House of Commons*, IX, 16.)

## Conventicle Act. 1670

140.

ALTHOUGH Parliament had passed a *Conventicle Act* in 1664 as part of the Clarendon Code, the present Act is included here in its stead because it more clearly states
Parliament's religious policies in this period, as well as the prejudices from which
they sprang.

[An Act] to Prevent and Suppress Seditious Conventicles.

For providing further and more speedy remedies against the growing and dangerous practices of seditious sectaries and other disloyal persons, who under pretence of tender consciences have or may at their meetings contrive insurrections . . . be it enacted . . . that if any person of the age of sixteen years or upwards, being a subject of this Realm, at any time after [10 May 1670] . . . shall be present at any assembly, conventicle or meeting under color or pretence of any exercise of religion in other manner than according to the liturgy and practice of the Church of England in any place within the Kingdom of England . . . at which conventicle, meeting or assembly there shall be five persons or more assembled together over and besides those of the same household, if it be in a house where there is a family inhabiting, or if it be in a house, field or place where there is no family inhabiting then where any five persons or more are so assembled as aforesaid, it shall and may be lawful to and for any one or more Justices of the Peace of the county . . . wherein the offence aforesaid shall be committed, or for the chief magistrate of the place where such offence shall be committed, and he and they are hereby required and enjoined upon proof to him or them respectively made of such offence, either by confession of the party or oath of two witnesses . . . or by notorious evidence and circumstance of the fact, to make a record of every such offence under his or their hands and seals . . . which record so made as aforesaid shall to all intents and purposes be in law taken and adjudged to be a full and perfect conviction of every such offender for such offence, which record and conviction shall be certified by the said Justice . . . at the next quarter-sessions. . . .

And be it further enacted . . . that if such offender so convicted as aforesaid shall at any time again commit the like offence or offences contrary to this Act, and be thereof in manner aforesaid convicted, then such offender so convict of such like offence . . . shall for every such offence incur the penalty of ten shillings, which fine and fines for the first and every other offence shall be levied by distress and sale of the offender's goods and chattels, or in case of the poverty of such offender upon the goods and chattels of any other person or persons who shall be then convicted in manner aforesaid of the like offence at the same conventicle, at the discretion of the said Justice. . . .

And be it further enacted . . . that every person who shall take upon him to preach or teach in any such meeting, assembly or conventicle, and shall thereof be convicted . . . shall forfeit for every such offence the sum of twenty pounds . . . and if the said preacher or teacher so convicted be a stranger, and his name and habitation not known, or is fled and cannot be found, or in the judgment of the Justice . . . before whom he shall be convicted shall be thought unable to pay the same, the said Justice . . . is hereby empowered and required to levy the same by warrant as aforesaid upon the goods and chattels of any such persons who shall be present at the same conventicle. . . .

And be it further enacted . . . that every person who shall wittingly and willingly suffer any such conventicle, meeting or unlawful assembly aforesaid to be held in his or her house, outhouse, barn, yard or back-side, and be convicted thereof in manner aforesaid, shall forfeit . . . twenty pounds. . . .

And be it further enacted . . . that the Justice of the Peace and chief magistrate respectively, or the . . . constables, head-boroughs and tithing-men by warrant from the said Justice . . . shall and may with what aid, force and assistance they shall think fit for the better execution of this Act, after refusal or denial to enter, break open and enter into any house or other place where they shall be informed any such conventicle as aforesaid is or shall be held . . . and take into their custody the persons there unlaw-fully assembled, to the intent they may be proceeded against according to this Act; and that the lieutenants or deputy lieutenants or any commissionated officer of the militia or other of his Majesty's forces with such troops or companies of horse and foot, and also the sheriffs and other magistrates and ministers of justice . . . with such other assistance as they shall think meet or can get in readiness with the soonest, on certificate made to them . . . under the hand and seal of any one Justice of the Peace or chief magistrate of his particular information or knowledge of such unlawful meeting or conventicle held or to be held in their respective counties or places, and that he with such assistance as he can get together is not able to suppress and dissolve the same, shall and may . . . repair unto the place where they are so held . . . and by the best means they can to dissolve, dissipate or prevent all such unlawful meet-ings, and take into their custody such and so many of the said persons so unlawfully as-sembled as they shall think fit. . . . (SR, V, 648: 22 Charles II, c.1.)

## The Articles of the Secret Treaty of Dover. 1670

**141.** THE enigmatic qualities of the treaty between Charles II and Louis XIV of France signed at Dover in 1670 have led to much confusion as to the real intent of Charles in religious matters. Judging by the King's promises alone, it seems reasonable to accept as true his intention to declare himself a Catholic, shatter the unity of the English people, and invite the French army into England to enforce his decisions on his sub-jects. When other criteria are considered in assaying the Dover Treaty it is apparent that Louis of France was not so much interested in an uncertain religious conversion as in securing England's neutrality in the war on the continent. Equally reasonable is the assumption that Charles, plagued by the old Stuart need of ready cash, was very much attracted by the yearly subsidy to be provided by the French King according to the provisions of the agreement, and that he was ready to promise almost anything without any real intention of keeping his word.

I. It is agreed, determined and concluded that there shall be for ever a good, secure, and firm peace, union, true fellowship, con-federacy, friendship, alliance and good cor-respondence between the Lord King of Great Britain, his heirs and successors on the one part, and the most Christian King Louis XIV on the other, and between all and every of their Kingdoms, states and territories, as also between their subjects and vassals, that they have or possess at present, or may have, hold and possess hereafter, as well by sea and fresh waters as by land. And as evidence that this peace shall remain inviolable, be-yond the capacity of anything in the world to disturb it, there follow articles of so great confidence, and also so advantageous to the said Lord Kings, that one will hardly find in any age more important provisions deter-mined and concluded.

II. The Lord King of Great Britain, be-ing convinced of the truth of the Catholic religion, and resolved to declare it and reconcile himself with the Church of Rome as soon as the welfare of his Kingdom will permit, has every reason to hope and expect from the affection and loyalty of his subjects that none of them, even of those upon whom God may not yet have conferred His divine grace so abundantly as to incline them by that august example to turn to the true faith, will ever fail in the obedience that all people owe to their Sovereigns, even of a different religion. Nevertheless, as there are sometimes mischievous and unquiet spirits who seek to disturb the public peace, especially when they can conceal their wicked designs under the plausible excuse of religion, his Majesty of Great Britain, who has nothing more at heart . . . than to confirm the peace which the mildness of his government has gained for his subjects, has concluded that the best means to prevent any alteration in it would be to make himself assured in case of need of the assistance of his most Christian Majesty, who, wishing in this case to give to the Lord King of Great Britain an unquestionable proof of the reality of his friendship, and to contribute to the success of so glorious a design, and one of such service not merely to his Majesty of Great Britain but also to the whole Catholic religion . . . promises to give for that purpose to the said Lord King of Great Britain the sum of two million *livres tournois.* . . . In addition the said most Christian King binds himself to assist his Majesty of Great Britain in case of need with troops to the number of 6,000 foot-soldiers, and even to raise and maintain them at his own expense, so far as the said Lord King of Great Britain finds need of them for the execution of his design; and the said troops shall be transported by ships of the King of Great Britain to such places and ports as he shall consider most convenient for the good of his service, and from the day of their embarkation shall be paid, as agreed, by his Most Christian Majesty, and shall obey the orders of the said Lord King of Great Britain. And the time of the said declaration of

Catholicism is left entirely to the choice of the said Lord King of Great Britain.

III. It has also been agreed . . . that the said most Christian King shall never break or infringe the peace which he has made with Spain. . . .

IV. It is also agreed and accepted that if there should hereafter fall to the most Christian King any new titles and rights to the Spanish Monarchy, the said Lord King of Great Britain shall assist his most Christian Majesty with all his forces . . . to facilitate the acquisition of the said rights. . . .

V. The said Lord Kings having each in his own right many more subjects than they would have any need of to justify to the world the resolution they have taken to humble the pride of the States General of the United Provinces of the Low Countries, and to reduce the power of a nation which has so often rendered itself odious by extreme ingratitude to its own founders and the creators of its republic, and which even has the insolence to aim now at setting itself up as sovereign arbiter and judge of all other potentates, it is agreed, decided and concluded that their Majesties will declare and wage war jointly with all their forces . . . on the said States General of the United Provinces of the Low Countries, and that neither of the said Lord Kings will make any treaty of peace, or truce, or suspension of arms with them without the knowledge and consent of the other, as also that all commerce between the subjects of the said Lord Kings and those of the said States shall be forbidden, and that the vessels and goods of those who carry on trade in defiance of this prohibition may be seized by the subjects of the other Lord King. . . .

VI. And for the purpose of waging and conducting the war . . . it is also agreed that his most Christian Majesty will undertake all the expense necessary for setting on foot, maintaining and supporting the operations of the armies required for delievering a powerful attack by land on the strongholds and territory of the said States, the said Lord

King of Great Britain binding himself only to contribute to the army of the said most Christian King, and to maintain there at his own expense, a body of 6,000 infantry....

VII. As to what concerns the war at sea, the said Lord King of Great Britain shall undertake that burden, and shall fit out at least fifty great ships and ten fire-ships, to which the said most Christian King shall bind himself to add a squadron of thirty good French vessels. . . . And in order that the said Lord King of Great Britain may more easily support the expense of the war, his most Christian Majesty binds himself to pay to the said King each year that the said war shall last the sum of three millions of *livres tournois*. . . . And of all the conquests which shall be made from the States Gen-

eral his Majesty of Great Britain shall be content with the following places, viz., the island of Walcheren, Sluys, with the island of Cadsand. . . . And inasmuch as the dissolution of the government of the States General might involve some prejudice to the Prince of Orange, nephew to the King of Great Britain, and also that some fortresses, towns and governments which belong to him are included in the proposed division of the country, it has been determined and concluded that the said Lord Kings shall do all they can to secure that the said Prince may find his advantage in the continuation and end of the war, as shall hereafter be provided in separate articles.... [all prior English-French agreements are void]. (J. Lingard, *History of England,* (ed. 1874), IX, 251.)

## The First Declaration of Indulgence. 1672

**142.** THE *Declaration of Indulgence,* which suspended the penal laws against non-Anglicans and permitted Protestant dissenters to worship in public and Catholics in private places, was far removed from the dangerous promises made by Charles in the Treaty of Dover. Charles's purpose in issuing the *Declaration* was twofold. He hoped to win by it the support of both Catholics and dissenters and thereby affect the composition and temper of the Parliament which was to meet the following year. Also, it is conceivable that in resorting to such action the King attempted to construct, out of the raw material of executive decree, something he could barter to Parliament for the supply necessary to conduct the war against the Dutch which had begun earlier in the year and which was not going well for the English. It is quite clear that the *Declaration,* along with the Treaty of Dover, was dictated by political expedience.

Our care and endeavors for the preservation of the rights and interests of the Church have been sufficiently manifested to the world by the whole course of our government since our happy restoration, and by the many and frequent ways of coercion that we have used for reducing all erring or dissenting persons, and for composing the unhappy differences in matters of religion which we found among our subjects upon our return. But it being evident by the sad experience of twelve years that there is very little fruit of all those forcible courses, we think ourself obliged to make use of that supreme power in ecclesiastical matters which is not only inherent in

us but has been declared and recognized to be so by several statutes and Acts of Parliament. And therefore we do now accordingly issue this our declaration, as well for the quieting the minds of our good subjects in these points, for inviting strangers in this conjuncture to come and live under us, and for the better encouragement of all to a cheerful following of their trade and callings, from whence we hope by the blessing of God to have many good and happy advantages to our government, as also for preventing for the future the danger that might otherwise arise from private meetings and seditious conventicles.

And in the first place, we declare our express resolution, meaning and intention to be that the Church of England be preserved and remain entire in its doctrine, discipline and government as now it stands established by law; and that this be taken to be, as it is, the basis, rule and standard of the general and public worship of God, and that the orthodox conformable clergy do receive and enjoy the revenues belonging thereunto; and that no person, though of a different opinion and persuasion, shall be exempt from paying his tithes or other dues whatsoever. And further we declare that no person shall be capable of holding any benefice, living or ecclesiastical dignity or preferment of any kind in this our Kingdom of England who is not exactly conformable.

We do in the next place declare our will and pleasure to be that the execution of all and all manner of penal laws in matters ecclesiastical, against whatsoever sort of nonconformists or recusants, be immediately suspended, and they are hereby suspended; and all judges, judges of assize and jail delivery, sheriffs, justices of the peace, mayors, bailiffs, and other officers whatsoever, whether ecclesiastical or civil, are to take notice of it, and pay due obedience thereunto.

And that there may be no pretence for any of our subjects to continue their illegal meetings and conventicles, we do declare that we shall from time to time allow a sufficient number of places, as they shall be desired, in all parts of this our Kingdom for the use of such as do not conform to the Church of England, to meet and assemble in, in order to their public worship and devotion, which places shall be open and free to all persons. But to prevent such disorders and inconveniences as may happen by this our indulgence, if not duly regulated, and that they may be the better protected by the civil magistrate, our express will and pleasure is that none of our subjects do presume to meet in any place until such place be allowed and the teacher of that congregation be approved by us.

And lest any should apprehend that this restriction should make our said allowance and approbation difficult to be obtained, we do further declare that this our indulgence, as to the allowance of the public places of worship and approbation of the teachers, shall extend to all sorts of nonconformists and recusants except the recusants of the Roman Catholic religion, to whom we shall in no wise allow public places of worship, but only indulge them in their share in the common exemption from the execution of the penal laws, and the exercise of their worship in their private houses only.

And if after this our clemency and indulgence any of our subjects shall presume to abuse this liberty, and shall preach seditiously, or to the derogation of the doctrine, discipline or government of the established Church, or shall meet in places not allowed by us, we do hereby give them warning, and declare we will proceed against them with all imaginable severity. And we will let them see we can be as severe to punish such offenders, when so justly provoked, as we are indulgent to truly tender consciences. (E. Cardwell, *Documentary Annals of the Reformed Church of England,* II, 282.)

## Charles II: Speech to Parliament Concerning the Declaration of Indulgence of 1672. 1673

THE Parliament of 1673 met in an atmosphere of suspicion and resentment. Charles's *Declaration of Indulgence* of the previous year gave substance to the persistent rumor that the forces raised by the King, ostensibly for the Dutch War, were really intended as a threat to Parliament. In explaining the *Declaration* to Parliament the King overlooked the fundamental cause of the Parliamentary dissatisfaction, the fact that he had resorted to suspension of statutory law. The House of Commons made this point

143.

clear in its next communication to the King, thus ignoring the substantive content of the document in favor of the constitutional point involved. Ten days later Charles answered Commons's communication by attempting to differentiate between the suspension of law and the mere lifting of penalties for private disobedience to law.

Sensing the defensive attitude of the Crown, Commons drew up a second reply within two days. The King had been "very much misinformed" as to the suspending power. He must not alter "the legislative power, which has always been acknowledged to reside in your Majesty and your two Houses of Parliament." Not satisfied with having raised the dispute to the level of a constitutional issue, the two Houses sent a joint message to Charles, the meaning of which was unmistakable. In language little less than contemptuous the King was informed that Parliament did not intend to bargain. The suspending power was unconstitutional and Catholics were to be barred from army service. Less than a week later Charles gave in and withdrew both the *Declaration of Indulgence* and his claimed right to suspend laws or free any from obedience to them.

My Lords and Gentlemen:

I am glad to see you here this day....

Since you were last here I have been forced to a most important, necessary and expensive war, and I make no doubt but you will give me suitable and effectual assistance to go through with it. I refer you to my declaration for the causes, and indeed the necessity, of this war, and shall now only tell you that I might have digested the indignities to my own person rather than have brought it to this extremity, if the interest as well as the honor of the whole Kingdom had not been at stake. . . .

You will find that the last supply you gave me did not answer expectation for the ends you gave it, the payment of our debts. Therefore I must in the next place recommend them again to your special care.

Some few days before I declared the war I put forth my declaration for indulgence to dissenters, and have hitherto found a good effect of it by securing peace at home when I had war abroad. There is one part of it that hath been subject to misconstruction, which is that concerning the papists, as if more liberty were granted them than to the other recusants, when it is plain there is less, for the others have public places allowed them, and I never intended that they should have any, but only have the freedom of their religion in their own houses, without any concern of others. And I could not grant

them less than this when I had extended so much more grace to others, most of them having been loyal and in the service of me and of the King my father. And in the whole course of this indulgence I do not intend that it shall any way prejudice the Church; but I will support its rights and it in its full power. Having said this, I shall take it very, very ill to receive contradiction in what I have done. And I will deal plainly with you: I am resolved to stick to my declaration.

There is one jealousy more that is maliciously spread abroad . . . and that is that the forces I have raised in this war were designed to control law and property. I wish I had had more forces the last summer. The want of them then convinces me I must raise more against this next spring, and I do not doubt but you will consider the charge of them in your supplies.

I will conclude with this assurance to you, that I will preserve the true reformed Protestant religion and the Church as it is now established in this Kingdom, and that no man's property or liberty shall ever be invaded.

*ANSWER OF THE HOUSE OF COMMONS TO THE KING'S SPEECH.*
[14 February 1673]

Most Gracious Sovereign,

We, your Majesty's most loyal and faithful subjects, the Commons assembled in Parliament, do in the first place, as in all duty bound, return your Majesty our most humble and hearty thanks for the many gracious promises and assurances which your Majesty has several times during this present Parliament given to us, that your Majesty would secure and maintain unto us the true reformed Protestant religion, our liberties and properties, which most gracious assurances your Majesty has out of your great goodness been pleased to renew unto us more particularly at the opening of this present session of Parliament.

And further we crave leave humbly to represent that we have, with all duty and expedition, taken into our consideration several parts of your Majesty's last speech to us, and withal the declaration therein mentioned for indulgence to dissenters . . . and we find ourselves bound in duty to inform your Majesty that penal statutes in matters ecclesiastical cannot be suspended but by Act of Parliament.

We therefore, the knights, citizens and burgesses of your Majesty's House of Commons, do most humbly beseech your Majesty that the said laws may have their free course until it shall be otherwise provided for by Act of Parliament, and that your Majesty would graciously be pleased to give such directions herein that no apprehensions or jealousies may remain in the hearts of your Majesty's good and faithful subjects.

*THE KING'S ANSWER.* [24 February 1673]

His Majesty has received an address from you; and he has seriously considered of it, and returneth you this answer:

That he is very much troubled that that declaration, which he put out for ends so necessary to the quiet of his Kingdom, and especially in that conjuncture, should have proved the case of disquiet in his House of Commons, and give occasion to the questioning of his power in ecclesiastics, which he finds not done in the reigns of any of his ancestors. He is sure he never had thoughts of using it otherwise than as it has been intrusted in him, to the peace and establishment of the Church of England and the ease of all his subjects in general. Neither does he pretend to the right of suspending any laws wherein the properties, rights or liberties of any of his subjects are concerned, nor to alter anything in the established doctrine or discipline of the Church of England. But his only design in this was to take off the penalties the statutes inflict upon dissenters, and which he believes, when well considered of, you yourselves would not wish executed according to the rigor and letter of the law.

Neither has he done this with any thought of avoiding or precluding the advice of his Parliament; and if any bill shall be offered him which shall appear more proper to attain the aforesaid ends, and secure the peace of the Church and Kingdom, when tendered in due manner to him, he will show how readily he will concur in all ways that shall appear good for the Kingdom.

*THE HOUSE OF COMMONS'S ANSWER.*

[26 February 1673]

Most Gracious Sovereign,

We, your Majesty's most humble . . . subjects, [etc.]. . . .

We do not in the least measure doubt but that your Majesty had the same gracious intentions in giving satisfaction to your subjects by your answer to our last petition and address. Yet upon a serious consideration thereof we find that the said answer is not sufficient to clear the apprehensions that may justly remain in the minds of your people, by your Majesty's having claimed a power to suspend penal statutes in matters ecclesiastical, and which your Majesty does still seem to assert in the said answer to be intrusted in the Crown, and never questioned in the reigns of any your ancestors; wherein we humbly conceive your Majesty has been very much misinformed, since no such power was ever claimed or exercised by any of your Majesty's predecessors, and if it should be admitted might tend to the interrupting of the free course of the laws, and altering the legislative power, which has always been acknowledged to reside in your Majesty and your two Houses of Parliament.

We do therefore with an unanimous consent become again most humble suitors unto your sacred Majesty, that you would be pleased to give us a full and satisfactory answer to our said petition and address. . . .

## STATEMENT OF THE TWO HOUSES.
[3 March, 1673]

Most Gracious Sovereign,

We, your Majesty's most loyal subjects, the Lords Spiritual and Temporal and Commons in this present Parliament assembled, being very sensible of the great dangers and mischiefs that may arise within this your Majesty's realm by the increase of popish recusants amongst us; and considering the great resort of priests and Jesuits into this Kingdom, who daily endeavor to seduce your Majesty's subjects from their religion and allegiance, and how desirous your loyal subjects are that no popish recusants be admitted into employments of trust and profit, and especially into military commands over the forces now in your Majesty's service; and having a tender regard to the preservation of your Majesty's person and the peace and tranquillity of his Kingdom, do in all humility desire that your Majesty would be pleased to issue out your royal proclamation to command all priests and Jesuits, other than such as, not being natural-born subjects to your Majesty, are obliged to attend upon your royal consort the Queen, to depart within thirty days out of this your Majesty's Kingdom; and that if any priest or Jesuit shall happen to be taken in England after the expiration of the said time, that the laws be put in due execution against them; and that your Majesty would please in the said proclamation to command all judges, justices of the peace, mayors, bailiffs, and other officers to put the said laws in execution accordingly.

That your Majesty would likewise be pleased that the Lord Chancellor of England shall . . . issue out commissions . . . to the judge advocate and commissaries of the musters and such other persons as he shall think fit . . . to tender the oaths of allegiance and supremacy to all officers and soldiers now in your Majesty's service and pay; and that such as refuse the said oaths may be immediately disbanded, and not allowed or continued in any pay or pension. . . .

That the said commissaries of the musters be commanded and enjoined by your Majesty's warrant, upon the penalty of losing their places, not to permit any officer to be mustered in the service and pay of your Majesty until he shall have taken the oaths of allegiance and supremacy and received the sacrament of the Lord's Supper according to the laws and usage of the Church of England; and that every soldier serving at land shall take the said oaths before his first muster, and receive the sacraments in such manner before his second muster.

## THE KING'S ANSWER TO THE JOINT STATEMENT. [8 March, 1673]

Yesterday you presented me an address as the best means for the satisfying and composing the minds of my subjects; to which I freely and readily agreed, and shall take care to see it performed accordingly. I hope, on the other side, you gentlemen of the House of Commons will do your part, for I must put you in mind it is near five weeks since I demanded a supply, and what you voted unanimously upon it did both give life to my affairs at home and disheartened my enemies abroad. But the seeming delay it has met with since has made them take new courage, and they are now preparing for this next summer a greater fleet . . . than ever they had yet, so that if the supply be not speedily dispatched it will be altogether ineffectual, and the safety, honor and interest of England must of necessity be exposed. Pray lay this to heart, and let not the fears and jealousies of some draw an inevitable ruin upon us all.

If there be any scruple remain yet with you concerning the suspension of penal laws,

I here faithfully promise you that what has been done in that particular shall not for the future be drawn into consequence or example. And as I daily expect from you a bill for my supply, so I assure you I shall as willingly receive and pass any other you shall offer me that may tend to the giving you satisfaction in all your just grievances. (*Journals of the House of Commons*, IX, 246.)

## The First Test Act. 1673

144.

THE *Test Act* was Parliament's angry and frightened statutory answer to the King's abortive attempt to suspend the penal laws and employ Catholics and dissenters in the armed forces. This law barred from civil and military office any who were unable to pass the test of religious soundness by publicly participating in the services of the Established Church, or who refused to deny the Catholic concept of transubstantiation, or who refused to swear the oaths of allegiance and supremacy.

The King's assent to the *Test Act* virtually surrendered Crown supremacy in the Church. And it had even deeper constitutional and political significance. The Act was a necessary preliminary to the later attempted exclusion of the Duke of York from the throne on grounds of his Catholicism.

An Act for preventing dangers which may happen from Popish Recusants.

For preventing dangers which may happen from popish recusants . . . be it enacted . . . that all and every person . . . as well peers as commoners, that shall bear any office or offices, civil or military, or shall receive any pay, salary, fee or wages by reason of any patent or grant from his Majesty, or shall have command or place of trust from or under his Majesty, or from any of his Majesty's predecessors, or by his or their authority or by authority derived from him or them within the Realm of England . . . or in his Majesty's navy . . . or shall be of the household or in the service or employment of his Majesty or of his Royal Highness the Duke of York, who shall inhabit, reside or be within the city of London or Westminster, or within thirty miles distant from the same, on the first day of Easter term that shall be in the year [1673] or at any time during the said term, all and every the said person and persons shall personally appear before the end of the said term, or of Trinity term next following, in his Majesty's High Court of Chancery, or in his Majesty's Court of King's Bench, and there in public and open court between the hours of nine of the clock and twelve in the forenoon take the several oaths of supremacy and allegiance . . . by law established; . . . and that all and every of the said respective persons and officers not having taken the said oaths in the said respective courts aforesaid shall on or before the first day of August [1673,] at the quarter-sessions for that county or place where he or they shall be, inhabit or reside on the twentieth day of May, take the said oaths in open court . . . and the said respective officers aforesaid shall also receive the sacrament of the Lord's Supper according to the usage of the Church of England at or before the first day of August in the year [1673] in some church upon some Lord's Day [Sunday]. . . .

And be it further enacted . . . that all and every person or persons that shall be admitted, entered, placed or taken into any office or offices [as above specified] . . . after the first day of Easter term aforesaid, and shall inhabit, or reside when he or they is or are so admitted or placed within the cities of London or Westminster or within thirty miles of the same, shall take the said oaths aforesaid in the said respective court or courts aforesaid in the next term after such his or their admittance . . . into the office or offices, employment or employments aforesaid, between the hours aforesaid and no other . . . and that all and every such person or persons to be admitted after the said first day of Easter term as aforesaid not having taken the said oaths in the said courts aforesaid shall, at the quarter-sessions for the county or place where he or they shall reside next after such his admittance or admittances into any of the said respective offices or employments aforesaid, take the said several and respective oaths as aforesaid; and all and every such person and persons so to be admitted as aforesaid shall also receive the sacrament of the Lord's Supper according to the usage of the Church of England within three months after his or their admittance in or receiving their said authority and employment, in some public church upon some Lord's Day. . . .

And be it further enacted . . . that all and every the person or persons aforesaid that do or shall neglect or refuse to take the said oaths and sacrament in the said courts and places and at the respective times aforesaid shall be *ipso facto* adjudged incapable and disabled in law to all intents and purposes whatsoever to have, occupy or enjoy the said office or offices. . . .

And be it further enacted, that all and every such person . . . that shall neglect or refuse to take the said oaths or the sacrament as aforesaid within the times and in the places aforesaid and in the manner aforesaid, and yet after such neglect and refusal shall execute any of the said offices or employments after the said times expired wherein he or they ought to have taken the same, and being thereupon lawfully convict . . . every such person . . . shall be disabled from thenceforth to sue, or use any action, bill, plaint or information in course of law, or to prosecute any suit in any court of equity, or to be guardian of any child or executor or administrator of any person, or capable of any legacy or deed of gift or to bear any office within this Realm of England . . . and shall forfeit the sum of five hundred pounds, to be recovered by him or them that shall sue for the same. . . .

And be it further enacted . . . that at the same time when the persons concerned in this Act shall take the aforesaid oaths of supremacy and allegiance they shall likewise make and subscribe this declaration following, under the same penalties and forfeitures as by this Act is appointed:

I, (name), do declare that I do believe that there is not any transubstantiation in the sacrament of the Lord's Supper, or in the elements of bread and wine, at or after the consecration thereof by any person whatsoever. (SR, V, 782: 25 Charles II, c.2.)

## The Second Test Act. 1678

**145.** THE second *Test Act* extended the political disabilities consequent to Protestant dissent and Catholicism to include membership in Parliament. Hereafter none who could not pass the tests established by Parliament in the first *Test Act* in matters of religious belief could be seated in either House. Thus the law and the constitution were used to enforce intolerance and narrowness to a degree seldom approached by the governments of the Commonwealth.

An Act for the more effectual preserving the King's person and Government by disabling papists from sitting in either House of Parliament.

Forasmuch as divers good laws have been made for preventing the increase and danger of popery in this Kingdom, which have not had the desired effects by reason of the free access which popish recusants have had to his Majesty's court, and by reason of the liberty which of late some of the recusants have had and taken to sit and vote in Parliament; wherefore, and for the safety of his Majesty's royal person and government, be it enacted . . . that from and after the first day of December which shall be in the year [1678] no person that now is or hereafter shall be a Peer of this Realm, or member of the House of Peers, shall vote or make his proxy in the House of Peers, or sit there during any debate in the said House of Peers, nor any person that now is or hereafter shall be a member of the House of Commons shall vote in the House of Commons, or sit there during any debate in the said House of Commons after their Speaker is chosen, until such Peer or member shall from time to time respectively and in manner following first take the several oaths of allegiance and supremacy, and make, subscribe and audibly repeat this declaration following:

I, (name), do solemnly and sincerely in the presence of God profess, testify and declare that I do believe that in the sacrament of the Lord's Supper there is not any transubstantiation of the elements of bread and wine into the body and blood of Christ at or after the consecration thereof by any person whatsoever; and that the invocation or adoration of the Virgin Mary or any other saint and the sacrifice of the mass, as they are now used in the Church of Rome, are superstitious and idolatrous. And I do solemnly in the presence of God profess, testify and declare that I do make this declaration and every part thereof in the plain and ordinary sense of the words read unto me, as they are commonly understood by English Protestants, without any evasion, equivocation or mental reservation whatsoever, and without any dispensation already granted me for this purpose by the Pope or any other authority or person whatsoever, or without any hope of any such dispensation . . . or without thinking that I am or can be acquitted before God or man or absolved of this declaration or any part thereof, although the Pope or any other person or persons or power whatsoever should dispense with or annul the same, or declare that it was null and void from the beginning.

Which said oaths and declaration shall be in this and every succeeding Parliament solemnly and publicly made and subscribed between the hours of nine in the morning and four in the afternoon by every such peer and member of the House of Peers at the table in the middle of the said House before he take his place in the said House of Peers, and while a full House of Peers is there with their Speaker in his place, and by every such member of the House of Commons at the table in the middle of the said House, and while a full House of Commons is there duly sitting with their Speaker in his chair, and that the same be done in either House in such like order or method as each House is called over by respectively.

And be it further enacted, that from and after the said first day of December every Peer of this Realm and member of the House of Peers, and every Peer of the Kingdom of Scotland or of the Kingdom of Ireland, being of the age of one and twenty years or upwards . . . and every member of the said House of Commons, not having as aforesaid taken the said oaths and made and subscribed the said declaration, and every person now or hereafter convicted of popish recusancy, who hereafter shall at any time after the said first day of December come advisedly into or remain in the presence of the King's Majesty or Queen's Majesty, or shall come into the court or house where they or any of them reside, as well during the reign of his present Majesty . . . as during the reigns of any his royal successors kings or queens of England, shall incur and suffer all the pains, penalties, forfeitures and disabilities in this Act mentioned or continued, unless such peer, member or person so convicted do respectively in the next term after such his coming or remaining take the said oaths and make and subscribe the said declaration. . . .

[The penalty for violating the Act to be the same as stated in the Test Act of 1673]

And be it further enacted . . . that . . . it shall . . . be lawful to and for the House of Peers and the House of Commons or either of them respectively, as often as they or either of them shall see occasion, either in this present Parliament or any other hereafter to be holden, to order and cause all or any of the members of their respective Houses of Parliament openly in their respective Houses of Parliament to take the said oaths, and to make and subscribe the said declaration, at such times and in such manner as they shall appoint. . . .

And be it enacted, that in every case where any member or members of the House of Commons shall by virtue of this Act be disabled to sit or vote in the House of Commons, then and in every such case, without any further conviction or other proceeding against such member or members, the place or places for which they or any of them were elected is hereby declared void, and a new writ or writs shall issue out of the High Court of Chancery by warrant . . . from the Speaker of the House of Commons . . . and by order of the said House, for the election of a new member . . . to serve in the House

of Commons in the place . . . of such member . . . so disable, to all intents and purposes as if such member . . . were naturally dead.

And be it further enacted . . . that every person . . . who . . . shall be, a sworn servant to the King's or Queen's Majesty, not having before that time duly taken the oaths and made and subscribed the declaration contained in [the *Test Act* of 1673] . . . shall take the said oaths and make and subscribe the declaration before expressed in his Majesty's High Court of Chancery . . . and if any such person shall refuse or neglect to do the same, and yet after such refusal or neglect shall advisedly come into or remain in the presence of the King's or Queen's Majesty, or shall come into the court or house where they or any of them reside, as well during the reign of his present Majesty [etc.] . . . every such person shall be disabled to hold any place as such sworn servant, and shall incur and suffer all the pains, [etc.] . . . .

Provided that nothing in this Act shall relate to or have any effect upon any person being a natural-born subject of the King of Portugal who now is or hereafter shall be a sworn servant to the Queen's Majesty, not exceeding nine in number at any one time. . . .

Provided always, that nothing in this Act contained shall extend to his Royal Highness the Duke of York. (SR, V, 894: 30 Charles II, s.2., c.1.)

## The Habeas Corpus Act. 1679

**146.** THE writ of *habeas corpus* had a long history in England prior to the reign of Charles II, extending as it did well back into the early middle ages. During the 16th century its use had become more widespread as the lawyers and judges of the Common Law courts fought to maintain their equality with the Prerogative courts. Nevertheless, the government had found many ways of nullifying the more benevolent aspects of *habeas corpus* writs. This was especially so in cases of arrest for political offenses. The Act of 1679 attempted to strengthen the writ's effectiveness in this respect.

An Act for the Better Securing the Liberty of the Subject and for Prevention of Imprisonments beyond the Seas.

Whereas great delays have been used by sheriffs, jailers, and other officers to whose custody any of the King's subjects have been committed for criminal or supposed criminal matters, in making returns of writs of *Habeas Corpus* to them directed, by standing out an Alias and *Pluries Habeas Corpus* and sometimes more, and by other shifts to avoid their yielding obedience to such writs, contrary to their duty and the known laws of the land, whereby many of the King's subjects have been and hereafter may be long detained in prison, in such cases where by law they are bailable, to their great charge and vexation; for the prevention whereof and the more speedy relief of all persons imprisoned for any such criminal or supposed criminal matters, be it enacted . . . that whensoever any person . . . shall bring any *Habeas Corpus* directed unto any sheriff or sheriffs, jailer . . . or other person whatsoever, for any person in his . . . custody, and the said writ shall be served upon the said officer or left at the jail or prison with any of the under-officers . . . or deputy of the said officers or keepers, that the said officer . . . shall within three days after the service thereof as aforesaid (unless the commitment aforesaid were for treason or felony plainly and specially expressed in the warrant of commitment), upon payment or tender of the charges of bringing the said prisoner, to be ascertained by the judge or court that awarded the same and endorsed upon the said writ, not exceeding twelve pence per mile, and upon security given by his own bond to pay the charges of carrying back the prisoner if he shall be remanded by the court of judge to which he shall be brought according to the true intent of this present Act, and that he will not make any escape by the way, make return of such writ, and bring . . . the body of the party so committed or restrained unto or before the Lord Chancellor or Lord Keeper of the Great Seal of England for the time being, or the judge or barons of the said court from whence the said writ shall issue, or unto and before such person . . . before whom the said writ is made returnable according to the command thereof, and shall then likewise certify the true causes of his detainer or imprisonment, unless the commitment of the said party be in any place beyond the distance of twenty miles from the place or places where such court or person is or shall be residing, and if beyond the distance of twenty miles and not above one hundred miles, then within the space of ten days, and if beyond the distance of one hundred miles then within the space of twenty days after such delivery aforesaid. . . .

And to the intent that no sheriff, jailer or other officer may pretend ignorance of the import of such writ, be it enacted . . . that all such writs shall be marked in this manner, *Per statutum tricesimo primo Caroli Secundi Regis,* and shall be signed by the person that awards the same; and if any person . . . shall be . . . committed . . . as aforesaid for any crime, unless for treason or felony plainly expressed in the warrant of commitment, in the vacation time and out of term, it shall and may be lawful to and for the person . . . so committed or detained (other than persons convict or in execution by legal process), or anyone on his or their behalf, to appeal or complain to the Lord Chancellor or Lord Keeper or any one of his Majesty's Justices, either of the one bench or of the other, or the barons of the Exchequer of the degree of the coif [the white silk cap denoting the wearer as a sergeant-at-law]; and the said Lord Chancellor, Lord Keeper, Justices or barons or any of them, upon view of the copy or copies of the warrant . . . of commitment . . . or otherwise upon oath made that such copy or copies were denied to be given by such person . . . in whose custody the prisoner . . . is . . . detained, are hereby authorized and required, upon request made in writing by such person . . . attested and subscribed by two witnesses who were present at the delivery of the same, to award and grant an *Habeas Corpus* under the seal of such court whereof he shall then be one of the judges, to be directed to the officer or officers in whose custody the party so committed . . .

shall be, returnable immediate before the said Lord Chancellor . . . or such Justice of any of the said courts; and upon service thereof as aforesaid the officer . . . [etc.] in whose custody the party is so committed . . . shall within the times respectively before limited bring such prisoner or prisoners before the said Lord Chancellor or Lord Keeper, [etc.] . . . before whom the said writ is made returnable, and in case of his absence before any other of them, with the return of such writ and the true causes of the commitment . . . and thereupon within two days after the party shall be brought before them the said Lord Chancellor [etc.] . . . shall discharge the said prisoner from his imprisonment, taking his or their recognizance with one or more surety or sureties in any sum according to their discretions, having regard to the quality of the prisoner and the nature of the offence, for his . . . appearance in the Court of the King's Bench the term following, or at the next assizes, sessions, or general jail delivery [a writ of jail delivery was a commission issued to a Justice to hear all cases in a particular jail-house and thus relieve the jail of some of its inhabitants and thereby "deliver" it from overcrowding] of and for such county, city or place where the commitment was, or where the offence was committed, or in such other court where the said offence is properly cognizable, as the case shall require, and then shall certify the said writ with the return thereof and the said recognizance or recognizances into the said court where such appearance is to be made, unless it shall appear unto the said Chancellor [etc.] . . . that the party so committed is detained upon a legal process, order or warrant out of some court that has jurisdiction of criminal matters, or by the some warrant signed and sealed with the hand and seal of any of the said Justices or barons, or some Justice or Justices of the peace, for such matters or offences for the which by the law the prisoner is not bailable. . . .

And be it further enacted [that any officer who shall refuse to free a person holding a writ of *Habeas Corpus,* or shall not deliver to the prisoner upon demand a copy of the warrant of commitment, shall forfeit to the prisoner £100 for the first and £200 for the second such offence and shall lose his office]. . . .

[No person delivered under a *Habeas Corpus* may be re-imprisoned for the same offense until after legal trial wherein he is convicted].

Provided always, that nothing in this Act shall extend to discharge out of prison any person charged in debt or other action, or with process in any civil case, but that after he shall be discharged of his imprisonment for such his criminal offence he shall be kept in custody according to law for such other suit. . . .

Provided also . . . that it shall and may be lawful to and for any prisoner . . . to move and obtain his or their *Habeas Corpus* as well out of the High Court of Chancery or Court of Exchequer as out of the Courts of King's Bench or Common Pleas or either of them; and if the said Lord Chancellor or Lord Keeper or any judge or judges, baron or barons for the time being of the degree of the coif of any of the courts aforesaid in the vacation time, upon view of the copy or copies of the warrant . . . of commitment . . . or upon oath made that such copy . . . were denied as aforesaid, shall deny any writ of *Habeas Corpus* by this Act required to be granted being moved for as aforesaid, they shall severally forfeit to the prisoner or party grieved the sum of £500. . . .

And for preventing illegal imprisonments in prisons beyond the seas, be it further enacted . . . that no subject of this Realm that now is or hereafter shall be an inhabitant or resident of this Kingdom of England, dominion of Wales or town of Berwick-upon-Tweed shall or may be sent prisoner into Scotland, Ireland, Jersey, Guernsey, Tangier or into any parts, garrisons, islands or places beyond the seas which are or at any time hereafter shall be within or without the dominions of his Majesty . . . and that every such imprisonment is hereby enacted and adjudged to be illegal. . . .

Provided also, that if any person . . . at any time resident in this Realm shall have committed any capital offence in Scotland or Ireland, or any of the islands or foreign plantations of the King . . . where he . . . ought to be tried for such offence, such person . . . may be sent to such place, there to receive such trial in such manner as the same might have been used before the making of this Act. . . . (SR, V, 935: 31 Charles II, c.2.)

## The Exclusion Bill. 1680

### 147.

THE "Exclusion Controversy," or the struggle wherein Shaftesbury's Whigs attempted to negate, and Halifax's Tories to defend, the hereditary succession, bore fruit in Commons's *Exclusion Bill* of 1680. Its defeat in the upper House was the result of the Anglican Churchmen's support of Charles. The price paid by the King for that support was the repudiation of his policies of religious toleration.

An Act for securing of the Protestant Religion by Disabling James, Duke of York, to inherit the Imperial Crown of England and Ireland and the dominions and territories thereunto belonging.

Whereas James, duke of York, is notoriously known to have been perverted from the Protestant to the popish religion, whereby not only great encouragement has been given to the popish party to enter into and carry on most devilish and horrid plots and conspiracies for the destruction of his Majesty's sacred person and government, and for the extirpation of the true Protestant religion, but also, if the said duke should succeed to the imperial crown of this Realm, nothing is more manifest than that a total change of religion within these Kingdoms would ensure, for the prevention whereof it be therefore enacted . . . that the said James, duke of York, shall be and is by authority of this present Parliament excluded and made forever incapable to inherit, possess or enjoy the imperial crown of this Realm and of the Kingdom of Ireland and the dominions and territories to them or either of them belonging, or to have, exercise or enjoy any dominion, power, jurisdiction or authority within the same Kingdoms, dominions or any of them.

And be it further enacted . . . that if the said James, duke of York, shall at any time hereafter challenge, claim or attempt to possess or enjoy, or shall take upon him to use or exercise any dominion, power, authority, or jurisdiction within the said Kingdoms, dominions or any of them as King or chief magistrate of the same, that then he the said James . . . for every such offence shall be deemed and adjudged guilty of high treason. . . .

[Any person assisting such attempt by James, or any person writing, declaring, or preaching that James has any right to the throne, shall also be adjudged in high treason.]

And be it further enacted . . . that if the said James . . . shall at any time [after 5 November 1680] . . . come into or within any of the Kingdoms or dominions aforesaid, that then he . . . shall be deemed and adjudged guilty of high treason . . . and further, that if any person . . . whatsoever shall be aiding or assisting unto such return . . . that then every such person shall be deemed and adjudged guilty of high treason.

And be it further enacted . . . that the said James . . . or any other person being guilty of any of the treasons aforesaid, shall not be capable of or receive benefit by any pardon otherwise than by Act of Parliament. . . .

Provided, and be it hereby declared, that nothing in this Act contained shall be construed, deemed or adjudged to disable any person from inheriting or enjoying the imperial crown of the Realm and dominions aforesaid (other than the said James), but that in case the said James . . . shall survive his now Majesty and the heirs of his Majesty's body, the said imperial crown shall descend to and be enjoyed by such person and persons successively during the lifetime of the said James, Duke of York, as should have inherited and enjoyed the same in case the said James . . . were naturally dead. . . . (*Manuscripts of the House of Lords, 1678–1688, 195.*)

## Sir Robert Filmer, *Patriarcha, or the Natural Power of Kings.* 1680. (Written c. 1652)

**148.** THE fundamental principles upon which Robert Filmer based his arguments proving the validity of the divine rights theory were not new in mid-17th century England. A host of political theorists—along with James I and Charles I—had much earlier developed the thesis that civil authority was placed by God in the hands of the monarch, and that men could have no sanctions against monarchs for that reason. However, devious as were Filmer's proofs, they were better ordered and more rational than those of his precursors. Filmer chose to base his contentions on the law of nature as the expression of God's will rather than on confusing scriptural evidence often used by monarchists. Thus, in Filmer, kingship is proven by historical evidence to be natural. Since God ordains and directs nature, kingship is of God. The entire structure of Filmer's theory rests upon the unsound identification of the political State with the primitive family—monarchy with fatherhood, and thus, kingly power with paternal *dominium*. Adam, the first sovereign, received absolute power from God to regulate his family and posterity through all future generations. As a gift of God this right of political dominion was also a property right. To Filmer it was the property right which continued in effect to bind subject to king.

Although Filmer was taken up by the Royalist groups of England it is doubtful that more than a few of them gave serious consideration to the historical evidences of the virtue of monarchy he set down in the *Patriarcha*. The real significance of that work was in its appeal as a propaganda device, for it had a marked effect on popular thought. The best evidence of Filmer's importance in his own day is to be found in the fact that John Locke dedicated the first of his two treatises on government to the end of denying Filmer's ideas.

Since the time School-Divinity began to flourish there has been a common opinion maintained, as well by divines as by other learned men, which affirms:

*Mankind is naturally endowed and born with freedom from all subjection, and at liberty to choose what form of government it please: And that the power which any one man has over others, was at first bestowed according to the direction of the multitude.*

This tenet was first hatched in the Schools, and has been fostered by all succeeding Papists for good divinity. The divines also of the Reformed Churches have understood it, and the common people everywhere tenderly embrace it . . . never remembering that the desire of liberty was the first cause of the fall of Adam.

But, however, this vulgar opinion has of late obtained a great reputation, yet it is not to be found in the ancient fathers and doctors of the primitive Church: it contradicts the doctrine and history of Holy Scripture, the constant practice of all ancient Monarchs, and the very principles of the Law of Nature. . . .

Yet upon the ground of this doctrine both *Jesuits,* and some other zealous favorers of the *Geneva* discipline, have built a perilous conclusion, which is, *that the people or multitude have power to punish, or deprive the Prince, if he transgress the law of the Kingdom; witness* [Robert] *Parsons* and [George] *Buchanan.* . . .

.    .    .    .    .    .

Creation made man Prince of his posterity. And indeed not only *Adam* but succeeding *Patriarchs* had, by right of father-hood, royal authority over their children . . . for as Adam was Lord of his children, so his children under him, had command and power over their own children. . . .

I see not then how the children of *Adam,* or of any man else can be free from subjection to their parents: and this subjection of children being of the foundation of all Regal authority, by the ordinance of God Himself, it follows that civil power . . . is by divine institution. . . .

This Lordship which *Adam* by command [of God] had over the whole world, and by right descending from him to the Patriarchs . . . was as large and ample as the absolute dominion of any Monarch which has been since creation: for dominion of life and death, we find that *Judah* the father pronounced death against *Thamar* his daughter-in-law, for playing the harlot. . . . Touching war, we see that *Abram* commanded an army. . . . For matter of peace, *Abraham* made a league with *Abimelech.* . . . These acts of judging in *capital crimes,* of making *war,* and concluding *peace,* are the chiefest marks of *sovereignty* that are found in any *Monarch.*

Not only until the *flood,* but after it, this *Patriarchal* power did continue. . . . The three sons of *Noah* had the whole world divided amongst them by their father; for of them was the whole world overspread. . . . Most of the civilized nations of the earth labor to fetch their original from some one of the sons or nephews of *Noah,* which were scattered abroad after the confusion of *Babel:* in this dispersion we must certainly find the establishment of *regal power* throughout the Kingdoms of the world.

.    .    .    .    .

We may trace this paternal government into the *Israelites* coming out of Egypt. . . . After the return . . . out of bondage, God out of a special care for them chose *Moses* and *Joshua* successively to govern as princes. . . . But when God gave the *Israelites* Kings, he reestablished the ancient and prime right of lineal succession to paternal government. And whensoever He made choice of any special person to be King, He intended that the issue [descendants] also should have benefit thereof. . . .

It may seem absurd to maintain that Kings now are the fathers of their people . . . yet they all either are, or are to be reputed the next heirs of those first progenitors, who were at first the natural parents of the whole people, and in their right succeed to the exercise of *supreme jurisdiction.* . . .

As long as the first fathers of families lived, the name of the Patriarchs did aptly belong to them; but after a few descents, when the true fatherhood itself was extinct, and only the *right* of the father descends to the true heir, then the title of *Prince* or *King* was more *significant,* to express the power of him who succeeds only to the right of that fatherhood which the ancestors did *naturally* enjoy. (Robert Filmer, *Patriarcha or the Natural Power of Kings,* 1680, 1-3, 11-16, 18-19. Although not published until the stated date the work was undoubtedly written prior to 1652).

# The Reign of James II
## 1685-1688

# DOCUMENTS OF THE REIGN OF JAMES II

# England, 1685-1688   Introduction

James II came to a throne as secure as any English King had ever ascended. The "Exclusionists" had been defeated by the Tory-Anglican legitimists, and the Whig doctrine which would make of Kings mere public servants having tenure at the will and whim of the constituency had proven to be as yet too weak to challenge seriously the right of the heir apparent to the Crown. Yet unluckily James had a personality very similar to that of his father, Charles I. By training and instinct a shrewd administrator, he had not the sensitivity or political sagacity necessary for his office. Where Charles II had proved resourceful in bending with the winds of violent politics James sought to follow a pattern of self-determined and austerely inflexible policies, not caring that the constitutional precedents which counted heavily in the thoughts of the English people were opposed to the arbitrariness of the Stuart principle of Divine Right.

It is clear that James was misled by the soothing tone of Tory talk of non-resistance into taking a position in no way geared to the sinister ambiguities of that doctrine. He did not understand that in repudiating the violence which had characterized Puritan political action the gentry had substituted passive, constitutional methods for resisting the expressions of the executive which did not agree with their own desires. Nor did he realize that basically Tory non-resistance was much the same as its Whig opponents' political doctrine of strict and enforceable limitations on the Monarchy.

The exclusion problem was fought out in Parliament and the defeated Whigs grudgingly accepted the legitimate succession without resorting to even the threat of violence. Thereafter the question of who should be king was relatively unimportant to constitutional theory, for Tory and Whig were in agreement as to the position of the Monarchy in the constitution. The primary difference between the two parties now concerned the degree of limitations Parliament had the right to construct and apply to the Crown. Despite the repeated public professions by the Cavalier Parliament of the sacred and awesome nature of that office, it is clear from their legislative actions that the Tories, like the Whigs, believed that the Crown must be limited, controlled, and inferior to the law of the land. The making of law was felt to be altogether a prerogative of Parliament. After 1685 even the Tories no longer attempted to deny the truth that Parliament, not the King, was the center of English constitutional life. The documents of the Tory settlement at the time of the Restoration show that the Cavalier Parliament, though noted for its royalism, granted less real power to royal possession than any of the Parliaments of James I or his successor. Experience had proved to even this most monarchist of all representative groups the obsolescence of the theories of government which placed an over-abundance of legal power in the hands of any single governmental institution other than the legislature. Thus, Tory non-resistance was a denial of the *extent* of Whig proposals for political limitations rather than the principles upon which Whig doctrines rested. In the final analysis both Whig and Tory looked to Parliament and the law as the constitutional factors limiting and controlling the Crown.

In this agreement on political theory Tory and Whig accepted a modified form of the sixteenth century humanistic principle of utilitarianism which had emphasized the necessity for obedience to constituted authority but rejected all arbitrariness on the part of governors as immoral. The Prince was bound to justice and righteousness by right reason and by the threat of divine punishment for immoral political action. This new concept of utility for both parties was based on the necessity for social and political stability. All political actions and every political principle must be dedicated to attaining harmony and domestic peace within the political state. Other rationalizations for authority might exist as aids in maintaining politically sound traditions, or as propaganda devices to keep a hold on the popular imagination, but these were regarded as politically fictive and of no real constitutional weight when compared to the limitations imposed by the theory of utility. Significantly, both parties carefully overlooked the fact that the legislature, too, might overreach its constitutional limitations. The point made by Richard Hooker to the effect that Parliament could not act against the truth because its mass basis would not allow it to be guided by anything but right reason was firmly imbedded in the constitutional thought of the Parliamentarians. Yet neither Tory nor Whig, at the end of the seventeenth century, was really much interested in the mystical concept of divinely directed right reason. Instead of reason, which grew out of divine grace, political philosophy openly accepted the doctrines of expediency and public utility; it was politically and socially good that monarchy be limited and that the representative institution have authority since the security of the commonwealth would find its strongest safeguards in that division of political power which gave voice to the mass of men through an elected assembly which would always do the bidding of the constituency.

In combining the sweet reasonableness of humanistic *naiveté* with the precise realism of Hooker the Parliamentarians established logical and moral grounds for limiting the monarchy. While maintaining the public fiction of non-resistance against that institution they left open the way of relieving the nation of a repugnant individual who might, because of the uncertainties of the succession or the vissicitudes of partisan politics, come to inhabit the throne. This solution documents the bankrupt state of Tory-Anglican political and constitutional theory, for once again the dominant class turned to the violent past for a solution to its problems. From the Republican period it winnowed out the article of Calvinistic faith that held that immoral Kings must be destroyed. Yet the alliance of conservative political leaders and confused churchmen was determined to use constitutional methods rather than force in crippling the prerogative. Such fallacious optimism overlooked the probability that a cornered King might, like Charles I, insist on his right of self-defense and force his opponents to cast away all the fine theories of peaceful, legal, and constitutionally applied limitations.

James II never understood these utilitarian theories which strove to limit his office on moral grounds. He accepted the Hobbesian concept of sovereignty as an indivisible and immutable right. He clung to an outdated concept of the constitution, not realizing that his own Tory party, though it made use of the terms of Divine Right and non-resistance for political purposes, interpreted them quite differently.

But assured of the initial good-will of the dominant Tory group and the primates of the Established Church, James might easily have made his position unassailable. Moreover he also had a very real claim to Whig support since, more than any monarch before him, he showed an abiding enthusiasm for the instruments of trade so dear to the material interest of the merchant class—the navy, colonial expansion, and the general development of continental and colonial commerce. If it is true that Whig appreciation of the political principles of kings was gauged by the effect of those principles on the ledgers, then indeed James was potentially secure. Yet his reign lasted less than four years.

In the last analysis, it was largely James's stubborn insistence on denying the religious desires of the majority of the English people that cost him his throne. The old fear of Rome was as acute in the last quarter of the seventeenth century as it had been in the first. Indeed, since James openly professed a Catholic preference, Anglican churchmen and non-conformist preachers were more than ever disposed to suspect insidious political designs in every Crown move towards easing the official Parliamentary policy of non-toleration. Thus James's indulgence toward the Catholics helped neither the Catholics nor the Monarchy itself, since it threatened the vested interest of the King's Tory-Anglican supporters and simultaneously stimulated Whig and non-conformist fear of a revival of political Catholicism. Parliamentary non-toleration disappeared in practice only when the supposed political alliance between the monarchy and the Catholics was broken by the accession of William and Mary.

It is doubtful, however, whether religious temper alone precipitated the Revolution of 1688, which for the second time in less than a half-century forcefully removed a Stuart King from the English throne. Practically every act of James in his short reign had results which were distasteful to his enemies and embarrassing to his friends. Six months after his accession James made the decision which sent his nephew, the Duke of Monmouth, to execution on grounds of treason. The charge was logical in the light of Monmouth's actions and justly rendered according to the law. However, the elimination of one pretender eventually resulted in gaining for William and Mary the undivided support of all who had advocated the exclusion of James from the throne. Thus in terms of political tactics the execution was a blunder of considerable magnitude. The cruelty of Lord Jeffreys in the Bloody Assizes following Monmouth's defeat aroused considerable popular antipathy toward the King, for such legal barbarism was more difficult to explain than the execution of one who had set himself up as King and made treasonous war against the State. The excesses of the military in punishing the guilty followers of Monmouth were partially the cause of Parliament's resistance to James's demand for a standing army to prevent future rebellions. Parliament shrewdly chose to use the question of the army as an excuse for attacking James's unconstitutional use of the prerogative in officering the army which had defeated Monmouth, and in peopling his councils, his courts, and the churches of the land, with Catholics. Here again was a religious problem having political corollaries; both Tory and Whig had a common interest in opposing the King's program of integrating Catholics into institutions of public responsibility.

Significantly, Parliament was more interested in James's denial of the constitutional limitations on his right to act as he did in this matter than in his use of Catholic army officers whose loyalty to the state was unquestionable. Parliament chose to struggle against the King on constitutional rather than religious grounds. As the first step the anti-Catholic factions instigated the test case of Godden vs. Hales in which the plaintiff challenged the validity of the Crown's suspending and dispensing powers. The judges unexpectedly decided against Parliament by stating that the laws were the King's laws and that he could dispense any person from obedience to them as he chose. From this decision the Parliamentarians, royalists and non-resistors though they might nominally be, could only deduce that all the statutory defenses set up against the Crown's unlimited and arbitrary authority could be one by one shattered on the reasoning of the judges of the King's courts; hence that, in the final analysis, non-resistance was a failure.

Tory realization of the inadequacy of the laws of Parliament to withstand the attacks of the King was the beginning of their rejection of James and the real commencement of the revolution of 1688. James failed because he allied his principles of toleration for the Catholics with what was considered to be unconstitutional government. This threatened destruction of Parliament and law, the elements of control absolutely necessary for the continued dominance of his own supporters, was James's undoing. The royalists chose to abandon the person of a king rather than their concept of what kingship should be and what part it should play in the political life of the nation.

## James II: Speech to Parliament Concerning Catholic Army Officers. 1685

**149.** THE victory of the Tories in the Exclusion crisis brought the power of the Whigs in Parliament temporarily to an end. By the time of his accession James II was in command of a sufficiently strong following in both Houses of Parliament to tempt him to override the *Test Acts* and appoint Catholics to both civil and military offices of responsibility. In this speech to Parliament James admitted having used the suspending prerogative to get around the penal laws in appointing men of his choice, regardless of their religious affiliations, to certain important positions in the army. Both the King and Parliament realized that the fundamental issue involved was the suspending power; and the King's admitted action produced another constitutional crisis.

My Lords and Gentlemen, after the storm that seemed to be coming upon us when we parted last, I am glad to meet you all again in so great peace and quietness. . . . When we reflect what an inconsiderable number of men began it, and how long they carried it on without any opposition, I hope everybody will be convinced that the militia, which has hitherto been so much depended on, is not sufficient for such occasions, and that there is nothing but a good force of well-disciplined troops in constant pay that can defend us from such as, either at home or abroad, are disposed to disturb us. And in truth, my concern for the peace and quiet of my subjects, as well as for the safety of the government, made me think it necessary to increase the number to the proportion I have done. This I owed as well to the honor as the security of the nation, whose reputation was so infinitely exposed to all our neighbors, by having so evidently lain open to this late wretched attempt, that it is not to be repaired without keeping such a body of men on foot that none may ever have the thought again of finding us so miserably unprovided.

It is for the support of this great charge, which is now more than double to what it was, that I ask your assistance in giving me a supply answerable to the expense it brings along with it. And I cannot doubt but what I have begun, so much for the honor and defence of the government, will be continued by you with all the cheerfulness that is requisite for a work of so great importance.

Let no man take exception that there are some officers in the army not qualified, according to the late *Test Acts,* for their employment. The gentlemen, I must tell you, are most of them well known to me, and having formerly served with me in several occasions, and always approved the loyalty of their principles by their practice, I think fit now to be employed under me. And I deal plainly with you, that after having had the

benefit of their service in such time of need and danger, I will neither expose them to disgrace, nor myself to want of them, if there should be another rebellion to make them necessary for me.

I am afraid some men may be so wicked to hope and expect that a difference may happen between you and me upon this occasion. But when you consider what advantages have arisen to us in a few months by the good understandings we have hitherto had; what wonderful effects it has already produced in the change of the whole scene of affairs abroad, so much more to the honor of this nation and the figure it ought to make in the world; and that nothing can hinder a further progress in this way, to all our satisfactions, but fears and jealousies amongst ourselves, I will not apprehend that such a misfortune can befall us as a division, or but a coldness, between me and you, nor that anything can shake you in your steadiness and loyalty to me who, by God's blessing, will ever make you returns of all kindness and protection, with a resolution to venture even my own life in the defence of the true interest of this Kingdom. (*Journals of the House of Commons,* IX, 756.)

## The Reply of the House of Commons to James's Defense of Catholic Army Officers. 1685

JAMES'S plea that the loyalty of the officers in question was sufficient to allow their service despite the *Test Acts* was not acceptable to Commons. The House offered to free the officers from whatever penalties they had already incurred by their service to the King but reminded James that only Parliament could change the law and that the King must comply and dismiss the officers from their employment.

**150.**

Most Gracious Sovereign, we, your Majesty's most loyal and faithful subjects, the Commons in Parliament assembled, do in the first place, as in duty bound, return your Majesty our most humble and hearty thanks for your great care and conduct in the suppression of the late rebellion, which threatened the overthrow of this government both in Church and State and the utter extirpa-

tion of our religion by law established, which is most dear unto us, and which your Majesty has been graciously pleased to give us repeated assurances you will always defend and support, which with all grateful hearts we shall ever acknowledge.

We further crave leave to acquaint your Majesty that we have with all duty and readiness taken into our consideration your

Majesty's gracious speech to us. And as to that part of it relating to the officers in the army not qualified for their employments according to an Act of Parliament made in the twenty-fifth year of the reign of your Majesty's royal brother of blessed memory, entitled, *An Act for Preventing dangers which may happen from popish recusants,* we do out of our bounden duty humbly represent unto your Majesty that those officers cannot by law be capable of their employments, and that the incapacities they bring upon themselves thereby can no ways be taken off but by an Act of Parliament.

Therefore out of that great deference and duty we owe unto your Majesty, who has been graciously pleased to take notice of their services to you, we are preparing a bill to pass both Houses for your Royal assent, to indemnify them from the penalties they have now incurred. And because the continuance of them in their employments may be taken to be a dispensing with that law without Act of Parliament (the consequence of which is of the greatest concern of the rights of all your Majesty's dutiful and loyal subjects, and to all the laws made for security of their religion), we therefore, the knights, citizens and burgesses of your Majesty's House of Commons, do most humbly beseech your Majesty that you would be graciously pleased to give such directions therein that no apprehensions or jealousies may remain in the hearts of your Majesty's good and faithful subjects. (*Journals of the House of Commons,* IX, 758.)

## Decision and Reasoning of the Court in the Case of Godden vs. Hales. 1686

**151.** THE plaintiff, Arthur Godden, charged Edward Hales, a Catholic officer in the army, with not having sworn the oaths requisite to such employment according to the provisions of the *Test Acts,* and demanded payment of the five hundred pounds penalty money as specified in the law. The judges' decision in denying Godden's plea and dismissing the action against Hales, although legally sound according to the constitution, upset all the statutory defenses constructed by Parliament against a revival of monarchial power. Should James press his advantage, no matter how righteous his stand and methods, he could only provoke bitter resistance among his opponents.

[Decision of Chief Justice Herbert]. . . . In the case of Godden and Hales, wherein the defendant pleads a dispensation from the King, it is doubted whether or no the King had such a prerogative. . . . Upon the argument before us, it appeared as clear a case as ever came before this court; but, because men fancy I know not what difficulty when really there is none, we were willing to give so much countenance to the question in the case as to take the advice of all the judges of England.

They were all assembled at Serjeants' Inn, and this case was put to them. . . . To these eleven judges there is one dissenter . . . who yet continues his opinion that the King cannot dispense in this case. But that is the opinion of one single judge against the opinion of eleven.

We were satisfied in our judgments before; and now, having the concurrence of eleven out of twelve, we think we may very well declare the opinion of the court to be that the King may dispense in this case.

And the Judges go upon these grounds:

That the Kings of England are Sovereign Princes,

That the laws of England are the King's laws,

That therefore it is an inseparable prerogative in the Kings of England to dispense with penal laws in particular cases and upon particular necessary reasons,

That of those reasons and those necessities, the King himself is sole judge; and then, which is consequent upon all,

That this is not a trust invested in, or granted to, the King by the people, but the ancient remains of the Sovereign power and prerogative of the Kings of England; which never yet was taken from them, nor can be.

And therefore, such a dispensation appearing upon record ... saves him from the forfeiture, and judgment ought to be given for the defendant. (Howell, *State Trials*, XI, 1197.)

## Declaration of Indulgence. 1687

## 152.

JAMES seemed bent on alienating the friends and supporters who had defeated the Exclusionist Whigs and insured his succession. The *Declaration*, encouraged by the Judges' decision in the case of Godden vs. Hales, suspended all limitations on religious worship and forbade any molestation of Catholic or non-conformist. All offices, civil and military, were thrown open to Catholics as well as to all types of Protestants, and every civil limitation on their service and employment was cancelled.

His Majesty's Gracious Declaration to all His Loving Subjects for Liberty of Conscience.

.... We cannot but heartily wish, as it will easily be believed, that all the people of our dominions were members of the Catholic Church. Yet we humbly thank Almighty God it is, and has of long time been, our constant sense and opinion (which upon divers occasions we have declared) that conscience ought not to be constrained, nor people forced in matters of mere religion; it has ever been directly contrary to our inclination, as we think it is to the interest of government, which it destroys by spoiling trade, depopulating countries and discouraging strangers; and finally, that it never obtained the end for which it was employed. And in this we are the more confirmed by the reflections we have made upon the conduct of the four last reigns; for after all the frequent and pressing endeavors that were used in each of them to reduce this Kingdom to an exact conformity in religion it is visible the success has not answered the design, and that the difficulty is invincible.

We therefore, out of our princely care and affection unto all our loving subjects, that they may live at ease and quiet, and for the increase of trade and encouragement of strangers, have thought fit by virtue of our royal prerogative to issue forth this our declaration of indulgence, making no doubt of the concurrence of our two Houses of Parliament when we shall think it convenient for them to meet.

In the first place we do declare that we will protect and maintain our archbishops, bishops and clergy, and all other our subjects of the Church of England in the free exercise of their religion as by law established, and in the quiet and full enjoyment of all their possessions, without any molestation or disturbance whatsoever.

We do likewise declare that it is our royal will and pleasure that from henceforth the execution of all and all manner of penal laws in matters ecclesiastical, for not coming to Church, or not receiving the sacrament, or for any other nonconformity to the religion established, or for or by reason of the exercise of religion in any manner whatsoever, be immediately suspended; and the further execution of the said penal laws and every of them is hereby suspended.

And to the end that by the liberty hereby granted the peace and security of our government in the practice thereof may not be endangered, we have thought fit, and do hereby straitly charge and command all our loving subjects, that as we do freely give them leave to meet and serve God after their own way and manner, be it in private houses or places purposely hired or built for that use, so that they take especial care that nothing be preached or taught amongst them which may any ways tend to alienate the hearts of our people from us or our government; and that their meetings and assemblies be peaceably, openly and publicly held, and all persons freely admitted to them; and that they do signify and make known to some one or more of the next justices of the peace what place or places they set apart for those uses.

And that all our subjects may enjoy such their religious assemblies with greater assurance and protection, we have thought it requisite, and do hereby command, that no disturbance of any kind be made or given unto them, under pain of our displeasure and to be further proceeded against with the utmost severity.

And forasmuch as we are desirous to have the benefit of the service of all our loving subjects, which by the law of nature is inseparably annexed to and inherent in our royal person, and that none of our subjects may for the future be under any discouragement or disability (who are otherwise well inclined and fit to serve us) by reason of some oaths or tests that have been usually administered on such occasions, we do hereby further declare that it is our royal will and pleasure that the oaths commonly called the oaths of supremacy and allegiance, and also the several tests and declarations mentioned in the Acts of Parliament made in the 25th and 30th years of the reign of our late royal brother King Charles II, shall not at any time hereafter be required to be

taken, declared or subscribed by any person ... whatsoever, who is or shall be employed in any office or place of trust, either civil or military, under us or in our government. And we do further declare it to be our pleasure and intention from time to time hereafter to grant our royal dispensations under our great seal to all our loving subjects so to be employed, who shall not take the said oaths, or subscribe or declare the said tests or declarations, in the above-mentioned Acts [The King's reference here is to all penal statutes imposing religious conformity.]. . . .

And to the end that all our loving subjects may receive and enjoy the full benefit and advantage of our gracious indulgence hereby intended, and may be acquitted and discharged from all pains, penalties, forfeitures and disabilities by them or any of them incurred or forfeited, or which they shall or may at any time hereafter be liable to, for or by reason of their nonconformity or the exercise of their religion, and from all suits, troubles or disturbances for the same, we do hereby give our free and ample pardon unto all nonconformists, recusants and other our loving subjects for all crimes and things by them committed or done contrary to the penal laws formerly made relating to religion and the profession or exercise thereof, hereby declaring that this our royal pardon and indemnity shall be as good and effectual to all intents and purposes as if every individual person had been therein particularly named, or had particular pardons under our great seal, which we do likewise declare shall from time to time be granted unto any person or persons desiring the same, willing and requiring our judges, justices and other officers to take notice of and obey our royal will and pleasure hereinbefore declared. . . .
(E. Cardwell, *Documentary Annals of the Reformed Church of England*, II, 308.)

## The Petition of the Seven Bishops. 1688

WHEN, in 1688, the churchmen were ordered by James to read his second *Declaration of Indulgence* from their pulpits, the bishops of the Established Church faced a trying situation. To obey the King meant destruction of their Church, while to disobey meant open repudiation of the ideal of non-resistance. Seven Bishops chose to disobey, and they drew up a petition protesting that the *Declaration* was illegal and pleading that the King would not insist on their distribution of it through Church channels.

**153.**

To the King's most Excellent Majesty; the humble petition of William, archbishop of Canterbury, and of divers of the suffragan Bishops of that province now present with him, in behalf of themselves and others of their absent brethern, and of the clergy of their respective dioceses.

Humbly showeth, that the great averseness they find in themselves to the distributing and publishing in all their churches your Majesty's late declaration for liberty of conscience proceedeth neither from any want of duty and obedience to your Majesty, our holy mother, the Church of England, being both in her principles and constant practice unquestionably loyal, and having to her great honor been more than once publicly acknowledged to be so by your gracious Majesty, nor yet from any want of due tenderness to dissenters, in relation to whom they are willing to come to such a temper as shall be thought fit when that matter shall be considered and settled in Parliament and Convocation, but among many other considerations from this especially, because that declaration is founded upon such a dispensing power as has often been declared illegal in Parliament, and particularly in the years 1662, 1672, and in the beginning of your Majesty's reign, and is a matter of so great moment and consequence to the whole nation, both in Church and State, that your petitioners cannot in prudence, honor or conscience so far make themselves parties to it as the distribution of it all over the nation, and the solemn publication of it once and again even in God's house and in the time of His divine service, must amount to in common and reasonable construction.

Your petitioners therefore most humbly and earnestly beseech your Majesty that you will be graciously pleased not to insist upon their distributing and reading your Majesty's said declaration. And your petitioners, as in duty bound, shall ever pray, etc.... (Howell, *State Trials*, XII, 318.)

## Decision and Reasoning of the Judges in the Case of the Seven Bishops. 1688

AS A result of their *Petition*, which James called "the standard of rebellion," the bishops were charged with libel and brought to trial in the Court of King's Bench. After consideration of the issues and evidence involved the judges were evenly divided. The **jury**, however, returned its verdict for the defendants.

**154.**

[Chief Justice Wright].... thus stands the case. It is an information against my lords the bishops, his grace my lord of Canterbury and the other six noble lords; and it is for preferring, composing, making and publishing, and causing to be published, a seditious libel. The way that the information goes is special, and it sets forth that the King was graciously pleased, by his royal power and prerogative, to set forth a declaration of indulgence for liberty of conscience in the third year of his reign; and afterwards ... orders in Council that this declaration should be published by my lords the bishops in their several dioceses; and after this was done my lords the bishops come and present a petition to the King, in which were contained the words which you have seen. . . .

. . . . Upon the point of the publication I have summed up all the evidence to you; and if you believe that the petition which these lords presented to the King was this petition, truly, I think, that is a publication sufficient. If you do not believe it was this petition, then my lords the bishops are not guilty of what is laid to their charge in this information, and consequently there needs no inquiry whether they are guilty of a libel. But if you do believe that this was the petition they presented to the King, then we must come to inquire whether this be a libel.

Now, gentlemen, anything that shall disturb the government, or make mischief and a stir among the people, is certainly within the case of *Libellis Famosis;* and I must in short ... take it to be a libel. . . .

[Justice Holloway]. . . . The question is, whether this petition of my lords the bishops be a libel or no. Gentlemen, the end and intention of every action is to be considered; and likewise in this case we are to consider the nature of the offence that these noble persons are charged with. It is for delivering a petition, which, according as they have made their defence, was with all the humility and decency that could be; so that if there was no ill intent, and they were not (as it is not nor can be pretended they were) men of evil lives or the like, to deliver a petition cannot be a fault, it being the right of every subject to petition. If you are satisfied there was an ill intention of sedition or the like, you ought to find them guilty. But if there be nothing in the case that you find, but only that they did deliver a petition to save themselves harmless, and to free themselves from blame, by showing the reason of their disobedience to the King's command, which they apprehended to be a grievance to them, and which they could not in conscience give obedience to, I cannot think it is a libel. . . . (Howell, *State Trials,* XII, 422, 426.)

## Secret Letter of Invitation to William and Mary to Invade England and Depose James II. 1688

155.  ON JULY, 1688, the Queen, Mary of Modena, a Catholic, gave birth to a son, an obvious Catholic heir to the English throne. On July 30, the day of the seven bishops' acquittal, four Whigs and three Tory spokesmen sent the invitation to William and Mary of Orange to bring an army to England and guarantee the restoration of English liberties by deposing Mary's father from the throne. Thus the Tories, admitting the failure of non-resistance, joined the group which had touched off the Exclusionist crisis. Shaftesbury was vindicated and the Whigs, having openly repudiated the constitution they had always claimed to defend, began to prepare for what appeared to be certain civil war. Thus all that remained of the Stuart constitution passed into oblivion.

We have great satisfaction to find [from reports by secret agents] ... that your Highness is so ready and willing to give us such assistance as they have related to us. We have great reason to believe we shall be every day in a worse condition than we are, and less

able to defend ourselves, and therefore we do earnestly wish we might be so happy as to find a remedy before it be too late for us to contribute to our own deliverance. But although these be our wishes, yet we will by no means put your Highness into any expectations which may misguide your own councils in this matter; so that the best advice we can give is to inform your Highness truly both of the state of things here at this time and of the difficulties which appear to us.

As to the first, the people are so generally dissatisfied with the present conduct of the government in relation to their religion, liberties and properties (all which have been greatly invaded), and they are in such expectation of their prospects being daily worse, that your Highness may be assured there are nineteen parts of twenty of the people throughout the Kingdom who are desirous of a change, and who, we believe, would willingly contribute to it, if they had such a protection to countenance their rising as would secure them from being destroyed before they could get to be in a posture able to defend themselves. It is no less certain that much the greatest part of the nobility and gentry are as much dissatisfied, although it be not safe to speak to many of them beforehand; and there is no doubt but that some of the most considerable of them would venture themselves with your Highness at your first landing, whose interests would be able to draw great numbers to them whenever they could protect them and the raising and drawing men together. And if such a strength could be landed as were able to defend itself and them till they could be got together into some order, we make no question but that strength would quickly be increased to a number double to the army here, although their army should all remain firm to them; whereas we do upon very good grounds believe that their army then would be very much divided among themselves, many of the officers being so discontented that they continue in their service only for a subsistence (besides that some of their minds are known already), and very many of the common soldiers do daily show such an aversion to the popish religion that there is the greatest probability imaginable of great numbers of deserters which would come from them should there be such an oc-

casion; and amongst the seamen it is almost certain there is not one in ten who would do them any service in such a war.

Besides all this, we do much doubt whether this present state of things will not yet be much changed to the worse before another year, by a great alteration which will probably be made both in the officers and soldiers of the army, and by such other changes as are not only to be expected from a packed Parliament, but what the meeting of any Parliament (in our present circumstances) may produce against those who will be looked upon as principal obstructors of their proceedings there, it being taken for granted that if things cannot then be carried to their wishes in a parliamentary way other measures will be put in execution by more violent means; and although such proceedings will then heighten the discontents, yet such courses will probably be taken at that time as will prevent all possible means of relieving ourselves.

These considerations make us of opinion that this is a season in which we may more probably contribute to our own safeties than hereafter (although we must own to your Highness there are some judgments differing from ours in this particular), insomuch that if the circumstances stand so with your Highness that you believe you can get here time enough, in a condition to give assistance this year sufficient for a relief under these circumstances which have been now represented, we who subscribe this will not fail to attend your Highness upon your landing and to do all that lies in our power to prepare others to be in as much readiness as such an action is capable of, where there is so much danger in communicating an affair of such a nature till it be near the time of its being made public. But, as we have already told your Highness, we must also lay our difficulties before your Highness, which are chiefly, that we know not what alarm your preparations for this expedition may give, or what notice it will be necessary for you to give the States beforehand, by either of which means their intelligence or suspicions here may be such as may cause us to be secured before your landing. And we must presume to inform your Highness that your compliment upon the birth of the child (which not one in a thousand here believes to be the queen's) has done you some injury, the false imposing of that upon the princess and the nation being not only an infinite exasperation of people's minds here, but being certainly one of the chief causes upon which the declaration of your entering the Kingdom in a hostile manner must be founded on your part, although many other reasons are to be given on ours.

If upon a due consideration of all these circumstances your Highness shall think fit to adventure upon the attempt, or at least to make such preparations for it as are necessary (which we wish you may), there must be no more time lost in letting us know your resolution concerning it, and in what time we may depend that all the preparations will be ready, as also whether your Highness does believe the preparations can be so managed as not to give them warning here, both to make them increase their force and to secure those they shall suspect would join with you. We need not say anything about ammunition, artillery, mortar pieces, spare arms, etc., because if you think fit to put anything in execution you will provide enough of these kinds, and will take care to bring some good engineers with you; and we have desired Mr. H. to consult you about all such matters, to whom we have communicated our thoughts in many particulars too tedious to have been written, and about which no certain resolutions can be taken till we have heard again from your Highness. . . . (J. Dalrymple, *Memoirs of Great Britain and Ireland,* I, 228)

# The Reign of William and Mary

## 1689-1702

## DOCUMENTS OF THE REIGN OF WILLIAM AND MARY

# England, 1689-1702   Introduction

The events of the reign of James II proved to Tory and Whig alike that their doctrines were not basically opposed. The Tories had accepted the principle that while statutory limitations could be applied to the political actions of kings the legitimate succession was inviolable. James's pro-Catholic policies rendered this contention untenable. The Whigs had argued that the constitution could not prevent the forcible dethronement of a monarch who exceeded the constitutional limitations on his right to act. The corollary to this power of removal was the necessity for popular choice of a new king. James's flight to the French enemies of the realm vindicated the Whig theory. Thus the parties were brought together in self-defense while the concept of popular resistance became crucial to the future development of the constitution. In 1688 the ideal of righteous resistance to immoral authority which had previously been fundamental to sectarian political theory was dignified with legal and moral acceptability and given lasting place among the primary rights of the English people.

Yet the lustrous implications of the phrase "Glorious Revolution" were justified neither by the events of 1688 nor by subsequent changes in the constitution. In focusing the attention of future generations on the concept of the subject's moral resistance against arbitrary government, Locke's *Treatises* distorted the historical picture in order to justify the political theories he preferred. Later constitutional crises in western Europe completed this distortion of this historic episode by apotheosizing the period as the historical precedent for vigorous popular action. The abundance of documentary materials will help to give a more exact idea of the constitutional meaning of the years from 1688 to 1701.

The change of kings brought little that was revolutionary to the structure of the English constitution or to the function of its various parts. The Tory-Whig alliance which unseated James and offered the throne to William and Mary was motivated by the conservative wish to defend the *status quo* of the settlement of 1660. It was James himself who triggered the revolution by challenging the order necessary to the traditional ruling class's monopoly of Parliament. In his toleration for Catholics James threatened a religious settlement which was acceptable to a majority of the people of all classes. Had the king been successful in re-establishing his supremacy over the law it is fairly certain that he would have ended by restoring the Catholic religion to England on a basis of equality with the established Church. Supported by a strong and grateful Catholic group the King's right to act would have been beyond the control of Parliament. Whig and Tory were thus allied to reassert and protect the supremacy of Church and Parliament. The so-called Revolution of 1688 did nothing more than to re-establish this supremacy.

Basic to the settlement of the revolution was the *Bill of Rights*. Not interested in the fine and devious concepts of political governance and constitutional theory which characterize so many of the earlier legislative documents, the Convention Parliament set down the conditions under which William and Mary could have the throne, adding to these an unflattering appraisal of James's actions and a list of the rights of the subject which the executive had no power to limit or deny. The dispensing and suspending powers, which Parliament had not accepted as constitutional even in the reign of James I, were expressly forbidden. The right of the King to maintain an army in time of peace was denied, Parliament reclaimed its freedom of speech in any area touching the common welfare, and the Stuart practice of interfering with Parliamentary elections was declared illegal. Yet none of these expressions was really new or revolutionary. The defenses against monarchial arbitrariness, for example, had been constructed by the Cavalier Parliament a generation before. In restating the doctrine of limitations in the *Bill of Rights,* and in forcing William and Mary to accept them publicly as parts of a binding contract between people and government, Parliament defined both limitations and the right of resistance as undeniable parts of the constitution. But to primate, gentleman, and parliamentarian this was a return to fundamental, established, and constitutional principles.

Although the *Bill* was thus conservative in tone and general content, two innovations were included. An oath of allegiance to the joint Monarchy was required of all subjects and the succession was regulated in two ways: Catholic claimants were excluded and future right to the throne was vested in the heirs of Mary, then in Anne and her heirs. In default of such heirs the succession was established in the descendants of William if, Mary being dead, he should rewed. In so asserting its authority over the succession Parliament gave way to the desires of the group which had demanded the exclusion of James II on grounds of his Catholicism in 1681, and it was only here that the settlement was somewhat revolutionary. Never before had the legislature gone so far as to claim the actual right of electing kings or the right to determine the religious preference of a king. After a century-long period of theologically-based struggle the English people had completely reversed the Reformation principle of "whose territory, his religion." Now it was the king who must conform to the dictates of a state Church beyond his control. However this was of only relative significance since once the succession was established Parliament could claim no further selective right.

In general the Parliaments of William and Mary were satisfied with the return to the 1660 settlement. The prevailing feeling was that experience and practice, rather than theory would lead to solution of the many constitutional problems that existed. More than ever the ruling class realized that the application of premature and enthusiastic political formulas to problems might, as during the Interregnum, result in conditions more distasteful than those which appeared in need of reform. This fear of innovation re-emphasized for the English people the virtue of compromise and of evolutionary development of political and constitutional institutions.

After 1689 Parliament had the right to interfere in almost every area of government. The army was brought under Parliament's control by the *Mutiny Act,* and the control of State finances overshadowed all minor powers which the settlement granted the crown. Thus the conception of kingship as an integral part of Parliament was brought to its fullest development. In the new unity of these two primary forces an ancient Parliamentary claim was finally fully realized; the way was opened to the tremendous constitutional developments of the eighteenth and nineteenth centuries.

The real significance of the Revolution of 1688 was not in the constitutional provisions which it produced, or in the changes in the statutory law which resulted, or in the shifting of the balance of powers from king to Parliament—but rather in the fact that subject and Crown established a contractual base for a new, productive, and agreeable relationship. The monarch accepted the principles set down in Locke's essays. He no longer had an uncontested title to the throne. As a servant of the state he had to respect the will of the people from whence stemmed all political authority. His obligations were established by law, and his rights were clearly defined. Nevertheless, when acting in accord with his Parliaments, there were no real limitations on the King; his voice became one with that of the nation, and his acts were the direct responsibility of the Parliament with which he acted. Thus after 1689 the monarchy was in certain respects stronger than it had been at any time during the Stuart period.

In joining forces King and Parliament admitted mutual defeat in the long struggle for political domination. Each institution possessed an inherent element of power which was necessary to the proper function of the other. Tradition had shaped the English constitution in such a way that harmonious interaction by the two parts was essential to political progress.

The revolution of 1688 brought people and king into closer union than had ever before existed, without subverting the rights of the one or destroying the dignity of the other. For this reason it is improper to speak of "parliamentary sovereignty" in this period, for this was to come in the eighteenth century when Parliament would by degrees eliminate the checking power of the crown and force the king from the legislative hall. Between 1689 and 1701 William and Parliament together brought to logical solution the problem of the position of the king relative to Parliament and the law. In statutes like the *Bill of Rights, Appropriation Act, Mutiny Act, Triennial Act,* the several *Place Acts,* and the *Civil List Act,* the basis of agreement was broadened and the sense of cooperation perfected. Each statute added to the equipoise and balance of the heretofore conflicting parts of the constitution. The culmination of such soundly constituted methods of interaction was the *Act of Settlement* of 1701.

This *Act* gave legal basis to ministerial responsibility. Foreign and domestic policies could no longer emanate from any single constitutional component. Crown and Parliament were to play an equal part in constructing national policy and both shared praise or blame for the outcome of any policy. With this common responsibility, legislature and executive came to realize the necessity of common cause even though at times undesirable compromises were found to be necessary.

The settlement of Church affairs during William's reign illustrates the determination of the opposed forces to reach agreements that would be mutually acceptable. James's loss of the throne was accompanied by the Tory's loss of their monopoly in religion. The Whigs were committed to toleration for all forms of Protestant worship, and William favored the broadest sort of comprehension. Yet the goodwill of all elements was requisite to national harmony. Therefore the Tories and the Anglican primates had to be won over to comprehension. This was done by insuring the position of the Anglican Church as the Established Church. The lot of the dissenters and non-conformists was eased by the Whig sponsored *Toleration Bill* of 1689 which granted religious freedom to a majority of the Protestant sects but still excluded them from state employment and franchise. Attention was paid to popular sentiments by the continued official intolerance of the government toward the Catholics. Thus the religious settlement was a compromise between the extremes of liberty desired by the Whigs and the narrow exclusiveness upon which the Anglican religious monopoly had been based. That it was unfair to the non-conformists and dissenters is of less importance than the fact that it was a fruitful precedent for later development of truly ethical toleration. In the early eighteenth century even the Catholics were to win a degree of liberty to worship while the intense religious passions of the earlier period were gradually replaced by more worldly colonial, and commercial considerations.

## John Locke, *Two Treatises of Government.* 1690

**156.** JOHN LOCKE'S political theory is contained in his *Two Treatises of Government.* Since Locke's purpose in writing of political society was to justify the Glorious Revolution, the first of the treatises was devoted to a refutation of the several fundamental principles upon which the Divine Rights theories of the Stuart monarchs had been based, most particularly in Filmer's *Patriarcha.* The second treatise—of greater significance to English constitutional thought—was dedicated to proving that political sovereignty existed only in the whole people and that Parliament constituted its best expression. However, Locke drew a clear line between Sir Thomas Smith's concept of Parliament wherein every man sat, and his own concept of Parliament as an instrument created by the sovereign people, and limited by the natural rights of the community of men to specific political purposes. The concept of Parliamentary omnicompetence had no place in John Locke's theory.

Modern political theorists tend to emphasize the areas of agreement between the political theories of Locke and Thomas Hobbes. However such agreement, if it truly exists, is unimportant since the two theories had directly opposite influences on the development of the English constitution. Generally, certainly, both saw society as inaugurated in a contract, and both accepted man's existence in a state of nature prior to the compact which begot order, security, and justice. Yet even here agreement was limited. In Locke's state of nature man was subject to the dictates of the reason inherent in every man. Violence, when present, was consequent to man's disregard of the laws of reason rather than to man's natural brutish affinity to war and dispute which Hobbes had assumed. Locke, then, saw mere inconvenience in the state of nature where Hobbes saw man's fatal inability to attain peace, harmony, and social-political progress. Where Hobbes held that society's only hope lay in civil government, Locke held that man exchanged a natural, and not necessarily evil, state for another where greater progress could be found.

Another major difference in the two theories is to be found in the definition of rights and liberties given by the contracting individuals into the hands of the government. Hobbes transferred the entire right of all the subjects to the *de facto* governor, or sovereign, who then assumed absolute prerogative. Locke denied that the individual gave to governor or government more of his natural right than was consonant with the desired ends. Indeed, in Locke it is found that political authority and right is given to the *community* rather than to a sovereign or governor. Also, to Locke the contract between the individual and the political community was specific in stating what is given to the community: solely the natural right of enforcing the law of reason which every man had as his personal possession in the pre-civil state of nature. All other rights are reserved to the individual as defenses against the political state. Thus, instead of regarding all of man's right as deriving from civil government as Hobbes did. Locke saw no rights in existence after the formation of government which had not been operative prior to its beginning.

In Hobbes' utilitarian theory there is found no concept of legitimate popular rebellion against a government or governor guilty of not fulfilling the trust for which the sovereign power was called into being. But the right of the subjects to exercise political recall is essential to the whole structure of Locke's system.

Countless historians have documented the tremendous impact of Locke's political theories on the constitutional and political thought of the people of England and America. Yet Locke's influence in England was less enduring than it was in the new world to the west. While his theories were well suited to the practical politics of 18th and 19th century England, they came into conflict with the changing constitutional concepts of that people in the period after the death of Queen Anne. At the moment when Parliament assumed an omnipotent position in direct denial of all theories opposed to political sovereignty the doctrines of John Locke were laid to rest.

If man in the state of Nature be so free as has been said, if he be absolute lord of his own person and possessions, equal to the greatest and subject to nobody, why will he part with his freedom ... and subject himself to the domination and control of any other Power? To which it is obvious to answer, that though in the state of Nature he hath such a right, yet the enjoyment of it is very uncertain and constantly exposed to the invasion of others; for all being kings as much as he, every man his equal, and the greater part no strict observers of equity and justice, the enjoyment of the property he has in this state is very unsafe, very insecure. This makes him willing to quit this condition which, however free, is full of fears and continual dangers; and it is not without reason that he seeks out and is willing to join in society with others who are already united, or have a mind to unite for the mutual preservation of their lives, liberties and estates, which I call by the general name —property.

The great and chief end, therefore, of men uniting into commonwealths and putting themselves under government, is the preservation of their property, to which in the state of Nature there are many other things wanting.

Firstly, there wants an established, settled, known law, received and allowed by common consent to be the standard of right and wrong, and the common measure to decide all controversies between them. For though the law of Nature be plain and intelligible to all rational creatures, yet men, being biased by their interest, as well as ignorant for want of study of it, are apt to allow of it as a law binding to them in the application of it to their particular cases.

Secondly, in the state of Nature there wants a known and indifferent judge, with authority to determine all differences according to the established law. For every one in that state being both judge and executioner of the law of Nature, men being partial to themselves, passion and revenge is very apt to carry them too far, and with too much heat in their own cases, as well as negligence and unconcernedness, makes them too remiss in other men's.

Thirdly, in the state of Nature there often wants power to back and support the sentence when right, and to give it due execution. They who by an injustice [are] offended will seldom fail where they are able by force to make good their injustice. Such resistance many times makes the punishment dangerous, and frequently destructive to those who attempt it.

Thus mankind, notwithstanding all the privileges of the state of Nature, being but in an ill condition while they remain in it, are quickly driven into society.... 'Tis this makes them so willingly give up every one his single power of punishing to be exercised by such alone as shall be appointed to it amongst them, and by such rules as the community, or those authorized by them to that purpose, shall agree on. And in this we have the original right and rise of both the legislative and executive power as well as of the governments and societies themselves.

For in the state of Nature, to omit the liberty he has of innocent delights, a man has two powers. The first is to do whatsoever he thinks fit for the preservation of himself and others within the permission of the law of Nature; by which law, common to them all, he and all the rest of mankind are one community, make up one society distinct from all other creatures, and were it not for the corruption and viciousness of degenerate men, there would be no need of any other, no necessity that men should separate from this great and natural community, and associate into lesser combinations. The other power a man has in the state of Nature is the power to punish the crimes committed against that law. Both these he gives up when he joins in a ... particular political society, and incorporates into any commonwealth separate from the rest of mankind.

The first power, *viz.,* of doing whatsoever he thought fit for the preservation of himself and the rest of mankind, he gives up to be regulated by laws made by the society, so far forth as the preservation of himself and the rest of that society shall require; which laws of the society in many things confine the liberty he had by the law of Nature.

Secondly, the power of punishing he wholly gives up, and engages his natural force, which he might before employ in the execution of the law of Nature, by his own single authority, as he thought fit, to assist the executive power of the society as the law thereof shall require. For being now in a new state, wherein he is to enjoy many conveniences from the labor, assistance, and society of others in the same community, as well as protection from its whole strength, he is to part also with as much of his natural liberty, in providing for himself, as the good, prosperity, and safety of the society shall require, which is not only necessary but just, since the other members of the society do the like.

But though men when they enter into society give up the equality, liberty, and executive power they had in the state of Nature into the hands of the society, to be so far disposed of by the legislative as the good of the society shall require, yet it being only with an intention in every one the better to preserve himself, his liberty and property (for no rational creature can be supposed to change his condition with an intention to be worse), the power of the society or legislative constituted by them, can never be supposed to extend farther than the common good; but is obliged to secure every one's property by providing against those three defects above mentioned that made the state of Nature so unsafe and uneasy. And so, whoever has the legislative or supreme power of any commonwealth, is bound to govern by established standing laws, promulgated and known to the people, and not by extemporary decrees, by indifferent and upright judges, who are to decide controversies by those laws; and to employ the force of the community at home only in the execution of such laws, or abroad to prevent or redress foreign injuries and secure the community from inroads and invasion. And all this to be directed to no other end but the peace, safety, and public good of the people. John Locke, *Two Treatises of Government: Concerning the True Original, Extent, and End of Civil Government,* Second Treatise, Ch. IX.)

## The Bill of Rights. 1689

AMONG other things, the *Bill of Rights* established the constitutional conditions under which the English Monarchy was to exist and function. All the rights claimed by Parliament in the long struggle against the Stuart Kings since 1603 were enumerated in the Bill as stemming from the Constitution, and all the limitations on the Crown were exactly stated in order to preclude future uncertainty and debate. But in a sense the *Bill of Rights* was a far more conservative document than the passions and tensions of the times might have produced. The Monarchy was limited, to be sure, and Parliament was given the legal right to interfere in every area of government, yet it would deny the spirit and content of the Bill to argue that it created Parliamentary sovereignty. Later the settlement made in the document was bulwarked with further legislative enactments, but each of them added to the harmonious interaction of executive and legislature. The general result of the whole mass of legislation during the period 1688-1701 was to elevate both of the constitutional components through the reasonable balance which that legislation brought into being.

### 157.

An Act Declaring the Rights and Liberties of the Subject and Settling the Succession of the Crown.

Whereas the Lords Spiritual and Temporal and Commons assembled at Westminster, lawfully, fully and freely representing all the estates of the people of this Realm, did upon the [13 February, 1688] present unto their Majesties, then called and known by the names and style of William and Mary, Prince and Princess of Orange, being present in their proper persons, a certain declaration in writing made by the said Lords and Commons in the words following:

Whereas the late King, James II, by the assistance of divers evil counsellors, judges and ministers employed by him, did endeavor to subvert and extirpate the Protestant religion and the laws and liberties of this Kingdom:

By assuming and exercising a power of dispensing with and suspending of laws and the execution of laws without consent of Parliament:

By committing and prosecuting divers worthy prelates for humbly petitioning to be excused from concurring to the said assumed power:

By issuing and causing to be executed a commission under the great seal for erecting a court called the Court of Commissioners for Ecclesiastical Causes:

By levying money for and to the use of the Crown by pretence of prerogative for other time and in other manner than the same was granted by Parliament:

By raising and keeping a standing army within this Kingdom in time of peace without consent of Parliament, and quartering soldiers contrary to law:

By causing several good subjects being Protestants to be disarmed at the same time when papists were both armed and employed contrary to law:

By violating the freedom of election of members to serve in Parliament:

By prosecutions in the Court of King's Bench for matters and causes cognizable only in Parliament, and by divers other arbitrary and illegal courses:

And whereas of late years partial corrupt and unqualified persons have been returned and served on juries in trials, and particularly divers jurors in trials for high treason which were not freeholders:

And excessive bail has been required of persons committed in criminal cases to elude the benefit of the laws made for the liberty of the subjects:

And excessive fines have been imposed:

And illegal and cruel punishments inflicted:

And several grants and promises made of fines and forfeitures before any conviction or judgment against the persons upon whom the same were to be levied:

All which are utterly and directly contrary to the known laws and statutes and freedom of this realm:

And whereas the late King James the Second having abdicated the government and the throne being thereby vacant, his Highness the Prince of Orange (whom it has pleased Almighty God to make the glorious instrument of delivering this Kingdom from popery and arbitrary power) did (by the advice of the Lords Spiritual and Temporal and divers principal persons of the Commons) cause letters to be written to the Lords Spiritual and Temporal being Protestants, and other letters to the several counties, cities, universities, boroughs and cinque ports, for the choosing of such persons to represent them as were of right to be sent to Parliament, to meet and sit at Westminster upon the two and twentieth day of January in this year [1688], in order to such an establishment as that their religion, laws and liberties might not again be in danger of being subverted, upon which letters elections having been accordingly made:

And thereupon the said Lords Spiritual and Temporal and Commons, pursuant to their respective letters and elections, being now assembled in a full and free representative of this nation, taking into their most serious consideration the best means for attaining the ends aforesaid, do in the first place (as their ancestors in like case have usually done) for the vindicating and asserting their ancient rights and liberties declare:

That the pretended power of suspending of laws or the execution of laws by regal authority without consent of Parliament is illegal:

That the pretended power of dispensing with laws or the execution of laws by regal authority, as it has been assumed and exercised of late, is illegal:

That the commission for erecting the late Court of Commissioners for Ecclesiastical Causes, and all other commissions and courts of like nature, are illegal and pernicious:

That levying money for or to the use of the Crown by pretence of prerogative without grant of Parliament, for longer time, or in other manner than the same is or shall be granted, is illegal:

That it is the right of the subjects to petition the King, and all commitments and prosecutions for such petitioning are illegal:

That the raising or keeping a standing army within the Kingdom in time of peace, unless it be with consent of Parliament, is against law:

That the subjects which are Protestants may have arms for their defence suitable to their conditions and as allowed by law:

That election of members of Parliament ought to be free:

That the freedom of speech and debates or proceedings in Parliament ought not to be impeached or questioned in any court or place out of Parliament:

That excessive bail ought not to be required, nor excessive fines imposed, nor cruel and unusual punishments inflicted:

That jurors ought to be duly impanelled and returned, and jurors which pass upon men in trials for high treason ought to be freeholders:

That all grants and promises of fines and forfeitures of particular persons before conviction are illegal and void:

And that for redress of all grievances, and for the amending, strengthening and preserving of the laws, Parliament ought to be held frequently.

And they do claim, demand and insist upon all and singular the premises as their undoubted rights and liberties, and that no declarations, judgments, doings or proceedings to the prejudice of the people in any of the said premises ought in any wise to be drawn hereafter into consequence or example; to which demand of their rights they are particularly encouraged by the declaration of his Highness the Prince of Orange as being the only means for obtaining a full redress and remedy therein. Having therefore an entire confidence that his said Highness ... will perfect the deliverance so far advanced by him, and will still preserve them from the violation of their rights which they have here asserted, and from all other attempts upon their religion, rights and liberties, the said Lords Spiritual and Temporal and Commons assembled at Westminster do resolve that William and Mary, Prince and Princess of Orange, be and be declared King and Queen of England, France and Ireland and the dominions thereunto belonging, to hold the Crown and royal dignity of the said Kingdoms and dominions to them, the said Prince and Princess, during their lives and the life of the survivor of them, and that the sole and full exercise of the regal power be only in and executed by the said Prince of Orange in the names of the said Prince and Princess during their joint lives, and after their deceases the said Crown and royal dignity of the said Kingdoms and dominions to be to the heirs of the body of the said Princess, and for default of such issue to the Princess Anne of Denmark and the heirs of her body, and for default of such issue to the heirs of the body of the said Prince of Orange. And Lords Spiritual [etc.] ... do pray the said Prince and Princess to accept the same accordingly.

And that the oaths hereafter mentioned be taken by all persons of whom the oaths of allegiance and supremacy might be required by law, instead of them; and that the said oaths of allegiance and supremacy be abrogated.

I, (name), do sincerely promise and swear that I will be faithful and bear true allegiance to their Majesties King William and Queen Mary. So help me God.

I, (name), do swear that I do from my heart abhor, detest and abjure as impious and heretical this damnable doctrine and position, that princes excommunicated or deprived by the Pope or any authority of the See of Rome may be deposed or murdered by their subjects or any other whatsoever. And I do declare that no foreign prince, person, prelate, state or potentate has or ought to have any jurisdiction, power, superiority, pre-eminence or authority, ecclesiastical or spiritual, within this Realm. So help me God.

Upon which their said Majesties did accept the Crown and royal dignity of the Kingdom of England, France and Ireland, and the dominions thereunto belonging, according to the resolution and desire of the said Lords and Commons contained in the said declaration. And thereupon their Majesties were pleased that the said Lords Spiritual and Temporal and Commons, being the two Houses of Parliament, should continue to sit, and with their Majesties' royal concurrence make effectual provision for the settlement of the religion, laws and liberties of this Kingdom, so that the same for the future might not be in danger again of being subverted, to which the said Lords Spiritual and Temporal and Commons did agree, and proceed to act accordingly. Now in pursuance of the premises the said Lords Spiritual and Temporal and Commons in Parliament assembled, for the ratifying, confirming and establishing the said declaration and the articles, clauses, matters and things therein contained by the force of a law made in due form by authority of Parliament, do pray that it may be declared and enacted that all and singular the rights and liberties asserted and claimed in the said declaration are the true, ancient and indubitable rights and liberties of the people of this Kingdom, and so shall be esteemed, allowed, adjudged, deemed and taken to be; and that all and every the particulars aforesaid shall be firmly and strictly holden and observed as they are expressed in the said declaration, and all officers and ministers whatsoever shall serve their Majesties and their successors according to the same in all times to come. And the said Lords Spiritual [etc.] . . . seriously considering how it has pleased Almighty God in his marvelous providence . . . to this nation to provide and preserve their said Majesties' royal persons most happily to reign over us upon the throne of their ancestors, for which they render unto him from the bottom of their hearts, their humblest thanks and praises, do truly, firmly, assuredly and in the sincerity of their hearts think, and do hereby recognize, acknowledge and declare, that King James II having abdicated the government, and their Majesties having accepted the Crown and royal dignity as aforesaid, their said Majesties did become, were, are and of right ought to be by the laws of this Realm our Sovereign Liege Lord and Lady, King and Queen of England, [etc.] . . . in and to whose Princely persons the royal state, Crown and dignity of the said Realms with all honors, styles, titles, regalities, prerogatives, powers, jurisdictions and authorities to the same belonging and appertaining are most fully, rightfully and entirely invested and incorporated, united and annexed. And for preventing all questions and divisions in this Realm by reason of any pretended titles to the Crown, and for preserving a certainty in the succession thereof, in and upon which the unity, peace, tranquillity and safety of this nation does under God wholly consist and depend, the said Lords Spiritual and Temporal and Commons do beseech their Majesties that it may be enacted, established and declared, that the Crown and regal government of the said Kingdoms and dominions, with all and singular the premises thereunto belonging and appertaining, shall be and continue to their said Majesties and the survivor of them during their lives and the life of the survivor of them, and that the entire, perfect and full exercise of the regal power and government be only in and executed by his Majesty in the names of both their Majesties during their joint lives; and after their deceases the said crown and premises shall be and remain to the heirs of the

body of her Majesty, and for default of such issue to her Royal Highness the Princess Anne of Denmark and the heirs of her body, and for default of such issue to the heirs of the body of his said Majesty; and thereunto the said Lords Spiritual and Temporal and Commons do in the name of all the people aforesaid most humbly and faithfully submit themselves, their heirs and posterities for ever, and do faithfully promise that they will stand to, maintain and defend their said Majesties, and also the limitation and succession of the Crown herein specified and contained, to the utmost of their powers and their lives and estates against all persons whatsoever that shall attempt anything to the contrary. And whereas it has been found by experience that it is inconsistent with the safety and welfare of this Protestant Kingdom to be governed by a popish prince, or by any King or Queen marrying a papist, the said Lords Spiritual [etc.] . . . do further pray that it may be enacted, that all and every person and persons that is, are or shall be reconciled to or shall hold communion with the See or Church of Rome, or shall profess the popish religion, or shall marry a papist, shall be excluded and be for ever incapable to inherit, possess or enjoy the crown and government of this Realm . . . or to have, use or exercise any regal power, authority or jurisdiction within the same; and in all and every such case or cases the people of these Realms shall be and are hereby absolved of their allegiance; and the said Crown and government shall from time to time descend to and be enjoyed by such person or persons being Protestants as should have inherited and enjoyed the same in case the said person or persons so reconciled, holding communion or professing or marrying as aforesaid were naturally dead; and that every King and Queen of this Realm who at any time hereafter shall come to and succeed in the imperial Crown of this Kingdom shall on the first day of the meeting of the first Parliament next after his or her coming to the Crown, sitting in his or her throne in the House of Peers in the presence of the Lords and Commons therein assembled, or at his or her coronation before such person or persons who shall administer the coronation oath to him or her at the time of his or her taking the said oath (which shall first happen), make, subscribe and audibly repeat the declaration mentioned in the statute made in the thirtieth year of the reign of King Charles II entitled, *An Act for the More Effectual Preserving the King's Person and Government by Disabling Papists from Sitting in either House of Parliament.* But if it shall happen that such King or Queen upon his or her succession to the Crown of this Realm shall be under the age of twelve years, then every such King or Queen shall make, subscribe and audibly repeat the said declaration at his or her coronation or the first day of the meeting of the first Parliament as aforesaid which shall first happen after such King or Queen shall have attained the said age of twelve years.... [as established and enacted by the authority of this present Parliament]. (SR, VI, 142: 1 William and Mary, s.2, c.2.)

## Act Legalizing the Convention. 1689

## 158.

THE Convention which welcomed William and Mary to England legalized its sitting as Parliament by a special Act which was accepted by the Monarchy which the Convention had created. Such legal by-play would be most difficult to explain according to the traditional constitutional concept of Parliament as a body which could only meet under King's writ. However, it would be even more difficult to argue the positive merits of the legality of the new Monarch's position since Parliament had never acquired the franchise to elect Kings. The fiction that James had abdicated his throne and deserted his people in a time of great need does not answer the many constitutional questions that arose from this situation.

An Act for Removing and Preventing all Questions and Disputes Concerning the Assembling and Sitting of this Present Parliament.

For preventing all doubts and scruples which may in any wise arise concerning the meeting, sitting and proceeding of this present Parliament, be it declared and enacted ... that the Lords ... and Commons convened at Westminster [22 January, 1688], and there sitting on [13 February] following, are the two Houses of Parliament, and so shall be and are hereby declared, enacted and adjudged to be, to all intents, constructions and purposes whatsoever, notwithstanding any want of writ or writs of summons or any other defect of form or default whatsoever, as if they had been summoned according to the usual form; and that this present Act and all other Acts to which the royal assent shall at any time be given before the next prorogation after the said [13 February] shall be understood, taken and adjudged in law to begin and commence upon the said [13 February], on which day their said Majesties, at the request and by the advice of the Lords and Commons, did accept the Crown and royal dignity of King and Queen of England....

And be it further enacted ... that the Act made in the thirtieth year of King Charles II entitled, *An Act for the More Effectual Preserving the King's Person and Government by Disabling of Papists from Sitting in either House of Parliament,* and all other Acts of Parliament, as to so much of the said Act or Acts only as concerns the taking the oaths of supremacy and allegiance or either of them in the said Act or Acts respectively mentioned by any member or members of either House of Parliament with relation to their sitting and voting in Parliament, shall be and are hereby repealed to all intents and purposes, anything in the said recited Act or Acts to the contrary notwithstanding.

And be it further enacted, that the taking the oaths hereinafter mentioned, and the making, subscribing and repeating the declaration in the said Act of the thirtieth year of King Charles II mentioned, by every member of either House of this present Parliament from and after the first day of March next ensuing, in such manner as the taking the said oaths of allegiance and supremacy and the making, subscribing and repeating the said declaration in the said last mentioned Act are required, shall be good and effectual to all intents and purposes as if the said oaths of allegiance and supremacy had been taken and the said declaration had been made, subscribed and repeated in such manner and at such time as by the said Act or Acts or any of them are required; and that in all future Parliaments the oaths hereinafter mentioned, and the declaration in the said Act made in the thirtieth year of King Charles

II mentioned, shall be taken, made, subscribed and repeated by every member of either House of Parliament within the time and in the same manner and form and under the penalties and disabilities as the said oaths of allegiance and supremacy and the said declaration by the said Act of the thirtieth year of King Charles II are limited, ordained and appointed to be taken, made, subscribed and repeated, and not at any other time or in any other manner, to enable them to sit and vote in Parliament....

And it is hereby ... enacted ... that the oaths above appointed by this Act to be taken in the stead and place of the oaths of allegiance and supremacy shall be in the words following and no other:

[The oaths that are here prescribed are identical to those oaths that were prescribed in the *Bill of Rights*].

Provided ... that this ... Parliament may be dissolved after the usual manner as if the same had been summoned ... by writ. (SR, VI, 23: 1 William and Mary, c.1.)

## The Mutiny Act. 1689

I59.   THE *Mutiny Act* was a further step in the sharing of power between King and Parliament. The Crown was given full authority to grant commissions, to assemble court-martials for punishment of mutineers and deserters, and to maintain general discipline. However, the Act was to be in force for only one calendar year. Thereafter Parliament must each year repass the Act. Thus Crown authority to control the army was contingent on the will and voice of the legislature.

An Act for Publishing Officers or Soldiers who shall Mutiny or Desert their Majesties' Service.

Whereas the raising or keeping a standing army within this Kingdom in time of peace, unless it be with consent of Parliament, is against law; and whereas it is judged necessary by their Majesties and this present Parliament that during this time of danger several of the forces which are now on foot should be continued and others raised for the safety of the Kingdom, for the common de-

fence of the Protestant religion and for the reducing of Ireland; and whereas no man may be forejudged of life or limb, or subjected to any kind of punishment by martial law, or in any other manner than by the judgment of his peers and according to the known and established laws of this Realm; yet nevertheless it being requisite for retaining such forces as are or shall be raised during this exigence of affairs in their duty an exact discipline be observed, and that soldiers who shall mutiny or stir up sedition or shall desert their Majesties' service be brought to a more exemplary and speedy punishment than the usual forms of law will allow.

Be it therefore enacted ... that from and after [12 April, 1689] every person being in their Majesties' service in the army, and being mustered and in pay as an officer or soldier, who shall at any time before [10 November, 1689] excite, cause or join in any mutiny or sedition in the army, or shall desert their Majesties' service in the army, shall suffer death or such other punishment as by a court-martial shall be inflicted.

And it is hereby further enacted and declared, that their Majesties, or the general of their army for the time being, may by virtue of this Act have full power and authority to grant commissions to any lieutenants-general or other officers not under the degree of colonels from time to time to call and assemble court-martials for punishing such offences as aforesaid.

And it is hereby further enacted and de-

clared, that no court-martial which shall have power to inflict any punishment by virtue of this Act for the offences aforesaid shall consist of fewer than thirteen, whereof none be under the degree of captains.

Provided always, that no field officer be tried by other than field officers, and that such court-martial shall have power and authority to administer an oath to any witness in order to the examination or trial of the offences aforesaid.

Provided always, that nothing in this Act ... shall extend or be construed to exempt any officer or soldier whatsoever from the ordinary process of law.

Provided ... that this Act or anything therein contained shall not extend or be any ways construed to extend to or concern any the militia forces of this Kingdom.

Provided also, that this Act shall continue and be in force until [10 November, 1689], and no longer.... (SR, VI, 55: 1 William and Mary, c.5.)

## Act Abolishing Hearth Tax. 1689

**160.**

THE taxing of hearths or heating stoves was not unusual during the reigns of Charles II and James II. Like windows, they were considered by common consent to be luxuries and were taxed as such. However, the payment of the tax rate was often avoided by fraudulent misrepresentation on the part of the householders, a condition which occasioned the searching of premises by tax officials who had the right to act without specific warrants. The government's power to search at will was a clear invasion of private property rights, and it was on this ground that Parliament nullified the principal statutes upon which hearth taxes rested.

An Act for the taking away the Revenue arising by Hearth Money.

Whereas his Majesty, having been informed that the revenue of Hearth Money was grievous to the people, was pleased ... to send to the Commons assembled in Parliament to signify his pleasure either to agree to a regulation of it or to the taking it wholly away, as should be thought most convenient by the said Commons; and whereas upon mature deliberation the said Commons do find that the said revenue cannot be so regulated but

that it will occasion many difficulties and questions, and that it is in itself not only a great oppression to the poorer sort but a badge of slavery upon the whole people, exposing every man's house to be entered into and searched at pleasure by persons unknown to him; we, your Majesty's ... Commons, being filled with a most humble and grateful sense of your Majesty's unparalleled grace and favor to your people, not only by restoring their rights and liberties, which have been invaded contrary to law, but in desiring to make them happy and at ease by taking away such burdens as by law were fixed upon them ... do most humbly beseech your Majesty that the said revenue of Hearth Money may be wholly taken away and abolished; and be it enacted ... that an Act ... entitled, *An Act for the Establishing an Additional Revenue upon his Majesty ... for the better Support of his ... Crown and Dignity* [14 Charles II, c.10., wherein Parliament had stated that ".... every dwelling and other house and edifice, and all lodgings and chambers ... shall be chargeable ... with the annual payment to the King's Majesty ... for every fire-hearth and stove within every such house, edifice, chambers and lodgings ... the sum of two shillings by the year...."] and another Act made in the second session of the said Parliament in the fifteenth year of his said late Majesty's reign, entitled, *An additional Act for the better Ordering and Collecting the Revenue arising by Hearth Money* [15 Charles II, c.13.], and another Act made in the sixteenth year of the reign of his said late Majesty, entitled, *An Act for Collecting the Duty arising by Hearth Money by the Officers to be appointed by his Majesty* [16 Charles II, c.3.], and all and every the articles, clauses and things in the said several Acts contained, shall be and are hereby wholly repealed, annulled and made void.... (SR, VI, 61: 1 William and Mary, c.10.)

## The Toleration Act. 1689

**161.** THIS ACT might well be viewed as the first real step toward religious liberty and toleration in England—less for its content than for the spirit of moderation and toleration which motivated Parliament in constructing it. After its passage only Catholics and Unitarians were forbidden to worship in their own ways. Dissenters and non-conformists, though still legally excluded from offices in local or national government, began quietly to accept such offices. They were seldom challenged. After the turn of the decade annual Acts of Indemnity and Acts of Occasional Conformity were passed which made such office-holding legal. Although their application was still far from perfect, the personal liberty and individual rights essential to the democratic nature of the English Constitution were clearly beginning to develop.

An Act for Exempting their Majesties' Protestant Subjects Dissenting from the Church of England from the Penalties of certain Laws.

Forasmuch as some ease to scrupulous consciences in the exercise of religion may be an effectual means to unite their Majesties' Protestant subjects in interest and affection, be it enacted ... that neither the statute made in the three and twentieth year of the reign of the late Queen Elizabeth entitled, *An Act to Retain the Queen's Majesty's Subjects in their due Obedience* [23 Eliz. c.1.], nor the statute made in the twenty-ninth year of the said Queen entitled, *An Act for the more Speedy and due Execution of certain Branches of the Statute made in the Three and Twentieth Year of the Queen's Majesty's Reign* [29 Eliz. c.6.], nor that branch or clause of a statute made in the first year of the reign of the said Queen entitled, *An Act for the Uniformity of Common Prayer and Service in the Church and Administration of the Sacraments* [1 Eliz. c.2.], whereby all persons having no lawful or reasonable excuse to be absent are required to resort to their parish church or chapel or some usual place where the common prayer shall be used, upon pain of punishment by the censures of the Church and also upon pain that every person so offending shall forfeit for every such offence twelve pence, nor the statute made in the third year of the reign of the late King James I entitled, *An Act for the better Discovering and Repressing Popish Recusants* [3 James I, c.1.], nor that other statute made in the same year entitled, *An Act to Prevent and Avoid Dangers which may grow by Popish Recusants* [3 James I, c.5.], nor any other law or statute of this Realm made against papists or popish recusants, except the statute made in the five and twentieth year of King Charles II entitled, *An Act for Preventing Dangers which may happen from Popish Recusants* [25 Charles II, c.2.], and except also the statute made in the thirtieth year of the said King Charles II entitled, *An Act for the more effectual Preserving the King's Person and Government by disabling Papists from Sitting in either House of Parliament* [30 Charles II, c.1.], shall be constructed to extend to any person or persons dissenting from the Church of England that shall take the oaths mentioned in a statute made by this present Parliament entitled, *An Act for Removing and Preventing all questions and Disputes concerning the Assembling and Sitting of this present Parliament* [1 William and Mary, c.1.,] and shall make and subscribe the declaration mentioned in a statute made in the thirtieth year of the reign of King Charles II entitled, [as above, 30 Charles II, c.1.], which oaths and declaration the Justices of Peace at the general sessions of the peace to be held for the county or place where such person shall live are hereby required to tender and administer to such persons as shall offer themselves to take, make and subscribe the same, and thereof to keep a register....

And be it further enacted ... that all and every person ... that shall as aforesaid take the said oaths, and make and subscribe the declaration aforesaid, shall not be liable to any pains, penalties or forfeitures mentioned in an Act made in the five and thirtieth year of the reign of the late Queen Elizabeth entitled, *An Act to retain the Queen's Majesty's Subjects in their Due Obedience* [35 Eliz., c.1.], nor in an Act made in the two and twentieth year of the reign of the late King Charles II entitled, *An Act to Prevent and Suppress Seditious Conventicles* [22 Charles II, c.1], nor shall any of the said persons be

prosecuted in any ecclesiastical court for or by reason of their non-conforming to the Church of England.

Provided always ... that if any assembly of persons dissenting from the Church of England shall be had in any place for religious worship with the doors locked, barred or bolted during any time of such meeting together, all and every person or persons that shall come to and be at such meetings shall not receive any benefit from this law, but be liable to all the pains and penalties of all the aforesaid laws recited in this Act for such their meeting, notwithstanding his taking the oaths and his making and subscribing the declaration aforesaid; provided always, that nothing herein contained shall be construed to exempt any of the persons aforesaid from paying of tithes or other parochial duties, or any other duties to the church or minister, nor from any prosecution in any ecclesiastical court or elsewhere for the same. . . .

And be it further enacted ... that no person dissenting from the Church of England in Holy Orders or pretended Holy Orders ... nor any preacher or teacher of any congregation of dissenting Protestants, that shall make and subscribe the declaration aforesaid, and take the said oaths at the general or quarter-sessions of the peace to be held for the county, town, parts or divisions where such person lives ... and shall also declare his approbation of and subscribe the articles of religion mentioned in the statute made in the thirteenth year of the reign of the late Queen Elizabeth [13 Eliz., c.12.], except the thirty-fourth, thirty-fifth and the thirty-sixth [articles], and these words of the twentieth article, *viz.,* "the Church hath power to decree rites or ceremonies, and authority in controversies of faith, and yet," shall be liable to any of the pains or penalties mentioned in an Act made in the seventeenth year of the reign of King Charles II entitled, *An Act for Restraining Nonconformists from Inhabiting in Corporations* [17 Charles II, c.2], nor the penalties mentioned in the aforesaid Act made in the two and twentieth year of his said late Majesty's reign, for or by reason of such persons preaching at any meeting for the exercise of religion, nor to the penalty of one hundred pounds mentioned in an Act made in the thirteenth and fourteenth years of King Charles II entitled, *An Act for the Uniformity of Public Prayers and Administration of Sacraments and other Rites and Ceremonies, and for Establishing the Form of Making, Ordaining and Consecrating of Bishops, Priests and Deacons in the Church of England* [14 Charles II, c.4.], for officiating in any congregation for the exercise of religion permitted and allowed by this Act. . . .

And whereas some dissenting Protestants scruple the baptizing of infants, be it enacted . . . that every person in pretended Holy Orders . . . or preacher or teacher, that shall subscribe the aforesaid articles of religion except before excepted, and also except part of the seven and twentieth article touching infant baptism, and shall take the said oaths and make and subscribe the declaration aforesaid in manner aforesaid, every such person shall enjoy all the privileges, benefits and advantages which any other dissenting minister as aforesaid might have or enjoy by virtue of this Act. . . .

And whereas there are certain other persons, dissenters from the Church of England, who scruple the taking of any oath, be it enacted . . . that every such person shall make and subscribe the aforesaid declaration and also this declaration of fidelity following, *viz.,*

I, (name), do sincerely promise and solemnly declare before God and the world that I will be true and faithful to King William and Queen Mary, and I do solemnly profess and declare that I do from my heart abhor, detest and renounce as impious and heretical that damnable doctrine and position that princes excommunicated or deprived by the Pope or any authority of the See of Rome may be deposed or murdered by their subjects or any other whatsoever, and I do

declare that no foreign prince, person, prelate, state or potentate has or ought to have any power, jurisdiction, superiority, pre-eminence or authority, ecclesiastical or spiritual within this Realm.

And shall subscribe a profession of their Christian belief in these words:

I, (name), profess faith in God the Father, and in Jesus Christ His Eternal Son, the true God, and in the Holy Spirit, one God blessed for evermore, and do acknowledge the Holy Scriptures of the Old and New Testament to be given by divine inspiration.

And every such person that shall make and subscribe the two declarations and profession aforesaid, being thereunto required, shall be exempted from all the pains and penalties of all and every the aforementioned statutes made against popish recusants or Protestant nonconformists, and also from the penalties of an Act made in the fifth year of the reign of the late Queen Elizabeth entitled, *An Act for the Assurance of the Queen's Royal Power over all Estates and Subjects within Her Dominions* [5 Eliz., c.1.], for or by reason of such persons not taking or refusing to take the oath mentioned in the said Act, and also from the penalties of an Act made in the thirteenth and fourteenth years of the reign of King Charles II entitled, *An Act for Preventing Mischiefs that may arise by certain persons called Quakers Refusing to take Lawful Oaths* [14 Charles II, c.1.], and enjoy all other the benefits, privileges and advantages under the like limitations, provisos and conditions which any other dissenters shall or ought to enjoy by virtue of this Act. . . .

Provided always, and it is the true intent and meaning of this Act, that all the laws made and provided for the frequenting of divine service on the Lord's Day, commonly called Sunday, shall be still in force and executed against all persons that offend against the said laws, except such persons come to some congregation or assembly of religious worship allowed or permitted by this Act.

Provided ... that neither this Act nor any clause, article or thing herein contained shall extend or be construed to extend to give any ease, benefit or advantage to any papist or popish recusant whatsoever, or any person that shall deny in his preaching or writing the doctrine of the Blessed Trinity as it is declared in the aforesaid articles of religion. ...

Provided ... that no congregation or assembly for religious worship shall be permitted ... until the place of such meeting shall be certified to the Bishop of the diocese, or to the archdeacon or that archdeaconry, or to the Justices of the Peace at the general or quarter-sessions of the peace for the county, city or place in which such meeting shall be held, and registered in the said Bishop's or archdeacon's court respectively, or recorded at the said general or quarter-sessions. ... (SR, VI, 74: 1 William and Mary, c.18.)

## Act Suspending the Habeas Corpus Act. 1689

### 162.

THIS ACT was a temporary measure passed by Parliament to deal with the unrest stemming from the threat of civil war. James II, safe at the court of the French King, was not without friends in England or the means to cause trouble. His very existence as claimant to the throne raised a great many constitutional and political problems for those of tender conscience. The suspension of the right of *habeas corpus* is included here because of the method used by Parliament to maintain the principle involved while temporarily suspending the operation of the statute giving it constitutional substance. To guard against the subject's loss of the protection of the writ, the suspension was to last only until a given date. The same principle of chronological limitation had been used in the *Mutiny Act*.

An Act for Empowering his Majesty to Apprehend and Detain such Persons as he shall find just Cause to Suspect are Conspiring against the Government.

For the securing the peace of the Kingdom in this time of imminent danger against the attempts and traitorous conspiracies of evil-disposed persons, be it enacted ... that every person ... that shall be committed by warrant of their Majesties' most honorably Privy Council, signed by six of the said Privy Council at least, for suspicion of high treason, may be detained in safe custody till [17 April, 1689], without bail ... and that no judge or other person shall bail or try any such person ... so committed without order from their said Majesties' Privy Council ... till the said [17 April]. ...

Provided always, that from and after the said [date] the said persons so committed shall have the benefit and advantage of an Act made in the one and thirtieth year of King Charles II entitled, *An Act for the better Securing the Liberty of the Subject and for Prevention of Imprisonment beyond the Seas* [31 Charles II, c.2.], and ... of all other laws and statutes any way relating to or providing for the liberty of the subjects of this Realm.

.... This present Act shall continue until the said [17 April, 1689] and no longer.

Provided always, and be it enacted, that nothing in this Act shall be construed to extend to the ancient rights and privileges of Parliament, or to the imprisonment or detaining of any member of either House of Parliament, until the matter of which he stands suspected be first communicated to the House of which he is a member, and the consent of the said House obtained for his commitment or detaining. (SR, VI, 24: 1 William and Mary, c.2.)

## The Act of Recognition of William and Mary. 1690

**163.** AFTER William and Mary had accepted the *Bill of Rights* they were declared King and Queen of England. It is interesting to note, however, that their claim to the throne was not stated to be hereditary or one of divine right. Rather their elevation was expressly stated as enacted by the Houses of Parliament.

An Act for Recognizing King William and Queen Mary, and for Avoiding all Questions touching the Acts made in the Parliament... at Westminster [13 February, 1688].

We, your Majesties' most humble and loyal subjects, the Lords Spiritual and Temporal and Commons in this present Parliament assembled, do beseech your most excellent Majesties that it may be published and declared in this high court of Parliament, and enacted by authority of the same, that we do recognize and acknowledge your Majesties were, are and of right ought to be by the laws of this Realm our Sovereign Liege Lord and Lady, King and Queen of England, France and Ireland and the dominions thereunto belonging, in and to whose princely persons the royal state, Crown and dignity of the said Realms, with all honors, styles, titles, regalities, prerogatives, powers,

jurisdictions and authorities to the same belonging and appertaining, are most fully, rightfully and entirely invested and incorporated, united and annexed. And for the avoiding of all disputes and questions concerning the being and authority of the late Parliament assembled at Westminster [on 13 February, 1688], we do most humbly beseech your Majesties that it may be enacted, and be it enacted by the King and Queen's most excellent Majesties, by and with the advice and consent of the Lords Spiritual and Temporal and Commons in this present Parliament... that all and singular the Acts made and enacted in the said Parliament were and are laws and statutes of this Kingdom, and as such ought to be reputed, taken and obeyed by all the people of this Kingdom. (SR, VI, 156: 2 William and Mary, s.1, c.1.)

## The Triennial Act. 1694

**164.** THIS ACT clarified the constitutional status of the problem of Parliamentary meetings. Politically the Act was unnecessary since the several statutes limiting Crown income and control of the army necessitated frequent Parliaments. However Parliament desired to reinforce its position as a constitutional institution, and the regularity of its sessions rather than its checking power on the Crown was in the end to determine its eventual position in the Constitution.

An Act for the Frequent Meeting and Calling of Parliaments.

Whereas by the ancient laws and statutes of this Kingdom frequent Parliaments ought to be held, and whereas frequent and new Parliaments tend very much to the happy union and good agreement of the King and people, we, your Majesties' most loyal and

obedient subjects the Lords Spiritual and Temporal and Commons in this present Parliament assembled, do most humbly beseech your most excellent Majesties that it may be declared and enacted in this present Parliament, and it is hereby declared and enacted ... that from henceforth a Parliament shall be held once in three years at the least.

And be it ... enacted ... that within three years at the farthest from and after the dissolution of this present Parliament, and so from time to time for ever hereafter within three years at the farthest from and after the determination of every other Parliament, legal writs under the great seal shall be issued by directions of your Majesties, your heirs and successors for calling, assembling and holding another new Parliament.

And be it further enacted ... that from henceforth no Parliament whatsoever that shall at any time hereafter be called, assembled or held shall have any continuance longer than for three years only at the farthest, to be accounted from the day on which by the writs of summons the said Parliament shall be appointed to meet.

And be it ... enacted ... that this present Parliament shall cease and determine on the first day of November, [1696], unless their Majesties shall think fit to dissolve it sooner. (SR, VI, 510: 6 and 7 William and Mary, c.2.)

## An Act for the Continued Sitting of Parliament. 1695

THE ancient custom under which Parliament was automatically dissolved by the death of the king had led to considerable uncertainty in the past and was terminated by this Act. Now Parliament continued in session regardless of the demise of the king. Its actions, however, remained mere bills rather than statutes and its measures had to be submitted to the succeeding monarch.

165.

An Act for the Continuing, Meeting and Sitting of a Parliament in Case of the Death or Demise of His Majesty, His Heirs and Successors.

Whereas this Kingdom of England may be exposed to great dangers by the invasion of foreigners, or by the traitorous conspiracies of wicked and ill-disposed persons, whenever it shall please God to afflict these Realms by the death of our gracious Sovereign King William ... or by the death of any of his heirs and successors, before a Parliament can be summoned and called by the next heir and successor to the Crown; for prevention whereof be it enacted ... that this present Parliament, or any other Parliament which shall hereafter be summoned and called by his Majesty King William, his heirs and successors, shall not determine or be dissolved by the death or demise of his said Majesty, his heirs and successors, but such Parliament shall and is hereby enacted to continue, and is hereby empowered and required immediately to meet, convene and sit, and to act, notwithstanding such death or demise, for and during the time of six months and no longer, unless the same shall be sooner prorogued or dissolved by such person who shall be next heir to the Crown of this Realm of England in succession, according to an Act of Parliament made in the first year of the reign of King William and Queen Mary, entitled, *An Act Declaring the Rights and Liberties of the Subject and Settling the Succession of the Crown:* and if the said Parliament shall be so prorogued then it shall meet and sit on and upon the day unto which it shall be prorogued, and continue for the residue of the said time of six months, unless sooner prorogued or dissolved as aforesaid.

And it is ... further enacted ... that in case there shall be no Parliament in being at the time of the death or demise of his Majesty, or any of his heirs and successors, then the last preceding Parliament shall immediately convene and sit, and is hereby empowered and required to act as aforesaid to all intents and purposes as if the said Parliament had never been dissolved.

Provided ... that nothing in this Act contained shall extend or be construed to extend to alter or abridge the power of the

King, his heirs and successors, to prorogue or dissolve Parliaments, nor to repeal or make void one Act of Parliament made in the sixth year of the reign of his present Majesty King William, entitled, *An Act for*

*the Frequent Meeting and Calling of Parliaments,* but that the said Act shall continue in force in everything that is not contrary to or inconsistent with the direction of this Act. (SR, VII, 84: 7 & 8 William III, c.15.)

## The Civil List Act. 1698

**166.** THIS ACT set aside a regular yearly income for Crown use. Certain custom rates on specified imports were established whereby the Crown was to receive a fixed annual return of seven hundred thousand pounds. However, this yearly income was to be collected only during William's life.

An Act for Granting to his Majesty a further Subsidy of Tunnage and Poundage towards raising the Yearly Sum of Seven Hundred Thousand Pounds, for the Service of his Majesty's Household and other Uses therein mentioned, during his Majesty's Life.

We . . . the Commons of England . . . being deeply sensible of the great blessings which by the goodness of Almighty God we . . . do fully enjoy under your Majesty's most auspicious government, and being desirous to make a grateful acknowledgment of your Majesty's unparalleled grace and favor to us your Commons . . . have therefore freely . . . resolved to increase your Majesty's revenue . . . and do give and grant unto your most excellent Majesty the further rates, duties and sums of money hereinafter mentioned, and do humbly beseech your Majesty that it may be enacted . . . that over and above all subsidies of tunnage and poundage . . . for or upon any wines, goods or merchandises whatsoever imported or to be imported, there shall be raised, levied, collected, paid and satisfied unto his Majesty one other subsidy called tunnage for and upon all wines which from and after [31 January, 1699], at any time or times during his Majesty's life, shall be imported or brought into the Kingdom of England . . . Wales, or town of Berwick-upon-Tweed, that is to say, of every tun of wine of the growth of France or of any the dominions of the French King or Crown of France that shall come into the port of

London and the members thereof by way of merchandise by his Majesty's natural born subjects, the sum of four pounds and ten shillings of current English Money [is levied]. . . .

And whereas it is intended that the yearly sum of seven hundred thousand pounds shall be supplied to his Majesty for the service of his household and family, and for other his necessary expenses and occasions, out of the hereditary rates and duties of excise upon beer, ale and other liquors which were granted to the Crown [by 12 Charles II, c.12.], and out of the rates and duties of excise of beer, ale and other liquors payable for the term of his Majesty's life by an Act of Parliament made and passed in the second year of the reign of his Majesty and the late Queen of blessed memory . . . and out of the revenue of the general letter office, or Post Office . . . and out of the small branches of his Majesty's revenue hereinafter mentioned and expressed, that is to say, the first fruits and tenths of the clergy, the fines for writs of covenant and writs of entry payable in the Alienation Office, the post fines, the revenue of the wine licenses, the moneys arising by sheriffs' proffers and compositions in the Exchequer and by the seizures of uncustomed and prohibited goods, the revenue of the duchy of Cornwall and any other revenue arising by rents of lands in England or Wales or for fines of leases of the same or any of them, and the duty of four and a half per cent in specie arising in Barbados and the Leeward Islands in America; and out of the moneys which from and after the commencement of this Act shall arise by the further subsidies and duties hereby granted; be it therefore further enacted . . . that if the said great and small branches and revenues hereinbefore mentioned . . . shall produce in clear money more than the yearly sum of seven hundred thousand pounds . . . that then the overplus of such produce . . . shall not be issued, disposed, made use of or applied to any use or purpose or upon any pretext whatsoever without the authority of Parliament. . . . (SR, VII, 382: 9 William III, c.23.)

## The Act of Settlement. 1701

### 167.

WITH the *Act of Settlement* the legislative phase of the Glorious Revolution came to an end. The primary purposes of the Act were two: to clarify and legalize the system regulating the royal succession, and to establish absolute barriers against a Stuart restoration.

Other considerations were incorporated which solidified certain constitutional concepts and made them part of English law. The Crown was forced to conduct the affairs of the State in the Privy Council. Also a "place" clause was inserted in the Act stating that no person who received any income from the Crown could serve simultaneously in the House of Commons.

An Act for the Further Limitation of the Crown and Better Securing the Rights and Liberties of the Subject.

[The first part of the present Act restates the portions of the *Bill of Rights* which established the royal succession and excluded Catholics from the Crown].

. . . . After the making of which statute and the settlement therein contained your Majesty's good subjects, who were restored to the full and free possession and enjoyment of their religion, rights and liberties by the providence of God giving success to your Majesty's just undertakings and unwearied endeavors for that purpose, had no greater temporal felicity to hope or wish for than to see a royal progeny descending from your Majesty, to whom . . . they owe their tranquillity, and whose ancestors have for many years been principal asserters of the reformed religion and the liberties of Europe, and from our said most gracious Sovereign Lady . . . and it having since pleased Almighty God to take away our said Sovereign Lady and also the most hopeful Prince William, Duke of Gloucester (the only surviving issue of her Royal Highness the Princess Anne of Denmark), to the unspeakable grief and sorrow of your Majesty and your said good subjects, who under such losses being sensibly put in mind that it stands wholly in the pleasure of Almighty God to prolong the lives of your Majesty and of her Royal Highness, and to grant to your Majesty or to her Royal Highness such issue as may be inheritable to the Crown and regal government aforesaid by the respective limitations in the said recited Act contained, do constantly implore the Divine mercy for those blessings, and your Majesty's said subjects having daily experience of your royal care and concern for the present and future welfare of these Kingdoms, and particularly recommending from your throne a further provision to be made for the succession of the Crown in the Protestant line for the happiness of the nation and the security of our religion, and it being absolutely necessary for the safety, peace and quiet of this Realm to obviate all doubts and contentions in the same by reason of any pretended titles to the Crown, and to maintain a certainty in the succession thereof to which your subjects may safely have recourse for their protection in case the limitations in the said recited Act should determine; therefore for a further provision of the succession of the Crown in the Protestant line, we your Majesty's most dutiful and loyal subjects ... in this present Parliament ... do beseech your Majesty that it may be enacted and declared, and be it enacted and declared by the King's most excellent Majesty, by and with the advice and consent of the Lords Spiritual [etc.] ... that the most excellent Princess Sophia, Electress and Duchess dowager of Hanover, daughter of the most excellent Princess Elizabeth, late Queen of Bohemia, daughter of our late Sovereign Lord King James I ... be ... declared to be the next in succession in the Protestant line to the imperial Crown and dignity of the said Realms of England, France and Ireland ... after his Majesty and the Princess Anne of Denmark and in default of issue of the said Princess Anne and of his Majesty respectively, and that from and after the deceases of his said Majesty our now Sovereign Lord, and of her Royal Highness the Princess Anne of Denmark, and for default of issue of the said Princess Anne and of his Majesty respectively, the Crown and regal government of the said Kingdoms of England etc. ... with the royal state and dignity of the said Realms, and all honors, styles, titles, regalities, prerogatives, powers, jurisdictions and authorities to the same belonging and appertaining, shall be, remain and continue to the said most excellent Princess Sophia and the heirs of her body being Protestants; and thereunto the said Lords ... and Commons shall and will in the name of all the people of this Realm most humbly and faithfully submit themselves, their heirs and posterities, and do faithfully promise that after the deceases of his Majesty and her Royal Highness, and the failure of the heirs of their respective bodies, to stand to, maintain and defend the said Princess Sophia and the heirs of her body being Protestants ac-

cording to the limitation and succession of the Crown in this Act specified and contained, to the utmost of their powers. ...

And whereas it is requisite and necessary that some further provision be made for securing our religion, laws and liberties from and after the death of his Majesty and the Princess Anne of Denmark, and in default of issue of the body of the said Princess and of his Majesty respectively, be it enacted by the King's most excellent Majesty, by and with the advice and consent of the Lords ... and Commons in Parliament assembled and by the authority of the same:

That whosoever shall hereafter come to the possession of this Crown shall join in communion with the Church of England as by law established.

That in case the Crown and imperial dignity of this Realm shall hereafter come to any person not being a native of this Kingdom of England this nation be not obliged to engage in any war for the defence of any dominions or territories which do not belong to the Crown of England without the consent of Parliament.

That no person who shall hereafter come to the possession of this Crown shall go out of the dominions of England, Scotland or Ireland without consent of Parliament.

That from and after the time that the further limitation by this Act shall take effect all matters and things relating to the well governing of this Kingdom which are properly cognizable in the Privy Council by the laws and customs of this Realm shall be transacted there, and all resolutions taken thereupon shall be signed by such of the Privy Council as shall advise and consent to the same.

That after the said limitation shall take effect as aforesaid no person born out of the Kingdoms of England, Scotland or Ireland, or the dominions thereunto belonging (although he be naturalized or made a denizen, except such as are born of English parents), shall be capable to be of the Privy Council, or a member of either House of Parliament, or to enjoy any office or place of trust either civil or military, or to have any grant of lands, tenements or hereditaments from the Crown to himself or to any other or others in trust for him.

That no person who has an office or place of profit under the King, or receives a pension from the Crown, shall be capable of serving as a member of the House of Commons.

That after the said limitation shall take effect as aforesaid Judges' commissions be made *quam diu se bene gesserint,* and their salaries ascertained and established, but upon the address of both Houses of Parliament it may be lawful to remove them.

That no pardon under the great seal of England be pleadable to an impeachment by the Commons in Parliament.

And whereas the laws of England are the birthright of the people thereof, and all the kings and queens who shall ascend the throne of this Realm ought to administer the government of the same according to the said laws, and all their officers and ministers ought to serve them respectively according to the same, the said Lords ... and Commons do therefore further humbly pray that all the laws and statutes of this Realm for securing the established religion and the rights and liberties of the people thereof, and all other laws and statutes of the same now in force, may be ratified and confirmed, and the same are by his Majesty, by and with the advice and consent of the said Lords ... and Commons, and by authority of the same ratified and confirmed accordingly. (SR, VII, 636: 12 & 13 William III, c.2.)

# The Reign of Anne

## 1702-1714

## DOCUMENTS OF THE REIGN OF ANNE

# England, 1702-1714    Introduction

In the sixteenth and seventeenth centuries constitutional change had been continuous and fruitful in terms of the construction and definition of institutions and legal-political concepts. Seeking security, the English people had modified their constitution many times to fit their shifting needs. Feudal interdependence, Tudor absolutism, divine right, republicanism, and finally the parliamentary supremacy leading to the sovereignty of the House of Commons in the nineteenth century, were all largely products of a native tendency toward trial and error in government. Nevertheless the fact of change itself was a result of popular awareness of the need for ordered and workable systems of social and political relationships which could raise society above that terrible primitivism described by Thomas Hobbes:

> Every man is the enemy to every man, wherein men live without other security than what their own strength ... furnish them. ... In such condition there is no industry ... no knowledge ... no account of time, no arts, no letters, no society; and which is worst of all, continual fear, and danger of violent death, and the life of man, solitary, poor, nasty, brutish, and short.

The struggle up and away from such a state was continuous throughout all of English history until the reign of Anne, last of the Stuart monarchs, when the coordination of desire for progress and political ability was replaced by a complacent self-satisfaction with the gains already achieved.

In truth, what appears as a radical loss of national initiative in the area of constitutional movement was the logical result of the circumstances and events of English history. It should first be remembered that national development had been as marked as constitutional change in the past two centuries. Since 1485 a medieval people had grown to be a nation—and England became a modern state among similar highly competitive states, all dedicated to self-expression as a first principle and self-aggrandizement as a fundamental necessity. The rise of the modern community of European states had brought to the fore novel conditions and absorbing problems for the English. Colonial and imperial development, commercial intercourse, and the shifting balance of forces on the continent involved the islanders in complex international relationships of which they were not sole arbiter. Little by little over the course of the two centuries England had been forced to set aside the Elizabethan ideal of political isolation from the continent. Once involved in the religious, dynastic, and national conflicts of France, Spain, and the Empire, England was free neither to withdraw on her own terms nor to act independently of her allies. Increasing involvement in continental problems meant a growing expenditure of English national energy and material substance on non-domestic affairs. This early eighteenth century preoccupation with foreign affairs coincided with the most violent manifestations of Louis XIV's militant program for continental domination, a possibility greatly feared by all Englishmen alike. Yet this was only one of the primary causes for diminishing activity in English constitutional development at the turn of the eighteenth century.

Another significant factor limiting constitutional interest during Anne's reign was precisely the result of the rapidity and breadth of development in prior times. The English were and are an essentially conservative people. With few precedents to point the way, every modification of the constitution, no matter how insignificant, was viewed as a task of some magnitude. By 1700 much of the work of constitution building was completed and a time for rest, for consolidation, and for digesting the social, material, and spiritual gains accruing from the actions of society in the seventeenth century was in order. The previous intense interest and precipitous action in every field of political development had brought the English people to a point past which they evidently would not go without a pause for re-orientation. Past changes had to be studied in the perspective of newly emerged political and economic patterns, and constitutional aspirations weighed for their soundness, moral validity, and social utility.

In looking to the past Anne's subjects must have found much both to encourage and depress them. Although English history had evolved the constitution, this evolution was punctuated with violent and destructive internecine conflicts. It was also apparent that these conflicts had not always been waged for unimpeachable motives; like all peoples, the English had sometimes relied upon morally dubious sanctions for political actions. But even so, the total meaning of that history was probably not displeasing. England was indisputably Protestant, and had attained that majority desire without permanently rejecting religious toleration. In the struggle for political dominance legislature and Crown had found common meeting ground in a new identity of purpose wherein each had a definite and necessary function. From republican experimentation with written constitutions the English people had learned that strict reliance on dogmatic first principles could lead to tyranny. In reacting against such political fundamentalism the people came in later times to seek change and progress through the less dramatic modes of "conventions" of the constitution, slow and modulated change in customs, and deliberate utilitarian compromise.

These were the cornerstones of the foundation of the constitution as it stood at the beginning of the eighteenth century. If it was far removed from its medieval counterpart of the period of Henry VII it was at least as far from ultimate perfection. One of the most glaring of the weaknesses of the constitution which became plainly visible during Anne's reign was its vulnerability to class control.

No matter how faulty the division of power had been under the old constitution the English monarchy had always been aware that no cleavage divided its basic interests from those of the nation at large. Yet once the Crown had been brought down to the level of the seventeenth-century ruling class, an at least theoretically objective arbiter between the various class interests was lost to the nation. The hollow pretense that Parliament consisted of the chosen representatives of the people needs no investigation here. It is sufficient to point out that the oft repeated appeal to the "sovereignty of the people" by the oligarchy of social position and material opulence was a mere euphemism adapted by that group to rationalize its usurpation of the political authority which the monarchy had once possessed.

## Regency Act, 1707

**168.**

THE *Regency Act* constituted Parliament, the Privy Council, and the high officers of State as a great body of regents in the event of the death of the Queen. Each body and each officer serving at the time of Anne's demise was to continue to function in their employment for the space of six months unless their service was terminated by the royal successor. In case the Queen died without heirs Parliament was directed to proclaim publicly the next Protestant successor according to the *Act of Settlement* of 1701.

An Act for the Security of Her Majesty's Person and Government and of the Succession to the Crown of Great Britain.

Whereas by the happy union of England and Scotland it is become necessary to make divers alterations in relation to an Act passed in the Parliament of England in the fourth year of the reign of her present Majesty... entitled, *An Act for the better Security of Her Majesty's Person and Government and of the Succession to the Crown of England in the Protestant line* [6 Anne, c.11.], and to extend the provisions of the said Act throughout the whole United Kingdom, for the better security of our most gracious Sovereign's person and government, and of the succession to the Crown of Great Britain in the Protestant line as it is now by the laws and statutes of this Realm settled, limited and appointed; be it therefore enacted... that if any person or persons shall maliciously, advisedly and directly, by writing or printing, maintain and affirm that our Sovereign Lady the Queen that now is, is not the lawful and rightful Queen of these Realms, or that the pretended Prince of Wales, who now styles himself King of Great Britain, or King of England by the name of James III, or King of Scotland by the name of James VIII, has any right or title to the Crown of these Realms, or that any other person or persons has or have any right or title to the same otherwise than according to an Act of Parliament made in England in the first year of the reign of their late Majesties King William and Queen Mary... entitled, *An Act Declaring the Rights and Liberties of the Subject and Settling the Succession of the Crown* [1 William & Mary, s.2, c.2.], and one other Act made in England in the twelfth year of the reign of his said late Majesty King William III, entitled, *An Act for the Further Limitation of the Crown and better Securing the Rights and Liberties of the Subject* [12 & 13 William III, c.2.], and the Acts lately made in England and Scotland mutually for the union of the two Kingdoms, or that the kings or queens of this Realm, with and by the authority of Parliament, are not able to make laws and statutes of sufficient force and validity to limit and bind the Crown and the descent, limitations, inheritance and government thereof, every such person or persons shall be guilty of high treason, and being thereof lawfully convicted... shall suffer pains of death....

And be it enacted... that this present Parliament or any other Parliament which shall hereafter be summoned and called by her Majesty... shall not be determined or dissolved by the death or demise of her said Majesty... but such Parliament shall and is hereby enacted to continue, and is hereby empowered and required, if sitting at the time of such demise, immediately to proceed to act, notwithstanding such death or demise, for and during the term of six months and no longer, unless the same be sooner prorogued or dissolved by such person to whom the Crown of this Realm... shall come....

And be it enacted... that if there be a Parliament in being at the time of the death of her Majesty... but the same happens to be separated by adjournment or prorogation, such Parliament shall immediately after such demise meet, convene and sit, and shall act, notwithstanding such death or demise, for and during the time of six months and no longer, unless ... sooner prorogued or dissolved as aforesaid.

And be it enacted ... that in case there is no Parliament in being at the time of such demise that has met and sat, then the last preceding Parliament shall immediately convene and sit at Westminster, and be a Parliament to continue as aforesaid ... but subject to be prorogued and dissolved as aforesaid.

Provided ... that nothing in this Act contained shall extend or be construed to extend to alter or abridge the power of the Queen, her heirs or successors, to prorogue or dissolve Parliaments, nor to repeal or make void one Act of Parliament made in England in the sixth year of the reign of their ... Majesties King William and Queen Mary, entitled, *An Act for the Frequent Meeting and Calling of Parliaments* [7 & 8 William and Mary, c.2.], but that the said Act shall continue in force in everything that is not contrary to or inconsistent with the direction of this Act; and the said *Act for the Frequent Meeting* [etc.] ... is hereby declared and enacted to extend to the Parliament of Great Britain as fully and effectually to all intents, constructions and purposes as if the same were herein and hereby particularly recited and enacted.

And be it enacted ... that the Privy Council of her Majesty, her heirs or successors, for the Kingdom of Great Britain shall not be determined or dissolved by the death or demise of her Majesty, her heirs or successors, but such Privy Council shall continue and act as such by the space of six months next after such demise, unless sooner determined by the next successor to whom the imperial Crown of this Realm is limited and appointed to go, remain and descend; nor shall the office or place of Lord Chancellor or Lord Keeper of the Great Seal of Great Britain, or of Lord High Treasurer of Great Britain, Lord President of the Council for Great Britain, Lord Privy Seal of Great Britain, Lord High Admiral of Great Britain, or of any of the great officers of the Queen or King's household for the time being; nor shall any office, place or employment, civil or military, within the Kingdoms of Great Britain or Ireland, dominion of Wales, town of Berwick-upon-Tweed, isles of Jersey, Guernsey, Alderney and Sark, or any of her Majesty's plantations become void by reason of the demise or death of her present Majesty, her heirs or successors, queens or kings of this Realm; but ... every ... person and persons in any of the offices, places and employments aforesaid shall continue in their respective offices, places and employments for the space of six months next after such death or demise, unless sooner removed and discharged by the next in succession as aforesaid. ...

And be it enacted ... that whensoever her Majesty ... shall happen to demise and depart this life without issue of her body, the Privy Council for Great Britain in being at the time of such demise of her Majesty shall with all convenient speed cause the next Protestant successor entitled to the Crown of Great Britain by virtue of the Acts before mentioned to be openly and solemnly proclaimed in Great Britain and Ireland, in such manner and form as the preceding kings and queens respectively have been usually proclaimed after the demise of their respective predecessors, and that all and every member and members of the said Privy Council wilfully neglecting or refusing to cause such proclamation to be made shall be guilty of high treason, and being thereof lawfully convicted shall ... suffer pains of death. ...

And because it may happen that the next Protestant successor may at the time of such demise of her Majesty be out of the Realm of Great Britain in parts beyond the seas, be it therefore enacted ... that for the continuing of the administration of the government in the name of such Protestant successor until her or his arrival in Great Britain the seven officers hereinafter named who shall be in the possession of their offices at the time of such demise of her Majesty, that is to say the Archbishop of Canterbury . . . the Lord Chancellor or Lord Keeper of the Great Seal of Great Britain . . . the Lord High Treasurer of Great Britain . . . the Lord President of the Council for Great Britain . . . the Lord Privy Seal of Great Britain . . . the Lord High Admiral of Great Britain . . . and the Lord Chief Justice of the Queen's Bench . . . shall be, and are by virtue of this Act constituted and appointed Lords Justice of Great Britain, and are and shall be by virtue of this Act empowered in the name of such successor . . . to use, exercise and execute all powers, authorities, matters and acts of government and administration of government in as full and ample manner as such next successor could use or execute the same if she or he were present in person . . . until such successor shall arrive. . . .

And be it further enacted . . . that no person shall have in his own name, or in the name of any person or persons in trust for him or for his benefit, any new office or place of profit whatsoever under the Crown, which at any time since [25 October, 1705] have been created or erected, or hereafter shall be created or erected, nor any person who shall be commissioner or sub-commissioner of prizes, secretary or receiver of the prizes, nor any comptroller of the accounts of the army, nor any commissioner of transports, nor any commissioner of the sick and wounded, nor any agent for any regiment, nor any commissioner for any wine licenses, nor any governor or deputy-governor of any of the plantations, nor any commissioners of the navy employed in any of the out-ports, nor any person having any pension from the Crown during pleasure, shall be capable of being elected, or of sitting or voting as a member of the House of Commons in any Parliament which shall be hereafter summoned and holden. . . . (SR, 6 Anne, c.41.)

## The Act for the Union of England and Scotland. 1707

169.

THE union of England and Scotland had been one of the major ambitions of James I from 1603 until his death. Parliament had denied his hopes for many reasons, but by 1707 the fears upon which Parliamentary rejection of the union had rested had disappeared. Scottish Presbyterianism was no longer a threat to the Established Church of England and the London merchants felt well able to protect their financial interests against the canny Scottish traders.

An Act for an Union of the two Kingdoms of England and Scotland.

Whereas articles of union were agreed on [22 July, 1706], by the commissioners nominated on behalf of the Kingdom of England . . . and the commissioners nominated on the behalf of the Kingdom of Scotland . . . and whereas an Act has passed in the Parliament of Scotland [16 January, 1706] wherein it is mentioned that the Estates of Parliament, considering the said articles of union of the two Kingdoms, had agreed to and approved of the said articles of union with some additions and explanations, and that your Majesty, with advice and consent of the Estates of Parliament . . . had passed in the same session of Parliament an Act entitled, *Act for Securing of the Protestant Religion and Presbyterian Church Government*, which by the tenor thereof was appointed to be inserted in any Act ratifying the treaty, and expressly declared to be a fundamental and essential condition of the said treaty or union in all times coming, the tenor of which articles as ratified and approved of with additions and explanations by the said Act of Parliament of Scotland follows;

*Article I.* That the two Kingdoms of England and Scotland shall upon [1 May, 1707],

and for ever after, be united into one Kingdom by the name of Great Britain; and that
the ensigns armorial of the said United
Kingdom be such as her Majesty shall appoint, and the crosses of St. George and St.
Andrew be conjoined in such manner as her
Majesty shall think fit, and used in all flags,
banners, standards and ensigns both at sea
and land.

*Article II.* That the succession to the
Monarchy of the United Kingdom of Great
Britain and of the dominions thereto belong-
ing, after her most sacred Majesty and in
default of issue of her Majesty, be, remain
and continue to the most excellent Princess
Sophia, electress and duchess dowager of
Hanover, and the heirs of her body being
Protestants. . . .

*Article III.* That the United Kingdom of
Great Britain be represented by one and the
same Parliament, to be styled the Parliament
of Great Britain.

*Article IV.* That all the subjects of the
United Kingdom of Great Britain shall from
and after the union have full freedom and
intercourse of trade and navigation to and
from any port or place within the said
United Kingdom and the dominions and
plantations thereunto belonging, and that
there be a communication of all other rights,
privileges and advantages which do or may
belong to the subjects of either Kingdom,
except where it is otherwise expressly agreed
in these articles.

*Article V.* That all ships or vessels belonging to her Majesty's subjects of Scotland at
the time of ratifying the treaty of union of
the two Kingdoms in the Parliament of Scotland, though foreign built, be deemed and
pass as ships of the build of Great Britain. . . .

*Article VI.* That all parts of the United
Kingdom for ever, from and after the union,
shall have the same allowances, encourage-
ments and drawbacks, and be under the
same prohibitions, restrictions and regulations of trade, and liable to the same customs
and duties on import and export; and that
the allowances, [etc.] . . . shall from and after

the union take place throughout the whole
United Kingdom, excepting and reserving
the duties upon export and import of such
particular commodities from which any persons the subjects of either Kingdom are specially liberated and exempted by their private rights, which after the union are to remain safe and entire to them in all respects
as before the same; and that from and after
the union no Scots cattle carried into England shall be liable to any other duties either
on the public or private accompts than those
duties to which the cattle of England are or
shall be liable within the said Kingdom. . . .

*Article VII.* That all parts of the United
Kingdom be for ever from and after the
union liable to the same excises upon all
excisable liquors . . . and that the excise
settled in England . . . when the union com-
mences take place throughout the whole
United Kingdom.

*Article VIII.* That from and after the
union all foreign salt which shall be imported into Scotland shall be charged at the
importation there with the same duties as
the like salt is now charged with being imported into England. . . .

*Article IX.* That whensoever the sum of
one million nine hundred ninety-seven thousand seven hundred and sixty-three pounds
eight shillings and fourpence halfpenny shall
be enacted by the Parliament of Great Britain to be raised in that part of the United
Kingdom now called England, on land and
other things usually charged in Acts of Parliament for granting an aid to the Crown by
a land tax, that part of the United Kingdom now called Scotland shall be charged
by the same Act with a further sum of forty-
eight thousand pounds free of all charges as
the quota of Scotland to such tax. . . .

*Article X.* That during the continuance of
the respective duties on stamped paper,
vellum and parchment by the several Acts
now in force in England, Scotland shall not
be charged with the same . . . duties.

*Article XI.* That during the continuance of
the duties payable in England on windows

and lights, which determine on [1 August, 1710], Scotland shall not be charged with the same duties.

*Article XII.* [The English tax on coal not to be paid by the Scots].

*Article XIII.* [The English tax on malt not to be paid by the Scots].

*Article XIV.* That the Kingdom of Scotland be not charged with any other duties laid on by the Parliament of England before the union except these consented to in this treaty, in regard it is agreed that all necessary provision shall be made by the Parliament of Scotland for the public charge and service of that Kingdom for the year [1707]; provided nevertheless that if the Parliament of England shall think fit to lay any further impositions by way of customs, or such excises with which by virtue of this treaty Scotland is to be charged equally with England, in such case Scotland shall be liable to the same customs and excises....

*Article XV.* That whereas by the terms of this treaty the subjects of Scotland, for preserving an equality of trade throughout the United Kingdom, will be liable to several customs and excises now payable in England which will be applicable towards payments of the debts of England contracted before the union, it is agreed that Scotland shall have an equivalent for what the subjects thereof shall be so charged towards payment of the said debts of England, in all particulars whatsoever in manner following; [complex provisions are here established in order to protect the Scottish people from the pre-union English national debt]....

*Article XVI.* That from and after the union the coin shall be of the same standard and value throughout the United Kingdom as now in England....

*Article XVII.* That from and after the union the same weights and measures shall be used throughout the United Kingdom as are now established in England....

*Article XVIII.* That the laws concerning regulation of trade, customs, and such excises to which Scotland is by virtue of this treaty to be liable, be the same in Scotland from and after the union as in England, and that all other laws in use within the Kingdom of Scotland do after the union... remain in the same force as before (except such as are contrary to or inconsistent with this treaty), but alterable by the Parliament of Great Britain, with this difference between the laws concerning public right, policy and civil government, and those which concern private right, that the laws which concern public right, policy and civil government may be made the same throughout the whole United Kingdom, but that no alteration be made in laws which concern private right except for evident utility of the subjects of Scotland.

*Article XIX.* That the Court of Session or College of Justice do after the union... remain in all time coming within Scotland as it is now constituted by the laws of that Kingdom, and with the same authority and privileges as before the union, subject nevertheless to such regulations for the better administration of justice as shall be made by the Parliament of Great Britain.... And that the Court of Justiciary do also after the union... remain in all time coming within Scotland as it is now constituted.... And that all Admiralty jurisdictions be under the Lord High Admiral or Commissioners for the Admiralty of Great Britain for the time being; and that the Court of Admiralty now established in Scotland be continued, and that all reviews, reductions or suspensions of the sentences in maritime cases competent to the jurisdiction of that court remain in the same manner after the union as now in Scotland, until the Parliament of Great Britain shall make such regulations and alterations as shall be judged expedient for the whole United Kingdom, so as there be always continued in Scotland a Court of Admiralty.... And that all other courts now in being within the Kingdom of Scotland do remain, but subject to alterations by the Parliament of Great Britain....

*Article XX.* That all heritable offices, superiorities, heritable jurisdictions, offices for life and jurisdictions for life be reserved to the owners thereof as rights of property. . . .

*Article XXI*. That the rights and privileges of the royal burghs in Scotland as they now are do remain entire after the union. . . .

*Article XXII*. That by virtue of this treaty, of the peers of Scotland at the time of the union sixteen shall be the number to sit and vote in the House of Lords, and forty-five the number of the representatives of Scotland in the House of Commons of the Parliament of Great Britain. . . .

*Article XXIII*. That the aforesaid sixteen peers of Scotland mentioned . . . to sit in the House of Lords of the Parliament of Great Britain shall have all privileges of Parliament with the peers of England. . . .

*Article XXIV*. That from and after the union there be one great seal for the United Kingdom of Great Britain, which shall be different from the great seal now used in either Kingdom . . . and that a seal in Scotland after the union be always kept and made use of in all things relating to private rights or grants which have usually passed the great seal of Scotland. . . .

*Article XXV*. That all laws and statutes in either Kingdom, so far as they are contrary to or inconsistent with the terms of these articles or any of them, shall from and after the union cease and become void, and shall be so declared to be by the respective Parliaments of the said Kingdoms. . . .

And the tenor of the *Act for Securing the Protestant Religion and Presbyterian Church Government* within the Kingdom of Scotland is as follows:

Our Sovereign Lady and the Estates of Parliament considering that by the late Act of Parliament for a treaty with England for an union of both Kingdoms it is provided that the commissioners for that treaty should not treat of or concerning any alteration of the worship, discipline and government of the Church of this Kingdom as now by law established, which treaty now being reported to Parliament, and it being reasonable and necessary that the true Protestant religion as presently professed within this Kingdom, with the worship, discipline and government of this Church, should be effectually and unalterably secured, therefore her Majesty, with advice and consent of the said Estates of Parliament, does hereby establish and confirm the said true Protestant religion and worship, discipline and government of this Church to continue without any alteration to the people of this land in all succeeding generations; and . . . her Majesty . . . ratifies, approves and for ever confirms the Act of the first Parliament of King William and Queen Mary entitled, *Act Ratifying the Confession of Faith and Settling Presbyterian Church Government*, with all other Acts of Parliament relating thereto, in prosecution of the declaration of the Estates of this Kingdom containing the *Claim of Rights* . . . and her Majesty . . . expressly provides and declares that the foresaid true Protestant religion contained in the above-mentioned Confession of Faith, with the form and purity of worship presently in use within this Church . . . shall remain and continue unalterable, and that the said Presbyterian government shall be the only government of the Church within the Kingdom of Scotland. . . . (SR, VIII, 566: 6 Anne, c.11.)

## Land Tax Act for Great Britain. 1707

**170.** ONE of the main issues in the century-long debates concerning possible union between England and Scotland had been the problem of division of taxation between the two areas. The present Act is clearly a sensible solution. Amounts of the national burden assigned to each were proportioned to wealth and ability to pay. It should be noted that this just division of responsibility became the pattern for all future Parliamentary acts involving these two areas.

An Act for Granting an Aid to her Majesty to be Raised by a Land Tax in Great Britain for the Service of the Year One Thousand Seven Hundred and Eight.

.... The Commons of Great Britain in Parliament assembled, finding it necessary for the preservation and good of this whole United Kingdom to furnish such ample supplies of money as may sufficiently enable your Majesty to carry on and finish the present war with success, have cheerfully and unanimously given and granted, and by this present Act ... do give and grant, unto your Majesty the several and respective rates and assessments hereafter mentioned; and we do humbly beseech your Majesty that it may be enacted, and be it enacted ... that the sum of two millions forty-three thousand eight hundred thirty-six pounds sixteen shillings and fivepence halfpenny shall be raised, levied and paid unto her Majesty within the Kingdom of Great Britain by such proportions and in such manner and form as are hereafter in this Act expressed.

And it is hereby declared and enacted ... that the sum of one million nine hundred ninety-five thousand eight hundred eighty-two pounds and fivepence halfpenny ... be raised, levied and paid unto her Majesty within the space of one year from [25 March, 1708], and shall be assessed and taxed in the several counties, cities, boroughs, towns and places of England, Wales and Berwick-upon-Tweed according to the proportions and in the manner following. ...

And be it enacted ... that the sum of forty-seven thousand nine hundred fifty-four pounds sixteen shillings, residue of [the sum of the total tax] ... by this Act granted, shall be raised and levied in that part of Great Britain called Scotland by an eight months cess of five thousand nine hundred ninety-four pounds seven shillings of lawful money of Great Britain for every month. ... (SR, VIII, 637: 6 Anne, c.35.)

## Treasons Act. 1708

THIS ACT was a successful attempt to make the treason laws of England and Scotland conform.

## 171.

An Act for Improving the Union of the Two Kingdoms.

Whereas nothing can more conduce to the improving the union of the two Kingdoms ... than that the laws of both parts of Great Britain should agree as near as may be, especially those laws which relate to high treason and the proceedings thereupon ... to the end therefore that the said union may be more effectually improved, be it enacted ... that from and after [1 July, 1709] such crimes and offences which are high treason or misprision of high treason within England shall be construed, adjudged and taken to be high treason and misprision of high treason within Scotland, and that from thenceforth no crimes or offences shall be high treason or misprision of high treason within Scotland but those that are high treason or misprision of high treason in England.

And that from and after the said [date] the Queen's Majesty ... may issue out commissions of oyer and terminer in Scotland under the seal of Great Britain to such persons as her Majesty ... shall think fit, and that three of the Lords of the Justiciary to be in the said commission of oyer and terminer, whereof one to be of the quorum, to inquire of, hear and determine such high treasons [etc.] ... in such manner as is used in England. ...

And be it ... enacted ... that from and after the said [date] the justice court and other courts having power to judge in cases of high treason [etc.] ... in Scotland shall have full power and authority, and are hereby required, to inquire by the oaths of twelve or more good and lawful men of the county, shire or stewartry where the respective courts shall sit of all high treasons [etc.] ... committed within the said counties, [etc.] ... and thereupon to proceed, hear and determine the said offences whereof any person shall be indicted before them in such manner as the Court of Queen's Bench or Justices of oyer and terminer in England may do by the laws of England. ...

And that from and after the said [date] all persons convicted or attainted of high treason [etc.] ... in Scotland shall be subject and liable to the same corruption of blood, pains, penalties and forfeitures as persons convicted or attainted of high treason [etc.] ... in England. ...

And that from and after the said [date] no person accused of any capital offence or other crime in Scotland shall suffer or be subject or liable to any torture, provided that this Act shall not extend to take away that judgment which is given in England against persons indicted of felony who shall refuse to plead or decline trial. ...

.... And be it further enacted ... that after the decease of the person who pretended to be Prince of Wales during the life of the late King James, and since pretends to be King of Great Britain, and at the end of the term of three years after the immediate

succession to the Crown upon the demise of her present Majesty shall take effect, as the same is and stands limited by an Act ... entitled, *An Act for Declaring the Rights and Liberties of the Subject and Settling the Succession of the Crown* [1 William & Mary, s.2, c.2.], and by one other Act ... entitled, *An Act for the Further Limitation of the Crown and better Securing the Rights and Liberties of the Subject* [12 & 13 William III, c.2.], no attainder for treason shall extend to the disheriting of any heir nor to the prejudice of the right or title of any person or persons other than the right or title of the offender or offenders during his, her or their natural lives only. ...

And be it further enacted ... that from and after the decease of the person who pretended to be Prince of Wales [etc.] ... when any person is indicted for high treason [etc.] ... a list of the witnesses that shall be produced on the trial for proving the said indictment, and of the jury, mentioning the names, profession and place of abode of the said witnesses and jurors, be also given at the same time that the copy of the indictment is delivered to the party indicted, and that copies of all indictments for the offences aforesaid with such lists shall be delivered to the party indicted ten days before the trial and in presence of two or more credible witnesses. ... (SR, IX, 93: 7 Anne, c.21.)

## The Occasional Conformity Act. 1711

**172.** THIS ACT was a further step in the increasing religious toleration which characterized the reigns of William and Mary and Anne.

An Act for Preserving the Protestant Religion by better Securing the Church of England as by Law Established, and for Confirming the Toleration Granted to Protestant Dissenters by an Act entitled, *An Act for Exempting their Majesties' Protestant Subjects Dissenting from the Church of England from the Penalties of Certain Laws* [1 William & Mary, c.18.], and for Supply-

ing the Defects Thereof, and for the Further Securing the Protestant Succession by Requiring the Practisers of the Law in North Britain to take the Oaths and Subscribe the Declaration therein Mentioned.

Whereas an Act was made in the thirteenth year of the reign of the late King Charles II entitled, *An Act for the Well Governing and Regulating of Corporations* [13 Charles II, s.2., c.1.], and another Act ... entitled, *An Act for the Preventing Dangers which may Happen from Popish Recusants* [25 Charles II, c.2.], both which Acts were made for the security of the Church of England as by law established, now for the better securing the said Church, and quieting the minds of her Majesty's Protestant subjects dissenting from the Church of England, and rendering them secure in the exercise of their religious worship, as also for the further strengthening of the provision already made for the security of the succession to the Crown in the House of Hanover, be it enacted ... that if any person or persons after [25 March, 1712], either peers or commoners, who have or shall have any office or offices, civil or military, or receive any pay, salary, fee or wages by reason of any patent or grant from or under her Majesty or any of her Majesty's predecessors or of her heirs or successors, or shall have any command or place of trust from or under her Majesty, [etc.] ... or by her or their authority ... within that part of Great Britain called England, the dominion of Wales or town of Berwick-upon-Tweed, or in the navy, or in the several islands of Jersey or Guernsey, or shall be admitted into any service or employment in the household or family of her Majesty, her heirs or successors, or if any mayor, alderman, recorder, bailiff, town clerk, common councilman or other person bearing any office of magistracy or place or trust or other employment relating to or concerning the government of any the respective cities, corporations, boroughs, cinque ports and their members or other port towns within that part of Great Britain called England, [etc.] ... who by the said recited Acts or either of them were or are obliged to receive the sacrament of the Lord's Supper according to the rites and usage of the Church of England as aforesaid, shall at any time after their admission into their respective offices or employments, or after having such patent or grant, command or place of trust as aforesaid, during his or their continuance in such office, [etc.]

... knowingly or willingly resort to or be present at any conventicle, assembly or meeting within England, [etc.] ... for the exercise of religion in other manner than according to the liturgy and practice of the Church of England in any place within that part of Great Britain called England, [etc.] ... at which conventicle, assembly or meeting there shall be ten persons or more assembled together over and besides those of the same household, if it be in any house where there is a family inhabiting, or if it be in an house or place where there is no family inhabiting then where any such ten persons are so assembled as aforesaid, or shall knowingly be present at any such meeting in such house or place as aforesaid, although the liturgy be there used, where her Majesty ... and the Princess Sophia, or such others as shall from time to time be lawfully appointed to be prayed for, shall not there be prayed for in express words according to the liturgy of the Church of England, except where such particular offices of the liturgy are used wherein there are no express directions to pray for her Majesty and the royal family, shall forfeit forty pounds, to be recovered by him or them that shall sue for the same. ...

And be it enacted, that every person convicted in any action to be brought as aforesaid, or upon any information, presentment or indictment in any of her Majesty's courts at Westminster, or at the Assizes, shall be disabled from thenceforth to hold such office or offices. ...

.... And be it enacted ... that if any person ... who shall have been convicted as aforesaid ... shall after such conviction conform to the Church of England for the space of one year ... and receive the sacrament of the Lord's Supper according to the rites and usage of the Church of England at least three times in the year, every such person ... shall be capable of the grant of any the offices ... aforesaid. ...

And it is ... enacted ... that the toleration granted to Protestant dissenters by the Act

... entitled, *An Act for Exempting their Majesties Protestant Subjects Dissenting from the Church of England from the Penalties of Certain Laws* [1 William & Mary, c.18.], shall be and is hereby ratified and confirmed ... [and is to be] inviolably observed for the exempting of such Protestant dissenters as are thereby intended from the pains and penalties therein mentioned.... (SR, IX, 551: 10 Anne, c.6.)

## The Parliamentary Qualifications Act. 1711

**I 73.** THE influence of the gentry is plainly visible in this Act which established landed wealth as the necessary economic qualification for membership in the House of Commons. Such class-oriented legislation had disturbing consequences in years to come, for it excluded from Parliament all the groups which were to be enriched by the Industrial Revolution later in the century. This Act may be considered the last successful attempt of the Tory gentry to maintain a firm hold on the reins of government.

An Act for Securing the Freedom of Parliaments by the farther qualifying the Members to Sit in the House of Commons.

For the better preserving the constitution and freedom of Parliaments, be it enacted ... that from and after the determination of this present Parliament no person shall be capable to sit or vote as a member of the House of Commons for any county, city, borough or cinque port within that part of Great Britain called England, the dominion of Wales and town of Berwick-upon-Tweed, who shall not have an estate, freehold or copyhold, for his own life or for some greater estate either in law or equity to and for his own use and benefit, of or in lands, tenements or hereditaments, over and above what will satisfy and clear all encumbrances that may affect the same, lying or being within that part of Great Britain called England, [etc.] ... of the respective annual value hereafter limited, *viz.*, the annual value of six hundred pounds above reprises for every knight of a shire and the annual value of three hundred pounds above reprises for every citizen, burgess or baron of the cinque ports; and that if any person who shall be elected or returned to serve in any Parliament as a knight of a shire or as a citizen, burgess or baron of the cinque ports shall not at the time of such election and return be seized of or entitled to such an estate in lands, tenements or hereditaments as for such knight or for such citizen, burgess or baron respectively as hereinbefore required or limited, such election shall be void.... [This Act not to apply to the returns of the Universities] (SR, IX, 365: 9 Anne, c.5.)

## The Schism Act. 1714

**I 74.** THE political and constitutional results of the religious toleration embodied in Parliamentary Acts of the past two decades become most apparent during the last years of Anne's reign. Although dissenters were barred from Parliament they were allowed in county and municipal offices. Even Catholic religious services were tolerated and Catholic schools permitted. In a momentary panic a Tory-dominated Parliament attempted with the *Schism Act* to deny this tacit toleration by imposing on all schoolmasters an oath of loyalty to the Established Church.

The Act had, however, no practical effect. As other problems increasingly absorbed the national interest, religious freedom became a minor issue. To all intents and purposes theological struggle was ended by the time of the death of Anne and thereafter the English people were free to seek solutions to the new political and economic problems of the eighteenth century.

An Act to Prevent the Growth of Schism, and for the further Security of the Churches of England and Ireland as by Law Established.

Whereas by an Act of Parliament ... entitled, *An Act for the Uniformity of Public Prayers and Administration of Sacraments and other Rites and Ceremonies, and for Establishing the Form of Making, Ordaining and Consecrating Bishops, Priests and Deacons in the Church of England* [14 Charles II, c.4.], it is ... enacted that every schoolmaster keeping any public or private school, and every person instructing or teaching any youth in any house or private family as a tutor or schoolmaster, should subscribe before his or their respective archbishop, bishop or ordinary of the diocese a declaration or acknowledgment, in which ... was contained as follows, *viz.,* "I, (name), do declare that I will conform to the liturgy of the Church of England as it is now by law established" ... and whereas notwithstanding the said Act sundry papists and other persons dissenting from the Church of England have taken upon them to instruct and teach youth as tutors or schoolmasters, and have for such purpose openly set up schools and seminaries, whereby if due and speedy remedy be not had great danger might ensue to this Church and State; for the making of the said recited Act more effectual and preventing the danger aforesaid, be it enacted ... that every person ... who shall from and after the first day of August next ensuing keep any public or private school or seminary, or teach and instruct any youth ... within that part of Great Britain called England, the dominion of Wales or town of Berwick-upon-Tweed, before such person or persons shall have subscribed so much of the said declaration and acknowledgment as is before recited, and shall have had and obtained a licence from the respective archbishop, bishop or ordinary of the place under his seal of office ... shall and may be committed to the common jail of such county ... there to remain without bail ... for the space of three months. ...

.... And be it ... enacted, that no licence shall be granted by any archbishop, [etc.] ... unless the person ... who shall sue for the same shall produce a certificate of his ... having received the sacrament according to the usage of the Church of England ... within the space of one year next before the grant of such licence ... nor until such person ... shall have taken and subscribed the oaths of allegiance and supremacy and abjuration as appointed by law, and shall have made and subscribed the declaration against transubstantiation contained in the Act ... entitled, *An Act for Preventing Dangers which may happen from Popish Recusants* [25 Charles II, c.2.]. ...

And be it ... enacted ... that any person who shall have obtained a licence and subscribed the declaration and taken and subscribed the oaths as above appointed, and shall at any time after, during the time of his ... keeping any public or private school or seminary or instructing any youth ... knowingly or willingly resort to or be present at any conventicle, assembly or meeting within England, [etc.] ... for the exercise of religion in any other manner than according to the liturgy and practice of the Church of England, or shall knowingly and willingly be present at any meeting or assembly for the exercise of religion, athough the liturgy be there used, where her Majesty ... and the Elector of Brunswick or such others as shall from time to time be lawfully appointed to be prayed for shall not there be prayed for in express words according to the liturgy of the Church of England, except where such particular offices of the liturgy are used wherein there are no express directions to pray for her Majesty and the royal family, shall be liable to the penalties in this Act. .... (SR, IX, 915: 13 Anne, c.7.)

# Additional Readings

The following is a list of works which are suggested as additional aids for the study of English history in the period from 1485 to 1714. Each volume has been chosen for its special pertinence to a particular area or problem. Availability in the average college or university library, quality of the work, and intrinsic interest have been taken into consideration in selecting material for the list. In the case of controversial subjects, authors of differing viewpoints are included in order to present varying approaches to the topic. Desire to avoid duplication necessitated the rejection of certain standard volumes. In no case, however, does omission imply criticism.

The categories into which the works are divided are the usual ones for the Tudor-Stuart period. It should be kept in mind that despite these convenient groupings, works on religious history will generally include constitutional and political facts and analysis, just as works primarily constitutional in nature include materials from almost every other area.

No attempt has been made to direct the student to the abundant pamphlet literature of the sixteenth and seventeenth centuries. While its constitutional and political significance is undeniable, its availability is questionable, since much of the labor of editing and reprinting the pamphlets is still to be done. The few pamphlets included are considered to be of such overriding significance that their omission seemed out of the question.

Where the editors cite an edition other than the first, it is with the realization that first editions of many works are either unobtainable or out-dated in form. Recent editions are in almost every instance better suited to the needs of the student. Where the editors do not cite an edition number it is because many sound editions of that work are available.

## Documents, Records, and Contemporary Works

Abbott, S. C. ed. *Writings and Speeches of Oliver Cromwell.* 4 vols. 1937.

Adair, E. R. ed. *The Sources for the History of the Council in the Sixteenth and Seventeenth Centuries.* 1924.

Birch, T. ed. *The Works of Sir Walter Raleigh.* 8 vols. 1829.

Bowyer, R. *The Parliamentary Diary of Robert Bowyer, 1606-1607.* Ed. D. H. Willson. 1931.

Brown, B. C. ed. *Letters and Diplomatic Instructions of Queen Anne.* 1935.

Browning, A. ed. *English Historical Documents: 1660-1714.* 1953.

Bruce, John. ed. *Letters of Queen Elizabeth and King James VI of Scotland.* 1918.

Bryant, A. ed. *The Letters, Speeches, and Declarations of King Charles II.* 1935.

Burnet, G. *History of His Own Time.* 1695. Edition of 1833.

*Calendar of State Papers: Domestic.*

Calvin, John. *The Institutes of the Christian Religion.* 1536. Edition of 1559.

Cardwell, E. ed. *Documentary Annals of the Reformed Church of England, 1546-1716.* 1839.

Cecil, Robert. *Correspondence of King James VI of Scotland with Sir Robert Cecil and Others in England During the Reign of Queen Elizabeth.* Ed. J. Bruce. 1861.

Chalmers, G. ed. *A Collection of Treaties Between Great Britain and Other Powers.* 2 vols. 1790.

Cheyney, E. P. ed. *Readings in English History Drawn from the Original Sources.* 1908.

Coke, Sir Edward. *The First Part of the Institutes of the Laws of England.* 2 vols. Edition of 1817.

────── *Fourth Part of the Institutes of the Laws of England, Concerning the Jurisdiction of the Courts.* Edition of 1789.

────── *Twelfth Report.* Edition of 1777.

Costin, W. C. and Watson, J. S. eds. *The Law and Working of the Constitution: Documents, 1660-1914.* 1952.

Dasent, F. R. *et al.* eds. *Acts of the Privy Council of England, 1542-1628.* 1890.

D'Ewes, Sir Simons. *A Complete Journal of Both Houses of Lords and Commons Throughout the Whole Reign of Queen Elizabeth.* 1693.

────── *The Journal of Sir Simon D'Ewes From the First Recess of Long Parliament to the Withdrawal of King Charles From London.* 1682. Ed. W. H. Coates. 1942.

Dobson, A. ed. *Diary of John Evelyn.* 1906.

Dudley, Edmund. *The Tree of Commonwealth.* 1509. (many editions)

Dykes, D. O. ed. *Source Book of English Constitutional History from 1660.* 1930.

Filmer, Sir Robert. *Patriarcha: Or the Natural Power of Kings.* 1642.

Firth, C. H. ed. *The Clarke Papers.* 1901.

Firth, C. H. and Rait, R. S. eds. *Acts and Ordinances of the Interregnum.* 1911.

Forster, J. ed. *Debates on the Grand Remonstrance, November and December, 1641.* 1860.

Fortescue, Sir John. *The Governance of England.* 1471. Ed. C. Plummer. 1885.

────── *De Laudibus Angliae; A Treatise in Commendation of the Laws of England.* 1468. Edition of 1874.

Fuller, Thomas. *The Church History of Britain.* 1655. Edition of 1837.

Gardiner, S. R. ed. *The Constitutional Documents of the Puritan Revolution, 1625-1660.* 1899.

────── ed. *Parliamentary Debates of 1610.* 1861.

────── ed. *Reports of Cases in Star Chamber and High Commission.* 1866.

Gee, H. and Hardy, W. J. eds. *Documents Illustrative of English Church History.* 1896.

Grant, W. L. and Munro, J. eds. *Acts of the Privy Council of England: Colonial Series.* 1909.

Haller, W. ed. *Tracts on Liberty in the Puritan Revolution, 1638-1647.* 2 vols. 1934.

Hobbes, Thomas. *Leviathan.* 1651.

Hooker, Richard. *The Laws of Ecclesiastical Polity.* c.1597.

Howell, T. B. ed. *A Complete Collection of State Trials to 1783: Continued to the Present Time.* 33 vols. 1816-26.

James I. *News from Scotland.* 1591. Ed. G. B. Harrison. 1924.

*Journals of the House of Commons, 1547-1714.* 117 vols. 1803-63.

*Journals of the House of Lords, 1578-1714.* 119 vols. 1846-87.

Knox, John. *The History of the Reformation in Scotland.* 1566.

Latimer, Hugh. *Sermons, 1548.* Edition of 1845.

Leadham, I. S. ed. *Select Cases in the Star Chamber, 1477-1544.* 1910.

────── ed. *Select Cases in the Court of Requests, 1497-1569.* 1898.

Locke, John. *Of Civil Government. Two Treatises.* 1690.

Lodge, E. and Thornton, G. eds. *English Constitutional Documents, 1307-1485.* 1935.

*Manuscripts of the House of Lords, 1678-1688.* Edition of 1895.

Molesworth, William. ed. *The English Works of Thomas Hobbes.* 1840.

More, Sir Thomas. *Utopia.* 1516 (many editions).

Nicholas, E. ed. *Proceedings and Debates in the House of Commons in 1620 and 1621.* 1766.

Notestein, Wallace. ed. *Commons Debates, 1621.* 7 vols. 1935.

—— ed. *The Journal of Sir Simon D'Ewes.* 1923.

Petrie, C. ed. *The Letters, Speeches, and Proclamations of King Charles I.* 1935.

Prothero, G. W. ed. *Select Statutes and Other Constitutional Documents Illustrative of the Reign of Elizabeth and James I.* 1934.

Rice, G. ed. *Public Speeches of Queen Elizabeth: Selections.* 1951.

Rushworth, John. ed. *Historical Collections.* ...1721.

Rymer, T. ed. *Foedera, Conventiones, Litterae, et... Acta Publica.* 17 vols. 1704-17.

Saint-German, Christopher. *Doctor and Student... a Dialogue....* Edition of 1761.

Scobel, H. ed. *Acts and Ordinances of Parliament.* 1649.

Scott, W. and Bliss, J. eds. *The Works of William Laud.* 7 vols. 1847-60.

Smith, Sir Thomas. *De Republica Anglorum: A Discourse of the Commonwealth of England.* c.1564. Ed. L. Alston. 1906.

State Papers: *Henry VIII.* 11 vols. 1830-52.

*Statutes of the Realm.* 11 vols. 1810-21.

*Statutes at Large.* 105 vols. 1762-1865.

Stephenson, C. and Marcham, G. eds. *Sources of English Constitutional History.* 1937.

Stubbs, W. ed. *Select Charters and Other Illustrations of English History.* 9th edition. 1913.

Tanner, J. R. ed. *English Constitutional Documents of the Seventeenth Century, 1603-1689.* 1947.

—— ed. *Tudor Constitutional Documents: 1485-1603.* 1948.

—— ed. *Constitutional Documents of the Reign of James I: 1603-1525.* 1952.

Tawney, R. H. and Power, I. eds. *Tudor Economic Documents.* 3 vols. 1924.

——, Brown, P. A., Bland, A. E. eds. *English Economic History: Select Documents.* 1914.

Townshend, Heywood. ed. *Historical Collections....* 1590.

Travelyan, G. M. ed. *Select Documents for Queen Anne's Reign.* 1929.

Woodhouse, A. S. P. ed. *Puritanism and Liberty, Being the Army Debates From the Clarke Papers; 1647-49.* 1938.

## Constitutional History

Adams, G. B. *Constitutional History of England.* Revised by R. L. Schuyler. 1934.

Allen, J. W. *A History of Political Thought in the Sixteenth Century.* 1928.

—— *English Political Theory, 1603-1640.* 1938.

Anson, W. R. *The Law and the Custom of the Constitution.* 2 vols. 1908.

Bagehot, W. *The English Constitution and Other Political Essays.* 1877.

Blackstone, William. *Commentaries on the Laws of England.* 4 vols. Edition of 1791.

Brodie, G. A. *A Constitutional History of the British Empire.* 3 vols. 1866.

Cam, H. M. and Turberville, A. S. eds. *A Bibliography of English Constitutional History.* 1929.

Campbell, Lord John. *Lives of the Lord Chancellors and Keepers of the Great Seal of England.* 10 vols. Edition of 1856.

Carlyle, A. J. *A History of Political Theory in the West.* 6 vols. 1936.

Cobbett, W. *Parliamentary History of England.* 1820.

Chrimes, S. B. *English Constitutional Ideas in the Fifteenth Century.* 1936.

Dalrymple, J. *Memoirs of Great Britain and Ireland.* 1771.

Dicey, A. V. *The Privy Council.* 1887.

—— *The Law and the Constitution.* 1885.

—— *Introduction to the Study of the Constitution.* 1902.

Figgis, J. N. *The Divine Right of Kings.* 1914.

Gilbert, G. *The History and Practice of the High Court of Chancery.* 1758.

Gooch, G. P. *English Democratic Ideas in the Seventeenth Century.* Edited by H. J. Laski. 1927.

—— *Political Thought in England From Bacon to Halifax.* 1914.

Hadley, James. *Introduction to Roman Law.* 1873.

Hallam, Henry. *The Constitutional History of England From the Accession of Henry VII to the Death of George II.* 1870.

Hastings, Margaret. *The Court of Common Pleas in Fifteenth Century England.* 1947.

Holdsworth, W. S. *Essays in Law and History.* 1946.

——— *A History of English Law.* 12 vols. 1903-38.

Inderwick, F. A. *The King's Peace: A Historical Sketch of English Law Courts.* 1895.

Jenks, E. *Parliamentary England. The Evolution of the Cabinet System.* 1903.

——— *A Short History of English Law.* 1922.

Judson, M. A. *The Crisis of the Constitution: An Essay in Constitutional and Political Thought in England, 1603-1645.* 1949.

Maitland, F. W. *The Constitutional History of England.* 1908.

——— *English Law and the Renaissance.* 1901.

McIlwain, C. H. *The High Court of Parliament and Its Supremacy.* 1910.

——— *The Growth of Political Thought in the West.* 1932.

Mosse, G. L. *The Struggle for Sovereignty in England.* 1951.

Petit-Dutaillis, Charles. *Studies and Notes Supplementary to Stubbs Constitutional History.* Ed. J. Tait. 2 vols. 1908.

Pike, L. O. *A Constitutional History of the House of Lords.* 1894.

Pollard, A. F. *The Evolution of Parliament.* 1920.

Pollock, F. *Essays in the Law.* 1922.

——— *The Expansion of the Common Law.* 1904.

Relf, F. H. *The Petition of Right.* 1917.

Scofield, C. L. *A Study of the Court of Star Chamber.* 1900.

Stubbs, William. *The Constitutional History of England.* 3 vols. 1891-96.

Tanner, J. R. *English Constitutional Conflicts of the Seventeenth Century, 1603-1625.* 1928.

Taswell-Langmead, T. P. *English Constitutional History.* 1946.

Thompson, Faith. *A Short History of Parliament, 1295-1642.* 1953.

Turner, E. R. *The Cabinet Council of England in the Seventeenth and Eighteenth Centuries.* 1932.

Vinogradoff, Paul. ed. *Essays in Legal History.* 1914.

White, A. B. *The Making of the English Constitution.* 1925.

Willson, D. H. *The Privy Councillors in the House of Commons, 1604-1629.* 1940.

## Religious History

Ashley, M. *The Greatness of Oliver Cromwell.* 1957.

Bainton, R. H. *The Reformation of the Sixteenth Century.* 1952.

Barker, A. E. *Milton and the Puritan Dilemma, 1641-1660.* 1942.

Baskerville, G. *English Monks and the Suppression of the Monasteries.* 1937.

Berens, L. H. *The Digger Movement in the Days of the Commonwealth.* 1906.

Brunton, D. B. *Members of the Long Parliament.* 1954.

Crook, Isaac. *John Knox the Reformer.* 1906.

Firth, C. H. *Oliver Cromwell and the Rule of the Puritans in England.* 1905.

Gardiner, S. R. *Oliver Cromwell's Place in History.* 1897.

——— *History of the Commonwealth and Protectorate.* 1901.

Gasquet, F. A. *Hampshire Recusants.* 1896.

Guizot, F. *The History of the English Revolution of 1640.* 1851.

Henson, H. H. *Puritanism in England.* 1912.

Hughes, Philip. *The Reformation in England.* 2 vols. 1950-54.

Hutchinson, F. E. *Cranmer and the English Reformation.* 1951.

Inderwick, F .A. *The Interregnum.* 1901.

Innes, A. *Cranmer and the Reformation in England.* 1900.

Jenks, E. *The Constitutional Experiments of the Commonwealth, 1649-1660.* 1890.

Kidd, B. J. *The Counter-Reformation, 1500-1600.* 1933.

Knappen, M. M. *Tudor Puritanism. A Chapter in the History of Idealism.* 1939.

Lee, M. *James Stewart, Earl of Moray. A Study of the Reformation in Scotland.* 1953.

Mackenzie, A. M. *The Scotland of Queen Mary and the Religious Wars, 1513-1638.* 1952.

Meyer, A. D. *The English Catholics in the Reign of Elizabeth.* 1916.

Mosse, G. L. *The Reformation.* 1953.

Mozley, J. F. *William Tyndale.* 1937.

Parker, T. M. *The English Reformation to 1558.* 1950.

Pease, T. C. *The Leveller Movement.* 1916.

Pennington, E. L. *The Church of England and the Reformation.* 1952.

Plum, H. G. *Restoration Puritanism.* 1943.

Pollard, A. F. *Thomas Cranmer and the English Reformation, 1489-1556.* 1904.

Powicke, F. M. *The Reformation in England.* 1938.

Rupp, E. G. *The English Protestant Tradition.* 1947.

Smith, H. M. *Pre-Reformation England.* 1938.

Smith, P. *The Age of the Reformation.* 1920.

Smyth, C. H. *Cranmer and the Reformation under Edward VI.* 1926.

Stoughton, J. *History of Religion in England From the Opening of Long Parliament.* 1881.

Strype, J. *Life and Acts of Matthew Parker.* 3 vols. 1821.

—— *Life and Acts of John Whitgift.* 3 vols. 1822.

Tatham, G. B. *The Puritans in Power.* 1913.

Tawney, R. H. *Religion and the Rise of Capitalism.* 1937.

Thompson, J. V. P. *Supreme Governor.* 1940.

Ward, F. P. *The Counter-Reformation.* 1893.

Waugh, E. *Edmund Campion.* 1935.

Whiting, C. E. *Studies in English Puritanism, 1660-1688.* 1931.

## Tudor History

Aubrey, John. *Aubrey's Brief Lives.* Ed. O. L. Dick. 1950.

Baumer, F. L. *The Early Tudor Theory of Kingship.* 1940.

Beesly, E. *Queen Elizabeth.* 1892.

Black, J. *The Reign of Elizabeth.* 1936.

Cam, H. *England Before Elizabeth.* 1950.

Caspari, Fritz. *Humanism and the Social Order in Tudor England.* 1954.

Cheyney, E. P. *History of England from the Defeat of the Armada to the Death of Elizabeth.* 2 vols. 1914-26.

Creighton, M. *Cardinal Wolsey.* 1898.

—— *The Age of Elizabeth.* 1887.

—— *Queen Elizabeth.* 1889.

Fisher, H. A. L. *History of England from the Accession of Henry VII to the Death of Henry VIII.* 1906.

Froude, J. A. *The Reign of Elizabeth.* 1911.

Gairdner, J. *The Houses of Lancaster and York.* 1886.

Gasquet, Cardinal. *Henry VIII and the English Monasteries.* 1889.

Hackett, F. *Henry VIII.* 1929.

Harrison, D. *Tudor England.* 2 vols. 1953.

Hay, Denys. *Polydore Virgil, Renaissance Historian and Man of Letters.* 1952.

Henderson, T. F. *Mary Queen of Scots.* 1905.

Innes, A. D. *England under the Tudors.* 1905.

Mackie, J. D. *The Earlier Tudors, 1485-1558.* 1952.

Madden, F. *The Privy Purse Expenses of the Princess Mary.* 1831.

Maitland, F. W. *Roman Canon Law in the Church of England.* 1898.

Mattingly, G. *Catherine of Aragon.* 1942.

Markam, C. R. *King Edward VI.* 1907.

Maynard, T. *Bloody Mary.* 1955.

—— *The Crown and the Cross: A Biography of Thomas Cromwell.* 1950.

Merriman, R. B. *Life and Letters of Thomas Cromwell.* 1902.

Neale, J. T. *Queen Elizabeth.* 1934.

—— *The Elizabethan House of Commons.* 1950.

Neale, J. T. *Elizabeth and Her Parliaments, 1559-1581.* 1953.

Nichols, John. *The Progresses and Public Processions of Queen Elizabeth.* 3 vols. 1823.

Pickthorn, K. W. M. *Early Tudor Government: Henry VII.* 1934.

—— *Early Tudor Government: Henry VIII.* 1934.

Pollard, A. F. *Henry VIII.* 1902.

—— *The Reign of Henry VII from Contemporary Sources.* 1919.

Prescott, H. F. M. *Mary Tudor.* 1952.

Read, Conyers. *Bibliography of British History: Tudor Period, 1485-1603.* 1933.

—— *The Tudors.* 1936.

—— *Mr. Secretary Walsingham and the Policy of Queen Elizabeth.* 3 vols. 1925.

Richardson, W. C. *Tudor Chamber Administration, 1485-1547.* 1952.

Routh, E. *Sir Thomas More and His Friends, 1477-1535.* 1934.

Rowse, A. L. *The England of Elizabeth.* 1951.

Salzman, L. F. *England in Tudor Times.* 1926.

Schenk, Wilhelm. *Reginold Pole.* 1950.

Seton-Watson, R. W. ed. *Tudor Studies.* 1924.

Smith, L. B. *Tudor Prelates and Politics.* 1953.

Strachey, Lytton. *Elizabeth and Essex.* 1928.

Strathman, E. A. *Sir Walter Raleigh: A Study in Elizabethan Skepticism.* 1951.

Temperely, G. *Henry VII.* 1914.

Williams, C. H. *The Making of Tudor Despotism.* 1935.

Williamson, J. A. *The Tudor Age.* 1953.

—— *The Age of Drake.* 1938.

Williamson, R. H. *Sir Walter Raleigh.* 1952.

Zeeveld, W. G. *The Foundations of Tudor Policy.* 1948.

## Stuart History

Airy, O. *The English Restoration and Louis XIV.* 1895.

Anthony, Irvin. *Raleigh and His World.* 1934.

Bryant, A. *King Charles II.* 1931.

Churchill, W. S. *Marlborough, His Life and Times.* 1938.

Coates, M. *Social Life in Stuart England.* 1925.

Creighton, Louise. *Life of Sir Walter Raleigh.* 1882.

Davies, G. *The Early Stuarts, 1603-1660.* 1937.

—— *The Restoration of Charles II.* 1955.

Firth, C. H. *The Last Years of the Protectorate.* 2 vols. 1929.

—— *The House of Lords During the Civil War.* 1910.

Gardiner, S. R. *A History of the Great Civil War.* 1893.

—— *History of England, 1603-1642.* 10 vols. 1883-85.

—— *History of the Commonwealth and Protectorate, 1649-1660.* 3 vols. 1894-1903.

—— *A History of England Under the Duke of Buckingham and Charles I, 1624-1628.* 1875.

Head, F. W. *The Fallen Stuarts.* 1901.

Holdsworth, W. *History of English Law.* 1938.

Jane, L. C. *The Coming of Parliament. England From 1350 to 1660.* 1905.

Macaulay, T. B. *The History of England from the Accession of James II.* Edition of 1915.

Mathew, D. *The Age of Charles I.* 1951.

Moir, T. L. *The Addled Parliament of 1614.* 1957.

Morgan, W. M. *English Political Parties and Leaders in the Reign of Queen Anne.* 1902.

Nichols, John. *The Progresses, Progressions, and Magnificant Festivities of King James I. . . .* 4 vols. 1928.

Nobbs, D. *England and Scotland, 1560-1707.* 1952.

Notestein, Wallace. *Winning of the Initiative by the House of Commons.* 1925.

Ogg, David. *England in the Reign of Charles II.* 1934.

Oldys, W. *The Life of Sir Walter Raleigh.* 1829.

Pepys, Samuel. *Diary.* (many editions).

Petrie, Charles. *The Jacobite Movement.* 1949.

Petrie, Charles. *The Stuarts.* 1937.

Pinkham, L. *William III and the Respectable Revolution. The Part Played by William of Orange in the Revolution of 1688.* 1954.

Pollard, A. F. *England Under the Protector Somerset.* 1900.

Pollock, J. *The Popish Plot. A Study of the History of the Reign of Charles II.* 1944.

Read, Conyers. *Bibliography of British History: Stuart Period.* 1933.

Reese, M. M. *The Tudors and Stuarts.* 1940.

Spedding, James. *An Account of the Life and Times of Francis Bacon.* 2 vols. 1878.

Stanhope, E. *The Reign of Queen Anne.* 1871.

Stone, J. M. *Mary the First Queen of England.* 1901.

Trevelyan, George. *England Under Queen Anne.* 1930.

—— *England Under the Stuarts.* 1904.

Turner, G. F. *James II.* 1938.

Wedgwood, C. V. *The Great Rebellion.* 1955.

Williams, J. R. *James I.* 1953.

Williamson, R. H. *The Gunpowder Plot.* 1952.

Willson, D. H. *King James VI and I.* 1956.

## General History

Ames, R. A. *Citizen Thomas More and His Utopia.* 1949.

Ashley, M. P. *Financial and Commercial Policies Under the Cromwellian Protectorate.* 1934.

Beard, C. A. *The Office of Justice of the Peace in England.* 1904.

Bosher, R. S. *The Making of the Restoration Settlement: The Influence of the Laudians, 1649-1662.* 1951.

*Cambridge History of the British Empire.* 8 vols. 1929-36.

Campbell, W. E. *Erasmus, Tyndale, and More.* 1949.

—— *More's Utopia and His Social Teaching.* 1930.

Chambers, R. *Thomas More.* 1935.

Dicey, A. V. *The Privy Council.* 1887.

Dietz, Frederick. *An Economic History of England.* 1942.

—— *English Public Finances, 1558-1641.* 1932.

Dunham, W. H. and Pargellis, S. *Complaint and Reform in England.* 1938.

Feiling, K. *A History of the Tory Party, 1640-1714.* 1924.

Fleming, D. H. *The Reformation in Scotland.* 1910.

Gilmore, M. P. *The World of Humanism, 1453-1517.* 1952.

Holdsworth, W. S. *A History of English Law.* 9 vols. 1903-26.

Kelsall, R. K. *Wage Regulation Under the Statute of Artificers.* 1938.

Knappen, M. M. *Constitutional and Legal History of England.* 1942.

Leonard, E. M. *Early History of English Poor Relief.* 1900.

Lingard, J. *History of England.* 12 vols. 1874.

Maitland, F. W. *The Collected Works of Frederick William Maitland.* Ed. H. A. L. Fisher. 3 vols. 1911.

Makower, F. *The Constitutional History and Constitution of the Church of England.* 1895.

Montague, F. C. *The Political History of England, 1603-1660.* 1907.

Morris, C. *Political Thought in England. Tyndale to Hooper.* 1952.

Onions, C. T. ed. *Shakespeare's England.* 2 vols. 1917.

Pollard, A. F. *Factors in Modern History.* 1907.

Shaw, W. *The English Church During the Civil Wars and Under the Commonwealth.* 1876.

Trevor-Roper, H. R. *The Gentry, 1540-1640.* 1953.

Usher, R. G. *The Rise and Fall of the High Commission.* 1913.

Webb, S. and Webb, B. *English Local Government from the Revolution to the Municipal Corporations Act.* 1919.

Willey, B. *The Seventeenth Century Background.* 1950.

# Index